# Communication and Change in American Religious History

*Edited by*

Leonard I. Sweet

WILLIAM B. EERDMANS PUBLISHING COMPANY
GRAND RAPIDS, MICHIGAN

*For Thomas E. Boomershine,*
*friend, colleague, and mentor*

Copyright © 1993 by Wm. B. Eerdmans Publishing Co.
255 Jefferson Ave. S.E., Grand Rapids, Mich. 49503

Printed in the United States of America

**Library of Congress Cataloging-in-Publication Data**

Communication and change in American religious history / edited by
  Leonard I. Sweet
     p.     cm.
  Includes bibliographical references.
  ISBN 0-8028-0682-1
  1. Communication — Religious aspects — Christianity — History.  2. United States —
Church history.  I. Sweet, Leonard I.
  BR517.C655   1993
  277.3 — dc20                  93-29150
                                           CIP

Most of the essays in this volume were originally prepared as papers presented at
a conference on communication and change funded by the Lilly Endowment.

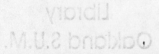

# Contents

*Communication and Change in American Religious
History: A Historiographical Probe*
Leonard I. Sweet
1

1. *Protestantism and Capitalism: Print Culture
and Individualism*
Martin E. Marty
91

2. *Religion, Communications, and the Career
of George Whitefield*
Harry S. Stout
108

3. *The Spirit of the Old Writers: Print Media,
the Great Awakening, and Continuity in New England*
Charles E. Hambrick-Stowe
126

4. *From Democratization to Domestication: The Transitional
Orality of the American Methodist Circuit Rider*
A. Gregory Schneider
141

5. *God, Rhetoric, and Logic in Antebellum American
Theological Education*
Glenn T. Miller
165

6. Technology and the Character of Community Life
   in Antebellum America: The Role of Story Papers          185
   Ronald J. Zboray

7. The Millennium and the Media          216
   James H. Moorhead

8. Systematic Benevolence: Religious Publishing and
   the Marketplace in Early Nineteenth-Century America          239
   David Paul Nord

9. The Evangelical Enlightenment and the Task
   of Theological Education          270
   Mark A. Noll

10. Preaching to the "Faith" of America          301
    David G. Buttrick

11. Oral Roberts: Religious Media Pioneer          320
    David Edwin Harrell, Jr.

12. From New Thought to New Vision:
    The Shamanic Paradigm in Contemporary Spirituality          335
    Catherine L. Albanese

13. American Christianity and the History
    of Communication: A Bibliographic Probe          355
    Elmer J. O'Brien

        I. Bibliographical Sources          355
       II. General Studies          371
      III. Colonial Period: 1640-1689          386
       IV. Colonial Period, Religious Ferment, and
           the New Nation: 1690-1799          405
        V. Growth of the Nation: 1800-1860          427
       VI. The Civil War and Rapid Technological
           Development: 1861-1919          445
      VII. The Modern Electronic Era: 1920 to the Present          452

Contributors          480

# Communication and Change in American Religious History: A Historiographical Probe

## Leonard I. Sweet

This collection of essays explores the interplay in American history between the emergence of new communication forms and religious and social change. It is a book that assumes that religion and communication should partake of each other's history. It seeks to move from fringe to focal concern the impact of new communication forms on the shape and development of American religious life and the syntax of tradition and innovation in American history.

More concretely, this volume is built around the "seminal question" of biblical scholar Thomas E. Boomershine, to whom this volume is dedicated, "whether changes in communications technology in the culture are of major importance for the Christian church in the late twentieth century."[1] A new mindscape and soulscape have been created by post-

---

1. Thomas E. Boomershine, "Christianity and the Communication of the Word," unpublished essay, 1991. Much of Boomershine's seminal work is still unpublished. Available now are "Biblical Megatrends: Towards a Paradigm for the Interpretation of the Bible in Electronic Media," *Society of Biblical Literature 1987 Seminar Papers* 26 (1987): 144-57; "Peter's Denial as Polemic or Confession: The Implications of Media Criticism for Biblical Hermeneutics," *Semeia* 39 (1987): 47-68; "Religious Education and Media Change: A Historical Sketch," *Religious Education* 82 (Spring 1987): 269-78; "Christian Community and Technologies of the Word," in *Communicating Faith in a Technological Age,* ed. James

---

This essay would not have been possible without the expert research assistance of Betty O'Brien, to whom I owe a huge debt of gratitude. Quentin Schultze and David Paul Nord also offered helpful criticism on portions of this essay.

1

modern electronic communications technologies, argues poststructuralist Mark Poster, as he distinguishes the new forms of intellectual and social interaction generated by electronic communication vis-à-vis modern culture's oral and print modes of communication.[2] Pierre Babin, Director of the Center for Research and Communication in Lyon, France, and a consultant for this Lilly-funded project, states the thesis in theological terms:

> The incarnation of the Christian message in different cultural epochs, each characterized by different media, has introduced not just a new way of transmitting a message (print or electronic, for example), but a new form of Christian existence and a new form of church. Unless there is this continual total transformation, the Christian message and Christ himself are not communicated.[3]

Historian Averil Cameron, along with sociologists Roger Finke and Rodney Stark, asks this question somewhat less spongily. How have some leaders and movements been able to capture the imagination of the society in which they lived? Their separate conclusion is that those religious leaders who have made the biggest advances have been those who worked out of their tradition to express their faith through innovative ways and means, idioms and technologies accessible and adapted to the times in which they lived.[4] Is it true, as Britisher Colin Morris contends, that "many of the exciting new twists in the Christian story over the centuries have occurred because advocates for Christianity have exploited developments in communications technology"?[5]

McDonnell and Frances Trampiets (Middlegreen, Slough, Eng.: St Paul Publications, 1989), 84-111; "A New Paradigm for Interpreting the Bible on Television," in *Changing Channels: The Church and the Television Revolution,* ed. Tyron Inbody (Dayton: Whale-prints, 1990), 61-76; and "Doing Theology in the Electronic Age: The Meeting of Orality and Electricity," *Journal of Theology* (United Theological Seminary) 95 (1991): 4-14.

2. Mark Poster, *The Mode of Information: Poststructuralism and Social Change* (Chicago: University of Chicago Press, 1990).

3. Pierre Babin, *A New Era in Religious Communication* (Minneapolis: Fortress Press, 1991), 8.

4. Averil Cameron, *Christianity and the Rhetoric of Empire: The Development of Christian Discourse* (Berkeley: University of California Press, 1991); Roger Finke and Rodney Stark, *The Churching of America, 1776-1990: Winners and Losers in Our Religious Economy* (New Brunswick, NJ: Rutgers University Press, 1992).

5. Colin Morris, *Wrestling With an Angel: Reflections on Christian Communications*

Media studies have heretofore largely inhabited the more sleepy hamlets of scholarly professions, where the light shed has been often oblique, the story itself fragmented and heavily encumbered, more backcloth than even backdrop. This anthology does not attempt to mount a single thesis or even to marshall a complex argument. Its method is kaleidoscopic and cinematic; its rangy essays together form more a mesh than a line of analysis. The introduction to this patchwork book attempts to sew together its pile of pieces by situating and assessing the many-sided contributions in this collection and placing them in a historiographical framework.

My introduction stands as froth in the wake of Elmer J. O'Brien's contribution to this volume, "American Christianity and the History of Communication: A Bibliographic Probe," which by itself ought to convince anyone to pick up this book. If bibliography is the sociology of texts, Elmer O'Brien is a master sociologist. His bibliography on "American Christianity and the History of Communication" is a landmark contribution. In a time when practicing librarians are loudly silent in scholarship, O'Brien has scrupulously schooled himself in the history of religious books and periodicals.[6] In a time when historiography has shut itself into denominational bunkers, O'Brien's absorbing and authoritative patrol through a variety of intellectual territories brings welcome coherence out of a bumpy mass of mappings and studies. Until now very little bibliographical first aid has been forthcoming for the scholar of religious communications (as his bibliography of bibliographies reveals).[7] O'Brien's "probe" is impressive and invaluable in covering as wide a range of bibliographic activity as possible.

O'Brien's bibliography, like Paul A. Soukup's stadium-sized reference volume before him, has only annotated those items that could be checked personally by the author. Unlike O'Brien's work, Soukup's chapter four on

---

(London: Collins, 1990), 63-64. An excellent text on the role of communication in history is *Communication in History: Technology, Culture, Society,* ed. David Crowley and Paul Heyer (New York: Longman, 1991), a collection of interdisciplinary essays organized into eight parts and covering 50,000 years, beginning with the cave markings and ending with the microelectronics of postmodern culture.

6. Paul Raabe extends an altar call for librarians to come forward as scholars in "Library History and the History of Books: Two Fields of Research for Librarians," in *Essays in Honor of James Edward Walsh on His Sixty-Fifth Birthday* (Cambridge, MA: Goethe Institute of Boston and Houghton Library, 1983), 7-22.

7. Of particular importance to this essay has been James A. Capo, "Annotated Bibliography on Electronic Media," *Religious Education* 82 (1987): 304-34. Capo's work focuses most tightly on the relationships between television and theological education.

historical materials includes titles in other languages. Unfortunately, Soukup gives only a representative rather than a comprehensive surveying of this historical field, although Soukup's 1,311 entries cover a tentacular range of communication forms, including the arts and dance, rhetoric and audience studies, computers and comic books.[8] Every narrative, even a bibliographic narrative, needs to knot its thread to produce designs in the carpet. Mark Fackler's essay on "evangelical scholarship in communication studies" knots as tight and bright a thread in as short a space as anyone could imagine possible.[9]

The value of any *omnium gatherum,* with all the inbuilt limitations of its nature, lies chiefly in the excellence of its parts. In *Communication and Change* there is to be found refreshingly different probes of the terrain of communications technology, which come from covering the subject from diverse vantage points, from high theoretical altitudes to close-focus empirical intensity. In moments of amusement, I divide historians into two types — those who go to a concert with ideas, and those who leave a concert with ideas. The latter were invited to contribute to this volume. The digging that goes on in it is both an exploration of new ground and a cultivation of that ground for further studies of the history by which ideas and knowledge are diffused.

## Communication in a Print Culture

To venture the kind of essay on communication and change that Martin E. Marty was asked to contribute to this volume is to agree to turn oneself into a turkey just in time for Thanksgiving. As we have come to expect from him, Marty brings perhaps his greatest strength to any turkeyshoot — his ability to relate both theory and practice to wider social and intellectual issues. It is a brave historian who can stand back from the flood

---

8. Paul A. Soukup, *Christian Communication: A Bibliographical Survey* (New York: Greenwood Press, 1989). See also Soukup, *Communication and Theology: Introduction and Review of the Literature* (London: WACC, 1983), and his excellent article on "Communication, Cultural Form and Theology," entitled "Communications, Media and Spirituality," *The Way* Supplement 57 (Autumn 1986): 77-89.

9. Mark Fackler, "A Short Story of Evangelical Scholarship in Communication Studies," in *American Evangelicals and the Mass Media: Perspectives on the Relationship Between American Evangelicals and the Mass Media,* ed. Quentin J. Schultze (Grand Rapids: Academie Books, 1990), 357-71.

and mass of studies on Protestantism, capitalism, print culture, and individualism, and then step forward to throw some refocusing light, which scholars so desperately need.

In "Protestantism and Capitalism: Print Culture and Individualism," Marty sets the pace for our exploration of the symbiotic relationship between Protestantism and mass media by interpreting communication as an umbrella term for oratory, literacy, printing, journalism, the book, and electronic media. From the church's role in retailing news and information in the colonial period to the dominant role of media and the imagistic values of postmodern culture — where the media no longer "cover" elections but *are* the very elections themselves — starting in Marty's essay there is the magic found in all good anthologies, forever luring the reader into deeper waters and unbeaten paths.

Continuing his Niebuhrian emphasis on "irony" as a very present help in this prowl through the discomforting territory of communication, a landscape crowded with incongruities, Marty shows how the Puritan investment in print culture could lead its youth not *in* to the covenanted community but *out* toward capitalist pursuits. More currently, liberalism's investment in "high-cultural literacy" yielded oppositional dividends as its market share declined and its cultural hegemony eroded. In other words, the reading worlds of biblical and individual literacy created a choice culture in which the seeds of subverting community loyalties and identities were in the very plantings designed to stabilize community loyalties and identities in the first place.

The Reformation "priesthood of all believers" meant a "priesthood of readers," readers of a book, as historian David Paul Nord put it at the conference that preceded this volume. The role of Protestantism in the emergence of the print industry, and vice versa, is the subject of much discussion. "Protestant doctrines harnessed an evangelical religion to a new capitalist industry aimed at expanding markets and increased book sales."[10] Of course, the book format was adopted by the Christian church long before the invention of printing and moveable type. Roots of print culture can be found in the medieval approach to Scripture and other forms of reading.[11]

10. Elizabeth L. Eisenstein, "The Emergence of Print Culture in the West," *Journal of Communication* 30 (Winter 1980): 103. See also her classic *The Printing Press as an Agent of Change: Communications and Cultural Transformations in Early-modern Europe* (Cambridge: Cambridge University Press, 1979). A totally different perspective on the Jesuits' success with print vis-à-vis the Puritans is James Axtell, "The Power of Print in the Eastern Woodlands," *William and Mary Quarterly* 3d ser., 44 (1987): 300-309.

11. Michael T. Clanchy, "Looking Back from the Invention of Printing," in *Literacy*

Protestants were masters of the printed word, which replaced face-to-face human exchanges as the primary medium of social communications and cultural currency. The interaction of print and sources of authority is a specialty of Elizabeth Eisenstein, who argues that "the most dynamic impetus to the development of printing was supplied by Christian evangelism."[12] She also makes the case for increased controls over authorship as one by-product of the invention of printing — controls that are now loosening and disappearing with the rise of copiers and faxes.

Marty shows the danger of trying to reduce complex social relationships to simple formulas, even formulas as nuanced as Eisenstein's. Marty does not allude to the academic dogfighting over Kenneth Lockridge's thesis about the "short-range" motivating force for the Puritan emphasis on literacy — not modernization but "the conservation of piety" and the reaffirmation of "traditional values in a time of social transition."[13] Marty keeps a cool head and a civil pen in areas of scholarly battlespeak. His knack for getting under the skin without irritating it is partly attributable to his staying acutely in touch with the unsettling ambivalences and fissures within history. Some people "used their literacy to go separate ways," as Marty succinctly puts it: "The very churches that taught reading and formed a print culture to promote the Protestant tradition were also on the whole providing adherents with the tools that gave them a means of exit from the confinements of that tradition."

For Marty the question almost becomes this: In what ways might media literacy become a communifying force rather than an isolating one? Here the ironic interpretation of the history of social form and function offers considerable pleasures. It seems that all technologies as well as all ideologies willy-nilly produce contradictory meanings. Might it be that times of tremendous technological change and transition release dual directions, even oxymoronic tendencies?

---

*in Historical Perspective,* ed. Daniel P. Resnick (Washington: Library of Congress, 1983), 7-22.

12. Elizabeth L. Eisenstein, "From Scriptoria to Printing Shops: Evolution and Revolution in the Early Printed Book Trade," in *Books and Society in History: Papers of the Association of College and Research Libraries Rare Books and Manuscripts Preconference, 24-28 June 1980, Boston, Massachusetts,* ed. Kenneth E. Carpenter (New York: R. R. Bowker, 1983), 32.

13. Kenneth Lockridge, *Literacy in Colonial New England: An Enquiry into the Social Context of Literacy in the Early Modern West* (New York: Norton, 1974). Lockridge has been taken to task by Richard Beale Davis, *A Colonial Southern Book Shelf: Reading in the Eighteenth Century* (Athens: University of Georgia Press, 1979).

"The book is an artifact that during the 500-odd years since 1450 has had a more profound effect on our history than any other invention."[14] Unfortunately, American scholars have lagged well behind European scholars in *l'histoire du livre* or *livre et société*.[15] Questions such as how books, paperbacks, and the ideas they embodied ended up in the hands of colonial America's community of readers have only begun to be asked by Americanists, while in Europe the "field" of book history is beginning to look, in Robert Darnton's words, "less like a field than a tropical rain forest."[16] By now historians, unable to ignore the social setting of religious history, are beginning to ask how communications technology has changed the face of religion in America.

There is perhaps no greater evidence that book culture is coming to an end, a vital but vestigial force in a predominantly electronic culture, than the explosion of scholarly interest in the history of the book.[17] The year 1983 alone saw the publication of three landmark publications on the history of the book, which itself is a subcategory of the larger history of reading, which in turn is a subcategory of the larger history of literacy.[18] Of the three literacy skills — signing, reading, and writing — historians have been turning the history of literacy into a history of reading. Literacy has been where many disciplines converge but generally

14. The words are those of Brown University's Thomas R. Adams, in *Papers of the Bibliographical Society of America* 79 (1985): 578. Adams is the former president of the Bibliographical Society of America, which along with the American Antiquarian Society has promoted the study of the history of the book in America.

15. See John Feather, "Cross-Channel Currents: Historical Bibliography and *l'Histoire du Livre*," *Library* 6th ser., 2 (1980): 1-15. For the history of the book in America, see *The Book in America: A History of the Making and Selling of Books in the United States,* ed. Helmut Lehmann-Haupt, Lawrence C. Wroth, and Rollo G. Silver (New York: R. R. Bowker, 1951).

16. Robert N. Darnton, "What Is the History of Books?" in *Reading in America,* ed. Cathy N. Davidson (Baltimore: Johns Hopkins University Press, 1989), 29. This is a slight revision of an essay that previously appeared in *Daedalus* 111 (Summer 1982): 65-83. See also Darnton's "First Steps Toward a History of Reading," in *The Kiss of Lamourette: Reflections in Cultural History* (New York: W. W. Norton, 1990).

17. Two excellent reviews of some of this literature are Paul Saenger's review essay of *Books and Society in History,* ed. Kenneth E. Carpenter, in *Eighteenth-Century Studies* 19 (Fall 1985): 94-99, and Richard L. Venezky, "Books, Readers, and Society," *History of Education Quarterly* 30 (Winter 1990): 645-56.

18. See *Books and Society in History,* ed. Carpenter; *Literacy in Historical Perspective,* ed. Resnick; and *Printing and Society in Early America,* ed. William L. Joyce, David D. Hall, Richard D. Brown, and John B. Hench (Worcester, MA: American Antiquarian Society, 1983).

do not meet — or at least have not met until the focus shifted to reading, following the work of Roger Chartier, Robert Darnton, Carl Kaestle, and others.

Reading stands as one of the most common, yet most complex, of modern cultural activities, encompassing newspapers, pamphlets, tracts, periodicals, posters, and other printed matter. On top of the diversity of reading materials there is the differentiation in readings — reading as a private, intimate activity, and reading as a social, public function taking place in public places (in restaurants, transits, libraries, even in family settings, which imply contact with others), with the one a more silent and the other a more oral activity. For over twenty years, reader-directed criticism has been showing us that literary texts cannot be understood without attention to the various functions of the reading process. Much of this work has been done on the antebellum period.[19] There is need for a more historical approach to reader-response criticism, such as that found in James L. Machor's work, which decries the "historical aporia" so pervasive in literary studies and wonderfully yokes the "return of the reader" to the "return to history."[20]

The primary terms of scholarly discussion about reading and the book have been those of literacy. The history of literacy and "cultural literacy" remains elusively out of focus between the various angles of vision — semiotics, ethnology, phenomenology, reception theory, deconstruction, feminist criticism, and so forth. The current convention is that the ability to read was more common than the ability to write, even to the point that there was little connection between the two, as T. C. Smout

19. Two excellent introductions to the field are *The Reader in the Text: Essays on Audience and Interpretation,* ed. Susan Suleiman and Inge Crosman (Princeton, NJ: Princeton University Press, 1980), and *Reader Response Criticism: From Formalism to Poststructuralism,* ed. Jane P. Tompkins (Baltimore: Johns Hopkins University Press, 1980). For the antebellum period, see, for example, Michael Denning, *Mechanic Accents: Dime Novels and Working-Class Culture in America* (London: Verso, 1987), or R. Laurence Moore, "Religion, Secularization, and the Shaping of the Culture Industry in Antebellum America," *American Quarterly* 41 (June 1989): 216-42.

20. James L. Machor, "Introduction: Readers/Texts/Contexts," in *Readers in History: Nineteenth-Century American Literature and the Contexts of Response,* ed. J. L. Machor (Baltimore: Johns Hopkins University Press, 1993), vii-xxix. See also Machor's contribution to the same collection, "Historical Hermeneutics and Antebellum Fiction: Gender, Response Theory, and Interpretive Contexts," 54-84, and an earlier version, "Fiction and Informed Reading in Early Nineteenth-Century America," *Nineteenth-Century Literature* 47 (December 1992): 320-48.

and David D. Hall argue.[21] Yet William G. Gilmore, who has "*Annales-ized*" the study of literacy through scrutiny of signature rates found on wills over four decades (1797-1830) in rural northwestern New England, has discovered near-total literacy for males (except those in the lowest fifth in wealth) and extremely high overall signature rates for females, a gender variance that had "declined dramatically" by the early 1790s.

Granted, what is being measured by Gilmore's multiple-moment research is only the skills of signing, directly, and rudimentary reading ability, indirectly. But his reminder that "no one was incapacitated by illiteracy in premodern America," that people lived and loved and communicated "far more directly than we will ever comprehend," is well taken. How did they do it? Gilmore isolates six methods of cultural expression between the 1780s and 1830s in rural New England: (1) oral communication; (2) music and singing; (3) visual arts and crafts; (4) dancing; (5) handwriting; and (6) the printed word.[22]

How did Americans participate in the world of print? What turned America into a nation of readers? One crucial means was through religious organizations, which created a network of print culture and multiplied it, especially after 1815. The role of the church in the cultural push toward basic literacy cannot be gainsaid. Surely the growth of a market economy, and its requirement of an educated population, conspired to make reading "a necessity of everyday life" for most people. But so, too, did religion, especially evangelical religion and its encouragement of reading through the targeting of audiences based on gender, class, and life passage. Both worked together to create an unprecedented mass reading public, with literacy rates higher than any other place in the world except Sweden and Finland.

To what extent did the evangelical Protestant culture of literacy center in the book, or in tracts, treatises, liturgy, literature, and the like? Most agree that Protestantism was a religion of The Book, an observation that scholars are finding is more than trivially true. Robert Darnton's sure-footed and stimulating essay on the way "books do not merely recount

---

21. T. C. Smout, "Born Again at Cambuslang: New Evidence on Popular Religion and Literacy in Eighteenth-Century Scotland," *Past and Present* 97 (1982): 121-27, and David D. Hall, *Worlds of Wonder, Days of Judgment: Popular Religious Beliefs in Early New England* (New York: Alfred A. Knopf, 1989).

22. William J. Gilmore, "Elementary Literacy on the Eve of the Industrial Revolution: Trends in Rural New England, 1760-1830," *Proceedings of the American Antiquarian Society* 92 (April 1982): 87-171; quotes are from p. 87.

history, they make it," speaks of the "communications circuit" encompassing author, publisher, printer, shipper, bookseller, and reader.[23] Each role needs treatment, although in the early days one person could play more than one role.

For example, Elizabeth Carroll Reilly has authored a pacesetting study of Boston bookseller/printer/publisher Jeremy Condy, a liberal Baptist minister during the "stormy" years of the Great Awakening who left the pastorate because of poor salary support. Reilly asks such questions as these: "What sociology of knowledge do we find in New England? How far did the ideas in such books filter into colonial society? What forms did they take?"[24]

Booksellers were key purveyors of religious ideas, and Condy's theological training made him a natural broker of print information. His clerical contacts already placed him in a literary network that he utilized in his entrepreneurial book trade business, which included catalogue listings of cloth, china, glassware, stationery stock, sealing wax, and other office supplies, catalogues that are often forgotten in discussions of bookselling competitions for control of popular almanacs and newspapers.

Condy specialized in reprinting English classics, brief and popular treatises written by those authors with whom he agreed. He thus had a role in disseminating liberal theological doctrines that stressed religion's rootedness in praxis more than dogma. Condy also published works written by friends and acquaintances. In other words, booksellers were part of a complex communications network that depended heavily on "patterns of friendship, family, and proximity."[25] Condy's intellectual community was highly integrated and focused. He knew his customers, and he knew his books.

### Awakenings and Communication Systems

The various Great Awakenings in American history, especially the first two, have been the sites of some of the most significant scholarship in

23. Darnton, "What Is the History of Books?" 27-52, esp. 47. See also chap. 7 in Darnton, *The Kiss of Lamourette*. Hall traces the colonial American "communications circuit" in his *Worlds of Wonder, Days of Judgment*. See also Hall's "The History of the Book: New Question? New Answers?" *Journal of Library History* 21 (1986): 27-36.

24. Elizabeth Carroll Reilly, "The Wages of Piety: The Boston Book Trade of Jeremy Condy," in *Printing and Society in Early America*, ed. Joyce et al., 83-131.

25. Reilly, "The Wages of Piety," 98-99, 114.

recent American religious history. Our interests here center in whether "looking back over the centuries, it is clear that a combination of evangelical fervor and media sophistication has always been explosive."[26] Harry S. Stout has been one of the key leaders (along with Elizabeth Carroll Reilly, Ian K. Steele, Richard D. Brown, William J. Gilmore, Nathan Hatch, Richard Kielbowicz, and others) in the scholarly movement to understand the communications revolution that occurred during the late eighteenth and early nineteenth centuries.

Was the First Great Awakening an "interpretative fiction" of the late nineteenth and early twentieth centuries, as one historian has suggested as part of a larger thesis that portrays American Christianity as the creation of a democratic folk culture that was contending with more than cooperating with modernity?[27] Or was the First Great Awakening the "invention" of the Second Great Awakening, as another recent argument goes?[28] Or was the Awakening, at least as it expressed itself in the middle colonies, but an extension of Scots-Irish revivalism?[29] Whatever case one argues, there is common agreement that the mushrooming religious periodical press and the burgeoning publication organs of denominations and voluntary societies were used to connect contemporary events with the colonial past and to create a historic revivalistic tradition. These evangelical organs of communication may have been at least as important as the use of popular print culture to democratize and decentralize religious and cultural authority, as Nathan Hatch argues.

In fact, as Charles E. Hambrick-Stowe's essay in this volume, "The Spirit of the Old Writers: Print Media, the Great Awakening, and Continuity in New England," exemplifies, it has been precisely the study of religious communications systems and networks created by evangelicals in the mid-eighteenth century that has led historians to challenge the novelty

---

26. Quentin J. Schultze, "The Wireless Gospel," *Christianity Today*, 15 January 1988, 18-23, esp. 23.

27. Jon Butler's scholarship, which has been criticized for loving to overturn shrines, is refreshing and rejuvenating to the field of American religion precisely for that reason. See his "Enthusiasm Described and Decried: The Great Awakening as Interpretative Fiction," *Journal of American History* 69 (1982): 305-25. His larger study is *Awash in a Sea of Faith: Christianizing the American People* (Cambridge, MA: Harvard University Press, 1990).

28. Joseph Conforti, "The Invention of the Great Awakening, 1795-1842," *Early American Literature* 26 (1991): 99-118.

29. Marilyn J. Westerkamp, *Triumph of the Laity: Scots-Irish Piety and the Great Awakening, 1625-1760* (New York: Oxford University Press, 1988).

of nineteenth-century revivals ("the eighteenth-century revivals should take their place on a continuum of Protestant evangelical development, with its starting point in the seventeenth century"), to ponder the "American-ness" of the First Great Awakening, and to argue for an international context for studying revivals in addition to the more fashionable local community studies to understand what is at base a transatlantic phenomenon.[30]

Hambrick-Stowe traces the tensions and twists in the communication story by focusing on the role played in the Awakening by America's first religious periodical, the weekly *Christian History.* New Light revivalists, who were known for their spontaneous, oral modes of address, adopted a "print-oriented" strategy to spread the revival. What is more, Hambrick-Stowe finds that these innovative technologies of print media were used to reclaim, republish, and reactivate some of the old devotional classics and old-fashioned themes and practices he earlier studied so carefully in *The Practice of Piety.*[31] New Light technological pioneers proved to be keepers of an ancient flame. This ancient-future phenomenon — of futurist technology combined with ancient literature, of new ways wedded to old works and old reading habits — happens so often in this history of media that it is almost as if tremendous change necessitates the harnessing of the new to the old.

Virtually every study of colonial communications reinforces the continuing need to study the North Atlantic framework to social-religious history.[32] Until the 1740s, information sources solidified transatlantic community sensibilities — with administrative control in London. Two scholars in particular, David Cressy and Ian K. Steele, have convinced

---

30. Susan [née Durden] O'Brien has generated a series of stunning essays on the communications networks of the First Awakening. See her "A Transatlantic Community of Saints: The Great Awakening and the First Evangelical Network, 1735-1755," *American Historical Review* 91 (1986): 811-32, the quote is from p. 815; Durden, "A Study of the First Evangelical Magazines, 1740-1748," *Journal of Ecclesiastical History* 27 (July 1976): 255-75. See also her dissertation, "Transatlantic Communications and Influence During the Great Awakening: A Comparative Study of British and American Revivalism" (Ph.D. diss., University of Hull, 1978).

31. Charles E. Hambrick-Stowe, *The Practice of Piety: Puritan Devotional Disciplines in Seventeenth-Century New England* (Chapel Hill: University of North Carolina Press, 1982).

32. This is accented as well in Mark Noll's review essay, "Evaluating North Atlantic Religious History, 1640-1859," *Comparative Studies in Society and History* 33 (April 1991): 415-25.

historians that communications systems in colonial culture were trans-atlantic phenomena.[33] The American book trade was part and parcel of the English provincial trade.[34] By the 1750s, colonists had begun to read of their common interests through colonial newspapers and broadsheets, until in 1776 print was decisive in appealing to popular sentiment among widely disparate congregations and communities.

There is still little agreement as to when reading became a mass phenomenon. Some historians, such as Michael Schudson, push the date for the rise of print culture to way after 1830.[35] The majority have focused on the years between 1780 and 1830, during which the American Revolution played a prominent role in the emergence of a mass reading public and a new style of reading was introduced.[36] The distinction between "intensive" and "extensive" reading experiences, which David Hall likes so much but which Ronald Zboray has challenged, draws a critical distinction between "necessary" legal and religious texts, such as psalm books, hymnals, sermons, and other moral works with an assured market ("intensive"), and a literature of choice (that included secular music) and style of reading ("extensive") that emerged during this period.[37] Other historians have argued that book culture was a smaller and more select social phenomenon than print culture, and that it needs to be analyzed accordingly with geographic specificity and a lookout for where those "centers of print culture" might be.[38]

33. David Cressy, *Coming Over: Migration and Communication Between England and New England in the Seventeenth Century* (New York: Cambridge University Press, 1987), and Ian K. Steele, *The English Atlantic, 1675-1740: An Exploration of Communication and Community* (New York: Oxford University Press, 1986).

34. See Stephen Botein, "The Anglo-American Book Trade before 1776: Personnel and Strategies," in *Printing and Society in Early America*, ed. Joyce et al., 48-82.

35. Michael Schudson, *Discovering the News: A Social History of American Newspapers* (New York: Basic Books, 1978).

36. Gordon S. Wood, "The Democratization of Mind in the American Revolution," in *The Moral Foundations of the American Republic*, ed. Robert Horwitz (Charlottesville: University of Virginia Press, 1977), 102-28; see also David D. Hall, "The Uses of Literacy in New England, 1600-1850," in *Printing and Society in Early America*, ed. Joyce et al., 1-47.

37. See Ronald J. Zboray, "Antebellum Reading and the Ironies of Technological Innovation," in *Reading in America*, ed. Davidson, 180-200. For the separate development of sacred and secular music, see Richard Crawford and D. W. Krummel, "Early American Music Printing and Publishing," in *Printing and Society in Early America*, ed. Joyce et al., 186-227.

38. Joseph F. Kett and Patricia A. McClung found "striking differences in book

Two historians' names in particular are associated with thickening our paper-thin knowledge of popular colonial religious communication through studies that consistently demonstrate high standards of originality, depth, and rigor: Harry S. Stout and David D. Hall. Schooled in the literature of the steeple and streets (including broadsides and ballads), both have advanced our understanding of how elites lost control over information through democratizing communication networks and wider accessibility to information.[39] Stout, illuminating and compelling in whatever he touches, has already demonstrated that the democratic structures of thought and action forged by republican revolutionaries proved to be powderkegs of protest against the status quo, and that they are inexplicable outside the context of evangelical sermons and communications.[40]

In his contribution to this collection, "Religion, Communications, and the Career of George Whitefield," Stout builds on his biography of

ownership between urban and rural areas," differences that were not attributable to differences in wealth. Specifically, "our evidence indicates that, while rural residents were as likely as inhabitants of cities to own books, they were much less likely to own substantial numbers of books." See their important article on the emergence in the late 1700s and early 1800s of a thriving "town literary culture" that transcended geographical boundaries, "Book Culture in Post-Revolutionary Virginia," *Proceedings of the American Antiquarian Society* 94 (1984): 97-147.

39. See the following works by Hall: *The Faithful Shepherd: A History of the New England Ministry in the Seventeenth Century* (Chapel Hill: University of North Carolina Press, 1972); "The World of Print and Collective Mentality in Seventeenth-Century New England," in *New Directions in American Intellectual History,* ed. John Higham and Paul K. Conkin (Baltimore: Johns Hopkins University Press, 1979), 166-80; "The Uses of Literacy in New England, 1600-1850"; "Toward a History of Popular Religion in Early New England," *William and Mary Quarterly* 3d ser., 41 (1984): 48-55; *Worlds of Wonder, Days of Judgment;* and "The Politics of Writing and Reading in Eighteenth-Century America," in *Publishing and Readership in Revolutionary France and America: A Symposium at the Library of Congress, Sponsored by the Center for the Book and the European Division,* ed. Carol Armbruster (Westport, CT: Greenwood Press, 1993), 151-66.

40. Harry S. Stout, "Religion, Communication, and the Ideological Origins of the American Revolution," *William and Mary Quarterly* 3d ser., 34 (1977): 519-41; Stout, "Word and Order in Colonial New England," in *The Bible in America: Essays in Cultural History,* ed. Nathan O. Hatch and Mark A. Noll (New York: Oxford University Press, 1982), 19-38; and Stout, *The New England Soul: Preaching and Religious Culture in Colonial New England* (New York: Oxford University Press, 1986). See also Rhys Isaac's essay on evangelicals' mastery of popular communication styles, "Preachers and Patriots: Popular Culture and the Revolution in Virginia," in *The American Revolution: Explorations in the History of American Radicalism,* ed. Alfred F. Young (DeKalb: Northern Illinois University Press, 1976), 125-56; also Isaac, *The Transformation of Virginia, 1740-1790* (Chapel Hill: University of North Carolina Press, 1982).

George Whitefield, the best we have to date, to help illumine further what it means when historians call Whitefield a "mass revivalist."[41] Whitefield used the popular press, mounted outdoor pulpits, mastered "mass marketing" techniques (that he borrowed from transatlantic merchants), and spoke in the vernacular of the common people. Whitefield's use of journalism and periodical publications, one historian argues, has earned the First Great Awakening the distinction of "launching a new literary genre." As part of the developing revival techniques, "the evangelical newspaper and magazine" was launched, literature that ironically, by the beginning of the nineteenth century, had been co-opted by denomination systems into official propaganda.[42] Whitefield even plundered the theater for ideas and inspiration throughout his thirty-three-year ministry. The growing Anglo-American market economy, which was already uniting the colonies, virtually commodified Whitefield until he became an "American icon — the first intercolonial hero," Stout argues, the precursor of modern-day evangelists.

Frank Lambert's historiographic refurbishment of Whitefield stresses his use of new commercial techniques as well as communications ones. It was Whitefield's employment of print, Lambert argues, especially his "print and preach" exploitation of the press using newspapers and other paperback items, that separated him from his predecessors and created the intercolonial Great Awakening. Whitefield's use of print created a new religious public sphere that was intercolonial. What had been "private and local" became with Whitefield "public and national."

Not afraid to abandon theological discourse for vernacular ad hominems and promotional language, Whitefield designed a "publicity campaign unprecedented in revivalism" and used "the printed word to prepare men and women to receive the spoken word."[43] Both Stout and Lambert stress Whitefield as a child of the Enlightenment who staked his revivalism on rational biblical interpretation. This was one reason why the charge of "enthusiasm" was so biting to him and to other revivalists — the accusation that they had abandoned reason struck at the heart of how they saw themselves. In the dispute over revivalism, "writers on both sides learned

41. Harry S. Stout, *The Divine Dramatist: George Whitefield and the Rise of Modern Evangelicalism* (Grand Rapids: Eerdmans, 1991).

42. See Durden [O'Brien], "A Study of the First Evangelical Magazines."

43. Frank Lambert, "The Great Awakening as Artifact: George Whitefield and the Construction of Intercolonial Revival, 1739-1745," *Church History* 60 (June 1991): 223-46, esp. 234; Lambert, " 'Peddlar in Divinity': George Whitefield and the Great Awakening, 1737-1745," *Journal of American History* 77 (1990): 812-37.

that the reading public demanded reasoned argumentation supported by evidence."[44] In "one of the greatest ironies of the Great Awakening," Lambert notes, a Calvinist was the one to embrace mass marketing and other innovative technologies in reaching the masses for Christ.

American culture as a system of communication is a huge topic on which much more can and must be said. But we will never again look at the topic with the same eyes thanks to Richard D. Brown's historico-cultural analysis, which has done so much to re-angle and jangle our awareness of the history of information flow from 1700 to 1865. The spread of mass communication and the decentralized patterns of information transmission both reflected and shaped the democratization and pluralization of American culture. Brown shows how a "common, coherent Christian culture" was possible in colonial society — only because "scarcity had all but required conformity of perceptions since nearly everyone shared access to the same information and to the same interpretive commentaries on it."[45] With "abundance" came a competitive market-oriented system and a choice culture, as a host of democratizing forces set about eroding the hierarchic control and role of the favored few. A print culture defused the power of traditional forms of face-to-face information transmission, influence, and communal cohesion.

Brown has his dissenters. Larzer Ziff's *Writing in the New Nation* (1991) focuses on literary culture from the mid-eighteenth to mid-nineteenth centuries, especially the relationship of literature to political theory and to conceptions of the self. David Brainerd and Jonathan Edwards figure prominently in Ziff's revisionist story of an almost criminal force lurking in American history — writing and print. Print culture set loose conservative social forces, he argues, that structured tight mechanisms of social control in American culture.[46]

Brown's study rightfully raises both cheers and hackles. His inattentiveness to religion in American life, especially the role of revivals in "modernizing" the rural South in particular and communications in the countryside in general, is particularly unfortunate.[47] As William J. Gil-

44. Lambert, "The Great Awakening as Artifact," 243.

45. Richard D. Brown, *Knowledge Is Power: The Diffusion of Information in Early America, 1700-1865* (New York: Oxford University Press, 1989), 294.

46. Larzer Ziff, *Writing in the New Nation: Prose, Print, and Politics in the Early United States* (New Haven: Yale University Press, 1991).

47. See John L. Brooke, "Talking and Reading in Early America," *Reviews in American History* 19 (1991): 31-36.

more has pointed out, "families and individuals participating actively in print culture and yet remaining chiefly interested in religious and other traditional forms of reading fare are missing from this analysis."[48] In fact, much of the "diffusion of information" reflected the ways in which religion itself was becoming more diffuse (individualistic and pluralistic). The church and clergy command of communications, which Brown himself has done so much to help us understand, had been supplemented by a variety of religious authorities and expressions (revivals, camp meetings, voluntary societies, and the like).[49] But the variety of information to which people could turn was still under religious control.

Brown has started any number of historiographical hares without running any to the ground: print reinforced social distinctions based on class and occupation; it led to specialization in the acquisition of information; it created two unique information marketplaces — one based on vocational need and the other based on recreation and leisure. Most importantly for our purposes, the ways in which "equal access" may itself be more a mirage than a reality, and the manner in which information was then (and is now) molded and shaped for public consumption, needs further exploration. Brown's argument that technology was less an agent of change than long-term social, ideological, and economic factors, especially the inexorable "secularization" process, remains the least satisfactory part of his thesis.

### Evangelical Mastery of Media

Where Brown is more likely to talk about the role print played in individuals' transition from a Christian culture to a market and pluralistic one, Mark Noll, Nathan Hatch, and others are more prone to discuss how print and reading have contributed to the making of America's religions. Mark Noll's essay in this volume, "The Evangelical Enlightenment and the Task of Theological Education," is important because it extends Brown's approach to evangelical culture. Perhaps there is no area of scholarship that makes the historian feel like a slow learner more than this one: the complex

48. William J. Gilmore, review of *Knowledge Is Power* by R. D. Brown, *Journal of the Early Republic* 10 (1990): 414.

49. For the movement of clergy from the hub of a community's information network to denominational oracles, see Richard D. Brown, "Spreading the Word: Rural Clergymen and the Communication Network of 18th-Century New England," *Proceedings of the Massachusetts Historical Society* 94 (1982): 1-14.

and confounding *nature* ("the most complex word in the language") of the interaction and *alienation* ("one of the most difficult words in the language") between faith and *culture* ("one of the two or three most complicated words in the English language").[50]

Exploring the evangelical Protestant mesh of tradition, transformation, and transcendence in the Christianization of American culture, Noll presents what amounts to an evangelical sixth alternative to H. Richard Niebuhr's five-fold typology of *Christ and Culture* (1951).[51] The absence in the evangelical tradition of a strong theology of culture, along with the presence in the evangelical tradition of what Clifford Christians calls a "culture mandate" to "convert cultural forms, not to eliminate them," both juxtaposed to a misguided evangelical philosophy of technology that presumes neutrality rather than moral embeddedness, has meant that evangelicals have been especially vulnerable to an encultural mythos.[52] In the case of the evangelical tradition, Noll sets forth what I am calling an in-cultural (or in Jesus' terms an "in-but-not-of-but-not-out-of-it-either," cf. John 17:11-16) mechanism of conceptual apparatus and mode of cultural interaction that contrasts with anticultural, countercultural, or encultural modes of engagement.

Evangelicals aspired to be true to their time. They were suspicious of the countercultural mode, which is temperamentally allergic to cultural institutions and in which any cultural involvement requires ceaseless scrutiny and ruthless theological hygiene. They eschewed the encultural mode (a la Dean Inge's dictum, "If you marry the spirit of the age you'll soon find yourself a widower"), and they denounced a church of golden retrievers where, when culture says fetch, it jumps in whatever direction culture has thrown the stick. They denounced the anticultural mode as unevangelistic and unbiblical.

Instead, they thought they could live with the times while living in the timeless — that is, in-culturate the gospel. In opening the tradition to transformation, however, evangelicals forgot the component of transcendence, the element of judgment that reads culture in terms of the gospel

---

50. Raymond Williams, *Keywords: A Vocabulary of Culture and Society* (New York: Oxford University Press, 1976), 184, 29, 76 respectively.

51. For a further attempt at exploring this sixth alternative, see Leonard I. Sweet, *Quantum Spirituality: A Postmodern Apologetic* (Dayton: Whaleprints, 1991).

52. Clifford G. Christians, "Redemptive Media as the Evangelical's Cultural Task," in *American Evangelicals and the Mass Media*, ed. Schultze, 331-56. Quentin J. Schultze, "The Mythos of the Electronic Church," *Critical Studies in Mass Communications* 4 (September 1987): 245-61.

and submits culture to the gospel. As Noll puts it, their in-the-flesh witness ended not in "incarnation" but in "enculturation." Evangelical trade-ins were not necessarily upgrades.

The function of history is to help us not to be ourselves. The historical perspective provides the only transcendent plane that can yoke distance to intimacy in order to yield the Shakespearean splendor of timelessness: "He was not of an age, but for all time." Evangelicals had become so intimate with the interpretive and media systems of one era that they could not achieve critical distance from those same systems. Evangelicals were in love, and as Roland Barthes once said, to be in love is to be "in the brazier of meaning."

Strapped in that "brazier of meaning," the timely never got lifted to the plane of the timeless. Evangelicals failed to exercise critical judgments of historical transcendence that might have enabled them to adjust to changing media forms and interpretive intellectual systems. For Noll, the connection between criticism and creativity seems almost constitutive. Or to put the story Noll tells more severely, once again in American history nothing fails like success. The loss of evangelical hegemony after the Civil War is a plotline that continues to unfold.[53]

For Noll, "mastery" is the right word for what evangelicals did to both the dominant communications systems and what he calls "interpretive systems" of the day. Indeed, more and more secularization theory hits the historian as sheer wind, at least when applied to patterns of life in the United States, where Christianization, not secularization, is the dominant religious fact of life.[54] The mastered interpretive system was "theistic Enlightenment science," and antebellum evangelical Protestantism became adept at using the argot of this, the nation's most powerful and prevailing interpretive system. In Noll's words: "Evangelical control of media provided the means, evangelical control of interpretation provided the rationale, evangelical energy drove both media and interpretation." In some of evangelicalism's most unlikely areas to house Enlightenment sensibilities — revivalism and Scripture — evangelicals appropriated the Christian tradition to modern categories and created the "Evangelical Enlightenment." The result was a "momentous creation": "Side by side with the

53. It is exceedingly well told in Mark Noll, *A History of American Christianity in the United States and Canada* (Grand Rapids: Eerdmans, 1992).

54. So argue Roger Finke and Rodney Stark in their "rational choice" history of *The Churching of America, 1776-1990.* There is no book that better demonstrates the differences between tradition-driven and market-driven religion in America.

evangelical media, the two bestrode American civilization for its first seventy-five years."

How did evangelical Protestantism come to "master" the media and meanings of American antebellum culture? Many of the essays in this collection strive to answer that question. But a key to every strategy was the evangelical in-cultural model of inventing parallel versions and alternative structures to virtually every social activity, organization, and product available. This "in-but-not-of-but-not-out-of-it" strategy of culture sacralization has yielded both the high kitsch and "Holy Gosh" of "Jesus Junque" so abundant in today's "Christian bookstores" and the plethora of voluntary societies and social movements that did so much to shape America's broad-based culture and commerce.

*Mastery #1* One way was through a new means of getting information to the people, specifically through circuit riders, all of whom were more than itinerant preachers. Circuit riders were also booksellers and colporteurs, the major propagandists of a new mass culture of reading and writing who carried in their saddlebags or locked pouches all manner of books, pamphlets, newspapers, and letters.[55] Book agents or "correspondents" followed in the wake of the circuit riders, until by 1859 three million families had been visited by some eight million volumes through these book distributors alone.[56] Evangelicals believed that "the proper deployment of an army of well-selected books would prove of major consequence in the battle for the minds and hearts of ordinary Americans."[57]

Circuit riders were simultaneously promoters of print culture and leaders of the oral epic tradition.[58] These traveling preachers were "margin-

55. See, as an example of a vast secondary literature, Betty I. Young, "A Missionary/Preacher as America Moved West: The Ministry of John Wesley Osborne," *Methodist History* 24 (July 1986): 195-215.

56. See Madeleine B. Stern, "Dissemination of Popular Books in the Midwest and Far West During the Nineteenth Century," in *Getting the Books Out: Papers of the Chicago Conference on the Book in 19th-Century America,* ed. Michael Hackenberg (Washington: Library of Congress, 1987), 76-97, esp. 77. See also Richardson Wright, *Hawkers and Walkers in Early America* (Philadelphia: Lippincott, 1927), and L. Wesley Norton, "Religious Newspapers on the American Frontier," *Journal of the West* 19 (April 1980): 16-21.

57. Michael H. Harris, "'Spiritual Cakes Upon the Waters': The Church as a Disseminator of the Printed Word on the Ohio Valley Frontier to 1850," in *Getting the Books Out,* ed. Hackenberg, 98.

58. See Julia Dagenais, "Frontier Preaching as Formulaic Poetry," *Mid-America Folklore* 19 (Fall 1991): 118-26.

ally literate," they preached extemporaneously, and they were experts in establishing an almost mystical rapport with listeners. They also pioneered the use of images conjoined to speech sounds. Some preachers "actually employed small boys as spies, paying them as much as a dime for catching a more successful colleague speaking from notes."[59] Bruce Rosenberg shows how contemporary African-American preachers have retained this earlier tradition of formulaic poetry using metrical and syntactical patterns.[60]

But circuit riders are good examples of the way silent, solitary reading was taking its place alongside earlier patterns of communal, oral reading. Peter Cartwright, perhaps the most famous circuit rider of them all and certainly never associated with habits of daily reading, wondered aloud whether more good had been done in his life by his legendary preaching or by his "sacred duty" of distributing religious literature.[61]

There is much more we need to know, especially if we are to escape the fundamental methodological mistake Jonathan Rose calls the "receptive fallacy" — assuming the reader takes from the text what the author or critic puts into it.[62] What about public reading? Where was it encouraged and for what reasons? How are people trained to read? How important has been the church's role in this? Were there other ways in which reading skills were maintained and honed apart from almanacs, weekly newspapers, hymnals, religious tracts, and after 1815, books and home libraries? What was the "social authority of learning"?[63] Ronald J. Zboray's work marks a significant advance in understanding many of these underlying issues.[64]

Noll wonders whether the triumph of evangelical Protestantism in

---

59. Dagenais, "Frontier Preaching as Formulaic Poetry," 119.

60. Bruce A. Rosenberg, *Can These Bones Live? The Art of the American Folk Preacher* (Urbana: University of Illinois Press, 1988).

61. Peter Cartwright, *Autobiography* (Nashville: Abingdon Press, 1956), 187.

62. Jonathan Rose, "Rereading the English Common Reader: A Preface to a History of Audiences," *Journal of the History of Ideas* 53 (1992): 47-70, esp. 49.

63. See Rhys Isaac's look at Devereux Jarratt's history of literacy in "Books and the Social Authority of Learning," in *Printing and Society in Early America*, ed. Joyce et al., 228-49.

64. See Ronald J. Zboray, "Antebellum Book Distribution and the Transportation Revolution Reconsidered," *American Quarterly* 38 (1986): 53-71; Zboray, "Antebellum Reading and the Ironies of Technological Innovation," *American Quarterly* 40 (1988): 68-74; Zboray, "Book Distribution and American Culture: A 150-Year Perspective," *Book Research Quarterly* 3 (1988): 37-59.

American culture could have been possible without this dual mastery of systems — communication and interpretation — and suggests that the interplay of orality and literacy in the history of Methodism may have the clues to unlocking this puzzle. A. Gregory Schneider's essay in this volume, "From Democratization to Domestication: The Transitional Orality of the American Methodist Circuit Rider," and Glenn T. Miller's contribution, "God, Rhetoric, and Logic in Antebellum American Theological Education," take up the challenge. Both demonstrate why Noll's pondering is a point of some importance, because Methodist preaching appears to work the opposite way to media mastery.

Contrary to stereotype, this new form of "sacred rhetoric" (Miller's phrase) called the "extemporaneous sermon" required extensive preparation and skill. Indeed, the phrase "off the cuff" referred to the way early masters of this form of oratory cribbed notes to themselves on their cuffs and used their sleeves as lecterns. The impact of this new homiletic, which required intimacy with the audience and strong narrative skills, was revolutionary: the "democratization of American Christianity" Nathan Hatch calls it.[65] It also helped shove aside the traditional sermon as the primary form of public discourse.

In one of the many ironies to appear in this collection, the early seminaries resisted this media form and bet their futures on the Puritan tradition of the scholarly pastor. It was not until after the Civil War, when evangelicals began losing ground to a new science and theology that required an embrace of the historical-critical method, that the seminaries' offer of a "new professional tradition" came into its own.[66] Miller is especially sensitive to the ways in which orality and textuality do not exist in simple binary opposition. Rather, they have a complex, sometimes complementary, at other times contradictory relationship.

Schneider confirms Miller's observations and extends them to encompass the uncertain relationship between oral and written communication. He demonstrates from the communications side that the Methodist mastery of the oral medium in preaching was not a dragging of the feet and a digging of the heels in the old order but a "transitional

65. See David S. Reynolds, "From Doctrine to Narrative: The Rise of Pulpit Storytelling in America," *American Quarterly* 32 (1980): 479-98; see also Nathan O. Hatch, *The Democratization of American Christianity* (New Haven: Yale University Press, 1989).

66. See Glenn T. Miller's history of the origins of theological education entitled *Piety and Intellect: The Aims and Purposes of Ante-Bellum Theological Education* (Atlanta: Scholar's Press, 1990).

orality" that lubricated the masses' slide into textuality. Where Hatch has found a buttressing of the word through "bundles of books and pamphlets," Schneider argues provocatively that oral modes of communication could undergird print modes of knowledge and "make textual consciousness the property of ordinary people rather than the preserve of elites." Listener-friendly could also be reader-friendly.

Rhys Isaac's stress on the ability of evangelicals to communicate with an orally biased populace while being adept at print culture, that is, to bridge both worlds, is underscored by Schneider.[67] Both Isaac's and Schneider's complex arguments on the textual base of Methodism and the circuit rider's promotion of "textual modes of consciousness" require careful reading. Circuit riders and class meetings pioneered forms of oral and aural rituals that undermined the old order of deference and hierarchy and modeled a new world of egalitarian individualism and market economies. Perhaps it was not accidental that Ivy Lee, the first public relations agent, was the son of a Methodist minister. When Methodism transformed itself into an "established" church after the Civil War and its decline as a social force began, it still continued to mix oral and print cultures. The Chautauqua movement, where oral readings and reviews were combined with America's first book-of-the-month club, virtually became a communications system itself, and needs to be studied as such.

The oral rituals fostered by the Methodists helped the common people contend with the enormous transformations in understandings of selfhood and identity that marked the period between the Revolution and the Civil War. There was a new conception of the self brought on by urbanization, market relations, and new technologies. With the loss of social group support systems, the maintenance of self became a lifetime preoccupation — hence the "therapeutic ethos" (Jackson Lears) where life became a relentless round of self-improvement and self-expression exercises.[68] Methodist preaching captured the imagination of ordinary people and helped them understand their daily, practical, transitional selves in transcendent terms.

*Mastery #2* Here Schneider enters a second world that the evangelicals were able to master: the home. As the self became more inward and less

67. See Isaac, *The Transformation of Virginia*, 122-29, 253-64.
68. See *The Culture of Consumption: Critical Essays in American History, 1800-1980*, ed. Richard Wrightman Fox and T. J. Jackson Lears (New York: Pantheon, 1983), 17-21.

communal, the self became an affair more of the heart and home than of the church. Schneider joins Colleen McDannell in emphasizing the way in which the home came to eclipse the church as the shrine of the spirit.[69] Evangelical Protestants, led in significant measure by women, shaped a domestic faith that made the home a medium of salvation and sanctification.[70] The history of the home, not too long ago consigned to the sidelines of cultural and intellectual history, is now center stage.

*Mastery #3* A third mastery that evangelicals accomplished was the Christianization of print and other forms of mass media. Roger Chartier has pointed out that the real Gutenberg revolution was not the printed book but the evolution over time from an oral or quasi-oral tradition of reading to a silent, visual, and personal relationship with a text that was possible with print. When did access to information and knowledge come to be seen as a basic democratic right? When did the psychological relation between readers and text become indissoluble, and what role did religion have in fashioning and in being fashioned by this linkage?

Two scholars have helped us the most: Nathan O. Hatch and David Paul Nord. Few historians have been so critically acclaimed as Hatch. It is not difficult to see why. His eye-opening, prize-winning *The Democratization of American Christianity* (1989) — "the most important study of [the so-called Second Great Awakening] ever published" (Turner); "one of the finest books on American religious history to appear" (Moorhead) — is so artful and fluent that it is tempting to make a discussion of Hatch into a bouquet of quotations.[71] Hatch thinks narrow and deep, and like a well, echoes widely.

The rise of a democratic religious print culture during the Second Great Awakening is at the heart of the Hatch thesis about America's distinctive pluralist and populist brand of Christianity. Hatch politely and carefully questions the theoretical strategies historians have used to uncover

69. Colleen McDannell, *The Christian Home in Victorian America, 1840-1900* (Bloomington: Indiana University Press, 1986).

70. See Leonard I. Sweet, *The Minister's Wife: Her Role in Nineteenth-Century American Evangelicalism* (Philadelphia: Temple University Press, 1983).

71. Hatch, *The Democratization of American Christianity*. For the quotes see the reviews by James Turner, *Journal of Interdisciplinary History* 22 (Autumn 1991): 352, and by James H. Moorhead, *Theology Today* 47 (1990-91): 90. Of the numerous other reviews of this book, one of the most memorable is Stephen J. Stein, "Radical Protestantism and Religious Populism," *American Quarterly* 44 (1992): 262-70.

evangelical history, while at the same time he sees evangelicalism, not as a countermodernization movement, or as Grant Wacker puts it, "not as a negative reaction to, but as an integral part of, the modernization process."[72] What Hatch has shown for the nineteenth century, and George Marsden and Joel Carpenter have shown for the twentieth, is that this is nowhere more apparent than in evangelicals' skillful and trendsetting use of the arts of communications.

What explains success in America's religious marketplace? Hatch says it is the ability of religious groups to adopt and adapt to the democratic and populist impulses of American culture, and to use popular forms of communication to reach the widest possible audience. The antebellum period stands out for the parallel rise of the popular press (newspaper and periodical publication targeted for American middle-class audiences in cities and towns) and fiction reading. In the early 1820s there were less than one hundred magazines. By 1850, that number had swelled to well over six hundred. The popular press cannot be understood, Hatch has argued well, without proper attention to its forerunner, the religious press, which had more influence on the shape of culture and religion in America than in Great Britain.

Religious journalism has been grievously understudied, with significant exceptions in Protestant sources and numerous studies on Catholic journalism, most of which are detailed in O'Brien's bibliography. Before Hatch, there were some signs of intelligent life in this field of study, but not too many.[73] Denominational periodical literature has been studied but has been insufficiently consulted by historians. The widest and wisest scholarship has been lavished on Methodism (thanks to John Wesley, one of the most "bookish" of all religions in America) and its official publishing house, and on Presbyterianism (especially on the West Coast) and its official publishing house, although some work has been done on the Lutherans, Baptists, Christian Church, and Mormons (who claim the "first successful religious

---

72. Grant Wacker, "Uneasy in Zion: Evangelicals in Postmodern Society," in *Evangelicalism and Modern America,* ed. George Marsden (Grand Rapids: Eerdmans, 1984), 20. See also Martin E. Marty, "The Revival of Evangelicalism and Southern Religion," in *Varieties of Southern Evangelicalism,* ed. David Harrell, Jr. (Macon: Mercer University Press, 1981), 7-21.

73. See Joan Jacobs Brumberg, "Does the Bibliomania Rage at Tavoy?" in her *Mission for Life* (New York: Free Press, 1980), 44-78, and John C. Nerone's important dissertation, "The Press and Popular Culture in the Early Republic: Cincinnati, 1793-1843" (Ph.D. diss., University of Notre Dame, 1982).

daily newspaper in the English language").[74] Roman Catholics displayed what one scholar calls a "profound ambivalence" toward popular mass media. The relationship of Catholic culture and media culture has been best explored by Robert White.[75] The African-American press — its periodicals and its books — as well as African-American readers themselves, are only beginning to be studied.[76] A marvelous example of denominational press literature bringing out the thews and sinews of cultural analysis is Sister Mary

74. John H. Ness, *One Hundred Fifty Years: A History of the Publishing in the Evangelical United Brethren Church* (Dayton: Board of Publication of the Evangelical United Brethren Church, 1966); Elmer J. O'Brien, "The *Methodist Quarterly Review:* Reflections on a Methodist Periodical," *Methodist History* 25 (1987): 76-90; Leland D. Case, "Origins of Methodist Publishing in America," *Papers of the Bibliographical Society of America* 59 (1965): 12-27; James Penn Pilkington, *The Methodist Publishing House: A History, Volume 1, Beginning to 1870* (Nashville: Abingdon Press, 1968); Walter N. Vernon, *The United Methodist Publishing House: A History, Volume 2, 1870-1988* (Nashville: Abingdon Press, 1989); Willard G. Roberts, "The Methodist Book Concern in the West, 1800-1870" (Ph.D. diss., University of Chicago, 1947). For Presbyterians see Willard M. Rice, *History of the Presbyterian Board of Publication and Sabbath School Work* (Philadelphia: Presbyterian Board of Publication and Sabbath School Work, 1889); Clifford M. Drury, "Presbyterian Journalism on the Pacific Coast," *Pacific Historical Review* 9 (1940): 461-69; and Jane Moyer, "The Making of Many Books: 125 Years of Presbyterian Publishing, 1838-1963," *Journal of Presbyterian History* 41 (1963): 124-40. For Lutherans see Daniel Nystrom, *A Ministry of Printing: History of the Publication House of Augustana Lutheran Church, 1889-1962* (Rock Island, IL: Augustana Press, 1962); Ernst W. Olson, *The Augustana Book Concern: A History of the Synodical Publishing House with Introductory Account of Earlier Publishing Enterprises* (Rock Island, IL: Augustana Book Concern, 1934); Vishwa M. Mishra, "The *Lutheran Standard:* 125 Years of Denominational Journalism," *Journalism Quarterly* 45 (1968): 71-76. For Baptists see Daniel Gurden Stevens and E. M. Stephenson, *The First Hundred Years of the American Baptist Publication Society* (Philadelphia: American Baptist Publication Society, 1924). For the Christian Church see *The Centennial of Religious Journalism,* ed. John P. Barrett (Dayton: Christian Publishing Association, 1908). For Mormons see Monte B. McLaws, *Spokesman for the Kingdom: Early Mormon Journalism and the "Desert News," 1830-1898* (Provo, UT: Brigham Young University Press, 1977).

75. Jerome Breunig, "Present Position of the Catholic Press," *America,* 19 February 1955, 532-35. For a historical overview see Appolinaris W. Baumgartner, *Catholic Journalism: A Study of Its Development in the United States, 1789-1930* (New York: Columbia University Press, 1931). Robert A. White, "Mass Media and Culture in Contemporary Catholicism," in *Vatican II: Assessment and Perspectives: Twenty-Five Years After (1962-1987),* ed. René Latourelle (New York: Paulist Press, 1989), 3:580-616.

76. Penelope L. Bullock, *The Afro-American Periodical Press, 1838-1909* (Baton Rouge: Louisiana State University Press, 1981). Donald Franklin Joyce, *Gatekeepers of Black Culture: Black-Owned Book Publishing in the United States, 1817-1981* (Westport, CT: Greenwood Press, 1983). For a rare look at black reading audiences, see Marva Banks, "*Uncle Tom's Cabin* and Antebellum Black Response," in *Readers in History,* ed. J. L. Machor, 209-27.

Patrice Thaman's survey of the religious press's reaction to the "manners and morals of the 1920's."[77]

If historians are to squeeze fresh juice from studies of the religious press, the cultural importance of editors — the ones most studied include William Lloyd Garrison and Elijah P. Lovejoy — needs immediate attention.[78] What is now available is noteworthy for its mere existence: a study of William G. Brownlow, editor of *Jonesboro (Tennessee) Whig and Independent Journal* (1839-1849); some treatments of James Monroe Buckley, powerful editor of the Methodist *Christian Advocate* for thirty-two years (1880-1912); an assessment of Swedenborg editor James C. Malin; a treatment of the religion journalism of James Gordon Bennett; a study of Eugene C. Routh's editorship of the Southern Baptist *Commission* in the twentieth century; and scattered looks at Charles Clayton Morrison, the influential editor of the *Christian Century.*[79]

Between 1800 and 1830, according to Hatch, religious periodicals had gone from almost nonexistence to "the grand engine of a burgeoning evangelical culture, the primary means of promotion for and bond of union within competing religious groups."[80] This tremendous spread of religious newspapers and tracts was part of the explosion of print consumption after

77. Mary Patrice Thaman, *Manners and Morals of the 1920's* (1954; repr. Westport, CT: Greenwood Press, 1977), completely omits the African-American periodical literature as well as Conservative and Orthodox Judaism and conservative Protestantism.

78. See David Paul Nord's entry on William Lloyd Garrison in *American Newspaper Journalists, 1690-1872,* ed. Perry J. Ashley, Dictionary of Literary Biography, 43 (Detroit: Gale Research, 1985), 232-47; John Gill, *Tide Without Turning: Elijah P. Lovejoy and Freedom of the Press* (Boston: Starr King, 1958).

79. R. Burt Lattimore, "A Survey of William Brownlow's Criticism of the Mormons, 1841-1857," *Tennessee Historical Quarterly* 27 (1968): 249-56. George Preston Mains, *James Monroe Buckley* (New York: Methodist Book Concern, 1917); Saranne Price O'Donnell, "Distress from the Press: Antifeminism as Expressed in the Editorial Opinions of James M. Buckley, Editor of the *Christian Advocate* (New York) 1880-1912," in *Women in New Worlds: Historical Perspectives on the Wesleyan Tradition,* ed. Hilah F. Thomas and Rosemary Skinner Keller (Nashville: Abingdon Press, 1981), 2:76-93. James C. Malin, "William Sutton White, Swedenborgian Publicist," *Kansas Historical Quarterly* 24 (1958): 68-103; 25 (1958): 197-227. Judith M. Buddenbaum, "'Judge . . . What Their Acts Will Justify': The Religion Journalism of James Gordon Bennett," *Journalism History* 14 (1987): 54-68. C. A. Vernon, *A Disciple Approach to the Church: A Critical Examination of the Writings of Charles Clayton Morrison* (B.D. thesis, Butler University, 1958); Linda M. Delloff, "C. C. Morrison: Shaping a Journal's Identity," *Christian Century,* 18 January 1984, 43-47; Harold E. Fey, "Ecumenists of Our Times: Charles Clayton Morrison," *Mid-Stream* 15 (July 1976): 263-69.

80. Nathan O. Hatch, "Elias Smith and the Rise of Religious Journalism in the Early Republic," in *Printing and Society in Early America,* ed. Joyce et al., 250-77.

1790 and the institutionalization of print culture. The printed page, a symbol and symptom of modernization (it would eventually replace the centering symbol of the chalice), created a new "communications environment" that William Gilmore calls the "modernization of knowledge."[81] From here on, one could live in the backwoods but still be part of the cultural mainstream; isolation was not mutually exclusive with association.

Gilmore's inassimilable style, raw accumulation of indigestible data, and bogged-down pages with slagheaps of mind-numbing jargon give his readers a pretty rough workout. But while thin on readerly pleasures, Gilmore offers a thick return on 538 pages of hard reading. Religion, government, and politics were the realms to benefit first from full-scale printing in books and pamphlets in the 1770s. In the 1780s, religion (sermons, autobiographies, theology treatises, devotional writings) constituted twenty-five percent of locally printed imprints. But this figure is deceiving, since the rest virtually were state government publications. Religious themes displayed remarkable consistency into the 1830s as one of the highest-in-demand subjects of print. If anything, religious reading increased market share in the 1820s and 1830s as evangelicals began to apply religion to daily life and the treatment of social problems. In fact, "the most significant development within Upper Valley [Vermont] printing in 1778-1830 was the diffusion of sacred works."[82]

To be sure, a literary explosion doesn't mean that people were reading more; it only means that a greater variety of reading material was available. Did technological change have a different impact on different social groupings? Gilmore's analysis is less differentiated here than that of Zboray, who argues that the early nineteenth century was a revolution for middle-class urban families only. The urban working class could not afford even the new inexpensive literature; and rural dwellers, he insists, were entirely left out of the exploding antebellum literary marketplace.[83] Future research that will referee this fight is needed.[84]

81. William J. Gilmore, *Reading Becomes a Necessity of Life: Material and Cultural Life in Rural New England, 1780-1835* (Knoxville: University of Tennessee Press, 1989), 346.

82. Gilmore, *Reading Becomes a Necessity*, 203.

83. Ronald J. Zboray, "Antebellum Reading and the Ironies of Technological Innovation," in *Reading in America*, ed. Davidson, 180-200; and Zboray, "Reading and the Ironies of Technological Innovation," in Zboray, *A Fictive People: Antebellum Economic Development and American Reading Public* (New York: Oxford University Press, 1992), 3-16.

84. Patricia Anderson's study of popular culture in mid-nineteenth-century Britain, *The Printed Image and the Transformation of Popular Culture, 1790-1860* (New York: Clarendon Press, 1992), argues for the widest spectrum of "mass" circulation.

Prior to the nineteenth century, books preserved beliefs and knowledge rather than disseminating new information or retailing opinion. Knowledge transmission by print rather than by oral means brought with it the privatization and democratization of knowledge. The individual accessed knowledge without need of family or friends or employers, and accessed it at will. Both Hatch and Gilmore have shown that babelian voices and choices made truth more contentious and cloudy. Both Hatch and Gilmore have found an increase in available religious reading matter, both in quantity and in diversity, during the early nineteenth century. But Gilmore, who sees himself as a social historian, does not relate the "democratization of mind" to the Second Great Awakening or revivalism. For the significance of his findings about the essentially religious reading culture of Vermont (rural habitats in particular allegedly had rich reading habits), and on evangelicalism's importance to the growth of print culture, Gilmore's book stammers when it ought to shine. He shows more how reading became a necessity of economic life than how reading became a necessity of religious or cultural life. He shows how extensive reading came in religious and secular form, but not how it helped to shape an evangelical culture.[85] In short, this is a flawed book — but do you know any book that isn't?

Hatch, on the other hand, knows his way around religion as well as around theory. Hatch features the role of ordinary laypeople and religious populists, their spirits resonating with the democratic spirit roaming to rule the early republic, who worked a democratic and demotic and decentralizing revolution on their respective bodies. How did they overcome the religious establishment and vested interests? They learned to address the masses through entrepreneurial ventures and vernacular communications of speech, text, and music.[86]

From 1810-1828 newspaper circulation in America increased twice as rapidly as the population, and religious periodicals kept pace with, if

---

85. Richard Rabinowitz's study *The Spiritual Self in Everyday Life: The Transformation of Personal Religious Experience in Nineteenth-Century New England* (Boston: Northeastern University Press, 1989) is extremely helpful here.

86. It is a major weakness of this essay that it pays no attention to music as a communication form, especially since music's importance is increasing rather than diminishing. But the literature is simply too intimidating for an essay that already has a heavy (top-heavy?) topdressing of bibliographic references. The best introduction to the issues involved is Sandra S. Sizer, *Gospel Hymns and Social Religion: The Rhetoric of Nineteenth-Century Revivalism* (Philadelphia: Temple University Press, 1978).

not exceeded, this advance. . . . If Jacksonian America witnessed the advent of 'an ERA OF PAPER, and the AGE OF PRINT,' as Grenville Nellen suggested to a Harvard audience in 1838, evangelical denominations were its most enthusiastic celebrants. They took a back seat to no one in their commitment to the transforming power of the printed word.[87]

In other words, evangelical propaganda was "audience" or "market driven." Whether this should properly be called "democratization" or "populariza-tion" needs further thought. The more people are told what they want to believe, the more effective the propaganda. What is clear, however, is that mastery of radical new communication forms is what made possible the spread of evangelical Christianity in America; it may still be what makes possible the spread and strength of evangelical Christianity. Indeed, if one wants to understand the amazing strength of evangelical religions and televangelism today, the best place to begin is with Hatch's book.

The key role of the 1780 to 1830 period, according to Hatch, cannot be overestimated. In the early republic a tidal wave of democratic principles and populist sentiments washed away the old hierarchical information flow in American Christianity. It was "a period of religious ferment, chaos, and originality unmatched in American history," and the "populist impulse" was the most dynamic element in American religious life in this period.[88] Religious populism is situated at the heart of the democratizing process. Populism continues to the present in the appeal of H. Ross Perot, and Hatch's jigsawing together of populism's antidemocratic, even demagogic streak into the puzzle of the "democratization" of religious belief and institutions is especially brilliant.[89] One wishes he had done the same for the contradictory tendencies of revivalism to decentralize (witness the fragmentation of American religion, which he emphasizes) and to central-ize (witness the formation and proliferation of voluntary societies).

Hatch sounds the death knell for the social control hypothesis of the Awakening as a means for conservatives to sustain their power, which has exerted such a crooked charm over previous generations of scholars.[90] Ironi-cally, the one area where communications and social control might produc-

87. Hatch, "Elias Smith and the Rise of Religious Journalism," 270.
88. Hatch, *The Democratization of American Christianity,* 64.
89. For Perot see Sean Wilentz, "Pox Populi," *New Republic,* 9 August 1993, 29-34.
90. For a fuller development of this discussion, see Leonard I. Sweet, "The Evan-gelical Tradition in America," in *The Evangelical Tradition in America,* ed. L. I. Sweet (Macon: Mercer University Press, 1984), 1-86.

tively be brought together is the history of slavery, and here the pickings are slim. The best available account depicts a communication system between master and slave that was complex and interactive, with slaves manipulating the judicial and patriarchal metaphors to their own advantage.[91]

Yet another early republic study, this one sprung unmessily from the loins of a prize-winning Yale doctoral thesis, stresses that continuity rather than change was the primary pulse that beat in the heart of Vermonters.[92] Vermonters' evangelical ardor stemmed from more than their desire for democratic order. The disestablishment of Protestantism necessitated other means to safeguard traditional social values — hence revivals and reform movements, which were movements of control for those who were undergoing economic uneasiness and social instability. Like his mentor Paul Johnson before him, Randolph Roth's social history of nine "burned-over" towns in Caledonia and Windsor portrays revival religion and reform movements as an attempt by community elites and the middle class to maintain their influence, which was being eroded by the democratic movements of the day unleashed by the Revolution.[93] His comparison between manufacturing and agricultural communities argues that religious and reform movements made their greatest headway among the middle-class residents of manufacturing towns. Roth's church members appear more socially mobile than non–church members, utilizing church membership for capitalist ventures and participating in revivals for social adhesion and business advantages.

Roth rejects the thesis that republicanism became liberalism in early nineteenth-century America. He argues that the vision of "a Christian reformed republic" stumbled, not because of revivalistic "exclusivity," but because of this "dilemma" whereby evangelicals struggled for tolerant and democratic principles while at the same time they yearned for the

91. Rhys Isaac, "Communication and Control: Authority Metaphors and Power Contests on Colonel Landon Carter's Virginia Plantation, 1752-1778," in *Rites of Power: Symbolism, Ritual, and Politics Since the Middle Ages,* ed. Sean Wilentz (Philadelphia: University of Pennsylvania Press, 1985), 275-301.

92. Randolph A. Roth, *The Democratic Dilemma: Religion, Reform, and the Social Order in the Connecticut River Valley of Vermont, 1791-1850* (Cambridge: Cambridge University Press, 1987).

93. The challenges of pluralism that eastern Vermont faced were confronted a century earlier by the Middle Colonies, according to Richard W. Pointer, *Protestant Pluralism and the New York Experience: A Study of Eighteenth-Century Religious Diversity* (Bloomington: Indiana University Press, 1988), and Randall Balmer, *A Perfect Babel of Confusion: Dutch Religion and English Culture in the Middle Colonies* (New York: Oxford University Press, 1989).

safeguarding of their standing order, their "orderly and pious way of life."[94]
Roth's "dilemma" is this republican thrust for order and the threat to order
posed by democratic individualism. By 1850, valley residents believed they
had created a democratic social order that permitted "discrimination, elite
rule, and collusion" behind the scenes, but that publicly stood proudly as
"the most Christian and democratic society on earth."

The value of Roth's study lies less in the answers to its questions than
in those questions that it stimulates us to ask. By looking at Wales and
Württemberg, Roth provides another valuable transatlantic perspective that
scholarship is fashionably into. His interpretation of the temperance crusade
as a successor to revivals deserves follow-up research, with special sensitivity
to the nap and nuance of temperance literature. Most unfortunately, there is
little recognition in Roth that women played a role in, much less led, the
evangelical movement, and that there can be wide differences between ideal
formulations and more confused realities. Elaborate intellectual edifices can
be constructed on some very narrow and tendentious arguments. Yet the fact
that it is possible to argue with Roth on almost every page is a tribute to the
breadth and depth this dissertation provides.

Aside from Hatch, no one is better able to tell us about the
beginnings of religious mass media in America than David Paul Nord.
Nord's work is now focused on the history of readers and on the question
of whether a text is ever complete, or is instead the history of its readings
and receptions by interpreters, readers, and all manner of adaptors.[95]
Heretofore Nord has specialized in the linkages between religion and
mass communications in American history. He has already shown that
the American heritage of freedom of expression had important religious
roots, that the style of newspaper journalism which emerged in eighteenth-century America, which grew into late nineteenth-century popular
("yellow") journalism, and which dominates today in news reporting
(even beyond tabloid journalism) is inexplicable outside of the institutions of public communication built by seventeenth-century New England Puritans around their doctrine of divine providence.[96]

94. Roth, *The Democratic Dilemma,* 6, 115.

95. See David Paul Nord's "sequel" to his essay in this collection entitled "Religious
Reading and Readers in Antebellum America," unpublished paper presented before the
fifteenth annual meeting of the Society for Historians of the Early American Republic,
July 1993.

96. For the religious roots of freedom of expression, see David Paul Nord, "The
Authority of Truth: Religion and the John Peter Zenger Case," *Journalism Quarterly* 62

*Mastery #4* Nord's greatest influence, however, has been his portrayal of the fourth media mastery: evangelicalism on the cutting edge of industrialism. In some pathbreaking research, he has studied the ways in which evangelical voluntary societies, which after 1815 distributed literature "like snow-flakes over the land,"[97] were pioneers in the use of mass media, as well as many people's first exposure to modern mass media. The vast benevolent empire evangelicals built in the nineteenth century was their fourth mastery of media form.

The early arrival of mass reading audiences in America vis-à-vis Europe and the forming and functioning of a "commercially exploitable reading public" in America are inexplicable outside Nord's work, which has been confirmed by Nathan Hatch, R. Laurence Moore, and Michael H. Harris for America and by Leslie Howsam for Great Britain.[98] Howsam's scholarship shows how the British Foreign Bible Society had a transforming influence on the whole field of book production.

> The BFBS acted in the name of God and mass production to challenge every conventional practice in book-making. It engineered a decisive shift towards the integration of printing and binding, enforced new standards of production, experimented with printing machinery and with new materials for making paper and covers, accelerated the development of typefaces, and placed itself in the forefront of the onslaught on pre-industrial trade practices.[99]

The irony of the fact that the use of sweated female labor in Bible production drove many women into brothels should not escape historians.

In his contribution to this collection entitled "Systematic

---

(Summer 1985): 227-35. For newspaper journalism, see Nord, "Teleology and News: The Religious Roots of American Journalism, 1630-1730," *Journal of American History* 77 (June 1990): 9-38.

97. The evangelical publishing thrust is best discussed in Harris, " 'Spiritual Cakes Upon the Waters,' " 98-129.

98. For America see Nathan O. Hatch, "Elias Smith and the Rise of Religious Journalism"; Moore, "Religion, Secularization, and the Shaping of the Culture Industry" — the phrase "commercially exploitable reading public" is from p. 227; and Harris, " 'Spiritual Cakes Upon the Waters.' " For Great Britain see Leslie Howsam, *Cheap Bibles: Nineteenth-Century Publishing and the British and Foreign Bible Society* (New York: Cambridge University Press, 1991).

99. David Vincent, "Scripture for the Masses" [review of Howsam's *Cheap Bibles*], *TLS: Times Literary Supplement*, 12 June 1992, 26.

Benevolence: Religious Publishing and the Marketplace in Early Nineteenth-Century America," Nord shows how the chaos of change stimulated evangelicals into new ways of thinking and acting that created organizational structures and styles of "systematic management" which pioneered modern business practices. In earlier articles Nord had featured the shaping role that evangelical enterprises such as the American Bible Society, the American Tract Society, and other voluntary associations, through their sophisticated use of new printing, papermaking, and stereo-typing technologies, played in the popularization of print and the creation of mass media in America.[100]

In "Systematic Benevolence," Nord shows how these voluntary organizations were innovators in mass communication and business management through distribution technologies that paved the way for modern business practices. The colportage system required tight, national administrative controls and a highly reticulated information network. If traveling agents were to work and evangelicals were to mount national public information campaigns, they would have to create new structures of accountability and information distribution as well as exploit cheap printing and cheap postage. In so doing, evangelicals pioneered modern forms of associations (from maternal associations to abolitionist societies) and led the way in using improvements in communication through supralocal communication systems that went beyond face-to-face community and

100. David Paul Nord, *The Evangelical Origins of Mass Media in America, 1815-1835* (Columbia, SC: Association for Education in Journalism and Mass Communication, 1984); see also Nord, "Working-Class Readers: Family, Community, and Reading in Late-Nineteenth-Century America," *Communication Research* 13 (April 1986): 156-81; and Nord, "A Republican Literature: A Study of Magazine Readers and Reading in Late-Eighteenth-Century New York," *American Quarterly* 40 (March 1988): 42-64. The standard history of the American Bible Society is Creighton Lacy, *The Word Carrying Giant: The Growth of the American Bible Society (1916-1966)* (South Pasadena, CA: William Carey Library, 1977). See also Peter J. Wosh, "Bibles, Benevolence and Emerging Bureaucracy: The Persistence of the American Bible Society" (Ph.D. diss., New York University, 1990); and John Alden, "The Bible as Printed Word," in *The Bible and Bibles in America,* ed. Ernest S. Frerichs (Atlanta: Scholars Press, 1988), 9-28. Crucial studies of the American Tract Society include Lawrence Thompson, "The Printing and Publishing Activities of the American Tract Society from 1825 to 1850," *Papers of the Bibliographical Society of America* 35 (1941): 81-114; Harvey George Neufeldt, "American Tract Society, 1825-1865: An Examination of Its Religious, Economic, Social and Political Ideas" (Ph.D. diss., Michigan State University, 1971); Stephen Elmer Slocum, "The American Tract Society: 1825-1975: An Evangelical Effort to Influence the Religious and Moral Life of the United States" (Ph.D. diss., New York University, 1977).

built specialized national constituencies (in other words, "special interest" communities).[101]

Two scholars in particular, Michael H. Harris and Paul Boyer, have issued clarion calls for scholars to attend to evangelicals' "supreme — or perhaps desperate? — faith in the power of the printed word to reshape social reality" if American reform movements are to be fully understood.[102] For example, the evangelical movement's communication campaigns trained individuals who adapted mass media techniques to the antislavery cause. Abolitionists launched a massive public information campaign in 1835, to mention but one instance, by flooding the mails with nearly a million pamphlets. Social reform movements and their strategies are inexplicable outside the ideological and sociological context of missionary, tract, Bible, and Sunday school associations.

Victor Neuburg argues that religious tracts do not belong, properly speaking, to the chapbook tradition, which provides us a rare window into the reading habits of the more rank-and-file American, although a goodly number of the chapbooks he identifies have religious themes. Between May 1814 and May 1824, the American Tract Society published over four million tracts, an astonishing number that reveals, if not the extent of readership, at least the existence of "a large reading public at the bottom end of the social scale," a finding thus confirming Gilmore over Zboray.[103] Some studies of religious tract movements, both former and contemporary (there are over 4,000 tract titles currently in circulation from forty-three known tract publishers, with total printings well into the billions), are marred by scholarly ignorance of evangelical theology.[104] Scholars unfamiliar with the tradition would do well to look first at John P. Ferré's perceptive work on contemporary book publishing and at Stephen Board's whirlwind tour of religious periodicals, which he estimates stand at ten percent of the total periodical literature.[105]

---

101. See also Moore, "Religion, Secularization, and the Shaping of the Culture Industry."

102. Paul Boyer, *Urban Masses and Moral Order in America, 1820-1920* (Cambridge, MA: Harvard University Press, 1978), 33; Harris, "'Spiritual Cakes Upon the Waters.'"

103. The quote is from Victor Neuburg, "Chapbooks in America: Reconstructing the Popular Reading of Early America," in *Reading in America,* ed. Davidson, 107.

104. An example of this is David Sonenschein, "Sharing the Good News: The Evangelical Tract," *Journal of American Culture* 5 (1982): 107-21.

105. John P. Ferré, "Searching for the Great Commission: Evangelical Book Publishing Since the 1970s," and Stephen Board, "Moving the World with Magazines: A

Up until recently, historians have been so busy mining the "transportation" revolution that they have spent little energy exploring the "communication" revolution and its impact on nineteenth-century American life.
One of the few historians besides Nord and Zboray to bring the two together
— as they originally were in the widespread use of the abstract general term
"communications" to describe physical facilities of roads, canals, and rail-
ways as well as information and ideas — is Richard B. Kielbowicz. Kielbowicz's study of the pivotal role of the post office in the communications
revolution concludes that it was the post office *and* the press together that
provided the chief public information source until the Civil War.[106]

Kielbowicz operates out of a very narrow view of "public information."
Where Richard D. Brown finds rich pickings among a sweeping and auda-
cious range of references (personal correspondence, gossip, orations, private
meditations, and the like), Kielbowicz mines only the technology that
brought news into American homes — the postal system, the primary
long-distance communications technology in America before the Civil War.

Religion and postal service forged a symbiotic relationship. The post
office's beneficent policy toward religious publications made the mail an
attractive delivery system. Congress in the 1790s gave preferred postal rates
to newspapers — that is why so many religious materials came out in
newspaper format. Religious magazines reached largest national circulations in the early 1800s, surpassing even newspapers, until by 1850 there
were 181 religious periodicals published in America, half of them newspapers. As Nord and others have shown, in antebellum postal operations,
religious publications predominate.[107]

For example, residents of Jacksonville, Illinois, received more religious than secular publications at the town post office in 1831/1832.
Sixty-eight secular and unidentified publications had 214 subscriptions in

Survey of Evangelical Periodicals," both in *American Evangelicals and the Mass Media,* ed.
Schultze, 99-117 and 119-42, respectively.

106. Richard B. Kielbowicz, *News in the Mail: The Press, Post Office, and Public
Information, 1700-1860s* (New York: Greenwood Press, 1989). A companion volume is
Culver H. Smith, *The Press, Politics, and Patronage: The American Government's Use of
Newspapers, 1789-1875* (Athens: University of Georgia Press, 1977). For Zboray's work
on the railroad's surprising intensification of regional differences in literary dissemination,
see his "The Transportation Revolution and Antebellum Book Distribution Reconsidered,"
*American Quarterly* 38 (1986): 53-71, and most importantly, Zboray, *A Fictive People.*

107. Wesley Norton, *Religious Newspapers in the Old Northwest to 1861: A History
and Record of Opinion* (Athens: Ohio University Press, 1977).

Jacksonville, compared to 54 religious publications with 243 subscriptions. Individuals in Jacksonville received up to eight different religious publications. Similarly, religious periodicals were among the most widely circulated nonlocal publications in Beekmantown, New York, and in Farmington, North Carolina. Surprisingly, northern towns proved more insular in their reading than southern towns. Southerners relied more heavily on national publications; northerners were more regional in their reading.

Kielbowicz stresses the role of routine operations of the post office in the formation of the press rather than legislation, policies, and so forth. He also confirms Nord's work on the "innovative fusion of postal and printing capabilities," which began with evangelicals' development of a means of internal communication — magazines — that used the mails and kept traveling agents in touch with one another.[108] The shaping influence of religious newspapers on the development of the American press is only beginning to be understood and appreciated.[109] In the summarial words of the field's most prolific scholar, Quentin J. Schultze, the author of the best single essay introduction to the entire arena of religion and the mass media, "early American evangelicals largely established the tone and style of mass communication in the United States" that is still with us to this day.[110]

*Mastery #5* A fifth mastery that evangelicals achieved was in one of the key purveyors of literacy: the Sunday school. Gilmore portrays three principal ways in which people acquired literacy during the early national period: (1) home parental instruction; (2) district summer and winter school sessions; and (3) Sunday schools, which emphasized reading, memorization, and rote recitation — with little if any writing instruction. Sunday schools became normative after 1815 in most areas, and they stood in communities as a major "zone of access" to print materials, which need to be analyzed as both material commodities and informational/cultural/moral transmitters.[111] "By midcentury nearly all American communities, even the hum-

108. Kielbowicz, *News in the Mail*, 66.

109. Marvin Olasky, "Journalism Historians and Religion," *American Journalism* 5 (1989): 41-53.

110. See Quentin J. Schultze, "Keeping the Faith: American Evangelicals and the Media," in *American Evangelicals and the Mass Media*, ed. Schultze, 23-45. The quote is from Schultze's introduction to the collection, p. 13.

111. Gilmore, "Elementary Literacy on the Eve of the Industrial Revolution," 87-171. The four key means for occupational instruction are listed on pp. 98-99.

blest, had felt some of the impact of the various evangelical associations'
literacy campaigns," Zboray writes in his discussion of the church's encouragement of literacy.[112]

The role of Sunday school in literacy education needs more vigorous
exploration.[113] Sunday school libraries, which may have been as important
to the transmission of religious traditions in early nineteenth-century
America as periodicals or books, have been virtually unstudied.[114] What
were their sizes? What were their contents? What percentage were religious
titles, and how did that differ from private libraries?[115] Do Sunday school
libraries evidence the same "democratization of mind" that other scholars
have found in family libraries of the early republic? At a time when access
to print sources was severely limited, libraries, lyceums, and lectures were
absolutely vital to the diffusion of knowledge.[116] The lyceum and lecture
circuit helped people find their way through this mass of information, as
oral communications and print worked together in ways that are still in
need of exploration.[117]

If reading had become a "necessity of life," Bible reading was "the

112. See Zboray, "Family, Church, and Academy," in his *A Fictive People,* 69-82;
the quote is on p. 91.

113. Thanks to Anne M. Boylan, we now have a superb introduction to the Sunday
school: *Sunday School: The Formation of an American Institution, 1790-1880* (New Haven:
Yale University Press, 1988).

114. Significant exceptions include Frank K. Walter, "A Poor but Respectable Relation: The Sunday School Library," *Library Quarterly* 12 (1942): 731-39, and F. Allen
Briggs, "Sunday School Libraries in the 19th Century," *Library Quarterly* 31 (1961):
166-77.

115. Kett and McClung's study, "Book Culture in Post-Revolutionary Virginia,"
121-22, found that "for all locations 70 percent of the books in small libraries (ten or
fewer itemized titles) were religious." In larger libraries, religious titles stood as the largest
single category, but they were a minority of all titles. These religious titles were more
practical, how-to books than theological treatises.

116. Stellar work on the lecture circuit has been done by Donald M. Scott, "The
Popular Lecture and the Creation of a Public in Mid-Nineteenth Century America," *Journal
of American History* 66 (1980): 791-809; and Scott, "Print and the Public Lecture System,
1840-1860," in *Printing and Society in Early America,* ed. Joyce et al., 278-99. An early
but still good study is Carl Bode, *The American Lyceum: Town Meeting of the Mind* (1956;
repr. Carbondale, IL: Southern Illinois University Press, 1968).

117. See Scott, "Print and the Public Lecture System." A recent moral prospectus
for newspapers features precisely this sifting function as "one of the primary services a
newspaper can render to the public in this age of instant communications." See Burl
Osborne, "Responsibilities of a Newspaper," in *The Morality of the Mass Media,* ed.
W. Lawson Taitte (Dallas: University of Texas at Dallas, 1993), 25-40.

most common reading experience in rural New England through 1835."[118] The Bible was the most commonly itemized title in inventories of libraries, the centerpiece of Sunday school libraries, and the most popular book in America.[119] Indeed, almanacs and Bibles were the most widely disseminated forms of print until the 1820s, when newspapers assumed ascendancy. Gilmore's work on private family libraries reveals that in the Windsor District there were 520 full Bibles and separate New Testaments (found in seventy-four percent of family libraries), with family Bibles serving as one-volume libraries for many rural families. The first great publishing house of the nineteenth century was built primarily on the back of its successful Bible sales.[120]

The authority of the church was marked by the place occupied by the Bible — in the home, where it was read aloud, and in the church, where it occupied a central and elevated position. Mary De Jong has even identified a genre of female Scripture biography that helped the biblical women come alive to white, middle-class Christians.[121] In colonial society, when a large proportion of the population could not read, the symbolic placing of the Bible in the home testified volumes about what governed their lives.

The degree to which the mid-nineteenth-century "Bible politics" of interpretation affected the act of reading itself is examined in Steven Mailloux's study of Margaret Fuller's 1845 review of Frederick Douglass's *Narrative of the Life*. After reading this provocative essay in "rhetorical hermeneutics," no historian can ever fail again to come to grips with the way reading is "historically contingent, politically situated, institutionally

118. Gilmore, *Reading Becomes a Necessity,* 257.

119. The best single study of the Bible in American culture is Mark A. Noll, *Between Faith and Criticism: Evangelicals, Scholarship, and the Bible in America,* 2d ed. (Grand Rapids: Baker Book House, 1991). See also *The Bible in America: Essays in Cultural History,* ed. Noll and Hatch. For more specialized work see Carlos Baker, "The Place of the Bible in American Fiction," in *Religious Perspectives in American Culture,* ed. James W. Smith and A. L. Jamison (Princeton: Princeton University Press, 1961), 243-72; and W. Harrison Daniel, "Biblical Publication and Procurement in the Confederacy," *Journal of Southern History* 24 (1958): 191-201.

120. James N. Green, "From Printer to Publisher: Mathew Carey and the Origins of Nineteenth-Century Book Publishing," in *Getting the Books Out,* ed. Hackenberg, 26-41. See also Green, *Mathew Carey, Publisher and Patriot* (Philadelphia: Library Company, 1985).

121. Mary De Jong, "Dark-Eyed Daughters: Nineteenth-Century Popular Portrayals of Biblical Women," *Women's Studies* 19 (1991): 283-308.

embedded, and materially conditioned."[122] Similarly, the debate over *The Woman's Bible* (1886 to 1895) demonstrated that the Scriptures continued to set much of the terms of discussion even for those who felt alienated by the tradition. The controversy also casts into doubt the theoretical capacity of "separate spheres" ideology to accommodate the tremendous diversity of viewpoints represented in the women's movement.[123]

To study Sunday school libraries — and their merging, along with parochial, social, and private libraries, into public libraries — is to stumble through thickets as diverse as the nature of the communications system in early America, the range of access to print culture in communities, or the functioning of popular juvenile literature.[124] Perhaps only dime novels are as ripe for the scholarly picking as Sunday school publications and children's literature.[125]

*Mastery #6* Evangelicals also mastered the arena known as "popular entertainment." Evangelicalism's "in-but-not-of" strategy of cultural inter-

122. Steven Mailloux, "Misreading as a Historical Act: Cultural Rhetoric, Bible Politics, and Fuller's 1845 Review of Douglass's *Narrative*," in *Readers in History*, ed. Machor, 3-31.

123. This is the argument of Kathi L. Kern, "Rereading Eve: Elizabeth Cady Stanton and *The Woman's Bible*, 1885-1896," *Women's Studies* 19 (1991): 371-83.

124. The importance of Sunday school libraries is emphasized in Robert W. Lynn and Eliot Wright, *The Big Little School: Two Hundred Years of the Sunday School* (Nashville: Abingdon Press, 1980). For parochial libraries see William D. Houlette, "Parish Libraries and the Work of the Reverend Thomas Bray," *Library Quarterly* 4 (1934): 583-609; and John Fletcher Hurst, "Parochial Libraries in the Colonial Period," in *Papers of the American Society of Church History*, ed. Samuel Macauley Jackson (New York: G. P. Putnam's Sons, 1890), 2:37-50. The study of denominational libraries is virtual virgin territory. For other libraries see Walter M. Whitehill, "The King's Chapel Library," *Publications of the Colonial Society of Massachusetts* 38 (1959): 274-89; George Smart, "Private Libraries in Colonial Virginia," *American Literature* 10 (1938): 24-52; Louis B. Wright, "The Gentleman's Library in Early Virginia," *Huntington Library Quarterly* 1 (1937): 3-61; Robert V. Williams, "George Whitefield's Bethesda: The Orphanage, the College and the Library," in *Library History Seminar No. 3, Proceedings, 1968*, ed. Martha Jane K. Zachert (Tallahassee: Journal of Library History, 1968), 47-72; Carl Bridenbaugh, "The Press and the Book in Eighteenth-Century Philadelphia," *Pennsylvania Magazine of History and Biography* 65 (1941): 1-30; and Michael H. Harris, "A Methodist Minister's Working Library in Mid-19th Century Illinois," *Wesleyan Quarterly Review* 4 (1967): 210-19.

125. Robert H. Canary holds his nose while probing "The Sunday School as Popular Culture," *Midcontinent American Studies Journal* 2 (Fall 1968): 5-13. By contrast see Ellen Schaffer, "The Children's Books of the American Sunday-School Union," *American Book Collector* 17 (1966): 21-28.

action doomed its early principled opposition to the rise of "culture industries" — novel-reading, theater-going, and concert-attending.[126] R. Laurence Moore, a preeningly odd but indispensable commentator on the American religious scene, analyzes the revivals as "religious theater" and camp meetings as a "form of carnival," both constituting "what was arguably the first, large-scale, popular entertainment in the United States."[127] Entertainment evangelism is not something created by televangelists today, as Stout has demonstrated, but by eighteenth- and nineteenth-century revivalists.

Antebellum Americans went to the theater and read novels not to escape from the humdrum into the exotic and strange so much as to escape a "truth-stranger-than-fiction" landscape of a strange and rapidly changing world. Fiction, of course, was highly problematic reading material in antebellum America. But evangelicals were not alone in deeming the novel a danger to religion, morality, and the country. Indeed, at first one was deemed slumming it morally and culturally when reading fiction. How did this intense opposition to "the weedy and the seedy" in the formal garden of literature, which dominated the scene early in the nineteenth century, collapse with a thud in the 1850s as evangelicals took to writing fiction with a vengeance?

In other words, how did the *Ladies' Repository* come to editorialize in 1865, "We live in a fiction reading age. . . . Hurrying, uncultured, everyday people . . . will not read heavy, labored, theological works. The . . . masses must have easy reading, or they will not read at all."[128] How did Mark Twain come to observe in 1871, "The gospel of Christ came filtered down to nineteenth-century Americans through stage plays and through the despised novel and Christmas story, rather than from the drowsy pulpit"?[129]

The evangelical tradition's in-cultural model was uneasy with cen-

---

126. The phrase is that of Moore in "Religion, Secularization, and the Shaping of the Culture Industry."

127. Moore, "Religion, Secularization, and the Shaping of the Culture Industry," 228ff. For the role of "religious holiday" and "holy fairs" in American evangelicalism, see Leigh Eric Schmidt, *Holy Fairs: Scottish Communions and American Revivals in the Early Modern Period* (Princeton, NJ: Princeton University Press, 1989).

128. As quoted in Machor, "Fiction and Informed Reading in Early Nineteenth-Century America," 329.

129. As quoted in David S. Reynolds, *Faith in Fiction: The Emergence of Religious Literature in America* (Cambridge, MA: Harvard University Press, 1981), 1.

sorship. As Nord has shown, evangelicals aimed "to foil the enemy at his own weapons," which were cheap, popular paperback publications. They believed more in competition than in censorship. Evangelicals sheltered themselves behind competitive parallel narrative structures and forms — religious newspapers, tracts, and Sunday school fiction, for example — that sacralized novels and secular newspapers. Evangelicals confidently believed that virtually no text or social artifact, however "worldly" or inhospitable, could not be rebaptized and redeployed to serve moral and religious purposes. Even novels.

Fiction's unifying force in American antebellum life, and the building of a modern sense of community based on the printed word, has been a major theme in Ronald J. Zboray's pioneering scholarship. Zboray, who is seemingly *au fait* with all the major trends in historiography, has already displayed his truly remarkable knowledge of antebellum culture in the reconstruction of the transition from letters to novels and the national fictionalization of community life. In this unique creation of a "fictive people," Zboray argues, one cannot escape the irony wherein "the strong motivations given to literacy in order to maintain traditional community life ultimately contributed to the destruction of that very way of life."[130]

In his contribution to this collection, "Technology and the Character of Community Life in Antebellum America: The Role of Story Papers," Zboray deftly explores the phenomenal circulations of "story papers," which were often lumped with sentimental literature and romantic novels in the evangelical mind. There has been a great deal of attention to "news papers" in recent years, but virtually no one has looked at the "story papers." Thanks to the doctoral work of sociologist Michael Schudson and the historical research into journalism of Marvin Olasky, we know that today's idea of "news" was a Calvinist offshoot (Nord calls Increase Mather America's first great journalist) that coalesced in the Jacksonian era's democratization of politics and the expansion of a market economy.[131]

In the 1830s the steam-powered "penny" press broke away from previous models and formed the ancestor of today's newspapers. "Penny news papers," perhaps the most significant technological innovation in

130. Ronald J. Zboray, "The Letter and the Fiction Reading Public in Antebellum America," *Journal of American Culture* 10 (1987): 27-34, esp. 33; and most importantly his masterful *A Fictive People*.

131. Marvin Olasky, "Democracy and the Secularization of the American Press," in *American Evangelicals and the Mass Media*, ed. Schultze, 47-67.

print culture during the first half of the nineteenth century, sought large circulation and advertising rather than subscriptions and subsidies from political parties. These dailies relied on market-based sales over social and political ties, and they reflected "not the affairs of an elite in a small trading society, but the activities of an increasingly varied, urban, and middle-class society of trade, transportation, and manufacturing."[132] Their advertising was now an economic exchange, not a moral stand as it had been earlier.

Indeed, the "news paper" was such a mass circulation success that it may be that Alexis de Tocqueville's image of the Michigan frontiersman, fighting for an existence in his log cabin, where he sat of an evening reading his Bible, Shakespeare, and newspaper, may not have been far off the mark. We need to know a lot more about these "news papers." How did clergy react to the emergence of this cheap, daily press? Earlier papers had refused to accept ads they did not agree with. Now everything was different. Did religious leaders embrace advertising that was more freewheeling, or did they resist it? If the penny press liberated the masses from control of the local elites and facilitated the breakdown of a hierarchic, ordered society, did clergy find themselves among those "elites"? Did newspaper reading become a democratic rage, and public speaking through word and print a patriotic duty, partly because evangelicals had fashioned mass communications in their own evangelistic image?

Between 1790 and 1810, the number of newspapers exploded from 90 to 370. More importantly, their nature changed as well as their numbers; they used leveling methods of discourse that were off-putting and even ridiculing of lawyers, physicians, and clergy. No wonder, as Hatch has shown, intellectuals and elites displayed widespread contempt for newspapers, equating their reading with "tavern-haunting, drinking, and gambling." Journalist James Gordon Bennett, founder of the *New York Herald*, is supposed to have been the first (1836) to inaugurate a religion beat in a newspaper designated for a general audience.[133] Ever since that day, reporters and believers have peered at each other suspiciously through a fog of mutual incomprehension.[134] Some erstwhile correspondents — Mike Maus, Wes-

132. Schudson, *Discovering the News,* 23.

133. Buddenbaum, " 'Judge . . . What Their Acts Will Justify.' "

134. The work of media historians Marvin N. Olasky and Judith M. Buddenbaum is absolutely seminal here. See Olasky, *The Prodigal Press: The Anti-Christian Bias of the American News Media* (Westchester, IL: Crossway, 1988); Buddenbaum, "Religion in the News: Factors Associated with the Selection of Stories from an International Denominational News Service" (Ph.D. diss., Indiana University, 1985); Buddenbaum, "Analysis

ley G. Pippert, and Judith M. Buddenbaum — have lowered competing drawbridges of illumination over this moat of misunderstanding and mistrust.[135] We need to study further the skeptical attitudes of the media toward religion itself, which the David Koresh fiasco made clear.

Zboray's work on the "story papers," which were the progenitors of the dime novel and soap opera, fills a huge gap in our knowledge. Story papers sold "a state of mind as much as a product for use." Zboray highlights the role of popular culture in general in addressing the needs of a people who felt a "sense of personal loss" from their diminished community life brought on by a world of industrial development filled with high stakes and high falls — he cites one recent estimate that "about one in every five antebellum Americans would go broke at some time in their lives." People subscribed to religious, agricultural, and general newspapers in larger numbers, but even these publications included fiction just like the story papers. "The synchrony between the rationalized, mechanical process of production in the fiction factories that produced the story papers and the technology of storytelling in the content of those publications cannot be underestimated," he warns as he probes the ubiquitous metaphor of the machine and its confidence in the "machine-built community."

Are reading practices affected by religious preferences, as by age, social status, region, and other conditions? What influenced the reading choices of evangelicals and nonevangelicals? How were the antebellum Christian reading experiences of sentimental fiction different from experiences of reading the Bible, or newspapers, or devotional literature, or sermons?[136] What moral dimensions of readerly engagement were encouraged by re-

---

of Religion News Coverage in Three Major Newspapers," *Journalism Quarterly* 63 (1986): 600-606; and Buddenbaum, "The Religion Beat at Daily Newspapers," *Newspaper Research Journal* 9 (1988): 57-69. Less historical and more strident is Cal Thomas, *Book Burning* (Westchester, IL: Crossway, 1983). For the catcalls in the electronic media, see Buddenbaum, "Religion News Coverage in Commercial Network Newscasts," in *Religious Television: Controversies and Conclusions,* ed. Robert Abelman and Stewart M. Hoover (Norwood, NJ: Ablex Pub. Corp., 1990), 249-63.

135. Mike Maus, "Believers as Behavers: News Coverage of Evangelicals by the Secular Media," and Wesley G. Pippert, "Worldly Reporters and Born-Again Believers: How Each Perceives the Other," both in *American Evangelicals and the Mass Media,* ed. Schultze, 253-73 and 275-86, respectively; Judith M. Buddenbaum, "Network News Coverage of Religion," in *Channels of Belief: Religion and American Commercial Television,* ed. John P. Ferré (Ames, IA: Iowa State University Press, 1990), 57-78.

136. See the pioneering study by Jane Tompkins, *Sensational Designs: The Cultural Work of American Fiction, 1790-1860* (New York: Oxford University Press, 1985), esp. 147-85.

viewers?[137] Were there gender or class differences in what religious literature men and women read? Michael Denning's presentation of evidence for class differences in reading dime novels raises as many questions as it answers.[138] Thanks to Zboray's work, we know that men were as likely (and in some cases more likely) to read prose fiction as women, contrary to stereotype, and that "reading patterns of men and women differed little."[139]

Evangelicals had so mastered the fictive form that they were generating best-selling novels in phenomenal numbers.[140] Women seemed especially aware of the genre's potential to convey as well as recast standard ideas about gender, race, ideology, and politics.[141] Jane Tompkins's study isolating the Christian woman reader of antebellum American fiction combines high theory with deep empirical enrichment. Susan Harris's study of women's subversive reading in mid-nineteenth-century America deserves much more discussion than it has received.[142]

Women's leadership in generating popular religious literature has been recently highlighted by the discovery of a regional variation of the evangelical domestic novel — most often associated with Harriet Beecher

137. An excellent beginning is Nina Baym, *Novels, Readers, and Reviewers: Responses to Fiction in Antebellum America* (Ithaca, NY: Cornell University Press, 1984).

138. Denning, *Mechanic Accents.*

139. Ronald J. Zboray, "Reading Patterns in Antebellum America: Evidence in the Charge Records of the New York Society Library," *Libraries and Culture* 26 (Spring 1991): 301-33, esp. 306.

140. An excellent general study of the novel has been done by Cathy N. Davidson, *Revolution and the Word: The Rise of the Novel in America* (New York: Oxford University Press, 1986).

141. For an excellent overview see Mary De Jong's introduction to a special theme issue on "Religion and Anglo-American Women" entitled "Protestantism and Its Discontents in the Eighteenth and Nineteenth Centuries," *Women's Studies* 19 (1991): 259-69. For evidence of the study of women's novels as a growth industry in scholarship, see Nina Baym, *Women's Fiction: A Guide to Novels By and About Women in America, 1820-1870* (Ithaca, NY: Cornell University Press, 1978); Linda K. Kerber, " 'We Own that Ladies Sometimes Read': Women's Reading in the Early Republic," in *Women of the Republic: Intellect and Ideology in Revolutionary America,* ed. L. K. Kerber (Chapel Hill: University of North Carolina Press, 1980), 233-64; Mary Kelley, *Private Women, Public Stage: Literary Domesticity in Nineteenth-Century America* (New York: Oxford University Press, 1984). The benchmark study everyone argues with is, of course, Ann Douglas, *The Feminization of America* (New York: Alfred A. Knopf, 1977), a book that scholars of reader-response criticism, such as Janice Radway, *Reading the Romance: Women, Patriarchy, and Popular Literature* (Chapel Hill: University of North Carolina Press, 1984), are beating into a pulp.

142. Tompkins, *Sensational Designs.* Susan K. Harris, *Nineteenth-Century American Women's Novels: Interpretive Strategies* (New York: Cambridge University Press, 1990).

Stowe, Susan Warner, Catherine Sedgwick, Sara Willis Parton, and the more liberal Adeline D. T. Whitney[143] — that was headquartered in the South and sought to defend southern culture.[144] Ann-Janine Morey has identified a lamentations genre of fiction written by ministers' wives that provides a healthy corrective to my own assessment of the role of ministers' wives in nineteenth-century Protestantism.[145] Of special need for further study are Catholic women novelists, who have been smartly studied by Colleen McDannell. McDannell has waged a virtual one-person crusade to bring gender considerations into Catholic history: "Women's history has essentially been Protestant women's history."[146]

How methodologically sophisticated the scholarship in "popular culture" studies has become is evident in a comparison of Louis Schneider and Sanford Dornbusch's early work on inspirational literature in American history with recent studies of the religious novel as a force for social justice issues.[147] John P. Ferré and Gary Scott Smith have studied bestselling social gospel novels as a window into mass culture with textured and textural savvy.[148] But their work is only a beginning, and the huge gap in this collection of essays symbolizes the work that needs to be done in the Victorian and Progressive periods, when, for example, the religious press became marginalized in the publishing industry while religious themes and leaders pervaded nonreligious journals and sources.

143. Shirley Marchalonis, "Leaving the Jargons: Adeline D. T. Whitney and the Sphere of God and Women," *Women's Studies* 19 (1991): 309-25.

144. Elizabeth Moss, *Domestic Novelists in the Old South: Defenders of Southern Culture* (Baton Rouge: Louisiana State University Press, 1992).

145. Ann-Janine Morey, "Lamentations for the Minister's Wife, by Herself," *Women's Studies* 19 (1991): 327-40; Sweet, *The Minister's Wife*.

146. Colleen McDannell, "Catholic Women Fiction Writers, 1840-1920," *Women's Studies* 19 (1991): 385-405, esp. 385. See also McDannell, " 'The Devil Was the First Protestant': Gender and Intolerance in Irish Catholic Fiction," *U.S. Catholic Historian* 8 (1989): 51-65; and McDannell, "Catholic Domesticity, 1860-1960," in *American Catholic Women: A Historical Exploration,* ed. Karen Kennelly (New York: Macmillan, 1989), 48-80.

147. Louis Schneider and Sanford Dornbusch, *Popular Religion: Inspirational Books in America* (Chicago: University of Chicago Press, 1958).

148. John P. Ferré, *A Social Gospel for Millions: The Religious Bestsellers of Charles Sheldon, Charles Gordon and Harold Bell Wright* (Bowling Green, OH: Bowling Green State University Press, 1988); Gary Scott Smith, "Charles M. Sheldon's *In His Steps* in the Context of Religion and Culture in Late Nineteenth-Century America," *Fides et Historia* 22 (Summer 1990): 47-69. A much less sophisticated approach is Elmer F. Suderman, "The Social-Gospel Novelists' Criticisms of American Society," *Midcontinent American Studies Journal* 7 (1966): 45-60.

The subject of censorship in particular and the repression of reading material in general demonstrates just how profound our ignorance of the history of communication and change really is. Might censorship and other restraints on publication work to help modernization as well as inhibit it?[149] Is artistic freedom or pietistic moralism the best category with which to understand the history of censorship, at least in the United States? Unfortunately, most historical overviews of censorship focus almost exclusively on press and print, not on electronic media.[150] Equally unfortunate is the absence to date of even a bad study of the "nut mail" letters associated ever since the Lanzman-Milam Decision (1975) with Madalyn Murray O'Hair's reputed attempts to deny broadcast space to religious programs.

*Mastery #7* A seventh mastery that evangelicals could claim was ideological. Ideas are journeys that one takes — life journeys, not just mind journeys. James H. Moorhead's contribution, "The Millennium and the Media," centers on the role of media in bringing apocalyptic themes to the marketplace and on the role of millennial ideology in the development of various media forms.[151] What a peculiar substance millennialism is proving to be — like a gas that fills any vessel into which it is introduced, some form of millennial ideology seems to pervade whatever social movement one is examining. In this case, Moorhead underscores millennialism as a motivating force in founding mass media enterprises such as Bible societies, tract societies, and periodicals.

In fact, evangelicals justified their use of the media of the day in millennial terms. Moorhead's tracing of evangelicals' use of telegraphy in the Union Prayer Meeting Revival of 1857 is especially interesting. Not coincidentally, the millennial age was a communications revolution — which helps explain why evangelicals picked up print so quickly. The use of print became an "eschatological imperative," as Moorhead calls it, as

149. This is the fascinating conclusion of Raymond Birn, "Book Production and Censorship in France, 1700-1715," in *Books and Society in History*, ed. Carpenter, 145-71.

150. See as an example the otherwise excellent essay by Andrew R. Cecil, "Censorship: Historical Background and Justifiable Forms," in *The Morality of the Mass Media*, ed. W. L. Taitte, 209-58. An exception that proves the rule is Mark Facker, "Religious Watchdog Groups and Prime-Time Programming," in *Channels of Belief*, ed. Ferré, 99-116.

151. See Michael Barkun, "The Language of Apocalypse: Premillennialists and Nuclear War," in *The God Pumpers: Religion in the Electronic Age*, ed. Marshall Fishwick and Ray B. Browne (Bowling Green, OH: Bowling Green State University Press, 1987), 159-73.

well as a civic duty. To be an American was to be well informed —
republican government required the universal diffusion of knowledge —
a theme that lyceums, lectures, and libraries voiced constantly in the 1820s
and 1830s.

The printed word was seen as the indispensable, even millennial lever
of social reform. The confidence of evangelicals in print as little levers that
could move great weights, as well as evangelicals' "those who read, lead"
trust in literacy, was unbounded. Books could usher in the new age —
"books could make a Christian" — a confidence that expressed itself in
what missionary John Mason Peck called the "bullet theory" of communication: the printed word was the magic bullet that, when fired, would
fell the mind of the West for Christ.[152] Moorhead skillfully traces the role
that improved knowledge and technology would play in the millennial
enterprise. The salvific potential of technology was assumed until after the
Civil War, when "building the kingdom of God became as much a matter
of efficient technique and program as it was of piety."

Moorhead's study delivers more than it promises. It raises questions
as to the religious contexts and effects of reading, about which we know
little. To what extent did technology reshape religious relations as it did
social relations? To what extent did religious leaders see technology as a
transforming agent that could broaden and deepen the moral sense as well
as produce other social miracles, such as altering the relationships between
class, gender, family, and so on? Proof of effects is hard to find, but most
suggestively, Moorhead observes that "in the final analysis, the communications revolution derived from an altered consciousness as much as
it did from the efficacy of technology." Yet he makes the theoretically
consequential observation that the power of the media could restructure
belief itself by turning our attention to media and apocalyptic as it
manifested itself in nineteenth-century Millerism.

Moorhead's essay raises for the historian the larger issue of the
interplay of intellectual and social history. In his study of theologies of
revelation, theologian Avery Dulles observes that evangelical theology is
best suited for the use of mass media.[153] Similarly, Robert White explores
the forces in Catholic culture that have made it distrust popular media as

152. Peck is quoted in Russell B. Nye, *Society and Culture in America, 1830-1860*
(New York: Harper & Row, 1974), 294. See also Harris, "'Spiritual Cakes Upon the
Waters,'" 101.

153. Avery Dulles, *Models of Revelation* (Garden City, NY: Doubleday, 1983).

being in conflict with Catholicism's theological integrity, although he sees this bias breaking down.[154] Pat Robertson has admitted publicly that in his mind the electronic church is nothing more than the "early Wesleyan movement."[155] Is there something symbiotic about print and Calvinism, or electronic broadcasting and Pentecostalism? Indeed, can one imagine Pentecostalism without electronic technology? Did they do more than grow up together?

And what about electronic media and "prosperity theology"? Does the health and wealth gospel, a perennial American fascination today touted by such powerful media personalities as Kenneth Hagin, Kenneth and Gloria Copeland, Jerry Savelle, and Fred Price, "resonate in profound ways with some of the deeply embedded cultural themes of American society," as more than one historian argues, even perhaps functioning as a form of American folk theology itself?[156] Jeffrey K. Hadden notes the tremendous irony in the fact that evangelicals' use of the media, their mix-and-match mastery of both "modern marketing and medieval indulgences," encouraged them to embrace a theology and psychology redolent of the liberal Protestant tradition of "positive thinking," which had its roots in the "mind cure" movement late in the nineteenth century.[157] Eugene F. Klug's work relating theological themes to media (mostly television) from a distinctively Lutheran perspective is, if not a catch, at least a cast in the right direction.[158]

---

154. White, "Mass Media and Culture in Contemporary Catholicism."

155. As quoted in Eugene F. Klug, "The Electronic Church," *Concordia Theological Quarterly* 45 (October 1981): 273.

156. Dennis Hollinger, "Enjoying God Forever: An Historical/Sociological Profile of the Health and Wealth Gospel," *Trinity Journal* 9 (Fall 1988): 131-49, esp. 149. See also Bruce Barron, *The Health and Wealth Gospel* (Downers Grove, IL: InterVarsity Press, 1987), and Joe E. Barnhart, "Prosperity Gospel: A New Folk Theology," in *Religious Television*, ed. Abelman and Hoover, 159-64. For prosperity theology as a synthesis of Peale's "positive thinking" program and classical Pentecostalism, see D. T. Williams, "Prosperity Teaching and Positive Thinking," *Evangelical Review of Theology* 11 (1987): 197-208.

157. Jeffrey K. Hadden, "Indemnity Lost, Indulgences Regained: Theological Convergence in American Televangelism," in *Restoring the Kingdom,* ed. Deane William Ferm (New York: Paragon House, 1984), 211-23.

158. Klug, "The Electronic Church," 260-80.

## Communication in an Electronic Culture

There are fourteen bays in New York's St. John the Divine Church, which when finished will have the greatest cubic footage of any Gothic cathedral in the world. Each of these fourteen bays features a mammoth stained-glass window, celebrating different arenas of human endeavor. One is the Communication Bay. Designed in 1985, it includes (besides Jack Benny) someone watching television.

Book culture and literary culture are giving way to an electronic culture. This is very basic. But it is not very simple. Communication structures are more than mediums of transmission, as Harold Adams Innis, Marshall McLuhan, and Walter J. Ong have taught us.[159] Media are also mediums of translation, affecting every nook and cranny of society, including the intellectual and social girders that underpin that society.

Innis, McLuhan, and Ong inhabit the footnotes like three genies in a bottle. To discover the power of the genies firsthand one has only to read Walter J. Ong's work on orality and literacy. In this masterpiece he explores the parameters of the sea change between oral cultures and cultures of the written word, and the transformations and transmissions of consciousness that are produced by the technology of the word.[160]

Will telecommunications change society more drastically than did printing, creating a new social order, not just a revision of the old

159. Harold Adams Innis is perhaps the most important scholar in the area of communication structures. Marshall McLuhan took Innis's insights, as found in *Empire and Communication* (Oxford: Clarendon Press, 1950; rev. ed. Toronto: University of Toronto Press, 1972) and in *The Bias of Communication* (Toronto: University of Toronto, 1951), and turned them on their head the way Marx did to Hegel's insights. For the McLuhan-Innis connection, see James W. Carey, *Communication as Culture: Essays on Media and Society* (Boston: Unwin Hyman, 1989), esp. chap. 6, and Carey, "Harold Adams Innis and Marshall McLuhan," *Antioch Review* 27 (Spring 1967): 5-39. Marshall McLuhan and Quentin Fiore, *The Medium Is the Message* (New York: Bantam Books, 1967); M. McLuhan and Eric McLuhan, *Laws of Media: The New Science* (Toronto: University of Toronto Press, 1988); M. McLuhan and Bruce R. Powers, *The Global Village: Transformations in World Life and Media in the 21st Century* (New York: Oxford University Press, 1989). Walter J. Ong, *Rhetoric, Romance, and Technology: Studies in the Interaction of Expression and Culture* (Ithaca, NY: Cornell University Press, 1971); Ong, *Orality and Literacy: The Technologization of the Word* (New York: Methuen, 1982). See also Joshua Meyrowitz, *No Sense of Place: The Impact of Electronic Media on Social Behavior* (New York: Oxford University Press, 1985). For an essay that is distinguished for its observations and evocations, see Kenneth Bedell, "The Use of Television by Interpretive Communities," in *Changing Channels*, ed. Inbody, 113-27.

160. Ong, *Orality and Literacy*.

order?[161] In the same way print encouraged analysis and rationality, so electronic media will change the structure of discourse. The ideology of representation, created by the modern era, is giving way to an ideology of participation, created by a postmodern electronic culture.[162] Who is helping us to understand these changes?

In discussions of "mass communications," radio and television are customarily where scholars of American religion walk in and where American religious leaders walk out.[163] Indeed, one is almost as likely to find a radio or television ministry etched in a stained-glass window as one is to find a radio or television ministry engaging a mainline church today.

In academic circles, media scholarship has been little more than grouting around the grousing. Intellectuals and religious leaders initially resisted electronic culture, and many still do.[164] The lengths we will go and the excuses we will come up with not to use electronic technologies are demonstrated by the academic receptions and reviews of the onset of computer Bibles.[165] Raymond Williams argues that there has always been strenuous objection to new modes of popular communication from the opinion makers, and that they are always wrong: they were wrong about Shakespeare in the 1590s, wrong about Austen in the 1810s, "wrong about circuses and quilts, vaudeville and narrowboat decoration, Marvel Comics and Hollywood, jazz and brass bands."[166]

Being wrong in the past did not stop Franco Ferrarotti from announcing in 1988 the "end of conversation" as a result of mass media.[167] Other scholars cannot resist a superior sneer.[168] Malcolm Muggeridge is

161. This is the argument of Meyrowitz, *No Sense of Place.*

162. An elaboration of the Enlightenment ideology of representation that replaced the Puritan ideology of "immanence" can be found in Ziff, *Writing in the New Nation.*

163. See, for example, William Martin, "Mass Communications," *Encyclopedia of the American Religious Experience,* ed. Charles H. Lippy and Peter W. Williams (New York: Charles Scribner's Sons, 1987), 3:1711-26.

164. For a helpful historical overview see James D. Nelson, "Crunching the Tradition: Christianity and Television in Historical Perspective," in *Changing Channels,* ed. Inbody, 43-60.

165. One article will suffice: Gary Gumpert and Katherine Kurs, "Captured RAM in a Thicket," *Books and Religion* 18 (Summer 1991): 1-2, 11.

166. As quoted in Brian Winston, *Misunderstanding Media* (Cambridge, MA: Harvard University Press, 1986), 5.

167. See Franco Ferrarotti, *The End of Conversation* (New York: Greenwood Press, 1988).

168. A wonderfully witty example is Robert Abelman, "Ten Commandments of the Electronic Church," *Channels* 4 (January/February 1985): 64, 67.

not the only possessor of a face frozen in a permanent rictus of rage over television. He doubts that "our Lord would accept the Devil's offer to prime time on television," carefully manipulating the answer by the question's formulation just as surely as electronic media can manipulate their audience.[169]

Only a few have been able to argue that television has altered the shape of human consciousness more than any invention since alcohol without holding their nose. Daniel Boorstin proved a prophet in his lauding of television "for its power to disband armies, to cashier presidents, to create a whole new democratic world — democratic in ways never before imagined, even in America."[170] But even those scholars who approve television in the church do so for much the same reason that Churchill gave for being a democrat: the alternatives seem even worse.

Scholars of media can be quite cavalier with their cavils and hopelessly "logocentric." Witness the bad-mood books by Neil Postman about electronic culture. Intellectuals clearly hate television, for all the usual reasons — the most lazy of which is television's transformation of America into hippo families gradually sinking into their couches and barkolounges like mud-bathing hippos. (Robert Wuthnow reminds us that "it is not only religious television that turns people to a passive faith. The institutional church has always had a stake in promoting passivity."[171]) In fact, Neil Postman has made virtually an entire career out of shouting out the evils of television, beginning with *Teaching as a Conserving Activity* (1979), but most eloquently in *The Disappearance of Childhood* (1982) and *Amusing Ourselves to Death* (1985), which features ten chapters of critique and ten pages of constructive analysis.

Most recently, Postman has finally named the evil: *Technopoly: The Surrender of Culture to Technology* (1992). "Technopoly" is a good word to identify the totalitarian powers of this new technology, although he focuses here on computers rather than on television. Where Walter Ong sees computers promising "a heightened possibility of renewed human intercourse," Postman sees only dehumanizing tendencies in the new

169. Malcolm Muggeridge, *Christ and the Media* (Grand Rapids: Eerdmans, 1977), 84. For the manipulation charge see William Kuhns, *The Electronic Gospel: Religion and Media* (New York: Herder & Herder, 1969), 121.

170. Daniel Boorstin, *The Republic of Technology: Reflections on Our Future Community* (New York: Harper & Row, 1978), 7.

171. Robert Wuthnow, "Religion and Television: The Public and the Private," in *American Evangelicals and the Mass Media*, ed. Schultze, 205.

media. (Whether computers are indeed media, if by media we mean interactive but mediated communication, is another matter.) The computer may be, however, the defining technology for our age, which means that its cultural and religious significance needs more exploration than we have given it.[172]

The two indispensable reference sources for the history of electronic religious communications are Judith S. Duke's atlas and survey, which makes up for in depth what it lacks in breadth, and Ben Armstrong's sourcebook on religious broadcasting.[173] There is still no good comprehensive history of electronic media ministries.[174] There is also no adequate, even brief history of Christian broadcasting, although Hal Erickson's alphabetical chronicling of American religious broadcasting, while marred by a somewhat patronizing tone, provides invaluable data and background information on programs and personalities for the person who will one

172. That the computer is the defining technology of our age is the argument of J. David Bolter, *Turing's Man: Western Culture in the Computer Age* (Chapel Hill: University of North Carolina Press, 1984). Much of the recent research on computer use by the church is found in Doctor of Ministry dissertations; see, for example, John W. Gannett, "Computer Communications and the Church: Communicating Theology through the Use of a New Medium" (D.Min. diss., Lutheran School of Theology, 1992). For a sampling of the literature on religion and computers, see Kenneth B. Bedell, *Using Personal Computers in the Church* (Valley Forge, PA: Judson Press, 1982); Bedell and Parker Rossman, *Computers: New Opportunities for Personalized Ministry* (Valley Forge, PA: Judson Press, 1982); Bedell, *The Role of Computers in Religious Education* (Nashville: Abingdon Press, 1986); Bedell and Norman E. Thomas, "The Use of Computers in Mission Research," *International Bulletin of Missionary Research* 12 (October 1988): 156-60; Rossman, "Computers and Ministry: A Look at the Possibilities of Computers in the Church," *Christian Ministry,* March 1984, 10-12; Rossman, "Computers and Religious Research: Fish Imaging Fire," *American Theological Library Association Proceedings* 40 (1986): 311-21; Rossman, *Computers, Bridges to the Future: The Effect of Tomorrow's Computer Tools on Religious Thought and Institutions* (Valley Forge, PA: Judson Press, 1985); Rossman and Richard Kirby, *Christians and the World of Computers: Professional and Social Excellence in the Computer World* (Philadelphia: Trinity Press International, 1990); Rossman, *The Emerging Worldwide Electronic University: Information Age Global Higher Education* (Westport, CT: Greenwood Press, 1992). See also Gary Gumpert, *Talking Tombstones and Other Tales of the Media Age,* esp. the essay "The Last Person Who Knew Everything" (New York: Oxford University Press, 1987), 140-66.

173. Judith S. Duke, *Religious Publishing and Communications* (White Plains, NY: Knowledge Industry Publications, 1981). *Religious Broadcasting Sourcebook,* ed. Ben Armstrong, rev. ed. (Morristown, NJ: National Religious Broadcasters, 1978).

174. An early attempt at compiling historical data is George H. Hill, *Airwaves to the Soul: The Influence and Growth of Religious Broadcasting in America* (Saratoga, CA: R and E Publishers, 1983).

day write it.[175] Besides offering an early history of the programs and personalities involved in religious broadcasting, J. Harold Ellens provides an invaluable look at attempts at "electronic education" by denominations.[176]

## Telegraphy and Telephony

"What Hath God Wrought?" With this question, tapped out on telegraph on 24 May 1844, Samuel F. B. Morse signaled the beginning of a communication revolution, and the beginnings of the electronic church. Wireless telegraphy and telephony constituted new forms of electronic communication in the middle and late nineteenth century. In these "proto–mass media" of telegraph, telephone, phonograph, and electric light there lies the origin of all electrical communications and the beginnings of our transition from print beings to electronic beings.

The emergence of the telegraph in the 1840s, and its role in the Union Prayer Meeting Revival of the late 1850s, is the source of numerous touchdowns in American religious historiography, but no landings.[177] The story behind the installation of telegraphic lines and transoceanic telegraph cables and their importance to the formation of religious practices, as well as to the entire transatlantic revivalist tradition, would richly repay its chroniclers as well as readers. Where this volume is weakest is unfortunately where the scholarship is most anemic. The beginnings of the electronic church in telegraphy and telephony is one of the most anxious of topics to which scholars bring some of the most anemic and anorexic of resources. The latter nineteenth and early twentieth centuries are key areas for future study of tradition and innovation.

The telephone emerged in the third quarter of the nineteenth century,

175. Hal Erickson, *Religious Radio and Television in the United States, 1921-1991* (Jefferson, NC: McFarland, 1992). His seventeen-page introductory essay is the best and most accurate single, short introduction to the subject. See the entry on Kathryn Kuhlman (pp. 111-12) as an example of Erickson's somewhat condescending approach.

176. J. Harold Ellens, *Models of Religious Broadcasting* (Grand Rapids: Eerdmans, 1974), 95-122.

177. See also Leonard I. Sweet, "A Nation Born Again: The Union Prayer Meeting Revival and Cultural Revitalization," in *In the Great Tradition: Essays on Pluralism, Volunteerism and Revivalism, in Honor of Winthrop S. Hudson*, ed. Joseph D. Ban and Paul R. Dekar (Valley Forge, PA: Judson Press, 1982), 193-221; Marvin D. Hoff, "The Fulton Street Prayer Meeting," *Reformed Review* 17 (September 1963): 26-37; and C. E. Autrey, "The Revival of 1858," *Southwestern Journal of Theology* 1 (1958): 9-20.

the next electric communications medium to develop after the telegraph. In the late nineteenth century, Carolyn Marvin has shown, church services were occasionally transmitted by telephone (as were baseball games, concerts, and plays) to groups of people in other cities. But the sizes of these telephonic church services were small.[178] Electronic technology created anxiety among many religious leaders, especially for its ability to secularize religious themes in unpredictable ways. It could also be seen as a "peril to piety," promoting absenteeism from worship, self-indulgence over self-sacrifice, and the like.[179] Yet many other religious leaders used the telegraph and telephone to exercise authority and to extend their influence.

Marvin's refreshingly different view of the terrain places media history within a larger framework than just institutions and artifacts and is especially adept at giving us tantalizing glimpses into the conflicting religious meanings and varied responses these new technologies evoked. Marvin is surely right in stressing the continuity between the telegraph and broadcasting, rather than the more traditional quantum leap approaches that jump from the telegraph to radio to television. Marvin also contradicts the rampant technological determinism that enables historians to circle questions in communications history without attempting any answers. What determined the future, she argues, was the way people thought about the communications process, the social meanings people attributed *to* new modes of technology, not simply the technology itself.

### Radio

The first wireless voice broadcast ever released was a Christian religious program on Christmas Eve, 1906. But a wireless world ruled by broadcast radio did not come to the fore until the 1920s, when radio became a true mass medium instead of a popular hobby (see Woody Allen's film *Radio Days*), and the golden age of radio, the 1930s and 1940s, when radio brought into American homes popular entertainment and the "live" immediacy of Franklin Delano Roosevelt's "fireside chats."

America's first religious broadcast was on Westinghouse's KDKA,

---

178. Carolyn Marvin, "Early Uses of the Telephone," in *Communication in History*, ed. Crowley and Heyer, 145.

179. Carolyn Marvin, *When Old Technologies Were New: Thinking about Electric Communication in the Late Nineteenth Century* (New York: Oxford University Press, 1988), 178, 215.

America's first commercial station. On 2 January 1921, barely two months after beginning its own regular programming, KDKA invited Pittsburgh's prestigious Calvary Episcopal Church to use the new technology. Ironically and paradigmatically, the liberal rector refused to compromise his ministry with media, echoing the many fundamentalists who were initially "skeptical of the new phenomenon of radio in its early days and were convinced that no force that trespassed on the realm of the 'Prince of the power of the air' could come to any good."[180] It was the junior pastor, Lewis B. Whittemore, who ended up preaching that first Sunday on the radio. After the services became a popular feature of KDKA, the senior rector, Edwin J. Van Etten, took them over and declared the "universality of radio religion."

By 1922, there were 218 licensed broadcasting stations in the United States. A year later, there were 556. Religious organizations became leading station owners. By 1925, local churches alone held one out of every fourteen licenses given by the Department of Commerce, and churches in addition to other religious organizations owned one out of every ten radio stations. If it was not, as Susan J. Douglas puts it, "the first technology that could bring religion into people's homes," radio was the first technology that generated immediate excitement for its potential of evangelizing American culture away from those things that had undermined religious authority.[181] Radio was greeted with comparatively little controversy in contrast to television partly because the broadcasting of sermons was an "early staple" of radio transmissions from stations owned by churches.[182]

Three scholars have best helped us understand the impact of radio and its role in shaping American Protestantism: Joel Carpenter, Dennis Voskuil, and Quentin J. Schultze. Indeed, for Carpenter, one cannot understand the nature of American evangelicalism without attention to religious broadcasting and especially radio.[183]

180. Larry K. Eskridge, "Evangelical Broadcasting: Its Meaning for Evangelicals," in *Transforming Faith: The Sacred and Secular in Modern American History,* ed. M. L. Bradbury and James B. Gilbert (New York: Greenwood Press, 1989), 128.

181. Susan J. Douglas, "Broadcasting Begins," in *Communication in History,* ed. Crowley and Heyer, 196.

182. Dave Berkman, "Long Before Falwell: Early Radio and Religion — As Reported by the Nation's Periodical Press," *Journal of Popular Culture* 21 (Spring 1988): 1-11. For an early look see Spencer Miller, Jr., "Radio and Religion," *Annals of the American Academy of Political and Social Science* 177 (January 1935): 135-40.

183. Joel A. Carpenter, "From Fundamentalism to the New Evangelical Coalition," in *Evangelicalism and Modern America,* ed. Marsden, 3-16; Carpenter, "Fundamentalist Institutions and the Rise of Evangelical Protestantism, 1929-1942," *Church History* 49 (1980): 62-75.

Evangelicals, if somewhat slow at first, were quick studies in the use of radio, as Schultze and others have shown.[184] "The electronic church" or "televangelism" of the 1960s and 1970s emerged from these early radio ministries, which Schultze calls "the invisible medium."[185] Here is where one begins to see constituencies and coalitions that transcended denominations and the formation of an evangelical identity and image that helped make evangelicalism such a powerful force in American culture.

But the tale of religious radio, replete with any number of "ironies and paradoxes," continues to the present. Schultze contends that "in sheer numbers, evangelical radio was the success story of the 1970s and 1980s," although behind the scenes evangelical radio had become a religious ghetto, with supporters not necessarily coterminous with listeners.[186] The way in which radio brought together orality and electricity in the charged atmosphere of evangelism is yet to be fully explored as a factor in the evangelical dominance of the airwaves, where today it is estimated that three-fourths of all religious broadcasting is either evangelical or fundamentalist.

If it is true that "evangelical radio is so poorly researched, compared with nonreligious broadcasting, that no one knows for certain where the industry has been, let alone where it is headed," the same is doubly true for establishment radio.[187] The abortive attempts by some mainline denominations to start their own radio stations during the 1920s is scarcely known, much less studied. There has been more attention to evangelical radio than to establishment Protestant or Roman Catholic radio, partly because evangelicals are writing the history nowadays and because evangelicals from the beginning exploited the media. Evangelicals were more opportunistic in the use of radio than their establishment peers.

But why were they more optimistic about its use as well, especially since they used radio to denounce other forms of media such as film and literary "best-sellers"?[188] How does one account for the likes of Moody Bible Institute, which could initially denounce religious use of radio and then became one

184. Quentin J. Schultze, "Evangelical Radio and the Rise of the Electronic Church, 1921-1948," *Journal of Broadcasting and Electronic Media* 32 (1988): 289-306.

185. Schultze, "Evangelical Radio," 301-2. See also Schultze, "The Wireless Gospel," and Schultze, "The Invisible Medium: Evangelical Radio," in *American Evangelicals and the Mass Media*, ed. Schultze, 171-95. This is also the argument of William C. Martin, "Giving the Winds a Mighty Voice," in *Religious Television*, ed. Abelman and Hoover, 63-70.

186. Schultze, "The Invisible Medium," 171, 178.

187. Schultze, "The Invisible Medium," 187.

188. Edward M. Berckman, "The Changing Attitudes of Protestant Churches to Movies and Television," *Encounter* 41 (1980): 293-306.

of the most creative in the use of electronic technology? This reversal has yet
to be understood.[189] The role that the bewildering variety of radio ministries
may have played in the very creation of the National Association of Evangelicals (NAE) in 1941 is also still fuzzy.[190] A fine study of the 1920s periodical
literature details the "coming together" of religion and radio.[191]

Aimee Semple McPherson and Charles E. Fuller brought radio beyond
the "suck and blow" preaching reputation of its early years. Both pioneered
in the use of radio in mass evangelization, although McPherson has received
far less credit and attention than she deserves.[192] A pioneer media preacher
who embraced new electronic media with quasi-religious fervor, McPherson
was "the first woman in the world to preach a sermon over the wireless
telephone," and the first to bring down the wrath of the government for her
"wandering wavelength." She was also the first woman to hold a Federal
Communications Commission broadcaster's license. Through station KFSG,
which she started in 1924 (a comparative history of successful early stations
such as KFSG, WMBI, and KFUO would be invaluable), she pioneered a
form of mass evangelism (for example, her "Cathedral of the Air"), and
became what David Edwin Harrell calls in his contribution to this book "the
first widely recognized pentecostal evangelist and a national celebrity."

McPherson was more a TV preacher than a radio one. In her "illustrated sermons," she began preaching TV sermons before TV.[193] Amaz-

189. Gene A. Getz, *MBI: The Story of the Moody Bible Institute* (Chicago: Moody
Press, 1969).
190. For the NAE's Code of Ethics for "Gospel Broadcasting" drafted in 1943, see
Ralph M. Jennings, "Policies and Practices of Selected National Religious Bodies as Related
to Broadcasting in the Public Interest, 1920-1950" (Ph.D. diss., New York University,
1968). Joel Carpenter alludes to the instrumental role that fear among fundamentalists
and other evangelicals of being shut out from the airwaves played in the formation of the
NAE in "The Fundamentalist Leave and the Rise of an Evangelical United Front," in *The
Evangelical Tradition in America*, ed. Sweet, 257-88, esp. 265ff.
191. Berkman, "Long Before Falwell."
192. For example, Barry C. Siedell's attempt at an exhaustive look at religious radio
fails even to mention McPherson. It lifts up John Zoller, Paul Rader, R. R. Brown,
Charles E. Fuller, Donald Grey Barnhouse, T. Myron Webb, Walter A. Maier, Clarence
Jones, Reuben Larson, Clarence Erickson, Paul Meyers, J. Harold Smith, M. R. DeHaan,
Theodore Epp, and Harry Schultze. But no McPherson — and in fact, no women. Siedell,
*Gospel Radio* (Lincoln, NE: Back to the Bible Broadcast, 1971).
193. These are explored very capably by John Lathan Hood, "The New Old-Time
Religion: Aimee Semple McPherson and the Original Electric Church" (Master's thesis,
Wheaton College, 1981). See also Mary H. Kendzora, "The Homiletics of Aimee Semple
McPherson" (M.Div. thesis, Asbury Theological Seminary, 1979), esp. 73-80.

ingly, McPherson foresaw radio's extension into the realm of music and movies.[194] She was touted in her day for boasting the second-largest listening audience in Los Angeles and for pastoring the "largest radio church in the world."[195] Daniel Mark Epstein's straightforward, index-less biography *Sister Aimee* gets the basic facts in order and should stimulate historians to revise upward their estimation of her skill and savvy.[196] Unlike Harry Emerson Fosdick and to a lesser extent S. Parkes Cadman, who were deeply ambivalent about the use of radio and who decried the cinema, stage, and other forms of mass culture,[197] McPherson before her death in 1944 purchased a site for the construction of a television transmitting station on Mt. Wilson, and had she lived she would have doubtless launched America's first television ministry.[198]

Fuller's role in shaping a national identity for evangelicals can hardly be overestimated and has only partially been told.[199] By 1932, almost ten percent of all radio programming in America was religious, and Fuller's "Old-Fashioned Revival Hour" became a benchmark symbol for evangeli-

194. David L. Clark, "Miracles for a Dime: From Chautauqua Tent to Radio Station with Sister Aimee," *California History* 57 (1978/79): 354-63. Also William G. McLoughlin, "Aimee Semple McPherson: 'Your Sister in the King's Glad Service,'" *Journal of Popular Culture* 1 (1967): 193-217.

195. As quoted by Schultze, "Evangelical Radio," 295.

196. Daniel Mark Epstein, *Sister Aimee: The Life of Aimee Semple McPherson* (New York: Harcourt Brace Jovanovich, 1993). See also L. DeAne Lagerquist, "Aimee Semple McPherson," in *Twentieth-Century Shapers of American Popular Religion,* ed. Charles H. Lippy (New York: Greenwood Press, 1989), 263-70. A new biography of McPherson is forthcoming from Eerdmans, the latest volume in their Library of Religious Biography series: Edith L. Blumhofer, *Aimee Semple McPherson: Everybody's Sister* (Grand Rapids: Eerdmans, 1993).

197. For Fosdick see Robert Moats Miller, *Harry Emerson Fosdick: Preacher, Pastor, Prophet* (New York: Oxford University Press, 1985), esp. "The Dean of All Ministers of the Air: Radio's 'National Vespers Hour' Reaches Millions," 379-89; and Leonard I. Sweet's review article, "Liberalism's Lost Days: A Re-evaluation of Fosdick," *Christian Century,* 18-25 December 1985, 1176-80. For Cadman see Fred S. Hamlin, *S. Parkes Cadman: Pioneer Radio Minister* (New York: Harper, 1930).

198. Gloria Ricci Lothrop, "West of Eden: Pioneer Media Evangelist Aimee Semple McPherson in Los Angeles," *Journal of the West* 27 (1988): 50-59.

199. George Marsden has the best treatment of Fuller to date, but it focuses on his role in founding Fuller Theological Seminary: *Reforming Fundamentalism: Fuller Seminary and the New Evangelicalism* (Grand Rapids: Eerdmans, 1987). See also the interpretive piece by Edward M. Berckman, "The Old-Time Gospel Hour and Fundamentalist Paradox," *Christian Century,* 29 March 1978, 330-32, and L. David Lewis, "Charles E. Fuller," *Twentieth-Century Shapers of American Popular Religion,* ed. Lippy, 148-55.

cals, especially among the male evangelical audience.[200] The role of Fuller and religious programming in putting the new network, Mutual Broadcasting System, on strong financial footing has yet to be told. By 1943, religious broadcasters accounted for over twenty-five percent of the network's purchased airtime.

Thanks to radio and TV personality Fulton J. Sheen, Family Rosary Crusade founder Father Patrick ("The family that prays together stays together") Peyton, and hit movies from the 1930s to the 1960s, such as *The Bells of St. Mary's, On the Waterfront, Boystown, The Nun's Story, The Cardinal, Going My Way,* and *I Confess,* there was a powerful presence of Catholic culture in the media that cries out for more study. There is a desperate need to understand Father Charles E. Coughlin, the pioneer radio preacher who combined Catholic doctrine with anticommunism in garnering a radio audience of more than 45 million, as more than a right-wing polemicist and anti-Semite who more than anyone else got Franklin D. Roosevelt elected to the presidency.[201]

Establishment figures such as S. Parkes Cadman, Ralph Sockman, Harry Emerson Fosdick, David H. C. Read, Norman Vincent Peale, Daniel A. Poling, and Rabbi Stephen S. Wise typify the way mainline religious leaders once had a virtual "market monopoly on religious radio."[202] In fact, in the very same year (1923) that fundamentalist preacher R. R. Brown started the first nondenominational radio weekly, "Radio Chapel Service," over Omaha station WOW, the Greater New York Federation of Churches established a radio division that featured popular Brooklyn pastor S. Parkes Cadman on what they called the

200. It is suggestive that by 1945 men preferred only news above religious broadcasts in daytime radio programming; as cited by Schultze, "Evangelical Radio," 297.

201. A modest beginning is Ellens's portrait in *Models of Religious Broadcasting,* 55-61, and D. P. Noonan, *The Catholic Communicators* (Huntington, IN: Our Sunday Visitor, 1990), 10-39. An early attempt at biography is L. B. Ward, *Father Charles E. Coughlin* (Detroit: Tower Publications, 1933). Unfortunately, Richard Akin Davis's "Radio Priest: The Public Career of Father Charles Edward Coughlin" (Ph.D. diss., University of North Carolina, 1974) remains unrevised and unpublished.

202. Dennis N. Voskuil, "Reaching Out: Mainline Protestantism and the Media," in *Between the Times: The Travail of the Protestant Establishment in America, 1900-1960,* ed. William R. Hutchison (Cambridge: Cambridge University Press, 1989), 86. For Fosdick see R. Scott Appleby, "Harry Emerson Fosdick," in *Twentieth-Century Shapers of American Popular Religion,* ed. Lippy, 141-48, and Sweet, "Liberalism's Lost Days." For Sockman see William B. Lawrence, "Ralph Washington Sockman," in *Twentieth-Century Shapers of American Popular Religion,* ed. Lippy, 27-42, and Lawrence, "Ralph Sockman: The Compleat Methodist," *Quarterly Review* 5 (Winter 1985): 27-42.

"National Radio Pulpit," which had the "distinction of being the first network religious series — before there was an official network" called NBC.[203] It was the "Big Three" religious groups (Protestant, Catholic, and Jewish) that helped write the self-regulatory protocols for religious broadcasting, a prominent feature of which was the distribution of free or "sustaining" network time to Federal Council of Churches' approved religious groups.[204] It was also the "Big Three" that contributed much to radio's success through their "National Radio Pulpit," "Lutheran Hour," "Catholic Hour," "Message of Israel," and "The Eternal Light" (emanating from Jewish Theological Seminary).

The story of the mainstream versus outsider struggle in religious broadcasting history, how the evangelicals beat out the liberals for the airwaves, is best told by Dennis Voskuil with good help from Richard Ostling.[205] It was evangelicals' use of communications technology, and their establishment of parachurch media networks, that was the key to the emergence of evangelicalism's cultural authority as the new mainstream Protestant tradition. Voskuil also gives us the best account of the decoupling of mainstream Protestantism between 1900 and 1960 from what Robert Lynn has called the "Media Society."[206] In Voskuil's words,

> Ironically, the mainline Protestants, who were most appreciative of modern science, most ebullient about the potential for human progress, and most willing to accommodate theology to modern thought forms, did not successfully exploit the new technologies of mass communication.[207]

The rest is not, as they say, history, but is very much of the present. Mainline Protestantism and Roman Catholicism seem intent on replaying in the twentieth century the Council of Trent's inability to see in the

203. Hal Erickson, *Religious Radio and Television in the United States, 1921-1991: The Programs and Personalities* (Jefferson, NC: McFarland, 1992), 2-3.

204. See Jennings, "Policies and Practices of Selected National Religious Bodies."

205. Dennis N. Voskuil, "The Power of the Air: Evangelicals and the Rise of Religious Broadcasting," in *American Evangelicals and the Mass Media*, ed. Schultze, 69-95. Richard N. Ostling, "Evangelical Publishing and Broadcasting," in *Evangelicalism and Modern America*, ed. Marsden, 46-55.

206. Voskuil, "Reaching Out," 72-92, and Robert W. Lynn, "The Unnoticed Revolution: Mainline Protestantism and the Media Society" (unpublished manuscript, presented at Claremont, CA, in 1974).

207. Voskuil, "Reaching Out," 72.

sixteenth century the consequences of the spread of literacy and print technologies.[208]

Far from historiography having withered into biography and sociology, as in some other areas of inquiry, there is a desperate need for monographic treatment of the radio days of both mainline and fundamentalist groups.[209] What good studies there are now have to be assembled piecemeal. The stories of these radio pioneers and their blockbuster broadcasts are worthy of independent treatments: R. R. Brown ("World Radio Congregation"); T. Myron Webb ("Bible Fellowship Hour"); Clarence Erickson ("Heaven and Home Hour"); J. Harold Smith ("Radio Bible Hour"); Theodore H. Epp ("Back to the Bible"); John Zoller ("America Back to God Hour"); Walter A. Maier ("The Lutheran Hour"), and America's first Christian-owned radio station KFUO in 1924; Paul Rader ("The March of Ages"); Donald Grey Barnhouse ("Bible Study Hour"); M. R. De Haan ("Radio Bible Class"); one of the most interesting personalities that ever took to the airwaves, "Fighting Bob" Shuler (KGEF for "Keep God Ever First"); Henry Schultze and Peter Eldersveld ("Back to God Hour"); and my personal favorite, Paul Myers ("Haven of Rest").[210]

208. This is the historical context in which to place Barbara G. Wheeler's call for denominations to step forward to safeguard serious theological publishing. See Wheeler, "Theological Publishing: In Need of a Mandate," *Christian Century,* 23 November 1988, 1066-70.

209. Siedell's minimally footnoted and uncritical history entitled *Gospel Radio* is surprisingly accurate, although its evangelistic thrust necessitates careful usage.

210. For the "Back to God Hour," see David DeGroot, *World's Beyond: The Story of the Back to God Hour, 1939-1979* (Palos Heights, IL: Back to God Hour, 1979), and Ellens, *Models of Religious Broadcasting,* 46-55. For Paul Rader see Larry K. Eskridge, "Only Believe: Paul Rader and the Chicago Gospel Tabernacle, 1922-1933" (Master's thesis, University of Maryland at College Park, 1985); also *Jazz Age Evangelism: Paul Rader and the Chicago Gospel Tabernacle, 1922-1933* (Wheaton, IL: Archives of the Billy Graham Center, Wheaton College, 1984). For De Haan see James R. Adair, *M. R. De Haan: The Man and His Ministry* (Grand Rapids: Zondervan, 1969). Charley Orbison gives a balanced and insightful look into the muckraker minister in "'Fighting Bob' Shuler: Early Radio Crusader," *Journal of Broadcasting* 21 (1977): 459. For Paul Myers see the memorial tribute booklet dated 28 January 1973, *"First Mate Bob": Paul Myers, Founder of "Haven of Rest"* (Hollywood: Haven of Rest, 1973). For Walter A. Maier see Guy C. Carter, "Walter A. Maier," in *Twentieth-Century Shapers of American Popular Religion,* ed. Lippy, 270-77.

## Television

The study of televangelism is a field of such noise and confusion that one goes near it only with gloves, goggles, and defoggers.[211] Televangelism has been analyzed in a dizzying variety of arenas — from the *Fundamentalist Journal* to *Forbes* to *Penthouse* and *Playboy* magazines. As a social movement that "has no obvious parallel anywhere else in the Western Hemisphere," it has been rated the reigning force of our day when measured in terms of "undisputed access to the airwaves."[212] As a theological movement, it has been rated one of the most technologically astute and theologically "antediluvian" forces at work in the world today: the "seemingly effortless employment of the most modern skills of the technological age in the service of the positively antediluvian ideal of a pre-enlightened mentality, and repelled by the unapologetic assertion of beliefs assumed dead since Darwin."[213] As a religious movement, it is "a farrago of preaching, personalities, promotions, and politics," making it as senseless to talk about the "electronic church" as the "American church."[214]

Everybody says how bad religious television is. Certainly there is much that is risible, and more that is shocking, about televangelism. But most who have written on it are unreliable guides to its curiosities. How good could it be? Can it be good? What is the answer to this question from within the Christian community?

From the evangelical side, Virginia Stem Owens seems to suggest that the answer is no. ("The answer to the question 'Can't we do it better?' is obviously no. Or at least we haven't.")[215] Malcolm Muggeridge and Jacques Ellul similarly portray modern mass communications as a form of

211. For the defogger see Stewart M. Hoover, "Ten Myths About Religious Broadcasting," in *Religious Television,* ed. Abelman and Hoover, 23-39.

212. At least this is the argument of Kimberly Neuendorf and Robert Abelman, "Televangelism: A Look at Communicator Style," *Journal of Religious Studies* 13 (1987): 41-57.

213. S. J. D. Green, "The Medium and the Message: Televangelism in America," *American Quarterly* 44 (March 1992): 136. Compare Robert S. Alley's rather incantational "Television, Religion and Fundamentalist Distortions," in *Religious Television,* ed. Abelman and Hoover, 265-73, with Tyron Inbody's provocative "Television as a Medium for Theology," in *Changing Channels,* ed. Inbody, 79-96.

214. This is the argument of Quentin J. Schultze, "Defining the Electronic Church," in *Religious Television,* ed. Abelman and Hoover, 41-51.

215. Virginia Stem Owens, *The Total Image, Or Selling Jesus in the Modern Age* (Grand Rapids: Eerdmans, 1980).

idolatry that willy-nilly compromises every religious movement that touches it.[216]

From the mainline side, in one of the strangest articles ever published on religion and communications, James A. Taylor argues at the same time that Jesus would never have used television as a medium for preaching the gospel, that no one can be converted through mass media since this can only be done by face-to-face exchanges (print was never used for conversion?), and that, just as the Protestant Reformation was the child of printing, so the future face of faith in the "new Reformation" will be the child of telecommunications, and liberal churches "might as well face the fact that more and more people who would otherwise have belonged to our churches are going to be born again out of television's experiential womb."[217] Harvey Cox also says no, that there is "something *in the television medium* itself," a "built-in dynamic" that makes religious television a threat to true faith and democratic societies.[218] John Black's textbook on communication studies devotes but eight pages to "mass media" and dismisses mass media as a vehicle of "limited usefulness" for social change.[219]

Clearly, much of the available scholarship shows tremendous distaste for the subject, especially that which emerges from liberal Protestantism. Peter G. Horsfield's *Religious Television* (1984) is a case in point, although Horsfield is of a different mind today. Similarly, William Fore's widely cited attacks on televangelism have kept up their intensity, although his attacks on television as a medium itself, particularly as a means of "pre-evangelism," have softened over the years.[220] Hors-

---

216. Muggeridge, *Christ and the Media;* Jacques Ellul, *Humiliation of the Word* (Grand Rapids: Eerdmans, 1985).

217. James A. Taylor, "Progeny of Programmers: Evangelical Religion and the Television Age," *Christian Century,* 20 April 1977, 379-82.

218. Harvey G. Cox, "Religion, Politics, Television," *Christianity and Crisis,* 17 November 1986, 408-9.

219. Black is quoting here a WACC study extrapolated from a third-world setting. John Black, *Christian Communication Reconsidered* (Geneva: WCC, 1989), 44-51, esp. 50.

220. See, for example, William F. Fore, "The Electronic Church," *Ministry* 1 (January 1979): 4-7; Fore, "Beyond the Electronic Church," *Christian Century,* 7-14 January 1981, 29-30; Fore, "A Critical Eye on Televangelism," *Christian Century,* 23 September 1981, 939-41; Fore, " 'Living Church' and 'Electronic Church' Compared," in *Religious Television,* ed. Abelman and Hoover, 135-46. One can see the difference simply in contrasting Fore's *Image and Impact: How Man Comes Through the Mass Media* (New York: Friendship Press, 1970) or his *Television and Religion: The Shaping of Faith, Values and Culture* (Minneapolis: Augsburg, 1987) with his more recent *Mythmakers: Gospel, Culture and the Media* (New York: Friendship Press, 1990).

field's book was as unapologetically antagonistic as Ben Armstrong's *The Electronic Church* (1979) was unabashedly apologetic and optimistic.[221]

Scholars like Horsfield have managed relatively unsuccessfully not to gag on the televangelist fare. Even when historians of "popular culture" explore the coming together of media, pop culture, and religion, although they try as hard as they can to take the subject seriously, it still comes out as *The God Pumpers,* with the "central" focus being "is this revival or rip off?"[222] Or as another historian puts the choice for "serious" study after a colleague explored televangelist images in editorial cartoons, "Electronic Church: Fearsome or Folly?"[223]

Aside from Schultze's penetrating and comprehensive *Televangelism and American Culture,* the most refreshingly different view of the terrain is Derrick de Kerckhove's analysis of televangelism as a neurological phenomenon of equal importance to its theological and liturgical and sociological implications. Clearly on the McLuhanesque side of the media debate, de Kerckhove takes McLuhan farther and argues that medium changes not only the style or the content of the message, but more importantly *"the programming and the accessing mode of the spectator"* as well.

> Television does not merely create an audience and considerably extend the impact of evangelism over greater numbers of people, thus furthering the impact of radio evangelism; it also modifies the nature of this audience and shapes the human nervous system according to its own very specific patterns.[224]

De Kerckhove argues for an ironic view of televangelism: it stands as one of the few "truly democratic" services still available today. It is funded solely and directly by the people who use it, and its continuation

221. Ben Armstrong, *The Electronic Church* (Nashville: Thomas Nelson, 1979).

222. Marshall Fishwick, "From Sea to Shining Sea," in *The God Pumpers,* ed. Fishwick and Browne, 15.

223. Edward H. Sewell, Jr., "Exorcism of Fools: Images of the Televangelist in Editorial Cartoons," and Nick Thorndike, "Electronic Church: Fearsome or Folly?" both in *The God Pumpers,* ed. Fishwick and Browne, 46-59 and 174-82, respectively.

224. Derrick de Kerckhove, "Televangelism: A Theology for the Central Nervous System," *Communio* 9 (Fall 1982): 260 and 258. See also Quentin J. Schultze, *Televangelism and American Culture: The Business of Popular Religion* (Grand Rapids: Baker Book House, 1991).

is at the discretion of the "consumer's good will and not by the producers' fixing the prices."[225]

Perhaps the greatest problem for historians is the imagistic values of postmodern culture. The anti-visual bias of scholars — where pictures are inferior to words, visual talking to verbal talking — is well established and entrenched. But there is also another reason for the academic distrust and dislike of images. In the *Annales*-school sense, "history" means something too narrow if it only encompasses society, law, religion, household, even ecobiology, and doesn't include visual images. Scholars have never forgiven electronic communications for holding so much promise as a "class medium" (art form) but quickly becoming a "mass medium."[226]

Nothing in print has matched the sheer sarcasm and snideness of Tim Luke's article "From Fundamentalism to Televangelism," which analyzes Christian fundamentalism from a Marxist perspective as an "audiovisual cult," created by corporate capitalism, that dispenses the "uppers of success, healing, and fulfillment to those many troubled, upwardly mobile people who are going through 'tough times' in the corporate marketplace."[227] As fundamentalism became a consumption community, prime dogmas were replaced by prima donnas.

> Average American consumers, as they matured and sought to know God, flipped the channel from "Mister Rogers' Neighborhood" to "Oral Roberts," quit the "Mickey Mouse Club" to join the "700 Club," and dropped "Ted Mack's Amateur Hour" to tune in to Jerry Falwell's "Old-Time Gospel Hour." In consumer society, Jesus or God, like Wonder Bread or Geritol, is sold telegenically as healing bodies, mending lives, renewing health, and changing attitudes.[228]

Is no one out there in the establishment world saying yes to mediated ministries? Dennis Benson, Donald Oberdorfer, John W. Bachman, and Stewart Hoover have been both inclusive and interpretive of mediated ministries, although too much of their creative energy has been spent on the one-

225. De Kerckhove, "Televangelism," 264.
226. This is suggested by William C. Martin, "Perspectives on the Electronic Church," in *Varieties of Southern Religious Experience,* ed. Samuel S. Hill (Baton Rouge: Louisiana State University Press, 1987), 173-89, esp. 180.
227. Tim Luke, "From Fundamentalism to Televangelism," *Telos* 16 (1983-84): 204-10, esp. 205.
228. Luke, "From Fundamentalism to Televangelism," 206.

handed "blessing or curse," "wasteland or wonderland" debate.[229] Robert A. White, research director for the London-based Centre for the Study of Communication and Culture, also responds affirmatively.[230] He and others, such as Martin Marty from the Protestant side and Ellwood E. Kieser from the Catholic side, offer blueprints to "wired ministries" in a world electronic community, even suggesting how the video camera might supplement the pen and pencil for composing postmodern ministry.[231] James McDonnell and French scholar Pierre Babin are calling for critical "discernment" and discrimination as well as affirmation of the role and place of media in contemporary society.[232] A new kind of spirituality is being born in an electronic culture: "Jesus spoke of salt; why should we not speak of radar?" Babin asks.

Perhaps the most theoretically sophisticated answer to the query comes from Mark Hulsether, who uses poststructuralist cultural criticism to show that mainstream evangelicalism, even as it is expressed through popular religious television, can have oppositional potential and "take the form of postmodern political resistance."[233]

Some of the most sophisticated studies of the mediatization of Amer-

229. Dennis C. Benson, *Electronic Evangelism* (Nashville: Abingdon, 1973), and Benson, *The Visible Church* (Nashville: Abingdon, 1988); Donald N. Oberdorfer, *Electronic Christianity: Myth or Ministry* (Taylor Falls, MN: Brekke, 1982); John W. Bachman, *Media: Wasteland or Wonderland* (Minneapolis: Augsburg, 1984); Stewart M. Hoover, *The Electronic Giant: A Critique of the Telecommunications Revolution from a Christian Perspective* (Elgin, IL: Brethren, 1982), and Hoover, *Mass Media Religion: The Social Sources of the Electronic Church* (Newbury Park, CA: Sage, 1988). See also the very early article "The Church Must Use Television" by Charles Brackbill, Jr., *Religion in Life* 22 (Winter 1952-53): 110-21.

230. Robert A. White, "Mass Communication and Culture: Transition to a New Paradigm," *Journal of Communication* 33 (1983): 279-301.

231. See Martin E. Marty, *The Improper Opinion: Mass Media and the Christian Faith* (Philadelphia: Westminster Press, 1961), and Ellwood E. Kieser, "Evangelism through Electronics," *America*, 6 May 1978, 358-61. See also Gene Jaberg and Louis G. Wargo, Jr., *The Video Pencil: Cable Communications for Church and Community* (Washington, DC: University Press of America, 1980); Donald N. Oberdorfer, *Electronic Christianity: Myth or Ministry* (Taylor Falls, MN: John L. Brekke, 1982). An early attempt at constructive theorizing about religion and electronic communication was Everett C. Parker, Elinor Iman, and Ross Syder, *Religious Radio: What to Do and How* (New York: Harper, 1948).

232. James McDonnell, "Christian Discernment in a Mass-Mediated Culture," and Pierre Babin, "The Spirituality of Media People," both in "Communications, Media and Spirituality," *Way* Supplement 57 (Autumn 1986): 36-45 and 46-54, respectively. See also Babin, *A New Era in Religious Communications*.

233. Mark Hulsether, "Evangelical Popular Religion as a Source for North American Liberation? Insights from Postmodern Popular Culture Theory," *American Studies* 33 (Spring 1992): 63-81.

ican life are occurring in the realm of culture studies. Robert Wuthnow explores the "paradox" of mediated ministry: television privatizes religious faith while it simultaneously and paradoxically drives religion into the public arena and turns private issues into public ones. Televised religion both pulls faith in more privatized directions and stimulates the role of religion in public life.[234] The way television is in and of itself a "new religion" that can fulfill religious functions in a person's life was first addressed by John Wiley Nelson, then successively by George Gerbner, former dean of the Annenberg School of Communication at the University of Pennsylvania; William Fore; Quentin Schultze; and most notably by Gregor T. Goethals, whose work on the sacramental aspects of television and its ritual functions and visual symbols is still underappreciated.[235]

Apart from Boomershine, Stewart Hoover and Quentin Schultze have been the loudest lone voices for televangelism in the land of faith, although Schultze admits that "only the fool would claim to know for certain what role [electronic media] should play in religious faith and practice."[236] While the kind of study that televangelism deserves has yet to be written, Hoover's study provides a model of how it may be done.[237]

234. Robert Wuthnow, "Religion and Television: The Public and the Private," in *American Evangelicals and the Mass Media,* ed. Schultze, 199-214, esp. 202, and Wuthnow, *The Struggle for America's Soul: Evangelicals, Liberals, and Secularism* (Grand Rapids: Eerdmans, 1989).

235. John Wiley Nelson, *Your God Is Alive and Well and Appearing in Popular Culture* (Philadelphia: Westminster Press, 1976). George Gerbner and Kathleen Connolly, "Television as New Religion," *New Catholic World,* March-April 1978, 52-56. Quentin J. Schultze, *Television: Manna from Hollywood* (Grand Rapids: Zondervan, 1986); Schultze, "Secular Television as Popular Religion," in *Religious Television,* ed. Abelman and Hoover, 239-48; Schultze, "Television Drama as a Sacred Text," in *Channels of Belief,* ed. Ferré, 3-28. Fore, *Television and Religion.* Gregor Goethals's first book, *The TV Ritual: Worship at the Video Altar* (Boston: Beacon Press, 1981), is widely quoted but seldom taken seriously. Even so, this volume has received much more attention than her subsequent work, *The Electronic Golden Calf: Images, Religion, and the Making of Meaning* (Cambridge, MA: Cowley Publications, 1990); see also Goethals, "Religious Communication and Popular Piety," *Journal of Communication* 35 (Winter 1985): 149-56; Goethals, "The Church and the Mass Media: Competing Architects of Our Dominant Symbols, Rituals and Myths," in *Communicating Faith in a Technological Age,* ed. McDonnell and Trampiets, 56-77; and Goethals, "Afterword," in *Changing Channels,* ed. Inbody, 157-60.

236. See Hoover, *The Electronic Giant,* and Quentin J. Schultze, *Redeeming Television: How TV Changes Christians — How Christians Can Change TV* (Downers Grove, IL: InterVarsity Press, 1992). The quote is from Schultze, "The Place of Television in the Church's Communication," in *Changing Channels,* ed. Inbody, 36.

237. Hoover, *Mass Media Religion.*

In challenging us to think institutionally about the production of telecommunications, Hoover plunges into waters few scholars have dared to disturb.[238] One of the most unusual and promising scholarly projects in recent years has been the multidisciplinary, collaborative analysis of religion and media by the faculty of United Theological Seminary funded by the Lilly Endowment. Approaching their task with critical flair, jigsawed sensibilities, and good humor, a group of scholars risked getting a bad name for good-mouthing a subject.[239]

Quentin J. Schultze's *Redeeming Television* (1992) is a welcome advance of the consumer-as-passive-victim account of the mass media. Designed as the answer to Neil Postman and all others who argue that television is inherently distorting of the truth, Schultze presents a hopeful case for the medium of television.[240] He bases his argument in Reformed theology's "cultural mandate," which stresses human responsibility for the care of all creation (Gen. 1:28).[241] Schultze wants to transform passive TV "watchers" into critical "viewers."[242] He and Robert A. White are writing extensively on how faith communities can help to shape what White calls the movement toward a New World Information and Communication Order (NWICO).[243]

Most scholars identify four types of religious programming on television, all of which need study. First and rarest are ecumenical and denominational programs, some of which are long running ("This Is the Life" [Lutherans], "Faith for Today" [Seventh-Day Adventists], "Insight"

238. See especially Hoover, *The Electronic Giant.*

239. The participating scholars included Donald B. Rogers, Pamela Mitchell, Tyron Inbody, Thomas E. Boomershine, James D. Nelson, Norman E. Thomas, Kenneth Bedell, Gregor Goethals, and consultant Quentin Schultze. The publication issuing from their efforts is *Changing Channels,* ed. Inbody. The need for media education in theological education is the theme of the special congress issue of *Media Development* on "Communication and Theological Education," October 1989. See esp. Paul A. J. Soukup's "Changing the Way Communication Is Taught in Seminaries," 2-5.

240. See also Coleen Cook, *All That Glitters: A Newsperson Explores the World of Television* (Chicago: Moody Press, 1992).

241. Schultze, *Redeeming Television.*

242. Quentin J. Schultze, "Religious Belief in a Technological World: The Implications of the Electronic Church," in *Communicating Faith in a Technological Age,* ed. McDonnell and Trampiets, 112-29; and Schultze, "The Place of Television in the Church's Communication," 23-42.

243. Robert A. White, "Christians Building a New Order of Communication," in *Communication for All: New World Information and Communication Order,* ed. Philip Lee (Maryknoll, NY: Orbis Books, 1986), 105-17.

[Paulists]). Second are the weekly worship services televised by local congregations. Third are the syndicated programs purchased by televangelism (by 1990 purchased airtime accounted for 92 percent of religious telecasting). Fourth are the cable and satellite networks, such as CBN, Trinity, the Jewish Television Network, ACTS/VISN. The whole of religious television programming, which is tremendously diverse and vibrant, has not achieved anywhere near the scholarly attention that televangelism has. Since the late 1960s, evangelicals have mastered media niche programming, offering something for the disabled ("Joni and Friends"), the sports enthusiasts ("Sports Forum"), the ideologues ("The John Ankerberg Show"), youth ("Christian Countdown"), the troubled ("Dial the Pastor"), the children ("Davey and Goliath"), the parents (James B. Dobson's "Focus on the Family" empire), and so forth. All of this programming, which addresses the pedagogical needs of the evangelical community, as well as its evangelistic ambitions, needs further study. The relationships between television and religious institutions have not been looked at enough from the vantage point of broadcasters themselves, which is what makes A. William Bluem's guidelines for religious programming so significant.[244]

## Televangelism

The historiography on televangelism has framed its subject primarily in political, social, economic, and religious terms.

*The Political Frame* There is a whole genre of scholarship worthy of an essay in and of itself that critiques televangelism for its propensity to venture into a variety of political arenas.[245] Sociologists Jeffrey K. Hadden

---

244. A. William Bluem, *Religious Television Programs* (New York: Hastings House, 1969). See also Horace M. Newcomb, "Religion on Television," in *Channels of Belief,* ed. Ferré, 29-44.

245. See, for example, Robert Abelman and Kimberly Neuendorf, "How Religious Is Religious Television Programming?" *Journal of Communication* 35 (1985): 98-110, and Robert Abelman and Gary R. Pettey, "How Political Is Religious Television Programming?" *Journalism Quarterly* 65 (1988): 313-19. The three essays on the separation or lack thereof between "electronic church and state" in *Religious Television,* ed. Abelman and Hoover, are especially helpful: Gary R. Pettey, "Bibles, Ballots, and Beatific Vision: The Cycle of Religious Activism in the 1980's," 197-205; Anthony T. Podesta and James S. Kurtzke, "Conflict Between the Electronic Church and State: The Religious Right's Crusade Against Pluralism," 207-26; and Larry Gross, "Religion, Television, and Politics: The Right Bank of the Mainstream," 227-36.

and Anson Shupe's *Televangelism,* despite an overreach and overbite in their assessment of the political power of the religious right, is a worthy follow-up to the earlier treatment by Hadden and Charles E. Swann called *Prime Time Preachers*.[246] Hadden makes evangelicalism too monolithic, and he overstates the case for the mobilizing influence of televangelism in the emergence of political movements. But Hadden has done scholars a tremendous service by his even-handed approach to televangelism, especially its relationship to politics. Thanks to Hadden, it is possible to be serious without simultaneously being snide, sarcastic, or sanctimonious about the phenomenon (a la Neil Postman's "the best things on television *are* its junk").

Hadden classifies four phases of mood and approach in media coverage of the New Christian Right (NCR), and especially its foremost instrument, Jerry Falwell's Moral Majority ("seldom in modern history has the emergence of an interest group attracted so much attention"): these phrases range from alarm to assessment to dismissal to assumption of their presence and power. Hadden emphasizes the role of televangelism in the formation of the NCR, the ability of the media to pump tremendous resources into the NCR political movement, and the shifting allegiance and alliance of evangelicals with the Republican Party.[247]

Hadden's employment of the conceptual model of resource mobilization theory in understanding Pat Robertson's 1988 presidential campaign has caused him to join Jeremy Rifkin in arguing that televangelists will have a major role in shaping America's political future.[248] Recent

246. Jeffrey K. Hadden and Anson Shupe, *Televangelism: Power and Politics on God's Frontier* (New York: Henry Holt, 1988). For a briefer treatment of their book, see Hadden and Shupe, "Televangelism in America," *Social Compass* 34 (1987): 61-74. Hadden and Charles E. Swann, *Prime Time Preachers: The Rising Power of Televangelism* (Reading, MA: Addison-Wesley Publishing Co., 1981). See also the less useful but better written study by James Morris, *The Preachers* (New York: St. Martin's Press, 1973).

247. He also makes the case for NCR in Hadden and Shupe, *Televangelism,* 291-92. Jeffrey K. Hadden, "Conservative Christians, Televangelism, and Politics: Taking Stock a Decade after the Founding of the Moral Majority," in *In Gods We Trust: New Patterns of Religious Pluralism in America,* ed. Thomas Robbins and Dick Anthony, 2d ed. (New Brunswick, NJ: Transaction Publishers, 1990), 463-72. The quote about the Moral Majority is taken from p. 464.

248. Jeremy Rifkin, *The Emerging Order* (New York: G. P. Putnam's Sons, 1979). For Jeffrey K. Hadden see "Televangelism and Political Mobilization," in *American Evangelicals and the Mass Media,* ed. Schultze, 215-29; Hadden, "Religious Broadcasting and the New Christian Right," *Journal for the Scientific Study of Religion* 26 (1987): 1-24; Hadden, "Televangelism and the Future of Politics," in *New Christian Politics,* ed. David G.

scholars are more prone to see the religious right as less political and more complex than heretofore thought.[249] There is a special need to place the religious right in broader historical context.[250] Historians have not "Fibber McGeed" every closet yet in the house of politics and televangelism, but they seem to have been trying.

*The Social Frame* Jeffrey Hadden calls televangelism "one of the most important social movements of the century," potentially "of the order and magnitude of the revolution that Martin Luther symbolized."[251] Unfortunately, as Stewart M. Hoover notes, "most religious broadcasting research has been dominated by the quantitative and functional approaches," which are as preoccupied with issues of audience size and composition as they are with the social phenomenon itself.[252] Of course, part of the reason for this preoccupation is the question of evangelicalism's power within American culture. But Hoover's call for "qualitative research of audience experiences," which he himself models in his anthropological study of the

---

Bromley and Anson Shupe (Macon: Mercer University Press, 1984),151-65, reprinted as "Television and Politics," in *Piety and Politics: Evangelicals and Fundamentalists Confront the World,* ed. Richard John Neuhaus and Michael Cromartie (Washington, DC: Ethics and Public Policy Center, 1987), 379-94.

249. See Jon Meacham, "What the Religious Right Can Teach the New Democrats," *Washington Monthly,* April 1993, 42-46.

250. George Marsden does this in an early essay, "Preachers of Paradox: The Religious New Right in Historical Perspective," in *Religion and America: Spirituality in a Secular Age,* ed. Mary Douglas and Steve Tipton (Boston: Beacon Press, 1982), 150-68.

251. As quoted in introduction to Jeffrey K. Hadden, "Televangelism and Politics," in *Piety and Politics,* ed. Neuhaus and Cromartie, 379.

252. Stewart M. Hoover, "The Meaning of Religious Television: The '700 Club' in the Lives of Its Viewers," in *American Evangelicals and the Mass Media,* ed. Schultze, 231. Hoover's own contribution to the discussion can be found in his *Mass Media Religion.* An excellent beginning look at "The Social Significance of Religious Television" is by Robert Wuthnow, in *Religious Television,* ed. Abelman and Hoover, 87-98. For a review of the debate over audience size, see Eskridge, "Evangelical Broadcasting," esp. 136-37 n. 6, and Hoover, "The Religious Television Audience: A Matter of Significance or Size?" in *Religious Television,* ed. Abelman and Hoover, 109-29. More specifically, see Everett Parker, David Barry, and Dallas Smythe, *The Television-Radio Audience and Religion* (New York: Harper, 1955); Jeffrey K. Hadden, "The Great Audience Size Debate," *Religious Broadcasting* 18 (January 1986): 20-22; and Hadden, "Getting to the Bottom of the Audience Size Debate," *Religious Broadcasting* 18 (February 1986): 88, 116, 122, 124, 126, 128. For an ethnographic study of PTL's reach in a small Ohio town, see Louise M. Bourgault, "The PTL Club and Protestant Viewers: An Ethnographic Study," *Journal of Communication* 35 (1985): 132-48.

"700 Club," needs to be followed up.[253] What is the social context of television viewing, and what are the social effects of that experience? The history of audience "appropriation" (Roger Chartier) of print messages suggests that no audience can be trusted simply to accept unedited any media offering. Electronic communications seem especially receptive to audience modulations.

The Annenberg-Gallup two-year study of religion and television asked such questions as these: "Is religion on television more religion than television or more television than religion?" What about the "electronic church" and its viewers? Who and how many are they? The value of this study was its placing the phenomenon within the larger social and cultural context of what is going on in American life.[254] The limited usefulness of the study inheres in its marked mainline bias and in the need to interpret and evaluate televangelism from a variety of standpoints.[255] The elderly, the disabled, and the isolated may use televangelism differently, for example, from active members of a local congregation.

In spite of this growing sociological literature on the subject, there is still a lot we don't know enough about, even the who and how many and what kind of people are watching on a regular basis.[256] Our best data to date suggests that televangelism's audience most likely peaked around 1978, and has remained there or declined slightly since then. The dimly understood world-class and transcultural credentials of evangelical broadcasting have been placed in historical perspective and ably assessed by Dennis A. Smith, Robert Fortner, and Peter Horsfield.[257]

253. Hoover, "The Meaning of Religious Television," 241.

254. *Religious Television Survey* (Princeton: The Gallup Organization, 1984); *Religion and Television: A Research Report by The Annenberg School of Communications, University of Pennsylvania and the Gallup Organization, Inc.,* ed. George Gerbner et al. (Philadelphia: Annenberg School of Communications, University of Pennsylvania, 1984). See William F. Fore's helpful analysis of this report in "Religion and Television: Report on the Research," *Christian Century,* 18-25 July 1984, 710-13.

255. Schultze's critique of the report is excellent. See his "Vindicating the Electronic Church? An Assessment of the Annenberg-Gallup Study," *Critical Studies in Mass Communication* 2 (Fall 1985): 283-90. See also the cautionary review by James F. Engel, "Caution: Data Subject to Interpretation," *Religious Broadcasting* 16 (June 1984): 26-27; and Harold Hostetler's second thoughts, "How Many Are Really Watching?" *Religious Broadcasting* 16 (September 1984): 18-19.

256. Robert Abelman, "Who's Watching, For What Reasons?" in *Religious Television,* ed. Abelman and Hoover, 99-108.

257. Dennis A. Smith, "The Gospel According to the United States: Evangelical Broadcasting in Central America," and Robert S. Fortner, "Saving the World? American

The area of most shoddy scholarship surrounds the "exposés" which followed the televangelism scandals that blew open the televangelism business beginning in March of 1987.[258] Not only did the scandals release a barrage of studies that turned up the lurid lights on "telescandals," even leading one scholar to argue that commentators such as Ted Koppel were doing more than "reporting" the telescandals; "they *co-authored* it, most spectacularly on TV."[259] Veteran religion reporter George W. Cornell argues that they also stimulated growth in religion news reporting in the mainstream press.[260]

Of course, religious scandals of media figures did not begin with the ubiquitous, uxorious Jim Bakker and his PTL Club cohorts, or with Jimmy Swaggart's red-light night visitations or Oral Roberts's death-defying fund-raising schemes or Rex Humbard's girdle factories.[261] For this, one has to reach back to Sister Aimee's "kidnapping" disappearance, A. A. Allen's drunk-driving charges, Billy James Hargis's sexual escapades with males and females (discovered by one young couple on their wedding night), and Leroy Jenkins's arson conviction and twelve-year prison term.

The best of the post-scandal scholarship assesses the "Bakker-Hahn"

Evangelicals and Transnational Broadcasting," both in *American Evangelicals and the Mass Media,* ed. Schultze, 289-305 and 307-28, respectively. Peter Horsfield, "American Religious Programs in Australia," in *Religious Television,* ed. Abelman and Hoover, 313-28. To compare an early and late international perspective, try Eugene Nida, *Message and Mission: The Communication of the Christian Faith,* rev. ed. (Pasadena, CA: William Carey Library, 1990), alongside Eric Shegog, "Religion and Media Imperialism: A European Perspective," in *Religious Television,* ed. Abelman and Hoover, 329-52. A recent prescriptive piece is Norman E. Thomas, "Television and the Church's Global Mission," in *Changing Channels,* ed. Inbody, 131-46.

258. Larry Martz et al., "TV Preachers on the Rocks," *Newsweek,* 11 July 1988, 26-28. For an excellent review article see Jacques Gutwirth, "Les Églíses Électroniques," *Archives de Sciences Sociales des Religions* 33 (October-December 1988): 201-14. A theme issue entitled "Religion and Popular Media," ed. Karl-Fritz Daiber, yielded seven essays in French and English in *Social Compass* 34, 1 (1987): 5-128.

259. See, for example, Joe E. Barnhart and Steven Winzenburg, *Jim and Tammy: Charismatic Intrigue Inside PTL* (Buffalo: Prometheus Books, 1988). Susan Harding's article on Ted Koppel's treatment of televangelism is brilliant; see her "The World of the Born-Again Telescandals," *Michigan Quarterly Review* 27 (1988): 527.

260. George W. Cornell, "The Evolution of the Religion Beat," in *Reporting Religion: Facts and Faith,* ed. Benjamin J. Hubbard (Sonoma, CA: Polebridge Press, 1990), 20-35.

261. Malise Ruthven, *The Divine Supermarket: Shopping for God in America* (New York: William Morrow, 1990), provides an entertaining look at the Bakker, Swaggart, Falwell mess. See also Carol Flake, "Sunday Night Live: The Electronic Kingdom," *New Republic,* 19 May 1982, 9-11; and Barnhart and Winzenburg, *Jim and Tammy.*

and "Swaggart-prostitute" effects on the movement itself.[262] It has been hard for all the televangelists not to be tarred with the same telescandal brush. Indeed, George Marsden notes the delicious irony that Pat Robertson saved himself with the public by moving "from evangelism to the cleaner field of politics."[263] Indeed, the telescandals led to an unexpected "scandal effect," which featured a decline in religious activity and in respect for clergy in particular and for organized religion in general. The only good news is that this effect seems to have been short-lived.[264]

*The Economic Frame*  The linkages between the history of religious television and economics are intimate, even intrinsic to the phenomenon itself. In the early days, the Federal Communications Commission policy of free airtime for religious groups "unofficially, but quite effectively" cut evangelicals off from access to the networks while it spoiled mainline denominations with the notion of airtime as a "right rather than a commodity."[265] Mainline Protestantism's media strategies backfired, to the extent that they had them, although initially they were better off: through the National Council of Churches, and fitting their establishment position in American religion, mainliners insisted on free airtime and in the early years occupied a privileged place on network radio and television.

Establishment Protestants did not have to fight the regulatory commissions' restrictions and broadcast industry barriers that ironically, much like the disestablishment of Protestantism itself, threw evangelical broadcasters on their own resources.[266] In short, bureaucratic discrimination forced evangelicals to look beyond religious stations, to turn to paid pro-

---

262. Larry Martz and Ginny Carroll, *Ministry of Greed: The Inside Story of the Televangelists and Their Holy Wars* (New York: Weidenfeld and Nicholson, 1988); Harding, "The World of the Born-Again Telescandals," 525-40; Jeffrey K. Hadden and Anson Shupe, "Elmer Gantry: Exemplar of American Televangelism," in *Religious Television*, ed. Abelman and Hoover, 13-22.

263. George Marsden, "Star Wars in Beulah Land," *Reformed Journal* 37 (April 1987): 2-3.

264. Tom W. Smith, "Religious Beliefs and Behaviors and the Televangelist Scandals of 1987-1988," *Public Opinion Quarterly* 56 (1990): 360-80.

265. Martin, "Mass Communications," 1711, 1717. For the modification of FCC policy, permitting commercial religious programming to meet public interest requirements of licensees, see Linda Jo Lacey, "The Electric Church: An FCC 'Established' Institution?" *Federal Communication Law Journal* 31 (Spring 1978): 235-75.

266. A good summary of early network broadcasting policies that favored establishment Protestantism can be found in Miller's applausive "Radio and Religion," 135-40.

gramming, to take advantage of marketing research and innovative fund-raising, and eventually to found the National Religious Broadcasters (NRB) in 1944 to fight these policies, another story that has yet to be written. The almost monopolistic place of evangelicals on airwaves today is partly because they adapted to the free enterprise system more readily than establishment groups, who had been on the government dole for broadcast time for so long that they had trouble adjusting to having to finance their media ministries.[267]

Some have analyzed televangelism in economic terms and have used the fact that televangelists must "buy time" to "buy time" for the church to point out that "Jesus was not for sale," and the church he founded must also not be "for sale."[268] Theologian Carl F. H. Henry means what he says in his essay on "Heresies in Evangelical Fund Raising."[269] Issues of financial accountability and fund-raising ethics have only increased since the televangelism scandals.[270] Researchers have found, for example, that "an average hour of religious programming includes requests for $189.52." If one watches two hours of religious TV a week (the average), one is being solicited for $19,710 on average in the course of a year. If one's two-hour fare consists only of revival and preaching programs, that figure skyrockets to an average of $33,361 per year.[271]

*The Religious Frame* What are the themes and topics of religious programming? How religious is religious TV? One study found a surprisingly wide array of social, political, and religious topics discussed, with "death, communism, and God" leading in that order.[272] Twenty-five percent of

---

267. Jeffrey K. Hadden, "Soul-Saving Via Video," *Christian Century,* 28 May 1980, 609-13.

268. Peter Elvy takes the reader on this journalistic journey in *Buying Time: The Foundations of the Electronic Church* (Mystic, CT: Twenty-Third Publications, 1987).

269. Carl F. H. Henry, "Heresies in Evangelical Fund Raising," in *Religious Television,* ed. Abelman and Hoover, 165-72.

270. Kimberly A. Neuendorf, "The Public Trust Versus the Almighty Dollar"; Robert Abelman, "The Selling of Salvation in the Electronic Church"; and Abelman, "In Conversation: Arthur C. Borden, Evangelical Council for Financial Accountability" — all in *Religious Television,* ed. Abelman and Hoover, 71-84, 173-85, and 185-92, respectively; Harry A. Flick, "Rhetorical Analysis of Jerry Falwell's Television Fund-Raising" (Ph.D. diss., Southern Illinois University at Carbondale, 1985).

271. Abelman and Neuendorf, "How Religious Is Religious Television Programming?" 108, 110.

272. Abelman and Neuendorf, "How Religious Is Religious Television Programming?"; Abelman and Neuendorf, "Themes and Topics in Religious Television Programming," *Review of Religious Research* 29 (Winter 1987): 152-74.

programming, however, did *not* have any religious theme. This study also agrees with Hadden and Swann's findings that not all religious programming is conservative and not all conservative programming is political.[273] These authors find more diversity in religious programming than do those who say that religious television promotes conservative ideology.

Colin Morris, in analyzing the prevalent charge that TV works to erode organized religion by seducing people away from church, counters that "paradoxically the medium may actually be stimulating human faculties that are hospitable to faith" through its heavy breathing in images and visual imagination — the staple of religious belief.[274] One of the few scholars to address the issue of broadcasting's importance within evangelical culture, and the functions that the media perform within evangelicalism, is Larry K. Eskridge.[275]

The focus of Steve Bruce's work has been on how old-fashioned beliefs can be communicated through new-fangled technology.[276] Bruce accents the defensive posture of televangelism — eroded spiritual values, moral slippage, embattled "them" versus "us" mentalities. Televangelism doesn't "convert," Bruce insists, it only "confirms." Few ever come to Christ through the media. We need to know more about how parachurch broadcast ministries are altering the interpretations of biblical texts and traditions, beyond the insight afforded by secularization theory, which tends to emphasize the obvious: that the medium alters the messenger as well as the message itself.

While studying the ways in which technologies have politics, we also need to look beyond the political arena and explore televangelism's impact on social and religious life, where according to one scholar it has provided a sense of identity and belonging to the aging that local congregations were derelict in providing.[277] Studies of the relationship between evangel-

273. Hadden and Swann, *Prime Time Preachers.*

274. Morris, *Wrestling With an Angel,* 74.

275. Eskridge, "Evangelical Broadcasting," 127-39.

276. Steve Bruce, *Pray TV: Televangelism in America* (New York: Routledge, Chapman and Hall, 1990).

277. For the political arena see Langdon Winner, "Do Artifacts Have Politics?" in his *The Whale and the Reactor: A Search for Limits in an Age of High Technology* (Chicago: University of Chicago Press, 1986), 19-39. For the social and religious arena, a pathbreaking empirical study that needs multiple duplications is the analysis of the impact of religious broadcasting on residents of New Haven, Connecticut, in the early 1950s, by Parker, Barry, and Smythe, *The Television-Radio Audience and Religion.* On aging see Jerry D. Cardwell, *Mass Media Christianity: Televangelism and the Great Commission* (New York: University

ical broadcasting and local congregational life would help us understand
the accommodations each made or did not make for the other, and may
make even more surprising the "electronic church's" lack of desire to
dominate or to down the local congregation. Many studies decry a choice
culture where people flip churches as fast as they can flip channels. But
there are others who claim that electronic evangelism actually supports
local church life by stimulating interest in things spiritual.[278]

Where Hadden provided an intellectual genealogy for televangelism,
Razelle Frankl did scholars a service by placing twentieth-century mass
media in historical perspective.[279] In her 1987 study, she traces the sociological and theological roots of religious television in American revivalism, as it was shaped by communication pioneers Charles Grandison
Finney, who rationalized and bureaucratized revivals; Dwight L. Moody,
who routinized the rituals of revivalism and incorporated economic entities
into the equation; and Billy Sunday, who pioneered a form of entertainment evangelism with a distinctly patriotic flavor.[280] Her failure to consider radio and the role of Charles E. Fuller seriously mars the book's value
in placing evangelical use of the media in the American revivalistic tradition.

Historians have argued over Frankl's overlooked ancestors of today's
televangelists, such as George Whitefield, Charles E. Fuller, Kathryn
Kuhlman, and others. But ironically her comparative look at nineteenth-
century urban revivalism and twentieth-century televangelism shows that
change, not continuity, is the hallmark of televangelism: "the electric
church has gone beyond a mere media switch, intentionally or uninten-

---

Press of America, 1984). Ben Armstrong also makes this case in *The Electronic Church,* 11.
For the question of televangelism and the local church, see Gary D. Gaddy and David
Pritchard, "When Watching Religious TV Is Like Attending Church," *Journal of Com-
munication* 35 (1985): 123-31.

278. See Richard A. Blake, "Catholic, Protestant, Electric," *America,* 15 March
1980, 212.

279. Another rare example of this approach is Marvin, *When Old Technologies Were
New.*

280. Razelle Frankl, *Televangelism: The Marketing of Popular Religion* (Carbondale:
Southern Illinois University Press, 1987), 33, 43, 61. See also her "A Hybrid Institution,"
in *Religious Television,* ed. Abelman and Hoover, 57-61. The two recent biographies of
Sunday are woefully inadequate in assessing Sunday's media strategies. See Roger A. Bruns,
*Preacher: Billy Sunday and Big-Time American Evangelism* (New York: W. W. Norton, 1992),
and the more helpful Lyle W. Dorsett, *Billy Sunday and the Redemption of Urban America*
(Grand Rapids: Eerdmans, 1991).

tionally, consciously or unconsciously, and created a new institution with its own goals, objectives, and procedures for carrying them out."[281]

### Televangelists

On Easter Sunday of 1940, Roman Catholic Archbishop Fulton J. Sheen, who had been well known since 1930 for his radio program "The Catholic Hour," was the first to telecast the Christian message.[282] "It was a Roman Catholic bishop, not a Protestant evangelical, who proved the value of personality and staging in the early days of television religion," as Bill J. Leonard reminds us in his interpretive look at televangelism and Sheen's shift to television in 1951.[283]

A second forerunner of televangelism is Billy Graham, whose "Hour of Decision" began on radio but later switched to television.[284] An even-handed, fair-minded comparative study of Bishop Sheen and Billy Graham would go a long way in emancipating scholarship from the preoccupations and curiously motivated agenda of a previous generation of scholars.

The absence of substantive treatments of Sheen highlights our desperate need for biographical assessments of key figures in the history of the electronic media.[285] The time is overdue for literally hundreds of such studies — scholarly assessments of more academic integrity than, for

281. Frankl, *Televangelism,* 100.

282. Both Roman Catholic and Protestant services were telecast that morning, although Sheen's service was the one discussed and debated. A month later a Jewish Passover service was telecast. It is somewhat misleading to say that "the Jews, however, have never had a national religious broadcast," as Bruce Abrams does in "Why Televangelists Are Bad for Judaism and Why Judaism Is Bad Televangelism," in *Religious Television,* ed. Abelman and Hoover, 147-51; the quote is on p. 147.

283. Bill J. Leonard, "The Electric Church: An Interpretive Essay," *Review and Expositor* 81 (Winter 1984): 43-57.

284. Frederick William Haas, "A Case Study of the Speech Situation Factors Involved in the Radio Preaching on 'The Hour of Decision' Broadcast" (Ph.D. diss., University of Wisconsin, 1964).

285. The little there is does not do justice to Sheen's media pioneering. See Kathleen Riley Fields, "Bishop Fulton J. Sheen: An American Catholic Response to the Twentieth Century" (Ph.D. diss., University of Notre Dame, 1988); William James Hanford, "A Rhetorical Study of the Radio and Television Speaking of Bishop Fulton John Sheen" (Ph.D. diss., 1965); and Mary Jude Yablonsky, "A Rhetorical Analysis of Selected Television Speeches of Archbishop Fulton J. Sheen on Communism, 1952-1956" (Ph.D. diss., 1975). The best treatments of Sheen to date are D. P. Noonan's *The Passion of Fulton Sheen* (New York: Dodd, Mead, 1972) and Peter W. Williams, "Fulton J. Sheen," in *Twentieth-Century Shapers of American Popular Religion,* ed. Lippy, 387-93.

example, the gripes-and-grumblings biographical sketches that some magazines seem prone to give televangelists, sketches that can bear scarcely a whiff of affirmation.[286] Some of the most promising beginnings have been generated by scholarly interest in Billy Graham. John Pollock, Marshall Frady, Charles Lippy, and William Martin are not scholars who can scarcely bear a whiff of affirmation.[287]

Other solid starts, unfortunately many of them encyclopedic, include Michael R. McCoy on the Armstrong dynasty; Dennis Voskuil on Robert Schuller;[288] Carol V. R. George and Thomas E. Frank on Norman Vincent Peale (whose importance as a new force on the American religious scene — "nondenominational, entrepreneurial, communications-savvy, pragmatic, populist" — has scarcely been appreciated, and whose media skills helped him capture the religious boom, where from 1940 to 1960 church membership went from 50 percent of the entire population to 63 percent);[289] Paul G.

286. See, for example, Sarah Comstock, "Aimee Semple McPherson: Prima Donna of Revivalism," *Harper's Monthly Magazine,* December 1927, 11-19; Hayes B. Jacobs, "Oral Roberts: High Priest of Faith Healing," *Harper's,* February 1962, 37-43; Dick Dabney, "God's Own Network: The TV Kingdom of Pat Robertson," *Harper's,* August 1980, 33-52. On the Armstrongs see William C. Martin, "Father, Son, and Mammon," *Atlantic,* March 1980, 58-65; Martin, "The Birth of a Media Myth," *Atlantic,* June 1981, 7-16.

287. Marshall Frady, *Billy Graham: A Parable of American Righteousness* (Boston: Little, Brown, 1979), and Leonard I. Sweet, "The Epic of Billy Graham," *Theology Today* 37 (April 1980): 85-92. Other favorable looks at Graham include William C. Martin, *Prophet with Honor: The Billy Graham Story* (New York: William Morrow, 1991); John Pollock, *Billy Graham, Evangelist to the World: The Authorized Biography of the Decisive Years* (London: Hodder & Stoughton, 1966); and Pollock, *To All the Nations: The Billy Graham Story* (San Francisco: Harper & Row, 1985). Marshall W. Fishwick, "The Blessings of Billy," approaches Graham as the dominant expression of American popular piety in the twentieth century; see *The God Pumpers,* ed. Fishwick and Browne, 60-74. Also see Bill J. Leonard, "Who Will Be the Next Billy Graham?" *Christian Century,* 8-15 June 1983, 574-75.

288. For Armstrong see Michael R. McCoy, "Herbert W. Armstrong," in *Twentieth-Century Shapers of American Popular Religion,* ed. Lippy, 9-14. For Schuller see Browne Barr, "Finding the Good at Garden Grove," *Christian Century,* 4 May 1977, 424-27; and Dennis Voskuil, "Robert Schuller," in *Twentieth-Century Shapers of American Popular Religion,* ed. Lippy, 364-71. By far the fairest treatment of Schuller to date is Voskuil, *Mountains into Goldmines: Robert Schuller and the Gospel of Success* (Grand Rapids: Eerdmans, 1983). For a harsh verdict on Schuller's ministry, see John M. Mulder, "The Possibility Preacher," *Theology Today* 31 (July 1974): 157-60.

289. See Carol V. R. George's probing biography, *God's Salesman: Norman Vincent Peale and the Power of Positive Thinking* (New York: Oxford University Press, 1993); Thomas Frank, "Norman Vincent Peale," in *Twentieth-Century Shapers of American Popular Religion,* ed. Lippy, 326-34; and Arthur Gordon, *One Man's Way: The Story and Message of Norman Vincent Peale* (Englewood Cliffs, NJ: Prentice-Hall, 1972).

Chappell on Jimmy Swaggart; Shelley Baranowski on Jerry Falwell (whose success, not failure, led him to kill Moral Majority); Stewart Hoover on Pat Robertson and his Christian Broadcasting Network;[290] Louise Bourgault on CBN employee Jim Bakker, a former puppeteer who introduced the talk-show format on something called the "PTL Club"; David Pilgrim on "the most boring televangelist," Lester Sumrall; and mere fragments on David H. C. Read and Frederick B. Eikerenkoetter II (aka "Reverend Ike").[291] The list of those on whom virtually nothing has been written, such as Rex Humbard, who build the first sanctuary designed to accommodate television cameras and communications technology and technicians, would fill a page. Composite studies of televangelists have revolved around their political

290. For Swaggart see Blan Maurice Stout, "Preaching through Television: An Examination of the Preaching of Jimmy Swaggart Based Upon the Aristotelian Triad" (Th.M. thesis, Harvard Divinity School, 1983); Elton Jerald Ogg, "An Analysis of the Political Content in the Televised Evangelism of Jimmy Swaggart" (M.J. thesis, Louisiana State University, Baton Rouge, 1987); Arthur Frederick Ide, *Heaven's Hustler: The Rise and Fall of Jimmy Swaggart* (Dallas: Monument Press, 1988); Ervin S. Cox, "An Assessment of Jimmy Swaggart's Responses to ABC's WBRZ Documentary from the Perspective of the 'Rhetorical Situation'" (Ph.D. diss., 1988); David A. Harvey, "TV Preacher Jimmy Swaggart: Why Does He Say Those Awful Things about Catholics," in *The God Pumpers*, ed. Fishwick and Browne, 87-100; Paul G. Chappell, "Jimmy Swaggart," in *Twentieth-Century Shapers of American Popular Religion*, ed. Lippy, 417-24. For Falwell see Jeffrey K. Hadden, Anson Shupe, James Hawdon, Kenneth Martin, "Why Jerry Falwell Killed the Moral Majority," in *The God Pumpers*, ed. Fishwick and Browne, 101-15; Elizabeth Miller Fitzgerald, "Jerry Falwell: As Portrayed on ABC Network and Local Lynchburg Television" (M.A. thesis, University of Virginia, 1988); and Shelley Baranowski, "Jerry Falwell," in *Twentieth-Century Shapers of American Popular Religion*, ed. Lippy, 133-41. For Robertson see Hoover, "The Meaning of Religious Television," 231-49.

291. For PTL and the Bakkers see Bourgault, "The 'PTL Club' and Protestant Viewers." See also J. Stilson, "Ratings High: The Bakkers Are a Hot Draw on TV Interview Programs," *Electronic Media*, 1 June 1987, 1, 39; "Jim and Tammy Bakker," in *Twentieth-Century Shapers of American Popular Religion*, ed. Lippy, 14-20; Gary Joseph Hobbins, "An Analysis of the Apologetic Rhetoric of Televangelist Jim Bakker" (M.A. thesis, University of Wisconsin-Oshkosh, 1992); Gary Tidwell, *Anatomy of a Fraud: Inside the Finances of the PTL Ministries* (New York: Wiley, 1993); Charles E. Shepard, *Forgiven: The Rise and Fall of Jim Bakker and the PTL Ministry* (New York: Atlantic Monthly Press, 1991); John Mark Stewart, *Holy War: An Inside Account of the Battle for PTL* (Enid, OK: Fireside Pub. and Communications, 1987). For Sumrall see David Pilgrim, "Mass Marketing the Lord: A Profile of Televangelist Lester Sumrall," *Journal of Religious Studies* 18 (1993): 145-53. For Read see Kendig Brubaker Cully, "The Preacher on Madison Avenue: David H. C. Read," *New Review of Books and Religion* 1 (December 1976): 5. For Reverend Ike see Perry C. Cotham, "The Electronic Church," in *The Bible and Popular Culture in America*, ed. Allene Stuart Phy (Philadelphia, PA: Fortress Press, 1985), 103-36.

efforts or their communications styles, which one study has found to be "highly divergent" and "wide-ranging."[292] Indeed, one study found as much variety in televangelists as in "non-electric churchmen."[293]

An analysis of Martin Luther King, Jr., as a media figure and as an architect of media use is long overdue. Even studies that purport to study this end up only looking at his rhetorical style.[294] In fact, it would be difficult to find any other way to interpret Jesse Jackson's life than in this context, since Jackson has no institutional base other than the media.

Especially absent from the historiography are studies of women media pioneers such as journalist Dorothy Day, whose work in *The Catholic Worker* was key to the success of the Catholic Worker movement.[295] Conspicuously

292. Neuendorf and Abelman, "Televangelism," 57. For composite treatments see James Vincent Dupree, "A Burkean Analysis of the Messages of Three Television Preachers: Jerry Falwell, Robert Schuller and Jimmy Swaggart" (Ph.D. diss., Pennsylvania State University, 1983); John Elmer Hayes, "The Electronic Church: A Survey of Its Viewership and an Example of Its Ministry through Pat Robertson, Jim Bakker, and Two Johnson City Tennessee Churches" (M.Div. thesis, Emmanuel School of Religion, 1986); Mark Lloyd, *Pioneers of Prime Time Religion: Jerry Falwell, Rex Humbard, Oral Roberts* (Dubuque, IA: Kendall/Hunt Pub. Co., 1988); Stephen Jackson Pullum, "A Rhetorical Profile of Pentecostal Televangelists: Accounting for the Mass Appeal of Oral Roberts, Jimmy Swaggart, Kenneth Copeland, and Ernest Angley" (Ph.D. diss., Indiana University, 1989); Virginia K. Martycz, "Identification as Process: A Rhetorical Study of Three Televangelists as Social Intervenors" (Ph.D. diss., Ohio State University, 1991); and Janice Peck, *The Gods of Televangelism* (Cresskill, NJ: Hampton Press, 1993).

293. Charles LeRoy Johnson, "The Rhetoric of Retailing Religion: A Comparative Analysis of the Rhetoric of Electric and Non-Electric Church Ministers" (Ph.D. diss., Purdue University, 1986). See also Lawrence Leland Lacour, "A Study of the Revival Method in America, 1920-1955, with Special Reference to Billy Sunday, Aimee Semple McPherson and Billy Graham" (Ph.D. diss., Northwestern University, 1956).

294. See as an example Dean Fadely and Ronald Greene, "A Man, a Prophet, a Dream," in *The God Pumpers,* ed. Fishwick and Browne, 75-86.

295. Of prime importance for a study of Dorothy Day is *The Long Loneliness: The Autobiography of Dorothy Day* (New York: Harper, 1952). While June O'Connor's *The Moral Vision of Dorothy Day: A Feminist Perspective* (New York: Crossroad, 1991) is more recent, Day's "advocacy journalism" and literary importance is featured in Nancy L. Roberts, *Dorothy Day and the Catholic Worker* (Albany: State University of New York Press, 1984). Day's chief biographer is William D. Miller, whose major work *Dorothy Day: A Biography* (San Francisco: Harper & Row, 1982) was preceded by his *A Harsh and Dreadful Love: Dorothy Day and the Catholic Worker Movement* (New York: Liveright, 1973) and precedes his *All Is Grace: The Spirituality of Dorothy Day* (Garden City, NY: Doubleday, 1987). A more popular presentation is Jim Forest, *Love Is the Measure: A Biography of Dorothy Day* (New York: Paulist Press, 1986). Anne Klejment and Alice Klejment have provided a valuable research tool with their *Dorothy Day and the Catholic Worker: A Bibliography and Index* (New York: Garland Publishing, 1986).

absent are studies on women evangelists ("electric sisters," Richard G. Peterson calls them), beginning with Aimee Semple McPherson and continuing with Kathryn Kuhlman, Marilyn Hickey, Tammy Bakker, Beverly LaHaye, Terry Cole-Whittaker, Mother Angelica and the Eternal Word Television Network, and New Ager Elizabeth Clare Prophet.[296]

David Edwin Harrell, Jr., provides us with a model of how biography should be done. Harrell's scholarship on Oral Roberts immediately gets us beyond the hype or hatchet mode that inevitably seems to greet every new leader. The hatchet mode, which began the Roberts and Robertson appraisals, was quickly followed by the gush and rush of unenlightenment that accompanies the hagiography genre.[297]

296. See Richard G. Peterson, "Electric Sisters," in *The God Pumpers,* ed. Fishwick and Browne, 116-40. Most of the best work done to date on Kuhlman is in the form of dissertations. See as an example Katherine Jane Leisering, "An Historical and Critical Study of the Pittsburgh Preaching Career of Kathryn Kuhlman" (Ph.D. diss., Ohio University, 1981). Also see Deborah Vansau McCauley, "Kathryn Kuhlman," in *Twentieth-Century Shapers of American Popular Religion,* ed. Lippy, 225-33; Louise Farr, "The Divine Ms K." *MS,* July 1975, 12-15; and James Morris, "Kathryn Kuhlman," in *The Preachers* (New York: St. Martin's Press, 1973), 235-52. There are some meaty dishes, if one doesn't mind scraping off the gooey sauce in which they are drenched, in Helen Kooiman Hosier, *Kathryn Kuhlman: The Life She Led, the Legacy She Left* (Old Tappan, NJ: Fleming H. Revell Co., 1976), and Allen Spraggett, *Kathryn Kuhlman: The Woman Who Believes in Miracles* (New York: World Pub. Co., 1970). For Bakker see Frances FitzGerald, "Reflections: Jim and Tammy," *New Yorker,* 23 April 1990, 45-50, 67-87. For LaHaye see David Garrison, "Tim and Beverly LaHaye," *Twentieth-Century Shapers of American Popular Religion,* ed. Lippy, 233-40. For Cole-Whittaker see Peterson, "Electric Sisters," and Peterson, "Stained Glass Television: A Female Evangelist Joins the Electronic Church," *Journal of Popular Culture* 19 (Spring 1986): 95-105. For Mother Angelica see Dan O'Neill, *Mother Angelica: Her Life Story* (New York: Crossroad, 1986); see also the essay on "Mother Angelica: Catholic Cable TV Network Pioneer," in Noonan, *The Catholic Communicators,* 102-21.

297. See the disaffected Jerry Sholes's account *Give Me That Prime-Time Religion: An Insider's Report on the Oral Roberts Evangelistic Association* (New York: Hawthorn Books, 1979) and Gerard Thomas Straub, *Salvation for Sale: An Insider's View of Pat Robertson,* new, updated ed. (Buffalo: Prometheus Books, 1988). For Fuller hagiography see historian son Daniel P. Fuller's treatment of his father, *Give the Winds a Mighty Voice* (Waco, TX: Word Books, 1972); or Wilbur M. Smith, *A Voice for God* (Boston: W. A. Wilde, 1949); or J. Elwin Wright, *The Old Fashioned Revival Hour and the Broadcasters* (Boston: Fellowship Press, 1940). Paul L. Maier strives memorably but unsuccessfully for critical distance from his father in *A Man Spoke, a World Listened: The Story of Walter A. Maier* (St. Louis: Concordia Publishing House, 1963). For Schuller hype see Michael and Donna Nason, *Robert Schuller: His Story* (Waco, TX: Word Books, 1983), and more recently James Penner's gargantuan volume *Goliath: The Life of Robert Schuller* (Anaheim, CA: New Hope, 1992), a shameless exercise in hero-worship but a volume filled with unforgettable pictures. Larry W. Gates, *Dwelling in Schullerland* (Nashville: Winston-Derek, 1985), provides an insider's perspective.

Harrell was the perfect candidate to write Oral Roberts's biography. Drawing on his remarkable knowledge of the immense periodical literature and complex communications network built up by Pentecostalism, Harrell's benchmark study of Pentecostal healing evangelists and revivalists who emerged in the late 1940s needs to be supplemented by a more general study of the broader-based charismatic movement that emerged after the *annus mirabilis* 1958 and by a more particularized study of the central but untold role that Kathryn Kuhlman played in the formation of new electronic ministries.[298]

Harrell's book gives Roberts his due beyond Pentecostal history. In fact, Harrell calls him "one of the most influential religious leaders in the world in the twentieth century."[299] In his essay in this collection, entitled "Oral Roberts: Religious Media Pioneer," Harrell builds on his case for Roberts's influence by stressing Roberts's innovative deployment of mass media, as his ministry expanded from tent to radio to television because of his incredible organizational abilities. Pentecostalism and electronic media grew up together, and a major weakness of Ben Armstrong's look at the "Electric Church," a phrase he originated, is the slighting of the Pentecostal wing of the phenomenon he is writing about.

Roberts "perfected many of the techniques that became the foundation for direct mail operations in the 1980s," Harrell contends, and his narrow-casting use of the media in the 1980s for fund-raising, even after he dismantled his television ministry, "signaled the direction likely to be taken by the electronic church in the 1990s." Harrell is at his best in his discussion of Roberts's revolutionary move away from his standard-fare television format to professionally produced prime-time specials that utilized contemporary music and celebrity guests, a move that single-handedly took religious television "out of the Sunday morning religious ghetto." Harrell stresses the key role of Ralph Carmichael, who deserves study in and of himself. Harrell's flat declaration that "the modern electronic church was born with the airing of Oral's first special in March 1969" will be the center of debate for the foreseeable future.

298. David Edwin Harrell, Jr., *All Things Are Possible: The Healing and Charismatic Revivals in Modern America* (Bloomington: Indiana University Press, 1976), esp. his "Bibliographical Essay," 240-54. For the Episcopal segment of the "charismatic renewal movement," see John Lankford's review essay of Harrell's book, in *Historical Magazine of the Protestant Episcopal Church* 46 (June 1977): 251-65.

299. David Edwin Harrell, Jr., *Oral Roberts: An American Life* (Bloomington: Indiana University Press, 1987).

For those who hear "serious TV" as an oxymoron, Harrell's essay will be difficult to swallow. The Postman thesis — that TV speaks in only one voice and reduces everything to entertainment — takes a page out of Huxley's *Brave New World* and makes it into a mission: "People will come to love their oppression," Huxley wrote, "and adore the technologies that undo their capacity to think." Postman argues that television is biased against exposition, memory, meaning, context, coherence, and continuity. TV fails to meet the needs of public discourse by its very nature, not by the way it is used. It is not the content that is corrupting, but the very nature of the medium alters our sense of reality. TV is obsessed with trivialities, displays no sense of the past, fosters limited attention spans, and speaks in only one voice, reducing everything it touches to entertainment.

Here is where Roberts has been most vulnerable. Entertainment evangelism or the "entertainment milieu" (William Kuhns) did not, of course, begin with Oral Roberts's prime-time specials.[300] Voltaire used to talk of the Lyons mob rushing to an execution as to a sermon because in both cases the entertainment was free. As we have already discussed, by the mid-1800s, public lectures and evangelical sermons had become popular entertainments, thanks in part to the Charles G. Finney principle of "the commonsense people will be entertained." But Roberts modeled how electronic entertainment evangelism could be conducted.

## Movies

The relations among the various media industries themselves can be almost as complex as research into the exponential relationships among and effects on the body of multiple prescription drugs. The orthodox history of hostility between motion pictures and radio first, and then television, for bragging rights to (and advertising rates for) the hearts and minds of the public, is now undergoing revisionist interpretation. William Boddy's *Fifties Television* is a model of how to analyze one media form in the context of other cultural institutions and media forms.[301] Boddy demonstrates how the "networks" developed as they did, and not differently, because of a complex of social, economic, cultural, and political factors. Alas, Boddy

300. For the thesis of the usurpation of truth by technology see Kuhns, *The Electronic Gospel.*

301. William Boddy, *Fifties Television: The Industry and Its Critics* (Urbana: University of Illinois Press, 1990).

does not delve into the role of the church in the 1950s critique of TV programming mediocrity. The "ratings consciousness" reflected in the pervasive Nielsen and Arbitron worship symbolizes the cultural role pollsters play as our searchers of consensus.

For some reason, scholars of American religion have seen the motion picture industry as largely outside their remit. What little is done is prone (like Boddy) to treat the media as a secondary source and not as a primary text. Too many scholars can write on motion pictures or television programming without ever having watched the shows they write about.[302] Lester and Barbara Keyser's work on *Hollywood and the Catholic Church* (1984) is notable for its refusal to disdain the subject it studies.[303]

Issues of censorship and content control of motion picture production dominate the discussions, usually under such headlines as "Hollywood Under Attack."[304] One study has recently argued that the encounter between the church and the movie industry was "less a struggle than a mutual embrace," as both the Catholic church and the movie industry sought respectability and mainstream acceptance in twentieth-century America. "An industry largely financed by Protestant bankers, operated by Jewish studio executives, and policed by Catholic bureaucrats, all the while claiming to represent grass-roots America, resists either heroic or demystifying narrative treatment."[305]

The moral dimension to viewing movies and television needs as much exploration as the moral dimension to the reading of various kinds of newspapers.[306] Do religious viewers "feel differently" about watching various quantities and qualities of television? Thanks to the technologies of the 1970s — cable, satellites, and home videos — movies have begun to compete with network broadcasting by getting their product directly to home receivers.[307]

302. Obvious and significant exceptions include James Wall's editorials in *Christian Century*, and Wall, *Church and Cinema: A Way of Viewing Film* (Grand Rapids: Eerdmans, 1971).

303. Lester and Barbara Keyser, *Hollywood and the Catholic Church: The Image of Roman Catholicism in American Movies* (Chicago: Loyola University Press, 1984).

304. Robert Henry Stanley, *Mediavisions: The Art and Industry of Mass Communication* (New York: Praeger, 1987), 103ff.

305. Francis G. Couvares, "Hollywood, Main Street, and the Church: Trying to Censor the Movies Before the Production Code," *American Quarterly* 44 (December 1992): 584-616, esp. 610.

306. See Schudson, *Discovering the News*, 116, for a fuller discussion of this issue.

307. Michele Hilmes, *Hollywood and Broadcasting: From Radio to Cable* (Urbana: University of Illinois Press, 1990). See also Christopher Anderson, "Revisionist Histories," *Journal of Communication* 41 (Summer 1991): 136.

## MTV

The 1990s have been tagged "the video decade." The rise of rock videos, and the telecomputer merger of sound, image, and text into a fast-paced visual style that can be transmitted at ease, was more than a new type of media. MTV marked the birth of a new postmodern language, a dedifferentiated language expressive of a dedifferentiated, multidimensional "look and feel" culture where barriers (even those that keep "commercials" and "programming" in airtight categories) are breaking down.[308] E. Ann Kaplan was the first to claim the new genre of MTV as the first truly "postmodern" communication.[309] She is right. Unless we begin to understand the MTV phenomenon, we cannot come to terms with postmodern culture, much less youth culture. For good reasons, scholars have been reluctant to plunge into this terrible quagmire of live issues and dead theories.

Joe Gow's intent to study the 138 most popular music videos of the 1980s as a means of communication ends up with MTV still more a means of musical performance than a means of storytelling or pedagogy.[310] With the exception of Karol Borowski and his study of alternative religion, historians have not taken much interest in the diversity of popular media — Christian rock, southern gospel and contemporary Christian music, posters, T-shirts, comic-strip literature, cards, and the like — for the propagation of new forms of religiosity much less the reconstitution of religious faith itself by mass-media communications.[311]

The basic thrust of the new communications technologies is toward

308. John Pettegrew, "A Post-Modernist Moment: 1980s Commercial Culture and the Founding of MTV," *Journal of American Culture* 15 (Winter 1992): 57-65. See also *Dancing in the Dark: Youth, Popular Culture, and the Electronic Media,* by Quentin J. Schultze et al. (Grand Rapids: Eerdmans, 1991), esp. chap. 7, "Rocking to Images: The Music Television Revolution," 178-210.

309. E. Ann Kaplan, *Rocking Around the Clock: Music Television, Postmodernism, and Consumer Culture* (New York: Routledge, 1988).

310. Joe Gow, "Music Video as Communication: Popular Formulas and Emerging Genres," *Journal of Popular Culture* 26 (Fall 1992): 41-70.

311. Karol Borowski, "The Renaissance Movement in the U.S.A. Today: An Account of Alternative Religion in Popular Media," *Social Compass* 34, 1 (1987): 33-40. The best of the essays on contemporary Christian music include William D. Romanowski's superb historical survey "Contemporary Christian Music: The Business of Music Ministry," in *American Evangelicals and the Mass Media,* ed. Schultze, 143-69; Bill Young, "Contemporary Christian Music: Rock the Flock," in *The God Pumpers,* ed. Fishwick and Browne, 141-58; and Paul Baker, *Contemporary Christian Music: Where It Came From, Where It Is, and Where It's Going* (Westchester, IL: Crossway Books, 1985).

decentralization, democratization, destabilization, demonopolization, diversity, and participation. Whether or not MTV constitutes a revolution in the nature of public communication, or, as James W. Carey sees it, a force that served to "deepen and intensify basic patterns of communications that came into existence with the birth of the national magazines and the modern newspapers," the church has been slow to register or reflect on these changes.[312] How slow the mainline church can be to become aware of these changes is evident in Edwin H. Maynard's 50th anniversary stocktaking of the United Methodist attempts at "keeping up with a revolution."[313] The church has even been behind the academic community in studying rock videos during the 1980s for their exploitation of violence and sex. Tipper Gore's book was published by a denominational press, but it created no movement in that denomination that shared the concerns of her Parents' Music Resource Center (PMRC).[314]

One of the most potentially significant developments in the history of American religion's changing communication structures was the 1989 decision of the American Bible Society (ABS) to embark on a multimedia translation of the Scriptures. With Thomas Boomershine serving as its chief consultant from 1990 to 1992, the ABS completed a pioneering multimedia interactive computer program on the story of the Gerasene demoniac. This state-of-the-art hypertext was geared not just for an electronic youth culture that "turns on, boots up, downloads" but for an entire postmodern electronic culture. Alas, to date only the "Out of the Tombs" musical video has been released, the rest mired down or lost in the legerdemain of a labyrinthine bureaucracy.[315]

### Preaching in an Electronic Culture

MTV reversed a trend that has prevailed ever since the fourteenth century, when Italian sculptor Pier Jacopo Alari-Bonacolsi of Mantua produced "identical replicas" of his small bronzes thanks to the advent of the new

---

312. James W. Carey, "Changing Communications Technology and the Nature of the Audience," *Journal of Advertising* 9 (1980): 3.

313. Edwin H. Maynard, *Keeping Up With a Revolution* (Nashville: United Methodist Communications, 1990).

314. See the chapter "Zappa Meets Gore: Evaluating Popular Art," in *Dancing in the Dark*, ed. Schultze et al., 278-309.

315. *Out of the Tombs: A Scripture Translation of Mark 5:1-20*, a videorecording produced and directed by Merle Worth; film concept developed by Merle Worth and Thomas E. Boomershine (New York: ABS, 1991).

technology of bronze casting. Until MTV, each new technological innovation of artistic medium brought with it a growing attenuation of intimacy among artist, object, and patron. The implications for preaching of the dominant role of electronic media in contemporary culture is the concern of two homileticians: Fred B. Craddock and David G. Buttrick. Craddock understands electronic culture's creation of an ethos of "intimate distance" and has proposed an inductive method of preaching that moves it closer to the way in which electronics condition people to perceive reality.[316] Electronic culture requires new forms of truth-telling that rely on different uses of the intellect and require alternative kinds of content.

The other scholar to propound and ground the preaching act in electronic culture is David Buttrick. Buttrick's essay in this volume, "Preaching to the 'Faith' of America," aims at "awareness." Is there anything more tragic than when a person misunderstands himself or misperceives herself? As Buttrick makes clear in his essay, the church today needs a unique cocktail of analysis, narrative, exhortation, and wit, to become fully and focally aware of where it is living — at the tail end of the tradition that produced the modern era. The context of modern Christian witness in North America was largely shaped by a Reformation/Enlightenment "cultural formulation" (Buttrick's word for "paradigm"), a Protestant mind-set embodying individualism, rationalism, skepticism, systematization, and optimism — perhaps best symbolized and shorthanded by the three monosyllabic but multilayered words "Here I Stand."

It is precisely the inability of mainline Protestantism to say the words "There We Go" rather than "Here I Stand," to "Let God's Spirit Go" and "let the mystery shine" (Wilhelm Pauck), that helps to explain the growing appeal of what Buttrick calls "mystery cults" or what Catherine L. Albanese calls "shamanic spirituality." In her contribution to this volume, "From New Thought to New Vision: The Shamanic Paradigm in Contemporary Spirituality," Albanese offers some cooling draughts of scholarly insight to damp down the overheating one often feels after exposure to "New Age" spirituality. Albanese is known (along with Jon Butler) for her genius at spinning gold out of what others take to be straw. Here she opens what others have tossed out as spiritual junk mail and junk messages (such as UFOs, Shirley MacLaine stuff), and she finds a treasurehouse of meaning about the changing course of American religiosity.

Albanese's "shamanic spirituality" is one way in which Americans

---

316. Fred B. Craddock, *As One without Authority: Essays on Inductive Preaching* (Enid, OK: Phillips University Press, 1971).

have developed a "spirituality that substitutes image for word, using the resources of the pictorial imagination" instead of verbal and abstract resources. Using the shamanic model in its widest sense, Albanese gives a fascinating look at the variety of religious expressions in America today where vision and sound have replaced word and reason as the primary sources of authority. Subjecting to critical scrutiny what others have simply dismissed, Albanese has us look afresh at people like Roberts and Bakker, as well as at mysticism, for their reliance on the "imagistic spirituality" of the shamanic model and for their shamanistic role in American culture.

Albanese points out the importance of the language of "energy" and "field," which have replaced the linear, mechanical imagery in popular spiritual parlance. Energy theology brings together mysticism and science with traditional theology into an ancient-future combination that will grow even stronger in the future.[317]

The problem of communication and change is especially acute, as Buttrick makes clear, for Protestantism. With Protestantism came a book religion: "American religious history began with a migration of books." Even "public discourse was decidedly bookish," Buttrick shows, and "speakers' language sounded written."

> People not only read books; they sounded like the books they read. They spoke a literate, linear language. Their speeches were above all rational. . . . By the beginning of the nineteenth century, America thought like a book!

How will Protestantism adapt to a nontypographical epistemology? This is the question with which Buttrick ends his paper, and with which this essay ends. "What happens to Protestantism, a religion of the book, in an electronic age?" he asks. Will preachers be able to adjust to an electronic epistemology, with its use of images as the primary unit of cultural currency — something Buttrick calls "the logic of consciousness"?

Buttrick doesn't reveal his current prognostications, though he confirms many of the reservations and some of the hopes about the church's ability to adapt responsively and responsibly to the change in consciousness that electronic media have inaugurated.

---

317. For the ancient-future phenomenon see Leonard I. Sweet, *Faithquakes* (Nashville: Abingdon, forthcoming 1994).

# Protestantism and Capitalism: Print Culture and Individualism

## Martin E. Marty

As a background to contemporary studies, I have been asked to make a brief comment somehow connecting concepts that usually receive book-length, if not library-scope, attention by scholars: "Protestantism," "Capitalism," "Print Culture," and "Individualism." If treatment is necessarily cursory, then when, one asks, can an author write *quod erat demonstrandum* based on empirical evidence? What will issue from such an example as this of cultural history, a genre that must depend, as Jacques Barzun put it, on "the gift of seeing a quantity of fine points in a given relation without ever being able to demonstrate it." This means that "the historian in general can only show, not prove; persuade, not convince; and the cultural historian more than any other occupies that characteristic position."[1]

That diffidence about demonstrated truth is based on wariness about two elements of the assignment. On one hand, the task of dealing with the four terms just cited tempts a historian to reckon with the titans: Tillich on the Protestant era; Weber and Tawney on capitalism; Eisenstein on print cultures; Hobbes and Locke or Smith and Bentham on individualism. Not to comment on them, knowing that many readers will be aware of them, would jeopardize the development of the theme; to concentrate on them at length would be to distract from the manifest design of the whole book.

---

1. Jacques Barzun, "Cultural History as a Synthesis," in *The Varieties of History, from Voltaire to the Present,* ed. Fritz Stern (New York: Meridian Books, 1956), 393.

The other element has to do with how one would make the case about the connections implied in the title of this essay. Would a historian, through the surviving sources, somehow in effect interview each child, or many children, who were growing up in Charleston or Charlestown in the eighteenth century, asking: How did you learn to read? Why did you learn? Why did people teach you? What did you read? If and insofar as your teachers were Protestant, what did they communicate to you as they taught? Did they give you texts and ways of reading them that promoted capitalism — a term you and they never used? Did they encourage you to be "individualists" in reading those texts, including sacred texts? Did they encourage you to read the texts in community or in isolation? Did reading change your mind and lead you closer to the Protestant communities of faith or further from them? Answers to such questions — some parts of which it is possible to retrieve from the sources and traces — would then have to be collated, generalized upon, and employed to show connections implied in the title. Yet the evidences are far too random, too scattered, to permit even a minimal claim for social scientific certainty about what is learned.

So I shall take and am already taking a third course: to reflect on a hypothesis advanced in this book, to speculate about what theological educators have in mind in encouraging this project. Something very important is at stake in the inquiry, and the results will point to creative and fateful elements in theological education, ministry, mass media, and our mixed "print culture." In short, this is a historical project whose contemporary relevance is manifest. Obversely, no doubt issues of contemporary urgency inspired this volume and set some boundaries around it.

The hypothesis, as condensed in a letter to the contributors to this volume from Thomas Boomershine and Leonard Sweet, proposed "that the task of the Church in every age is to train leaders who are masters of the most powerful communications systems of that age and the systems of interpretation that make the primary traditions of Christianity meaningful in the context of that culture." I shall assume that whoever takes up this subject will argue about the meaning of "masters" and the implied mastery. A more modest view would suggest that leaders must show an awareness of and have an ability to interpret existence in the context of communications and interpretation systems of their age. I am not sure that the Christians in the Pauline era were "masters" of the *exousiae,* the powers and principalities of their day. Yet they survived and thrived in the face of these, and outlasted them. But this is not the place to quibble about the details of the hypothesis but to test it in general.

My preliminary testing, biased no doubt by what I take to be part of and to be influenced by a biblical, Christian, and Niebuhrian interpretation of history, suggests that here, as often if not always in history, the colonial American record displays ironic outcomes.

The irony in question is not literary irony but historical irony, the irony of situation — in *Oxford English Dictionary* terms, "a condition of affairs or events as if in mockery of the promise and fitness of things." Not an irony of fate, it "occurs when the consequences of an act are diametrically opposed to the original intention," and when "the fundamental cause of the disparity lies in the actor himself, and his original purpose" (Gene Wise). Niebuhrian, or what Richard Reinitz called "humane," irony, however, does not use the superior insight that historians bring by the accident of their appearance after the events about which they write, in order to generate apathy or cynicism about the follies of mortals and the worthlessness of human endeavor. Instead, it sees history moving under "a divine judge who laughs at human pretensions without being hostile to human aspirations."

For Niebuhr, in his essay on irony, this means that the historian has to be "an observer who is not so hostile to the victim of irony as to deny the element of virtue which must constitute a part of the ironic situation," while not being "so sympathetic as to discount the weakness, the vanity and pretension which constitute another element." The same "divine judge" charters and calls forth human responsibility and creativity.[2] The ironic element in colonial American Protestantism's reliance on literacy and development of a print culture lies in this: publishing, bookselling, and reading were intended by the Protestant leaders to build the covenanted community of faith. Ironically, however, the form their propagation of literacy took led to the development of individualisms that often led young aspirants from continued participation in that community and toward isolated and competitive pursuits of their good through capitalism. Capitalism is a code word for complex and partly self-contradictory ways of life, but in the present context at least it represents what were not only partly *compatible* (with evangelical Protestant) injunctions but also *distractions* from them.

Concentration on this theme in colonial America will evoke analogies

---

2. For references to Gene Wise, Richard Reinitz, Reinhold Niebuhr, and, implicitly, the Psalmist, see the argument in Martin E. Marty, *Modern American Religion*, vol. 1: *The Irony of It All, 1893-1919* (Chicago: University of Chicago Press, 1986), 3-7.

and comparisons with similar religious intentions and outcomes elsewhere. Among those that come to mind and that will illuminate this point are at least the following: In Victorian England, the Protestant clergy, Anglican established or dissenting alike, promoted the use of the printed page. Yet as they did so they also saw many of their young experience a loss of Christian faith and a replacement for it in the form of literature. (Those who did *not* promote literacy — for example, among the industrial workers — also saw loss of faith and commitment to Christian community, but that is a different story for a different day.) What resulted fulfilled Matthew Arnold's prophecy: "More and more mankind will discover that we have to turn to poetry to interpret life for us . . . and most of what now passes for religion and philosophy will be replaced by poetry."[3] In the German and French Enlightenments, something similar went on among literate elites in their passage from theology to philosophy.

Similarly, the twentieth-century American Jewish community often sees itself making "poetry," literature, a virtual replacement for the Torah, Talmud, Mishnah, and other sacred texts that once gave shape to that community. Or, in the Jewish case, the regard for sacred texts and religious literacy long nurtured in the European ghetto and shtetl and transferred to America with the baggage of immigrants, a literacy made possible and encouraged in many cases by the rabbi at *shul,* soon became the instrument for quick advancement by a more secular generation in intellectual and commercial ventures.[4]

A third illustration is more nearly contemporary: the decline in devotion to serious Catholic reading after the Second Vatican Council. More than anecdotal evidence indicates that before the Council the numerically stronger priesthood and the community of convent and monastery inhabitants, along with intact lay communities, produced a market and readership for theology and Catholic literature which evapo-

3. Matthew Arnold, "The Study of Poetry," in *Criticism: The Major Statements,* ed. Charles Kaplan (New York: St. Martin's Press, 1964), 403-4.
4. For the contexts of this Jewish experience, see Samuel C. Heilman, *The People of the Book: Drama, Fellowship, and Religion* (Chicago: University of Chicago Press, 1983); part 3, "Judaism Secularized," in Moses Rischin, *The Promised City: New York's Jews, 1870-1914* (New York: Corinth, 1964), 115-70; Arthur A. Goren, "Education as a Community Responsibility" and "Education: The Professionals and the Orthodox," chaps. 5 and 6 in *New York Jews and the Quest for Community: The Kehillah Experiment, 1908-1922* (New York: Columbia University Press, 1970), 86-109, 110-33; and Calvin Goldscheider and Alan S. Zuckerman, "Education and New Bases of Cohesion," in *The Transformation of the Jews* (Chicago: University of Chicago Press, 1984), 167-71.

rated as there was decline in these ranks and "liberation" from inherited pieties. Those who remained with the priesthood and in the active parish life evidently took their tastes for literature into secular channels. Left behind was a very large market for spiritual books of a conservative and charismatic character for those to whom parish life remained the norm.

A fourth locating point that illumines the recovery of the colonial plot has to do with contemporary Protestantism. The reports on Christian Booksellers Association conventions, spiritual weekend retreats, para-church movements, and best-seller lists are consistent: the larger market for Protestant books, a market that runs into the hundreds of thousands and sometimes the millions per best-seller, is in the conservative-evangel-ical-fundamentalist-pentecostal flank where there are more defined and confining cognitive boundaries around the community. The moderate and liberal churches, which had always done so much to encourage literacy, have seen much of their market decline while their potential readership presumably has shifted its reading tastes toward the more secular or at least the less specifically evangelical Protestant and even Christian-at-large products of a print culture.

To close this short comment on the contemporary relevance of this study and the ironic interpretation — as well as to introduce the notion of a clue as to how to address the unsought outcome of Protestant high-cultural literacy — there is reason to turn to the argument, partly speculative and partly grounded in firm data, of Robert Wuthnow. The Princeton sociologist in his research does not separate literacy education from scientific and practical education, but he does document outcomes of growth in American education among church members in general, and we may infer from these findings many corollaries to the specific literacy theme.

Wuthnow sets readers up for the ironic outcome by reporting accurately on the serious educational intention of religious leaders. They advocated literacy in religious writings as one way "to resist the challenges of secularism" by equipping individual believers to discern and speak for themselves, as well as to give moral shape to the culture. Yet Wuthnow found that along with increasing education there came more denominational switching, which meant less loyalty to extant inherited communities of faith. Higher levels of education also meant more marrying outside the community of faith, another factor in the lessening of loyalties. As higher education expanded, the role and influence of religion in higher education declined, even though clergy gave great encouragement to that expansion. "College educated young people fled the churches in droves during the 1960s," and thenceforth. Rising levels of education "contributed importantly to the growing turmoil that was beginning to be evident in the churches." While in the 1950s college-educated people were more likely than others to be involved with the churches, two decades later they were less so. In the same period, such people also changed from being conventionally religious to being more likely experimental in their spiritual searches. A new cultural cleavage had formed; the less educated, the less literate, were more likely to make up the body of the committed in believing communities. Wuthnow also saw some of these trends operating within the evangelical community as it literarily and socially "moved to the left" from the base in intact fundamentalism that had been among its antecedents.[5] James Davison Hunter has developed this understanding of change within evangelicalism as well.[6]

Having pointed to those corollaries and exposed their outcomes, it might seem that the conclusion of this inquiry about colonial America might be the advice to theological educators, clergy, and religious leadership to minimize literacy, not to encourage print culture, in order to "keep people dumb," as it were, and thus loyal. Instead — since a learned clergy and an informed laity do belong to the theology of most churches and educational institutions in any way connected with a project like this book — one would better put energies into questions of another sort. What does it take to promote literacy *and* keep communities intact using expressions of authority and coercion (for example, through the Roman Catholic versions, the *Index* and imprimatur; or through censorship and approved reading lists in Protestant religious communities)? Positively, what aspects of community kept many colonials from abandoning religious community for the sake of developing competitive individualisms in the face of capitalism, which means from making the move described in Richard Bushman's book title, *From Puritan to Yankee?* How nurture such aspects now?

At this point the theme will take one of its decisive turns, in dependence upon options turned up in scholarship of recent decades. Two schools of thought have addressed the question, Why did colonials, particularly New Englanders — who usually crowd the center of the stage in

5. Robert Wuthnow, *The Restructuring of American Religion: Society and Faith Since World War II* (Princeton: Princeton University Press, 1988), 68, 89, 90, 160-63, 185-91.

6. James Davison Hunter, "Accommodation: The Domestication of Belief," chap. 6 in *American Evangelicalism: Conservative Religion and the Quandary of Modernity* (New Brunswick: Rutgers University Press, 1983), 73-101.

this plot about print cultures — strenuously advocate writing, publishing, marketing, and reading of books and journals?

The long prevailing school, as described by one critic, we might call the "wilderness" school. Kenneth A. Lockridge says that this "prevailing hypothesis holds that Americans responded to the dissolving effects of the wilderness with a uniquely conscious desire to protect the transmission of culture through formal provisions for education." Thus in New England the settlers built on imported Puritan love for education when they passed their school laws. "The widespread reaction to the wilderness ultimately combined with social mobility and social diversification to produce everywhere in colonial America an educational ethos which was a powerful force for social change, and as well a source of 'typical' American optimism, individualism, and enterprise."

Lockridge associates this wilderness approach with Bernard Bailyn, who, he says, advocated a "more than Puritan" understanding in New England. Bailyn spoke of individualism and enterprise produced by this impulse "everywhere in colonial America." But Lockridge shows that Bailyn's assumption about widespread literacy does not stand up well to scrutiny in New England or in the rest of America. Lawrence Cremin also supported this wilderness notion, adding in his writing a stress on "social mobility as a causal force behind high literacy and 'liberated' attitudes." Lockridge also in a convincing way confutes that assumption.[7]

The quantifiers of colonial American literacy rates, including Lockridge, have to be modest and are frustrated by the character and quality of their evidence. They rely on the legal records, which reveal what percentage of the population could sign their own wills, an act of ability that provides a basic if minimal test of literacy. Yet on the basis of these frustrating inquiries into the subject in the larger context, Lockridge presents an alternative thesis that now meets with considerable acceptance. The wilderness, he says, never was much of a threat to maintaining literacy and socialization in New England. He agrees more with Samuel Eliot Morison about the transmission of cultural intentions: "Emigration [to America] enabled the Puritans to carry out in education, as in religion,

---

7. Kenneth A. Lockridge, *Literacy in Colonial New England: An Enquiry into the Social Context of Literacy in the Early Modern West* (New York: Norton, 1974), 43, 44, 141 (n. 63). He refers to Bernard Bailyn, *Education in the Forming of American Society: Needs and Opportunities for Study* (Chapel Hill: University of North Carolina Press, 1960), and Lawrence A. Cremin, *American Education: The Colonial Experience, 1607-1783* (New York: Harper & Row, 1970).

the system which they thought best."[8] At first they were slow to carry out
their educational intentions, perhaps because school laws could have little
effect when settlement was sparse. (The wilderness was thus a handicap,
not an asset, for the spread of literacy!) But they kept the Puritan ideal
and put it in practice where and when they could.

Lockridge concludes: "Protestantism, then, lay behind the eventual
advance in male literacy in colonial New England." It intended to preserve
a "world of the past," and remained traditional for men and out of range
for most women. "Within this more subdued world it is possible to hold
great respect for the Protestant impulse as the sole force powerful enough
to work a transformation in the level of literacy." Perhaps justifiably, he
adds, this religion helped pave the way to modernity, and it did interact
with lesser forces than this Protestant impulse. The evidence does not *prove*
his hypothesis, but it *suggests* that this hypothesis may explain the evolution
of literacy within the sample and open the door to a more realistic view
of the forces involved. It also advances the inquiries about Protestantism
insofar as it was a factor among others.[9]

When Puritans passed the school laws, their preambles often expressed concern that "learning may be buried in the graves of our fore-
fathers in Church and Commonwealth." Bailyn thought that such prefaces
were inspired by "the fear of imminent loss of cultural standards, of the
possibility that civilization itself would be buried"; hence, the wilderness
was the agent of literary development. But the larger context of the phrase
in the preamble merits full quotation, for it leaves out all reference to the
natural environment or to maimed families; it better matches what Morison said about transplanted intentions by Puritans:

> It being one chief project of that old deluder, Satan, to keep men from
> the knowledge of the Scriptures, as in former times keeping them in an
> unknown tongue, so in these later times by persuading them from the
> use of tongues, that so at least the true sense and meaning of the original
> might be clouded with false glosses of Saint-seeming-deceivers; and that
> learning may not be buried in the graves of our fore-fathers in Church
> and Commonwealth, the Lord assisting our indeavours.[10]

8. Samuel Eliot Morison, *Puritan Pronaos: Studies in the Intellectual Life of New
England in the Seventeenth Century* (New York: New York University Press, 1936), 59.
9. Lockridge, *Literacy in Colonial New England,* 45.
10. Lockridge, *Literacy in Colonial New England,* referring to Bailyn, *Education in the
Forming of American Society,* 27; the preamble is quoted by Morison, *Puritan Pronaos,* 67-68.

The story was not quite so focused as this in all of the colonies. "Beneath New England's burning Protestantism and consequent universal male literacy," Lockridge adds, "Anglo-America was a world in which literacy moved glacially at a middling level." Many men were illiterate and consequently of low social status; women's literacy was even lower. "The story, then, is simple and returns full circle to Protestantism. In New England Protestantism was instrumental in whatever major changes took place in literacy." Lockridge knew that he was expected to move on from there to connect his hypothesis and tentative findings to the Weberian implications and the steps toward modernity. Yet on the short range the intention was, and the evidence points to, "the conservation of piety" as "the prime motive force" behind encouragement of literacy, which "by all available measures appears to have succeeded." He extrapolates on the basis of this argument and suggests that Protestantism was not intended to be a "transitional ideology which mobilized men behind traditional values in order to ease the painful passage into a more modern social era," as Michael Walzer would have it. Instead, one could infer that among the forces behind the rise in literacy in the modern era there is often "a similar and equally effective desire to use literacy to reaffirm traditional values in a time of social transition."[11]

Insofar as this traditional impulse to develop learning in the context of support for and by a community of piety is a major factor — and our task is not to show why colonial America was a "print culture" but to ask why Protestantism helped to produce it — we then have to ask what happened to the original intention. Here is where an ironic interpretation helps, since among the outcomes were some unintended and even contradictory expressions. Among these were certain forms of individualism, which took shape in certain kinds of capitalism. Some of these may have been compatible with Puritan and other colonial religion, and they may often have drawn theological support from latter-day Puritans who favor capitalism as an ideology. But these did deny some, or shall we say much, of the original intention. How did this come about?

What did the colonial Puritans know about print culture? As traditionalists and preservers, they saw themselves as heirs and would-be completers of the Protestant Reformation. They knew the role that printing

11. Lockridge, *Literacy in Colonial New England*, 97, 100-101; see also Michael Walzer, *Revolution of the Saints: A Study in the Origins of Radical Politics* (Cambridge, MA: Harvard University Press, 1965).

and literacy had played in Puritanism, the English Reformation, and, behind that, the whole Protestant movement. Martin Luther had pictured printing as "God's highest and extremest act of grace, whereby the business of the Gospel is driven forward." He and the Germans tried to tie this business to German national chosenness, a connection that had no appeal for New Englanders. But Elizabethan England had picked up the same themes and applied them to its own Reformation and nation. John Foxe, in the colonial best-selling *Book of Martyrs,* spoke for many: "The Lord began to work for His Church not with sword and target to subdue his exalted adversary, but with printing, writing and reading." Elizabeth L. Eisenstein pronounces a summary judgment that seems to be universally accepted: "Printing and Protestantism seem to go together naturally." Further, "the advent of printing was an important precondition for the Protestant Reformation taken as a whole; for without it one could not implement a 'priesthood of all believers.'"[12]

Eisenstein argues quite properly that Roman Catholicism saw a threat in this spread of print culture and literacy, and at the Council of Trent (1546-63) began to set the precedents that kept Catholicism from being an advocate of reading, as Protestants in Old and New England and especially among the Puritans turned out to be. Trent tried to hold in confinement the new functions of the printed word. There were to be no new editions of the Bible. The laity had to accept clerical restrictions on their reading. They were not to read books on the *index librorum prohibitorum* or religious volumes that lacked the official *imprimatur.* The official and only licit public Bible was the Vulgate in Latin, not the vernacular. (Hence, *Latin* America contrasts with New England and its vernacular Bibles and literature. Catholicism feared both lay elite scholars and popular readers alike.)[13] The English Protestant and particularly Puritan tradition on both sides of the Atlantic, however, put confidence in promoting reading of the Bible and religious literature as a way of providing an alternative to Catholic authority — but not without showing interest in setting up an authority of its own. The doctrine of the universal priesthood of believers was never intended to lead to chaotic autonomous individualism. Christians were supposed to do their reading in the context of a rather conformist and bounded covenantal community.

12. Elizabeth L. Eisenstein, *The Printing Revolution in Early Modern Europe* (Cambridge: Cambridge University Press, 1983), 147-48, 151; she also provides the Luther and Foxe quotations.

13. Eisenstein, *Printing Revolution,* 157-63.

One way to see how the Protestant and Puritan assumptions complicated the life of the community and helped lead to individualism and other than communal religious life is to evoke a context described by Walter J. Ong, S.J., in his influential work on oral and literate cultures. Ong's introductory dictum is this: "Sight isolates, sound incorporates." Reading a book is thus an isolating act; participating in a liturgy or hearing a sermon is an incorporating one. Vision is "a dissecting sense," while sound is a unifying one. Picture, with Ong, what happens when the two kinds of culture meet, as they did in educational and ritual settings in New England or other colonies where there was a premium on literacy:

> When a speaker is addressing an audience, the members of the audience normally become a unity, with themselves and with the speaker. If the speaker asks the audience to read a handout provided for them, as each reader enters into his or her own private reading world, the unity of the audience is shattered, to be reestablished only when oral speech begins again. Writing and print isolate. There is no collective noun or concept for readers corresponding to 'audience.' . . . To think of readers as a united group, we have to fall back on calling them an 'audience,' as though they were in fact listeners. . . . The interiorizing force of the oral word relates in a special way to the sacral, to the ultimate concerns for existence. In most religions the spoken word functions integrally in ceremonial and devotional life. Eventually in the larger world religions sacred texts develop, too, in which the sense of the sacral is attached also to the written word. Still, a textually supported religious tradition can continue to authenticate the primacy of the oral in many ways. In Christianity, for example, the Bible is read aloud at liturgical services. For God is thought of always as 'speaking' to human beings, not as writing to them.[14]

The New England and other Protestant advocates of literacy and developers of a print culture, for all their distancing from "the larger world religions" in many approaches to ritual and for all their leaning toward the notion that God was "writing to them," did place great emphasis on the communal activity of the preached word, the rhetoric of communication being the central liturgical element. It was designed to gather and strengthen the covenanted community, and it did so. But all the while

14. Walter J. Ong, *Orality and Literacy: The Technologizing of the Word* (New York: Methuen, 1982), 72, 74-75.

one element of the evangelical message, which somehow gets to be translated as a combination of "the universal priesthood of all believers" and
"the right of private judgment" when conscientious Christians read scriptures and other sacral writings, served as competition, undercutting, and
instrumentalization of forces that worked *against* the community. Here is
where individualism developed.

Where the public congregation and the private readerships reinforced
each other, they successful engendered a Protestant worldview. Thus David D.
Hall, introducing essays on colonial print cultures, shows how much of the
reading concentrated on promoting such reinforcement. From the stories of
readers — who remained a minority, and who, we are often told, read the
same works repeatedly and slowly — we learn that "these books were read in
a special manner that befit their religious or devotional contents," with "awe"
and "reverence," as Samuel Goodrich in the nineteenth century would have
it. Robert Keayne, the colonial Boston merchant who was torn between
community and capitalism, spoke of reading a book on 1 Corinthians 11:27-
28 "100 and 100 times." His example shows how traditional literacy "evokes
a world view." In the colonial case, this view was full of portents and prodigies
of God's warnings, Protestant antipapal self-awareness, and counsel for death
and dying. "By one route or another, the world view of these texts became the
world view of most New Englanders."[15]

In due course, pluralism and diversity developed, and this development led to jarring elements within worldviews. There were now a culture
of the alehouse, which relied on its own texts; almanacs for families; and
new genres and topics, among them those which reinforced the world of
merchants and nascent capitalists. In Episcopalian Virginia, the "sound"
that unified worshipers in the churches, the centers for community assembly, was confined to the reading of the services in the Book of Common
Prayer, behind which stood the force of civil law. Rhys Isaac quotes an
English bishop to provide the rationale for this practice in the face of those
who promoted "creative individualism":

> Whatsoever good things we hear only once, or now and then, though
> perhaps upon the hearing of them, they may swim for a while in our

15. See David D. Hall, "The Uses of Literacy in New England, 1600-1850," in
*Printing and Society in Early America*, ed. William L. Joyce, David D. Hall, Richard D.
Brown, and John B. Hench (Worcester, MA: American Antiquarian Society, 1983), 31-36;
see also *The Apologia of Robert Keayne*, ed. Bernard Bailyn (New York: Harper & Row,
1965), 28-29.

brains, yet they seldom sink down into our hearts, so as to move and sway the affections, as it is necessary they should do in order to our being edified by them; whereas by a set form of public devotions rightly composed, we are continually put in mind of all things necessary for us to know or do, so that it is always done by the same words and expressions, which, by their constant use, will imprint the things themselves so firmly in our minds, that . . . they will still occur upon all occasions, which cannot but be very much for our Christian education.[16]

The bishop was giving expression to a still hegemonous oral culture, one soon to be challenged in Virginia. Walter Ong's "traditional" peoples might have sat still for such community-building events, but restless individualists of Thomas Jefferson's generation were bored and resentful in the face of such assumptions. They used their literacy to go separate ways, apart from church community, even when they remained nominal adherents.

Puritanism in New England was itself a halfway house between meeting house and counting house. One student of individualism, Ralph Ketcham, depicts how the individualizing itch was present in the heart of Puritanism, which was "particularly important in the shaping of American individualism."

Articulated and espoused by a host of powerful writers and preachers from Knox and Christopher Goodman to Milton and Bunyan, Puritanism in Britain loosened ties to traditional institutions . . . and released diverging streams of religious and moral energy. By insisting on the sainthood of all believers (eventually *masses* of believers), and on active membership in society as well as in churches, the Puritans and other Calvinists intensified citizenship and, potentially, vastly broadened it. Intent on the primacy of conscience, devoted to the individual study of the Scriptures, tending toward congregational rather than episcopal church government, keen on the disciplines of work and devotion to calling, and quick to challenge secular authority, the Puritans became the premier ideologues of individualism in seventeenth-century Anglo-America.[17]

16. Rhys Isaac, "Books and the Social Authority of Learning," in *Printing and Society in Early America*, 228-49; he quotes Bishop William Beveridge.

17. Ralph Ketcham, *Individualism and Public Life: A Modern Dilemma* (New York: Basil Blackwell, 1987), 46-47.

The encouragement of Bible reading and individual literacy efforts not only "congregationalized" religion; it also helped "denominational-ize" it, and denominationalization is a religious part of the rise of individualism. No longer was there reliance on a religious establishment; affiliation was no longer a product of fate or the accident of geography and governance. Now the consumer was in command, picking and choosing his prayers and ideology, often on the basis of utterly private reading. The Episcopalian world of Virginia, where religion generally seemed to be less a pervasive force than in New England, held off dissent and individualism in religion more than did the Congregationalism of those northern colonies. Yet in the end, in all thirteen Protestant colo-nies, the congregational, denominational, voluntaryistic pattern was to prevail, and the reading by individuals always played its part in the development.

The "Latin" American world, like the Mediterranean Catholic cul-tures in general, took a different course. Robert Dealy in *The Public Man* illustrates how in the Protestant world, where one is encouraged to follow one's own "priesthood" and "private judgment," one vocational goal was to accumulate possessions and then to depend upon them. God might disappear as the transcendent source behind the transaction, but eventually the transaction came to have a meaning of its own. In Latin Catholic cultures, however, where Dealy says a *caudijalle* ethic (as in *caudillo*) prevails, the person seeks to accumulate not possessions but friends, a company on whom he or she can then depend. Such a goal relies more on word of mouth than on contract; on voice more than sight; on oral rather than literate cultural transactions.[18]

As the company of individualists, dissenters, and absenters from the covenanted community grew in New England, it was the literate who could most contribute to and profit from nascent and developing capital-ism. Just as access to the printed word made possible religious choice, so those who were capable of reading also had the advantage when it came to economic choice, the latter being an integral element in capitalism. David Apter, chronicling the rise of capitalism, sees "modernity as choice." "Thus, modernization as the process leading to the state of modernity, begins when man tries to solve the allocation problem," and the act of doing so implies literacy and a print culture. Modernization as a non-

18. Glen Caudill Dealy, *The Public Man: An Interpretation of Latin American and Other Catholic Countries* (Amherst, MA: University of Massachusetts Press, 1977), xii-xiii.

economic process "originates when a culture embodies an attitude of inquiry and questioning about how men make choices — moral (or normative), social (or structural), and personal (or behavioral). The problem of choice is central for modern men." It implies rationality, the making of priorities, "experiment and invention," and forms of collectivity.[19] To transcend localism and the mere acceptance of fate, one must be able to read. The very churches that taught reading and formed a print culture to promote the Protestant tradition were also on the whole providing adherents with the tools that gave them a means of exit from the confinements of that tradition.

That white Protestants knew how empowering literacy can be is evident from their approaches to Native Americans and African-American slaves. While justifying their migration to America in part as an effort to convert the Indians, few of the immigrants pursued the task zealously. Their English condescension, to say nothing of their ready resort to arms, left them poorly poised to be effective. Exceptions were few. As Henry Warner Bowden reminds us:

> As an alternative to sacraments [with which Catholics in the hemisphere were more successful converters], the nonliterate natives were taught to read in their own language. Once the Praying Indians had reached that crucial plateau, they could read edifying tracts, books, and especially the Bible to improve their behavior. Reading was the chief Puritan means of acquiring practical guidelines for spiritual improvement.[20]

In a way this approach was an effective blocker of Native American development and liberation. Agents of literacy were few; translated writings were rare; motives for producing literate, praying Indians were weak.

Meanwhile, in southern colonies where slavery was institutionalized, white Protestants feared the effects of literacy in colonial slave populations. All the histories of slavery stress how eager slaves were to learn to read, especially to read the Bible, and how few were given the chance to do so. Indeed, slaveholders often systematically deprived slaves of teachers and resisted efforts, even by Christian educators, to give them the basic tools of literacy. As inhabitants of oral cultures, they were more easily dominated

19. David Apter, *The Politics of Modernization* (Chicago: University of Chicago Press, 1965), 9-11.
20. Henry Warner Bowden, *American Indians and Christian Missions: Studies in Cultural Conflict* (Chicago: University of Chicago Press, 1981), 125.

and directed; literates, on the other hand, were more ready for individualistic styles of dissent, though not very often for capitalist accumulation.
Some revivalists, especially in the North, advocated literacy as a means of
reinforcing the conversion experience, but they were discouraged. Literacy
is an enabling instrument, and Native Americans and African-American
slaves were not supposed to be enabled to rise.[21]

Individualism and community are not necessarily contradictory, even
if they happen to be in some tension; nor, except in the eyes of socialist
ideologues or literalists about biblical warnings against Mammon, are
capitalism and Christianity at all points in necessary and constant conflict.
Yet in the promotion of literate or print cultures at the expense of the oral,
the Protestant leadership, motivated by desires to retain a declining Protestant structure and ethos, was giving many of its adherents instruments
that they could soon use apart from community, toward personal and
individualistic ends. Therein lay the irony of this use of mass communications long ago, and therein it lies today.

The Council of Trent, some forms of Jewish Orthodoxy, antimodern-
ist Catholicism, and modern Protestant fundamentalisms all took pains
to see that there were some boundaries around and coherences within the
believing community as it gained literacy. The Protestants who remained
loyal, who did not figuratively "join the alumni association" of the church
through the centuries after the inventing of printing, have found ways to
make communal existence alluring even as they encourage individual
reading, the making of choices, and participation in both the life of the
church and the commercial sector.

Some may do all this through aesthetic or sacramental evocations of
tradition among sophisticated and otherwise innovative people. Others
may have learned to keep community together while encouraging united
response to the sense of a transcendental authority or a supernatural
revelation that demands response. This "sense of the presence of God" can
serve as a magnet calling the community to worship, discipline, and some
kinds of conformity, without discouraging individual pursuits, including
those of diverse economic patterns. This does not mean that theological
educators who want to learn from colonial America's exploitation of a
print culture should try to replicate attempts to invoke heteronomous

21. Among many examples, see Eugene D. Genovese, "Reading, Writing, and
Prospects," in *Roll, Jordan, Roll: The World the Slaves Made* (New York: Pantheon, 1974),
561-66.

authority or to breed docility and to discourage enterprise among adherents. It does mean that leadership does not *simply* put faith in exposure to the printed word, on which Protestantism has from the beginning relied, without taking compensatory steps to reinforce the use of print media. To keep the integrity of the believing, worshiping, interpreting, and activating community it is necessary to do more than encourage the rise of individualist domains where the pursuit of personal wealth alone dominates life — at the expense of the word of God, which presumably inspired the whole process whose hoped-for fulfillment was to determine the goal of Christian existence.

# Religion, Communications, and the Career of George Whitefield

## Harry S. Stout

Perhaps no eighteenth-century religious figure has been better known to church historians and less known to secular historians than George Whitefield. Over the centuries, church historians have revered him as the greatest Anglo-American revivalist and the Paul of his age. For them, he represented a timeless saint located along a vast continuum of faith and powerful preachers.[1] But secular history has been a different matter. There saints do not count. And having no clear place as a colonial founder, like John Winthrop or William Penn, and no literary identity as a powerful intellectual, like Jonathan Edwards or Ralph Waldo Emerson, he tended to be consigned to the ranks of sideshow. Echoing the conventional wisdom of the field, Perry Miller contrasted his sympathetic portrayal of Jonathan Edwards, the "American Augustine," with scorn for Whitefield the clown. Of Whitefield, Miller concluded: "a more repulsive individual never influenced history . . . he was reckless and irresponsible, whining and sanctimonious." To understand Whitefield, Miller continued, "we must go to such analogies as Peter the Hermit or Savonarola, or possibly the Pied Piper."[2]

American historians' neglect — or ridicule — of Whitefield was

---

1. See esp. Luke Tyerman, *The Life of the Rev. George Whitefield,* 2 vols. (London: Hodder and Stoughton, 1890); and Arnold A. Dallimore, *George Whitefield: The Life and Times of the Great Evangelist of the Eighteenth-Century Revival,* 2 vols. (Westchester, IL: Crossway Books, 1970, 1979).

2. Perry Miller, *Jonathan Edwards* (1949; repr. Amherst: University of Massachusetts Press, 1981), 142.

symptomatic of professional historians' neglect of religious history generally. In the formative phase of American history writing, there was no integration of religious history into American history, no sense that it constituted a "main theme" in the profession's priorities. Other ideological and environmental forces were used to explain the main course of American history.

In the past decade, however, this neglect has been replaced with a remarkable resurgence of interest in religious history in general American history. Indeed, in a recent essay, Jon Butler goes so far as to describe an "evangelical paradigm" in recent historiography that functions very much like the older Beardian or Turnerian paradigms. Citing a wide variety of works, from colonial slavery to "ethno-cultural" political behavior in the nineteenth century to twentieth-century foreign policy, Butler shows how far-reaching religion — and more particularly evangelical Protestantism — has become in shaping recent explanations of American history. From being "recovered" in the 1960s, the religious factor has now grown to virtually take over the field.[3]

The prime movers in this triumph of religious history have been the "New Social History," beginning in the 1970s, and the field of Women's Studies, which reached maturity in the 1980s. In reconstructing the worlds of "ordinary" men and women, both of these burgeoning fields have discovered that religion played a primary role in giving scope to ever-expanding liberties and public roles denied in other spheres.[4]

Outside the history profession, other more interdisciplinary fields have also contributed to a renewed interest in religion. Of these, the field of communications has been especially interesting. Scholars interested in communications theory and practice have found in eighteenth- and nineteenth-century religion and social reform prototypes for modern communications networks that would achieve secular dominance in the twentieth century. In a recent article, David Nord goes so far as to describe the evangelical origins of mass media.[5]

---

3. Jon Butler, "Born-Again History? A Critique of the New Evangelical Thesis in American Historiography" (Unpublished paper, American Historical Association, December 1992).

4. This literature is traced in Harry S. Stout and Catherine A. Brekus, "Declension, Gender, and the 'New Religious History,'" in *Belief and Behavior: Essays in the New Religious History,* ed. Philip J. Vandermeer and Robert P. Swierenga (New Brunswick: Rutgers University Press, 1991), 15-37.

5. David Paul Nord, "The Evangelical Origins of Mass Media in America, 1815-

Given the new respect accorded American religious history, it is time to reexamine Whitefield's contributions to Anglo-American culture and accord him the central role he deserves in shaping evangelical forces that, for better and worse, would come to triumph in the nineteenth century. Instead of hagiographic studies that abstract Whitefield from his times, it is important to examine him in the context of his age — the age of David Garrick, Benjamin Franklin, and Thomas Paine. Such was the scope of his fame and popularity that he rightly can be labeled Anglo-America's first modern celebrity, a preacher capable of commanding mass audiences (and offerings) across two continents, without any institutional support, through the sheer power of his personality. In this essay I would like to trace the roots of this celebrity-in-the-making by examining Whitefield's novel use of media and public relations. Then I would like briefly to explore some of the consequences of this creation for religious history and, more particularly, the history of evangelical revivals.

To understand Whitefield's remarkable innovations in pulpit media and public relations we need to understand both the personality of the man and the transitional times in which he lived. Earlier church historians have rightly fastened on Whitefield's deep piety and charismatic pulpit manner, but they have not sufficiently appreciated his deviation from the "typical" evangelical ministerial profile. Whitefield did not grow up in a particularly pious household, and his early training was more taken up with the stage than with biblical devotions or the liberal arts.[6] Long before his Oxford conversion he was caught up in a self-made dramatic world that brought with it insatiable needs for recognition and individual stardom. These needs — and the techniques of the theater — would stay with Whitefield long after his conversion. Indeed, they would shape his pulpit career in innovative ways that had no precedent in the annals of English-speaking, educated ministers.

Whitefield's uniquely dramatic, egocentric personality formed a new breed of preacher — one with the instincts and ego needs of the great actor together with the deep piety of a Methodist exhorter. Where other churchmen would seek fame as preacher-theologians, reconciling faith to

1835," *Journalism Monographs* 88 (1984): 1-30. See also Nord's "Theology and News: The Religious Roots of American Journalism, 1630-1730," *Journal of American History* 77 (1990): 9-38.

6. For an outstanding brief survey of Whitefield's childhood, youth, and subsequent career, see Stuart Henry, *George Whitefield: Wayfaring Witness* (Nashville: Abingdon Press, 1957).

the world of letters, or as institution builders, creating new denominations, Whitefield would seek fame as a preacher/actor, alone at the center stage of his own traveling revival. His personality and background drove him away from limiting denominational connections toward the largest crowds possible. Partly by calculation, partly by instinct, and partly by his own dramatic need for self-expression and self-promotion, Whitefield represented what might be termed the prototypical modern revivalist, detached from denominational affiliations and building a movement around himself and the experiential message of free grace that he proclaimed.[7]

Instead of building his revivals around the traditional institutional supports in the established or nonconforming churches, Whitefield built his revivals around the press. Whitefield discovered the press at the start of his preaching career in London during the summer of 1737 as he awaited travel orders to the newly founded Georgia colony. Following a series of wildly popular sermons in which his dramatic, embodied performances enthralled hundreds, publishers began clamoring for copies of his sermons to print. In his *Journal,* Whitefield recalled with satisfaction how his early sermon "Regeneration" was published and "sold well to persons of all denominations . . . at home and abroad."[8]

Advertisements for the young phenom's sermons appeared everywhere, including the skeptical — and soon overtly hostile — *Weekly Miscellany,* publishing organ for the Church of England. Soon the offices of Whitefield's publishing friend and fellow Methodist James Hutton strained to meet the demands. New sermons were called for, and Whitefield eagerly complied. "The Almost Christian" and "The Nature and Necessity of Society" were advertised widely and marketed throughout England, Scotland, and North America. Whitefield knew that many Anglican churchmen begrudged his popular successes, but instead of keeping silence he openly gloated, creating a storm of controversy that would later play well in papers throughout the Anglo-American world.[9]

Before leaving London, Whitefield rushed into print everything he had. Although collections of his sermons would be marketed throughout the eighteenth and nineteenth centuries, most of them were composed and first

7. For a fuller explication of this theme, see Harry S. Stout, *The Divine Dramatist: George Whitefield and the Rise of Modern Evangelicalism* (Grand Rapids: Eerdmans, 1991).

8. George Whitefield, *George Whitefield's Journals* (London, 1960), 86.

9. See Frank Lambert, " 'Pedlar in Divinity': George Whitefield and the Great Awakening, 1737-1745," *Journal of American History* 77 (1990): 812-37.

printed in the early years of his career. Of sixty-three printed sermons, forty-six originated in this period before he was twenty-five. In the same way that he would repeat extemporaneous sermons from stop to stop, he would reprint sermons in various combinations and issues for the remainder of his career, mixing in the old with an occasional new contribution.

While printed sermons were important promoters of Whitefield's fame in the pious and clerical communities, they could not, in themselves, create a celebrity. By their very nature, printed sermons hearkened back to an earlier, more elitist age marked by traditional standards of clerical decorum. In addition, their primary audiences tended to be the already converted. Printed sermons could memorialize preachers to their congregations and spread intellectual fame among their peers, but they could not penetrate the larger marketplace of print surfacing in urban centers throughout the Anglo-American world. For a preacher to become a celebrity, more popular media would have to be utilized. That meant, above all else, the newspapers, which were just beginning to proliferate in urban centers throughout Anglo-America.

Before Whitefield, the newspapers did not include religion in their subject matter. For the most part, news was taken up with secular concerns of business, government, and recreation. To traditional churchmen it represented an alien presence, at best indifferent and at worst a threat to traditional religious print. But to Whitefield it represented the perfect form of public outreach, for it reached precisely the "customers" who eluded the nets of printed sermons and settled churches. Acting more instinctively than methodically, Whitefield eagerly embraced the popular press as an essential ally for his own pursuit of mass audiences.[10]

Of course, there was a reason why religion was not primary in the news, and that was because it was not popular or useful in the marketplace. In utilizing the secular news, Whitefield was at once presenting religion as a popular commodity that could compete not so much against other churches as against the goods and services of this world. Not by accident, his greatest preaching successes would take place outside of traditional churches in the secular "fields" of the marketplace.

10. In surveying Whitefield's role in the eighteenth-century press, I have consulted all references to Whitefield in the following newspapers and magazines: *Weekly Miscellany* (London), *The Weekly History* (London), *Christian History* (Boston), *Glasgow Weekly History*, *Pennsylvania Gazette*, *American Weekly Mercury*, *Pennsylvania Journal*, *Boston Gazette*, *Boston News-Letter*, *Boston Post-Boy*, *Boston Evening Post*, *New England Weekly Journal*, *South-Carolina Gazette*, *Georgia Gazette*, and the *Providence Gazette*.

Whitefield learned how to make *himself* news. In part this was a simple function of his popularity. By September 1737, he noted with satisfaction how "my name was first put into the public papers." Later, following a fund-raising sermon series at St. Swithin's in London, the press recorded the astounding success of a "young gentleman going volunteer to Georgia" who had raised the staggering offering of £28, most of which was collected "in half-pence" from innumerable working-class supporters. Although professing unhappiness that the press dwelt on money instead of message and "would not lose two shillings for anybody," Whitefield was nevertheless pleased. He had made the news.

Whitefield discovered that the press built audiences as effectively as word of mouth. From this point forward, he would use the press even as it used him, to promote and stage his preaching performances. In fact, the two discovered in one another perfect foils for their insatiable search for mass attention. Instead of invoking authority as a means of popular control and influence, Whitefield would make himself popular and, on the basis of that popularity, claim authority and status.

For the first time in the eighteenth century, a preacher joined the ranks of generals, governors, and actors as a news event. "The tide of popularity," a young Whitefield gloated in 1737, "now began to run very high." The obligatory humility required of his profession could not suppress the exhilarating fact that "I could no longer walk on foot as usual, but was constrained to go in a coach, from place to place, to avoid the hosannas of the multitude." So enamored was he of his own successes that contemporaries and later readers had trouble accepting his accompanying Methodist codicil that God "gave me to see the vanity of all commendations but His own."[11]

While Whitefield's dramatic preaching was one important component of his newspaper appeal, it did not stand alone. Alongside it was a penchant for controversy that would place Whitefield in an antagonistic position to his own Anglican church. By distancing himself from his own church, Whitefield was in an ideal position to transcend denominational limitations and attract the largest crowd possible. His controversy with the church also had the advantage of winning the loyalties of ordinary people alienated from traditional authority.[12]

11. *George Whitefield's Journals,* 89.
12. See William H. Kenney, "George Whitefield; Dissenter Priest of the Great Awakening," *William and Mary Quarterly* 26 (1969): 75-93.

Throughout his career, Whitefield was no social radical bent on overturning society, nor was he in the habit of challenging civil authority — indeed, the crown always elicited his highest praise. But bishops were another matter. Whitefield could challenge them on religious grounds without calling the establishment itself into question. This would invariably provoke controversy, and controversy, he soon discovered, merely swelled the crowds, who in turn aroused the interests of the press. With controversy and the press in mind, Whitefield learned to "stage" preaching events in ways that would vault him to the forefront of media attention. He grasped intuitively the power of the press, regardless of whether the notices were praising or damning. In either case, he saw his name set before the public eye, and "peoples curiosity was stirred up more and more."

When Whitefield's accusations and criticisms came to the attention of the Bishop of London, the bishop complained publicly, setting in motion an endless round of controversy that played perfectly into the young Whitefield's hand. No authority figure has ever won a contest in the popular press, as the bishop soon discovered. The more the controversy was played out in the press, the more Whitefield emerged as the heroic victim. In a technique that would reap endless rewards, Whitefield portrayed any public criticism as "persecution" from on high, fueling popular antagonism to authority and identifying himself as the beleaguered underdog. By fall of 1737, while his voyage to Georgia was postponed, Whitefield reported that "thousands and thousands came to hear. My sermons were everywhere called for."[13]

Whitefield's media explorations did not stop with the newspapers and sermons. While en route to Georgia he began composing a journal and autobiography that would soon make him a household name on both sides of the ocean. The Georgia diary and the subsequently written autobiography would be his first attempts at journalistic self-promotion and, in their own context, were pioneering works of genius. Earlier than most, Whitefield perceived how the journal — once confined to the private and inner world of the diarist — could become an ideal vehicle for creating a public image. Instead of composing reflections within a context of devotional privacy, one could carefully select entries with a view toward constructing a persona — the person one wanted to be, or the person one thought would edify unknown readers — rather than presenting the self

13. *George Whitefield's Journal*, 90-91. See the sermons collected in *Sermons on Various Important Subjects* (London, 1939).

as he "really was." Unlike the Puritans or Methodists who separated private diary from public journal, Whitefield abolished the distinction in ways that anticipated the artful autobiography of his soon-to-be friend and publisher Benjamin Franklin.[14]

Again, in the case of the journal, we see how Whitefield's personality informed his instincts in ways that courted self-promotion and mythmaking. Most young ministers in their twenties would shy away from publishing their "personal" journals or advertising their controversies with their elders in the church. But not Whitefield. While conceding that past conventions dictated that private publications ought to "be deferred til after my death, or written by some other persons," Whitefield nevertheless broke from the convention by allowing the publication and serialization of his *Journal.* In the process, he transformed spiritual autobiography from its devotional context to a powerful form of self-promotion.

For his first journalistic entry, Whitefield told the story of his New World voyage and his successful campaign to convert the soldiers on board the ship. A brief examination of the journal confirms its appeal to popular audiences. As a teller of tales the young Whitefield had few equals. He had an ear for language and, though never a scholar or polite essayist, he produced colloquial prose ideally suited to the popular press. Reports on weather, course headings, and winds he deftly interspersed with nail-biting accounts of storms at sea, cascading waves, split sails, and imminent danger. Readers could easily imagine the situation when Whitefield awoke to a fierce gale. The ensuing moments were terrifying: "I went on deck; but surely a more noble, awful sight my eyes never beheld! For the waves rose mountains high and sometimes came on the quarter-deck. I endeavored all the while to magnify God, for thus making His power to be known. Then creeping on my knees (for I knew not how to go otherwise), I followed my friend between decks, and sang songs and comforted the poor wet people."[15] In fact, Whitefield was notorious for his timidity in the face of danger (often conceding that his wife was braver than he). But in the journal he became something different: a fearless voyager braving wind and storm to fulfill his appointed calling.

Action was the common theme throughout the journal. In place of

14. This theme is developed more fully in Harry S. Stout, "George Whitefield and Benjamin Franklin: Thoughts on a Peculiar Friendship," in *Proceedings* of the Massachusetts Historical Society, forthcoming, 1993.

15. *George Whitefield's Journals,* 103-6.

spiritual meditations and soliloquies of praise to God, Whitefield kept the journal moving with all the pace and skill of a superb storyteller. Unlike the accounts of other travelers, this travelogue would move effortlessly beyond nature to supernature. In the end, it wasn't so much about travel to the mysterious new colony of Georgia as it was about the mysteries of the New Birth. Like the Puritan founders of old, but with a new journalistic style, Whitefield saw the ocean crossing as a metaphor of the Christian's spiritual pilgrimage across a dangerous sea to a strange new world. For his journal, it resulted in a language of providence and power — all centered around himself, the storyteller. The result was a new literary type, simultaneously evangelistic and mythic in its self-promotion.

As the journal progressed, Whitefield carried both his heroic persona and his theme of evangelical piety into an accompanying story of even greater excitement and personal legend: the conversion of the crew and soldiers. The jagged progress of the ship in winter voyage became a metaphor for Whitefield's progress with the soldiers. Engaged readers learned of a gradual alteration in the attitudes and actions of the troops: "I perceived the soldiers were attentive to hear me, when I applied myself to those around the sick persons." Increasingly their hearts "softened" to his ministry and he won them over.

The *Journal* was printed during Whitefield's first American sojourn to great approval, going through six editions in six months. With nothing but the persona of the *Journal* to fill the public imagination he became more beloved to his friends and more despised by his foes. The journals, he discovered, would be his medium for public reputation, making him omnipresent to reading audiences throughout England, Scotland, and America, so that while he was absent he was yet present. As Whitefield continued to itinerate, his reputation continued to grow. By the time of his second and most sensational tour of the colonies in 1740, he was already a household name. The *Journal* had succeeded in whetting the public appetite for his preaching and in interesting American newsprinters.

In America, Whitefield's relationship to the press would be even more important than it had been in England. In fundamental ways, the two would grow up together. Whitefield would teach the American newspapers how to make religion *news,* and the press would respond with almost universal acclaim and adulation, trumpeting the name of Whitefield wherever he appeared.

In Philadelphia, where the "Great Awakening" of 1740 began, Whitefield worked closely with printers publicizing his two favorite subjects: the New Birth and himself. His most significant supporter was the enterprising printer Benjamin Franklin, who eagerly supported the young itinerant and marketed his *Journal* — now augmented by a hugely popular autobiography — throughout the middle colonies and in New England. But Franklin would not have the field to himself. Alongside his *Pennsylvania Gazette* was Andrew and William Bradford's *American Weekly Mercury,* which devoted front-page coverage to Whitefield from his first visit in November 1739 throughout the next year in virtually every issue. For the fledgling American newspapers, whose primary subjects had been largely limited to political and economic commentary, Whitefield represented a new avenue of inquiry. For the first time, religion became part of the exchange of information in the infant American press. The press was so generous in praising Whitefield that the Anglican Commissary Cummings complained openly — and correctly — that the printers conspired with Whitefield to trumpet his name at the expense of established religious and economic institutions.[16]

Soon American news printers throughout the colonies learned to pick up on any Whitefield materials that came to their attention. Throughout all of this, Whitefield was an active partner, channeling information to them about his preaching itineraries, his dramatic successes, and his confrontations with authority. With the support of his wealthy Methodist friend William Seward, he constructed a primitive publicity department that would employ letters and newspaper accounts throughout the Anglo-American world.

Controversy continued to play a major role in Whitefield's world of evangelical news. Readers throughout the colonies and abroad thrilled to accounts of his contests with Anglican and slave-owning authorities in the South. Early on, Franklin reprinted several letters of Whitefield that attacked traditional authorities. One, particularly obnoxious to Anglicans, asserted that the venerable Archbishop Tillotson knew no more about grace than "Mohamet." Southern slave owners also came under fire for refusing to evangelize their slaves.[17] Publicity, print, advance word, and Whitefield's own charismatic and controversial presence soon created a cause célèbre. In the primarily Calvinist colonies where Anglicans were few and where

16. See Frank Lambert, "The Great Awakening as Artifact: George Whitefield and the Construction of Intercolonial Revival, 1739-1745," *Church History* 69 (1991): 223-46.

17. See George Whitefield, *Sermons on Various Important Subjects by the Rev. George Whitefield, A.M.* (Boston, 1741).

resistance to institutional "authority" was an environmental given, White-field became an American hero. In Whitefield, colonial Americans dis-covered their first intercolonial hero, the first in a long line of public figures whose claims to influence would rest on celebrity and popularity rather than birth, breeding, or institutional fiat. For his part, Whitefield played the role of pious celebrity to perfection, careful never to offend civil authority and invariably recording lunches and meetings with governors, proprietors, and other local dignitaries in his journals and letters. Only non-Christian slave owners and the Church of England would feel the sting of his criticism, and they returned the favor by closing their pulpits and parishes, never realizing how perfectly their attempts at suppression fed Whitefield's popularity. Closed pulpits simply "forced" Whitefield into the public square, where he could compete in the marketplace for unprec-edented religious audiences. Whitefield was not unobservant of this "ser-vice," and once gloated: "Little do my enemies think what service they do me. If they did one would think, out of spite they would even desist from opposing me."[18]

When not preaching the New Birth to rapt audiences, Whitefield and his growing band of friends and supporters worked to build an Anglo-American Calvinist network, with Whitefield as the traveling center. Seward's journal provides a glimpse of religious publicity in the making. On April 22, 1740, he received news of a sloop going to Georgia. Imme-diately he sat down and "wrote letters to Savannah, Charlestown, Freder-ica, Virginia, Cape-Fear, New Brunswick, and New York." In that day alone he sent out over a hundred letters containing news of Whitefield's tour. In many of the letters, he "Inclosed our Brother's Letters against [Archbishop] Tillotson, and about the Negroes, and also sundry News-paper [accounts]." Along with reports on Whitefield's successes in Philadel-phia, Seward "wrote paragraphs for the News, where our Brother was to preach and had preached." A widening network of correspondents and printers was being created even as Whitefield traveled from place to place. Together, they were investing Whitefield with the status of a cultural myth of powerful and ever-growing proportions.[19]

Before Whitefield's arrival in New England in 1740, readers there knew all about the impending visit from the "marvel of the age." In an

18. *George Whitefield's Journals*, 423.
19. See William Seward, *Journal of a Voyage from Savannah to Philadelphia* (London, 1740).

age that had not yet established copyright laws, New England newspapers borrowed verbatim from accounts in the Philadelphia and New York newspapers and from letters that Whitefield and Seward had sent north. As early as April 1740, the *New England Weekly Journal* carried front-page coverage of Whitefield's attacks on Tillotson and Southern slave owners and applauded both. New England readers anticipated seeing "a man of middle stature, of a slender body, of a fair complexion, and of a comely appearance." He was "sprightly" and "cheerful" in temperament, and they understood that he moved "with great agility and life." The *Boston Gazette* described a Whitefield sermon at the Philadelphia courthouse in which "the pulpit seem'd almost to be the Tribunal, if the comparison may be pardon'd, of the great Judge, clothed in Flames, and adjudging a guilty world to penal Fire."

Soon the Boston printers got into the act. Samuel Kneeland and Thomas Green printed Whitefield's *Account* of orphan house management and disbursements, which he had written to allay public suspicion concerning his offerings. The major Boston publishers Draper, Rogers, and Fowle picked up Whitefield's sermons, while booksellers such as Daniel Henchman imported Franklin's edition of the *Journals* to meet widespread public demand.

As always, controversy was Whitefield's best friend, and New England accommodated with at least one outspoken skeptic, the conservative and thoroughly anglicized publisher Thomas Fleet. Fleet's audience aspired to gentility, so he chose as his journalistic model those fashionable London magazines that heaped abuse on the "field preacher," identifying him with methodism and mayhem. Fleet would maintain a staunch antagonism in his *Boston Evening Post* throughout Whitefield's early tours of New England. But, like other opposition, he simply fueled public curiosity. After reading Fleet's reprinting of Commissary Garden's harsh strictures against Whitefield, audiences became all the more intent on seeing the field phenomenon for themselves.

From America, Whitefield traveled to Scotland, fusing print, letter writing, and dramatic oral performance into mass events that had no precedent in religious assembly. By traveling constantly, Whitefield could structure all of his preaching around the cathartic and highly emotive experience of the New Birth. Theology, denomination, social duty, and sacraments were left behind for "settled" preachers. For Whitefield, all was passion and the experience of regeneration. Again Whitefield concentrated his attention on the urban centers, especially Edinburgh and Glasgow, where both print and marketplace attracted audiences from far and wide. Many in these audiences did not know one another and were caught up in a new religious association with Whitefield at the center.

The unprecedented enthusiasm and support of Scottish audiences convinced Whitefield that the transatlantic revival had become a reality. To cement the growing transatlantic "Calvinist Connexion," Whitefield exploited yet another media innovation: the religious magazine. His *Journals* had taught him the value of popular print. A magazine could do all that his *Journals* had done and more. Already in April 1741, on the eve of his first tour of Scotland, he had taken over a magazine entitled *The Weekly History; or, An Account of the Most Remarkable Particulars Relating to the Present Progress of the Gospel.* The first issue appeared on April 11, 1741. It bore the name of Whitefield's printer friend John Lewis on the masthead. But in reality it was a Whitefield production, filled with news of his revivals and charitable enterprises. In subject matter and style it paralleled the *Journal* and anticipated features that would become commonplace in nineteenth-century religious journalism. In format, the paper appealed to a popular audience with anticipated features geared to popular interest. Unlike more elite magazines sold by annual subscription, *The Weekly History* was sold on a cheap-for-cash format that would later be adopted by the secular penny press. Distribution came through local societies and through Whitefield's preexistent letter-writing network. For those unable to afford even the cheap cost of an issue, Whitefield provided a lending service where interested readers could "repair to the Printer's House to read 'em gratis."[20]

In effect, Whitefield was using the magazine to record a new history in the making: the history of the transatlantic revival. Unlike the "new age" of the Enlightenment, this new history was not recorded in scholarly essays and treatises by intellectual elites but in news-sheets and magazines. The central characters in this history were ordinary people who, for the first time, saw themselves as news.

Always at the center of this new revival was Whitefield. Besides recording revivals throughout the empire and in Europe, the magazine served as advance publicity for his speaking tours. Already in the spring issue, *The Weekly History* published accounts of Whitefield's upcoming

20. See Susan O'Brien, "A Transatlantic Community of Saints: The Great Awakening and the First Evangelical Network, 1735-1755," *American Historical Review* 91 (1986): 811-32.

visit to Scotland. In addition, it reprinted letters Whitefield received from other ministers and leaders in the transatlantic network, including Josiah Smith in Charleston, the merchant Thomas Noble in New York, the Tennents in Pennsylvania, and Benjamin Colman and William Cooper in Boston. News from Whitefield's Georgia orphan house also figured prominently. Regular reports from superintendent James Habersham described the building projects and youthful inhabitants. Alongside these accounts, the paper included conversion narratives penned by the ten- and eleven-year-old residents of the orphan house. To lend authenticity and poignancy, their testimonies were "spell'd precisely as they wrote them."

Whitefield recognized a good idea when he saw one, and he urged his Scottish and American co-laborers to begin journalistic endeavors of their own. Almost immediately, widely read imitators appeared. The first was the *Glasgow Weekly History*, begun by the Scottish revivalist and Whitefield supporter William Macculloch in December 1741. Most of Macculloch's stories were lifted directly from *The Weekly History*, with special emphasis on items of interest to Scottish readers. By early spring of 1742, Macculloch had strange and exciting news of his own from the small village of Cambuslang. Through letters and press, an international audience began following the progress of a "great awakening" that sounded like another Northampton in the making. Whitefield himself traveled to Cambuslang in time to participate in a series of revivals that drew thousands to the communion table. These events were then described in letters and accounts that had the effect of cementing a Scottish-American evangelical connection that would thrive throughout the remainder of the eighteenth century and beyond.[21]

Besides Macculloch's Scottish magazine, the Rev. James Robe established a similar imitator in Edinburgh with the *Christian Monthly History*. In America, Thomas Prince's *Christian History* began publication in Boston in 1743, through the publishing offices of Kneeland and Green. Although all of these magazines would prove to be short-lived, they served the indispensable function of recording a new history in the making. At the same time, they reinforced the ordinary participants' sense of international significance. For the first time, ordinary men and women were taking actions that placed them at the forefront of *news*. Perfect strangers spanning two continents were drawn increasingly into a common movement that

21. On Cambuslang, see esp. Arthur Fawcett, *The Cambuslang Revival: The Scottish Evangelical Revival of the Eighteenth Century* (London: Banner of Truth Trust, 1971).

transcended particular time and space. Like Whitefield and his evangelical associates, they were all "somebodies" in a glorious cause. Their first halting steps in the direction of a religious journalism transcended their immediate impact, however, for they would represent the foundation of an evangelical publishing empire destined to dominate Anglo-American print culture in the next century.

Inevitably, new culture heroes produce new myths. Even as White-field elevated himself to mythic status and became the first modern religious celebrity, his revivals also transformed the meaning of religion in profound ways that would persist into the twentieth century. In closing, I would like to return to the subject of religion as a main theme in Anglo-American history and suggest how Whitefield's mass revivals transformed the meaning of religious experience and association in ways that are recognizably "modern" and "evangelical."

Whitefield's religious vision was profound not in its theological depth but in its very popularity. His mass revivals were not really a church, nor were they connected to local communities and congregations. The audiences changed with every meeting, evidencing no permanent structure or leadership aside from Whitefield's own charismatic ministry and his network of media promoters. In addition, the audiences were routinely enjoined to support their local congregations and parishes, even as they were assured of bigger things afoot. In reality, Whitefield's audiences, publishers, and loyal supporters represented powerful new "parachurches" — groups of otherwise disconnected individuals bound in voluntary religious associations based on a marketplace organization and destined to characterize pan-Protestant "evangelical" organizations in the nineteenth and twentieth centuries.

In an ironic process that Whitefield could not have foreseen, and may not have realized, his media-enhanced revivals had become, in effect, an institution. More than any other eighteenth-century figure, he had brought new meaning to the term "revival."[22] What had initially been a convulsive and mysterious force upsetting ordinary life and catching participants by surprise had become, after 1745, something different — a familiar event that could be planned in advance, executed flawlessly, and then repeated at the next stop. By 1750, with the divisions of the first "Great Awakening" safely behind, Whitefield was no longer threatening.

22. For a fuller explication, see Michael J. Crawford, *Seasons of Grace: Colonial New England's Revival Tradition in Its British Context* (New York: Oxford University Press, 1991).

Just as he severed ties with Anglican bishops, so also did he distance himself from "Separatists" in Scotland and America who threatened the Presbyterian and Congregational establishments. The more he lined up with civil and ecclesiastical authorities, the more it became clear that his new revivals were not going to turn the world upside down. By 1765, even the *Boston Evening Post* sang his praises as a voice of faith and charity. Audiences everywhere, highbrow and lowbrow, paid tribute to the evangelical "marvel of the age." People could leave his revivals spiritually refreshed and leave the world unchanged. Whitefield's revivals had become, in effect, a form of entertainment, that is, a series of trans-local, staged events that could be repeated with predictable — and no longer frightening — regularity.

In one sense, Whitefield's vision of a revival-driven, transatlantic parachurch committed to the individual experience of the New Birth was nontheological. By not calling his revivals a denomination, he did not need to craft credal statements of faith or establish doctrinal requirements for membership that would set one group of Christians off from another. Yet in another sense, Whitefield's conception was profoundly theological. He avoided creeds and denominations in the revivals, but at the same time he presented a new theological perspective contained less in his own Calvinist convictions than in the radical new significance ascribed to religious experience and spiritual legitimacy.

In Whitefield's evangelical parachurch, individual experience became the ultimate arbiter of authentic religious faith. Experience — or, in Lockean terminology, "sensation" — came to be the legitimating mark of religion over against family, communal covenants, traditional church memberships, credal formulations, or sacraments. As sensation represented the only avenue for natural knowledge in Lockean epistemology, so the supernatural experience of the New Birth became the sole authentic entrée to spiritual knowledge in the evangelical revivals.[23] Both were of a piece with the eighteenth-century world in which they emerged; both were compatible with the increasingly individualized and impersonal world of the marketplace and its new order.

The parachurch emerging around Whitefield's revivals was not so much a school for communal nurture and theological indoctrination as it was a context for individual experience. In it, the conversion experience engulfed all else. Revivalists might argue about the "means" of the New

---

23. In theoretical terms, it was Jonathan Edwards who fused Locke's sensory epistemology to the doctrine of regeneration, but in homiletical terms, it was Whitefield who, more than anyone else, embodied the fusion Edwards described.

Birth and the respective roles of human will and supernatural grace in regeneration, but the experience itself ruled supreme. If there was no new denomination with a capitalized name reflecting its establishment, the New Birth itself assumed capital letters as the institutional and theological embodiment of a new religious movement.

Experience. It all came back, in every revival, to this. Seventeenth-century dissenters had spoken often of regeneration and the new birth, but always in the context of local congregations and weekly education in the sermon. When pressed, they had denied that true conversion could be experienced by those who were ignorant of the theological terms on which it rested. This meant that the teaching function of the church had always received primary emphasis. In a subtle but profound transformation, Whitefield reversed this emphasis. Instead of theological indoctrination being the foundation of spiritual experience, individual experience became the ground for a shared theology of revival. As long as the foundation was individual experience and the sensation of grace, whatever — or whoever — created it received theological legitimacy at once. Whitefield's stated theological preferences were, of course, Calvinist and predestinarian. But other revivalists could, and did, build quite different theological frameworks that enjoyed the same experiential legitimation.[24]

In the new revivals rooted in celebrity preaching and media packaging, theology counted for less. In the end, the revivals that Whitefield did so much to shape were simply not about theology, but about experience. And in that transformation we see the most far-reaching consequence of his revivals. Calvinists, Moravians, Methodists, Whitefield — and the evangelical heirs of later generations — would all discover legitimization in the experiences they produced and the revivals they orchestrated. All would ask the same question: Would God bless a counterfeit movement with true, saving grace? The answer would always be no. By their experiential fruits they would be known.

Clearly, Whitefield was not single-handedly responsible for all the changes and transformations that would take a century and more to work out fully. But by examining his career in the context of communications we can see how, in a remarkable number of instances, he anticipated many of the defining characteristics of evangelical, heart-centered religion in a modern democratic age.[25] Whitefield showed, in a word, how religion

24. This theme is worked out more fully in Stout, *The Divine Dramatist*, 113-32.
25. On nineteenth-century evangelicalism, see esp. Patricia U. Bonomi, *Under the*

could be made popular, built to compete in a morally neutral and voluntaristic marketplace environment alongside all the goods and services of this world. Entertainment, packaging, and profoundly individual experiences of grace together represented a religious "product" that could win audiences and support. As such, in his very lack of theological depth or acumen, Whitefield more than any other eighteenth-century figure best represents the prophet of evangelical modernity. He was indeed a pied piper, but one of such immense power and influence that evangelical Protestants have marched to his tune ever since.

*Cope of Heaven: Religion, Society, and Politics in Colonial America* (New York: Oxford University Press, 1986); Jon Butler, *Awash in a Sea of Faith: Christianizing the American People* (Cambridge, MA: Harvard University Press, 1990); and Nathan O. Hatch, *The Democratization of American Christianity* (New Haven: Yale University Press, 1989).

# The Spirit of the Old Writers:
## Print Media, the Great Awakening, and Continuity in New England

Charles E. Hambrick-Stowe

Scores of Congregational pastors from throughout New England responded to Thomas Prince's 1743 invitation to submit accounts of local manifestations of the "happy revival of religion" for publication in America's first religious periodical, *The Christian History.* Prince's correspondents not only reported on the numbers of souls converted and the circumstances surrounding the awakening; they also offered a reassuring, conservative interpretation of what to the more genteel and rationalist of the day seemed an unruly outburst of "enthusiasm, delusion, and disorder." To New Light clergy, the Great Awakening at its best vindicated what we could call "old-time religion," basic seventeenth-century Puritan principles and spirituality. In issue after issue of the weekly magazine, they concluded that the work of revival "was essentially the same" as that put forth in "the writings of Messirs, Shepard, Willard, Stoddard, and numberless other Divines of that Stamp and Principle" who had "rightly understood the Way of Salvation." This analysis was solidly in line with Prince's objectives in publishing *The Christian History.* The journal was an unwieldy collection of *(a)* extracts from the devotional-theological writings of "the most famous Old Writers" of Puritan England, Scotland, and "the first Settlers of new-England and their Children"; *(b)* "Manuscript original Letters now in the Hands of the Rev. Mr. Prince" written by ministers and other observers of mini-revivals "in almost all Parts of the Land" between 1660 and 1720; and *(c)* reports from Scotland and the British North American colonies concerning the Great Awakening of the 1730s and 1740s. By printing these three types of materials, Prince sought to illustrate the traditionalism of the Awakening. Specifically, he wished to demonstrate that "the pious Principles and Spirit" of the "Old Writers" were "at this Day revived," and "also [to] guard against all extremes."[1]

This conservative and print-oriented approach of pro-revival clergy casts a different light on our general understanding of the Great Awakening as an oral and present- or future-oriented phenomenon. According to much historical scholarship, the revival brought something entirely new to colonial American society. Words such as "crucial turning point," "watershed," "final break with the Middle Ages," and "crisis" sprinkle the writings of historians who have effectively described the changes wrought by this pre-Revolutionary spiritual upheaval. As Richard Bushman interpreted it, in what has become a classic description, "The converted were new men, with new attitudes toward themselves, their religion, their neighbors, and their rulers in church and state. A psychological earthquake had reshaped the human landscape." These changes have to do with individualism and democracy (over against Puritanism's hierarchical communalism), with a Lockean spirit of innovation (over against, in Perry Miller's words, Puritanism's "basically medieval" static worldview), with the rise of an emotion-laden heart religion (as opposed to Puritan scholasticism), and with the rise of a distinctly American identity. The innovation of extemporaneous sermon delivery, according to Harry S. Stout, was linked with the ministry's need to win the loyalty of the laity in an increasingly competitive market. Richard D. Brown, in his recent study of how information was diffused within American society from the colonial to the early national period, states that "in the Great Awakening the notion of individual choice was forcefully asserted, together with the exercise of personal preference by ordinary people who announced that they would henceforth decide what religious information they would choose to hear." Martin Marty astutely summarizes: "The Awakening can be seen as an event or a process in the course of which the religion of the colonial way of life was supplanted by a second way — the evangelical route through which, ever since, a person might become a fervent American believer." Many evangelical preachers themselves promoted the impression that God was now doing a new thing.

1. Thomas Prince, Jr., *The Christian History, Containing Accounts of the Revival and Propagation of Religion in Great-Britain and America for the Year 1743* (Boston, 1744), 1-2, 113, 155, 162, 185. The weekly was edited by the younger Prince, who nevertheless asked contributors to send manuscripts to his father, pastor of Boston's Third Church.

Jonathan Edwards himself referred to the Northampton revival of 1734 as "the Surprising Work of God."[2]

Jon Butler has recently taken a radically different view of the Great Awakening, which corresponds at certain points with the conservative agenda apparent in Thomas Prince's *The Christian History.* Prince's inclusion of accounts of spiritual awakenings from the generations between 1660 and 1720 demonstrates his own sense of, or desire for, continuity. Butler, arguing that the notion of a single event called the "Great Awakening" is artificial, similarly observes that "revivals linked to it started in New England long before 1730 yet did not appear with force in Virginia until the 1760s." Further, the revivals of the 1730s and 1740s were neither as geographically pervasive nor as enduring in influence as is commonly portrayed. Revivals were spawned not so much in an environment of spiritual depression, or the failure of traditional religion, as within the context of a gradual renaissance of "the state church tradition" of Anglicanism and Congregationalism and of ecclesiastical and clerical authority, even among dissenting revival-born groups, over an extended period from about 1680 to 1760. "In general, revivalism embraced conservative rather than radical or egalitarian approaches to the question of authority." For Butler the idea of the "Great Awakening" is the construct of nineteenth-century religious historians trying to promote revivals in their own day — that is, using the events of the 1730s and 1740s in the same way as Thomas Prince and other New Light clergy used seventeenth-century Puritanism. Butler thus thinks of the Great Awak-

2. Richard L. Bushman, *From Puritan to Yankee: Character and the Social Order in Connecticut, 1690-1765* (Cambridge, MA: Harvard University Press, 1967), 207. Perry Miller, "Jonathan Edwards and the Great Awakening," *Errand into the Wilderness* (Cambridge, MA: Harvard University Press, 1956), 153-66. Edwin Scott Gaustad, *The Great Awakening in New England* (New York: Harper, 1957), 1-15, 102-40. Alan Heimert, *Religion and the American Mind: From the Great Awakening to the Revolution* (Cambridge, MA: Harvard University Press, 1966), esp. 27-94. Wesley N. Gewehr, *The Great Awakening in Virginia, 1740-1790* (1930; Gloucester, MA: P. Smith, 1965), 3-18. David S. Lovejoy, *Religious Enthusiasm in the New World: Heresy to Revolution* (Cambridge, MA: Harvard University Press, 1985), 178-214. William G. McLoughlin, " 'Enthusiasm for Liberty': The Great Awakening as the Key to the Revolution," in *Preachers and Politicians,* ed. Jack P. Greene (Worcester, MA: American Antiquarian Society, 1977), 47-73. Harry S. Stout, *The New England Soul: Preaching and Religious Culture in Colonial New England* (New York: Oxford University Press, 1986), 185-211. Richard D. Brown, *Knowledge Is Power: The Diffusion of Information in Early America, 1700-1865* (New York: Oxford University Press, 1989), 273. Martin E. Marty, *Religion, Awakening, and Revolution* ([Wilmington, NC]: Consortium, 1977), 79-80, 93. Jonathan Edwards, *A Faithful Narrative of the Surprising Work of God* (London, 1737).

ening as "an interpretive fiction . . . an American equivalent of the Roman Empire's Donation of Constantine." Whether or not this conclusion is too extreme, it has become evident that the revivals of the 1730s and 1740s embodied tradition as well as innovation.[3]

Several other scholars have specifically identified themes of continuity in the Great Awakening with earlier Presbyterian-Congregational experience. Marilyn J. Westerkamp has shown that middle colony revivalism was a traditional, not an innovative, form of religious expression rooted in seventeenth-century Old World Scots-Irish piety. Leigh Eric Schmidt demonstrates that a particular Scottish tradition of "sacramental seasons," large outdoor protracted gatherings (typically eight days in duration) for preaching and the celebration of Holy Communion, shaped some of the major contours of American revivalism and gave birth to the supposedly uniquely "frontier" camp meeting. "From at least the 1730s," Schmidt shows, "though far removed from Ulster or Scotland," the "holy faires" of the communion seasons "provided a notable portion" of the force that invigorated the evangelical revivals in the middle colonies. Since at least one high-profile New Englander, David Brainerd, was mightily affected by his experience of these ritual exercises in 1745, the practice may well have influenced the revivalist spirit subsequently in New England.[4]

Proponents of the revival in New England similarly drew upon long-established English and seventeenth-century American Puritan devotional practices and patterns of spiritual experience both to fuel and to guide the Great Awakening in their region.[5] These efforts took place

3. Jon Butler, *Awash in a Sea of Faith: Christianizing the American People* (Cambridge, MA: Harvard University Press, 1990), 128, 164-66, 170-74, 179-81. See also Gregory H. Nobles, *Divisions Throughout the Whole: Politics and Society in Hampshire County, Mass., 1740-1775* (New York: Cambridge University Press, 1983). Nobles demonstrates the presence of a conservative impulse among Connecticut Valley clergy eager for "a stable ecclesiastical and social order" (37).

4. Marilyn J. Westerkamp, *Triumph of the Laity: Scots-Irish Piety and the Great Awakening, 1625-1760* (New York: Oxford University Press, 1988). Leigh Eric Schmidt, *Holy Fairs: Scottish Communions and American Revivals in the Early Modern Period* (Princeton: Princeton University Press, 1989), 54-56.

5. I have analyzed these foundational Puritan devotional practices and spiritual experience in *The Practice of Piety: Puritan Devotional Disciplines in Seventeenth-Century New England* (Chapel Hill: University of North Carolina Press, 1982) and in *Early New England Meditative Poetry: Anne Bradstreet and Edward Taylor* (New York: Paulist Press, 1988). See Michael J. Crawford, *Seasons of Grace: Colonial New England's Revival Tradition in Its British Context* (New York: Oxford University Press, 1991), for a discussion of "the transatlantic prorevival connection" and its roots in the late seventeenth century.

locally in the pulpit and in the context of pastoral work. On a broader, regional scale, New Light leaders specifically promoted the revivals of the 1730s and 1740s through their use of print media. The types of material included by Prince in *The Christian History* are mirrored in the lists of books published in Boston during this period. Although the mass publication of books and the advent of the religious periodical magazine were technologically innovative, the strong presence of traditional themes and old titles raises questions about how much underlying continuity accompanied the undeniable changes wrought in the Great Awakening decades. The motives behind this publishing effort included those identified by Prince in *The Christian History:* to reestablish a spiritual foundation and to guard against the excesses of enthusiasm.

Among the books published during this period one finds an astonishing number of reprints of seventeenth-century devotional tracts and manuals. Many of these were old favorites by English Nonconformist giants, such as John Owen, John Flavel, John Bunyan, James Janeway, Benjamin Keach, Thomas Gouge, Thomas Doolittle, William Burkitt, Thomas Vincent, Mordecai Matthews, Richard Baxter, Richard Standfast, and many others, all of whom died before 1710. William Dyer's *Christ's Famous Titles, and A Believer's Golden Chain,* the pseudonymous Andrew Jones's *The Black Book of Conscience,* Alleine's *Heaven's Alarm to Unconverted Sinners,* and John Rawlet's *The Christian Monitor* are just a few of the genuine blockbusters from the mid-seventeenth century (they enjoyed ten, twenty, and even more printings) that still commanded a large market when they appeared in the 1730s and 1740s. The influence of English dissenter John Corbet, who died in 1680, was likewise not limited to his own century. Fresh reprints of *Self-Employment in Secret* (first published in London in 1681 and in Boston in 1684), a record of his devotional practices, persisted through the 1740s. Similarly popular was Thomas Wilcox's *A Choice Drop of Honey, From the Rock of Christ,* an early seventeenth-century chestnut first published in Massachusetts in 1667, which saw several new editions during the Great Awakening. Jeremiah Burroughs's *The Rare Jewel of Christian Contentment,* first published in London in 1648, was also circulating again.[6] These "steady-sellers," as David Hall

6. William Dyer, *Christ's Famous Titles, and A Believer's Golden Chain* (Boston, 1731). Andrew Jones, *The Black Book of Conscience* (Boston, 1732). Joseph Alleine, *Heaven's Alarm to Unconverted Sinners* (Boston, 1727, 1739, 1743; Philadelphia, 1741). John Rawlet, *The Christian Monitor, Containing an Earnest Exhortation to a Holy Life* (Boston, 1733, 1743).

has described them in his study of seventeenth-century popular religion, thrived in the mid-eighteenth-century marketplace, some of them even until the early 1800s (and in the cases of Bunyan and Baxter until our own time). Although their publication both predated and (in the case of some) postdated the Great Awakening, it is also true that the appearance of editions of Puritan devotional classics during the 1730s and 1740s was part of a New Light strategy to guide the Awakening.[7]

Spiritual autobiography was also a staple of the religious book trade spanning the Puritan and Great Awakening eras. Elizabeth White's *The Experiences of God's Gracious Dealing,* for example, had appeared in numerous London and Glasgow editions from 1671 on and into the new century before being published in Boston in 1741. This work was mistaken as a product of colonial New England by Daniel Shea in his study *Spiritual Autobiography in Early America* (1968). In his "Preface and Retrospect" in a 1988 reprinting of his monograph Shea acknowledges the error and defers to Patricia Caldwell's "suggestive explorations" of how different White's Old World spirituality really was from the distinctly American forms of "national autobiographical expression" she sees developing almost immediately after immigration. Yet Mrs. White's *Experiences* was republished in America almost a century after and an ocean away from its time and place of origin, Shea notes, "as part of the promotional literature associated with the Great Awakening." The historical question of why this work was still so popular and/or useful in the New England of the 1740s is at least as significant as the question, raised by literary scholarship, of its stylistic differences from indigenous New World autobiographies. Whatever the differences that made the Great Awakening uniquely "American," the phenomenon was also part of an international transatlantic evangelical revival. The influence of George Whitefield in America, the near-simultaneous publication of *The Christian History* in Edinburgh and

---

[Joshua Scottow], *Old Men's Tears* (Boston, 1691; repr. 1733). John Corbet, *Enquiry into the State of His Own Soul: Or Self-Employment in Secret* (Boston, 1743). [Thomas Wilcox], *A Choice Drop of Honey, From the Rock Christ* (Boston, 1734, 1741). Jeremiah Borroughs, *The Rare Jewel of Christian Contentment* (Boston, 1731).

7. David D. Hall, *Worlds of Wonder, Days of Judgment* (New York: Knopf, 1989), 21-70. See also Margaret Spufford, *Small Books and Pleasant Histories: Popular Fiction and Its Readership in Seventeenth-Century England* (Athens: University of Georgia Press, 1981), esp. the chapter entitled "Small Godly Books: Popular Religion," 194-218; William L. Joyce et al., eds., *Printing and Society in Early America* (Worcester, MA: American Antiquarian Society, 1983), 1-173; and David D. Hall, *On Native Ground: From the History of Printing to the History of the Book* (Worcester, MA: American Antiquarian Society, 1984).

Boston, and the republication of so many older English devotional manuals and tracts in America attest to this fact. The New Light leaders used the print media to strengthen their Old World links and the traditionalism of their movement.[8]

The devotional classics published in New England during the decades of the Great Awakening re-presented the major themes of Puritan spirituality, including the essentially medieval techniques of meditation. This was a spirituality of the heart and not merely of rational understanding or proper behavior. Thomas Doolittle's seventeenth-century devotional treatise *Captives Bound in Chains,* which appeared again in a 1742 Boston edition, included a crescendo of arguments in order "yet more to affect your heart." These included acts of meditation: "Consider, that Christ did ransom you from your Captivity when you were an enemy unto him." The underlying spirituality of self-abasement preparatory to receiving the grace of God was once more set before the people. Thomas Wilcox in his *Choice Drop of Honey* wrote: "Thou who hast seen Christ all, and self nothing, who makes Christ thy life, and art dead to all righteousness besides, thou art the Christian who hath found favor with God." Mordecai Matthews's *The Christian's Daily Exercise* (Boston, 1730) and John Corbet's *Self-Employment in Secret,* among others, outlined the familiar regimen of reading, meditation, and prayer in private and family settings, morning and night. Matthews followed the convention of including meditative poetry with prose sections of exhortation and sample meditations. In the morning, for example:

> Rouze up thy sluggish Soul, O man
> When first awake thou art;
> And then let God and his concerns
> Be next unto thy heart.

And at the start of the workday:

> Imagine this same day to be
> Thy last and dying day;
> And God this night for ought thou knowst
> Should take thy breath away.

---

8. Daniel B. Shea, *Spiritual Autobiography in Early America* (1968; Madison: University of Wisconsin Press, 1988), x, 183-87. Patricia Caldwell, *The Puritan Conversion Narrative* (New York: Cambridge University Press, 1983), 1-8, 34-41. Hambrick-Stowe, *Practice of Piety,* 5n.

The medieval tradition of preparation for death was thus re-presented to the Great Awakening generation. Matthews exhorted: "Write in thy Book, or rather Heart, Against a Dying day." Richard Standfast's *A New-Years-Gift for Fainting Souls* (seventh edition, Boston, 1733) instructed its readers on traditional methods of self-examination, a fundamental exercise in Puritan preparationist spirituality. Cotton Mather augmented James Janeway's manual for children, *A Token for Children* (originally published in London in 1671-72), with case material from the deaths of pious New England children. This 1700 Boston edition was reprinted in 1728 and several times more in the 1740s and later. Its successful combination of the traditions of *ars moriendi* (meditative preparation for death) and the exemplar (meditative use of the lives of exemplary believers) demonstrates the continued vitality of age-old devotional conventions in the pre-Revolutionary "age of reason."[9]

Reprinted seventeenth-century books on sacramental meditation, such as Samuel Willard's *Some Brief Sacramental Meditations* (second edition, Boston, 1743), Thomas Vincent's *A Companion for Communicants* (Boston, 1730), and John Quick's *The Young Man's Claim Unto the Sacrament of the Lord's Supper* (Boston, 1741), put forth the well-worn disciplines for preparation to receive the sacrament in familiar manual or catechetical form. William Burkitt's *The Poor Man's Help, and Young Man's Guide,* for example, advised: "The Consideration of our Baptismal Vows, renewed and ratified by many Sacramental Engagements at the Holy Table, is certainly one of the strongest ties that Christianity lays upon us to oblige us to the Love and Practice of Universal Holiness." Vincent provided sample meditations for daily preparations during the week prior to the Supper and for minute-by-minute contemplation during Communion itself. The republication in Boston of the eucharistic manual by John Quick, a seventeenth-century minister in London, addressed issues that divided some New Englanders in the 1740s. Against the position associated with Solomon Stoddard, Quick asserted: "All that are baptized, have no more a Right to the blessed Sacrament of the Eucharist" than did unclean but circumcised Israelites to the Passover. He called for believers to be "refreshed and revived" and set forth rigorous spiritual self-examination as the means of such revival.[10]

---

9. Thomas Doolittle, *Captives Bound in Chains, Made Free by Christ Their Surety* (Boston, 1742), 211. [Thomas Wilcox], *A Choice Drop of Honey, From the Rock Christ,* 8th ed. (Boston, 1741), 23. Mordecai Matthews, *The Christian's Daily Exercise* (Boston, 1730), 2, 11.

10. William Burkitt, *The Poor Man's Help, and Young Man's Guide,* 8th ed. (Boston,

Works by the old Congregational authors also cautioned against some of the dangers of the revival's excesses. As one late-seventeenth-century manual, reprinted in a 1731 Boston edition, put it, "it is hard to say, from which Religion suffers most, whether from the want of Zeal in some, or from the Mistakes of Zeal in others." Some specific problems of the Great Awakening, such as the splintering of congregations, had been addressed authoritatively in the earlier period. John Owen, for example, wrote that "it is convenient that all Believers of one Place should joyne themselves in one Congregation . . . Which Order cannot be disturbed without Danger, Strife, Emulation, and Breach of Love." His "Rules of Walking in Fellowship, with Reference to the Pastor or Minister that watcheth for our Souls" stressed the need for respect for and submission to clerical authority. As reprinted in 1744, this argument for a homogenous, village-based congregationalism can only be read as a response to the tendency for Separate congregations and itinerant preachers to splinter New England society. The word "rule," derived from medieval monastic spirituality, took on new meaning as settled ministers struggled to retain control in a freer society. Jeremiah Burroughs's classic *The Rare Jewel of Christian Contentment* consisted of "eighteen rules for the obtaining of [the] excellent grace" of assurance. In an age of enthusiasm, such talk of rules bespoke a desire among clergy for order. Daniel Burgess's *Rules for Hearing the Word of God* (reprinted, Boston, 1742) urged that "when these rules shall be observed, Ministers shall be joyful [both] Fathers and Nurses." Another manual advised believers to "have frequent recourse to your Minister, our Spiritual Guide, desire his Advice, and follow his Instructions." The message could also be couched in fearful terms. *The Black Book of Conscience,* an extraordinary piece whose twenty-sixth edition was reprinted in Boston in 1732, warned against the "dreadful Terror" that will befall "all those that live and die in their Sins" as they "go to Hell without control." New Light clergy thus hoped to guard against emotional excess and loss of clerical authority in the very Awakening they otherwise promoted.[11]

At the same time, the old works gave voice to the central theme of the

---

1731), 134. Thomas Vincent, *A Companion for Communicants* (Boston, 1730), 8. John Quick, *The Young Man's Claim Unto the Sacrament of the Lord's Supper* (Boston, 1741), iv, vi.

11. Burkitt, *Poor Man's Help,* 1, 137. John Owen, *Eshcol: A Cluster of the Fruit of Canaan,* 7th ed. (Boston, 1744), 4, 7. Jeremiah Burroughs, *The Rare Jewel of Christian Contentment* (Boston, 1731). Daniel Burgess, *Rules for Hearing the Word of God* (Boston, 1742), 18. Andrew Jones, *The Black Book of Conscience, or God's High Court of Justice in the Soul,* 26th ed. (Boston, 1732), 13, 15.

Great Awakening, the rebirth of the soul from sin. Thomas Gouge (1609-1681), whose *The Young Man's Guide* was republished in 1742, argued: "It is necessary to be converted, that so thou mayest live. Thou dyest without Remedy, thou dyest without Mercy, if thou turn not." The directness associated with New Light preaching could readily be found in the classics. Thus, James Janeway (1636-1674): "What say you to all this? . . . If you will not be acquainted with God, you shall be acquainted with the Devil, and know whose Company is best by woeful Experience." Richard Baxter (1615-1691), known for his irenic temperament, nevertheless brought a message of immediacy and ultimacy, of both warning and promise. The very title of one of his devotional works, reprinted in Boston in 1731 (in its thirty-second edition!), has a distinctively Great Awakening tone: *A Call to the Unconverted to Turn and Live.* The words on the page can be imagined from a New England pulpit: "I beseech thee, I charge thee, to hear and obey the Call of God, and resolvedly to turn, that thou mayst live. But if thou wilt not . . . I summon thee answer for it before the Lord." In a prayer for use in family devotions, Baxter humbles the reader: "O woe to us that ever we were born, if thou forgive not our sins, and make us not holy before this short uncertain Life be at an end." His "Prayer for a Penitent Sinner" contains the language of the later revivalism: "Thou knowest my secret sins. . . . My sins, O Lord, have found me out. Fears and Sorrows overwhelm me! . . . O God, be merciful to me a Sinner. . . ." Janeway challenged all "that as yet are Strangers to God" whether they have "such a Friend as he is, that will always be at your Elbow . . . ? And if not, why then will *you* not *now accept* of his Acquaintance, who will be such a friend to all that love him?" (emphasis added). The directness of Janeway's personal, evangelical address to the reader is identical with that put forth by the New Light preacher. "Come away, poor Soul, for all this it is not yet quite too late. . . . Once more I make such an offer to thee, as I am sure none but a mad Man will refuse." And finally, he paints salvation in vivid colors borrowed from the Song of Solomon: "O the sweet Pleasure of Divine Love, infinitely transcending all carnal Affections."[12]

These devotional classics did not stint on the traditional "use of terror," nor did they shrink from proclaiming the urgent need for a personal conversion experience. Their republication reinforced a shift back

12. Thomas Gouge, *The Young Man's Guide* (Boston, 1742), 52. James Janeway, *Heaven Upon Earth* (Boston, 1730), 125, 133, 144, 205, 260. Richard Baxter, *A Call to the Unconverted to Turn and Live,* 32nd ed. (Boston, 1731), sig. D4, 149, 158.

in this direction in New Light pulpits. Between 1690 and 1730, Congregationalist preachers had typically adopted a kinder, gentler evangelistic style. Jon Butler, building on the work of Harry Stout, states that the presentation of the biblical promise of salvation from sin by God's grace through faith was reduced to a "commonplace exposition" of the message. "Preachers did not terrorize. Nor did they ignore. They simply assumed that their listeners should hear about the necessity of salvation and proceeded to tell them in thoroughly mundane ways."[13] Preachers seeking to promote the revival through their own revival of evangelistic preaching, with renewed emphasis on the "use of terror" and the immediate call for repentance and faith, found support for their "innovations" in the writings of their Puritan forebears.

Ministers such as Thomas Prince, continuing an editorial tradition established by Cotton Mather, likewise dedicated much energy to reprinting old works of reliable New Englanders and to publishing exemplary personal devotional manuscripts in danger of being lost. In the first category, the works of Thomas Shepard were always both influential in the thinking of preachers such as Jonathan Edwards and popular among New England readers. John E. Smith showed how Edwards built his *A Treatise Concerning Religious Affections* (1746) on the foundation of Shepard's theology of conversion, especially as enunciated in *The Parable of the Ten Virgins*. Edwards cited "Mr. Shepard's principles" with greater frequency than he did any other author, though not uncritically, often including lengthy quotations from his works. Moreover, new editions of Shepard's *The Sound Believer; or, A Treatise of Evangelical Conversion* (1736, 1742), *The Sincere Convert* (1735, 1742, 1743), *The Saints' Jewel* (1743), and *Three Valuable Pieces* (1747) were published in Boston during the period associated with the Great Awakening. A reprinting of Thomas Hooker's *The Poor Doubting Christian Drawn to Christ*, which had enjoyed a powerful influence upon the founding generation in New England, appeared again in 1743. Samuel Willard's writings, such as the monumental *Compleat Body of Divinity* (1726) and his *Brief Directions to a Young Scholar Designing the Ministry for the Study of Divinity* (1735), were limited in their direct influence on the clergy, though a collection of sermons, *Spiritual Dissertions Discovered and Remedied* (1741), and *Some Brief Sacramental Meditations* (1743) because of their content probably found a wider audience. These books may have seemed old-fashioned to some, but for

13. Butler, *Awash in a Sea of Faith*, 172. Stout, *New England Soul*, chap. 8.

others they provided theological and spiritual moorings during a time of rapid change, increasing diversity, and secularization. To those who saw New England's only hope in spiritual awakening, Joshua Scottow's popular jeremiad *Old Men's Tears for Their Own Declensions* carried the same message when reissued in the 1730s as it did on its first appearance in 1691: "It is time for our churches to remember from whence they are fallen, repent and do their first works."[14]

A prime example of the second category, newly published devotional writing, is Thomas Prince's edition of *The Memoirs of Capt. Roger Clap* (Boston, 1731). Clap, who had come to Boston as a pious youth in 1630, recalled how in those early years "the Lord Jesus Christ was so plainly held out in the Preaching of the Gospel unto poor lost Sinners, and the absolute Necessity of the New Birth, and God's Holy Spirit in those Days was pleased to accompany the Word with such Efficacy upon the Hearts of many" that many souls were converted. The language of "poor lost Sinners," "New Birth," and heart religion resonates strikingly with the spiritual tenor of the 1730s and 1740s. That the narrative was written by an elderly Clap in the late seventeenth century as he looked back on the earliest years of the founding of the Massachusetts Bay Colony served Prince's purposes to a tee. Here he could show that the emotional conversion of individuals within the context of general revival was in continuity with early New England experience, and that excess could be controlled by theological orthodoxy.[15]

Jonathan Edwards, Thomas Prince, and others were similarly intent on gathering and publishing firsthand narratives of contemporary spiritual experience, in part to demonstrate that the soul-searching and spiritual ecstasy of the Awakening were not new but something very old. Edwards edited and published *The Life of David Brainerd,* the famous missionary to the Indians who died at age 30, wishing it to serve as a model of piety for the mid-eighteenth century. The value for Edwards lay in its correlation with Puritan prototypes of journals and spiritual autobiographies. Brainerd himself overtly strove to replicate this traditional devotionalism in his own life and diaries and to advance it for others. Since the practice of journal

14. Jonathan Edwards, *Religious Affections,* ed. John E. Smith (New Haven: Yale University Press, 1959), 53-57, 475, index under "Shepard, Thomas." Joshua Scottow, *Old Men's Tears* (Boston, 1733), 11.

15. *Memoirs of Capt. Roger Clap,* Dorchester Antiquarian and Historical Society, Collections, I (Boston, 1854; orig. Boston, 1731), 17-20. Hambrick-Stowe, *Practice of Piety,* 5-7. Shea, *Spiritual Autobiography in Early America,* 118-26.

keeping was a living part of the Puritan legacy in Brainerd's day, he was familiar with the personal writings of the earlier generations and certainly conscious of their format. Cotton Mather had preserved many samples for just this purpose in his *Magnalia Christi Americana* (1702). Toward the end of Brainerd's life he was specifically aware of the journal of Thomas Shepard as a model, not only for his own interior life, but for others as well. "While I was confined at Boston," he recorded, "I read with care and attention some papers of old Mr. Shepard's, lately come to light and designed for the press." Brainerd helped with the editorial work on this diary of Thomas Shepard and later, at Edwards's Northampton parsonage, wrote a preface. Thomas Prince published the volume, along with Brainerd's preface, as *Meditations and Spiritual Experiences of Mr. Thomas Shepard* in 1747, at the very time that Edwards was editing the just-deceased Brainerd's own journals. The message could not be more clear that the piety of David Brainerd, whom Edwards viewed as an exemplar of the Great Awakening at its best, was of a piece with that of Thomas Shepard, one of the greatest representatives of the Old Puritan spirituality. This is the viewpoint consistently put forth by New Light clergy through their entire use of print media.[16]

The dynamics of the colonial publishing and bookselling business are only gradually coming to light. Stephen Botein has shown in reference to book importation that until the Revolutionary War "the Anglo-American book trade took form within networks of religious affiliation." Likewise, the seventeenth century's "shifting coalition of ministers, printers, and booksellers" no doubt continued through the period of the Awakening, in spite of increasing secularization of the business. Richard D. Brown observes that while in the seventeenth and early eighteenth centuries "public speech and printing" were fairly tightly controlled by "the right sort of people" — namely, the ministers, magistrates, and leading merchants — by the 1720s this "closed and confined" communications system could no longer be so fully monopolized by the elite: "the union of class and culture was dissolving." Nevertheless, Brown expresses doubt that "a

16. Jonathan Edwards, *The Life of David Brainerd*, ed. Norman Pettit (New Haven: Yale University Press, 1985), 451, 460, 513. *An Account of the Life of the Late Reverend Mr. David Brainerd* was originally published in Boston, 1749. Prince published the portions of Shepard's "Private Diary" which had been edited as part of his collection of *Three Valuable Pieces* by Shepard (Boston, 1747). Shepard's journal and autobiography are available in a modern edition: *God's Plot: The Paradoxes of Puritan Piety*, ed. Michael McGiffert (Amherst, MA: University of Massachusetts Press, 1972).

single movement, even one so profound and so extensive as the Great Awakening, could shatter the common culture and information system that sustained it, since both were closely attached to the actual circumstances and customary social functions of so many people." Although with the Awakening "the information system could never again be quite so unitary and deferential as before . . . the common culture and its restricted information system survived." Compared with the far more extensive social changes of the early nineteenth century, Brown states, "the Great Awakening, which might seem to have changed so much theoretically, made little practical difference."[17]

On the one hand, decisions concerning publication were market driven throughout the colonial period and cannot simply be chalked up to authoritarian motives of clerical or political elites. On the other hand, the clergy's role in determining what got published did not vanish with the rise of secular-minded printers like the Franklins. By the 1730s and 1740s Boston publishers were freely coming out with Anglican and Quaker works, so it is not that the Congregational clergy, much less the New Light faction, maintained control over the press. Clerical involvement in publishing was of necessity exercised within the context of multivalent market forces. During the Great Awakening the worlds of publishing and religious life were both becoming increasingly competitive; that is, colonial society itself, of which religion and publishing were manifestations, was becoming more free and competitive. It was natural, then, that when theological lines were drawn, battles were fought through the printed word, as revealed by the famous exchange between Jonathan Edwards (*Some Thoughts Concerning the Present Revival of Religion,* Boston, 1742) and Charles Chauncy (*Seasonable Thoughts on the State of Religion,* Boston, 1743).

New Light leaders responded to this challenge of modernity by aggressively employing print media in their strategy to promote and guide the revival. Their effort was a direct appeal for popular support. The use

17. Stephen Botein, "The Anglo-American Book Trade Before 1776: Personnel and Strategies," in *Printing and Society in Early America,* 51. Hall, *Worlds of Wonder,* 49, 244. Michael G. Hall sheds light on the matter as he describes Increase Mather's life-long relationship with the publishing business in *The Last American Puritan: The Life of Increase Mather* (Middletown, CT: Wesleyan University Press, 1988), passim. For Anglican and Quaker books, see, e.g., the "List of Books Sold by T. Cox at the Lamb on the South-side of the Town House in Boston," printed at the end of John Rawlet, *The Christian Monitor,* 25th ed. (Boston, 1733), 69-70. Brown, *Knowledge Is Power,* 40, 272-73. See also Edwin Wolf II, *The Book Culture of a Colonial American City: Philadelphia Books, Bookmen, and Booksellers* (Oxford: Oxford University Press, 1988).

of traditional materials — republication of devotional classics by English and American Puritan "Old Writers" and the printing of personal spiritual writings from both seventeenth-century and contemporary believers — in fact played to certain strengths in the popular marketplace. David Hall and Jon Butler suggest that during the period of the Great Awakening, as society was becoming more secular, the old "mentality of wonders, the story line of deliverance and confession, and the moral allegory of a land swept clean of sin . . . flourished once more among ordinary people." Hall explains that "for them printers continued to publish . . . books like Alleine's *Alarm to Unconverted Sinners.*" The persistence of a popular market, for example, helps to explain why in 1749 Benjamin Franklin would come out with yet another edition of Janeway's *A Token for Children* with Cotton Mather's by then traditional *Token for the Children of New-England.* Printers were not simply responding to economic opportunity, however. The books were published at the urging, under the editorship, and sometimes with the financial sponsorship of New Light clergy and their friends.[18]

What New England Congregationalist promoters of the Great Awakening sought, therefore, was truly a "*revival* of religion." Along with all that was undeniably "new" in the 1730s and 1740s — including a freer use of print media by spokespersons of every religious persuasion — New Light leaders played to the persistent market appeal of old devotional works and newer works displaying old themes. They prayed specifically, in Prince's words, that "the pious Principles and Spirit" of the "Old Writers" might be renewed in their time. Their goal was to encourage the spiritual awakening and to channel it along lines congruent with basic tenets of seventeenth-century Puritanism. In that evangelical Christianity did secure an authoritative and traditional role in American society during these decades leading up to the Revolution, New Light prayers — and efforts — were rewarded with success in the popular marketplace.

18. Hall, *Worlds of Wonder,* 244. Butler, *Awash in a Sea of Faith,* 182-85. James Janeway, *A Token for Children . . . To Which is added, A Token for the Children of New-England* (Philadelphia, 1749).

# From Democratization to Domestication: The Transitional Orality of the American Methodist Circuit Rider

A. Gregory Schneider

## I

Methodist circuit riders in the early national period got their education in what they liked to call "Bush College," a seminary as large as the great outdoors with a curriculum as broad as the range of human character they encountered in their travels. Bush College was an apprenticeship system in which older itinerants recruited and trained younger men into the ministry as they went about their regular tasks on the circuit. It was a face-to-face, word-of-mouth training where the basic criterion of success was getting people converted.

Bush College, if historians such as Notre Dame's Nathan Hatch are right, was also a school for democracy, for the circuit rider was a major player in what Hatch has termed the democratization of American Christianity. A major means of democratization was the oral medium of popular vernacular preaching. Once, in colonial America, the sermon had been a literary form, a prepared text delivered by a settled, university-trained clergyman at regular occasions. Now, as the colonies became a nation, the sermon became much more an oral form, an extemporaneous harangue delivered by an itinerant, unschooled preacher at whatever times he could gather a congregation. More and more of the people defected from the

Portions of this essay are from my book *The Way of the Cross Leads Home: The Domestication of American Methodism* (Bloomington: Indiana University Press, 1993).

hierarchical church communities dominated by the trained clergy and joined the religious movements that recognized and catered to the sovereignty of the audience. The Methodists became such masters of this popular oral medium that the circuit rider has earned a place in American legend. His preaching helped to create powerful motivations for spiritual liberty in non-elite audiences.[1] Indeed, according to other students of the early republic, evangelical preaching to the masses became a model for the new democratic oratory of republican revolutionaries bent on overturning British rule.[2]

One might infer from such interpretations that popular orality was a polar opposite of elite literacy and that the latter kind of culture and consciousness lost out, relatively speaking, to the oral culture of the untutored masses. Bush College, on this view, would have been the educational system of choice for a sort of throwback to what Walter Ong has termed "primary oral cultures."[3] However, as Nathan Hatch has pointed out, the democratic faiths of the American national period mastered not only the popular orality of vernacular preaching but also the mass literacy of the popular press.[4] The logic of Methodism's democratizing dynamic pointed rather toward a popular mass literacy, a new textuality available to all those aspiring to a new middle-class respectability. The mass religious culture eventually created through print required a domesticated discourse, one that was bound to supersede the popular orality that was the early medium of American Methodism and its Bush College. The orality of the circuit rider was transitional, then, a medium of the gospel that freed people from the dominance of patriarchal elites only to constrain them within new boundaries of self-control and self-exploration.

We can best see the transitional nature of this variety of orality by drawing two contrasts. The first contrast is that between Methodist oral

1. Nathan O. Hatch, *The Democratization of American Christianity* (New Haven: Yale University Press, 1989), 133-41.
2. Harry S. Stout, "Religion, Communications, and the Ideological Origins of the American Revolution," *William and Mary Quarterly*, 3rd ser., 34 (Oct. 1977): 519-41; Rhys Isaac, *The Transformation of Virginia, 1740-1790* (Chapel Hill: University of North Carolina Press, 1982), 245-69; Donald G. Mathews, "Evangelical America — The Methodist Ideology," in *Rethinking Methodist History: A Bicentennial Historical Consultation*, ed. Russell E. Richey and Kenneth E. Rowe (Nashville: United Methodist Publishing House, Kingswood Books, 1985), 91-99.
3. Walter J. Ong, *Orality and Literacy: The Technologizing of the Word* (London: Methuen, 1982), 11.
4. Hatch, *Democratization of American Christianity*, 141-46.

rituals like the class meeting and those ritual forms dominated by traditional elites in late colonial America. This contrast will illustrate the democratizing dynamic of early Methodist orality and suggest how Methodism helped to make textual consciousness the property of ordinary people rather than the preserve of elites. The second contrast is that between the orality of Methodist rituals and what Walter Ong has called "primary orality," the oral discourse and consciousness characteristic of cultures that have no acquaintance with writing or print.[5] Of course, these two oralities had points in common. The accent here, however, falls on their differences, because these differences explain how the circuit rider, who was steeped in the ethos of Methodist oral ritual, helped to domesticate American Christianity.

Circuit riders were creatures of class meeting and similar oral rituals because these rituals were the first points of enrollment for those who wanted to enter Bush College. He who would master the art of vernacular preaching and become a member of the Methodist itinerant brotherhood had first to speak well in class. Such performance lay at the foundation of effective ministry. As novelist and former circuit rider Edward Eggleston observed, "The early preacher's universal refuge was his own experience. It was a sure key to the sympathies of the audience."[6] The early preacher first learned in class to know and to use his experience. Only then did he pass on to higher lessons. We need to understand the nature of class meeting ritual, therefore, in order to understand the training of the early circuit rider.

## II

The culture of the late colonial Upper South, where American Methodism first flourished, was still largely an oral culture, but an oral culture interacting with forms of literacy belonging mostly to the gentry class. Primarily a classical literacy, gentry literacy reflected the oral patterns of Latin rhetoric. It was writing in service of speech. The speech was disputatious and agonistically toned — the kind taught to public men to equip them to debate, deliberate, and lead. This variety of oral-textual interaction was of long

5. Ong, *Orality and Literacy*, 31-75.
6. Edward Eggleston, *The Circuit-Rider: A Tale of the Heroic Age* (New York: J. B. Ford and Co., 1874), 127.

standing in Western culture; it dated from the days of Cicero and extended into the nineteenth century. The popular oral culture of the Upper South was structured also by certain "speaking books," such as the Bible and documents of common law, which had originated in oral performance, the constant recitation of which in church and law court made them powerful sources of authority in the oral culture of common people. Finally, for the few who had privilege, leisure, and inclination, there was a body of polite literature that had only recently come into print. This literature might be read in seclusion and thus might foster a private personality, a genuine individuality freed from the pressures of the immediate presence of others.[7] Only this literacy represented a genuinely textual culture and consciousness. For most people, both gentry and common folk, this private, textual individuality was not a live option. Their world was conveyed to them primarily through the immediate presence and spoken words of others.

The world these oral messages conveyed was a hierarchical world. At the most general philosophical level, the colonial southerners, like many other colonists, understood the cosmos to be a vast, continuous hierarchy of parts, each with its own degree of honor. Fathers were by nature of greater honor than children, men were by nature of greater honor than women, whites were of greater honor than blacks, and gentry were of greater honor than common planters.[8] The central symbol of this cosmos was the patriarch. Pure patriarchy counts as wealth the particular personal ties that obligate dependents to show submission, render service, and supply needs. The gentry patriarch stood at the center of a web of dependents — slaves, bond servants, children, wife — who were tied to him not by impersonal wage-for-labor contract but by the conditions of living under his "roof" and partaking of his "Meat, Drink, or Wages." On this condition they owed him deference and service. To strike him down was not mere murder but petit treason. As God was Father, so the King was Father, so the head of the household was Father. The highest level of cosmology incorporated the everyday experiences of dependence and deference and sanctified the authority of the planter patriarch.[9]

7. Isaac, *Transformation of Virginia*, 121-31; Bertram Wyatt-Brown, *Southern Honor: Ethics and Behavior in the Old South* (New York: Oxford University Press, 1982), 92-99; Ong, *Orality and Literacy*, 108-16.

8. Isaac, *Transformation of Virginia*, 308-9; Philip Graven, *The Protestant Temperament: Patterns of Child-Rearing, Religious Experience, and the Self in Early America* (New York: Alfred A. Knopf, 1977), 194-95, 297.

9. Isaac, *Transformation of Virginia*, 20-21.

This deferential world relied upon particular settings and events for its plausibility. The community of the Upper South was made up of a rhythm of events such as court days, militia musters, Sunday services, horse races, dances, cock fights, and burgess election contests. The gentry demonstrated their honor, manliness, wealth, and generosity in these events, many of which had the character of a contest or of a treat provided for the lower orders by the upper. As the lower orders played the part of fascinated observers in these ritual dramas, or directly participated in their own more rustic imitations, they experienced a constant socialization into the outlook and interests of the gentry. This traditional ritual economy conveyed what has become known as the "ethos of honor." The ethos of honor implied an understanding of self in which external appearance and performance and the judgments of others constituted the center of personal identity and self-worth. The central questions of social order were those of sovereignty and deference: Who was to defer to whom? Who was the superior? Who the inferior?

Perhaps no event communicated this hierarchical outlook more clearly than Sunday services in the parish church. The gentry owned their own pews at the front of the church, and they exhibited their superiority of property and social standing as they entered in a group just before services began, walking past the common sorts in regal self-assurance. In one church, space was so limited that only the greatest families could sit all together. The heads of lesser houses represented the honor of their families in single places as close to the front as possible, while their wives sat further back.[10] Recitation of liturgy from the Book of Common Prayer and the rank-ordering of seated personages constituted a powerful representation whereby the people might discern and internalize the divine hierarchical ordering of their lives. However, the meaning of such worship also derived from what happened before and after church. Sundays were not Puritan Sabbaths. They were times for a variety of diversions for all ranks of society. Church itself was a place for gentlemen and their ladies to show off their clothes, discuss tobacco prices, debate the relative lineages and qualities of their favorite horses, and invite one another home to dine. Worldly worship forged an identification of church and world. Residing at the top of the community hierarchy, the gentry embodied the spirit of the community, and in their public acts at church they identified them-

10. Rhys Isaac, "Evangelical Revolt: The Nature of the Baptists' Challenge to Traditional Order in Virginia, 1765-1775," *William and Mary Quarterly,* 3rd ser., 31 (July 1974): 349-50.

selves and their world with the spiritual realm.[11] Literacy and learning belonged chiefly to these gentlemen, and their speech, sprinkled with classical allusions and with recited portions of the Bible or of documents of the law, rendered their superiority all the more plausible.

The early Methodist circuit rider knew little or nothing of this kind of literacy or learning. The Anglican (later Episcopalian) priest or the Presbyterian minister had been to college. They could uphold the dignity of their office with the kind of speech that commanded deference. The Methodist preacher, however, had to elicit a different sort of response. Bush College demanded that he speak the vernacular and learn to use it to lead his congregations in the direction they wished to go. The audience was sovereign. Before the Methodist ministry was open to a man, he had to demonstrate to his audience that the Holy Spirit was moving him to preach.

But what demonstrated, or even began to suggest, to the prospective preacher or to his audience that he might be one whom the Spirit was calling to preach? The cues were diverse and subtle and included promptings within the candidate as well as the perceptions and responses of his congregations. The Methodist *Discipline,* however, specified three criteria by which to try those who thought themselves called to preach. First, did they know God as a pardoning God whose love dwelt in them and made them holy in all manner of conversation? Second, did they have the gifts for the task: sound understanding, right judgment, proper concepts of salvation, clear and ready speech? Third, did their preaching convince people of sin and convert them to God?[12] These criteria did help to identify the prospective preacher. They could be useful, however, only if there were some social setting, some pattern of human interaction, in which he might reveal his knowledge of God, his gifts, and his evangelistic effectiveness.

The same John Wesley who had provided the criteria for judging the fledgling preacher also designed the setting in which he might first try his wings. That setting was the class meeting. The *Discipline,* Methodism's manual of belief and practice, stated that every society of Methodists was

11. Isaac, *Transformation of Virginia,* 58-68; Graven, *The Protestant Temperament,* 328-29; Donald G. Mathews, *Religion in the Old South* (Chicago: University of Chicago Press, 1977), 3-10.

12. Robert Emory, *History of the Discipline of the Methodist Episcopal Church* (New York: G. Lane and C. B. Tippett, 1845), 62-63.

to be composed of one or more classes of twelve persons each, one of whom was designated the leader by the circuit preacher. They were to meet weekly, and the leader was to inquire into the religious behavior and experience of each member. Did they pray daily? Did they have family prayer if they were heads of families? Did they daily read the Scriptures? Did they avoid worldly involvements like drinking liquor, gambling, dancing, or the wearing of costly apparel? What was the state of their souls? What temptations had they met with, and how had they been delivered? Did they have forgiveness of their sins and peace with God in Christ? Did the Spirit bear witness with their spirits that they were children of God? As he conducted such inquiry the leader was to advise, reprove, comfort, or exhort as the occasion suggested. He was also to receive what members were willing to give for the relief of the poor.[13]

The purposes of the class meeting were several: pastoral oversight, fund-raising, enforcement of rules, and so forth. The main purpose, however, was fellowship. The early American bishops, in their notes on the *Discipline,* made fellowship the sine qua non of the class meeting. They further contended that the best "exercise" for such fellowship was inquiry into the state of the heart and the sharing of Christian experience. Thus the class meeting was a ritual of testimony, where those who had religion and those who were seeking religion came together and shared their various experiences in the effort to live Christian lives. This concern for fellowship carried through into a larger Methodist ritual of testimony called the "love feast." Love feasts generally took place at the quarterly meetings of a circuit, and they extended the fellowship of the saints to all church members on the circuit who were in good standing. The sharing of experiences was an important reason why persons who were not members of the Methodist society were restricted in the number of times they were allowed to visit a class meeting or love feast.[14] As the bishops put it, to allow unreligious persons frequent access to the meetings of the society would "throw a damp on these profitable assemblies, and cramp, if not entirely destroy, *that liberty of speech*" which had always been a blessing to believers and to those seeking salvation.[15]

Liberty of speech in class meeting was indeed a medium of great spiritual power and blessing. In class meeting, members testified un-

13. Emory, *History of the Discipline,* 177-78.
14. Emory, *History of the Discipline,* 327-28, 330-31.
15. Emory, *History of the Discipline,* 304.

ashamed by the disdain or mockery of the worldly. They spoke spontaneously of their religious feelings, both joyful and sorrowful. As a result, unbelievers were converted, believers were strengthened, and everyone was bound closer together in fellowship. One preacher's journal records many instances of classes in which he and the people "had a shout and a cry."[16] Shouting and crying in early Methodist meetings were evidence that the spoken words of the gospel, whether in the preacher's sermon or in the people's testimonies, were having their intended effect. Future bishop Thomas A. Morris held a class meeting for just five people, one of whom did not profess to be religious. "They all wept, one shouted for joy, and the non-professor being seriously affected, we finished with a prayer meeting for her special benefit."[17] Class meeting was a bond of unity among early believers. John Kobler reminisced about how the people would go to the class meeting and tell of their trials and God's work in their souls in ways so affecting "that the hardest heart could not remain unmoved."[18] These conditions in class meeting, if sustained, were a sign to sensitive pastors that their people were generating the sort of love that would flame up into revival and draw in more converts.[19] When the saints had liberty of speech in their class meetings, they created a sort of fusion reactor of the Spirit, generating light and love that overcame the world.

Class meeting and love feast, then, provided good opportunities for the would-be preacher to discover for himself and reveal to others the evidence of his call to preach. As a member of the class, he was expected to respond to questions about the state of his soul with the story of how he had been converted and how this experience had put the love of God in his heart. If he had the gifts of clear understanding and ready speech, they would show in his testimony. And if his testimony in class or love feast moved the hearts and minds of his hearers, perhaps convincing members of the class or visitors of their sinfulness or of God's pardoning

16. Thomas Mann, "Journal," 7 Apr. 1805 to 14 Jan. 1806, Thomas Mann Papers, Manuscript Department, Duke University Library, Durham, NC.

17. T. A. Morris, "Historical Scraps," *Western Christian Advocate* (Cincinnati), 4 Oct. 1839, 93.

18. Quoted in James B. Finley, *Sketches of Western Methodism: Biographical, Historical, and Miscellaneous, Illustrative of Pioneer Life,* ed. W. P. Strickland (Cincinnati, 1854), 174.

19. Isaac Crawford, "Journal," 16 Nov. and 16 Dec. 1837, Isaac Crawford Papers, Indiana State Library; [Samuel?] Fisk, "Diary," 27 Sept. 1840 and 1 Aug. 1841, Fisk Papers, Illinois State Historical Library; George S. Phillips, "Diary," 22 Oct. 1841, George Shane Phillips Collection, Huntington Library, San Marino, CA.

love, then that was yet further evidence that he seemed to meet the criteria for one called to the ministry. Of course, his religious conversation in class would have to harmonize with his conduct and conversation in other settings as he moved about his neighborhood. His fellow Methodists would watch and note and begin to talk among themselves and to the circuit preacher. The circuit preacher would hear and watch. Soon he would make the candidate a class leader. Then he might make him an exhorter, one who went to the pulpit after the preacher, made some applications of the sermon appropriate to neighborhood circumstances, and appealed to his hearers to seek religion. The next steps to the itinerancy usually included filling preaching appointments in or near the neighborhood, and then taking to the road in company with the circuit preacher. Soon the new preacher would be accepted on trial into the traveling brotherhood, eventually becoming a full-fledged minister of the church.[20]

The demand for a personal religious experience narrated convincingly in the oral medium, a demand made in class meeting, remained at the foundation of the early Methodist preacher's training. Of course, preachers were expected to carry books of theology in their saddlebags and to read them — on the floor of a cabin and by firelight, if necessary. They were expected to develop their homiletic skill and to conform their preaching to sound scriptural and theological standards. But it is a sign of the centrality of oral testimony that neophyte preachers were counseled to tell their experience if they forgot their sermons. The counsel only made explicit what came intuitively to many. James Finley, at only his second appointment as a green circuit preacher, found an old lawyer acquaintance who was prepared to take down in shorthand every word of the sermon. The young preacher panicked. His thoughts became confused, and his memory went blank. Then it occurred to him that although this lawyer knew "the sciences" far better than he did, he did not know the science of salvation. There Finley had the upper hand. So he chose a text on the new birth and used it as a platform for telling the story of his religious experience. He made a good impression.[21]

---

20. There are many accounts, with variations, of this sort of route to the ministry in the biographies and autobiographies of early Methodist preachers. One of the best known is James B. Finley, *Autobiography of Rev. James B. Finley,* ed. W. P. Strickland (Cincinnati: Methodist Book Concern, 1854), 180-93. For evidence that class leader to exhorter to preacher was a typical pattern, see also Joseph Tarkington, *Autobiography of Rev. Joseph Tarkington, One of the Pioneer Methodist Preachers of Indiana,* with an introduction by T. A. Godwin (Cincinnati: Curtis and Jennings, 1899), 7.

21. Finley, *Autobiography,* 190-91.

Circuit riders like Finley presided over a community different from the one over which the gentry class had ruled in late colonial times. In class meeting and similar rituals, Methodist preachers nurtured a community of intense feeling, of love to God and man. The model of community to be derived from Methodist experience was not that of a web of sovereignty and deference. Sovereignty and deference belonged to the hierarchical world of the gentry. Rather, the model of community embodied in Methodist oral ritual was one of a sacred circle of Christian affection set over against a sinful world. It was a democratic community in the sense that all persons within the circle were equal in the sight of God because all had sinned, repented of their sin, and experienced the love of God in their hearts. There was no room for the claims of honor or preeminence that had made the gentry a rank above the common order of humanity.

The ritual economy of Methodism, to review its contrasts with the rituals of the traditional elites, eschewed the outward demonstration of honor and rank. It affirmed instead a testimony to the inward workings of God's Spirit. It secluded members from the eyes and ears of worldlings, who expected demonstrations of honor, in order to grant believers liberty of speech, a speech that conveyed a transformative spiritual power. Within this special kind of oral culture the prospective Methodist preacher got his start, learning first to speak effectively in class before he rose to more advanced lessons. The community that he learned to lead moved away from patriarchy as the metaphor for human relations and turned toward another, more egalitarian metaphor that better suited their experience.

The metaphor the Methodists appropriated was the biblical metaphor of the family of God. The biblical usage of this metaphor does not necessarily preclude patriarchal understandings, of course. Indeed, Methodists spoke seriously of fathers in the gospel and gave them considerable deference. Still, the aspect of family life they lifted up with the metaphor of the family of God was not the sovereignty of the patriarch but the mutual affection of the family members. Such a metaphor, joined with experiences of intimate affection secluded from the world, had domestic implications that should not be ignored. Such implications will become clearer as we proceed to the contrast between primary orality and the transitional orality of Methodism.

# III

At first blush, of course, it must seem odd to claim that the oral discourse mastered by the circuit riders in Bush College helped to domesticate American Christianity. The idea of domesticity centers upon images of quietness and order, while accounts of early Methodist meetings abound in images of tumult — of shouting and crying, running and fainting, even barking and jerking. Some husbands and fathers of the early national period, furthermore, might doubt that Methodism promoted domestic order. For Methodists readily, even gleefully, sought the conversions of wives and children over resistance of their husbands and parents. An unreligious patriarch accustomed to sovereignty over his household certainly had his domestic tranquility disturbed when Methodists in the neighborhood carried off his wife or children into their evangelical fervor. From the standpoint of the old order, then, Methodism was indeed a disruptive influence. Its oral culture of testimony did dissolve some of the constraints of the patriarchal ethos of honor, including the hegemony of learned gentlemen over authoritative texts like the Bible. It was primarily in its similarities to primary oral cultures that this power to dissolve old bonds was most evident. In its dissimilarities to primary orality, however, Methodism pointed toward a new mode of organizing experience, one that stressed individualism, tender feeling, and distance from "the world."

Class meeting and love feast reflected the dynamics of oral cultures in several ways. The most obvious way was the empathetic and participatory mode of sharing knowledge. Primary oral cultures, which have no means of written communication at all, convey their lore through the recitation of stories, frequently in the form of epic poetry. In the act of recitation, the narrator, the audience, and the heroes of the epic are welded together in a single felt unit. Spoken words, after all, are not experienced as inert objects in space but as dynamic powers in time. They issue from the inside of the speaker and penetrate to the inside of the hearers. They do not make room for personal disengagement, distance, or objectivity. They demand response. The response of each individual, moreover, is encased in the community created by these powers.

The testimonies of the saints seem to have had this sort of effect. They brought the whole community to a felt unity and a participatory knowledge of religion through spoken performances. While the rituals of inquiry and testimony were happening, they did not seem to allow for much personal distance or neutrality. One either immersed oneself in the event or fled from it. The lack of space for neutrality was especially evident in a story about a visitor to a class meeting who obviously had no idea of what he had let himself in for. As the close and personal inquiry threatened to come around to him, he leapt from his seat. The cabin was so crowded that he could not get to the door. He scrambled up the chimney instead.[22] James Finley told of a class meeting in which the first few testimonies quickly aroused the saints to shouts of praise and the seekers of religion to cries for mercy and tears of contrition. The people became so excited that the noise could be heard a mile distant. As it happened, a whiskey distiller had gathered a gang outside the house, intending to break up the meeting. He stormed in among the believers, but a sentry at the door managed to shut out his companions. The distiller could not withstand the spiritual contagion around him and soon fell to the floor, apparently in conviction of sin. At the same moment, the holy tumult in the room crescendoed to its peak. Finley declared that "it seemed that heaven and earth had come together."[23] The sense of God's power and presence was palpable to those who participated in such moments.

The testimonies of the saints also reflected oral culture in that they were formulaic and episodic, relying upon a fund of memorized combinations of words from which to put together a performance, and recounting only episodes of their experience rather than putting together a fully developed narrative of their lives. Stock phrases like "a feast of reason and a flow of soul," "praise the Lord, brethren, I'm happy," "pleasant grief and mournful joy," as well as a wealth of scriptural quotes and allusions, all seem to have helped the faithful construct their testimonies. Short episodes like conversion experiences or providential deliverances were really the only sort of stories appropriate to class meeting or love feast, because there were always others with things to share. The assumption was, however, that these episodes epitomized the life organization of those who told them. This assumption leads to the next similarity.

The ritual dramas of social religion also reflected oral conventions in their encouragement of self-presentation in the mode of the "type" or "flat" character. In literary terms, a flat character is a thoroughly predictable one who fulfills our expectations repeatedly in various circumstances and episodes. Oral cultures organize their lore about appropriate virtues around

22. Walter B. Posey, *The Development of Methodism in the Old Southwest: 1783-1824* (Tuskaloosa, AL: Weatherford Printing Co., 1933), 116.

23. Finley, *Autobiography,* 240-41.

such type characters: the clever Br'er Rabbit, the wise Nestor, or, in the evangelical case, the pious Sister Love. The pious sister who testified in the love feast testified predictably, relating episodes of her life that reliably exemplified the religious experience and practice expected of all good Methodists. From the repeated testimony of such exemplary saints, the new members and converts learned how to tell their own stories and how to shape their lives accordingly. This learning by listening was a spiritual apprenticeship that all the believers served and that was also the foundation of the circuit rider's education. Such apprenticeship was yet another similarity to oral cultures.[24]

The dissimilarities between oral cultures and the practices of class meeting and love feast, however, are more important. The fundamental dissimilarity lies side by side with the fundamental similarity. The intense unity and community of class meeting and love feast were produced by individuals telling not simply the standard story of their evangelical subculture but their own individualized incarnations of that story. In analogy with the oral epic and its hero, one might say that they told the epic of Jesus, the Christian hero. But the conventions of the testimony rituals required each person individually to claim Jesus as his or her hero and to tell how he or she had personally come to identify with and follow him. This individualized appropriation of the Jesus story implied a change in the sense of the ownership of words. In primary oral cultures, the epic belongs to the community as a whole. In personal testimony, one's story is one's own, however much it may resemble the stories of others.

This insistence upon owning one's own story of finding Jesus as a personal, present Savior required an exploration of the inner life that is foreign to primary oral cultures. Such exploration was "consciousness raising" in a manner similar to the way in which the internalization of writing and of print heightens consciousness. The Rules of the Methodist Societies required that members spend time in private and family prayer and that they come apart into secluded spaces to tell of the exercises of their hearts. These requirements both separated people from the natural flow of ordinary face-to-face interaction and turned them inward upon themselves in self-examination. Writing and reading require a similar distancing from the natural oral milieu, encouraging a heightened awareness, especially in the act of writing, of the self who is writing and of the distance and difference between the writing self and the "audience" to

24. Ong, *Orality and Literacy,* 31-36, 43-46, 151-55.

which it is addressing itself. People of primary oral cultures resist or fail to comprehend requests for self-analysis or self-description. "What can I say about my own heart?" queried one illiterate peasant man. "Ask others; they can tell you about me."[25] The point of class meeting and other such rituals, of course, was precisely to teach people what they must come to know and speak about their own hearts.

The requirements of the Methodist societies reflected the origins of the Methodist movement in modes of consciousness and religious experience cultivated by long acquaintance with the technologies of writing and print. The Wesleys, of course, were highly educated and literate for their day. Both John Wesley and Francis Asbury kept meticulous journals and published portions of them during their own lifetimes, thus providing public models of the sort of private self-examination and self-awareness they expected of their spiritual children. The founding of a local Methodist society involved an amalgam of written and oral discourse. Preachers read the Rules of the Societies to those who wished to become members and obtained the promise of all present to keeping them. These rules were printed in the *Discipline,* which, along with the Bible, was the constant companion of every Methodist preacher. The Methodist societies had a textual foundation, even as the class meeting, the heart of each society's ritual practice, promoted textual modes of consciousness. Thus, even though early Methodist discourse was largely oral, the Methodist movement from its beginnings incorporated textual ways of organizing experience. It is a striking example of a cultural product that was forged in relatively elite textual contexts and that adapted to popular oral contexts and transformed them.

This last conclusion harmonizes with Walter J. Ong's description of what is occurring when language is committed to writing. Writing is a technology, he asserts, that implements "the reduction of dynamic sound to quiescent space."[26] This reduction is analogous in form to the curious transformations of Methodist piety. In such piety the dynamic noise of preaching, praying, testifying, shouting, and crying was part of a process that opened up a "space" within the self where the soul dwelt in quiescent repose, secure in constant communion with God and secluded from the storms of the world. The world, asserted a theorist of "Vital Religion,"

25. Ong, *Orality and Literacy,* 54-55; on the consciousness-raising dynamics of writing and print, see pp. 81-83, 101-8.
26. Ong, *Orality and Literacy,* 82.

was filled with "the glare of riches, the tinsel of honor, the gaudy show of pleasure," influences that set the ungodly "in high fermentation." Religion, on the other hand, removed the soul into the "calm regions of resignation and peace divine" where "the temper becomes mild, the dispositions assume a heavenly frame, the passions are reduced to order and harmonious operation and a fountain of pleasure is opened within, springing up into eternal life."[27] This inner center of communion is what Methodists referred to in their doctrine of the "Witness of the Spirit" that invoked Romans 8:16: "The Spirit beareth witness with our spirit that we are the children of God."[28]

People learned to seek and establish this inner center within themselves in the context of rituals, like class meeting, which were inner circles removed from the world and in which participants enjoyed among themselves an intense communion that felt divine. The shape of the social context was homologous to the shape of the self. The sharing of Christian experience in the rhetoric of oral testimony brought about this communion and unity among God, self, and others.

The intimacy of this kind of religious conversation suggests a further dissimilarity between Methodist orality and the discourses of both primary oral cultures and traditional cultures in which literacy was still in service of classical rhetoric. In contrast to the unity sought by evangelicals through their testimonies, primary and public oral discourse was agonistically toned, lending itself to verbal combat. Situated in the concrete world in which people struggle with one another for material comfort, power, and attention, this variety of oral expression ran to extremes of praise and blame. The Methodists had ample opportunity to observe this kind of orality in the banter and bravado of men trying to sustain their honor in the tavern or on the muster field. They saw it, too, in the literate grandiloquence of political oration and debate. Their religious experience, however, devalued both of these traditional modes of discourse. To be sure, Methodist preachers did engage in combative discourse, and they enjoyed telling tales of how they had bested hecklers or debating opponents on the rhetorical jousting field. In their denunciations of worldliness and in their appeals to the realities of heaven and hell, their extremes of praise

27. "Vital Religion — No. 2," *Western Christian Monitor* (Chillicothe, OH), Feb. 1816, 54-55.
28. C. R. Lovell, *Methodist Family Manual* (Cincinnati: Swormstedt and Poe, 1852), 191-94.

and blame echoed the agonistic tone of public rhetoric. The center of Methodist rhetoric, however, was the simplicity and incontrovertibility of personal testimony. Such testimony was incontrovertible in the sense that it did not invite dialectical combat or debate. The testifying witness did not present herself as an adversary to be bested in a contest, but as a model to be either rejected or accepted.

To the Methodists, the rhetoric of personal testimony was superior to the tradition of public speech sustained by the literate elites of early American society. An apologist for love feasts highlighted the contrast when he wrote that, compared with the love feast, "all worldly festivals are empty parade." No matter how much had been said in praise of distinguished orators of the day, the most thrilling words ever to fall on his ears and sink into his heart, the Bible excepted, were spoken in the love feast "by those whose hearts burned with love to God and man." "Their words were not those of studied elegance; they were the spontaneous effusion of the heart, when the power of the Holy Spirit was upon them, filling the house with glory, melting, subduing, renewing, and transforming the moral features of the whole."[29] The rhetoric of personal testimony, in the view of this witness, transformed one's heart and morals, not just one's party loyalties. An Ohio circuit rider named Leonard Gurley learned the difference between the two rhetorical styles by hard experience. He had acquired his first public-speaking skills in a club of young men who, on Saturdays, had taken their books and lunches out to a ridge between two prairies and spent the day in debate. When converted, however, he attempted to relate his experience in class meeting in his accustomed grandiloquent debating style. "The good people stared," he recalled with a wince, "and I was much mortified and humbled; and it required effort and time before I could shake off the cumbersome verbiage."[30]

If the public festivals and oratory of the world were empty things to be avoided or unlearned, so was the "formality" by which the worldly conducted their social affairs. A devout young Methodist woman named Harriet Stubbs gave an example of the tension between worldly and evangelical sociability in a letter she wrote to her friend and mentor James Finley. She had been thrust, through no choice of her own, into the gay and fashionable society of 1820s

29. "Love Feasts," *Western Christian Advocate,* 9 May 1834, 5.

30. Leonard B. Gurley, "A Memorial Discourse Delivered before the Central Ohio Annual Conference of the Methodist Episcopal Church, at Wauseon, Ohio, September 20, 1878, by Rev. Leonard B. Gurley, D.D., on the Fiftieth Anniversary of His Ministry," 5-6. This document was published with the *Minutes of the Central Ohio Annual Conference of the M. E. Church, 1878,* after p. 338 of the regular minutes.

Washington, D.C. "I fear I shall never become reconciled to the change," she confided. She described how visits were arranged almost entirely by the sending and receiving of cards — a convenience, she admitted, since it meant that one might receive company or not just as one wished. Potential visitors drove their carriages to one's door, sent a servant to inquire if the lady was at home, and understood perfectly if the lady sent word by her servant that she was indisposed or engaged. If the lady did receive them, her servant ushered them into a room, gave them her compliments, and told them she would do herself the honor to wait on them in a few minutes. When the lady appeared, the visitors conversed with her for ten or fifteen minutes and then took their leave. After describing this elaborate protocol, Miss Stubbs remarked that she had been obliged to receive a dozen such visits between the hours of ten and one o'clock, the fashionable time. *"O how I despise such formality,"* exploded the simple Methodist woman. She confessed to feeling "extremely awequerd [sic] and unhappy" in such company. The Methodist society in Georgetown, however, afforded her some respite. There she had found two or three Methodist families to whom she had become "very much attached" and whom she often visited "in sociable way." "After a morning spent in receiving such visits as I have before hinted at," she sighed, "you have no idea of the pleasure and relief there sweet society afford me [sic]."[31]

Thirty years after Harriet Stubbs penned her complaint, Bishop Thomas Asbury Morris pilloried in print the worldly style of visiting. He was explicit, where Harriet Stubbs had been only allusive, about the emotional contrast between worldly and Methodist styles of sociability. For him, the audience gained through the elaborate process required by polite society was an audience "dearly bought with loss of time and sacrifice of feeling." He much preferred the experiences he had had as a circuit rider when he simply knocked at the door, received "the warm hand of friendship," and felt perfectly at home. This was a simple-hearted, honest friendship, a social life unembarrassed by the affected and heartless etiquette of polite society.[32]

31. Harriet Stubbs to J. B. Finley, 13 Sept. 1823, James Bradley Finley Letters, Ohio Conference Archives of United Methodism, Ohio Wesleyan University, Delaware, OH.

32. T. A. Morris, *Miscellany: Consisting of Essays, Biographical Sketches, and Notes of Travel* (Cincinnati: Swormstedt and Poe, 1852), 92-93. See also Angeline Sears's complaints about the worldliness and dissipation of mind that came with much formal visiting, in Melinda Hamline, *Memoirs of Angeline Sears* (Cincinnati: Swormstedt and Power, 1851), 47-50.

This concern for a simple, heartfelt style of social contact and its corresponding hostility to formality was of a piece with the Methodist concern for authentic outward demonstration of inward feeling in the rituals of testimony. If true Christian fellowship in class meeting and love feast required a "liberty of speech" freed from the dampening influence of "unawakened persons," true sociability among Christians required a simplicity of manners freed from the awkwardness that the unfeeling etiquette of the worldly might create. Early Methodist religion aimed at the mystery of intimacy. It shunned those circumspect gestures that preserve the mystery of mutual distance.

Gestures of mutual distance were important primarily to a literate elite who needed to mitigate the agonism of the still largely oral culture over which they exercised hegemony. Such gestures embodied attitudes of respect that refined, but did not eliminate, the imperative to maintain honor or "save face" for oneself and one's house among one's neighbors. In rejecting both the agonism of primary oral culture and the hegemony of genteel literate culture, Methodist evangelicals turned to the warmth and spontaneity of their inner spaces and established a more absolute distance between themselves and the world. It was a moral and spiritual distance between different kinds of souls rather than a mere social distance between different classes of personae.

This new moral distance between the family of God and the world, coupled with the new intimacy among members of the family of God, required its own sort of discourse, a new kind of oral-textual interaction. It seems clear that Methodist orality was neither a survival of nor a throwback to the primary orality of cultures unacquainted with writing. It seems equally clear that interaction of orality and literacy in Methodism was of a different order than the interaction sustained by traditions of classical learning, disputation, and rhetoric among elite classes of Western culture. Methodist discourse was its own kind of medium, an orality and a literacy that cultivated a greater level of self-consciousness, a sense of greater distance between the self and its world, and a greater disposition to change and control both the self and the world. Methodist religious experience, both individual and social, implied two kinds of souls, each in its different social realm. There was a religious realm shared with the converted where one might turn inward to pursue the knowledge and transformation of the self, and there was a worldly realm shared with the unconverted where one must turn outward to pursue the transformation of the world, or at least of the worldlings. The experienced differences between these two realms became the foundation for the domestication of American Methodism.

This domestication consisted in a process of bifurcation in which the knowledge and transformation of the self became something largely beyond the reach of the church and more the main business of the home. On the other side of the bifurcation, the transformation of the world became something largely beyond the reach of the home and more the main business of the church. The history of American Methodism in the nineteenth century might be schematized in terms of this bifurcation. Leonard Gurley, whose ministerial career spanned fifty years in the middle of the century, seems to have done just that when he remarked,

> Early Methodism was *subjective;* personal conversion, personal experience, was the theme of pulpit, class, and love-feast. Modern Methodism is more *objective:* it does not undervalue personal experience, but it devotes its attention more fully to Christian activities.[33]

This objective Methodism included activities of great domestic significance, such as working in Sunday school. Rev. Gurley remarked, in fact, that modern Methodists spoke less in class, but worked more in Sunday school. But the replacement of class meeting by Sunday school implied that the church had ceded the work of the intimate shaping of the self to institutions which superintended the self in the course of its natural development — to the home in particular. When it came to inculcating and sustaining many of the fundamental meanings and values of American Protestantism — individualism, self-control, sentiment, piety — the church had become only an adjunct to the home.[34]

## IV

In the meantime there had arisen within Methodism a variety of world-transforming activities. There was the missionary cause, the temperance cause, the tract cause, the Bible cause, the Sunday school cause, the freedmen's cause, and numerous other causes, all of which usually had

33. Gurley, "Memorial Discourse," 12-13.
34. Colleen McDannell, *The Christian Home in Victorian America, 1840-1900* (Bloomington: Indiana University Press, 1986), 48-49.

specialized organizations to promote them. These causes often demanded attention from standing committees within the annual conference structures of church governance. Just six years before Rev. Gurley celebrated the modern "objective" character of Methodism, many of the national organizations for these causes had been made official agencies of the General Conference of the northern Methodist Episcopal Church. The growth of Methodism into a denominational bureaucracy was well underway.[35] Bureaucracies, denominational or not, tend to be experienced as "objective" realities unconcerned with and unfazed by one's "subjective" states of mind or any expression of them. It is not difficult to imagine how the orality of testimony might have begun to seem unnecessary or even inappropriate in such settings.

The class meeting, in fact, seems to have been a casualty of the bifurcation of the "subjective" and "objective" aspects of Methodism. By the 1820s and 1830s the rule requiring attendance at class meeting for continuing church membership was falling into disuse. Within a generation afterward the rule was almost entirely abandoned. In early Methodism the class meeting had elicited personal experience at the same time as it had excited the powers of revival and evangelism. Self-transformation and world-transformation had gone hand-in-hand. With the bifurcation of these two aspects of Methodist motivation, the class meeting and its distinctive brand of orality were stretched beyond their capacity to serve either motive adequately. Rituals of testimony were inappropriate in the ambience of the objective rational planning that began to characterize the various benevolent agencies of the church. They were also inadequate to fathom the depth and complexity of selfhood that revealed itself to those who were growing in the self-consciousness that the orality of testimony itself had encouraged. Still tied to the oral penchant for formulaic expression and "flat" characterization, testimony rituals could not well serve the continued growth of individualism.

It seems more than coincidental that the class meeting was beginning to decline and the Methodist benevolent agencies were beginning to proliferate at about the same time that the Methodist popular press was beginning to prosper — all occurred in the 1820s and 1830s. As Ong has told us, writing and print increase the distance between the knower — the

35. William McGuire King, "Denominational Modernization and Religious Identity: The Case of the Methodist Episcopal Church," *Methodist History* 20 (Jan. 1982): 75-89.

one who writes or reads — and the known — the persons or phenomena written or read about. This distance not only allows a more "objective" rendering of the world written or read about but also allows a greater introspective self-knowledge on the part of the reader or writer. It facilitates a deepened subjectivity at the same time that it allows a wider objectivity.[36]

On the side of objectivity, Methodism's weekly *Christian Advocate* allowed greater collective awareness of the church through its extensive commentary and reportage upon the doctrines, organization, and usages of the church. Many preachers contributed historical reminiscences that reduced their personal testimonies to print and made them adjuncts to the effort to construct more objectified accounts of the rise and progress of the church. Reportage of current events in the wider world beyond the church also contributed to a greater objectivity and analysis. The proliferation of print in American Methodism, then, may well have been a major agent in encouraging the development of Rev. Gurley's "objective" Methodism. This same proliferation of print recorded the decline of the class meeting.

On the subjective side, the growing availability of printed biographical and autobiographical narratives in books or periodicals provided models better able to encompass the sort of selves that the class meeting had begun to bring to light. The moral tales and exhortations found in the various domestic "Departments" of the *Advocate* — Ladies', Parents', Youths', Children's — and in the publications of the Tract and Sunday School Societies provided still further resources for a domesticated self-understanding. The Cincinnati *Ladies Repository,* a Methodist-sponsored monthly and American Protestantism's most successful women's magazine, provided an especially important medium for feminine self-exploration and self-definition. Eventually, even the novel, at first rigidly proscribed by the Methodist moralists, began to acquire some official respectability and favor, providing a still more sophisticated medium for self-knowledge, better attuned to the nuances of inner life.

In 1859, in fact, one Miriam Fletcher published a two-volume novel, *The Methodist,* that illustrates clearly not only the growing acceptance of such literature but also the domestication of Methodism.[37] The novel is

---

36. Ong, *Orality and Literacy,* 103-8.

37. Miriam Fletcher, *The Methodist; or, Incidents and Characters from Life in the Baltimore Conference,* 2 vols., with an introduction by W. P. Strickland (New York: Derby and Jackson, 1859). Persisting ambivalence over the novel is evident in Strickland's introduction and in the review of the novel in "Belles-Lettres: *The Methodist* (New York)," *Methodist Quarterly Review* 41 (Apr. 1859): 338-39. Both pieces take pains to vindicate

set in the old Baltimore Conference of the Methodist Episcopal Church, which included both tidewater and backcountry regions of Maryland and Virginia. The plot centers on the coming of age of a young man named Harry Bradford, a lineal descendant, on his father's side, of the famous Puritan by that name, and, on his mother's side, of an old Virginia family named Hunter.

The plot evinces something of the democratizing dynamic of Methodism in that it pits the humble Methodist piety of Harry and his mother against the fashionable society and high-toned Episcopalian faith of their Virginia ancestors and kin. Fletcher modulates this theme, however, in an effort to demonstrate that Methodism's respectability is on a par with that of the Episcopalians. She has both Harry and his mother, for instance, explain to their amazed relatives how it is that the Methodist preachers at an annual conference they attend in Baltimore have come to be so eloquent, dignified, and well informed. The answer, of course, is that "Bush College" has made them so. This is the best education for men in their calling, as good as or better than the formal theological training the snobbish Virginians and Marylanders have assumed to be essential to the ministry.[38] Indeed, Harry's first sojourn in Bush College makes him so much "more handsome, more manly and dignified in manners," that one of his lady cousins declares that she will invite him to walk down Baltimore's Market Street with her so she can show him off and let everybody know he is her cousin.[39] These efforts to demonstrate respectability may be taken as one evidence of the domestication of Fletcher's Methodism.

The best such evidence, however, comes from the role in the plot of Harry's mother, Mrs. Sophey Bradford. Mrs. Bradford, the wise, principled, discerning, and, above all, praying mother, is the spiritual center of Fletcher's domestic Methodism. She is the very embodiment of the ideals of motherhood and "female influence" that pervaded the didactic literature that poured out of the Methodist popular press from the 1830s onward. The novel's depiction of the Methodist church, furthermore, makes all the usages and officials of the church refer back to Mrs. Bradford

---

"true-to-life" fiction and distinguish it from the popular fiction of the day. See also the article by Daniel Curry, "The Modern Novel," *Methodist Quarterly Review* 42 (Apr. 1860): 181-200.

38. Fletcher, *The Methodist,* 2:29-44.
39. Fletcher, *The Methodist,* 2:28.

and her influence. The impress of her spirit is the lodestone that guides Harry through all his experiences among his fashionable relatives and among the various scenes and characters he encounters in his early itinerant ministry. Especially it is she and his internalization of her presence and judgment that allow him to rightly discern the subtleties of motive surrounding his difficult decisions about whom to marry. She helps him see the mistake of his engagement to Rose Carter, a physically beautiful but spoiled child of old Virginia's culture of honor. It is his self-sacrificing adherence to duty, a quality modeled for him and supported in him by his mother, that eventually causes Rose to break off their engagement. Mrs. Bradford then helps Harry understand his persistent attachment to Susan Allington, a pious, sensible girl-next-door who reminds him of his mother.

It is Mrs. Bradford, in fact, who accounts for the real difference between her son's religious experience and that of Rose Carter. Harry, Fletcher tells us, had been so well prepared for God's grace that unskillful observers might have mistaken the natural fruits of character for "the planting of the Lord." Rose, on the other hand, had been so flattered and petted from infancy, and so caught up with trivial matters of pleasure, that selfishness had become deeply rooted in her whole being. Christian self-denial and benevolence might look desirable from a distance, but she shrank from any present inconvenience. Poor Harry, who had entered his ill-starred engagement with Rose only after she had been converted, looked for religion to do for her what, according to Fletcher, it never promises to do. "It had not at once given strength and richness to a mind previously neglected and habituated to trivial pursuits."[40] In short, the spiritual excellence of Fletcher's Methodist hero is due not so much to the work of the Spirit, who presumably worked on Rose as much as on Harry, as to the domestic influence of the mother.

Mrs. Bradford provided a model for Methodist mothers as they took up the burden for spiritual growth and self-awareness in themselves and in their children. They were in a position to carry this burden into regions more intimate and intricate than a class meeting structure ever could have managed. The extent to which particular mothers actually bore such burdens depended, of course, upon their individual circumstances. The rise of popular literature like Fletcher's novel, however, meant that increasing numbers of middle-class people, rather than just an elite, had access

40. Fletcher, *The Methodist*, 2:125-26, 132-34.

to a new literacy. It was a literacy that, by its form, abetted the progress of a privatizing self-awareness and, by its content, recommended a domestic religion that nurtured this more private self. Methodist rituals of testimony had modeled such domesticity and had begun to foster such self-awareness, but because of their still too public and oral-formulaic character, they could not finish what they had begun.


## V

It may seem a long distance, culturally, from Bush College to the quiet domestic circles and bureaucratizing voluntary benevolent agencies of late-nineteenth-century Methodism. It was, in fact, a long distance temporally. But the seeds of such domestication were already being planted along with the disposition to tell one's personal experience of Jesus as Savior. The ground had first to be cleared of the older plantings of patriarchy, hierarchy, and the culture of honor. Once this democratic uprooting was accomplished, the graduates of Bush College faithfully cultivated the new growth. The tools of their husbandry were at first the oral forms of discourse best suited to the culture of the common people among whom they labored. The seeds they planted, however, were patterns of experience that originated in textuality and that cried out for textual forms in which to be expressed. Methodism's popular didactic literature and eventually even domestic fiction were produced both to meet the demand and to stimulate it further.

The domestic consciousness is still with us, ministered to today not only by vastly expanded popular print but also by electronic media. The specific effects of these newer technologies of the word are beyond the scope of this essay. One may at least ask in conclusion, however, whether these new media enhance or subvert the domestic patterns that graduates of Bush College labored so faithfully to put in place.

# God, Rhetoric, and Logic in Antebellum American Theological Education

## Glenn T. Miller

In his essay "Theological Education and Media," Thomas Boomershine argued an evocative thesis:

> the primary task in the education of the Church's primary leaders is the mastery of the most powerful medium of communication and of the interpretative systems by which the Word of God can be made present in that medium.[1]

Boomershine's thesis is straightforward. In any given society, the dominant means of communication will determine the standards that educators set for their students. The commitment to these standards, in turn, shapes the education environment. Thus, whenever new methods of communication become popular, theological education changes.

When Boomershine discussed actual societies, however, he introduced some needed complications into his analysis. Individuals within societies do not change at a uniform rate. One segment of society will adopt a new form of communication, such as the manuscript. Another segment, perhaps the poorer, will continue to use the older media for a season. Further, forms of media do not follow one another as numbers in a series of integers. The society that employs writing, for example, retains a place for other, earlier media. The older modes "do not go away but are

---

1. Thomas Boomershine, "Theological Education and Media" (1989; privately distributed).

reintegrated into new functional roles."[2] Every human community communicates with itself through a media mix.

Early nineteenth-century America provides an excellent case study for Boomershine's thesis. The society was in the midst of massive intellectual, governmental, and religious change. These alterations included shifts in the relative influence of different media. In theory, we should be able to identify the dominant media, note the changes in the relative position of these modes of communication, and examine the relationship between communication and theological education.

## I. The World of Words

As Sidney Mead noted, nineteenth-century America was a land best described by spatial metaphors.[3] To its citizens, the nation appeared almost infinite. When the Mexican-American War ended, the United States stretched from the Atlantic to the Pacific. The traveler did not quickly meet natural or political boundaries. The nation rolled on and on and on.

The conquest of space was one of the major achievements of the early national period. New forms of transportation rapidly followed one another. The turnpike succeeded the Indian trail; the canal followed the turnpike; the steamboat replaced the canal. Finally, the railroad conquered everything as its steel rails spun an iron web east and west, north and south.

The ease of communication varied with the speed of transportation. As mechanized transportation improved, the nation developed a thriving publishing industry that produced newspapers, magazines, and books. Print was, however, too slow for the nation's burgeoning commerce. In 1844 Samuel F. B. Morse (1791-1872) demonstrated that André Ampère's proposed electrical telegraph was workable. By varying the length of a pulse of electricity, an operator could send information almost instantaneously over vast distances. Traders knew the prices of stocks on the New York Exchange before the close of business in Chicago. Many a young businessman's career began with a good ear and a loose wrist.

Americans were remaking their inherited language. The drive was for simplicity. Americans may have adopted Noah Webster's new orthography because it made sense, because it made them feel special, or because

2. Boomershine, "Theological Education and Media," 10.
3. Sidney Mead, *The Lively Experiment* (New York: Harper & Row, 1963).

Webster's *Dictionary* was the only one readily available to printers. For whatever reason, the brash changes in spelling signaled the new nation's determination to transform English into a more easily understood language. The popular press began to use shorter, verb-packed sentences to communicate with its audience. Sound was often superseded by sight. The newly popular crisp, terse style moved the reader's eyes across the page before the mind remembered the sounds.

The new nation worshiped words. Voters elected people to the House or to the Senate largely because of their verbal skills. The great leaders of the early republic were all orators: Clay, Calhoun, Douglas, Webster, Houston, and Lincoln. Despite the artistic conventions of the time, we cannot envision these titans with their mouths closed. Words bore the new republic toward its future. Daniel Boorstin noted:

> In this first national era, the "great orations" were widely recognized as the levers of American history and the formulae of American purpose. The signposts of a national destiny that was gradually becoming visible were public speeches of one kind or another.[4]

John Adams planned to compile a history of the United States by collecting important speeches and writing commentaries on them.[5]

The nineteenth century was a period of innovation in printing and publishing. The iron press, the stereotype, the use of steam power, and the mechanized production of paper made the century an age of print. The amount of material published was astronomical. The increasing size of the market led to specialization that separated bookselling from publishing and publishing from printing. Merchants, door-to-door salesmen, and small vendors sold contemporary books and cheap editions of the classics (priced at a penny or two). Newspapers became an important part of American life. Every small town and county seat had its own weekly,[6] and the larger towns and cities had dailies. When Horace Greeley decided to begin his *Tribune* in 1840, New York already had seven papers, most selling for a penny.[7] Greeley's was the eighth.

4. Daniel Boorstin, *The Americans: The National Experience* (New York: Random House, 1965), 308.

5. Boorstin, *The Americans*, 310.

6. So great was the lure of print that Boorstin (*The Americans*, 124-33) notes that some places had a paper before they had a town!

7. For an account of the competition among newspapers in New York, see William Harlan Hale, *Horace Greeley: Voice of the People* (New York: Harper & Row, 1950).

Magazines also flourished. In 1794 the government authorized the postal service to carry magazines. As the mail system expanded, so did the number of periodicals. The nation had five in 1794, forty in 1810, one hundred in 1825, and six hundred in 1850.[8] Although the average journal died in its first two years, publishers quickly replaced it with another. The reviews covered every topic from serious theology and science to house-keeping and agriculture.

Americans were discovering the magic of print. The newspaper, the journal, and the cheap book impacted all areas of American life. Although education in the North expanded rapidly for many reasons, the availability of inexpensive reading matter helped to popularize learning. Since print media were the most popular forms of entertainment, people had to be trained to use their leisure.

The new technology of transportation and communication arrived just in time. The American miracle was that the nation — despite sectional, religious, and economic diversity — had only one civil war. The widely used nickname "the Union" was fiction. The United States was anything but united. Americans built their nation on foundations riddled by many deep fissures. One fault line ran between farmers in the agrarian South and West who believed in free trade and Yankee traders and man-ufacturers who worshiped high tariffs and protection.

Additional friction was caused by the national passion for moralizing, which inspired wave after wave of clerical reformers to hit the hustings. One righteous army or another crusaded for the extermination of every vice from tobacco and alcohol to white bread. The clergy injected these campaigns into the national bloodstream. The Sunday school, the local embodiment of the American Protestant conscience, trumpeted them one after another. Whenever individuals were more committed to a cause than their friends and neighbors, they formed societies to achieve their stated good or to fight their favorite evil. In turn, these societies combined into state and national organizations to carry each crusade forward. Naturally, each new ethical imperative angered, embarrassed, or chided someone. The offended were within their democratic rights to form their own associations to combat militant virtue.

Another dangerous fault ran along the line separating Protestant and Catholic. Colonial America bristled with the dissonance of dissent. The

8. Frank Luther Mott, *A History of American Magazines* (Cambridge, MA: Harvard University Press, 1930, 1957), I:120, 342.

denunciation of Antichrist and all his minions was common pulpit fare. In the nineteenth century, however, Catholicism became the nation's largest denomination. To nervous Protestants the waves of immigrants that fueled this numerical growth were as unending as the misery of the European peasantry. Protestant pastors responded to the crisis by publishing tracts against the pope, preaching sermons about the dangers of barbarism, and creating new political parties.

If the struggle between Catholic and Protestant was bitter, an even more volatile issue was the existence of slavery. Given American assumptions about property, liberty, and race, the problem was politically unsolvable. Democracy sped toward the exhaustion of legislative alternatives. Since no compromise could address the deeper issues or resolve the conflicts, Congressional attempts only postponed the conflict. Sooner or later, someone would substitute violence for reasoned deliberation.

The revolution in transportation and communication did not end these tensions. In the short run, the new technology may have aggravated them. American disagreements required wordsmiths continually to replenish the nation's supply. Orators discussed every issue almost endlessly. The new technologies of transportation and communication hurled these arguments across the American space. No sooner, for instance, had Lincoln uttered his prophecy that a nation could not survive half slave and half free than a South Carolina planter muttered, "So be it." However, in the long run, these technical advances promoted understanding. If they did not prevent one civil war, they may have stopped others.

## II. The Protestant Love of Words

St. Paul asserted that "faith comes by hearing" (Rom. 10:17). Although all Protestants lived by this admonition, both Lutheran and Episcopalian Christianity compromised this belief. The singing of prepubescent boy choirs occasionally interrupted these denominations' carefully metered liturgies. Further, Episcopalian and Lutheran church buildings often contained valuable works of art and other signs of the "beauty of holiness." Those worshipers who had eyes to see but not ears to hear easily escaped the stream of words flowing from the pulpit.

The British Reformed churches[9] made no such aesthetic concessions.

9. I use this term to refer to the broadly Puritan tradition represented in America

A large central pulpit or desk[10] that reached high above the worshipers' heads, usually crowned with a carved sounding board, dominated their services. The British Reformed preferred an architectural style that avoided any attempt at decoration or beauty. The earliest colonial meetinghouses resembled barns; the later ones, merchants' halls. Even steeples appeared only gradually. Harry S. Stout writes:

> if we see in their . . . architecture only the negation of what the Puritans opposed, we miss the thrust of their message and the source of their appeal. Puritan speech and architecture reflected an elaborate cultural and theological system whose expressed goal was the creation of a Bible commonwealth governed in all regards by the precepts of Holy Scripture.[11]

The Puritans constructed their sermons around a democratic rhetoric. The logic and rhetoric of Peter Ramus was "consistent with Puritan sentiments about preaching and plain speaking."[12] Ramus had advised speakers not to worry about all elements of traditional rhetoric, especially disposition, memory, and invention. Instead, Ramus urged orators to concentrate on the more important elements of style and delivery.[13] The result was a form of public discourse eloquently simple. Unlike Parliamentary speeches or sermons in the Queen's chapel, Puritan sermons were shaped around the capacity of the "average" person in the pew.[14] Like the biblical seers they so admired, Puritan prophets discovered their similes in nature, the home, and business life.

William Perkins's analysis of this style in the *Art of Prophesying* is somewhat arid and cold. From Perkins's manual, a reader might suppose that the Puritan sermon marched relentlessly from exegesis to application.

by the Presbyterians, the Congregationalists, and the Baptists. Although these groups often argued passionately among themselves, they were far closer to each other than they usually admitted.

10. The pulpit was clearly a desk and the pastor often looked more like a school teacher or judge than like a priest.

11. Harry S. Stout, *The New England Soul: Preaching and Religious Culture in Colonial New England* (Oxford: Oxford University Press, 1986), 15.

12. George A. Kennedy, *Classical Rhetoric and Its Christian and Secular Tradition from Ancient to Modern Times* (Chapel Hill: University of North Carolina Press, 1980).

13. Wilbur Samuel Howell, *Logic and Rhetoric in England, 1500-1700* (Princeton: Princeton University Press, 1956), 248.

14. The Puritans believed that they were preaching to the "average man," but they really seem primarily to have addressed people in the lower middle and middle classes, "average" in the sense that they did not have too much or too little.

However, the average Puritan sermon did not always follow Perkins's prescriptions. John Preston, one of the masters of the genre, saw the real fulcrum of the sermon as the appeal to the affections or inclinations. The purpose of every part of the sermon was more to turn the will than it was to convince the reason.

> All affections, as you know, are nothing else but the divers motions and turnings of the will. As the will turns this way or that way; so a man is said to be affected, to love or to hate, to grieve or to rejoice. Now love is that act of the will, whereby it turns itself to a thing, as hatred is that whereby it turns itself from a thing.[15]

William Haller notes that the Puritan sermon competed in the marketplace for the attention of the same individuals that might attend a play by Marlowe or Shakespeare.[16] This rivalry may have contributed to the Puritan love of the personal story or anecdote. The preacher wanted the people to see their struggle for grace mirrored in the life of an example who was similar to their father or mother, sister or brother. Above all, the minister himself was a living parable of grace whose words and acts were one. If few pastors openly boasted of their personal experience of grace, other Puritans recorded the details of their spiritual quests for them.

Religious alchemy transferred the mystique of the spoken word to the written text as well. The Puritans saw the Bible as a talking book, and their ears responded to what their eyes saw. David Hall puts it this way:

> In keeping with the Protestant vernacular tradition, they supposed that to read was to hear, to hear was to see, and to see was to receive truth (or light) communicated to the inner self, the heart. In presuming this near-identity between printed text and (spoken) Word, these texts also imposed on their readers the manner of their use. Nothing separated books from life or action; books transformed the inner self or "heart" in ways that carried over into everyday behavior. Willing a godly book to one of his sons, a minister affirmed: "I doubt not my book will give him a hart of all sound doctrine."[17]

15. John Preston, *The Breastplate of Faith and Love* (London: N. Bourne, 1634; repr. Edinburgh: Banner of Truth Trust, 1979), "Love," 9.

16. William Haller, *The Rise of Puritanism* (New York: Columbia University Press, 1938), 33.

17. David D. Hall, *Worlds of Wonder, Days of Judgment* (New York: Knopf, 1989), 39.

Thus the published sermon, one of the most important Puritan literary genres, existed on an important media boundary. To be sure, these sermons — like the Bible — were printed, but this did not eliminate their oral character. Printed sermons were silent speech.[18]

The long-term survival of the basic Puritan form of preaching in British North America was remarkable. Although the genre lost its monopoly about 1660, other styles of preaching never completely replaced it. Harry S. Stout suggests that ministers from Harvard were more likely to choose an essay form, complete with a detailed outline or full manuscript. In contrast, Yale-trained pastors favored the older style.[19] Further, Stout notes that establishment "evangelicals" prided themselves on speaking from brief outlines. The establishment awakeners' use of metaphor, parable, and anecdote differed little from that employed by the Puritans a century earlier.

Jonathan Edwards was a master of the inherited Puritan sermon. Looking back at Edwards's Enfield sermon a century later, Joseph Tracy noted:

> His plain, unpretending manner, both in language and delivery, and his established reputation for holiness and knowledge of the truth forbade the suspicion that any trick of oratory would be used to mislead the hearers.[20]

Edwards's traditional sermons, however, were already somewhat dated. While Presbyterian and Congregationalist awakeners would continue this type of pulpit oratory, the younger, more sectarian revivalists developed a more radical religious rhetoric.

## III. The New Rhetoric of Religion

Whitefield, Wesley, and their imitators created a new sacred rhetoric.[21] The central feature of this homiletics was the extemporaneous sermon. The ideal revivalist did not deliver his extemporaneous messages "off the

18. Much of Puritan literature was neither text nor oral communication but a combination of the two based on the apprehension of the word.

19. Stout, *New England Soul*, 220.

20. Joseph Tracy, *The Great Awakening* (Boston, 1842), 216.

21. I use the word *new* in a relative sense here. I believe that the Methodist exhorters of the eighteenth century continued a folk pattern of preaching that reached from the Baptist exhorters of the seventeenth century back through the ages to Wycliffe and the Lollards.

cuff"; he was to meditate about his Scripture, his doctrine, and his application for weeks before it was preached. Good extemporaneous preaching required a stockpile of knowledge, ideas, and phrases. Both Whitefield and Wesley stressed the need for their followers to study. Wesley in a fit of administrative idealism ordered his circuit riders to read five hours a day. Whitefield helped to found Trevecca, an early school for "lay preachers," to prepare Calvinist exhorters.

Whitefield was the uncontested master of the new form. When the Grand Itinerant stood up to speak, Whitefield allowed the biblical text to flow from the page into his body and soul. In this rational trance, Whitefield moved from one side of the podium to the other. All the while, the evangelist's eyes darted around the audience, pegging first one soul and then another. Whitefield's goal was a public intimacy in which each auditor heard the sermon as if it were being preached to them alone. The audience stirred Whitefield's imagination.

> Moved in his inmost soul by the sight of his fellow men, ready to perish and yet ignorant of their danger, he could not fetter himself with the rules by which ordinary men were taught to construct dull sermons; he must pour forth the desires of his heart and the convictions of his mind. And he did pour them forth in a style natural and clear, animated and pathetic.[22]

Whitefield's voice was a majestic instrument, ideally suited to his style. The evangelist colored his voice until his message was an emotional tapestry that wove together the bright hues of forgiveness and the dark shadows of despair. When his hearers' attention flagged, Whitefield transposed the scriptural text into a dialogue or play in which the evangelist acted the major roles. Whitefield's hearers experienced the biblical truths that the revivalist depicted.

Wesley was not as accomplished a pulpiteer as Whitefield. His upper-class reserve prevented him from achieving the same mystical relationship with his audience that Whitefield had with his hearers. Nonetheless, Wesley made an important contribution to the new rhetoric. Wesley encouraged ordinary men and a few extraordinary women to exercise the gifts of the Spirit. The effects of this admonition were dramatic. Soon Wesley's exhorters had set England aflame. Wherever the circuit riders preached, they organized their hearers and began the search for new prophets to spread the Word.

Whitefield introduced the new rhetoric into America. While some

22. Tracy, *Great Awakening*, 45.

of the sons of the Puritans, including Jonathan Edwards,[23] tried to imitate his methods, Whitefield's real imitators were the Separates.[24] Despite the active opposition of the Standing Order and of the state, the Separate preachers adopted Whitefield's methods and something of his mannerisms. Their own reading of the Scriptures convinced many of them to become Baptists (immersers).

Although the Separate preachers harvested many souls in New England, they scored their greatest triumph in the American South. The church at Sandy Creek, North Carolina, led by Daniel Marshall and Shubal Stearns, spearheaded their advance. Working from this base, these exhorters fanned out from Georgia in the South to Virginia in the North. Wherever the Separate preachers stopped, they planted a new congregation. Although it was not the Baptists' intention, the Separates also spread Whitefield's new rhetoric. In the eyes of many people, the Separates had set a new standard for oral sincerity.

As Isaac Rhys has shown, the new evangelical rhetoric was potent.[25] The Ciceronian phrases and well-balanced clauses of a Jefferson might stir the souls of Massachusetts' merchants and Virginia's grandees. But only the oral tenderness of the Whitefieldians could inspire Culpepper and Essex County yeomen to leave home, suffer, and die for freedom.[26]

23. Edwards's sermon "Sinners in the Hands of an Angry God" was an imitation of Whitefield. Edwards, even more than Wesley, could never completely surrender to the moment. He continued to preach more or less from fairly complete notes. Nonetheless, Edwards understood the power of the new rhetoric. Alan Heimert observes:

> Edwards noted Whitefield's historic role in the *Thoughts on the Revival,* but he did so by pointing to his *"zeal* and *resolution."* The same virtues, Edwards observed, had made possible the "great things that *Oliver Cromwell* did." In almost the same breath Edwards allowed Britain only "one generation more" before it would "sink under the weight" of its vice and selfishness. . . . Edwards declared, it was necessary for all the "people of God" . . . to be filled with the spirit of Whitefield and of Cromwell. (*Religion and the American Mind* [Cambridge, MA: Harvard University Press, 1966], 58)

24. Bruce Rosenberg in *The Art of the American Folk Preacher* (New York: Oxford University Press, 1970) has noted that many elements in this "popular" style may date back to the early friars and their style of preaching.

25. Isaac Rhys, *The Transformation of Virginia* (Chapel Hill: University of North Carolina Press, 1982). Rhys argues that those who heard the new preaching were strong supporters of the Revolution.

26. Alan Heimert in his *Religion and the American Mind* has correctly noted that there was a link between the Great Awakening and the Revolution, although he tends to link it too much to formal theology.

The very similar preaching of the Methodists soon augmented that of the Baptists. While Methodism entered the colonies in the 1760s, the denomination's first major season of growth followed its formal organization at the Christmas Conference in 1784. American Methodist exhorters used a rhetoric similar to that of the Baptists. The sermon was extemporaneous, often delivered in meter, and designed to appeal to the heart. Armed with this rhetoric, Methodists spread scriptural holiness over the land. The denomination even had its own form of revival. Although Presbyterians contributed to the development of the first camp meetings, this type of revival became almost exclusively Methodist.

The users of the new rhetoric of religion delighted in the give-and-take of debate. Peter Cartwright (1795-1872) described encounter after encounter with the opposition (usually Baptists) as he preached on the frontier in Kentucky and in Illinois.[27] As Cartwright described these forensic confrontations, the fireworks usually began when one party or the other issued a public challenge. Once an audience gathered, the two sides were free to argue their points as long as they could hold the public's attention. Cartwright claimed that he spoke once for three hours during one such exchange with the Shakers.

At times, Cartwright implies, the prize was the souls of the audience. The auditors allowed the more powerful debater to baptize them and to form a congregation. In many ways, the religious debate was analogous to the political debates of the time. At times the two overlapped. In 1846 Abraham Lincoln bested Cartwright in a contest for a congressional seat.

The Methodists and their rhetoric were everywhere. Under the leadership of Francis Asbury — a gaunt, determined apostle of discipline — the Methodists fulfilled their commitment to bring "scriptural holiness" into every corner of the country. The new rhetoric was a flexible instrument that the speaker might adjust to the circumstances of any region of the country.

> They sent their laborers into every corner of the country; if they hear of any particular attention to religion in a place, they double the number of laborers in those circuits, and place their best men there, and endeavor generally, to adapt the character of their preachers, to the character of the people among whom they are to labor.[28]

27. For these debates, see *The Autobiography of Peter Cartwright,* ed. Charles Wallis (New York and Nashville: Abingdon Press, 1956).

28. John Schermerhorn and Samuel J. Mills, *A Correct View of That Part of the United States Which Lies West of the Allegheny Mountains . . . ,* cited in Nathan Hatch, *The Democratization of American Christianity* (New Haven: Yale University Press, 1989), 89.

Charles Finney's 1834 *Lectures on Revivals* summarized the assumptions (whether conscious or not) behind the new rhetoric. The most important of these was the conviction that souls could be won. For Finney, the doctrine of inability served to protect both sinners and ministers from their own unwillingness to accept the gospel's promises.

> A minister may be very learned and not wise. There are many ministers possessed of great learning; they understand all the sciences, physical, moral, and theological; they may know the dead languages, and possess all learning, and not be wise in relation to the great end [winning souls] for which they were called.[29]

Finney also recognized that ministers needed to have the right rhetoric in order to bring souls to the Master. In a withering paragraph, he wrote:

> I know a minister who held an anxious meeting and went to attend it with a *written discourse* [italics Finney's] which he had prepared for the occasion. Just as wise as it would be if a physician going out to visit his patients, should sit down at his leisure and write all his prescriptions before he had seen them.[30]

The real need was for a preacher to turn to the language of the business classes and use it to present his message.

> This accounts for the fact that some plain men, that have been brought up to business, and acquainted with human nature, are ten times better qualified to win souls than two that are educated . . . and are in fact ten times as well-acquainted with the proper business of the ministry.[31]

Nathan Hatch has referred to the impact of the new rhetoric as the "democratization of American Christianity."[32] The phrase is rich with intended and unintended ironies. Like democracy itself, the new forms of religion both built community and destroyed it. America had become the

29. Charles Finney, *Lectures on Revivals* (Boston, 1868), 177.
30. Finney, *Lectures*, 175. People with an ear for language will notice how much closer Finney's rhetoric is to modern educated English than, say, the language of Jonathan Edwards.
31. Finney, *Lectures*, 179.
32. Hatch, *Democratization of American Christianity*.

home of many "one true" churches that competed with one another. Within the walls of a local meetinghouse, the fellowship of kindred spirits might strangely warm the believer's heart; outside the door, the warmth came from the emotional insistence on one's own point of view.

The new rhetoric raised important questions about theological education. Was it possible to teach the new sacred oratory and the assumptions behind it? Was this an art that could only be learned by imitation? Did the new style generate its own institutions?

## IV. The Traditional Education of the Ministry

Theological education was a newly rediscovered idea in antebellum America. The traditional form of ministerial preparation among English Protestants was the public college. Nineteenth-century churches were inveterate college builders. Boorstin wrote:

> Of the hundred-eighty odd colleges founded in these years that survived into the twentieth century, well over a hundred appeared outside the original thirteen colonies. The proportion is all the more impressive since population has remained concentrated on the eastern seaboard.[33]

How did this inherited form of education fit into the new media society of nineteenth-century religious America? Did it support the new evangelical rhetoric, sponsor a continuation of the older Puritan forms, or point to something of a different order? To answer this question, we must understand what the "old-time" college was and what it was not.

Despite some minor adjustments, the college had changed little since the Renaissance.[34] The purpose of the liberal arts college was to train public men who were able to assume positions of leadership in church and state. Although all liberal arts degrees included a smattering of science and

33. Boorstin, *The Americans,* 153.
34. The full story of the development of Oxford and Cambridge from their medieval to their Renaissance form is beyond the scope of this essay. The most important part of this evolution was the central place of the colleges, which, unlike the universities themselves, were not bound by elaborate regulations. First Puritans and then various shades of Anglicans took advantage of this to tailor education to their own needs. For an excellent discussion of the Puritan contribution to this process, see John Morgan, *Godly Learning: Puritan Attitudes Towards Reason, Learning, and Education, 1560-1640* (Cambridge: Cambridge University Press, 1986).

mathematics, the primary function of the curriculum was to transmit knowledge from the past.[35] In particular, the college's stock-in-trade was the intensive study of Latin and Greek literature.

Religion made up only a small proportion of the college student's total program. Seventeenth-century Harvard College held theology classes only two hours a week on Saturday mornings. Yale's program was similar. In the early national period, the colleges replaced this modicum with a course in moral philosophy taught by the president.[36] At Williams, the catalogue described the course in the following way:

> The work . . . is so arranged that the principal studies of senior year relate to man himself as a physical, intellectual, and moral, and religious being. In an important sense the studies of the senior year are a system by themselves.[37]

While these "philosophy" courses were usually more religious than a present-day philosophical ethics course might be, the teachers avoided denominational particularities. The course was a system by itself, since it usually consisted of a college president's reflections on his own reading and experience.

The traditional college taught religion indirectly. Collegiate education, like the education of a boarding school, relied heavily on residence to teach its most important lessons. By living with other young gentlemen, the college student learned the manners and conversation expected of a member of the ruling class. Since church membership was part of a leader's customary behavior, the college taught good religious manners through the steady habits of the chapel. The churches supplemented these customary religious exercises with periodic student revivals that awakened some to their lost condition and enlisted others in Christian service.

The college taught effective written and spoken English by indirection. Although some instructors were capable persons whose classes made Rome and Greece live again, such inspired teachers appear to have been rare.

35. Mark A. Curtis, *Oxford and Cambridge in Transition: 1558-1642* (Oxford: Clarendon Press, 1959), esp. 149-227.

36. Ironically, prospective ministers may have been exposed to more theology in the college toward the end of the nineteenth century when the "elective system" permitted students to choose courses that were more directly related to their future vocational plans.

37. Cited in George E. Peterson, *The New England College in the Age of the University* (Amherst: Amherst College Press, 1964).

Professors usually taught their classes by the recitation method. The pedagogue, perched behind his high desk, hurled questions rapidly at selected class members. The named student was then to stand and answer quickly with a more or less verbatim quotation from the textbook.[38] Many educators devoted their entire class time to the almost endless task of explicating the grammar, illustrating the vocabulary, and parsing the irregular verbs in the assigned texts. Perhaps the popular nineteenth-century phrase "mental discipline" captures the meaning of much contemporary collegiate education. College was the intellectual equivalent of pumping iron. People believed that the exercise was highly beneficial, but nothing could make it interesting.

The literary and debating societies were the places where young men learned the arts of eloquence. The students directed and organized these societies, and the faculties allowed them considerable freedom. Although the students' writings and speeches were not subject to professional critique, mutual criticism was part of almost every meeting. The debates, of course, tested the students' wit and knowledge and their knowledge of particular topics.

The college suited the older traditional Puritan rhetoric. Presbyterians, Congregationalists, and Episcopalians shared the Renaissance tradition of the learned minister. The schools followed this standard. The Bachelor of Arts curriculum produced a minister who had a general knowledge of the world, who was learned enough to be intellectually superior to much of his congregation, and whose sermons were carefully organized.

The colleges wanted also to train ministers who would be social and religious models. Even on the frontier, many college-trained ministers hoped to be resident gentlemen whose labors might raise the standard of the whole region. In some cases, these dedicated people achieved their purposes. Many of the first state superintendents of schools in the Midwest were Reformed ministers. The Midwest quickly achieved a higher educational level than the eastern South.[39]

In contrast, the practitioners of the new rhetoric were profoundly

38. Few collegiate instructors had any real advanced study, and scholarship was not a criterion for appointment or retention. Mark Hopkins's often-quoted statement that he never read anything but the newspapers was hopefully an exaggeration, but it may not have fallen far from the mark.

39. Samuel Taylor Coleridge defended the nineteenth-century establishment on the grounds that it provided England with a "clerisy" or class of educated men who encouraged the development of arts and sciences. The role of clergymen — and particularly the role of the children of clergymen — in the development of German culture was similar.

ambivalent about college education. Although the Baptists and Methodists built many colleges, their leaders had difficulty explaining the value of these institutions to their people.[40]

Methodist leaders justified their colleges by an appeal to the general health of the community. Education was part of the task of nation building, and American Methodists wanted to shape their nation's future. The committee that recommended the founding of Indiana Asbury reported:

> Next to the religion of the Son of God your committee consider the light of science calculated to lessen the sum of human woe and to increase the sum of human happiness. Therefore we are of the opinion that the means of education ought to be placed within the reach of every community in general, so that all may have an opportunity of obtaining an ordinary and necessary education. From observation and information, your committee are convinced that where superior schools and colleges are neglect[ed] ordinary schools are almost universally in a languished state.[41]

Education was a reform, similar to temperance, that Christians advocated for the sake of their fellows.

The Christian Church (Disciples of Christ) justified colleges with a similar argument. Alexander Campbell's commonsense hermeneutics stressed the ability of the average man to read and interpret the Bible. Although the fiery democrat had no use for seminaries or preacher factories, Campbell was a supporter of liberal arts colleges. Like the Methodists, Campbell believed that the nation needed education to support democracy. For him, the college helped to create an educated electorate.

Baptists had more difficulty in justifying the college. The Baptists were the most sectarian of America's major denominations. In the colonial period, Baptists[42] founded and contributed to the College of Rhode Island

40. The actual motives behind the founding of particular schools were diverse. The "boosters" helped to establish many. The boosters' motives were clear: they believed that a college might raise the status of a town or (more likely) the value of real estate near the campus. Others, such as the members of the Yale Band and the Iowa Association, wanted to bring Christianity to the West. In addition, denominationalists believed that schools increased the reputation of their churches. Some founders acted because they believed that a market for a school existed in a given area.

41. Cited in William Warren Sweet, *Indiana Asbury–DePauw University: 1837-1937* (New York: Abingdon Press, 1938).

42. The college was established by an improbable alliance of Philadelphia or confessional Baptists and Separate or revivalistic churches.

(1767; present-day Brown University). Although the charter specified that a Baptist was to be president, the colonial legislature granted other denominations representation on the Board. Baptists were always a minority among the students. Later Baptist colleges had much the same composition. When Wake Forest College opened in 1834, for example, the student body of seventy-two only contained sixteen professors of religion.

Antebellum Baptists never developed a clear rationale for their colleges or for those school ties to the denomination. The Baptists found theological and literary institutes easier to support than colleges or seminaries. Most early nineteenth-century Baptist schools began as preacher's academies. After all, the institute was an academy where ministers studied the Bible;[43] the college was a school that created gentlemen. Not surprisingly, the denomination's colleges depended heavily on the public for students and donations.[44]

How were the practitioners of the new rhetoric trained? Although stories of unlettered preachers abound, most of those who served were able to read the Scriptures. Almost all had some literary skills and were effective communicators. Once a candidate had acquired basic literacy, the nineteenth-century publishing revolution provided the minister with readily available and inexpensive resources.

By reading widely, ministers gained knowledge of the world and of their own denomination and its theology. For those willing to invest the time, the theological journals published by the various churches provided an up-to-date summary of contemporary theology. Most Methodist ministers were also agents for the Methodist book concern. Likewise, ministers of other denominations served as colporteurs for their denomination's press. In short, most ministers acquired their education from the mass media of the nineteenth century, especially the new publishing industry.

Further, democratic evangelicalism was an educational movement. Members of Baptist, Methodist, Christian (Disciples), Presbyterian, and

43. The charter of Newton Theological School in New England prohibited the teaching of systematic theology because of that discipline's relationship to the older state church system of credal subscription.

44. Baptists were very loose organizationally, and many churches were not active in the new "conventions" that were formed to support education and missions. The only reason why Baptists were able to fund so many colleges was that many and perhaps most Baptists did not participate in the convention or give to the support of convention causes. At this time, all Baptist causes were financed by agents who personally canvassed the churches for donations.

Congregational[45] churches attended or taught in Sunday school, read missionary journals, went to meetings of missionary societies, and distributed tracts. Each of these organizations added something to the minister's cache of skills and knowledge.

## V. A Minority Report

Historians have an advantage: they know how the story ends and read the past from the perspective of later events. This apparent benefit, however, has its drawbacks. The most serious is that historians often distort the relative importance of certain events in their own context. Because historians know that Prussia eventually united Germany, for example, we emphasize the importance of Prussia in earlier periods in German history.

In writing the history of American religion, we are in danger of a similar fallacy. Because twentieth-century American Protestants frequently prepare their ministers in seminaries, we assume that the seminary was always an important part of American education. Further, we see some of the schools that existed before the seminary as somehow John the Baptist to the theological school's blessed Advent. Unfortunately, such a perception of the seminary's history is faulty.

Antebellum seminaries trained only a small proportion of American Protestant ministers. In part, this was the result of the American free market in religion. Since few British denominations demanded seminary for ordination, there was no economic or professional pressure to earn a seminary diploma. Churches hired able young ministers shortly after they responded to God's call. Few attended seminary; far fewer completed the full three-year program. Why should an able and industrious person sacrifice three years of earnings for a professional status available elsewhere? If a minister wanted to serve a rich church, the Bachelor of Arts degree was enough for him to be known as a learned gentleman.

The relative unimportance of the seminary was not only economic. Many nineteenth-century ministerial candidates did not attend seminary because they knew what the new institutions offered. The seminaries were theological schools that stressed the minute points of traditional theology. Seminary advocates had difficulty explaining to a student how the mastery

---

45. Of course, not all churches in these denominations were evangelical, although all had many evangelical churches among their membership.

of Gesenius's *Grammar* might attract a committee from a socially prominent church. They had equal difficulty explaining the program to such a
committee. Although the schools usually offered one course in homiletics
(also called "sacred rhetoric" or occasionally "preaching"), the course was
usually offered in the last year, after many students had returned home.

Another way to describe the seminary's irrelevance might be in terms of
the media. In the midst of the expansion of the new rhetoric and the new
publishing industry, the nineteenth-century seminary was isolated from the
contemporary means of communication. The school's emphasis on Greek and
Hebrew made little sense, for example, in a world in which only professional
scholars had a sufficient grasp of those languages to read the Bible easily.

At best, the mechanization of the book trade enabled nineteenth-
century professors to publish more works than might have been possible
earlier. Ironically, the schools held the excitement of the Awakening at bay.
Although some seminary student organizations were devoted to missions,
the schools themselves were very sober-minded institutions.

What, then, was this new institution? The seminary represented a
new professional tradition in American theology.[46] American church
leaders inherited their earlier theological form from England, where custom had caused the theological faculties of the universities to be discon-
tinued.[47] When an important theological issue was current, a minister
would address the question, often in the form of a published sermon.
Another minister then replied. The process continued until the authors
resolved the issue or until one of the writers weakened.

The seminary was a quantum leap forward from this older tradition. In the place of the gentleman scholar, who worked long hours in
his garret and invested his meager finances in a private library, the
seminary offered substantial facilities. Although seminary libraries were
small, they were much larger than a private individual could collect.
Moreover, the better seminaries purchased significant libraries in Europe
that bolstered their collections.[48] The seminary was a place where cir-

46. See my book *Piety and Intellect* (Atlanta: Scholar's Press, 1990).

47. Many positions in these schools of theology, however, continued to exist as
sinecures, which were often at the disposal of the ruling party. Until late in the nineteenth
century, corruption was almost a necessary part of the English constitution.

48. The best account of antebellum seminary libraries is Norman Kansfield, " 'Study
the Most Approved Authors': The Role of the Seminary Library in Nineteenth Century
American Protestant Theological Education" (Ph.D. diss., University of Chicago, Graduate
School of Library Science, 1981).

cumstances encouraged both students and faculty to form a community of learning.[49]

Above all, the seminary offered a chance for specialization. Moses Stuart (1780-1832) never completed a full course in Hebrew. Yet Stuart exploited the new opportunities that his specialized teaching position provided. He mastered Hebrew, wrote valuable (albeit conservative) books on Old Testament criticism, and corresponded with scholars in England and Germany on scholarly issues. While Stuart did not establish a modern research degree, he did found a post-seminary program of biblical study that trained many of the period's biblical critics.

In effect, seminaries were a bet that Americans might improve their religious and intellectual horizons in the future. It was a daring gamble. Few people saw the need for scholarly theology. Most Christian leaders believed that the revival or something like it would serve the American churches for centuries to come. Had it not been for the new intellectual excitement generated by the rise of higher criticism and the new theology, perhaps the common wisdom would have been correct. But new occasions teach new duties, and the seminaries had a more central role in the coming intellectual climate.

49. One of the hallmarks of any advance in education is the establishment of an educational community where communication can take place. This was the significance of Plato's "school" near the grave of Academos in Athens. The thought of one could be improved by dialogue with others.

# Technology and the Character of Community Life in Antebellum America: The Role of Story Papers

Ronald J. Zboray

*MONOMANIA. — "A fellow in New Orleans the other day drew a crowd around him, fancying himself the* clock *of the old cathedral! and he kept moving his hands in the most ludicrous manner around his face, knocking his head, whenever the hour struck, against an old damaged steamboat boiler which lay alongside him."*

*Universal Yankee Nation*[1]

Such sad scenes of mental disintegration have become so common in modern American cities as to be "newsworthless." Today's urbanites shrug, avert their eyes, and deem the particular expression of madness meaningless.[2]

1. *Universal Yankee Nation* 3 (29 Oct. 1842): 304.
2. On the moral indifference accorded the modern American underclass, see Richard Sennett, *The Conscience of the Eye: The Design and Social Life of Cities* (New York: Alfred A. Knopf, 1990). The social construction of meaning and insignificance is treated in the following works: Susan Stewart, *Nonsense: Aspects of Intertextuality in Folklore and Literature* (Baltimore: Johns Hopkins University Press, 1978); Jean-Jacques Lecercle, *Philosophy through the Looking Glass: Language, Nonsense, Desire* (La Salle, IL: Open Court, 1985); and, with broader application for the discussion below, Erving Goffman, *Behavior in Public Places: Notes on the Social Organization of Gatherings* (New York: Free Press, 1963).

Research for this essay was funded in part by the Albert S. Boni Fellowship (1983) of the American Antiquarian Society.

In 1842, many Americans saw this event as significant, maybe a little amusing, and — just perhaps — cathartic. Around the unfortunate man several "crowds" gathered: the one described in the anecdote, the readers who collectively shared in the event in the local paper, and at least the Northeastern readers of the *Universal Yankee Nation,* if not that nation itself, whether it be universal or Yankee.[3] For an instant, his personal tragedy had become a centerpiece of community construction, at first in a face-to-face setting, then within a local print culture, and finally fifteen hundred miles away in a circle of readership emanating from Boston, the place of ultimate publication. And yet, through these distinct levels of reception, some kernel of significance remained in the story.[4]

What interpretive conventions linked these audiences?[5] Certainly these onlookers shared some of the dislocations, confusions, and anxieties inspired by the rapid advance of industrial capitalism in antebellum America. In the anecdote, the man had become a machine, a timepiece, in an era of increasing consciousness of temporal economy, when the phrase "time is money" echoed constantly in the press.[6] In some of the emerging factories, the clanking bells of a watchtower rigidly organized the day of "operatives" — the job title itself connotes the expectation of mechanistic

3. The New Orleans *Daily Picayune* reported the incident on October 16, 1842. The item appeared in almost identical form in the *Universal Yankee Nation*'s later reprint. The latter paper substituted "in New Orleans" for "on the Levee" and deleted the last line of the *Picayune*'s report: "We believe this is the latest case to be recorded."

4. Scholarly considerations of literary reception abound. For an introduction to the topic, see Hans Robert Jauss, *Toward an Aesthetic of Reception,* vol. 2: *Theory and History of Literature,* trans. Timothy Bahti (Minneapolis: University of Minnesota Press, 1982); *The Reader in the Text: Essays on Audience and Interpretation,* ed. Susan Suleiman and Inge Crossman (Princeton: Princeton University Press, 1980); and Stanley Fish, *Is There a Text in this Class? The Authority of Interpretive Communities* (Cambridge, MA: Harvard University Press, 1980).

5. Steven Mailloux, *Interpretive Conventions: The Reader in the Study of American Fiction* (Ithaca, NY: Cornell University Press, 1982).

6. The embourgeoisement of rural New England is treated in Robert A. Gross, "Culture and Cultivation: Agriculture and Society in Thoreau's Concord," *Journal of American History* 69 (June 1982): 42-61. See also the excellent essays in Peter Benes et al., *The Farm,* Annual Proceedings of the Dublin Seminar for New England Folklife, no. 11 (Boston: Boston University Press, 1988). An overview of temporal consciousness in America can be found in Michael O'Malley, *A History of American Time* (New York: Viking, 1990). For a specific consideration of the social aspects of horological mechanism in early modern English culture (with obvious ramifications for the later United States), see Samuel L. Macey, *Clocks and the Cosmos: Time in Western Life and Thought* (Hamden, CT: Archon Books, 1980).

behavior.[7] In railway stations across the country, the peal of a bell on the roof noted the imminent arrival and departure of a tightly scheduled train.[8] The man's hands (another term used for factory worker) had themselves become the appendages of the clock mechanism, and the movement of them is dubbed "ludicrous." How outrageous that a man should move like a machine!

The man did not choose to become just any clock, however, but that of the old St. Louis Cathedral in the *Vieux carré*, the scene of community focus in the French Quarter. The hourly chimes of the cathedral had, since the late eighteenth century, organized life in the locale and served as an exemplum of mechanical accuracy. "As methodical as the hands of the Cathedral clock perform their evolutions" — that was the way the New Orleans *Daily Picayune* described, during the same week in which it reported the "monomania," the plodding journey to the graveyard of a lugubrious hearse driver.[9] For a moment, the man and his imitation of the clock had grabbed from the cathedral bell the center of attention in that part of town.

But more lay beneath this appeal to an older, preindustrial communal order. For the man banged his head against the quintessential symbol of antebellum prosperity in New Orleans, a steamboat boiler. Steam-powered vessels, by cutting the upriver journey by nearly twenty times over earlier keelboats, had encouraged a reciprocal rather than merely a downriver pattern of trade between the Crescent City and the many towns of the Mississippi and Ohio River valleys. Upon the enormous expansion of commerce that resulted, New Orleans became the fourth largest city in

7. Thomas Dublin, *Women at Work: The Transformation of Work and Community in Lowell, Massachusetts, 1826-1860* (New York: Columbia University Press, 1979). The problems the mill girls had in adjusting to the regime of the clock can be seen throughout their own writings in *Farm to Factory: Women's Letters, 1839-1860,* ed. T. Dublin (New York: Columbia University Press, 1979) and *The Lowell Offering: Writings by New England Mill Women, 1840-1845,* ed. Benita Eisler (New York: Harper & Row, 1965). Other considerations of the intensification of labor under industrialism include Alan Dawley, *Class and Community: The Industrial Revolution in Lynn* (Cambridge, MA: Harvard University Press, 1979); Paul Faler, *Mechanics and Manufacturers in the Early Industrial Revolution: Lynn, Massachusetts, 1780-1860* (Albany: State University of New York Press, 1981); and Judith McGaw, *Most Wonderful Machine: Mechanization and Social Change in Berkshire Papermaking, 1801-1885* (Princeton: Princeton University Press, 1987).

8. Ronald J. Zboray, "The Railroad, the Community, and the Book," *Southwest Review* 71 (1986): 474-87.

9. "A Wedding and a Funeral," *Daily Picayune,* 16 October 1842, 2.

America, and in 1840 its people had average incomes forty-four percent above the national average and nine percent higher than that of the principal eastern cities of New York, Philadelphia, Boston, and Baltimore.[10]

The damaged, discarded, and rusting boilers of steamboats represented the downside of prosperity, however. Owners of these vessels employed cheap and flimsy high-pressure engines that, along with the competitive drive of captains to push their ships to the limit of their speed, led to an astounding number of accidents due to bursting boilers.[11] Lurid accounts of these tragedies that took thousands of passenger lives frequently appeared in the antebellum press and at times provoked public outcry. In fact, two such disasters, the sinking of the steamboats *Houma* and *Osage Valley*, occurred on the Lower Mississippi River in the week before the monomania incident.[12] These types of fatal accidents seemed to most antebellum Americans but one necessary price of rapid economic development.[13] Still, this attitude gave cold comfort to the victims.

When the deranged man in New Orleans banged his head against the damaged hull of one of these exploded boilers, his audiences may well have sensed an implicit criticism of the less savory aspects of technology in the age of steam.[14] The madness was meaningful: in his desperate demonstration, the man had welded an audience together out of an all-too-human frustration with the new time-discipline, the malignancy of machines, and the attitude that profits should come before human safety.[15] For as the "go-ahead people" — so described by a flood of visitors

10. Albert Fishlow, "Antebellum Regional Trade Reconsidered," *American Economic Review* 59 (May 1964): 325-64; Lawrence A. Herbst, "Interregional Commodity Trade from the North to the South and American Economic Development in the Antebellum Period," *Journal of Economic History* 35 (March 1975): 264-70.

11. Louis C. Hunter, *Steamboats on the Western Rivers* (Cambridge, MA: Harvard University Press, 1949). James G. Burke, "Bursting Boilers and Federal Power," *Technology and Culture* 7 (1966): 1-23.

12. *Daily Picayune,* 12 October 1842, 2; and 13 October 1842, 2.

13. Daniel Boorstin, *The Americans: The National Experience* (New York: Random House, 1965), 100-105, 465; George Rogers Taylor, *The Transportation Revolution, 1815-1861* (New York: Reinhardt, 1951), 65-66; Max Berger, *The British Traveller in America, 1836-1860* (Gloucester, MA: Peter Smith, 1964), 75-76.

14. A depressed local economy and a raging yellow fever epidemic probably added to the social anxieties of the onlookers. John Duffy, *Sword of Pestilence: The New Orleans Yellow Fever Epidemic of 1853* (Baton Rouge: Louisiana State University Press, 1966).

15. The classic statements of the difficulty workers had in adjusting to the new work and time discipline are E. P. Thompson, "Time, Work-Discipline, and Industrial Capitalism," *Past and Present* 38 (1967): 59-97; and Herbert Gutman, *Work, Culture, and*

to the antebellum United States — rushed headlong into industrial capitalism, they felt they had left behind "something." Americans variably identified that loss as "the sense of past," "expectancy," "belonging," "warmth," and a host of other fading positive attributes, catalogued in nineteenth-century melodrama.[16]

These "somethings" may be subsumed under the broad category "community,"[17] for it was within specific, personally memorialized, face-to-face groupings that this sense of loss registered. In 1840, eighty-nine percent of Americans still lived in towns with 2,500 or fewer people.[18] In such small-scale settings, the community differed little from the local population. Within the local dispositions (and limitations) of class, ethnicity, age, and gender,[19] a person certainly could be "known," in some way, by most people in the town, even if, with time, the individual or the family made a move or two in search of economic opportunity.[20]

---

*Society in Industrializing America: Essays in American Working-Class and Social History* (New York: Vintage, 1977).

16. Traditional sources include Fred Lewis Pattee, *The Feminine Fifties* (New York: D. Appleton, 1940); Helen Waite Papashvily, *All the Happy Endings* (New York: Harpers, 1956); Douglas E. Branch, *The Sentimental Years, 1836-1860* (New York: Hill and Wang, 1936).

17. The normative use of the concept of community has damaged its analytical value. The classic formulation and obfuscation is, of course, Ferdinand Tonniës, *Community and Society*, trans. Charles P. Loomis (East Lansing: Michigan State University Press, 1957). More recent attempts at rescuing the concept include the following: Mancur Olson, *The Logic of Collective Action: Public Good and the Theory of Groups* (Cambridge, MA: Harvard University Press, 1965); Lyn Lofland, *A World of Strangers: Order and Action in Urban Public Space* (New York: Basic Books, 1973); and Michael Taylor, *Community, Anarchy, and Liberty* (Cambridge: Cambridge University Press, 1982). For a recent challenge to traditional formulations of familism within communities, see Jan E. Dizard and Howard Gadlin, *The Minimal Family* (Amherst: University of Massachusetts Press, 1992).

18. United States Bureau of Census, *Census of Population: 1970* (Washington, DC: Government Printing Office, 1971), vol. 1, pt. A, sec. 1, p. 62.

19. For an excellent analysis of "knowing" across gender boundaries in these small communities, see Nancy Grey Osterud, "Strategies of Mutuality: Relations among Men and Women in an Agricultural Community" (Ph.D. diss., Brown University, 1984).

20. The personal acceptance of economic opportunism as a motive for geographical mobility may itself be an important indication of the erosion of community, but this must be distinguished from Malthusian pressure. Daniel Scott Smith, "A Malthusian-Frontier Interpretation of United States Demographic History before c. 1815," in Woodrow Borah, Jorge Hardoy, and Gilbert A. Stelter, *Urbanization in the Americas: The Background in Comparative Perspective* (Ottawa: History Division, National Museum of Man, 1980). This distinction, of course, touches on the fierce debate in early American studies concerning the *mentalité* of agrarian Americans: When did they become self-consciously profit maxi-

Despite the public clamor of buoyancy for "prospects" in the Yankee nation, the rate of failure was appallingly high. According to one estimate, about one in every five antebellum Americans would go broke at some time in their lives.[21] It must be remembered that no government-supported income floor protected the breadwinner from these bouts of economic calamity.[22] The Americans on the move tended to be less successful and thus particularly vulnerable.[23] The lifeline of old relationships maintained through correspondence often became critical to survival, as evidenced in the following letter from a would-be western immigrant from Massachusetts, who made it only to New York before he ran out of money:

> Had Uncle Mathew sent me enough I should have left [for Cincinnati] this afternoon, but now I shall have to remain in New York, to do what God only knows. The prospect for me in this world grows darker. I am completely broken down with misfortune and anxiety of mind. I would

---

mizing? See, e.g., James Henretta, "Families and Farms: *Mentalité* in Pre-Industrial America," *William and Mary Quarterly* 25 (1978): 3-32; Christopher Clark, "Household Economy, Market Exchange, and the Rise of Capitalism in the Connecticut River Valley, 1800-1860," *Journal of Social History* 13 (1979): 169-89; and, for the opposing view, James T. Lemon, "Early Americans and Their Social Environment," *Journal of Historical Geography* 6 (1980): 115-31. In other words, the relative balance of "pull" and "push" factors, *in the mind of the migrant,* may give important clues concerning the nature of community life. Ironically, evidence in the anthropological literature of "non-coercive" hunter-gatherer bands suggests that low-density population, an easily achieved subsistence level, and easy movement out of the group might drastically lessen the need for negative sanctions, sometimes a defining characteristic of community. Elman Service, *The Hunters* (Englewood Cliffs, NJ: Prentice-Hall, 1966); *Man the Hunter,* ed. Richard Lee and Irven DeVore (Chicago: Wenner-Grenn Foundation, 1968). Applied to America, this would mean that some of the conditions of early industrial capitalism as experienced in newer areas may have encouraged a greater feeling of community than in older settled communities, where we find population pressure upon resources and, in New England, the existence of the closed corporate town.

21. Peter J. Coleman, *Debtors and Creditors in America: Insolvency, Imprisonment for Debt, and Bankruptcy, 1607-1900* (Madison: State Historical Society of Wisconsin, 1974), 287. In one contemporary estimation, only seven out of one hundred early nineteenth-century New York City merchants did not at some time fail financially; see Robert G. Albion, *The Rise of the Port of New York, 1815-1860* (New York: Scribner's, 1939), 285-86.

22. On the ways in which Americans coped without these protections, see Richard L. Bushman, "Family Security in the Transition from Farm to City, 1750-1850," *Journal of Family History* 6 (1981): 238-52.

23. Stephan Thernstrom and Peter R. Knights, "Men in Motion: Some Data and Speculations about Urban Population Mobility in Nineteenth Century America," *Journal of Interdisciplinary History* 1 (1970): 7-35.

not pass through the ordeal that I have for the past six months again for Worlds but I am afraid the worse is to come. I did hope I should be able to try my fortune in the West, but it seemed that this failed me. I know not what I am to do, every day and every hour is adding to my difficulties and I cannot lift a finger to help myself. [E]mployment I cannot get[;] indeed if I now had a situation offered me, I should not have the heart to accept it. The transition from hope to utter despair is enough to drive me mad. For your kindness toward me I will always be grateful, for gratitude is all I have left to show. And should you see Uncle Mathew be so kind as to thank him for me. At the end of another week I know not where I shall be. I shudder to think of it. Probably in the grave. . . . I can write no more. My heart is ready to burst.[24]

A timely remittance from the family in this case averted tragedy. Others, without wealthy relatives to whom they could write for help, were not so fortunate.[25]

For successful migrants, the task of community re-formation would begin upon arrival in the new home.[26] Adults, of course, would never recapture that sense of parallel development of the self and the locale, that sense that the places one saw every day were the first places seen in one's life. Yet new friends could be made, and the process of settling into a new place — usually a dramatic departure from the former pattern of day-to-day life — took on a special history of its own. After a year or two, immersion in the life of the community would create new emotional bonds, perhaps different from the old ones in that they lacked personal and familial historicity, but nevertheless the basis for a feeling of social engagement and participation.[27]

Whether stable or mobile, most rural Americans had many chances for encountering other townsfolk. Farms as yet remained small enough to allow easy intercourse with the village center or with neighbors — and the

24. William S. Parker to West, Richardson, and Lord, 12 January 1838, West, Richardson, and Lord Papers, courtesy American Antiquarian Society.
25. The emotional importance of personal correspondence is treated in Marilyn Ferris Motz, *True Sisterhood: Michigan Women and Their Kin, 1820-1920* (Albany: State University of New York Press, 1983); and Ronald J. Zboray, "The Letter and the Fiction Reading Public," *Journal of American Culture* 10 (1987): 27-34.
26. Caroline Matilda Kirkland, in *A New Home — Who'll Follow? Or, Glimpses of Western Life* (New York: C. S. Francis, 1839) and *Western Clearings* (New York: Wiley and Putnam, 1845), describes this process of community re-formation.
27. Doyl Don Harrison, "Chaos and Community in a Frontier Town: Jacksonville, Illinois, 1825-1860" (Ph.D. diss., Northwestern University, 1973).

emerging farm labor market made occasional stints on other farms or even in rural trades increasingly common for younger people. Church services, court days, and a wide variety of social events provided even more occasions for the construction of community.[28]

The sense of separation from community must be distinguished from the day-to-day realities of participation in it. Few Americans wrote paeans to community life during the time when they lived there. Absence may well have made the heart grow fonder — and forgetful of the slaying gossip, the ancient prejudices, and the stultifying resistance to outside influence that all too commonly afflicted traditional communities. Yet one could also say that the new vexations encountered in the age of antebellum enterprise made the old limitations of local community life seem comparatively less galling.

On a deeper level, if retrospective assessments of community can be believed, people experienced it as more or less "oceanic." "There was a child went forth every day," Whitman wrote in 1855, "And the first object he looked upon, that object he became." He goes on to list as such subjectified objects the natural setting of the community and its social relations, including "the old drunkard . . . , the school mistress . . . , the friendly boys . . . , and the quarrelsome boys . . . , the tidy and fresh-cheeked girls — and the barefoot negro boy and girl."[29] The construction of self required little individual effort. The community remembered individuals and reminded them of their identity. Some modern social psychologists might even call this an arrested state of development, a persistent infantilization in which individuals resist erecting solid walls between the self and the surrounding familial and social milieu.[30]

Such a view goes a long way to explaining the hostility with which some current scholarship treats community as an analytical tool,[31] but it

28. On the importance of the church for community, see T. Scott Miyakawa, *Protestants and Pioneers: Individualism and Conformity in the American Frontier* (Chicago: University of Chicago Press, 1964); and Hal S. Barron, *Those Who Stayed Behind: Rural Society in Nineteenth-Century New England* (New York: Cambridge University Press, 1984).

29. Walt Whitman, *Walt Whitman's Blue Book, The 1860-1861 Leaves of Grass Containing his Manuscript Additions and Revisions* (New York: New York Public Library, 1968), 221-22.

30. This is the view taken by Howard F. Stein, *Developmental Time and Cultural Space: Studies in Psychogeography* (Norman, OK: University of Oklahoma Press, 1987).

31. See esp. Mary Tew Douglas, *How Institutions Think* (Syracuse, NY: Syracuse University Press, 1986), 21-30; and Richard Sennett, *The Fall of Public Man* (New York: Alfred Knopf, 1977), 219-55, 294-312. The arguments for and against the community concept are judiciously pondered in Thomas Bender, *Community and Social Change in America* (New

fails to accept nineteenth-century Americans on their own terms. In any case, the sense of loss of community may have defined the self, at least in its more modern usage, through a crisis of separation. And it would be the separated self who would find it necessary to mourn the loss, to recognize it, in order to deal with it and to keep a link to a memory of the community-oriented past.

Ironically, the real locale that provided the experience of community increasingly differed from its static remembrance, for the coming of industrial capitalism left few places untouched. Rip Van Winkle's poignant experience of returning after decades to his well-known hometown only to find it unrecognizable played out countless times in the nineteenth century. "The place where I drew my first breath and formed my most endearing attachments, had to me become a land of strangers," George Robert Twelves Hewes remarked on his first return to Boston nearly half a century after the Revolution. "Strange to me now are the forms I meet / When I visit the dear old town," Longfellow wrote in "My Lost Youth" (1855). With the intensification of industrial capitalism at mid-century, the pace of change only quickened in severity and widened in scope.[32]

The need for belonging and acceptance thus emerged early on as a common American characteristic, often noted by travelers. "The Americans are almost universally known to be a sensitive people," Alexander Mackay noted; "they are more than this; they are over-sensitive." Harriet Martineau remarked: "The fear of opinion takes many forms. There is the fear of vulgarity, fear of responsibility; and above all, the fear of singularity."[33]

---

Brunswick: Rutgers University Press, 1978). See also Maurice R. Stein, *The Eclipse of Community: An Interpretation of American Studies* (Princeton: Princeton University Press, 1960).

32. Hewes is quoted in James Hawkes, *A Retrospect of the Boston Tea-Party with a Memoir of George R. T. Hewes* . . . (New York: Bliss, 1834), 77. Alfred Young, "George Robert Twelves Hewes (1742-1840): A Boston Shoemaker and the Memory of the American Revolution," *William and Mary Quarterly* 38 (1981): 561-623. Henry Wadsworth Longfellow, *Poetical Works* (New York: AMS Press, 1966), 3:41.

33. Alexander Mackay, *The Western World; or, Travels in the United States in 1846-1847* (1850; repr. New York: Negro Universities Press, 1961), 319; Harriet Martineau, *Society in America* (1837; repr. New York: AMS Press, 1966), 14. Aleksandr Borisovich Lakier had another opinion of why Americans feared to voice their uncensored feelings: "The usual plan to obtain redress for libel . . . is summary and effective. The party who perceives himself aggrieved provides himself with either a cowhide, a Boey [sic] knife, or perhaps shoulders his rifle . . . and at once proceeds against the delinquent, who, if he should be taken unawares, expiates his offence by having his throat cut, or body drilled with a rifle bullet." Lakier, *A Russian Looks at America: The Journey of Aleksandr Borisovich Lakier,* ed. Arnold Schrier and Joyce Story (Chicago: University of Chicago Press, 1979), 141.

The experience of the loss of community thus had a social as much as a personal quality. For most Americans had to confront these feelings and see other people going through the same ordeal. The specificity of the locale and its relationships, however, needed to be sacrificed in order to achieve this shared mourning. The sense of loss becomes the vague "Old Folks at Home" — schematized into a universal Mother or Brother. Sometimes the specifics of the past become hidden beneath a fetish, as in the case of the weepy "The Old Oaken Bucket" (in which the iron-bound bucket serves as focal point for nostalgia) or the defensive "Woodman Spare that Tree."[34]

These songs, and a welter of similar therapeutic poems and stories, suggest the contribution of popular culture to creating a socialized response to this personal sense of community loss.[35] The very processes of economic change that set "men in motion"[36] in the nineteenth century also opened avenues of dissemination of an ideology for dealing with the change from smaller, more stable, subsistence-based agricultural communities to a larger, more complex, and highly commercialized society.

The anecdote about the New Orleans human clock was only one of thousands of attempts by publishers to find something to hold the attention of the heterogeneous American reading public. "Amongst a people so widely scattered, and living under such different circumstances," Alexander Mackay observed in 1837, "one may naturally expect to meet with every

34. Stephen Foster, "Old Folks at Home" (1851); Samuel Woodworth, "The Old Oaken Bucket" (1843); George P. Morris, "Woodman Spare that Tree" (1837).

35. The use of the word here derives from T. J. Jackson Lears, "From Salvation to Self-Realization: Advertising and the Therapeutic Roots of Consumer Culture," in *The Culture of Consumption,* ed. Richard Wrightman Fox and T. J. Jackson Lears (New York: Pantheon, 1983); and Philip Rieff, *The Triumph of the Therapeutic: The Uses of Faith after Freud* (1965; repr. Chicago: University of Chicago Press, 1987). Obviously, the discussion here places the development of such therapeutic devices much earlier. See, e.g., Ann Douglas, "Consolation Literature in the Northern United States, 1830-1880," *American Quarterly* 26 (1974): 496-515; and Jane Tompkins, *Sensational Designs: The Cultural Work of American Fiction, 1790-1860* (New York: Oxford University Press, 1985).

36. The phrase is from Thernstrom and Knights, "Men in Motion," and refers to the enormous amount of spatial mobility in nineteenth-century America. See, however, J. Morgan Kousser, Gary W. Cox, and David W. Galenson, "Log-Linear Analysis of Contingency Tables: An Introduction for Historians with an Application to Thernstrom on the 'Floating Proletariat,'" *Historical Methods* 15 (1982): 152-69; Donald Parkerson, "How Mobile Were Nineteenth Century Americans?" *Historical Methods* 15 (1982): 99-109; David Paul Davenport, "Duration of Residence in the 1855 Census of New York State," *Historical Methods* 18 (1985): 5-12; and David Paul Davenport, "Tracing Rural New York's Out-Migrants, 1855-1860," *Historical Methods* 17 (1984): 59-67.

variety of character, and every stage of social development."[37] Of course, even to maintain the belief in a seeming oxymoron like "heterogeneous public" required a leap in imagination on the part of publishers — a cultural equivalent of the mystical political motto *e pluribus unum.*[38]

Yet publishers, in the wake of rapid industrialization, faced a problem of overproduction. Their entrepreneurial visions refused to curb their ambitions of reaching the widest market possible for the least per-unit cost. As early as 1836, the intensification of labor under industrial capitalism and its consequent specializations met with the enormous productive potential of steam power. The steam press replaced the arduous human labor required to pull the bar of the press. (Even horses had been put to this purpose, with only limited success.) The steam-powered press, coupled with the adoption of integrated factory production techniques, provided newspaper publishers with an almost limitless production capability, and it encouraged them to seek fittingly enormous circulations. The publisher Frederick Gleason described the application of machinery and division of labor in his Boston newspaper and book factory in 1849:

> The Flag of Our Union is now printed on two of Adams' largest power presses by steam, and in order to issue our edition of over forty thousand copies, it requires that these presses work constantly from sunrise to sunset everyday of the week. It makes a busy scene of our publishing hall. The lower floor, or cellar, is devoted to the boiler and steam engine; the second story to the press room, where the papers are printed; the third floor to our business and packing offices; and the fourth floor to our bindery and printing office, where the matter is set up for the paper. Each room forms a department of itself, and altogether gives employment to thirty-five individuals, viz., a fireman, an engineer, two pressmen, three feeders for the presses, who lay on the sheets, a porter, a foreman to the printing office, and ten compositors. The bindery gives employment to some ten persons. . . . There are six clerks besides the publisher and editor. Add to this as many more able contributors. . . . Then we keep one paper mill, with all its apparatus and numerous attendants, constantly at work.[39]

37. Mackay, *The Western World,* 224.

38. For a discussion of this topic, bearing on an earlier period, see Michael Warner, *Letters of the Republic: Publication and the Public Sphere in Eighteenth-Century America* (Cambridge, MA: Harvard University Press, 1990).

39. [Frederick Gleason], "Local Matters," *Flag of Our Union* 4 (10 March 1849): 3.

Thus, for Gleason and other publishers for the mass market, technology and a new industrial organization of labor had lifted the constraints of scale of earlier artisan shops, which seldom employed more than ten people and had difficulty producing press runs of more than a few thousand.[40]

The cost of "getting up a paper" — the writing and editing of copy and its typesetting — remained largely unaffected by technology and hence expensive, however. Highly paid and very literate compositors still had to set manually every letter, em, and punctuation mark and had to proof the copy. Electrotyping and stereotyping — the processes by which a permanent impression of the typeset text was recorded in plate form — could insure that subsequent editions would not have to be reset, but the cost of typesetting a first edition differed little from those of earlier artisan shops.

Publishers faced a more daunting problem in finding copy for mass printing. They did this sometimes by outright plagiarism of other newspapers, both domestic and foreign, or by cultivating stables of incredibly prolific, if not equally talented, writers. Two of these, Timothy Shay Arthur and Joseph Holt Ingraham, produced between them in the two decades after the Panic of 1837 at least one hundred eighty-nine novels, or almost ten percent of all adult fiction in book form written by Americans during those years.[41]

The peculiar relationship among the various factors of production, in which the costs of designing the product and tooling the factory to produce it (i.e., writing and typesetting copy and creating the plates) continued to be very high relative to the expense of actual production, opened up economies of scale to publishers. The per-unit cost of a small press run thus far outweighed that of mass production of a single unit (a book or an issue of a periodical).[42] Seen another way, if the nation had then possessed a popular

40. Ronald J. Zboray, "Antebellum Reading and the Ironies of Technological Innovation," *American Quarterly* 40 (1988): 68-74; Ralph Green, "Early American Power Presses," *Studies in Bibliography* 4 (1951-52): 143-53. Cf. Rollo G. Silver, *The American Printer, 1787-1825* (Charlottesville: University Press of Virginia, 1967). Mid-century printer manuals give an idea of the specialization of tasks, supervision of labor, and desire for cost control in these factories. See, e.g., Thomas F. Adams, *Typographia; or The Printer's Instructor* (New York: R. Hoe, 1856).

41. Based on Lyle Wright, *American Fiction, 1774-1850: A Contribution toward a Bibliography* (San Marino, CA: Huntington Library, 1969), and Wright, *American Fiction, 1851-1875: A Contribution toward a Bibliography* (San Marino, CA: Huntington Library, 1965). Ingraham's work is evaluated in Robert W. Weathersby II, *J. H. Ingraham* (Boston: Twayne, 1980).

42. As an example of the productive power of the transformation, in 1852, by hand, it took 3,170 man hours to print 10,000 copies of a magazine at a total labor cost of

tradition of literary creation, rather than having depended for so long upon European writers,[43] and if industrialism had affected typesetting,[44] publishers may have found "narrowcasting" (intensive cultivation of a small but highly select audience) to be an economically attractive option. Hundreds of local print cultures could have flourished in this environment rather than the four literary worlds of the mid-nineteenth century: New York, Boston, Philadelphia, and, very weakly, Cincinnati.[45] As it turned out, however, publishers in those four cities had to create inexpensive, large press runs that somehow had to sell well beyond their metropolitan areas.[46] But what type of content might appeal to this broader, highly differentiated audience?

The Boston story papers — including *Flag of Our Union, Universal*

---

$302.50. To print the same number of magazines by machine in 1896 required only 14 hours and 56 minutes at a labor cost of $4.63. Elizabeth Faulkner Baker, *Printers and Technology* (New York: Columbia University Press, 1957).

43. Some, but certainly not all, of this was due to the fact that American publishers tended to pirate European works for free, but American authors had the protection of federal copyright and hence presumably would have to be paid. Bruce W. Bugbee, *The Early American Law of Intellectual Property: Genesis of American Patent and Copyright Law* (Washington, DC: Public Affairs Press, 1967); R. R. Bowker, *Copyright: Its History and Its Law* (Boston: Houghton Mifflin, 1912).

44. Workable automatic composing machines had already been invented. John Smith Thompson, *History of Composing Machines: A Complete Record of the Art of Composing Type By Machinery* (Chicago: Inland Printer, 1904).

45. This seemed to be happening in the early nineteenth century, as small but vibrant literary centers could be found in places such as Hartford, CT; Lexington, KY; Bangor and Portland, ME; Walpole, NH; Windsor, VT; Albany, NY; and especially the New York burnt-over district: Auburn, Buffalo, Rochester, Utica. Cincinnati may well have been one of the last if not the largest of these. See Walter Sutton, *The Western Booktrade: Cincinnati as a Nineteenth-Century Publishing Center* (Columbus: Ohio State University Press, 1961).

46. This is not to revise the old Whig school of publishing that credits innovations in printing technology with enormous, mostly salutary, social changes. That tradition, the roots of which can be traced back to the Protestant Reformation, reached its culmination, of course, in Marshall McLuhan, *The Gutenberg Galaxy* (Toronto: University of Toronto Press, 1965), only one of his more cogent cogitations. See also Elizabeth L. Eisenstein, *The Printing Press as an Agent of Change, Communications, and Cultural Transformation in Early Modern Europe* (Cambridge, MA: Harvard University Press, 1979). In recent years, the scholarly interest has swung in the opposite direction, imbedding printing technology in larger cultural considerations and thus diminishing its force as an independent agent. A recent example of the reassertion of human agency over the world of print is Warner, *Letters of the Republic*. Yet it would be going too far to suggest that capitalist development as concretely expressed in nineteenth-century America did not follow patterns, a seeming logic all of its own. If the opportunities existed for profit making, as they did with the productive and distributive potentials of publishing, these entrepreneurs would avail themselves of them (within the expansive limits of their ethics, of course).

*Yankee Nation, Uncle Sam, Yankee Blade,* and *True Flag* — pioneered the
use of fictional material, much of it authored by Americans, in order to
maximize sales.[47] The very nationalistic names of the papers advertised
their claim to a reading public that encompassed North and South and
stretched from sea to sea. Their editors knew they had to seek such a
wideflung market. "A paper of this sort should be as various as the *nation,*"
the *Universal Yankee Nation* recommended.[48]

Mid-century transportation improvements encouraged publishers to
cultivate markets well beyond their immediate urban hinterland.[49] In the
1830s, various shipping companies emerged to guide small luxury items
such as books and newspapers through the maze of land and water conveyances that served as the first serviceable national transportation network. Invoices from these firms fill the extant records of antebellum
publishers and suggest a high level of sophistication in transport services.
For example, an 1837 bill among the papers of the Philadelphia publisher
McCarty and Davis shows an engraving of the Pittsburg [sic] Transportation Line's "Rail Road Line of Portable Car Bodies, in which goods are
carried from Philadelphia to Pittsburg [sic], without being re-packed,
handled, or separated on the way" — a forerunner of modern container-
oriented shipping.[50]

The economic structure of the period, however, created only the
possibility and not the inevitability of mass production for a national
market.[51] The cheap fiction publishers had to conjure means to stimulate

47. For background on the story papers see Mary Noel, *Villains Galore . . . : The
Heyday of the Popular Story Weekly* (New York: Macmillan, 1954). David S. Reynolds notes
some of the confluences between story paper fiction and the classical literature of the
American Renaissance in *Beneath the American Renaissance: The Subversive Imagination in
the Age of Emerson and Melville* (New York: Alfred A. Knopf, 1988). For biographies of
individual firms, see Madeleine Bettina Stern, ed., *Publishers for Mass Entertainment in
Nineteenth Century America* (Boston: G. K. Hall, 1980).

48. *Universal Yankee Nation* 1 (9 Jan. 1841): 2.

49. For background on the postal system through which these publications circulated, see Richard B. Kielbowicz, *News in the Mail: The Press, Post Office, and Public
Information* (Westport, CT: Greenwood Press, 1989).

50. Invoice, T. S. Clarke Co., Zanesville, Ohio, to McCarty and Davis, 17 May
1837, McCarty and Davis Papers, courtesy American Antiquarian Society. The shipment
was for "Five Boxes Books." Alfred Chandler, *The Visible Hand: The Managerial Revolution
in American Business* (Cambridge, MA: Harvard University Press, 1977), 126-28.

51. Business historians have traditionally overlooked the importance of publishing
in developing modern business practices. Chandler's *Visible Hand* (81-144) places the "first
modern business enterprises" in the 1850s with the emergence of rail systems. He does

national demand,[52] a challenge that put publishers in the avant garde of industrialism.[53]

To address this problem, the cheap publishers tried to adjust the content of their goods to reflect national rather than local priorities and to aim for mass without sacrificing class. A manuscript copy of an 1843 prospectus written by Horace B. Wallace for the new series of the weekly

---

not consider publishing at all in his discussion of traditional enterprise. Apart from "armories and textile mills," he writes, "in all manufacturing enterprises the volume of production was not enough to bring the subdivision of labor nor the integration of several processes of production within a single establishment" (75). The tens of thousands of papers printed each week in a single establishment certainly presented a large enough volume for specialization and integrated factory production.

52. Religious publishing, as David Paul Nord argues persuasively in this volume (see pp. 149-79 below), was also at the forefront of managerial control of large enterprises. The search of mass religious publishers for control over market forces and competition poses an interesting contrast to the out-and-out entrepreneurial spirit of the commercial houses. The roots of the story papers and other secular mass media publications in the religious press is too large and complex a topic to be treated here. See David Paul Nord, "The Evangelical Origins of Mass Media in America, 1815-1835," *Journalism Monographs* 88 (1984). See also R. Laurence Moore, "Religion, Secularization, and the Shaping of the Culture Industry in Antebellum America," *American Quarterly* 41 (1989): 216-42. On the overlap of content between religious and secular fiction, see David S. Reynolds, *Faith in Fiction* (Cambridge, MA: Harvard University Press, 1981). Certainly, evangelical religion, whether expressed in the press or at revivals, contributed another powerful form of therapy — and the potential for a nationalization of personal consciousness — for the disruptions of local community life.

53. Publishers of all sorts had to face the problems of mass distribution much earlier than other businessmen. Publishing houses were among the first specialized businesses to engage regularly in advertising. In 1805, for example, the publishing industry contributed thirty-nine percent of all commercial notices appearing in Philadelphia's *United States Gazette.* All other specialized businesses added but another twenty percent, or half as much. Stuart Blumin, "From Black Coats to White Collars," in *Small Business in American Life,* ed. Stuart Bruchey (New York: Columbia University Press, 1980). By the middle of the nineteenth century, the publishing industry had already pioneered full-page ads with the liberal use of testimonials and psychological appeals, as well as full-blown campaigns involving various forms of publicity. See William Charvat, "James T. Fields and the Beginnings of Book Promotion," *Huntington Library Quarterly* 8 (1944-45): 82-94; Susan Geary, "The Domestic Novel as a Commercial Commodity: Making a Best Seller in the 1850's," *Papers of the Bibliographical Society of America* 70 (1976): 365-95; and Geary, "Harriet Beecher Stowe, John P. Jewett, and Author-Publisher Relations in 1853," *Studies in the American Renaissance* 1 (1977): 345-67. These campaigns were national in scope, as can be seen in the analysis of the Harper advertising records in Ronald J. Zboray, "The Transportation Revolution and Antebellum Book Distribution Reconsidered," *American Quarterly* 38 (1986): 53-71. The same article also discusses national wholesale distributors for books, another forward-looking innovation in distribution.

*New York Mirror* shows some of the dilemmas of pitching the proper tone to the mass market. "The contents will *invariably* be entirely *original*," the prospectus promised, and will "unite, in one definite purpose, *all* the force of *American* talent, — be thoroughly American in its tone, character, & interests, — & be fitted, by the power, variety, & brilliance of its matter, to satisfy all the demands of our national taste." The text goes on, in similarly bloated prose, to argue:

> The genius of this country admits, & the character, temper & habits of the people seem to call for, the development of a richer, more vivid & more attractive order of literature; which, stamped with the freshest interests of the passing hour, & wide in its range as society itself, shall animate and exalt the concerns it deals with; shall be at once familiar & elevating, — domestic in its tone, lofty in its tendencies; which shall cheer, excite, & gratify.

The author of these sublime vagaries enclosed a note to the publisher: "there, my dear fellow, you have one of the 9 & 30 advertisements which I have written for the Mirror — each worse than the other." In disgust, he confessed that he tried several styles, the "ranting & the refined; the boasting & the beautiful," but rejected them all because he could "find none that is not objectionable in some quarter." He advised the publisher: "you must agitate the pothouses without offending the parlours."[54]

A simple claim to national and democratic content was not enough, however, and the cheap publishers found that they quickly saturated local markets. To realize the full potential of production and its economies of scale, publishers had to get the goods to distant markets and induce consumers to buy these items. Some publishers assumed that the papers would simply sell themselves, that local readers would exchange the papers with relatives and acquaintances in distant places. *The Flag of Our Union* urged: "city people could not possibly make their country friends so acceptable a present in any other way imaginable" than to give a gift subscription to the paper. Hoping to induce backcountry folk visiting Boston to take up subscriptions, the papers placed newsboys on the trains bound to and from the city. The publishers ran advertisements in papers especially designed for travelers, like the Boston *Pathfinder*. The editors of

54. Horace B. Wallace to General George P. Morris, 6 January 1843, Book Trades Collection, courtesy American Antiquarian Society.

the story papers encouraged readers to pool their resources for the two-or three-dollar yearly subscription or to accumulate individual local subscriptions and receive their own for free. The *Star Spangled Banner* offered: "any person, who will obtain six subscribers . . . , and forward us $12, shall have a seventh copy gratis, and a complete set of all publications named in our catalogue."[55]

These more informal ways of creating demand gave way to the hard sell of armies of roving subscription agents, who would use the young transportation system to canvass, on commission, remote areas. In April 1851, the *Yankee Blade* published a lengthy piece on working the market in this manner. The *Blade* acknowledged special skills it took to get subscribers: "it requires about as much nerve to face a gruff, burly citizen, and convince him against his own most stubborn will that he wants the magazine or paper you have the honor of presenting for his consideration, as it does to face a bellowing cannon on the field of battle." Against "freezing indifference or a bullying manner, all their courage melts down like a cabbage plant under a hot sun." But the good agent has the "tenaciousness . . . of a bulldog" which "cannot be shaken off when they fasten on the button of a victim." He will have dozens of responses to the prospective customers' single objections. He will have bribed the hotel owner or postmaster to give him information about customers' reputations and finances. For customers with credit problems, he "knows several friends who will lend . . . the prospective sum." The skilled seller "could make a bet with an outsider upon the 'time,' he will make with [the customer], with a moral certainty of winning." If customers' friends come to their defense, he will convince them, too. "Your struggles grow fainter and fainter, and when . . . you go into your 'flurry,'" the article concluded, "he places his prospectus in your hand, you mechanically affix your sign[ature] to the document and it is over."[56]

55. "An Idea for the Reader," *Flag of Our Union* 3 (18 Dec. 1847): 3; "An Offer," *Star Spangled Banner* 3 (23 June 1849): 3; "To Businessmen," *Boston Pathfinder* 3 (22 June 1848): 2.

56. "Getting Subscribers," *Yankee Blade* 34 (12 Apr. 1851): 2. The papers constantly contended with bogus agents lapping up subscription money that never found its way to the paper. For example: "We have learned that an individual, calling himself J. H. Ford, is now, or was during the last month, travelling in the neighborhood of Jackson, Tennessee, representing himself as an authorized agent for the *Yankee Blade,* and that he has been quite successful in obtaining advance pay for our paper. This is to notify our friends, and the public generally, that we have no such person travelling for us." "Caution to the Public,"

With the means of national distribution for excess production in place, the story papers managed to obtain extensive circulations. The *Flag of Our Union*, for example, a weekly, boasted a circulation of 40,000 in 1849, more than any New York daily except the New York *Sun*, with a reported 55,000 in 1851. As early as 1842, when the clock anecdote appeared, the *Universal Yankee Nation* had already reached 23,000 copies per run. These circulations, while densest in Boston and its suburbs, did in fact stretch out across the country. For example, as early as 1842, the *Universal Yankee Nation* had agents in thirty-three Massachusetts towns outside Boston, eight in Maine, one in Vermont, three each in New Hampshire, New York, and Pennsylvania, two each in Rhode Island and Connecticut, and regional agents in Cincinnati, Baltimore, Washington, Louisville, Charleston, Mobile, New Orleans, and St. Louis.[57] In 1849, the *Flag of Our Union* boasted, "the present circulation of the Flag west of New York City, *is over ten thousand copies.*"[58]

As part of their wide appeal, the story papers sold, in a manner foreshadowing modern advertising, a state of mind as much as a product for use.[59] The papers offered the reader flattery as part of their therapy. "We are informed, and we have good reason to believe," *Uncle Sam* mused in 1844, "that there is not a pretty girl within thirty miles that will not sit down to her Sunday morning breakfast before she has looked over the Uncle Sam." The editorial added, "Moreover children cry for Uncle Sam as they do for Sherman's Lozenges." Two years later the same paper made a direct appeal to vanity: "The fair sex are requested to take the 'Uncle Sam' . . . — Come blue eyes, and black eyes, walk up and put down your purses. What is it? Caroline, Mary, Jane, Maria, Esther, Angelina — Goodness! What pretty names!"[60]

---

*Yankee Blade* 8 (26 May 1849): 3. For a similar situation with book canvassers, see Ronald J. Zboray, "Book Distribution and American Culture: A 150-Year Perspective," *Book Research Quarterly* 3 (1987): 55-57. Of course, book peddlers have a long history in America, but these should be distinguished from subscription agents. See Ronald J. Zboray, "The Book Peddler and Literary Distribution: The Case of Parson Weems," *Publishing History* 25 (1989): 27-44.

57. "Agents," *Universal Yankee Nation* 3 (21 May 1842): 31.

58. *Flag of Our Union* 4 (15 Aug. 1849): 3.

59. Cf., for a later period, Roland Marchand, *Advertising the American Dream: Making Way for Modernity, 1920-1940* (Berkeley: University of California Press, 1985); Stuart Ewen, *Captains of Consciousness: Advertising and the Social Roots of the Consumer Culture* (New York: McGraw-Hill, 1976).

60. *Uncle Sam* 4 (21 Sept. 1844): 2; and 5 (2 May 1846): 2.

Above all, the story papers eschewed controversy. In this, they observed Martineau's rule about the fear of opinion, as *Uncle Sam* boasted:

There are some folks who get a living by minding their own business, and Uncle Sam is one of them. That is the reason he never meddles with politics which we take to mean the science of living by minding every body's business but one's own. Uncle Sam has no religion *to talk about*[,] thinking that folks who have most of it in their mouths usually have least of it in their hearts, he keeps his lips closed on the subject, and lives in charity with all man and woman kind.[61]

By avoiding "singularities" of party and piety, the story papers hoped to find their way into many different types of households. The *Literary World* slyly commented on this strategy of audience building when, in 1850, it published a bestiary of readers. Along with browsing giraffes, wallowing hippopotami, and sighing and indolent musk deer, the editorial gave special notice to the following type of reader: "Wild turkeys, before proceeding [to read a book,] assemble on an eminence, and remain in consultation one or two days. At length the leader gives the signal note, and taking a particular direction, is followed by the rest. Common in America."[62] The story papers in their search for readers, in short, went turkey hunting, so to speak. They did so, by the end of the 1840s, with enormous sheets that gave the papers the name of "mammouths." The *Yankee Blade,* itself one of these, complained against its gargantuan competition: "every new paper that is started looms up at once to the bed blanket size, and bases its claim of support not on the quality of its contents, but on the number of square feet it displays." The *Blade* saw, in a comic light, how size enhanced self-esteem. "It is amazing nowadays to mark the apparent connection between every man's self-importance and the size of his newspapers," the paper editorialized; "we have known several little fellows who had felt themselves to be but diminutive vegetables before, to have been transformed into Belgian giants, by their own estimation." It then goes on to report the manner in which townsfolk across America turned out in wonder to watch these papers being unfolded and read.[63]

61. *Uncle Sam* 5 (2 May 1846): 2.
62. "Readers," *Literary World* 7, no. 201 (7 Dec. 1850): 453.
63. [William Mathews], "Mammouth Newspapers," *Yankee Blade* 6 (14 Aug. 1847).

The story papers played an important and often forgotten role in the "media mix" of rural towns, especially in New England. Postmasters' lists of local subscriptions to newspapers give clues about the various types of papers coming into the locale. For example, one such account, that of T. H. Lamson of New Boston, New Hampshire, in 1853, shows the townsfolk receiving religious, agricultural, story, and general news-papers. Nearly a third of the eighty-three subscriptions in the town went to story papers: *The True Flag* (1), *Flag of Our Union* (3), *American Union* (10), and *Gleason's Pictorial Drawing Room Companion* (11). Agricultural newspapers had the second greatest number of subscribers, but even these publications — as well as the general and religious ones — sometimes carried fiction similar to that of the story papers. Although young men and women were more likely to subscribe to the story papers, it would be misleading to think that they always engaged in solitary reading or that the papers did not circulate among kin, neighbors, and, through mail exchanges, among more distant relatives and friends. One estimate put the number of readers of a single copy of a story paper at about ten. Charles Lyell, in his tour of the United States in the 1840s, noted the family setting of reading: "if I went into the houses of persons of the middle and even humblest class, I should often find the father of a family . . . reading to his wife and four or five children one of the best modern novels, which he has purchased for twenty-five cents." He took special note of cheap story papers: "they often buy in two or three successive numbers of a penny newspaper" featuring this type of fiction.[64]

Diaries occasionally give a glimpse of the way in which fiction interplayed with fact in these relatively isolated communities. Edward Jenner Carpenter, a cabinetmaker's apprentice in Greenfield, Massa-chusetts, recorded in 1844-45 several instances of this relationship, among them one surrounding a fire in a nearby town:

64. T. H. Lamson, Memorandum Book, 22 October 1853, Book Trades Collection, courtesy American Antiquarian Society. The town's population in 1850 was 1,477, accord-ing to *The Seventh Census of the United States: 1850,* comp. J. D. B. DeBow (Washington, DC: Robert Armstrong, 1853), 21. For the estimate of readers of each copy of a story paper, see *Gleason's Pictorial Drawing Room Companion* 1 (3 May 1851): 13. Charles Lyell, *A Second Visit to the United States of North America* (New York: Harper and Brothers, 1849), 152-53. For an interesting consideration of group reading patterns in the late nineteenth century, see Barbara Sicherman, "Sense and Sensibility: A Case Study of Women's Reading in Late-Victorian America," in *Reading in America: Literature and Social History,* ed. Cathy N. Davidson (Baltimore: Johns Hopkins University Press, 1989), 201-25.

I heard today that it was a brush heap that was burnt over in Deerfield last night, a good large one I guess. I went into the Democrat Office [the local paper that doubled as bookstore] this noon & bought a book called the Burglars or the Mysteries of the League of Honor. I think it is first rate. The scene is laid in Deerfield and Boston.[65]

Apparently the "hard news" — or gossip? — about the fire in Deerfield (about which there was some suspicion of arson) had some influence on Carpenter's decision to purchase a cheap (twelve and a half cents) pamphlet novel partially set in the same town and with a conspiratorial theme. Was this a way in which he tried to deal with the fear of incendiarism, or did it add a touch of romance and mystery to a common local occurrence — or, with the paradoxical logic of popular culture, was it a little bit of both? Whatever the case, the ramifications for local community life ring clear: a new "visitor" from Boston, the story paper, had come into the midst of village life and had introduced an alien voice into the interpretation of close-at-hand events.[66]

Not all towns welcomed this stranger, the story paper. For although these publications often strove to avoid offending local taste, they did so anyway, simply because sex, violence, and sensation sold papers. Throughout the 1840s, the story papers tried to balance the attraction of these topics with the preciousness of Victorian morality. The early story papers carried advertisements for abortionists and for various drugs for "female problems," unwanted pregnancy presumably being in those days the foremost.[67] In 1847, *The Yankee Blade* editorialized against New York's

65. Edward Jenner Carpenter, Journal, 1844-45, diary entry for 6 September 1844, courtesy American Antiquarian Society. The novel to which he refers is by Justin Jones (founder of the *Star Spangled Banner*) writing under the pseudonym Harry Hazel, *The Burglars; or, The Mysteries of the League of Honor. An American Tale* (Boston: Hatch and Company, 1844), and it was reprinted by another Boston story paper publisher, Frederick Gleason, a year later. On Carpenter, see Winifred C. Gates, "Journal of a Cabinet-Maker's Apprentice," *The Chronicle of the Early American Industries Association* 15 (1962): 23-24, 35-36. Christopher Clark, ed., "Edward Jenner Carpenter's 'Journal,' 1844-1845," *Proceedings of the American Antiquarian Society* 98, 2 (1989): 303-94.

66. The personification of periodicals and books occurs frequently in antebellum America. T. B. Minor, for example, published his *Farmer's Monthly Visitor* out of the Burnt-Over District in Upstate New York. There were several periodicals with similar titles, including *Musical Visitor* (1840), *Friendly Visitor* (1825), and *Christian Visitor* (1823).

67. One issue of *Uncle Sam* (3 [24 Aug. 1844]), for example, carried the following advertisements with sexual content: "Dr. Heintzelman's Concentrated syrup of Sarsaparilla [sic] . . . [ — ] Biles which arise from an impure habit of the body"; "Dr Carswell" for

infamous carriage-trade abortionist, Madame Restell (who was standing trial for what was then a misdemeanor), along with "hundreds of others, great and small, engaged in the business and . . . even medical men who claim high position." The paper pointed to the "influx of French literature, and the consequent copying of French morals and customs," as the reason for this "change of moral sentiments among women." The editorial singled out Eugene Sue's *Mysteries of Paris,* asserting that the book,

> republished, with and without plates, by cart loads in this city [New York], by the very highly reputable house of Harper and Brothers, and sent to every village in the land, details a scene in which one of the distinguished ladies of the book goes to the hotel of a physician, (which is the seat of many scenes) and there procures an abortion upon her person, and which is described with a fidelity not surpassed by the revelations in the recent trial of Madame Restall [sic].[68]

This incident suggests the emergence, among the urban middle classes, of a new ethic of family limitation, for Restell's trial revealed that prominent married women had great resort to her. Of course, the mere discussion of this scandal provided its own titillation — "to inculcate a high sense of

---

unmentioned "difficult and protracted disease"; "Pipsissewa for cure of Scrofulaoe, King's Evil"; "Goodwill's Gonnorrhoea [sic] . . . detergent"; "Dr. Peter's . . . Office of Health: diseases of a scrofulous description arising from excessive indulgence in sensual gratification"; "French Renovating Pills for obstruction of menses"; "Dr. Carswell — Gonorrhea, Gleets, Strictures, Seminal Weakness, and also Syphilis"; "The Physiology of the Wedding Night"; "Dr. Dow: married ladies laboring under obstruction from natural courses, had better consult him personally for unnatural result might follow from taking some of his medicine" [!]; "Female Medical Office, Madame Restell, Female Monthly Pills, Preventive Powders, for Married Ladies in Delicate Health"; "Dr. Dow . . . private diseases"; a testimony from a woman cured of gonorrhea; "French Periodical Pills — the only precaution necessary to be observed is that married ladies should not take them if they have reason to believe they are en                   , as they are sure to produce abortions, almost without the knowledge of the patient, so gentle yet so active are they." The advertisements with sexual content numbered 14 among 27, or almost 52 percent.

68. "Letter from New York," *Yankee Blade* 7 (27 Nov. 1847): 3. James C. Mohr, *Abortion in America: The Origins and Evolution of a National Policy, 1800-1900* (New York: Oxford University Press, 1978). Allan Keller, *Scandalous Lady: The Life and Times of Madame Restell, New York's Most Notorious Abortionist* (New York: Atheneum, 1981). By the early 1850s, the story papers were eliminating the advertisements with sexual content. For example, the *True Flag* promised its readers it would print "no advertisement of business; and none, of course, of yellow covered novelletes [sic], quack medicine, or other trash." *True Flag* 1 (1 Nov. 1851): 3.

morality, and to show, by contrast, the hideousness of vice," as the *Flag of Our Union* put it in 1849 — but readers could well draw the conclusion that they required natively written fiction to protect their morals from the corrupting influence of outsiders. Indeed, the Harpers built their fortune on the reprints of the major European popular novelists.[69] In an oblique reference to that firm, one 1836 view of literary hell ("books have souls as well as men") reserved a "worse place than all" for "American reprints of English Publications."[70]

The nationalistic story paper editors wanted to make sure that the "visitor" that came into the community spoke in a distinctly American voice — although they did not hesitate to print cheap knock-offs of European fiction and occasionally to serialize the novels themselves. But the Boston papers in particular, by the mid-1840s, began to crow about their "original," native fiction. *Uncle Sam* celebrated its fifth anniversary in 1845 by reminding its readers: "we have published more original matter, we believe, than any other paper in the Union." The prospectus for the third volume (1848) of the *Star Spangled Banner* promised, in headlines, "Great Local Novelettes." Of course, the Boston papers may have simply turned to original productions because the New York and Philadelphia publishers consistently scooped them on reprinting the latest European novels. But the issue of moral control consistently crept into the justification for native fiction: "we shall continue to give the same large amount of original matter from the pens of the best American writers; and the same strict regard will be had for the high literary tone of the paper, and the christian spirit and unexceptionable morals it inculcates," *Gleason's Pictorial Drawing Room Companion* told its readers in 1852.[71]

In search of native fiction, many of the story papers openly solicited submissions from readers and went so far as to run contests with inflated awards for the best original work.[72] The papers' editors thus became, much against their will, the recipients of a flood of written material from com-

---

69. Although the Harpers did publish nearly as much American fiction as anyone, the percentage of native material in their enormous list remained relatively small. See Eugene Exman, *The Brothers Harper: A Unique Publishing Partnership and Its Impact on the Cultural Life of America from 1817 to 1853* (New York: Harper and Row, 1965).

70. *Booksellers' Advertiser and Monthly Register of New Publications, American and Foreign* 2 (1 March 1836): 2.

71. "Courteous Readers," *Uncle Sam* 5 (20 Sept. 1845): 2; "Prospectus for Volume 3 of the Star Spangled Banner," *Star Spangled Banner* 3 (1848): 3; "Volume Second," *Gleason's Pictorial Drawing Room Companion* 2 (1852): 477.

72. In October 1848, for example, *The Flag of Our Union* ran a competition offering

mon people. "One of our prominent Boston publishing houses received on average, an application daily from authors who were desirous of bringing out books under their auspices," the *True Flag* reported in 1854. "Of course, nine tenths of these were declined."[73] From their position of power at the head of a large, rationalized factory, story paper editors began to preach to readers the virtues of the new industrial discipline applied to prose:

> Correspondents, generally, are requested to be brief. Recollect that this is the age of steam, telegraph, and phonography.[74] Time is precious, and readers want their thoughts in quintessence. Apply the hydraulic pressure, then, and condense — condense — condense. Give us none of your weak diluted mixtures. We want the very apices rerum — the tops and sums — the spirit and the life of things, extracted and abridged. Short articles take little room — give a chance for variety — look better — have more pungency and point — and, above all, are *sure to be read.* Therefore, be brief, brief, brief.[75]

The *True Flag*, in 1852, agreed with this assessment — "we would also suggest to our more youthful contributors, to study *conciseness*" — but added another note of efficiency: "amateurs and professional writers should be careful to make correct manuscripts."[76] It was becoming too expensive to invest the editorial time required to make these illiterate pieces publishable.

The *Monthly Rose* in 1849 printed a comic tale of a semi-literate

---

a $1,000 prize for the best short story — the equivalent of more than three years' wages for a skilled, white worker in antebellum America. Noel, *Villains Galore,* 33.

73. "The Book Trade," *True Flag* 3 (22 Apr. 1854): 3.

74. That is, shorthand — notably the Pitman system. The advantages of the system were consistently phrased in terms of modern technology: "Although for a long time [the genius of invention and improvement has] confined her skill to building steamboats and making railroads, constructing machinery and teaching lightning how to talk, she has not altogether forgotten the world of the intellect; and PHONOGRAPHY, her last, most promising and beneficent boon . . . afford[s] a system of writing as much superior to that of the old script alphabet, as railroads are to the ancient truck-wheeled wagon, or the electric telegraph to the post-boy's plodding gait." Elias Longley, *American Manual of Phonography, Being a Complete Guide to the Acquisition of Pitman Phonetic Shorthand* (Cincinnati: Longley Brothers, 1857).

75. Given the number of words the editor himself used to make his simple point, the sins of his authors must have been mortal indeed. *Yankee Blade* 8 (26 May 1849): 3.

76. *True Flag,* 22 May 1852, 3.

novelist trying to get a manuscript published at the "Stars and Stripes of Our Beloved Country." The lad appeared on the publishing premises with "a pseudo-Byronic air" — meaning a poet's shirt revealing an expanse of chest that qualified him for more than "ordinary" inattention. The manuscript bore the title: "The Mesteryous Organest, or the Weevers daughter [sic]." On the promise of this, the house puzzled over it that night, in a useless attempt "to discover the plot." The editor returned it to him the next day, saying he could not use it "owing to an overstock in the market." He advised him to go to a "publisher of cheap novels" where he was certain to get "a round sum for his labors."[77]

The *True Flag* in 1849 went so far as to give its readers advice on writing stories. The message followed Edgar Allan Poe's doctrine of the single effect achieved with attention to the slightest detail. "The author should commence deliberately and build up not a shapeless, rugged structure, but a well arranged pile, in which every gem and ornament has its proper place, and which increases in beauty, or grandeur, as it arrives at the pointed, glittering spire." Although Poe wrote but "three or four good stories," the tutorial continued, he understood better than anyone "the mechanism of a good story."[78]

The synchrony between the rationalized, mechanical process of production in the fiction factories that produced the story papers and the technology of storytelling in the content of those publications cannot be underestimated. In the ordered rhythms of machines can be found the rationale for modern rituals of cultural construction — attempts at building new illusions of community based on common reception of media.[79] The machinery of prose conveyed the authority of technique, an "operational aesthetic," to an audience that would pay to be humbugged by a Barnum . . . and then shell out more to hear him tell them how he did it.[80]

77. "A Novel Writer," *Monthly Rose: A Flower of Home Culture for All Seasons,* "Bouquet" 4 (March 1849): 2.

78. "Story Telling," *True Flag,* 7 Feb. 1852, 3.

79. For its integrity as a usable concept for social scientists, "community," which requires a good deal of face-to-face interaction, must not be confused with its various analogues in which communication might be conducted through letter writing, print, or other media. For a fuller discussion, see Ronald J. Zboray, *A Fictive People: Antebellum Economic Development and the American Reading Public* (New York: Oxford University Press, 1992), 231n.37.

80. See the chapter "The Operational Aesthetic" in Neil Harris, *Humbug: The Art of P. T. Barnum* (Boston: Little, Brown, 1973). Phineas T. Barnum, *The Humbugs of the World: An Account of the Humbugs, Delusions, Impositions, Quackeries, Deceits and Deceivers Generally, in All Ages* (New York: Carleton, 1866).

Technological change thus stood for much more in antebellum America than mere improvements in the physical expression of capital and the resultant increase in output.[81] Most other nations have industrialized without enshrining technology in their public consciousness.[82] In other countries cultural traditions make an uneasy peace at best with technical innovation. But the consistent enthusiasm with which most Americans embraced mechanization suggests a deeper, healing use of the metaphor of the machine, one that goes beyond nuts, bolts, and profits.[83]

The press of the time, for example, describes many fictitious inventions that act as often humorous metaphorical solutions to problems. A typical article of this sort appeared in the New Orleans *Daily Picayune* the same month in which it reported "monomania." The article begins by holding out the hope that the embryonic inventions it describes will "impel" economically depressed New Orleans to "prosperity so fast forward, that the only thing to be feared is, that men cannot keep pace with the accumulation of their fortunes." One "wonderful piece of mechanism" had the ability to clear forests, plant corn, bake buckwheat cakes, and ship

81. Actually, the gains in productivity between the artisanal and industrial modes may have been much smaller than previously thought. See Kenneth L. Sokoloff, "Was the Transition from the Artisanal Shop to the Small Factory Associated With a Gain in Efficiency? Evidence from the U.S. Manufacturing Censuses of 1820 and 1850," *Explorations in Economic History* 21 (1984): 351-82; Bruce Laurie and Mark Schmitz, "Manufacture and Productivity: The Making of an Industrial Base, Philadelphia, 1850-1880," in *Philadelphia: Work, Space, Family, and Group Experience in the Nineteenth Century,* ed. Theodore Hershberg (New York: Oxford University Press, 1981); and John A. James, "Structural Change in U.S. Manufacturing, 1850-1890," *Journal of Economic History* 43 (1983): 443-60. For a different view, consult Jeremy Atack, "Economies of Scale and Efficiency Gains in the Rise of the Factory in America, 1820-1900," in *Quantity and Quiddity: Essays in United States Economic History,* ed. Peter Kilby (Middletown, CT: Wesleyan University Press, 1987).

82. Thomas P. Hughes's *American Genesis: A Century of Invention and Technological Enthusiasm, 1870-1970* (New York: Viking, 1989) is only one of the latest works to argue for the centrality of technology in defining the character of American civilization.

83. With a different, but not necessarily opposing view, Leo Marx in his classic *Machine in the Garden: Technology and the Pastoral Ideal in America* (New York: Oxford University Press, 1964), 145-226, discusses the nuances of the public reception of the machine metaphor in America. See also John Kasson, *Civilizing the Machine: Technology and Republican Values in America* (New York: Grossman, 1976); Daniel Boorstin, *The Republic of Technology: Reflections on Our Future Community* (New York: Harper & Row, 1978); and, for the political and social importance of the machine metaphor, Dolores Greenberg, "Energy, Power, and Perceptions of Social Change in the Early Nineteenth Century," *American Historical Review* 95 (1990): 693-714.

American flour to England "all at the same time!" Another, called "A Universal Currency Provider, or Varying Vegetable Producer," could turn cabbage into a wide array of other vegetables. The third invention promised "to convert clams into clucking hens, Mother Cary's chickens into hard-boiled eggs, and 'Pease's hoarhound candy' into apple dumplings." The paper concluded the article with a simple marriage of two contemporary clichés: "Go ahead, humbug!"[84]

These visions of transformational devices — the first seemed to be intended to replace slave labor — suggest the therapeutic uses of the image of the machine in its classic guise of order, system, and predictability. In situations in which a chaotic or threatening condition affected several people, the literary performance of humorously mechanizing a solution momentarily united them into an audience, a group of "hearers." The fanciful invention acknowledged the shared problem — in this case the real local economic woes belying the go-ahead spirit — by imaginatively solving it within the context of public faith in the machine. The catharsis of humor, insofar as it makes the hearers chuckle, unites them into an illusionary community of reception. From many, one: the machine metaphor, understood equally by all, brought together for a moment a "community" of people whose own viewpoints would have clashed had they been expressed in the social and political solutions that the machine metaphor finesses.[85]

For example, the fictive slave machine discussed above subtly comments on the frustrations of the inefficiencies of bonded labor without arousing opposing interpretations of solutions to the problem. Logical approaches would include the following: punish the slaves more, reward them with incentives, or end slavery altogether and replace it with wage labor. Yet the perceived necessity of the peculiar institution of slavery in the South essentially foreclosed meaningful public discussion. Each of these solutions to the problem represented a critical viewpoint toward

84. "Enterprise," *Daily Picayune*, 7 Oct. 1842, 2.
85. This is not to say that the specific reality of mechanization was always easily accepted, especially by those workers whom it might affect most intimately. See Merritt Roe Smith, *Harpers Ferry Armory and the New Technology: The Challenge of Change* (Ithaca, NY: Cornell University Press, 1977). For the acceptance of the machine, see Anthony F. C. Wallace, *Rockdale: The Growth of an American Village in the Early Industrial Revolution* (New York: Alfred A. Knopf, 1978). Rosalind Williams's work is ushering in a new sophistication in the socially symbolic analysis of technology; see her *Dream Worlds: Mass Consumption in Late Nineteenth Century France* (Berkeley: University of California Press, 1982) and *Notes on the Underground: An Essay on Technology, Society, and Imagination* (Cambridge, MA: Harvard University Press, 1990).

slavery that might estrange the others. In short, discussion in this case would lead more to community division than to cohesion. Yet the humorous metaphor of the machine worked the magic of transcending such oppositional views while acknowledging the existence of a problem, one perceived mutually by parties who might otherwise disagree. The machine metaphor, in this case, forged a symbolic community.

Little wonder that contemporary speeches, songs, and print culture brim with references to the age of steam, the railroad, and the telegraph. The machine promised therapy for Americans experiencing the shocks of early industrial capitalism.[86] The nation went through this transformation without the buffer of a unified, traditional culture, supported by an un-equivocal locus of authority. As part of the American democratic political paradox as it evolved after the Revolution, authority became depersonal-ized and derived from an abstraction, the "people" — a trope that more or less inverted downward the divine right of kings but indeed largely ignored the pluralistic, civic definition of the sum of people in the United States.[87] The "people mystical" required few rituals, however, as long as persistent community structures assured an operational authority grounded in the everyday material life of the family and the locale.[88]

As a popular legacy of the Enlightenment, most people still had faith in Reason and the underlying order of the universe set in motion by God, the Creator. (Some Christian denominations added varying degrees of interven-tionism to his role.) Like a watch or an orrery, the universe spun its course calmly and predictably. In this environment, knowledge could well be power, and people could pursue extensive patterns of reading of non-fiction printed material and still hope to remain mentally centered in the community.[89]

---

86. Most Americans would feel the maturation of industrial capitalism first not through direct contact with mechanization (i.e., as wage-remunerated operators of machin-ery) but through the reorganization and intensification of work, the growth of the wage labor market, the commercialization of agriculture, and the emerging patterns of national distribution.

87. In this regard, it is telling that Edmund S. Morgan uses "invention" as a key concept in his penetrating analysis of these themes, *Inventing the People: The Rise of Popular Sovereignty in England and America* (New York: Norton, 1988).

88. On the rituals of nationality, see Wilbur Zelinsky, *Nation into State: The Shifting Symbolic Foundations of American Nationalism* (Chapel Hill: University of North Carolina Press, 1988); and for the way in which reading played into these, see Zboray, *A Fictive People.*

89. "Knowledge is Power" is, of course, from Francis Bacon (1597). Richard D. Brown, *Knowledge Is Power: The Diffusion of Information in Early America, 1700-1865*

But with the rapid development of antebellum America, knowledge — too much of the wrong sort — could also mean loneliness, alienation, irreligion, immorality, a lack of patriotism, and, perhaps, madness, a Mephistophelian accompaniment to the demise of community and its replacement by singularity. "People disparage knowing and the intellectual life, and urge doing," Emerson commented in 1850; "I am very content with knowing, if only I could know."[90] Under the democratic ethos, the individual was supposed to be a "representative man," the standard bearer of common sense that, if sound, could lead others to the future empire of reason. The mid-nineteenth century is littered with pathetic geniuses or poets of the Democratic Spirit who moved forward expecting the "nation" to follow, only to look behind them and discover they were quite alone. Truth and democracy did not necessarily coincide. Industrialization had fractured the commonality of "sense" and left only divergent, self-seeking opinion and social distrust. Knowledge could simply reduce to pretending to it but not possessing it. Cultural leadership could devolve to mere hopeless candidacy.

To triumph over the vagaries of circumstance and to prove their public trustworthiness, the confidence men and painted women of the period sought a portable, self-contained, yet socially validated "character."[91] But that attainment itself implied a fictional, almost mechanistic, and widely apprehendable social construction — something that the fiction in story papers and elsewhere could readily provide. For the audience drew from characters the expectation of plot. For example, the mere appearance in a story of a roué and a poor, virtuous milliner summons up the likelihood of attempted seduction. The specific characters thus embody only a limited range of future action and reaction. So, too, could individuals achieve "continent, persisting, immovable" character (adjectives Emerson applied) in the face of the power of mass forces and distracting passions. Emerson himself realized the mechanistic metaphor and extended it: people of character "have in this phlegm or gravity of their nature a quality which answers to the fly-wheel in a mill which distributes

(New York: Oxford University Press, 1989); and William S. Gilmore, *Reading Becomes a Necessity of Life: Material and Cultural Life in New England, 1780-1835* (Knoxville: University of Tennessee Press, 1989).

90. Ralph Waldo Emerson, "Experience," in *Essays: Second Series* (Boston: Phillips, Sampson, 1850), 85.

91. Karen Halttunen, *Confidence Men and Painted Women: A Study of Middle-Class Culture in America, 1830-1870* (New Haven: Yale University Press, 1982).

the motion equably over all the wheels and hinders it from falling un-
equally and suddenly in destructive shocks."[92]

The machine's various manifestations — whether in the formulaic
plots of the story papers,[93] or in the character consciously achieved by
self-repressive Victorians, or in the various contraptions that put in ap-
pearances in lyceums, or in the physical expressions of capitalist development such as railroad and steamboat — all carried, to some extent, a script
of consensus building, the construction of surrogate communities for those
lost during economic development. For in front of everyone's eyes stood
"mechanism" — an embodiment of order that all could appraise on a
utilitarian basis: Did it work? Did the story emotionally affect the reader?
Did the man of character impress his solidity upon others? Did the electric
demonstration illuminate the audience? Did the conveyance get travelers
where they wanted to go in reasonable time and with comfort?

The metaphor of the machine, applied so liberally throughout the
culture, helped Americans to reconstruct a human assemblage akin to the
old communities that industrialism undermined. The commonality of
understanding that Americans found in the authority they delegated to
mechanism proved to be a physical expression of a newly formulated
"common" sense. As the price of this machine-built community, antebellum Americans sloughed off the dread of singularity, the threat of division,
and — not just a little — the integrity of personal vision. In so doing,
they could walk together into the modern, impersonal, and increasingly
technological universal Yankee nation.

That nation, in late October 1842, received word of some obscure
man in New Orleans who decided to impersonate a clock. His name is
now forgotten, as are the conditions that led to his self-destructive behavior. The crowd of onlookers saw a story in it, the story papers reported
it, and their readers probably shook their heads and smiled. They "knew"
the story as much as they knew themselves. In this larger view, the mechanistic beating of this man's head against the steamboat boiler reverberates
through the industrial epoch, as people learned to act — and to treat their
fellow humans — like machines.

A few years later, Aleksandr Lakier, a Russian visiting New York City,

92. Emerson, 17 January 1841, in A. W. Plumstead and Harrison Hayford, *The
Journals and Miscellaneous Notes of Ralph Waldo Emerson*, vol. 7, 1838-1842 (Cambridge,
MA: Harvard University Press, 1969).

93. For a discussion of the formulas, see John G. Cawelti, *Adventure, Mystery,
Romance* (Chicago: University of Chicago Press, 1976).

was disturbed at the number of "people on the street running about with preoccupied expressions," and the absence of "stroller[s] among them who might have come out for a bit of fresh air, or to admire the clear sky, or to dream a bit." With the new work-time discipline, an older sense of community — even as elusively expressed in casual gestures on a boulevard — had withered. It was replaced by a scarcely analogous, technologically rooted mass culture, of which the story papers were but one early expression.

Lakier, however, wisely refused to believe that people could be so devoid of the most fundamental human tendencies. He wondered, "perhaps they dream on the run here."[94] To help them run faster into industrial capitalism, while assuaging their sense of loss from the world left behind, the story papers and their progeny — from dime novels to television sitcoms — would indeed bequeath to future Americans a shared dream or two.

94. Lakier, *A Russian Looks at America*, 141.

# The Millennium and the Media

## James H. Moorhead

In 1793, the year in which the second administration of President George Washington began, the Reverend Samuel Hopkins of Newport, Rhode Island, published *A Treatise on the Millennium*. Most of Hopkins's description of the coming happy time stressed its religious features, especially the nearly universal piety that would reign then; but the *Treatise* also indicated that the millennium would include a revolution in knowledge. The thousand years would bring "a great increase of light and knowledge to a degree vastly beyond what has been before," even children surpassing "the highest attainments in these things, of the oldest men who have lived in former ages." The happy result of increased knowledge would be unity of sentiment, the end of denominational squabbles, and a shared faith based on a common understanding of the Bible. Improved material and technological conditions would play a role in bringing about these results. Due to advances in mechanical arts, the denizens of the millennium would need to spend only two or three hours a day in physical toil. "And the rest of their time they will be disposed to spend in reading and conversation, and in all those exercises which are necessary and proper, in order to improve their minds, and make progress in knowledge, especially in the knowledge of divinity." Hopkins assumed that there would also be more efficient ways to teach children to read and write — tasks that would be simplified by the fact that a universal language would be adopted. He expected that means would become available for people "by which they will be able to communicate their ideas, and hold intercourse and correspondence with each other, who live in different parts of the world, with much less expense of time and labour, perhaps a hundred times less, than that with which men now correspond." Hopkins also anticipated that advances in printing would render books "very cheap" and that every person would own at least one Bible. In short, Samuel Hopkins predicted a communications revolution, rooted in technological advance, as one of the marks of the latter-day glory.[1]

Although he regarded these events as ancillary features of the coming age, Hopkins had nevertheless evoked themes that resonated ever more insistently in Protestant thought down to the Civil War. Writing of features of the millennium in 1818, the Reverend Joseph Emerson asked: "May we not expect that every cottage will be irradiated with science, as well as with religion; and that every peasant will be able not only to read the Bible but to read the stars? — to read the stars with more than Newtonian eyes?"[2] Nearly forty years later, when Presbyterian minister Nathan L. Rice commented on the "signs of the times," he saw evidence of the impending millennium in the "rapidity of travel, the consequent increase of intercourse between the different nations, and the amazing facility of communicating intelligence." In this "providential arrangement" lay the means of history's consummation. "From the more enlightened, free and prosperous [nations], light will be diffused through the darker masses, and liberal principles will triumph, in spite of the efforts of tyranny[,] and every important change will become universal in its consequences."[3] Inspired by such visions, many Protestants avidly seized upon the medium of print to help inaugurate the millennium. Others, believing that human agency could not establish the kingdom of God on earth, no less gladly turned to the technology of communication. If they could not use the medium to establish the kingdom of God, they could at least employ it to sound the alarm that the coming of the Lord was at hand. Either way, the use of the latest, most efficient means of communication — and in the nineteenth century this of course meant print — had become an eschatological imperative.

---

1. *The Works of Samuel Hopkins,* 3 vols., ed. Bruce Kuklick (1865; repr. New York and London: Garland Publishing, 1987), 2:273, 274, 276, 287, 290-91.

2. Joseph Emerson, *Lectures on the Millennium* (Boston: Samuel T. Armstrong, 1818), 78.

3. Nathan L. Rice, *The Signs of the Times* (St. Louis: Keith and Woods, 1855), 17, 18-19.

# I

The zeal with which Protestants turned to the use of printed matter in the early nineteenth century was perhaps to be expected. From the beginning, Protestantism had emphasized a theology of the Word; and the sixteenth-century Reformers had used print as a major weapon in their struggle to reform Christendom. Belief in the religious importance of that medium persisted in colonial America, where in New England, for example, literacy was stressed in order that the Scriptures might be accessible. Between the late 1700s and the mid-1800s, however, the culture of print altered significantly. Improved printing and paper-making technologies encouraged mass production at cheaper prices. New labor arrangements in printing shops increased efficiency; and improved transportation — especially the introduction of the railroad — as well as the development of the postal service permitted a wider distribution of reading materials at less expense. The world of print, in short, moved from a condition of relative scarcity to abundance. Using newspapers alone as an example, one may point to a dramatic increase in numbers, from fewer than 100 in 1790 to over 370 twenty years later.

The change was apparent not only in the increased volume of printed matter but also in the diversity of the material. In the colonial period, persons had been restricted to a few staples of reading — perhaps a Bible, an almanac, a devotional classic or two, a newspaper or journal. Now, in addition to these, there were great numbers of novels, self-help treatises, and etiquette books, to name only a few of the available options. Moreover, persons in the early national period had a heightened awareness of the power of print, especially of newspapers and pamphlets, to mobilize popular opinion — a power that had been amply demonstrated by the press during the Revolutionary crisis. The nineteenth century reconfirmed that lesson, as political parties won adherents through partisan newspapers, and as abolitionists, despite their relatively small numbers, gained notoriety via the medium of print. But in the final analysis, the communications revolution derived from an altered consciousness as much as it did from the efficacy of technology. As Americans became enthusiastic republicans, they believed a well-informed citizenry to be a necessity and the attainment of knowledge to be a patriotic duty.[4] Or as the Reverend Robert Baird

4. Richard D. Brown, *Knowledge Is Power: The Diffusion of Information in Early America, 1700-1865* (New York: Oxford University Press, 1989); Bernard Bailyn and

explained in 1844: "Ignorance is incompatible with the acquisition or preservation of any freedom worth possessing; and above all, such a republic as that of the United States must depend for its very existence on the wide diffusion of sound knowledge and religious principles among all classes of the people."[5]

Most Protestants, sharing Baird's sentiments and committed to extending Christian influence, recognized the necessity of coming to terms with the communications revolution. To be sure, they were not willing to endorse every genre of literature and considered some beyond redemptive use. Despite the increasing popularity of religious fiction, for example, many felt uneasy with it and regarded it as subversive of moral purity.[6] Likewise, many thought that the secular newspaper was hopelessly corrupt — a "stepping-stone to hell" the Presbyterian Board of Publication called it near mid-century.[7] Along with Philip Schaff, some even had misgivings about religious periodicals and feared that "such reading," while tending "to diffuse a kind of culture among all classes of the people . . . kills taste for the study of solid books, and dissipates the mind almost as much as novel reading." But Schaff also spoke for most when he acknowledged that, for weal or woe, the popular press was there to stay and that the only realistic strategy was "to labor to make it more and more the vehicle and lever of truth and virtue."[8]

Protestants sought this end through religious newspapers, tracts, and Sunday school materials. In 1800, the religious newspaper was an oddity; within several decades it was ubiquitous. In his study of the religious

---

John B. Hench, eds., *The Press and the American Revolution* (Boston: Northeastern University Press, 1980); William L. Joyce, David D. Hall, Richard D. Brown, and John B. Hench, eds., *Printing and Society in Early America* (Worcester: American Antiquarian Society, 1983); Leonard L. Richards, *"Gentlemen of Property and Standing": Anti-Abolition Mobs in Jacksonian America* (New York: Oxford University Press, 1970); William J. Gilmore, *Reading Becomes a Necessity of Life: Material and Cultural Life in Rural New England, 1780-1835* (Knoxville: University of Tennessee Press, 1989).

5. Robert Baird, *Religion in America*, ed. Henry Warner Bowden (1844; New York: Harper & Row, 1970), 136-37.

6. For an account of the triumph of the religious novel, see David S. Reynolds, *Faith in Fiction: The Emergence of Religious Literature in America* (Cambridge, MA: Harvard University Press, 1981).

7. Quoted in Anna Jane Moyer, "The Making of Many Books: 125 Years of Presbyterian Publishing, 1838-1963," *Journal of Presbyterian History* 41 (Sept. 1963): 125.

8. Philip Schaff, *America: A Sketch of Its Political, Social and Religious Characteristics*, ed. Perry Miller (1855; repr. Cambridge, MA: Belknap Press of Harvard University Press, 1961), 65.

newspaper in the Old Northwest, for example, Wesley Norton discovered that in that region alone such papers had a circulation of 40,000 by 1840 and approximately five times that figure twenty years later. By 1850, the Methodist Book Concern, the most successful publisher in the region, employed twenty-five printers and forty-six binders in order to publish five periodicals. The New England Tract Society, founded in 1814 and later fashioned into the American Tract Society, provided vast quantities of religious literature at cheap prices and subsequently began a systematic and immensely successful program of colportage to distribute its materials. The denominations followed suit. For example, Old School Presbyterians had by 1850 created their own publishing enterprise, with over sixty colporteurs in the field. Similarly, the American Sunday School Union issued several magazines, produced scores of cheap books, and through a system of missionaries and auxiliary organizations secured the dissemination of those items.[9] The list of antebellum publishing ventures could be extended almost indefinitely. What Anne Boylan has written of the Sunday School Union's program might stand as an assessment of religious publishing in general in the antebellum period:

> At a time when the United States had few national institutions, virtually no national communications network . . . , and no national corporations, the management of the American Sunday School Union established the framework for what was, in effect, a national evangelical corporation. In their mind's eye, the union was the center of an evangelical community whose members, though widely scattered, were bound together by participation in a common institution and use of a common literature.[10]

Despite lingering fears of the evil potential of popular print, Protestants frequently placed their forays in the medium within a millennial perspective. For example, the ninth report of the New England Tract Society in 1823 urged potential contributors to consider how their efforts might shape a grand future. "Look down the lapse of ages; see numerous

9. David Paul Nord, "The Evangelical Origins of Mass Media, 1815-1835," *Journalism Monographs* 88 (1984); Wesley Norton, *Religious Newspapers in the Old Northwest to 1861: A History, Bibliography, and Record of Opinion* (Athens: Ohio University Press, 1977), 4-5; Moyer, "The Making of Many Books," 130; Anne M. Boylan, *Sunday School: The Formation of an American Institution* (New Haven: Yale University Press, 1988), 68-73.

10. Boylan, *Sunday School,* 73.

generations rising up in the fear of the Lord, as fruits of the seed you are now sowing." Seven years later the annual report sounded the millennial theme even more explicitly: those who disseminated tracts — or paid for this endeavor — were laying "the foundation for millions and millions of silent but pungent preachers of righteousness to go forth and speak each one to an individual, a family, a neighborhood, till they shall have no need to say any more, 'Know ye the Lord, for all shall know him from the least to the greatest;' and the whole 'earth be filled with the knowledge of the glory of the Lord, as the waters fill the sea.'"[11]

In 1833 William Cogswell, Secretary of the American Education Society, argued the same case more systematically in his appropriately titled *Harbinger of the Millennium.* The book reviewed the panoply of benevolent and evangelical enterprises sponsored by Protestants and concluded that these were portents of the coming kingdom of God. Among these evidences printed matter played a major role. Foremost was the distribution of the Bible, which, thanks to technological improvements, could now be sold at an extraordinarily cheap rate "till it shall reach every clime and nation under Heaven." Almost as important as the dissemination of the Scriptures was the spread of the tract.

> "The Bible Society is often and appropriately compared to the sun. But if the Bible society is the sun, the Tract society is the atmospheric medium that reflects the glorious rays, and throws them into every dark corner of the earth." Tracts impart pious instruction in a perspicuous, concise, and interesting manner. They must, therefore, be productive of the happiest effects. In these unassuming advocates of the cross, may be found a word in season, for the intemperate, the profane, and the Sabbath-breaker; for parents and children; for the high and the low, the rich and the poor, the righteous, and unrighteous, the civilized and uncivilized. . . . Are not these things a sign of the Millennium's approach?[12]

When the invention of the telegraph promised to speed communications even further and to permit the rapid printing of information from

---

11. *Proceedings of the First Ten Years of the American Tract Society* (Boston: Flagg and Gould, 1824), 102. The New England Tract Society changed its name to the American Tract Society in 1823; two years later it merged with other groups to form a national organization by the same name.

12. William Cogswell, *The Harbinger of the Millennium* (Boston: Peirce and Parker, 1833), 34, 55-66.

around the globe, many Protestants responded with equal zeal. A writer in a Methodist magazine for women observed in 1850: "This noble invention is to be the means of extending civilization, republicanism and Christianity over the earth. . . . Then will wrong and injustice be forever banished. Every yoke shall be broken, and the oppressed go free. . . . Then shall come to pass the millennium" — a happy time described by the author in the familiar verse: "all shall know him, from the least of them unto the greatest."[13] In 1858, at the fiftieth anniversary celebration of Andover Seminary, word arrived that a transatlantic telegraph cable had been successfully laid. Amid cheers, the waving of hats, and thumping on tables, those assembled joyfully sang, "Jesus shall reign where e'er the sun."[14]

Such confidence in the media appeared to find corroboration in religious revivals. As early as the Great Awakening of the 1740s, newly founded evangelical magazines, such as Thomas Prince's *The Christian History*, served as "clearinghouses for tidings about the revival."[15] In reporting awakenings in various communities, these organs were not merely conveying information; they were also providing models for imitation and thereby acting as instruments for the extension of the revival. Although Prince's paper was short-lived and probably occupied only a minor place in the Awakening (still largely dominated by oral communication), the role of the religious press in subsequent revivals and in the evangelical activity of the Second Great Awakening was more pronounced. The press promoted the various benevolent activities so characteristic of evangelical Protestantism in the antebellum period. Without the religious press to disseminate stories of struggling missionaries, successful conversions, and the like, the various voluntary and denominational organizations probably could not have mobilized a clientele sufficient to support their endeavors.[16]

13. Joseph Brady, "The Magnetic Telegraph," *Ladies' Repository* 10 (Feb. 1850): 61-62.

14. D. H. Meyer, *The Instructed Conscience: The Shaping of the American National Ethic* (Philadelphia: University of Pennsylvania Press, 1972), 123-24.

15. "Editor's Introduction," in Jonathan Edwards, *Apocalyptic Writings,* ed. Stephen J. Stein (New Haven: Yale University Press, 1977), 31; John E. Van de Wetering, "The *Christian History* of the Great Awakening," *Journal of Presbyterian History* 44 (June 1966): 122-29.

16. On the importance of oral style to the Great Awakening, see Harry S. Stout, "Religion, Communications, and the Ideological Origins of the American Revolution," *William and Mary Quarterly* 34 (Oct. 1977): 519-40. A thoughtful analysis of the role of printing in the evangelical activities of the early nineteenth century is provided by Joan

By the mid-nineteenth century, the press appeared powerful enough to generate a nationwide revival of religion almost by itself. In 1857, a prayer meeting began in the Dutch Reformed Church on Fulton Street, New York City. Other churches in the area soon followed suit. When Horace Greeley's *Tribune* and other papers (secular and religious) picked up the story, the Prayer Meeting Revival became a national event, prompting similar worship services in other cities and towns across the United States. The press in turn reported the success of these derivative meetings and thereby spawned further imitation. The revival was dominated by no single figure. No Whitefield, Finney, or Moody stood in the vanguard — though the latter two labored as foot soldiers in the revival, in Boston and Chicago, respectively. The Prayer Meeting Revival of 1857-58, however, needed no such charismatic leaders, for once begun it continued via the power of newspaper and telegraph. Therefore, it was highly appropriate that the first history of the revival was drawn largely from reports in Horace Greeley's *New York Tribune*.[17] Surveying this scene in late 1858, one writer was moved to declare: "The very newspapers, cleansed from defilement, have been polished into mirrors which reflect the divine glory to the darkest and most distant parts of the country. . . . In light of these great facts, is not our age a modern Pentecost, and our republic a modern Jerusalem, from which shall issue streams of converting power destined to exert a mighty influence in purifying our corrupted world?"[18]

In short, many Protestants in the antebellum period had deepened their faith in the media's role relative to the latter-day glory. Whereas Samuel Hopkins believed that improved printing and widespread diffusion of knowledge would be marks of the kingdom of God, his nineteenth-century successors viewed these as instruments by which the church could inaugurate the millennium, and that optimistic assessment merged with faith in the saving potential of technology in general. Such notions, of

Jacobs Brumberg, *Mission for Life: The Story of the Family of Adoniram Judson* (New York: Free Press, 1980), 44-78.

17. Timothy L. Smith, *Revivalism and Social Reform: American Protestantism on the Eve of the Civil War* (1957; repr. New York: Harper & Row, 1965), 63-79; Russell E. Francis, "Pentecost: 1858. A Study in Religious Revivals" (Ph.D. diss., University of Pennsylvania, 1948); William C. Conant, *Narratives of Remarkable Conversions and Revival Incidents* (New York: Derby and Jackson, 1858), 357-441.

18. J. M. Leavitt, "The Relation of Our Republic to Other Nations," *Ladies' Repository* 18 (Nov. 1858): 660.

course, comported well with the postmillennialism which was the dominant eschatology among leading Protestant spokespersons before the Civil War and which Methodist Bishop Leonidas L. Hamline described so succinctly:

> Although Divine power will effect this new creation [i.e., the millennium], it will not be by miracle. It will be a gradual, not an instantaneous work. It will be, not like the springing up of worlds from chaos, but like the stealing dawn or the cautious tread of Spring, its march will be clandestine, and its gentle, noiseless conquests will be almost unobserved among the nations. . . . The knowledge of God, or of his truth diffused throughout the earth is to transform it into holiness and beauty.[19]

And it was the diffusion of the knowledge of God that the new technology promised.

Yet it would be a serious error to infer that only those of postmillennial persuasion could appreciate the eschatological significance of the media. For example, George Duffield, one of the best-known expositors of premillennialism in the antebellum period, believed that the "great increase of knowledge" in the nineteenth century was a sign of the latter days. Although he had in mind chiefly the flourishing of biblical studies (especially the study of prophecy), Duffield also included as a sign of the times a more generalized increase of knowledge. "Never was there a day so marked with advancement in science, improvement in the arts, and the diffusion of general intelligence, by the pulpit, the press, and the public lecturers, as the present." But unlike many postmillennialists who saw this burgeoning knowledge as likely to help inaugurate the kingdom of God, Duffield offered the jaundiced assessment that these "improvements . . . instead of promoting general virtue and religion, are leading men away from God." Yet even in this negative fashion, the media contributed a sign that the end was near. Moreover, Duffield's own practice of writing on the subject of the Second Coming implied that the media had another eschatological function: to proclaim the end as a witness to the ends of the earth.[20]

Premillennialism owed its dissemination chiefly to the medium of

19. *Works of Rev. Leonidas L. Hamline, D.D.: Sermons,* ed. F. G. Hibbard (Cincinnati: Hitchcock and Walden, 1869), 337.

20. George Duffield, *Dissertations on the Prophecies Relative to the Second Coming of Jesus Christ* (New York: Dayton and Newman, 1842), 375-76.

print. Initially persons of this persuasion resorted to the publication of occasional books, sermons, or pamphlets. By the early nineteenth century, these means began to receive a supplement through newspapers and magazines. For example, Elias Smith, a leader of the Christian Connection in New England, started in 1808 the biweekly *Herald of Gospel Liberty,* which promoted, among other causes, premillennialism.[21] The British millenarian revival, originating in large measure as an attempt to fit the cataclysmic events of the French Revolution into the scheme of biblical prophecy, also exerted influence in the United States through the wide circulation of its books and periodicals. *The Literalist* provides a case in point. Published in Philadelphia between 1840 and 1842, the magazine filled its pages with republications of British millenarian works. The same decade also witnessed two other important premillennial ventures: *The American Millenarian and Prophetic Review* (1842-44) and David Lord's *Theological and Literary Journal,* beginning in 1848.[22]

Yet these publications, while important as forerunners of the premillennialism that would become increasingly common after the Civil War, remained inconsequential by comparison to the greatest millenarian publishing venture of the antebellum era: the Millerite campaign to sound the midnight cry. William Miller, a prosperous farmer from New York and Vermont, was converted to Christianity from Deism in the years after the War of 1812. Devoting himself to the study of biblical prophecy, he concluded that Christ would return about 1843. For a number of years, Miller said little regarding his views; but after a Baptist congregation issued him a license to preach in 1832, he began expounding his theories from various pulpits and in print. His audience remained limited until he encountered Joshua Himes in 1839. A Christian Connection minister with strong ties to William Lloyd Garrison, Himes systematically organized a media campaign to advertise the Adventist message. He prepared an edition of Miller's works and founded several newspapers, the best-known being *The Midnight Cry,* which claimed to have distributed 600,000 copies during five months in 1842. In addition, Himes started Adventist libraries — collections of Adventist books and pamphlets — available at cheap prices; and by encouraging the formation of local Adventist associations,

21. Nathan Hatch, "Elias Smith and the Rise of Religious Journalism in the Early Republic," in *Printing and Society,* ed. Joyce et al., 25-77.
22. Ernest R. Sandeen, *The Roots of Fundamentalism: British and American Millenarianism, 1800-1930* (Chicago: University of Chicago Press, 1970), 55, 90.

he created a distribution network for these works. He also aroused popular interest by holding camp meetings and by constructing a great tent that could hold several thousand persons. Carted about the Northeast to various meeting sites in 1842, the tent served as a powerful gimmick to draw the curious. How successful Himes was in focusing public attention on the Millerite message may be judged from the fact that Greeley's *New York Tribune* issued an extra number on 2 March 1843 to explore the Adventist message.[23] Although Millerism subsided into fragments of its former self after the failure of the prediction of the End, Himes had demonstrated more convincingly than any other contemporary figure the extraordinary potential of the press to mobilize a mass movement around millennial symbolism.

## II

The medium of print, however, did more than disseminate eschatological ideas; it also helped to reshape millennialism itself. One may discern at least four changes in the millennial thought of the antebellum period: an increasing fascination with technique and technology, a greater emphasis in certain quarters upon the most vivid or dramatic images of the last things, a growing diversity of millennial interpretations, and the first hints of a major schism between learned approaches to millennialism and its popular versions.

Fascination with technique and technology was readily apparent among postmillennialists. To understand this fact, one needs to recall the context in which postmillennialism arose and flourished. Although the eschatology existed before the 1790s, it did not emerge as a distinct philosophy of history until that time; and it did so at precisely the moment when Protestants began systematically organizing a variety of benevolent organizations to conquer the world for Christ. In fact, many of the writers of postmillennial treatises were intimately connected with one or more of these societies and saw in that eschatology exactly what was needed to win support for the benevolent empire. It reminded individuals that they must

23. Ronald L. Numbers and Jonathan M. Butler, eds., *The Disappointed: Millerism and Millennialism in the Nineteenth Century* (Bloomington: Indiana University Press, 1987), esp. 17-58; Edwin Scott Gaustad, *The Rise of Adventism: A Commentary on the Social and Religious Ferment of Mid-Nineteenth Century America* (New York: Harper & Row, 1974), 154-72.

serve as God's co-workers, for "all this [i.e., the millennium] is to be accomplished . . . not by miracles, but by the blessing of God accompanying the use of suitable means." Those "suitable means" entailed careful human planning, efficient use of resources, and careful cost-benefit analyses.[24] Publishing the gospel via print met those criteria. Or, in the words of one journal of the era: "A well conducted religious periodical is like a thousand preachers, flying in almost as many directions by means of horses, mailstages, steamboats, railroad cars, ships . . . offering life and salvation to the sons of men in almost every clime."[25] Similarly, the Tract Society emphasized that its publications enabled Christians to reach large numbers of people more swiftly and cheaply than they could do in any other way. Thus reports of the organization often dwelt at great length on the number of pages printed, the new technologies used to produce those reams, and the expanding number of local auxiliaries formed to distribute the materials.[26] Of course, evangelical motivation remained preeminent, and efficient use of the media was redemptive only if it confronted men and women with the claims of Christ. Nevertheless, the heightened role of the media — along with technology in general — foretokened changes that would occur in the post–Civil War period, when for many Protestants building the kingdom of God became as much a matter of efficient technique and program as it was of piety.[27] The seeds of that transformation had already been planted in the antebellum period.

Nor were the premillennialists immune to the blandishments of effective technique. Although their eschatology may have prevented them from believing that the media could bring in the kingdom of God, it did not discourage faith in the power of the printed word to warn multitudes of the wrath to come. Indeed, the sheer power of the media to evoke a response from the masses sometimes even appeared to reshape the message itself. For example, William Miller initially hesitated to set a specific date for the second advent; but a public aroused by the movement's successful publishing ventures clamored for a more definite time. Miller finally succumbed, endorsing 22 October 1844 as the likely date of Christ's return. Noting the popular stir created by the Millerite press once that

24. Cogswell, *Harbinger of the Millennium,* 59.
25. Quoted in Brumberg, *Mission for Life,* 68.
26. *Proceedings of the First Ten Years of the American Tract Society,* 28-29, 32, 42, 48, 54, 65, 75-76.
27. See, e.g., James H. Moorhead, "The Erosion of Postmillennialism in American Religious Thought," *Church History* 53 (March 1984): esp. 72-76.

action had been taken, Joshua Himes declared: "The fruits are glorious. . . .
The worldly minded have been quickened and made alive — and all classes
have been blessed beyond anything we have seen in times past. With this
view of the matter, I dare not oppose it, although I do not yet get the
light as to the month and day." As David Rowe has noted of this episode,
Himes appeared "more interested in its [the theory's] effectiveness than its
correctness"; and that effectiveness, one might add, was largely the result
of Adventism's massive printing campaign and the product of publicity
provided by the secular press.[28] The power of the media had, in short,
altered the form of Millerism itself; and subsequent premillennial movements followed the precedent. In the postbellum era, Charles T. Russell
announced the imminent return of Christ and built a movement on reams
of printed matter. He wrote approximately 50,000 printed pages and
distributed nearly 20,000,000 copies of his work. The major institutional
link among his congregations was not a formal ecclesiastical structure but
a publishing house — Zion's Watch Tower Tract Society. Likewise, the
rising cohort of dispensational premillennialists relied on a network of
printing efforts, such as the newsletters of Bible institutes and the widely
distributed Scofield Reference Bible.[29]

The success of newspapers and magazines in disseminating premillennialism raises the intriguing possibility that something about that
eschatology was especially suited to transmission by the mass media.
Popular print was most effective when it communicated a simple dramatic
message. What one person said of tracts in 1814 could stand as a description of the imperatives of mass publishing in general. The tract should be
"plain" and "entertaining," he observed. "However good a tract may be,
as to purity of doctrine, and perspicuity of style, if it be not so composed
as to interest the reader in a more than ordinary degree, it is in danger of
being thrown aside without a perusal. There is a way of representing divine
truth, which renders it striking, and makes it penetrate the mind, and
arrest the attention." Hence the tract should rely on "strong, pithy expression" and "lively representations of truth."[30]

28. David L. Rowe, *Thunder and Trumpets: The Millerites and Dissenting Religion
in Upstate New York, 1800-1850* (Chico, CA: Scholars Press, 1985), 135.

29. M. James Penton, *Apocalypse Delayed: The Story of Jehovah's Witnesses* (Toronto:
University of Toronto Press, 1985), 26, 29; Timothy D. Weber, *Living in the Shadow of
the Second Coming: American Premillennialism, 1875-1982,* enl. ed. (Chicago: University
of Chicago Press, 1987), 17, 33-55.

30. *Proceedings of the First Ten Years of the American Tract Society,* 19.

Premillennialism met these criteria. Although millenarian systems often rested on complex exegetical convolutions, the central message and images of the faith were "striking" and "lively": Jesus coming soon on the clouds with legions of angels amid supernatural signs and wonders. Moreover, in an age in which the literal truth of the Bible was an axiom for the vast majority of Protestants, the premillennialist had the advantage of presenting a message that seemed to treat the eschatology of the New Testament in precisely this fashion. By contrast, postmillennialism tended to be more complex, lacking the dramatic imagery and unambiguous literalism of its counterpart. Postmillennialism was a compromise between a progressive, evolutionary view of history and the apocalyptic outlook of the book of Revelation. It affirmed the Second Coming, but not until centuries of Christian progress had prepared the way for it. Like a theological Janus, it had one face turned toward the literal fulfillment of prophecy but the other averted, slightly embarrassed by such crudities.[31] One must wonder how readily these complexities lent themselves to translation through a popular communications medium.

Of course, the religious newspapers of major denominations — to the extent that they expressed an eschatological preference — generally leaned toward postmillennialism; but this fact does not indicate how thoroughly readers adopted the message. There is suggestive (though far from conclusive) evidence that they did not accede uncritically. Surveying numerous diaries and letters of obscure Americans in the antebellum period, Lewis Saum finds little evidence of an explicit postmillennialism. "When millennial intimations surfaced in the writings of the common folk," Saum writes, "they often did so as little more than predictions of cataclysmic retribution"; in other words, these intimations appear to have resembled premillennial more than postmillennial convictions.[32] Similarly, William J. Gilmore, after an extensive canvass of records of personal libraries in the estates of persons in Vermont during the early nineteenth

31. Ruth Bloch, in *Visionary Republic: Millennial Themes in American Thought, 1756-1800* (Cambridge: Cambridge University Press, 1985), remarks: "On the level of popular culture, the image of Christ appearing in the flesh had probably always dominated over the idea of a purely spiritual coming, both because of its greater dramatic power and because of its greater faithfulness to the literal biblical word" (33). On the ambiguous character of postmillennialism, see James H. Moorhead, "Between Progress and Apocalypse: A Reassessment of Millennialism in American Religious Thought, 1800-1880," *Journal of American History* 71 (Dec. 1984): 524-42.

32. Lewis O. Saum, *The Popular Mood of Pre–Civil War America* (Westport, CT: Greenwood Press, 1980), 74.

century, has noted that premillennial works tended to outnumber post-millennial ones among rank-and-file Protestants.[33]

To make these observations is not to suggest that the so-called average person was either a confirmed post- or premillennialist. Most persons probably had not sorted out their views so clearly but lived with a mental hodgepodge of images of the last things, which they had not ordered into a distinct or coherent theory. They might alternately hope for the gradual conquest of the world to Christ and for the sudden return of the Lord. Many were no doubt like Baptist William Newton Clarke, who as a youth approved postmillennial theories that "put the end indefinitely far away and yet . . . [he] listened trembling for the trump of God in every thunder-storm."[34] The genius of premillennialism was that it cut through these ambiguities to offer a clear-cut message — Jesus is coming; and the new mass print medium, trading in such "plain" and "striking" themes, could readily turn that message into a powerful agent of popular mobilization.

The success of Miller and of later dispensationalists in creating extensive popular movements raises a larger question. Did the advances in print contribute to the creation of a mass religious culture, evidences of which can be discerned in millennialism? At one level, the answer must be affirmative. Millerite propaganda attracted a widely dispersed community of believers; and those who did not heed the midnight cry could scarcely be unaware of it. They may have smiled at adventist credulity or laughed at doubtful stories of Millerites clad in ascension robes; but even as scoffers, they were caught up in the same event as the believers. That large numbers of Protestants felt compelled to refute Millerism and that major authors such as Poe and Hawthorne alluded to the movement in their fiction testified that Millerism constituted a common defining event for American religious culture in the 1840s — a condition that would have been unlikely if not impossible without the revolution in print.[35]

One must not, however, overstate the extent to which print created a common culture. While certain of the new printing techniques — for example, stereotyping and the steam-driven presses — did ultimately tend toward the consolidation of printing in the hands of large firms in urban areas, the print culture of the second quarter of the century was still largely

33. Gilmore, *Reading Becomes a Necessity of Life*, 316, 323, 338.
34. William Newton Clarke, *Sixty Years with the Bible: A Record of Experience* (New York: Charles Scribner's Sons, 1909), 102.
35. Gary Scharnhorst, "Images of the Millerites in American Literature," *American Quarterly* 32 (Spring 1980): 19-36.

decentralized. Papers, often with small readerships, grew up all across the country; and this proliferation occurred as American Christianity experienced a massive democratization.[36] By the early 1800s, this democratization manifested itself through assaults on the prerogatives of ruling elites of every sort and in general through a vaunting of the claims of the "people" to be their own masters. The result was what Gordon Wood has called "the time of the greatest religious chaos and originality in American history."[37] The numerous decentralized religious periodicals of the age fully reflected that chaos and originality.

So, too, did the millennial visions that these various papers presented, for they conveyed visions of the end as diverse as their editors and clienteles. For example, in January 1830 Alexander Campbell launched his *Millennial Harbinger*, which for the next forty-one years would be the most powerful journalistic voice of the "Christian" or restoration movement. Especially in the early years of its life, that magazine argued that the latter-day glory would come once Christians abandoned all creeds and denominational distinctives to embrace the Bible alone. Through this restoration would arise the "Millennial Church," which would "be the instrument of converting the whole human race, and of uniting all Christians upon one and the same foundation."[38] The year after Campbell began his paper, a struggling religious community in Missouri started its own newspaper under the banner *The Evening and the Morning Star.* It, too, offered a platform of restoration as the first step toward the millennium; but the restoration it envisioned was very different from Campbell's. This community believed that God had once again worked wonders as he had in the days of the apostles, that he had delivered new revelations through the prophet Joseph Smith, and that he was calling the Latter-day Saints to build Zion in America.[39] But persons other than "Christians" and Mormons also used the press to advance their own unique visions of the

36. Nathan O. Hatch, *The Democratization of American Christianity* (New Haven: Yale University Press, 1989), esp. 17-46.

37. Gordon Wood, "Evangelical America and Early Mormonism," *New York History* 61 (Oct. 1980): 362. See also Wood, "The Democratization of Mind in the American Revolution," in *Leadership in the American Revolution* (Washington, DC: Library of Congress, 1974), 63-89.

38. Quoted in Richard T. Hughes and C. Leonard Allen, *Illusions of Innocence: Protestant Primitivism in America, 1630-1875* (Chicago: University of Chicago Press, 1988), 173, 174.

39. Leonard J. Arrington and Davis Bitton, *The Mormon Experience: A History of the Latter-day Saints* (New York: Random House, 1979), 268.

millennium. Even some close to the so-called mainstream of Protestant evangelicalism founded newspapers offering interesting permutations of millennial thought. A case in point was *The Advocate of Moral Reform,* started by the New York Female Moral Reform Society in 1834 and achieving subscriber circulation of over 16,000 within several years. The Society drew much of its inspiration from the Finneyite style of revivalistic Christianity — indeed, the evangelist's wife was the first director of the Society. Building on the common postmillennial assumption of the benevolent societies that "the work of Moral Reform will be one of the mighty engines to usher in the millennial day," the *Advocate* gave that confidence a proto-feminist twist: Woman "is designed by her gracious Creator to act a conspicuous part in bringing in the millennial glory of his kingdom, not as a subordinate agent to man, but as a being who is standing immediately under the government of Jehovah."[40] In short, the popular press of the early 1800s often gave as many different versions of the millennial hope as there were editors.

The widespread discussion of millennialism in magazines, pamphlets, and newspapers also raises another question. How did popular evocations of millennial themes relate to more learned approaches? To answer that question one must begin by noting that millennialism from its origin had often had a learned cast. When the apocalyptic genre arose in the ancient Near East, it was the handiwork of a literate elite. In subsequent centuries, those who elaborated millennial systems on the basis of those Scriptures likewise needed a considerable measure of learning. They had to know the appropriate biblical texts in order to exegete them; and, if they attempted to read scriptural prophecies as a commentary on actual historical events, they also needed substantial acquaintance with secular chronology.[41] Learned millennialism, if we are to trust the booksellers' catalogues, also found ample representation on many Americans' shelves during the early nineteenth century. Scholarly exegetical works such as Jonathan Edwards's *History of the Work of Redemption,* Samuel Hopkins's *Treatise on the Millennium,* and Daniel Whitby's *Paraphrase and Commen-*

---

40. Cited in Cynthia Jurisson, "Evangelical Protestantism and the Roots of the Nineteenth Century Woman's Rights Movement" (Ph.D. seminar paper, Princeton Theological Seminary, 1987).

41. See, e.g., David S. Russell, *The Method and Message of Jewish Apocalypticism: 200 BC–AD 100* (Philadelphia: Westminster, 1964), 119; Bernard McGinn, ed., *Visions of the End: Apocalyptic Traditions in the Middle Ages* (New York: Columbia University Press, 1979), 1-36.

*tary on the New Testament* appeared frequently in the catalogues. An especially common entry was Thomas Newton's *Dissertation on the Prophecies,* which in 1787 started a long American career in the first of many editions.[42] Even William Miller, who claimed to be a self-taught interpreter and to believe that anyone with common sense and a willingness to study the Bible could verify his calculations, showed the influence of the learned millennial ideal. The first issue of *The Midnight Cry* boasted that Miller had been since childhood "a prodigy for learning . . . anxious to obtain books to read." Through the generosity of a few friends who opened their libraries to him, Miller

> was enabled to store his mind with a vast collection of historical facts, which have since been of so much service to him in the illustration of the prophecies. Possessing a strong mind and a retentive memory, he appropriated the contents of those gentlemen's libraries to his own use; and even now, after a lapse of more than thirty years, it is astonishing to observe the correctness of his frequent references to these historical facts and dates in his extemporaneous lectures.[43]

It is difficult to be certain how fully the learned works of Edwards, Whitby, and Newton — or even the specifics of William Miller's calculations — were understood by those who read them. One suspects that these readers did not always follow the intricacies of the argument, or that they often regarded them as subsidiary concerns. For these people the millennial faith was probably less a carefully wrought scenario than it was a confirmation of more simple convictions: that Christ would return soon on the clouds, that the preaching of the gospel would convert all humankind, or that the present moment was in some mysterious sense pregnant with eschatological significance. Sometimes even the proponents of carefully wrought millennial schemes admitted as much. The Adventist Josiah Litch, for example, cautioned that minute exegetical timetables were not the whole of Millerites' faith. The burden of their message, he said, was that the world had "approached a crisis"; therefore, "no disappointment respecting a definite point of time can move them, or drive them from their position."[44] How then

42. Ruth Bloch, "The Social and Political Base of Millennial Literature in Late Eighteenth-Century America," *American Quarterly* 40 (Sept. 1988): 385.

43. "Memoir of William Miller," *The Midnight Cry,* 17 November 1842.

44. Cited by Eric Anderson, "The Millerite Use of Prophecy: A Case Study of 'Striking Fulfillment,'" in *The Disappointed,* ed. Numbers and Butler, 88.

should one assess the relationship between learned exhibitions of millennialism and popular manifestations of the hope? Most likely learned millennialism, while different from popular hopes, also served to reinforce them. Even when persons did not fully understand the minutiae of a millennial scenario, it endowed their own pictures of the End with the authority of learning based on the sacred book. In these respects, popular and learned millennialism were partly separate, but also overlapping and mutually reinforcing.

But by the 1840s, a new sort of distinction between the two had just begun to emerge in America — a difference whereby learned approaches to the Apocalypse might call into question the very legitimacy of their popular counterparts. The career of Moses Stuart as biblical interpreter illustrates the rupture. After serving a brief pastorate at New Haven's Center Church (Congregational), Stuart was called in 1809 as professor of sacred literature at Andover Seminary, only two years after the founding of that institution. One of the many seminaries established in antebellum America as theological education became professionalized, Andover was deeply rooted in orthodox Congregationalism and, in fact, was created to serve as a breakwater against the spread of Unitarianism in New England. Along with other members of the faculty, Stuart every five years renewed an oath of loyalty to the Westminster Shorter Catechism as well as to a strict Andover creed. He also engaged with eagerness in pamphlet wars on behalf of orthodoxy — a fact that testified to the depth of his participation in the popular print culture of early nineteenth-century evangelicalism. But Stuart also had another community of reference embodied in a different culture of print. Eager to master all sources relevant to his area of academic specialization, he became enamored of German biblical scholarship and taught himself that language in order to reap its fruits. These German works, now more readily available in America, represented a culture very different from the parochial, ecclesiastical milieu that had spawned Andover. The German writers, almost to a man professors in the German universities, were writing in a setting partly divorced from communities of faith and governed instead by the canons of scholarly research and objectivity. Although Stuart remained largely faithful to the conservative religious ideas on which Andover was founded, his use of the work of another world of print culture was potentially subversive of the tradition in which he stood.[45]

45. On Moses Stuart's work in general and on his indebtedness to specialized German scholarship in particular, see John H. Giltner, *Moses Stuart: The Father of Biblical Science in America* (Atlanta: Scholars Press, 1988); and Jerry Wayne Brown, *The Rise of*

When Stuart wrote *Hints on the Interpretation of Prophecy* (1842) and *A Commentary on the Apocalypse* (1845), he illustrated the beginnings of that subversion. On one hand, he espoused a fairly standard postmillennial view that a spiritual reign of Christ would exist within history

> when all Christians, or at least the great body of them, come up to the standard of duty, or come very near to this standard, in their efforts to diffuse among the nations of the earth the knowledge of salvation. . . . Every Christian, then, and every Society for propagating the knowledge of Christianity, is helping to usher in the millennial day, when they ply this work to the best of their ability.

Yet Stuart also strongly assailed the way in which premillennialists and many postmillennialists commonly interpreted the Apocalypse. They assumed that the Revelation predicted events in the history of the church and world until the end of time. On the basis of his historical research, informed by his German readings, Stuart insisted that all of the Apocalypse through chapter 19 referred to events in the first century C.E. Only the remaining portions of the book predicted subsequent history — and then in exceedingly general terms that made no reference to particular historical events. In short, there were no prophetic signposts between ancient times and the End — signposts that the exegete could use to figure where one stood in a foreordained chronology. While Stuart stated his position cautiously, he had in effect delivered a serious blow to traditional Protestant millennialism.[46]

In the decades after the Civil War, other biblical scholars would advance beyond Stuart. Students of the Apocalypse who were even more enthralled by the research emanating from Germany would actually treat the Apocalypse with a measure of contempt. They would argue that it offered "a millennial mirage," that no modern person could take the book seriously, and that at best John's Revelation provided "the shell of a great truth" — a shell now to be sloughed off.[47] Although Moses Stuart was far

---

*Biblical Criticism in America, 1800-1870: The New England Scholars* (Middletown, CT: Wesleyan University Press, 1969), 45-59, 94-110.

46. Moses Stuart, *Hints on the Interpretation of Prophecy* (Andover, MA: Allen, Morrill and Wardwell, 1842), 140; Stuart, *A Commentary on the Apocalypse,* 2 vols. (Andover, MA: Allen, Morrill and Wardwell, 1845), 2:353-95.

47. Shirley Jackson Case, *Millennial Hope* (Chicago: University of Chicago Press, 1918), 215-25; Case, *The Revelation of St. John* (Chicago: University of Chicago Press, 1919), 407.

too conservative to say anything so bold, he had already sketched out in embryo the logic that led to such conclusions. The case of Moses Stuart serves as a reminder that improved transportation and communications not only encouraged the expression of a multitude of views at the popular level; these changes also permitted the flourishing of a specialized, learned culture of print that increasingly diverged from — and was sometimes antagonistic to — popular manifestations.

Protestants who eagerly used the media had not, of course, foreseen this result. They anticipated neither the plethora of eschatological inter-pretations among the rank and file nor the gulf between learned and popular millennialism. They had expected to use the technological revo-lution in communications to create a consensus of views. In part, they premised that hope upon what Perry Miller in a slightly different context called the "concordance of dissent."[48] Out of the free exchange of com-peting ideas a higher agreement would emerge. Hopkins anticipated this end when he predicted that increased knowledge would yield a Christian understanding that transcended denominational differences. The lords of the Tract and Bible Societies assumed that they could, amidst the rough-and-tumble of printed polemics, impress a common religious culture upon America. Schaff believed that out of the mélange of Christian bodies interacting with one another a higher form of Christianity was emerging. Campbell thought that the call to return to the all-sufficient truths of the Bible would end sectarian bickering and promote universal harmony. Even William Miller assumed that once his calculations were set before the world their self-evident logic would command the assent of all Bible-believing Christians. And Moses Stuart, writing near the height of the Millerite frenzy, hoped that his appeal to "the sober and considerate portion of our religious community" would counteract the babble of millennial interpretations in which "every man says 'what is right in his own eyes.' "[49] Perhaps Nathan L. Rice most succinctly stated the governing assumption when he avowed that the ability to contest ideas openly was the ultimate ground of stability and consensus. His illustration was drawn from the political realm but was equally applicable to what Protestants believed about the religious realm:

48. Perry Miller, *The Life of the Mind in America: From the Revolution to the Civil War* (New York: Harcourt, Brace and World, 1965), 43-48.
49. Stuart, *Hints on the Interpretation of Prophecy,* 144, 146.

But in countries where a rigid censorship is exercised over the press, abuses are perpetuated, because no complaint can be uttered against them. Discontent spreads silently; whilst civil rulers, surrounded by unprincipled sycophants, dream not of the extent and depth of it. In the end, revolution furnishes the remedy, or plunges the country into deeper troubles. Our country is filled with news-papers and pamphlets, in which every public measure is freely discussed. By means of the press and oral discussion, public sentiment is formed; and at the polls it finds a free expression, and makes its power felt. With us it is next to impossible, that a bloody revolution can occur.[50]

In view of the fact that Americans would fight the bloodiest war of their history within a few years of those remarks, Rice's comment was profoundly ironic; but it testified to the extraordinary faith of his generation that the free interplay of ideas through the medium of print could ultimately transmute discords into harmony.

There was, however, an even deeper irony in the hopes of Rice and his contemporaries. Despite all of their paeans to a free and vigorous communication of differing ideas, their faith in the power of print to create a consensus was not shaped by the realities of the communications revolution. That faith looked back toward an older culture of print — the culture of scarcity — wherein people read the few widely circulated books intensively, even reverently, and could thus be expected to achieve something approaching a common culture.[51]

But that assumption was misplaced in an era when a multitude of viewpoints could find expression in print. As Nathan Hatch has pointedly observed: "A profound irony, in fact, surrounds the success of religious printing. Instead of the press serving as truth's herald, it often amplified a welter of competing voices, proving, if anything, that no truth had inherent power."[52] Or, to state the issue in the terms already presented, the religious press of the antebellum period did not achieve a single mass culture but rather spawned a variety of religious subcultures, each with its own vision of the millennium.

50. Rice, *Signs of the Times,* 153.

51. For an excellent discussion of the culture of scarcity in print and the transition to abundance, see David D. Hall, "Introduction: The Uses of Literacy in New England, 1600-1850," in *Printing and Society,* ed. Joyce et al., 1-47.

52. Hatch, "Elias Smith," 277. See also Hatch, *Democratization of American Christianity.*

To be sure, the press would shortly contribute to something approaching a common millennial culture — at least on a sectional basis. During the crisis of the Union in the 1860s, most Northern Protestants rallied behind the federal government. Through reams of printed sermons and the denominational papers, they united in the conviction that the struggle for the Union had millennial significance and that the Civil War was an Armageddon of the Republic. In the South, similar convictions were espoused, but with a different view of whose armies were advancing the coming of the Lord.[53] But these sectionally based unities were scarcely a token of the triumph of the free exchange of ideas. If anything, they were confessions of failure. For decades, contesting voices had spoken through platform and press, and the result was not a higher agreement or shared millennial purpose but rather moral confusion and political disorder. The debates yielded unity only once their sound was submerged in the roar of cannons. Horace Bushnell, who in 1844 had criticized those acting "as if God would offer man a mechanical engine for converting the world, . . . or as if types of lead and sheets of paper may be the light of the world," summed up succinctly at the close of the Civil War: "No argument transmutes a discord, or composes a unity where there was none. The matter wanted here was blood, not logic."[54] Surely Samuel Hopkins, the leaders of the Tract Society, William Miller, Alexander Campbell, and Moses Stuart had a better idea of unity and consensus when they entrusted their arguments to printer's type.

53. See, e.g., James H. Moorhead, *American Apocalypse: Yankee Protestants and the Civil War, 1860-1869* (New Haven: Yale University Press, 1978).

54. The first quote from Bushnell is cited in Brumberg, *Mission for Life,* 67; the second appears in "Our Obligations to the Dead" (1865), reprinted in *Democratic Vistas: 1860-1880,* ed. Alan Trachtenberg (New York: George Braziller, 1970), 41.

# Systematic Benevolence: Religious Publishing and the Marketplace in Early Nineteenth-Century America

David Paul Nord

Selling books is one thing; giving them away is quite another. This essay is about the marketing effects of that difference. It is a study of religious publishing in antebellum America, with emphasis on the work of the American Tract Society. Its theme is how the benevolent mission of religious publishers — especially their goal of reaching *everyone* with printed material — shaped their business practices. Though religious publishers borrowed much from commercial publishing and bookselling, they were innovators as well. Because they refused to depend upon market forces to guide the distribution of their books and tracts, they came to rely on administration instead. Indeed, religious publishers were early adopters of techniques of internal organization and communication that would become, by the end of the century, standard operating procedures of the modern American business firm.

## The Market Revolution

*We live, fellow citizens, at an eventful period of the world.*[1]

1. *The Address of the Executive Committee of the American Tract Society to the Christian Public: Together with a Brief Account of the Formation of the Society* (New York: American Tract Society, 1825), 14, reprinted in facsimile in *The American Tract Society Documents, 1824-1925* (New York: Arno Press, 1972).

American life in the early nineteenth century was transformed by what Sean Wilentz has termed "the market revolution."[2] In the decades after 1815, transportation and commerce, agriculture and manufacturing shaped and were shaped by the steady growth of regional and national markets. Major cities were linked more closely, and the traditional isolation of small towns and rural communities was penetrated. Throughout the land, urban and rural people alike were drawn into an increasingly integrated national economy. For some Americans — from incipient capitalist to frontiersman to runaway apprentice — these were exhilarating changes and liberating times. For others, they were frightening changes and "end times," times that signaled the loss of the fundamental virtues that had made republican America a special historical place.[3]

For religious leaders the times could be both frightening and exhilarating. The marketplace could appear as problem or solution. On the one hand, the market revolution, as well as the sheer physical growth of the country, helped to undermine traditional religious authority. The standing order of religious orthodoxy was assailed by rising secularism from one side and rising religious democracy from the other. To the conservators of traditional values and authority, enthusiastic commercialism and enthusiastic religious populism seemed equally horrifying.[4] On the other hand, the expanding marketplace and the increasing availability of modern commercial and marketing techniques provided new opportunities for religious organization and evangelism. In other words, while the rise of market capitalism shook the hegemony of traditional religious elites, it also empowered them (as it did their competitors) to think and act in novel ways.[5]

2. Sean Wilentz, "Society, Politics, and the Market Revolution, 1815-1848," in *The New American History,* ed. Eric Foner (Philadelphia: Temple University Press, 1990), 52. See also Charles Sellers, *The Market Revolution: Jacksonian America, 1815-1846* (New York: Oxford University Press, 1991).

3. For a general discussion of these tensions, see Robert H. Wiebe, *The Opening of American Society: From the Adoption of the Constitution to the Eve of Disunion* (New York: Alfred A. Knopf, 1984); and Richard D. Brown, *Modernization: The Transformation of American Life, 1600-1865* (New York: Hill and Wang, 1976), chap. 6.

4. Nathan O. Hatch, *The Democratization of American Christianity* (New Haven: Yale University Press, 1989), chap. 2; Jean V. Matthews, *Toward a New Society: American Thought and Culture, 1800-1830* (Boston: Twayne Publishers, 1991), chap. 2. By "standing order" I mean the mainline denominations of the Calvinist and Reformed traditions, especially the Congregationalists and Presbyterians.

5. Thomas L. Haskell, "Capitalism and the Origins of the Humanitarian Sensibility,

One such novel way of thinking and acting was the application of mass publication to evangelism and religious community building. When mainstream religious leaders took to the popular press, they understood that they were fighting fire with fire, for they viewed the rise of mass printing as perhaps the most pernicious manifestation of the market revolution. And it was. Nothing symbolized (or embodied) the market revolution so clearly as the explosion of the print culture in early nineteenth-century America. This explosion shook the standing order in two ways. First, purely secular publication expanded dramatically, and much of this material — especially newspapers, novels, and political tracts — was viewed by traditional religious elites as subversive to morality and authority.[6] Second, though religious publication also expanded, much of this material fueled the work of religious radicals and populists bent upon destroying the standing order.[7]

In the face of this two-front assault — by secularism and religious radicalism — some conservative religious leaders chose to fight back with the weapon of their enemies: the printing press. Indeed, in their efforts to adapt modern methods to the maintenance of traditional hegemony, the leaders of the standing order emerged in the early nineteenth century as important innovators of popular publication. They entered the very market they feared, and in some ways they mastered it. I have argued elsewhere that the publishing enterprises of the standing order — especially the

---

Part 1," *American Historical Review* 90 (April 1985): 356-57; Haskell, "Capitalism and the Origins of the Humanitarian Sensibility, Part 2," *American Historical Review* 90 (June 1985): 548. See also Jon Butler, *Awash in a Sea of Faith: Christianizing the American People* (Cambridge, MA: Harvard University Press, 1990), 268-88; Ronald G. Walters, *American Reformers, 1815-1860* (New York: Hill and Wang, 1978), chap. 1; and Peter Dobkin Hall, *The Organization of American Culture, 1700-1900: Private Institutions, Elites, and the Origins of American Nationality* (New York: New York University Press, 1982).

6. Cathy N. Davidson, *Revolution and the Word: The Rise of the Novel in America* (New York: Oxford University Press, 1986), 38-41; William J. Gilmore, *Reading Becomes a Necessity of Life: Material and Cultural Life in Rural New England, 1780-1835* (Knoxville: University of Tennessee Press, 1989), chap. 10; Michael Denning, *Mechanic Accents: Dime Novels and Working-Class Culture in America* (London: Verso, 1987), part 1. See also David D. Hall, "The Uses of Literacy in New England, 1600-1850," in *Printing and Society in Early America*, ed. William L. Joyce et al. (Worcester, MA: American Antiquarian Society, 1983); and Linda K. Kerber, " 'We Own that Ladies Sometimes Read': Women's Reading in the Early Republic," chap. 8 of *Women of the Republic: Intellect and Ideology in Revolutionary America* (Chapel Hill: University of North Carolina Press, 1980).

7. Hatch, *Democratization of American Christianity*, 22-25. See also Butler, *Awash in a Sea of Faith*, chap. 8.

union Bible and tract societies — were key developers of the new technologies of print, including machine papermaking, stereotyping, and
steam-powered printing.[8] These printing activities were market driven, in
the sense that they were built on centralization, capitalization, mechanization, division of labor, and economies of scale. In other words, in their
printing enterprises, the religious publishers, like other great commercial
publishing houses in New York, Philadelphia, and Boston, sought to print
as efficiently and economically as possible.

Their distribution activities, on the other hand, were different.
Though they entered the marketplace of popular publication, they resisted
what they took to be its fundamental corrupting principle: the adjustment
of supply to popular demand. The religious publishers, especially the union
societies, had a purer and grander vision for mass media in America: They
proposed to supply reading material to *everyone,* regardless of demand,
regardless of location, regardless of ability to pay.

The effort to reach everyone required new forms of organization
different from those of the commercial popular press. This essay is about
that difference, especially as it is revealed in the work of the largest religious
publisher in the early nineteenth century, the American Tract Society.

8. David Paul Nord, "The Evangelical Origins of Mass Media in America, 1815-
1835," *Journalism Monographs* 88 (May 1984). See also R. Laurence Moore, "Religion,
Secularization, and the Shaping of the Culture Industry in Antebellum America," *American
Quarterly* 41 (June 1989): 216-42; and Lawrence Thompson, "The Printing and Publishing
Activities of the American Tract Society from 1825 to 1850," *Papers of the Bibliographical
Society of America* 35 (2nd quarter 1941): 81-114. For a recent study of pioneering religious
printing efforts in England, see Leslie Howsam, *Cheap Bibles: Nineteenth-Century Publishing
and the British and Foreign Bible Society* (Cambridge: Cambridge University Press, 1991).
By "union societies" I mean those organizations formed through the cooperative efforts of
the Congregational and Presbyterian (and to some extent the Episcopal, Dutch Reformed,
and Baptist) denominations. These include the American Tract Society, the American Bible
Society, the American Home Missionary Society, and the American Sunday School Union.
The standard histories of this "sisterhood of reform" are Charles I. Foster, *An Errand of
Mercy: The Evangelical United Front, 1790-1837* (Chapel Hill: University of North Carolina
Press, 1960), and Clifford S. Griffin, *Their Brothers' Keepers: Moral Stewardship in the United
States, 1800-1865* (New Brunswick: Rutgers University Press, 1960). Of denominations
outside this tradition, the Methodists were the leading publishers. See James Penn Pilking-
ton, *The Methodist Publishing House: A History,* vol. 1: *Beginnings to 1870* (Nashville:
Abingdon Press, 1968).

## The Power of Print

*The world has gone to reading, and read they will, for weal or for woe.*[9]

The men who founded the American Tract Society (ATS) were appalled by modern life but not terrified by it. Following the lead of their English brethren who had organized the Religious Tract Society of London in 1799, the founders of the American Tract Society resolved at the outset "to foil the enemy at his own weapons."[10] The enemy was cheap, popular publications; the weapon was the cheap, popular press.

Throughout the early decades of the nineteenth century, the leaders of the American Tract Society were obsessed with the morally corrosive power of the press. Tirades against the "satanic press" appear in virtually all publications of the Society, from annual reports to children's magazines, from the 1820s to the 1850s. The enemy included "infidel books" (Voltaire, Paine, and others), "foul and exciting romances," adventure stories of "war, piracy, and murder," and books of "mere fiction and fancy."[11] The metaphors were

9. *American Messenger,* May 1849, 18.
10. *Proceedings of the First Ten Years of the American Tract Society, Instituted at Boston, 1814* (Boston: American Tract Society, 1824), 8, reprinted in *American Tract Society Documents.* See also *Proceedings of the First Twenty Years of the Religious Tract Society* (London: Religious Tract Society, 1820), 6; and *Address of the Executive Committee,* 11-12. The first society to be called the American Tract Society was founded in Massachusetts in 1814 under the name New England Tract Society. In 1823 this society changed its name to American Tract Society. In 1825 the Boston-based ATS joined with several other regional tract societies (notably the New-York Religious Tract Society) to found the national institution known thereafter as the American Tract Society. This society was based in New York City for 150 years. Today it is located in Garland, Texas. For general histories of the ATS, see Elizabeth Twaddell, "American Tract Society, 1814-1860," *Church History* 15 (June 1946): 116-32; Stephen E. Slocum, Jr., "The American Tract Society, 1825-1975: An Evangelical Effort to Influence the Religious and Moral Life of the United States" (Ph.D. diss., New York University, 1975); and Harvey George Neufeldt, "The American Tract Society, 1825-1865: An Examination of Its Religious, Economic, Social, and Political Ideas" (Ph.D. diss., Michigan State University, 1971).
11. *American Messenger,* February 1847, 6; July 1849, 26. See also American Tract Society, *First Annual Report* (New York, 1826), 22; and "Prospectus" in *The Child's Paper,* January 1852, 4. The *American Messenger* and *The Child's Paper* were two successful efforts by the ATS in the antebellum era to produce mass-circulation periodicals. *American Messenger* was a four-page monthly newspaper begun in 1843; it achieved a circulation of 200,000 by 1853. *The Child's Paper,* an illustrated monthly for children begun in January 1852, reached a circulation of 100,000 within six months.

apocalyptic: poison, disease, pestilence, war, and death. "We have had a deep and increasing conviction," the editor of the *American Messenger* lamented in 1844, "that there is in this direction an invasion of the private virtue and public morals of the nation, more insidious, but not less formidable, than the approach of a foreign army, with all the demoralizing influence of war." The first book-length account of the society's activities declared that "the plagues of Egypt were tolerable, compared with this coming up into our dwellings of the loathsome swarms of literary vermin to 'corrupt the land,' to deprave the hearts, and ruin the souls of our citizens."[12]

In this putrid tide of "vicious literature," the novel loomed as the most insidious and dangerous pollutant of all. Tract Society writers likened novel reading to intoxication, and the imaginary world of fiction to the alcoholic stupor. For the ATS, novels were dangerous precisely because of their apparently innocent and innocuous charm, as the *American Messenger* warned:

> To yield to such a hellish charm is like the voluntary sacrifice of one's body and soul on the drunkard's altar. *Mental delirium tremens* is as certain a consequence of habitual intoxication from such reading, as is that awful disease the certain end of the inebriate. Beware of it![13]

Of course, many did not beware. And the ATS from time to time told the sad stories of young men and women laid low by novels, their lives launched in romantic adventure but invariably sunk in delusion, dissipation, and death. In a typical narrative, the *American Messenger* told of a runaway girl who "assumed the name of the most depraved French novelist; wandered away with a shoemaker; and ended her days on the Braintree 'Common' by the side of her suicide-murderer, with a copy of the most vicious of the novels of her French namesake on her person!"[14]

12. *American Messenger,* February 1844, 6; [R. S. Cook], *Home Evangelization: View of the Wants and Prospects of Our Country, Based on the Facts and Relations of Colportage* (New York: American Tract Society, 1849), 41. The denominational publishers made similar arguments. See, e.g., *Plan for Circulating the Books of the Presbyterian Board of Publication* (Philadelphia: Presbyterian Board of Publication, n.d.); *The Home and Foreign Record, of the Presbyterian Church in the United States of America,* July 1852, 111, and September 1852, 142; and *The Principles and Purposes of the American Baptist Publication Society* (Philadelphia: American Baptist Publication Society, n.d.).

13. *American Messenger,* February 1847, 6; November 1847, 42. See also ATS, *Ninth Annual Report* (1834), 16; and ATS, *Twenty-First Annual Report* (1846), 89.

14. *American Messenger,* May 1851, 18; January 1852, 4. For an overview of the opposition to novel reading in America, see Davidson, *Revolution and the Word,* chap. 3.

Modern communication and transportation spread the pestilence. "The press teems and the mails groan with fiction and trash," a Tract Society secretary proclaimed to a public mass meeting in late 1842. "Every steamship brings 'the latest novel' from Europe. Every steamboat carries large editions to the interior. . . . Whether it will end in any thing short of the indecencies, obscenity, and infidelity of France remains to be seen." Another speaker at the same meeting declared:

> The whole land is a vast school. The rail car, the steamboat, the man-ufactory, the work-shop, and the farm-yard, the mines of the Schuylkill and of Galena, are all *schools*. The printer is the daily teacher. Cunard's mail to-day brings the 'latest' from London and Liverpool, Paris and Canton; all night the presses of New-York and Boston groan with their labor, and to-morrow the car and the steamer are bearing every descrip-tion of news, and of moral and pernicious influences towards every point of the compass.[15]

Yet despite its abhorrence of the licentious products of the popular press, the American Tract Society venerated the press itself and its potential for religious, moral, and political reformation. Indeed, the officers and editors of the ATS were wide-eyed boosters of every sort of modern technology. Of course, the technology of *printing* was paramount. From the beginning, the Society not only helped to develop the "mighty engine" of the press directly in its publishing work; it also constantly praised the press in its publications. Annual reports frequently commented on the wonders of modern printing, and the power of the press was always a main theme in the Society's newspapers.[16] But the Society's love of technology

15. R. S. Cook, "The Power of the Press," in *Proceedings of a Public Deliberative Meeting of the Board and Friends of the American Tract Society, Held in Broadway Tabernacle, New York, October 25, 26, and 27, 1842* (New York: American Tract Society, 1843), 41-42.

16. See, e.g., ATS, *First Annual Report* (1826), 22; ATS, *Second Annual Report* (1827), 23; *American Messenger,* January 1843, 1; March 1843, 9; *Child's Paper,* March 1852, 7. On the Tract Society's contribution to the development of printing technology, see Nord, "Evangelical Origins." Denominational publishers also sang praises to the power of the press. See, e.g., Presbyterian Board of Publication, *Twelfth Annual Report* (1850), 39-40, and *Seventeenth Annual Report* (1855), 4-5; American Baptist Publication and Sunday School Society, *Fourth Annual Report* (1843), 16; American Baptist Publication Society, *Thirty-Second Annual Report* (1856), 48-49; Tract Society of the Methodist Epis-copal Church, *First Annual Report* (1854), 41, and *Sixth Annual Report* (1859), 17. Standard histories of these societies include Willard M. Rice, *History of the Presbyterian Board of Publication and Sabbath School Work* (Philadelphia: Presbyterian Board of Publication and

extended beyond printing — to railroads, to steamships, and, in the 1840s, to the magnetic telegraph. "We had already said of unusual speed, 'It is swift as lightning!'" the *American Messenger* remarked; "and now, when the lightning itself is made our messenger, metaphor fails. We can only look and wonder."[17] One writer imagined the voice of God enjoining Christians to take up the new technology and to make it their own:

> "I the Lord have given you power and wealth, mountains of iron and valleys of gold, a boundless territory and a free government. . . . I have added the ocean steamer, and the rail-way, and the steam printing-press, and the telegraph; employ all these for my glory and for the establishment of my kingdom! Use them all, till it shall be announced along the lightning wires that encircle the globe, 'Their line is gone out through all the earth, and their words to the end of the world.'"[18]

The managers of the American Tract Society believed that the satanic press must be supplanted by the "sanctified press." To this end, they urged not censorship but competition. In none of its screeds did the ATS propose that wicked literature be banned. The Society sought no protestant inquisition.[19] The 1845 annual report explicitly denounced the "Romanist" slogan of the Reformation era: "We must put *down* printing, or printing will put us down." Instead, the ATS proposed the converse: "We must put *up* printing, or printing will put us down." Though rejecting censorship, the Society did seek to engage its enemy in battle. "Though it would be foolhardy in us to attempt an 'index prohibitorium' or an official 'imprimatur,' yet it would be Christian prudence to make the press labor

---

Sabbath School Work, [1889]); Daniel Gurden Stevens, *The First Hundred Years of the American Baptist Publication Society* (Philadelphia: American Baptist Publication Society, [1924]); and Pilkington, *Methodist Publishing House.* For a general discussion of evangelical enthusiasm for publication, see Michael H. Harris, "'Spiritual Cakes Upon the Waters': The Church as a Disseminator of the Printed Word on the Ohio Valley Frontier to 1850," in *Getting the Books Out: Papers of the Chicago Conference on the Book in 19th-Century America,* ed. Michael Hackenberg (Washington: Library of Congress, 1987).

17. *American Messenger,* November 1847, 42; August 1846, 30; May 1847, 18; January 1850, 2.

18. *Home Evangelization,* 140; *American Messenger,* June 1851, 22.

19. Some of the ATS rhetoric about no censorship and open competition was surely disingenuous. In some of these proclamations, there is more than a hint of nostalgia for the good old days when bad literature *was* suppressed by the community. Public opinion now, unfortunately, would not allow such direct action; so the ATS did not call for it. See, e.g., Cook, "Power of the Press," 42-43.

prolifically with 'the true Gospel.'" Every form of the new technology must be marshaled for war:

> Shall we content ourselves with the post-coach speed of the eighteenth century, in schemes for evangelization, while all worldly schemes are propelled with the locomotive speed of the nineteenth century? Shall we creep along the beaten path our fathers trod, and *because* they trod it, eschewing or neglecting all the increased facilities Providence has given us for publishing the great salvation, while steam, and electricity, and the printing-press are left to be the agents of ambition, avarice, and revolution?[20]

Again and again, from the 1820s on, the answer was repeated: If the devil works fast, let us work faster.[21]

Although the Tract Society was eager to enter the marketplace of ideas, it was unwilling to depend upon the ordinary marketplace of trade. For the managers of the ATS, private enterprise — selling books according to the law of supply and demand — was the problem, not the solution. The Tract Society was conducted by the leading merchants and capitalists of the day, men who were making New York the great commercial city of America.[22] They understood how markets worked, and they could see that the task of religious publishing was to fight against the market, not follow it. "What has private enterprise done?" the 1849 annual report asked. For millions of people who had no religious books, especially people scattered throughout the West, the answer was obvious: nothing. This theme was emphasized routinely in Society publications, including *Home Evangelization:*

> No nation on the globe, perhaps, has so large a reading population; and in none is the press more active, or more influential. What the reading matter prepared for such a nation would be, if left solely to private enterprise, may be inferred from an examination of the catalogues of

20. *American Messenger,* May 1849, 18; *Home Evangelization,* 139-40; ATS, *Eighteenth Annual Report* (1843), 25-26.

21. *American Messenger,* April 1846, 15. See also ATS, *Second Annual Report* (1827), 23-24; *American Messenger,* July 1843, 29.

22. For example, one of the key figures in the ATS was Arthur Tappan, a radical reformer but also a merchant/importer of the first rank. See Bertram Wyatt-Brown, *Lewis Tappan and the Evangelical War on Slavery* (Cleveland: Press of Case Western Reserve University, 1969), chap. 3; Lewis Tappan, *The Life of Arthur Tappan* (New York: Hurd and Houghton, 1871; reprinted in facsimile by Negro Universities Press, 1970).

some of the respectable and even Christian publishing houses. Self-interest would shape the supply to the demand; and the mightiest agent God has given to the world for moulding public opinion and sanctifying the public taste, would be moulded by it, and be made to reflect its character, were there no conservative, redeeming influences.[23]

The problem was that the market-driven popular press was merely following public sentiment, rather than leading it. The *American Messenger* argued in 1844 that "if the public taste be wrong, the press with its indescribable power perpetuates and extends the injury thus inflicted on vital interests. The question is, *What will sell?* and as in other shambles and markets, so here, supply responds to demand, although souls are included in the traffic." The Tract Society proposed instead that supply drive demand, and by the 1850s they believed that this reversal of market forces was working. "There are facts of exceeding interest which show that the *supply of publications is increasing the demand,*" the *American Messenger* declared, "not only for the Society's books, but for all kinds of religious books."[24]

How could the force of the marketplace be reversed? How could supply be made to drive demand? How could *everyone* be reached with religious publications, whether they desired them or not, and whether they lived within reach of the book trade or not? The American Tract Society's answer to these questions was *organization.* The invisible hand of the market must be replaced by the visible hand of administration — what would later in the century be called "systematic management."[25]

## Organization: Phase One

> *True religion is aggressive.*[26]

The American Tract Society was founded in 1825 mainly to capture economies of scale in *printing.* In its initial address to the public, the

23. ATS, *Twenty-Fourth Annual Report* (1849), 54; *Home Evangelization,* 107.

24. *American Messenger,* February 1844, 5; October 1845, 42; July 1852, 26. The publishers of dime novels later brought this same logic into commercial book publishing.

25. Alfred D. Chandler, Jr., *The Visible Hand: The Managerial Revolution in American Business* (Cambridge, MA: Belknap Press of Harvard University Press, 1977), 8-12; JoAnne Yates, *Control Through Communication: The Rise of System in American Management* (Baltimore: Johns Hopkins University Press, 1989), 9-13.

26. ATS, *Fifteenth Annual Report* (1841), 24-25.

founders declared that the centralization of printing work, including stereotyping and engraving, was a powerful argument for a unified national society. "Tracts are now exceedingly cheap," they said, "but the Committee are greatly deceived if the formation of the American Tract Society does not render them cheaper." But from the beginning the Society envisioned economies in *distribution* as well. That is why the Society located its headquarters in New York, "where there are greater facilities of ingress and egress, and more extended, constant, and direct intercommunications with foreign ports, and every part of our interior, than are to be found in any other locality in the nation." Though men had built the wharfs and dug the Erie Canal, God had made the magnificent harbor and the water-level route to the West. Thus, "the City of New-York . . . seems destined, in the wisdom of Divine Providence, to become the centre of these extended operations."[27]

Though committed from the beginning to energy, efficiency, and economy in distribution, the Tract Society's early administrative efforts were not systematic. The distribution network set up in 1825 was decentralized and dependent upon the voluntary efforts of local "auxiliaries" and the unplanned, fortuitous travels of supportive merchants in and out of New York. The executive committee of the Society quickly realized that more systematic organization was needed, and during the 1830s they developed increasingly elaborate management techniques and structures.

In the early years, the Tract Society did business rather like other book publishers of the time. In essence, the Society operated as a printer and wholesaler, selling tracts and books at discount to local societies, to individual members, and to other benevolent associations, and (rarely) to bookstores. The idea was to sell a product "very nearly at cost" to others, who would in turn sell at a slightly higher price or (commonly) distribute gratis. The key players in this process were the many local tract societies that already existed in 1825 and that now were becoming auxiliaries of the New York–based American Tract Society. In 1825-26, when ATS leaders dreamed of delivering tracts to everyone in the county, they envisioned local auxiliaries, organized in every country, carrying forth the work. Promoting auxiliary societies was, therefore, as important as printing tracts.[28]

27. *Address of the Executive Committee*, 12-13. On the role of New York, see Nord, "Evangelical Origins," 14.

28. "Address of the Rev. Justin Edwards," in ATS, *First Annual Report* (1826), 32.

Quickly, however, the national society found it difficult to control the activities of these auxiliaries. Essentially, they were independent agencies. Though the Society tried to regulate them through constitutional provisions, in reality the power of the central office was limited almost entirely to the control of the discounted prices of tracts and books.[29] In these early years after 1825, then, the American Tract Society operated in a marketplace separate from but analogous to the market for commercial publications. Though the retailers were societies rather than booksellers, the ATS's relationship with them was the same: It was a price system, a marketplace.[30]

This decentralized wholesale system, operating through independent auxiliaries, did not produce the results the Society wanted. In the second annual report, the executive committee lamented the fact that so few tracts were going to the West. Of more than $25,000 in sales in the first two years of business, only $107 worth of tracts had gone to Kentucky, $58 to Ohio, and $178 to Indiana, Michigan, and Missouri combined. The problem was obvious. Though the West was the field most "destitute" of religious publications, the vast majority of auxiliaries were in the settled areas of the Northeast. The Tract Society believed that the people of the western frontier needed religious publications more because they had so few settled ministers, churches, and other religious institutions. They also needed "grants" (free tracts) more than sales, because they were often so poor. But for these same reasons they also lacked auxiliary societies to buy and distribute the tracts and Bibles they needed.[31] Many local societies in the East did send tracts west. But the overall market forces of the

29. ATS, *Third Annual Report* (1828), 11-12; "Address on the Formation of an Auxiliary Society," bound with ATS, *Second Annual Report* (1827). This includes a model constitution and an explanation of the discount system. For a full account of the discount system, see ATS, *Fifth Annual Report* (1830), 21-25, 91-92.

30. Recent overviews of the commercial book trade in this era include James Gilreath, "American Book Distribution," in *Needs and Opportunities in the History of the Book: America, 1839-1876*, ed. David D. Hall and John B. Hench (Worcester, MA: American Antiquarian Society, 1987); Ronald J. Zboray, "Book Distribution and American Culture: A 150-Year Perspective," *Book Research Quarterly* 3 (Fall 1987): 37-59; Rosalind Remer, "The Creation of an American Book Trade: Philadelphia Publishing in the Early Republic" (Ph.D. diss., University of California–Los Angeles, 1991); and the essays in Hackenberg, ed., *Getting the Books Out.*

31. ATS, *Second Annual Report* (1827), 19-23; ATS, *First Annual Report* (1826), 20; ATS, *Third Annual Report* (1828), 14. See also Helen Genevive Leavitt, "The American Tract Society, 1825-1850" (M.A. thesis, University of Chicago, 1936), 23-24.

wholesale/auxiliary system worked against the professed aim of the society to reach those most destitute of the means of grace. Instead, the market directed the flow of tracts and books to the East, to the wealthy local societies — in short, to those least in need.

Clearly, the Tract Society had to overcome not only the external market forces of "satan's press" but also the internal market forces of its own distribution system. If the Society hoped to deliver religious publications to everyone across the country, it would have to substitute organization for market forces at every step beyond the printing process. In the late 1820s, the Society tried to do this in two ways: by appointing paid agents in the West and by assisting local societies (especially in large cities in the East) to set up organizations for the "systematic monthly distribution of tracts." In each case, the general idea was the same: to organize the mass delivery of tracts to people who were not being reached by the auxiliary society arrangement — new settlers in the West and urban poor in the East.

In 1828 the Tract Society dispatched its first paid agent to the Mississippi Valley. By 1830 the Society had nine agents at work in the West (four in the East), and more than five percent of the society's expenses were going to the support of agents in the field.[32] In the 1830s, the Society employed two types of agents: general agents, in charge of all the work in a specified region; and volume agents, in charge of the distribution of books. (The ATS had begun to publish full-size books, in addition to standard tracts, in 1827.) These agents were widely scattered. In 1833, for example, the Society had sixteen agents in the field, including one in Ohio, two in Indiana, two in Kentucky, three in Illinois, one in Missouri, and so on. Agents traveled constantly, but they could not hope to cover the territories assigned to them. Their reports were filled with expressions of joy in the work but despair over the magnitude of it. Even the Society's own optimistic plans called for only thirty agencies, each embracing a territory 100 by 180 miles, each with 300,000 people.[33]

Largely because of the size of their territories, the Society's agents still operated largely as middlemen, wholesaling tracts and books to local societies, churches, Sabbath schools, and volunteer distributors. They had no choice but to depend heavily on volunteer support. For example, the

---

32. ATS, *Fourth Annual Report* (1829), 22; ATS, *Fifth Annual Report* (1830), 21, 34-41.

33. ATS, *Eighth Annual Report* (1833), 32-38.

first formal plan to distribute a book to *every* household over a large
geographical area originated in 1834 with the local clergymen and tract
men of Virginia, not with the national office. The ATS enthusiastically
endorsed this plan to supply books to everyone in the southeastern states,
but the national Society had neither the funds nor the agents to do the
job without massive local volunteer organization and support.[34] In 1834
the work still had to go where the support was. Similarly, though the
Society's agents did do some direct door-to-door selling in the 1830s, the
evidence suggests that most of these sales were in settled towns, rather
than in the religiously destitute countryside.[35] In these ways (wholesaling
and town sales), the agents of the American Tract Society in the 1830s
still worked much like the traveling agents of commercial booksellers.[36]
Despite the efforts of the national office to spread agents around the
country and to deny "the mere principles of merchandise," the Society's
agents in the 1830s could not extricate themselves from the power of the
marketplace.

The agent system was an effort to make tract distribution more
*extensive* geographically. The other early attempt by the ATS to foil the
marketplace was the organization of *intensive* distribution efforts within
limited geographical areas, a project called "the systematic monthly distribution." This plan, like systematic volume distribution in the Southeast,
originated with a local society. In 1829 the New York City Tract Society
resolved to deliver at least one tract each month to every family in the
city. Under the plan, the city's fourteen wards were divided into 500
districts, each with approximately 60 families. Each ward had a committee

34. *Proposed Circulation of the Standard Evangelical Volumes of the American Tract
Society to the Southern Atlantic States* (New York: American Tract Society, 1834). For a
general account of evangelical work in the South, see John W. Kuykendall, *Southern
Enterprize: The Work of National Evangelical Societies in the Antebellum South* (Westport,
CT: Greenwood Press, 1982).

35. In the annual reports, figures on sales and grants were usually broken down
only by state. But a few scattered lists of sales and grants *within* states were published. One
such list for Ohio shows that nearly all sales and grants were in the settled towns. See ATS,
*Fourteenth Annual Report* (1839), 36, 27-44 passim.

36. On the use of traveling agents for bookselling, see Zboray, "Book Distribution
and American Culture," 53-57; Zboray, *A Fictive People: Antebellum Economic Development
and the American Reading Public* (New York: Oxford University Press, 1993), chap. 3; James
Gilreath, "Mason Weems, Mathew Carey, and the Southern Booktrade, 1794-1810,"
*Publishing History* 10 (1981): 27-49; and several essays in Hackenberg, ed., *Getting the
Books Out.*

and a superintendent; each district had at least one distributor. During the first canvass, in March 1829, the society's distributors visited every one of the 28,383 families that they had determined lived in the city. Though conducted by volunteers, the New York project was indeed systematic. The superintendents trained the volunteer "tract visitors," provided them with printed instruction cards, supervised the punctual delivery of tracts by the 15th of each month, and required detailed and standardized monthly reports.[37]

The New York project worked fairly well. In 1831 the New York City Tract Society delivered nearly six million pages of tracts to the city's 36,000 families, and nearly two million more to seamen and other transients.[38] This record impressed the national Society very much, and the executive committee regularly encouraged other local societies to follow the lead of New York. General agents, too, were urged to get "systematic monthly distributions" going in their fields. Many did. But, as usual, the work progressed more steadily in the East than in the West and South. By 1831 some two or three hundred towns in New England had monthly distributions, and monthly projects were common in New York, Pennsylvania, and New Jersey. But few were in operation in the South and West.[39] Western agents' reports often mentioned monthly distribution efforts, but such efforts reached only a tiny fraction of the people in the 1830s. And, once again, they were usually the people in the settled towns, those least in need. As one agent explained in 1833, "Of the nine counties already visited, perhaps one-fifth of the population are monthly supplied, but they are generally those best supplied with the other means of grace." This agent was unusually lucky, by the way. One-fifth was an enormous proportion compared with other agents' experience. One said that one in twenty families in his district had received any tracts; another said one in fifty. Yet another put the situation in telling comparison: "The fact is, this field is about as much Missionary ground as Burmah."[40]

37. ATS, *Fourth Annual Report* (1829), 28-29, 74-76; ATS, *Fifth Annual Report* (1830), 31. The New York society's "Card of Instructions to Tract Missionaries" is reprinted in ATS, *Eighth Annual Report* (1833), 32-33. On the Tract Society's work in big cities during these years, see Paul Boyer, *Urban Masses and Moral Order in America, 1820-1920* (Cambridge, MA: Harvard University Press, 1978), chap. 2.

38. ATS, *Sixth Annual Report* (1831), 16.

39. ATS, *Sixth Annual Report* (1831), 24-28.

40. ATS, *Eighth Annual Report* (1833), 33-37; ATS, *Sixth Annual Report* (1831), 20-23; ATS, *Thirteenth Annual Report* (1838), 18.

The goal of systematic monthly distribution was the same as that of the western agents: to foil the marketplace, to "tender the message of the Gospel to *all* — high and low, rich and poor."[41] But the marketplace, like hell, was not easily overcome. Any dependence upon volunteers — for financial support or for distribution — distorted the work of the Society, directing it away from the low and the poor, away from the rural West and South. The leaders of the Tract Society recognized the failure, and in 1841 they decided that the major work of the Society must be removed entirely from forces beyond their administrative control.[42] They set about to build a national distribution system based upon salaried line employees, geographical administrative divisions, and a hierarchy of salaried managers. This was the beginning of the American Tract Society's famous system of colportage.

## Organization: Phase Two

> *I visited a vile little place, and went to every family; sold about a dozen volumes and gave several.*[43]

The word *colporteur* is a French term for an itinerant hawker of religious tracts or books. It derived from the pack the peddler carried ("portered") over his shoulder or neck ("col"). Though the roots of colportage reach back to the Reformation, the American Tract Society was the first to develop the system on a large scale in America. In August 1841 the Society commissioned its first two colporteurs and dispatched them to Indiana and Kentucky. From that small beginning, the project grew rapidly. At the end of five years, the Society had 175 colporteurs in the field; after ten years, more than 500. In the first ten years, Tract Society colporteurs visited

· 41. ATS, *Fifth Annual Report* (1830), 28-29.

42. In its report to a special auditing committee appointed in 1857, the ATS executive committee admitted that by 1841 the system of auxiliaries, agents, and monthly distributions had failed, and that "millions of the most destitute, neglected, and needy of our population were not thus reached." See *Report of the Special Committee Appointed at the Annual Meeting of the American Tract Society, May 7, 1857, to Inquire into and Review the Proceedings of the Society's Executive Committee* (New York: American Tract Society, 1857), 15. See also the ATS's *Home Appeal* of 23 June 1941, excerpted in ATS, *Twenty-Sixth Annual Report* (1851), 47.

43. Colporteur's report from Indiana, in ATS, *Eighteenth Annual Report* (1843), 46.

more than two million families (eleven million individuals), nearly half the population of the country. They sold 2.4 million books, granted 650,000 books, and gave away "several million" tracts.[44]

Of course, the effort did not realize the Society's grandest hopes — "to visit *every abode*," to provide "the gospel for everybody." Colporteurs and agents in the West and South frequently wrote that the needs far exceeded their resources.[45] But the work that was done was impressive. By 1856 the executive committee could boast:

> When we record the fact, from carefully kept statistics, that more than five millions of families have been visited at their firesides on a gospel errand, and that alone — more than are embraced in the census returns of the United States — it implies toil for Christ, such as no other nation on the globe ever witnessed.

Under the colportage system, the committee declared, tracts "have fallen like snow-flakes over the land."[46]

The principle of colportage was simple. In the first full report on the project in the annual report of 1843, the executive committee explained the idea: "Colporteurs go indiscriminately to every family; and whenever a family is found in need of a volume to guide them to heaven, and is unable to purchase, one is furnished gratuitously."[47] "Indiscriminately to every family" — that was the key. Whether a family would be likely to buy a book was beside the point. To make such a system work colporteurs

---

44. ATS, *Twenty-First Annual Report* (1846), 21; ATS, *Twenty-Sixth Annual Report* (1851), 46-47, 64-65. Each annual report after 1841 reviewed the colportage effort for the year. For general accounts of ATS colportage, see the special report "Ten Years of Colportage in America," in ATS, *Twenty-Sixth Annual Report* (1851), 45-72; *The American Colporteur System* (New York: American Tract Society, 1843), reprinted in *American Tract Society Documents; Home Evangelization;* R. S. Cook, "The Colporteur System," in *Proceedings of a Public Deliberative Meeting;* [Jonathan Cross], *Five Years in the Alleghenies* (New York: American Tract Society, 1863); and *Toils and Triumphs of Union Missionary Colportage for Twenty-Five Years,* by one of the Secretaries of the American Tract Society (New York: American Tract Society, 1866).

45. *Home Evangelization,* 19; *American Messenger,* September 1851, 34. For examples of laments from the South and West, see ATS, *Twenty-Third Annual Report* (1848), 70, 73.

46. ATS, *Thirty-First Annual Report* (1856), 41; ATS, *Twenty-Seventh Annual Report* (1852), 53. Denominational publishers also adopted the colportage system, though the ATS remained the leader for many years.

47. ATS, *Eighteenth Annual Report* (1843), 28.

had to be salaried employees (no commissions or discounts); their travel expenses had to be paid; they had to be supplied in the field with sufficient materials; they had to have detailed information about their territories; they had to be trained and motivated; and they had to be closely supervised. In other words, colportage required systematic management, from top to bottom. The American Tract Society worked out such a management system in the 1840s. It involved eight key elements: (1) centralized budgeting and accounting; (2) decentralized middle-level management by region; (3) systematic statistical fact gathering; (4) formal recruitment and training of line workers (colporteurs); (5) in-service training; (6) printed handbooks and instructions; (7) standardized financial reporting methods and report forms; and (8) a monthly magazine and other in-house communication media.

## 1. Budgeting and Accounting

Put in fiscal terms, the business of the American Tract Society was to move wealth westward. In the 1840s, the money for benevolent work lay largely in the East; the most economical printing resources lay in the East; but the need lay in the West. Thus, the budgeting and accounting systems had to be national. And they were. All money, like all tracts and books, flowed through New York. Disbursements and receipts from both sales and donations were handled by the treasurer and assistant treasurer at the national office. Each month the accounts were published in the *American Messenger,* and they were regularly audited by the executive committee. In its publications, the committee frequently reminded employees that "the same minute accuracy in all the business transactions of the Society is aimed at that to be found in systematic commercial establishments."[48] In the 1850s, a special outside auditing committee reviewed the financial management of the ATS and declared that it had met this standard with "economy and fidelity."[49]

In its financial accounting, the ATS was typical of businesses of the era. In budgeting and cost accounting, however, the Society was somewhat different and perhaps even ahead of its time. For example, in an era when

---

48. *American Colporteur System,* 22.

49. *Report of the Special Committee,* 5-7. This report includes a letter from three prominent New York publishers (John Harper, Robert Carter, and John Wiley), who examined the printing operations of the Society and concluded that "great care and economy are exercised in each department" (6).

most businesses were fairly conservative, the Tract Society was a reckless spender. The Society maintained no endowment, no investments, no cash reserves, no material stock reserves. They simply spent money as fast as they could get it and shipped books and tracts as fast as they could print them. "Thus the Society, with all existing facilities," the treasurer wrote in 1857, "lives 'from hand to mouth,' asking for 'daily bread,' every week's obligations being usually beyond the means at hand." Of course, many businesses, including perhaps most publishers, lived on the brink of financial disaster. But for the Tract Society this style of budgeting was born of policy, not exigency. At the outset, the executive committee announced that they would never look to the treasury and adjust their efforts accordingly. They said they would never accumulate reserves. Instead, they vowed they would always press onward, "knowing, that the cause is God's, and that he will never suffer it to fail." The Society needed "no Bank but the hearts of the people of God."[50] When money ran out, as it regularly did, the executive committeemen appealed for donations, or they covered the deficits out of their own pockets.[51]

Though rash and risk-taking in spending, the Society was unusually careful and systematic in accounting costs. Indeed, the methods that the ATS used to standardize and measure the cost of the product and the cost of distribution were similar to the most sophisticated cost-accounting methods developed in this era by the new textile mills of New England and elaborated later by American railroad companies. The ATS routinely figured costs for all products (tracts and books) in terms of pages per cent (penny). This standardized cost measure allowed the Society to make cost comparisons across product lines and over time. Just as the railroads would later speak of cost per ton/mile, the Tract Society spoke of cost per printed page. For example, the cost of tracts as early as the 1820s was figured at 13 pages per cent and falling. Similarly, the Society calculated the cost of colportage on another standard measure, cents per family visit. This permitted comparisons across individuals and regions. In 1850, for example, the average cost of colportage nationwide was fifteen cents per visit.[52]

The business historian Alfred Chandler has written that not before

50. *Report of the Special Committee,* 13; ATS, *First Annual Report* (1826), 17; ATS, *Third Annual Report* (1828), 15; *Home Evangelization,* 61.

51. *American Messenger,* February 1846, 7; January 1847, 1; January 1850, 2; ATS, *Third Annual Report* (1828), 14-15; *Report of the Special Committee,* 13.

52. Every annual report included cost data of this sort. See, e.g., ATS, *Third Annual Report* (1828), 15-16; ATS, *Fifth Annual Report* (1830), 64. For a twenty-five year summary, see ATS, *Twenty-Fifth Annual Report* (1850), 30-32.

the 1850s did American businessmen begin to use their accounts to determine unit costs, and that the railroads led the way. Historians of accounting, however, have found evidence of the use of cost accounting as early as 1815 by the Boston Manufacturing Company of Waltham, Massachusetts, the first of the mechanized, multi-process textile mills in New England. In these new functionally integrated factories, cost accounting for internal administration ("management accounting") grew from the same managerial pressures that were at work within the Tract Society, including the substitution of wage labor for market-priced labor (contract piecework). Very few businesses before the railroads, however, used cost accounting to manage geographically dispersed operations. The American Tract Society seems to have been one of the few. The Society's system of cost accounting was fairly rudimentary; it did not take into account depreciation of capital. But it did permit the calculation of simple and comparative unit costs, across functional departments and across vast distances.[53]

## 2. Middle-level Management

Alfred Chandler has also argued that in the 1840s there were virtually no middle-level managers in American business.[54] This is another generalization that does not strictly apply to the American Tract Society. In the 1840s, with the growth of colportage, the Society set up a managerial hierarchy of the sort that would later become standard in American businesses with national operations. Within the central office in New York, the work was divided among several functional departments, each with a manager reporting to the executive committee. The society also had regionally based "general agents" to raise funds, work with auxiliaries, and promote the tract cause in other ways. The key middle managers, though, were the "superintendents of colportage," also based in regional offices. By the 1850s, the Society had eight large colportage agencies, including four in the West at Cincinnati, Chicago, St. Louis, and New Orleans. Each was operated by a salaried superintendent who supervised the work

---

53. Chandler, *Visible Hand,* 39, 71, 109-11; H. Thomas Johnson and Robert S. Kaplan, *Relevance Lost: The Rise and Fall of Management Accounting* (Boston: Harvard Business School Press, 1987), 21-24. The Society's system for figuring costs is explained in *Report of the Special Committee,* 17-18.
54. Chandler, *Visible Hand,* 3.

of a clerk, sometimes an assistant manager, and from 42 to 120 colporteurs in the field. These superintendents of colportage were paid salaries that were substantial for benevolent work (up to $2,000); in some cases these salaries were equal to or greater than those of department heads in New York.[55]

### 3. Statistical Fact Gathering

Like many Americans in the early nineteenth century, the managers of the American Tract Society were obsessed with statistics.[56] Not surprisingly, they found their own production statistics especially fascinating. Every annual report brimmed with numbers — numbers of books and tracts printed, numbers sold and granted, numbers of dollars donated, numbers of miles traveled, numbers of families visited. Every year the columns of statistics grew longer and the numbers more impressive. At the end of its first twenty-five years, the Society could boast that it had raised $2.8 million and circulated 2.5 *billion* pages of tracts and books. The *American Messenger* regularly dazzled its readers with numbers. For example, feature stories about the work at Society headquarters were typically built around statistics: 236 printers and binders hard at work turning out 3,500 books and 30,000 tracts and pamphlets, *every day,* at a cost of nearly $1,000. The statistical puffery never let up. In 1850, the executive committee reported that "the number of books thus placed in the hands of the people in a single year, is believed to be greater than the aggregate of volumes in all the public libraries in this country."[57]

Besides tracking its own statistics, the Society also gathered a variety of statistics from the field. A good deal of effort was devoted to the compilation of what the executive committee called "a *moral census* of the United States." Annual reports and newspaper stories frequently drew on U.S. census data and other official statistics on population, immigration, trade, and welfare. But most important were the data gathered by the Society's own agents and colporteurs. Each colporteur was required to

55. ATS, *Twenty-Ninth Annual Report* (1854), 64-65; ATS, *Thirty-First Annual Report* (1856), 42-43. Salaries are reported in *Report of the Special Committee,* 23-24.

56. Patricia Cline Cohen, *A Calculating People: The Spread of Numeracy in Early America* (Chicago: University of Chicago Press, 1982), 205-7.

57. All the annual reports have detailed statistical tables. See, e.g., ATS, *Twenty-Fifth Annual Report* (1850), 30-31, 42-52, 68-71 (quote, 69). See also *American Messenger,* January 1850, 2.

report numbers of families visited, families without Bibles, families without other religious books, and so on. These data were aggregated and analyzed by the regional superintendents and the New York office to guide decisions about book allocations and colportage assignments and to support public pleas for money.[58] "Our aim," the executive committee declared in 1845, "has been in the prosecution of the colporteur enterprise, to gather authentic facts, which should in the aggregate present a fair and accurate view of *the country as it is.*" The committee's simple faith in numbers never flagged. At the end of a detailed statistical report on colportage in *Home Evangelization,* the author wrote, with typical nineteenth-century confidence, "We leave the naked statistics to speak for themselves."[59]

## 4. Recruitment and Training

Because colporteurs were salaried employees, not commission agents, the Tract Society believed that close supervision was essential. This supervision began with recruitment and training. Recruitment of colporteurs was a major responsibility of both superintendents of colportage and general agents. The salary of colporteurs was deliberately set low (initially $150 plus expenses) to insure that only dedicated evangelical Christians would apply. Applicants were then screened carefully, beginning with a formal interview by the superintendent or agent. The Society's handbook, *Instructions of the Executive Committee of the American Tract Society, to Colporteurs and Agents,* lists eighteen specific questions that the candidate was required to answer in detail. The topics ranged from the candidate's education to his religious faith to his business habits. Next, each application was reviewed by the executive committee in New York. The committee made it clear to agents and superintendents that they carried great authority in hiring, but that the application must be standardized and complete:

58. ATS, *Twentieth Annual Report* (1845), 73; ATS, *Twenty-Second Annual Report* (1847), 39; ATS, *Twenty-Fourth Annual Report* (1849), 52-55; *American Messenger,* January 1846, 3; October 1848, 38; December 1847, 47; September 1851, 34. For examples of the "moral census" approach and the use of statistics in the reports of individual colporteurs, see *Colporteur Reports to the American Tract Society, 1841-1846* (Newark, NJ: Historical Records Survey Project, Work Projects Administration, 1940). This is a mimeograph report, part of the larger project "Transcriptions of Early Church Records of New Jersey." The manuscript reports from which this transcription was made are located in the Presbyterian Historical Society, Philadelphia. This small collection is the only set of manuscript ATS colporteur reports that I have found.

59. ATS, *Twentieth Annual Report* (1845), 73; *Home Evangelization,* 92.

A mere recommendation, without the data on which it is based, is insufficient; nor can the Committee act unless there is, with the data, the express recommendation of the Agent or Superintendent. No colporteur can claim compensation for services unless commissioned by the Committee.[60]

Before finally handing the candidate his commission, the superintendent was required to put him through several weeks of training, emphasizing careful study of the Society's publications. Once commissioned, the new colporteur was to be eased into the work by spending a few weeks on the road with the superintendent or with an experienced colporteur. The idea was to prepare the colporteur in two ways: to teach him the substance of the books and tracts he would be distributing, and to show him how the daily work of colportage must be done. The goal, of course, was to reach everyone; and the key principle, as usual, was system. "It is only by proceeding *systematically*," the executive committee admonished new colporteurs, "that the whole work can be successfully prosecuted."[61]

## 5. In-service Training

To tighten supervision and to boost morale, the ATS also introduced a program of formal in-service training for colporteurs. Naturally, the Society urged agents and superintendents to visit informally with the workers in the field. But very early in the history of colportage, the Society also began regular colporteur conventions. The first two of these were held in 1844 in Michigan and Pennsylvania, and the idea quickly caught on. By 1850 the Society was organizing and funding both small meetings of colporteurs within one- or two-state areas and large, week-long conventions that drew colporteurs, agents, superintendents, and ATS officials from large geographical regions.[62]

60. *Instructions of the Executive Committee of the American Tract Society, to Colporteurs and Agents, With Statements of the History, Character, and Object of the Society* (New York: American Tract Society, 1868), reprinted in *American Tract Society Documents*, 19-20, 26-28. Editions of this book were published from the early 1840s into the late nineteenth century. I have looked at two editions from the 1850s at the American Antiquarian Society, Worcester, MA. They are nearly identical to the one cited here. I have cited the 1868 edition for convenience; it is available in reprint form. See also *Home Evangelization*, 76-77.
61. *Instructions of the Executive Committee*, 20-21, 28-45 (quote, 33). See also *American Colporteur System*, 21-23; and *Home Evangelization*, 79.
62. *Home Evangelization*, 82; ATS, *Twenty-First Annual Report* (1846), 22-23; ATS,

The conventions mixed the inspirational and the practical. They usually began with a day or two devoted to individual narratives of faith. ("The convention was more than once bathed in tears," according to the minutes of the Cleveland convention of 1850.) Then the participants turned to reports on the work itself. An account of a convention in Cincinnati in 1845 explained:

> The design of these reports was not merely to elicit the facts respecting the spiritual condition of the population; the amount of labor performed, and the apparent results; but to draw out minutely *the manner of performing the work,* that each might profit by the experience of the other, and that any mistakes might be pointed out and corrected.

At the Cincinnati convention, and at others as well, Society officials then shared with the colporteurs "practical hints" on selling books, making grants, conversing with families, handling book and tract orders, keeping accounts, and filing reports.[63] The published reports suggest that the colporteurs, whose daily work was ordinarily so solitary, valued these conventions highly. And so did the executive committee, despite — as they felt constrained to point out — the considerable expense involved.[64]

### 6. Handbooks and Instructions

From at least the early 1830s, the Tract Society used formal, printed instructions to communicate with workers in the field. Even before the colportage enterprise was launched in 1841, the ATS published guides for volunteers working in local systematic monthly distributions. These ranged from one-page cards to small pamphlets.[65] After 1841 the Society published a substantial handbook called *Instructions of the Executive Committee of the American*

Twenty-Sixth Annual Report (1851), 59-63; American Messenger, October 1848, 38; February 1853, 6.

63. ATS, *Twenty-Sixth Annual Report* (1851), 60; *Meetings of Colporteurs and Agents of the American Tract Society at Syracuse, Detroit, Cincinnati, Pittsburgh, and New-York* (New York: American Tract Society, 1845), 9, 19-20.

64. ATS, *Twenty-Sixth Annual Report* (1851), 63.

65. See, e.g., "Instructions for Christian Efforts, in Connection with the Monthly Tract Distribution," "Hints for Christian Effort, Connected with Tract Distribution," "Directions to Tract Visitors," and "Personal Christian Effort; or, Way-Marks for Tract Visitors." These are reprinted in ATS, *Ninth Annual Report* (1834), 126-28; ATS, *Twelfth Annual Report* (1837), 183-84; and ATS, *Thirteenth Annual Report* (1838), 33-39.

*Tract Society, to Colporteurs and Agents.* The Society also supplied colporteurs with annual reports and with copies of *Home Evangelization, Proceedings of the Public Deliberative Meeting,* and other documents. And the ATS insisted that these publications be studied diligently, with pen in hand.[66]

The few surviving colporteur reports suggest that these guides were available and followed, at least in part. Several of the colporteurs who worked in the Pine Barrens of New Jersey in the summer of 1843 marked their monthly reports as "per *'Instructions'* of the Executive Committee." Though the reports were largely narratives, all supplied the kind of statistical data demanded by the executive committee, and some used the tabular format recommended in the *Instructions.* Clearly these colporteurs felt the weight of the Society's directives. One wrote: "Your reporter, *according to request,* has endeavored to be very minute in this narrative — and therefore no apology is needed for its length."[67]

### 7. Reporting Methods and Forms

The Tract Society was very strict about how accounts were to be kept and how information was to be reported to New York. The executive committee put the matter nicely in its instructions to general agents:

> The first requisite for a successful agency is to be *qualified for the work;* the second, to *perform it;* the third, accurately to *report it when done.* The last point is utterly essential. In the neglect of it, the Committee have not the data for wisely directing the Agent's proceedings, nor judging of his usefulness, nor knowing what he has accomplished with reference to guiding the future operations of the Society within the same field.[68]

Of course, the same obligations of accounting and reporting rested upon superintendents of colportage. But even the lowliest colporteur on the frontier was required to keep detailed accounts and to make monthly,

---

66. *Instructions of the Executive Committee,* 29; *Home Evangelization,* 83.

67. *Colporteur Reports to the American Tract Society,* 14-15, 38, 42, 92, 113. These young men were students at the Princeton Theological Seminary and were devoting their summers to colportage for the ATS. See note 58 above. The *American Messenger* and the annual reports have hundreds of excerpts from colporteur reports, but the manuscript reports themselves have not been saved by the Society. The archive at the American Tract Society headquarters in Garland, Texas, has only published materials from the nineteenth century.

68. *Instructions of the Executive Committee,* 90.

quarterly, and annual reports to his superintendent. In its book of *Instructions* and in sessions at the colporteur conventions, Tract Society officials explained in minute detail how records were to be kept and reported — both financial accounts and social statistics for the Society's on-going "moral census" of America.[69]

To standardize the reporting process and to ease the burden on colporteurs, who had better things to do, the Society provided each man with two account books and a set of preprinted forms. One account book served as a daily log; the other as a running summary for monthly, quarterly, and annual reports. For each of these reports, the Society provided "blanks" to be filled in and mailed to the superintendent. In its instructions, the executive committee made it clear that accounting was part of the work of colportage: "However excellent the spirit and efficient the labors of the Colporteur, he will fail in the discharge of essential duty, if, having done his work, he neglects to report his labors properly, or to adjust his accounts accurately."[70]

As might be expected, the Society was most concerned to account for free grants of books — a very costly enterprise. Tracts were almost always given freely; most books were sold. But the colporteur was also expected to make free grants of books to families who had no religious books, desired them, but had no money to buy. The Society insisted that free grants be made, and it left the decision to the "sound discretion" of each colporteur. At the same time, the Society required an especially careful accounting and justification of all grants. The *Instructions* laid out the rules for making grants and for reporting them; these rules were also reinforced at the colporteur conventions.[71]

The surviving records suggest that colporteurs were careful to follow the rules, or at least to say that they had. "In every instance where these grants have been made," wrote one of the New Jersey colporteurs, "the families had no evangelical religious books, save a Bible and hymn book:

69. *Instructions of the Executive Committee,* 47-61; *Meetings of Colporteurs and Agents,* 20.

70. *Instructions of the Executive Committee,* 46-56 (quote, 46-47). For reprinted samples of forms, see 70-75.

71. *Instructions of the Executive Committee,* 40-41; ATS, *Twenty-Fifth Annual Report* (1850), 51; *Meetings of Colporteurs and Agents,* 10. In 1850, for example, colporteurs sold 417,939 books, granted 113,891 books, and gave away several million tracts. Altogether the free grants of books and tracts in the year before the 1850 annual meeting totaled 35 million pages. See ATS, *Twenty-Fifth Annual Report* (1850), 69.

and had not the money to buy — but expressed a desire to get them."
Other colporteurs wrote that they sometimes paid for a book out of their
own pockets if they felt a person could afford to buy but would not. The
executive committee regretted that the Society's strict rules sometimes
produced this extra burden on colporteurs. The committee sometimes
argued that a more free distribution of books, like tracts, would be best
— were the funds available.[72] But they were not. And with limited funds,
strict supervision of accounts was essential for systematic management of
a national operation: "The monthly or quarterly report of each [colporteur]
is before the Committee, who can readily direct the contraction or expansion of the gratuitous issues, if their interposition seems necessary."[73]

### 8. Magazine and In-house Media

To support the work of colportage, the Tract Society founded the *American
Messenger,* a monthly newspaper/magazine, in 1843. The *American Messenger*
was not a house organ; indeed, it became a popular American monthly in the
1840s, achieving a circulation of 100,000 by 1848 and 200,000 by 1853.[74]
It was designed to promote the colportage cause as widely as possible. But it
was also aimed at colporteurs, agents, and volunteer tract workers around the
country. It provided encouragement and instruction from the top down, from
management to employees; it also allowed low-level employees in different
parts of the country to share their experiences with each other. The paper
routinely carried lengthy narratives of colportage work as well as official
proceedings, reports, and announcements. The *American Messenger* became,
in effect, an ongoing colporteur convention-in-print. The Society also provided colporteurs with copies of a variety of other publications, which
recounted the inspirational histories of tract societies, of the ATS, and of
colportage, and in other ways drew the worker in the field into the larger
community of religious tract work.[75]

72. *Colporteur Reports to the American Tract Society,* 18; ATS, *Twenty-Seventh Annual
Report* (1852), 53; *Home Evangelization,* 86-87.
73. ATS, *Twenty-Fifth Annual Report* (1850), 51.
74. ATS, *Twenty-Sixth Annual Report* (1851), 49; *American Messenger,* January 1848,
2; October 1850, 38; January 1853, 2.
75. *American Messenger,* January 1843, 1; December 1846, 45; October 1848, 38;
May 1849, 18. See also *Instructions of the Executive Committee,* 29. The link between
American colportage and the larger and grander history of religious publishing, going back
to Luther, was a steady theme in ATS publications.

*　　　*　　　*

In the business practice of the American Tract Society, supervision was the word. Five years into the colportage project, the executive committee explained that "at an early period of the work it became apparent that a plan of thorough *supervision* was indispensable to the safe and successful prosecution of the enterprise." Ten years into the project, the committee declared that the goal of thorough supervision had been realized:

> With unwearied watchfulness in the investigation of the character and qualifications of candidates; with documents clearly defining the relations and duties of laborers; with a system of rigid accountability in all business transactions; with experienced supervisory agencies; with friends in all parts of the country to report any delinquency, and, above all, with the grace of God to direct, restrain, and control, we see not but there are as many safeguards around this as any other human agency. And with this growing conviction, we see few obstacles to the speedy enlistment of vastly increased numbers of evangelical laborers in this and various enterprises appropriate to laymen; thus speeding on the work of the world's conversion to God.[76]

## "Systematic Benevolence"

> *By aggressive effort, at great expense, and by forced and largely gratuitous circulation, such as benevolence alone would prompt, it deposits an average of one or two small volumes in each family.*[77]

The business methods of the American Tract Society in the 1830s and 1840s were different from the methods of the commercial book trade. During this era, many book publishers did use traveling agents in a way that seems at first glance similar to the Tract Society's system of colportage. But in fact the methods were quite different. The agents for commercial booksellers (and, indeed, for most religious publishers as well) worked on a discount system; they received books at discounted prices and sold them at a markup. Or they handled "subscription" sales, taking orders for books

---

76. ATS, *Twenty-First Annual Report* (1846), 22; ATS, *Twenty-Sixth Annual Report* (1851), 67.

77. *Home Evangelization*, 109.

not yet published.[78] Both types of agents were paid by commission. Thus, a good deal of risk devolved upon them, and their faithful performance was enforced by the discipline of the marketplace. The letter files of publishing houses show how the system worked: publishers fixed discounts, assigned territories to agents, took orders, and shipped books. No supervision was provided; the profit motive of the agent was all.[79] Indeed, many publishers in this era were moving away from the use of retail agents altogether, preferring instead to place books into the market wholesale and leave direct consumer sales to others.[80]

The American Tract Society simply operated a different sort of business. Theirs was "no mere book-selling scheme," as the executive committee put it. Indeed, the managers of the ATS held most of their fellow publishers in contempt. "It is most clear," they wrote in 1836, "that the tremendous influence of the public press in this country *may not be left* solely to the operation and influence of sales for the purpose of gain." This was the never-ending theme. In his report to the special auditing committee of 1857, the treasurer sounded it yet again: "The aim of issuing books for the sake of *profit on the sales,* has never entered into the counsels of the Committee."[81] The success of the ATS in undercutting the market

78. See essays in Hackenberg, ed., *Getting the Books Out;* and Walter Sutton, *The Western Book Trade: Cincinnati as a Nineteenth-Century Publishing and Book-Trade Center* (Columbus: Ohio State University Press, 1961). I don't mean to suggest here that no commercial publisher had ever tried to use salaried agents in this way. The famous traveling bookseller Mason Locke Weems worked on salary on at least one occasion; he also proposed around the turn of the century some of the other techniques used by the ATS much later. But such experiments seem to have been quite rare. James N. Green, in a personal letter to the author, December 19, 1990. See also James N. Green, *Mathew Carey: Publisher and Patriot* (Philadelphia: The Library Company, 1985); and Lewis Leary, *The Book-Peddling Parson: An Account of the Life and Works of Mason Locke Weems* (Chapel Hill, NC: Algonquin Books, 1984).

79. The manuscript papers of booksellers at the American Antiquarian Society contain a good deal of correspondence between publishers and agents. See, e.g., the Edward Livermore Letterbooks, several letters from April 1851; and the James Munroe & Co. Correspondence, several letters from the mid-1840s. See also Zboray, "Book Distribution and American Culture," 53-57. Desultory correspondence with agents was typical of premodern manufacturing firms, too. See Yates, *Control Through Communication,* 3.

80. W. S. Tryon, "Book Distribution in Mid-Nineteenth Century America: Illustrated by the Publishing Records of Ticknor and Fields, Boston," *Papers of the Bibliographical Society of America* 41 (1947): 219-20. See also Gilreath, "American Book Distribution," 153.

81. ATS, *Twenty-Ninth Annual Report* (1854), 59; ATS, *Eleventh Annual Report* (1836), 41; *Report of the Special Committee,* 16; ATS, *Twenty-Fifth Annual Report* (1850),

is suggested by the heated criticisms that commercial booksellers some-times leveled at the Society and at other religious publishers. In 1849, one author and marketer of religious books put out a diatribe against "charity publication societies," charging that their efforts had effectively destroyed the market for religious books in the ordinary commercial book trade. And the chief malefactor was the American Tract Society.[82]

In *The Visible Hand,* his classic study of the rise of modern business in America, Alfred Chandler associates modern business practice with the extension of administrative control over market forces. He writes that "modern business enterprise appeared for the first time in history when the volume of economic activities reached a level that made administrative coordination more efficient and more profitable than market coordina-tion." JoAnne Yates has refined Chandler's argument by showing how this new administrative control was exercised. She defines the theory and practice of "systematic management," which emerged in the late nineteenth century, as "control through communication." In this era, she says, American businesses learned to use middle-level managers, written instructions to employees, systematic reports, printed forms, improved record keeping, statistical analysis, meetings and conferences, in-house magazines, and other new communication techniques to impose the visible hand of management on the far-flung operations of a national firm.[83]

This, of course, describes precisely the business of the American Tract Society. And it describes, to some extent, other religious publishing firms in the first half of the nineteenth century. The ATS was unusually systematic in its national administration and unusually aggressive in its colportage work;

---

65. Denominational publishers sometimes made similar statements that their work was no mere bookselling venture. But they were usually self-supporting (through sales) and thus much more wedded to the market than was the ATS. See Presbyterian Board of Publication, *Fifth Annual Report* (1843), 8-9; *Principles and Plans of the Board of Publication of the Presbyterian Church in the United States of America* (Philadelphia: Presbyterian Board of Publication, 1854), 8; American Baptist Publication Society, *Principles and Purposes,* 7-12; J. Newton Brown, *History of the American Baptist Publication Society, From Its Origin in 1824, to Its Thirty-Second Anniversary in 1856* (Philadelphia: American Baptist Publishing Society, 1856), 170-71; Methodist Episcopal Church, *Journal of the General Conference* (1852), 120, 123; and *Journal of the General Conference* (1856), 229.

82. Herman Hooker, *An Appeal to the Christian Public, on the Evil and Impolicy of the Church Engaging in Merchandise: Setting Forth the Wrong Done to Booksellers, and the Extravagance, Inutility, and Evil-Working, of Charity Publication Societies* (Philadelphia: King & Baird, 1849), 3-4.

83. Chandler, *Visible Hand,* 8; Yates, *Control Through Communication,* chaps. 1-2. See also Johnson and Kaplan, *Relevance Lost,* chaps. 2-3.

but it was not unique. Some of the same methods were used by the American Bible Society, the Presbyterian Board of Publication, the American Baptist Publication Society, the Methodist Book Concern, and other publishers.[84] Other nonpublishing religious and benevolent organizations also drew on these same management techniques. The American Home Missionary Society (AHMS), for example, employed systematic accounting and reporting methods, statistical fact gathering, printed instructions, and employee periodicals. The annual reports of the AHMS and the files of the *Home Missionary* are strikingly similar to the reports and periodicals of the American Tract Society.[85] In other words, in their business practices as well as in their ideology, these groups were indeed a great sisterhood of evangelical reform.

Religious publishers and reform organizations are usually overlooked by business historians because they stood apart from the main current of market capitalism in nineteenth-century America. But precisely because they operated *against* the marketplace, they were very early forced to gather their entire business enterprise within the purview of administration. If this is what modern business management is all about, then these organizations — especially the American Tract Society — may well have been progenitors of it. The contribution of businessmen to benevolent reform is a common story; perhaps the contribution of systematic benevolence to business practice is an equally important one.

84. Hatch, *Democratization of American Christianity,* 11, 142-44, 202-4; Harris, " 'Spiritual Cakes Upon the Waters' "; Nord, "Evangelical Origins." Though the denominational publishers usually retained the discount/commission system of sales (even in colportage), they did adopt many of the other administrative methods that the ATS used, including statistical fact gathering, formal record keeping and reporting, and organizational media. See, e.g., John Leyburn, *Presbyterian Board of Publication: Its Present Operations and Plans* (Philadelphia: Presbyterian Board of Publication, 1848); *Instructions for Colporteurs of the Presbyterian Board of Publication* (Philadelphia: Presbyterian Board of Publication, n.d.); "General Circular," in American Baptist Publication Society, *Fourth Annual Report* (1843), 16-19; American Baptist Publication Society, *Sixth Annual Report* (1845), 38-39; *Instructions to Colporteurs* (New York: Tract Society of the Methodist Episcopal Church, n.d.); and *Documents of the Tract Society of the Methodist Episcopal Church* (New York: Carlton & Phillips, 1853).

85. The annual reports of the American Home Missionary Society (first report, 1827) looked very much like the reports of the ATS, carried similar information, and were even printed by the Tract Society's printer, Daniel Fanshaw. The *Home Missionary, and American Pastor's Journal* was designed to be a periodical mainly for workers in home missions. It first appeared in 1828. The standard history of the AHMS is Colin B. Goodykoontz, *Home Missions on the American Frontier: With Particular Reference to the American Home Missionary Society* (Caldwell, ID: Caxton Printers, 1939). See also Anne M. Boylan, *Sunday School: The Formation of an American Institution, 1790-1880* (New Haven: Yale University Press, 1988).

# The Evangelical Enlightenment
## and the Task of Theological Education

Mark A. Noll

I n the decades after the Revolution, American Protestants so effectively mastered the new nation's most powerful communication systems and its most pervasive system of interpretation that, by the time of the Civil War, the United States had become a Christian nation. In the same decades, American Protestants were so thoroughly mastered by the nation's most pervasive system of interpretation that, by the start of the first World War, they had lost their intellectual way.

An essay that deals primarily with the prevailing antebellum system of interpretation — with the combination of evangelical and Enlightenment convictions that came to dominate public thought in the new United States — cannot adequately defend this pair of assertions.[1] It can, however, briefly suggest something about the magnitude of the Protestant achievement before the Civil War and the scope of the mastery exerted by Protestants over communications and interpretive systems, before turning at greater length to questions concerning the interpretive system itself: why mastering an interpretive system of theistic Enlightenment science made Christianity powerful in the context of early national culture; what it meant theologically for Protestants to embrace this system of interpretation; and how mastery of this system contributed to both Protestantism's

1. On the theological and historical ambiguities attending notions of a Christian nation, see Mark A. Noll, George M. Marsden, and Nathan O. Hatch, *The Search for Christian America*, expanded ed. (Colorado Springs: Helmers & Howard, 1989); and Mark A. Noll, *One Nation Under God? Christian Faith and Political Action in America* (San Francisco: Harper & Row, 1988), 3-13.

spectacular rise in the antebellum period and its manifold intellectual uncertainties after the Civil War. Review of these circumstances may also suggest something about the ideal goals of theological education more generally — that mastery of the most powerful communications and interpretive systems of an age is a necessary condition for making the primary traditions of Christianity meaningful in the context of a culture, but that such mastery is not a sufficient condition unless it also includes some capacity for criticizing both media and interpretive frameworks themselves.

# I

The importance of evangelical Protestantism in American public life before the Civil War is a historical commonplace. Recently, however, a number of unusually effective works have underscored the drama that attended the rise of evangelical Protestantism in the public landscape. Demographers now describe with heightened accuracy the rise of church membership from a low of about seventeen percent of the population in 1776 to over thirty-seven percent in 1860,[2] and have thereby drawn fresh attention to the mighty engines of mobilization that achieved these results.[3] Comparative historians of missionary outreach now treat the early United States as a marvel, not so much for American success in sending the gospel overseas as for events in the United States itself. "The evangelization of North America was the most signal success of the great [nineteenth] century of missions," the British missiologist Andrew Walls concludes.[4] At least one school of political historians, their computers whirring away on once neglected conjunctions, has reached the conclusion that sometime fairly early in the nineteenth century "patterns of Christian allegiance" became "the key variable in voting behavior" where churches as "primary value-generating institutions" and religious beliefs as politically energetic con-

---

2. Roger Finke and Rodney Stark, "How the Upstart Sects Won America: 1776-1850," *Journal for the Scientific Study of Religion* 28 (1989): 30; Finke and Stark, "Turning Pews Into People: Estimating 19th Century Church Membership," *Journal for the Scientific Study of Religion* 25 (1986): 187.

3. For a still useful account of this sort of mobilization, see Donald G. Mathews, "The Second Great Awakening as an Organizing Process," *American Quarterly* 21 (1969): 23-43.

4. Andrew F. Walls, "The American Dimension in the History of the Missionary Movement," in *Earthen Vessels: American Evangelicals and Foreign Missions, 1880-1980,* ed. Joel A. Carpenter and Wilbert R. Shenk (Grand Rapids: Eerdmans, 1990), 19.

structs profoundly "affected political choices and goals."[5] Fresh regional
studies show that, between the Revolution and the Civil War, Christianization did involve significant ethical trade-offs that softened the dis-
ruptively hard edges of the gospel for the sake of social cohesion. They
also show, nonetheless, that in various ways, many sections of the South,
New England, and the expanding West were either being conquered by
the forces of Christian civilization or were successfully renovating hereditary forms of the faith for modern conditions.[6] Even the greatest literary
minds of the period, though they might keep their distance from the
churches, could not escape the all-pervasive pull of Christian discourse.[7]

    These recent studies provide, in effect, an academic chorus for the
more impressionistic judgments made at the time by foreign visitors and
recent immigrants. Best known is Tocqueville's paired praise for the Christianity of America and for Christianity itself: "there is no country in the
world where the Christian religion retains a greater influence over the souls
of men than in America; and there can be no greater proof of its utility
and of its conformity to human nature than that its influence is powerfully
felt over the most enlightened and free nation of the earth."[8] Philip Schaff's
verdict is less familiar but more detailed:

    5. Robert Swierenga, "Ethnoreligious Political Behavior in the Mid-Nineteenth
Century: Voting, Values, Cultures," in *Religion and American Politics from the Colonial
Period to the 1980s*, ed. Mark A. Noll (New York: Oxford University Press, 1989), 146,
163. Further depths of these antebellum religious-political connections are explored ex-
pertly in Daniel Walker Howe, "Religion and Politics in the Antebellum North," in Noll,
ed., *Religion and American Politics*, 121-45.

    6. See, e.g., Donald G. Mathews, *Religion in the Old South* (Chicago: University of
Chicago Press, 1977); Robert M. Calhoon, *Evangelicals and Conservatives in the Early South,
1740-1861* (Columbia: University of South Carolina Press, 1988); Paul K. Conkin, *Cane
Ridge: America's Pentecost* (Madison: University of Wisconsin Press, 1990); Curtis D. John-
son, *Islands of Holiness: Rural Religion in Upstate New York, 1790-1860* (Ithaca: Cornell
University Press, 1989); and Randolph A. Roth, *The Democratic Dilemma: Religion, Reform,
and the Social Order in the Connecticut River Valley of Vermont, 1791-1850* (New York:
Cambridge University Press, 1987). Slavery constituted a different sort of "region," but it,
too, witnessed the spread of evangelicalism; see Albert J. Raboteau, *Slave Religion: The
"Invisible Institution" in the Antebellum South* (New York: Oxford University Press, 1978).

    7. For works suggesting such ties, see Agnes McNeill Donohue, *Hawthorne: Calvin's
Ironic Stepchild* (Kent, OH: Kent State University Press, 1985); and John Patrick Diggins,
*The Lost Soul of American Politics: Virtue, Self-Interest, and the Foundations of Liberalism*
(New York: Basic, 1984), chap. 9, "Return of the Sacred to Political Thought: Herman
Melville and Abraham Lincoln."

    8. Alexis de Tocqueville, *Democracy in America*, ed. Thomas Bender (New York:
Modern Library, 1945), 182-83.

Christianity, as the free expression of personal conviction and of the national character, has even greater power over the mind, than when enjoined by civil laws and upheld by police regulations.

This appears practically in the strict observance of the Sabbath, the countless churches and religious schools, the zealous support of Bible and Tract societies, of domestic and foreign missions, the numerous revivals, the general attendance on divine worship, and the custom of family devotion — all expressions of the general Christian character of the people, in which the Americans are already in advance of most of the old Christian nations of Europe.[9]

In the early United States, the goal of Protestants — East and West; North and South; elite and populist; men and women; Methodist, Presbyterian, Congregationalist, Disciple, Millerite, "Christian," maybe even Episcopalian and Lutheran — was to Christianize and evangelize, and to accomplish these tasks together. In large measure they succeeded.[10] It is hard to think of a better way of accounting for that success than to conclude that the triumph of Christianity in antebellum America was due to Protestant mastery of the culture's most powerful means of communication and its most compelling interpretive system.[11]

Evangelical mastery of the media extended from technologies of information creation to organization for information dispersal. As David Paul Nord has shown, evangelical tract and Bible societies created a "mass media" driven by "the missionary impulse."[12] Whether those creations were cause or effect, the result was a radical democratization and thorough

9. Philip Schaff, *America*, ed. Perry Miller (1855; Cambridge, MA: Harvard University Press, 1961), 76.

10. Jon Butler does not regard the christianization that was apparent by 1850 as the result of intentional strategies by conventionally religious groups, but his chapter "Christian Power in the American Republic" still testifies to the prevalence of Christian values in the American population at mid-century. *Awash in a Sea of Faith: Christianizing the American People* (Cambridge, MA: Harvard University Press, 1990), 257-88.

11. Although this essay concentrates on Protestants, it is also possible to see some of the same processes working in roughly the same period among American Roman Catholics, who also sought to master communication and interpretive systems. For the media, see Jay P. Dolan, *Catholic Revivalism: The American Experience, 1830-1900* (Notre Dame: University of Notre Dame Press, 1978); and for the interpretive system, see Patrick W. Carey, ed., *American Catholic Religious Thought* (New York: Paulist, 1987), parts 1 and 2, "The Enlightenment" and "Romantic Catholicism."

12. David Paul Nord, "The Evangelical Origins of Mass Media in America," *Journalism Monographs* 88 (1984): 2.

christianization of print, with effects that are now just beginning to be appreciated.[13] Even more significant for the spread of Christianity may have been the evangelicals' mastery of organizations for information dispersal. The Methodist system of itinerancy was probably most important, though its effects have never been adequately studied. Voluntary associations developed by descendents of the older American denominations chipped in by putting new technologies to use, breaking through cumbersome denominational barriers, and raising vast amounts of money.[14] The Sunday School movement enlisted legions of men and, especially, women for the causes of literacy, morality, and faith.[15] Theological seminaries proliferated as means for providing theological training and for socializing earnest recruits into the tumults of professional ministry.[16] In contrast to the situation in England, where the most influential churches failed to promote itinerancy, the Sunday School, and mass lay mobilization, the churches in America took to these new patterns of organization with a vengeance.[17] The result was coverage, penetration, revival, hegemony, market dominance, the spread of the Kingdom — the metaphor is less important than the fact.

Mastering the technology and organization of information was, however, incomplete without a message to convey. In antebellum America that message was evangelical Protestantism. Success in spreading that message is indicated by the fact that in 1850, something like one-third of America's

13. See Nathan O. Hatch, *The Democratization of American Christianity* (New Haven: Yale University Press, 1989), 141-46. The christianization of print in the new republic is suggested by the proportion of titles not from governmental agencies (as listed in Evans, Bristol, and Shaw-Shoemaker) dealing with religious subjects. In the colonial period, the proportion is always at least a third, often much more than half. That proportion (counted at ten-year intervals) is at 38 percent in 1770, but drops to 4 percent in 1780, rises to 21 percent in 1790, drops again to 12 percent in 1800, but rises to 24 percent in 1810. Meanwhile, the number of individual titles not from governmental agencies rises dramatically from the pre-revolutionary to early national periods: 1770 (504); 1780 (1,510); 1790 (832); 1800 (2,336); 1810 (2,358). Figures courtesy of David Malone, M.A. student, Wheaton College, 1990.

14. See Nord, "Evangelical Origins."

15. Anne M. Boylan, *Sunday School: The Formation of an American Institution, 1790-1880* (New Haven: Yale University Press, 1988).

16. The best study of the antebellum seminary is Glenn T. Miller, *Piety and Intellect: The Aims and Purposes of Ante-Bellum Theological Education* (Atlanta: Scholars Press, 1990).

17. The contrast is drawn explicitly in W. R. Ward, "The Religion of the People and the Problem of Control, 1790-1830," in *Popular Belief and Practice*, ed. G. J. Cuming and Derek Baker (Cambridge: Cambridge University Press, 1972), 238.

church adherents were Methodists, another one-third were Baptists or Presbyterians, and a further one-sixth belonged to some other variety of mostly evangelical Protestantism.[18] Although the adherence rate had not yet climbed over forty percent, no other articulated system of values could challenge the sway of the evangelical churches. This was indeed the era of Sydney Ahlstrom's "golden day of democratic evangelicalism."[19]

The evangelicalism of this era was a faith singularly adapted to the American environment. Although it shared in a common stream that flowed from the English Reformation, through channels recut by Wesley, Whitefield, and Edwards, and out over the English-speaking world, this American evangelicalism was less ecclesiastical and more revivalistic than the English, less confessional and more voluntaristic than the Scottish, less historical and more individualistic than the Canadian, less musical and more socially active than the Welsh, less Calvinistic and more republican than in Northern Ireland.[20] The difference was not so much in theology or ecclesiology narrowly considered, though important variations existed. It was rather a difference explainable in terms of cultural adaptation.

This adaptation involved mastering the dominant system of interpretation in the new American nation. For that purpose two tasks were necessary: first, internalizing the conceptual "languages" of America's distinctive political and social experience; and second, providing compelling demonstration in those "languages" for the Christian message. It is not necessary slavishly to follow historians of political discourse like Quentin Skinner, J. G. A. Pocock, or John Dunn to see that the process they describe for political convictions obtains almost as clearly for religious beliefs. What such interpreters show is that identifiable conceptual lan-

18. Finke and Stark, "Upstart Sects," 31.

19. Sydney E. Ahlstrom, *A Religious History of the American People* (New Haven: Yale University Press, 1972), 385ff.

20. Evidence pointing to these contrasts is found in David W. Bebbington, *Evangelicalism in Modern Britain: A History from the 1730s to the 1980s* (Boston: Unwin Hyman, 1989), 20-104; Stewart J. Brown, *Thomas Chalmers and the Godly Commonwealth in Scotland* (New York: Oxford University Press, 1982); John Webster Grant, *A Profusion of Spires: Religion in Nineteenth-Century Ontario* (Toronto: University of Toronto Press, 1988), 152-85; Gwyn A. Williams, "Romanticism in Wales," in *Romanticism in National Context*, ed. Roy Porter and Mikulas Teich (Cambridge: Cambridge University Press, 1988), 25-27; and R. F. G. Holmes, "United Irishmen and Unions: Irish Presbyterians 1791 and 1886," and T. C. F. Stunt, "Evangelical Cross-Currents in the Church of Ireland, 1820-1833," in *The Churches, Ireland and the Irish*, ed. W. J. Sheils and Diana Wood (Oxford: Basil Blackwell, 1989).

guages become the means by which communities describe, evaluate, prescribe for, and protest against their cultural circumstances. Or in Skinner's words,

> it is evident that the nature and limits of the normative vocabulary available at any given time will also help to determine the ways in which particular questions come to be singled out and discussed. . . . The problem facing an agent who wishes to legitimate what he is doing at the same time as gaining what he wants cannot simply be the instrumental problem of tailoring his normative language in order to fit his projects. It must in part be the problem of tailoring his projects in order to fit the available normative language.[21]

In these terms, evangelical Protestantism became a powerful conceptual language in antebellum America because its advocates had absorbed into their vision of normative Christianity certain critical ideals of the national experience. These elements included republican political instincts (which themselves were evolving from classical to liberal forms), modern political economy (in process of shrugging off the last effects of earlier mercantile restraints), and, above all, the authority of Enlightenment demonstration. The result was a set of convictions still indisputably evangelical Protestant, but now enculturated as an *American* evangelicalism. The circumstances that led to this distinct variety of evangelicalism may have been largely passive, as war, Constitution writing, a popular "contagion of liberty," frontier expansion, and the felt need for economic self-sufficiency exerted their influence on inherited Christian beliefs. But advocates of this American evangelical faith were anything but passive as they put to use the conceptual language that emerged out of the American experience of revival, Revolution, nation formation, and westward expansion. An American evangelicalism rose to prominence during the decades after 1787, in other words, not just because evangelicals were mastering communications systems, but also because they had mastered the new nation's most pervasive interpretive system and because they knew how to put it to use. For our purposes, we may call that interpretive system "theistic Enlightenment science."

21. Quentin Skinner, *The Foundations of Modern Political Thought*, vol. 1: *The Renaissance* (Cambridge: Cambridge University Press, 1978), xi-xii. A fuller presentation of Skinner's views, with probing critical responses, is provided in James Tully, ed., *Meaning and Context: Quentin Skinner and His Critics* (Princeton: Princeton University Press, 1988).

## II

The reason why theistic Enlightenment science made Christianity meaningful in antebellum America is tautological: American culture was such that theistic Enlightenment science spoke in it with power. The story behind that situation is, however, more complex.

The definitional discriminations of Henry F. May are the place to begin an account of how theistic Enlightenment science came to be the prevailing interpretive system in the early United States. The key is May's suggestion that eighteenth-century Americans perceived several Enlightenments, rather than just one.[22] Americans in general held in high regard, but from afar, what May calls the *moderate* Enlightenment, exemplified by Isaac Newton and John Locke. By contrast, Protestants in America repudiated two other forms of European Enlightenment: the *skeptical*, as defined by Voltaire and David Hume, and the *revolutionary*, as in the work of Rousseau, William Godwin, and (after 1780) Tom Paine. A fourth variety of Enlightenment, however, received a very different reception in Protestant America. This *didactic* Enlightenment was largely a product of Scotland, where three generations of philosophers and moralists had struggled to rescue the intellectual and social goals of the earlier moderates from the taints of radicalism or skepticism. With other varieties of European Enlightenment thinkers, the Scots did hold (1) that the world of nature, known "experimentally" through the senses, was the foundation of reality; (2) that detached, rational, scientific inquiry was the ultimate arbiter of genuine knowledge; and (3) that by pursuing a more disciplined inquiry into the experience opened by the senses, humanity could progress to new heights of glory.[23] But the Scots' special

---

22. Henry F. May, *The Enlightenment in America* (New York: Oxford University Press, 1976). Similarly discriminating are D. H. Meyer, *The Democratic Enlightenment* (New York: G. P. Putnam's Sons, 1976); and J. R. Pole, "Enlightenment and the Politics of American Nature," in *The Enlightenment in National Context*, ed. R. Porter and M. Teich (Cambridge: Cambridge University Press, 1981), 192-214. The next several paragraphs are abridged from Mark A. Noll, "The Rise and Long Life of the Protestant Enlightenment in America," in *Knowledge and Belief in America*, ed. William Shea and Michael Lacey (forthcoming).

23. The best definitions of the Enlightenment in America are the following:

Let us say that the Enlightenment consists of all those who believe two propositions: first, that the present age is more enlightened than the past; and second, that we understand nature and man best through the use of our natural faculties. (May, *Enlightenment in America*, xiv)

At its very center the Enlightenment represents the philosophical assimilation of the scientific revolution of the sixteenth and seventeenth centuries . . . there was,

contribution was to show how these convictions could be employed in the
service of Christianity — along with social stability and scientific progress
— and not as a replacement for Christianity. That ability was the feature that
recommended the Scots' didactic Enlightenment to the new United States.

A wealth of outstanding writing has recently shown how thoroughly
America's Protestant evangelicals embraced this way of looking at the world.
But still there is something of a mystery about its acceptance. Evangelicalism
was a Protestant tradition rooted in the Reformation and shaped by the New
Light revivalism of John Wesley, George Whitefield, and Jonathan Edwards.
In other words, it arose from traditions that stressed human disability as
much as human capability, noetic deficiency as much as epistemic capacity,
historical realism as much as social optimism. How this tradition came to
express itself so thoroughly in a language of optimistic, progressive
humanism requires attention to the American context.

The answer to this problem is that the didactic Enlightenment of
Scotland offered Americans exactly what they needed to make sense out of
the tumults of the revolutionary era. Two great political tasks confronted the
revolutionary generation, and a third equally great difficulty faced the evangelicals who joined the patriot cause. The first was to justify the break with
Great Britain — that is, to define an ideology for Revolution strong enough
to dispel the sacred aura of British liberty that had enraptured the colonists
only short years before during war with France. The second was to establish
principles of social order for a new nation that was repudiating autocratic
government, hierarchical political assumptions, and automatic deference to

---

above all, a new faith in science . . . a heightened interest in the natural world,
including, significantly, human nature . . . a growing impatience with mystery and
"metaphysics" . . . [and] new hope for man. (Meyer, *Democratic Enlightenment,*
xii-xiv)

Alike in the Old World and the New, [the Enlightenment] had its roots in the same
intellectual soil, and produced a common harvest of ideas, attitudes, and even of
programs: recognition of a cosmic system governed by the laws of Nature and
Nature's God; faith in Reason as competent to penetrate to the meaning of those
laws and to induce conformity to them among societies in many ways irrational;
commitment to what Jefferson called "the illimitable freedom of the human mind,"
to the doctrine of progress, and — with some reservations — to the concept of the
perfectibility of Man; an ardent humanitarianism that attacked torture, slavery, war,
poverty, and disease; and confidence that Providence and Nature had decreed
happiness for mankind. (Henry Steele Commager, *The Empire of Reason: How Europe
Imagined and America Realized the Enlightenment* [Garden City, NY: Anchor Doubleday, 1977], xi-xii)

tradition. A third task, for Protestant leaders, was to preserve the hereditary position of Christianity in a culture that denied absolute sovereignty to any authority and that was turning against the structures of traditional religion as actively as it was turning against other inherited authorities.[24]

For each of these tasks, the reasoning of the Scottish Enlightenment proved irresistibly appealing — especially its ability to make public virtue scientifically credible and to do so for all people by nature without the need for a special revelation from God. The achievement was to create a stable theory for epistemology and society that was not tainted by the factionalism, the tyranny, or the corruption of inherited European traditions. The general influence of the Revolution on American thought was such that the form of reasoning by which patriots justified their rebellion against the crown instinctively became also the form of reasoning by which political and religious leaders sought a stable social order for the new nation. Even more germane for our purposes, it also became the conceptual language by which Protestant spokesmen defended the place of traditional faith in a traditionless society.[25]

24. Outstanding works on the ideological climate of the revolutionary period include Bernard Bailyn, *The Ideological Origins of the American Revolution* (Cambridge, MA: Harvard University Press, 1967), 26-30; Gordon S. Wood, *The Creation of the American Republic, 1776-1787* (Chapel Hill: University of North Carolina Press, 1969); Wood, "Conspiracy and the Paranoid Style: Causality and Deceit in the Eighteenth Century," *William and Mary Quarterly* 39 (1982): 401-41; Douglass Adair, " 'That Politics May Be Reduced to a Science': David Hume, James Madison, and the Tenth Federalist," in *Fame and the Founding Fathers,* ed. Trevor Colburn (New York: Norton, 1974); Daniel Walker Howe, "The Political Psychology of *The Federalist,*" *William and Mary Quarterly* 44 (1987): 485-509; and Joyce Appleby, *Capitalism and a New Social Order: The Republican Vision of the 1790s* (New York: New York University Press, 1984).

25. Of the many works concerning the "fit" of the Scottish Enlightenment in revolutionary America, among the best are May, *Enlightenment in America;* D. H. Meyer, *The Instructed Conscience: The Shaping of the American National Ethic* (Philadelphia: University of Pennsylvania Press, 1972); Garry Wills, *Inventing America: Jefferson's Declaration of Independence* (Garden City, NY: Doubleday, 1978); as modified by Ronald Hamowy, "Jefferson and the Scottish Enlightenment: A Critique of Garry Wills's *Inventing America,*" *William and Mary Quarterly* 36 (1979): 503-23; John C. Greene, *American Science in the Age of Jefferson* (Ames: Iowa State University Press, 1984), 12-36, 411-12; Sydney E. Ahlstrom, "The Scottish Philosophy and American Theology," *Church History* 24 (1955): 257-72; Theodore Dwight Bozeman, *Protestants in an Age of Science: The Baconian Ideal and Antebellum American Religious Thought* (Chapel Hill: University of North Carolina Press, 1977); Daniel Walker Howe, *The Unitarian Conscience: Harvard Moral Philosophy, 1805-1861* (Cambridge, MA: Harvard University Press, 1970); E. Brooks Holifield, *The Gentlemen Theologians: American Theology in Southern Culture, 1795-1860* (Durham, NC:

The particularly Enlightenment character of this reasoning was its reliance on objective scientific inquiry as an alternative to the authority of history, deference, and tradition. Protestant commitment to this form of the Enlightenment was thoroughgoing because it worked so well — it did justify the rebellion, it did establish social order (politically in a Constitution infused with the principles of moral philosophy, intellectually through a collegiate curriculum devoted to the teaching of moral philosophy), and it did make way for nearly a century's triumphant vindication of traditional Protestantism. Protestant commitment to this form of the Enlightenment became deeply engrained, not only because it was so successful, but also because, in the American environment, it appeared to be self-evident. For much of the early history of the United States, Protestants denied that they had a system of interpretation. They were merely pursuing common sense.

For Protestants, Enlightenment patterns of thought had even more uses than they did for statesmen. Some were social. Guardians of American public virtue could now rely on the "moral sense" to restate traditional morality in a scientific form without having recourse to traditional props for ethics, including even the special revelation of the Bible. Solid books by Wilson Smith, Daniel Walker Howe, and D. H. Meyer have shown how widespread and deeply engrained this trust in Enlightenment procedure became.[26] Explicit in the lectures and textbooks of the nation's academic leaders — the vast majority of whom were evangelical Protestants — was the Enlightenment belief that Americans could find within themselves resources, compatible with Christianity, to create a moral social order out of the rootlessness and confusion of the new nation.[27]

The extent of Protestant incorporation of the Enlightenment, however, went much further than merely its utility for the moral direction of

Duke University Press, 1978), 96-101, 110-54; Fred J. Hood, *Reformed America: The Middle and Southern States, 1783-1837* (University, AL: University of Alabama Press, 1980), 1-67, 88-112; and I. Woodbridge Riley, *American Philosophy: The Early Schools* (New York: Russell & Russell, orig. 1907), 475-79.

26. Wilson Smith, *Professors and Public Ethics: Studies of Northern Moral Philosophers before the Civil War* (Ithaca: Cornell University Press, 1956); Howe, *Unitarian Conscience;* and Meyer, *The Instructed Conscience.*

27. On that confusion, see John M. Murrin, "The Great Inversion; or, Court Versus Country: A Comparison of the Revolution Settlements in England (1688-1721) and America (1776-1816)," in *Three British Revolutions: 1641, 1688, 1776,* ed. J. G. A. Pocock (Princeton: Princeton University Press, 1980), 376; David Hackett Fischer, *Growing Old in America,* expanded ed. (New York: Oxford University Press, 1973), 112; and Gordon S. Wood, "Evangelical America and Early Mormonism," *New York History* 61 (1980): 361.

society. The interpretive system that evangelicals mastered during and after the Revolution also provided a conceptual language for expressing their faith. The message proclaimed by Sunday School volunteers, Methodist itinerants, and an avalanche of religious print may have emphasized spiritual experience at the expense of conceptual order. But the enduring power of the message depended also on its usefulness for establishing Christian civilization in the wake of the New Birth, and for doing so in a conceptual language fitting the intellectual environment of the early United States. At these formal levels, theistic Enlightenment science was overwhelmingly the argot of antebellum American evangelicalism.

This interpretive system prevailed when Americans formulated apologetics and theology. It also shaped the way in which both common people and the elite discussed revival and appropriated the Bible. As a simple exercise in theological contextualization, it is worth noting in some detail what it meant for American evangelicals to rely upon contemporary demonstration rather than historical precedent to defend their faith. But, while also preparing the way for a brief examination of the evangelicals' intellectual discontents after the Civil War, such an exercise also raises questions about mastery of an interpretive system in relationship to mastery of communications media. First, however, it is useful to observe the success of evangelicals in expressing their faith in terms of the new nation's most widely prevailing system of interpretation.

# III

### Apologetics

For Protestant leaders, theistic Enlightenment science arrived just in time. The circumstances of revolutionary America made a modern, respectable defense of the faith absolutely essential. The American Revolution differed from the later Revolution in France in large part because of the ability of American Protestants to make that defense. The great goal of Protestants in the struggle against the irreligion and disorder of the revolutionary period was, in the words of Princeton's John Witherspoon, "to meet [infidels] upon their own ground, and to show them from reason itself, the fallacy of their principles." Witherspoon's first proof for Christianity was the "sublimity" of "the doctrine contained in Scripture concerning God, his works, and creatures, and his relations to them," because such a quality "must necessarily have the approbation of unprejudiced reason."[28] In the 1790s and for several decades thereafter, Protestants relied heavily on the imported apologetics of William Paley to secure their case.[29]

Later, as they began to develop their own defenses for Christianity, American Protestants drew ever more directly on the methods of the didactic Enlightenment. Examples of apologetics grounded on scientific rationality abounded in the early national period. It was a part of Timothy Dwight's armament that proved immediately useful when he became president of Yale in 1795 and confronted undergraduate doubts about the veracity of the Bible. It was also a staple in the lengthy arguments of New England Unitarians against trinitarians, and vice versa.[30] Widespread as the recourse to scientific demonstration was among the Congregationalists, it was the Presbyterians who excelled at what T. D. Bozeman has called a "Baconian" approach to the faith.[31] In divinity, rigorous empiricism became the standard for justifying belief in God, revelation, and the Trinity. In the moral sciences, it marked out the royal road to ethical certainty. It also provided a key for using physical science itself as a demonstration of religious truths.[32] In every case the appeal was, as Witherspoon's successor, Stanhope Smith, put it, "to the evidence of facts, and to conclusions resulting from these facts which . . . every genuine disciple of nature will acknowledge to be legitimately drawn from her own fountain."[33] Among

28. John Witherspoon, "Moral Philosophy," in *The Works of the Rev. John Witherspoon,* 2nd ed., 4 vols. (Philadelphia, 1802), 3:368; "Lectures on Divinity," in *Works,* 4:28.

29. Wilson Smith, "William Paley's Theological Utilitarianism in America," *William and Mary Quarterly* 11 (1954): 402-24; and Bruce Kuklick, *Churchmen and Philosophers from Jonathan Edwards to John Dewey* (New Haven: Yale University Press, 1985), 53.

30. Sereno E. Dwight, "Memoir," in Timothy Dwight, *Theology Explained and Defended,* 4 vols. (New Haven: S. Converse, 1823), 1:22-23. On the Unitarian debate, see Frank Hugh Foster, *A Genetic History of the New England Theology* (Chicago: University of Chicago Press, 1907), 273-315.

31. Bozeman, *Protestants in an Age of Science,* 3-31.

32. For examples in divinity, see Witherspoon, "Lectures on Divinity," *Works,* 4:22-75; Samuel Stanhope Smith, *A Comprehensive View of the Leading and Most Important Principles of Natural and Revealed Religion* (New Brunswick, NJ: Deare & Myer, 1815); Archibald Alexander, *A Brief Outline of the Evidences of the Christian Religion* (Princeton: D. A. Borrenstein, 1825); Nathaniel W. Taylor, *Lectures on the Moral Government of God,* 2 vols. (New York: Clark, Austin & Smith, 1859). For harmonizations with science, see Bozeman, *Protestants in an Age of Science,* 71-159; and Herbert Hovenkamp, *Science and Religion in America, 1800-1860* (Philadelphia: University of Pennsylvania Press, 1978).

33. Stanhope Smith, *An Essay on the Causes of the Variety of Complexion and Figure in the Human Species,* ed. Winthrop Jordan (1810; Cambridge, MA: Harvard University Press, 1965), 3.

both Congregationalists and Presbyterians, the most theologically articulate Protestants in the early republic, this approach guided responses to Paine's *Age of Reason* in the 1790s, and to other infidels thereafter.[34] This kind of "supernatural rationalism" was also useful for counteracting the impious use of science by making possible the harmonization first of the Bible and astronomy and then of Scripture and geology.[35] And when the Methodists began to write apologetics, it was the note they struck, too, as in a treatise on salvation from Asa Shinn in 1813:

> Thus it appears, that it is not only right, but our sacred duty to think and judge each one for himself, by those methods and rules of judgment, which God has appointed to direct his intelligent creatures to truth and happiness. . . . It affords me unspeakable pleasure to find I can screen myself under the authority of a Reid, a Beatty, and a Campbell, among philosophers; and under the authority of a Baxter, a Wesley, a Fletcher, and others, among divines. . . . Not that I intend to follow any of these, with a blind submission.[36]

Closely related to the orthodox reliance upon scientific reason was dependence upon intuitive common sense, for common sense was everywhere considered the basis for reliable knowledge of the external world, trustworthy employment of logic, and empirical understanding of human nature. Nothing worked better at squelching the Deism that Tom Paine promoted, said Elias Boudinot, first president of the American Bible Society, than simply "the rules of common sense."[37] Timothy Dwight praised common sense as "the most valuable faculty . . . of man," and he

34. See Gary B. Nash, "The American Clergy and the French Revolution," *William and Mary Quarterly* 22 (July 1965): 402-4; and James H. Smylie, "Clerical Perspectives on Deism: Paine's *Age of Reason* in Virginia," *Eighteenth-Century Studies* 6 (1972-73): 203-20.

35. For a good discussion of "supernatural rationalism," see Kuklick, *Churchmen and Philosophers,* 87. On the harmonizations, see Ronald L. Numbers, *Creation by Natural Law: Laplace's Nebular Hypothesis in American Thought* (Seattle: University of Washington Press, 1977), 55-66; Bozeman, *Protestants in an Age of Science,* 96-97; and Hovenkamp, *Science and Religion in America,* 119-46.

36. Asa Shinn, *An Essay on the Plan of Salvation; in which the Several Sources of Evidence are Examined, and Applied to the Interesting Doctrine of Redemption, in its Relation to the Government and Moral Attributes of the Deity* (Baltimore: Neal, Wills and Cole, 1813), 108-9.

37. Elias Boudinot, *The Age of Revelation: Or, the Age of Reason Shewn to be an Age of Infidelity* (Philadelphia: Asbury Dickens, 1801), 30.

regularly used it both to begin and to sustain arguments.[38] The same faith in intuition served the New Haven Theology as it counterattacked the Unitarians and improved upon Jonathan Edwards's theory of the will. To accomplish the latter task, Nathaniel William Taylor urged, "Let a man look into his own breast, and he cannot but perceive . . . *inward freedom* — for if freedom be not in the *mind* it is nowhere. And liberty in the mind implies self-determination."[39]

So basic did this kind of reasoning become — a reasoning that used the impulses of consciousness as scientists put to use the impulses of the physical senses — that even self-consciously orthodox Protestants had no qualms about resting the entire edifice of the faith on the principles of theistic Enlightenment science. Archibald Alexander, longtime professor at the confessional Presbyterian seminary in Princeton, year by year told the first-year students:

> To prove that our faculties are not so constituted as to misguide us, some have had recourse to the *goodness* and *truth of God*, our creator, but this argument is unnecessary. We are as certain of these intuitive truths as we can be. . . . Besides, we must be sure that we exist, and that the world exists, before we can be certain that there is a God, for it is from these *data* that we prove his existence.[40]

Only rarely did a voice rise in this exuberant age of demonstration to question the limits of empirical neutrality when confronting arguments of fundamental religious significance. In 1836 John Henry Newman, from across the water, called to task just such an assumption, with special

38. Timothy Dwight, *Theology Explained and Defended*, 4 vols. (New Haven, 1825), 4:55, 260-61, as quoted in George M. Marsden, "Everyone One's Own Interpreter? The Bible, Science, and Authority in Mid-Nineteenth-Century America," in *The Bible in America*, ed. Nathan O. Hatch and Mark A. Noll (New York: Oxford University Press, 1982), 85. For a similar quotation and solid discussion, see Conrad Wright, *The Beginnings of Unitarianism in America* (Boston: Starr King, 1955), 92.

39. N. W. Taylor, undocumented quotation from William G. McLoughlin, *Revivals, Awakenings, and Reform* (Chicago: University of Chicago Press, 1978), 119. See also Taylor's essay "On the Authority of Reason in Theology," *Quarterly Christian Spectator*, 3rd ser., 9 (March 1837), which is quoted and discussed in George M. Marsden, *The Evangelical Mind and the New School Presbyterian Experience* (New Haven: Yale University Press, 1970), 47.

40. Archibald Alexander, "Theological Lectures, Nature and Evidence of Truth" (1812ff.), in *The Princeton Theology, 1812-1921*, ed. Mark A. Noll (Grand Rapids: Baker, 1983), 65.

reference to Paley's *View of the Evidences of Christianity* (1794), which even then was still regularly assigned as a text in America.

> Nothing is so common . . . as for young men to approach serious subjects as judges — to study them as mere sciences. . . . The study of the Evidences as now popular (such as Paley's) encourages this evil frame of mind — the learner is supposed external to the system. . . . In all these cases the student is supposed to look upon the system from without, and to have to choose it by an act of reason before he submits to it — whereas the great lesson of the gospel is faith, and obeying prior to reason, and *proving* its reasonableness by making experiment of it.[41]

Newman, as did also a few Americans, eventually fled from Protestant scientism to Catholic authority.[42] Jonathan Edwards, especially in his reasoning on free will and true virtue, had made similar objections in the previous century, only in favor of a Protestant conception of the Holy Spirit.[43] But between the Great Awakening and the Oxford Movement, almost no one in the mainstream of American Protestantism seconded the opinions of Newman or Edwards. Demonstration by means of science was what the age required, and that is what Protestant spokesmen provided.

### Revival

Revivalism, perhaps the least likely feature of antebellum Protestant life to reflect the influence of the Enlightenment, nonetheless also took on a new shape because of that influence. The push, even in the realms of the Spirit, was toward rationality and scientific predictability.[44] Early Methodists may have transcended the need for formal explication. But by the time of Charles G. Finney, the greatest evangelist of the antebellum period and one of the most influential Americans of his generation, theistic

41. John Henry Newman to Arthur Perceval, 11 January 1836, as quoted in Marvin R. O'Connell, *The Oxford Conspirators: A History of the Oxford Movement, 1833-45* (New York: Macmillan, 1969).

42. One American was Isaac Hecker; for his story, see John Farina, *An American Experience of God: The Spirituality of Isaac Hecker* (New York: Paulist, 1981).

43. Jonathan Edwards, *The Nature of True Virtue,* ed. William K. Frankena (Ann Arbor: University of Michigan Press, 1960), 12.

44. A good discussion of Enlightenment revivalism is found in C. Leonard Allen, Richard T. Hughes, and Michael R. Weed, *The Worldly Church* (Abilene: ACU Press, 1988), 27-31.

Enlightenment science had begun to shape attitudes toward revival. Finney's *Lectures on Revivals of Religion* (1835) summarized a new approach to evangelism. Since God has established reliable laws in the natural world, we know that he has also done so in the spiritual world. To activate the proper causes for revivals was to produce the proper effect. "The connection between the right use of means for a revival and a revival is as philosophically [i.e., scientifically] sure as between the right use of means to raise grain and a crop of wheat. I believe, in fact, it is more certain, and there are fewer instances of failure."[45] Because the spiritual world is analogous to the natural world, observable cause and effect must work in religion as well as in physics. The wine of revival — confidence in God's supernatural ability to convert the sinner — may have tasted the same in antebellum America as it had in earlier centuries, but now it was being poured from a new wineskin.

### Scripture

Nowhere did the marriage between Protestantism and the Enlightenment produce more lively offspring than in the American appropriation of the Bible. Traditional interpretations of Scripture may have come under attack in the new United States, elitist traditions of biblical exposition and elitist assumptions about how much study was necessary before a man could publicly preach the Bible were gleefully disregarded, but there was no retreat from Scripture itself. For reasons that have yet to be probed with the attention the subject deserves, the "Bible alone" (in both senses of the phrase) survived the assault on tradition that characterized the era. What Nathan Hatch has written about populist religion in the early republic was true as well for almost all other Protestants: "In a culture that mounted a frontal assault upon tradition, mediating elites, and institutions, the Bible very easily became . . . 'a book dropped from the skies for all sorts of men to use in their own way.' "[46]

Virtually every aspect of the profound Protestant attachment to the Bible and almost every level of evangelical culture was shaped by theistic

45. Charles G. Finney, *Lectures on Revivals of Religion*, ed. William G. McLoughlin (1835; Cambridge, MA: Harvard University Press, 1960), 33.

46. Hatch, *Democratization of American Christianity*, 182; the quotation is from John W. Nevin. See also Hatch, *"Sola Scriptura* and *Novus Ordo Seclorum,"* in Hatch and Noll, eds., *The Bible in America*, 59-78.

Enlightenment science. Convincing theological arguments, such as Andover's Moses Stuart's 1833 rebuttal of the notion of innate inheritable depravity, could rest on the fact that the erroneous view was "plainly at variance with the explicit declarations of the Scriptures . . . and with the first dictates of our unbiased feelings and our reason."[47] The orthodox Congregationalist Leonard Woods, Jr., wrote in 1822 that the best method of Bible study was "that which is pursued in the science of physics," regulated "by the maxims of *Bacon* and *Newton.*" Newtonian method, Woods said, "is as applicable in theology as in physics, although in theology we have an extra-aid, the revelation of the Bible. But in each science reasoning is the same — we inquire for facts and from them arrive at general truths."[48] Southern Presbyterian Robert Breckinridge wrote in 1847 that theology derived from the Bible could be a science expressed as "uncontrovertibly as I would write Geometry."[49] The best-known statement of Enlightenment biblicism appeared after the Civil War in Charles Hodge's *Systematic Theology,* but it was a position that he, with others, had been asserting for over fifty years:

> The Bible is to the theologian what nature is to the man of science. It is his store-house of facts; and his method of ascertaining what the Bible teaches, is the same as that which the natural philosopher adopts to ascertain what nature teaches. . . . The duty of the Christian theologian is to ascertain, collect, and combine all the facts which God has revealed concerning himself and our relation to him. These facts are all in the Bible.[50]

Methodist theology, though always more observant of the experiential prerogatives of the Holy Spirit, nonetheless followed the lead of British mentors away from the biblically infused and philosophically nuanced experientialism of John Wesley and John Fletcher toward the increasing moral rationalism of Richard Watson.[51] Eventually, Methodist

47. Moses Stuart, *Commentary on Romans* (1832), 541, as quoted in John H. Giltner, *Moses Stuart: The Father of Biblical Science in America* (Atlanta: Scholars Press, 1988), 115.

48. Leonard Woods, as quoted in Hovenkamp, *Science and Religion in America,* 61, and in Kuklick, *Churchmen and Philosophers,* 89.

49. Robert Breckinridge, quoted in Holifield, *Gentlemen Theologians,* 203.

50. Hodge, *Systematic Theology,* 3 vols. (1872-73; Grand Rapids: Eerdmans, n.d.), 1:10-11.

51. See Robert E. Chiles, *Theological Transition in American Methodism, 1790-1935* (New York: Abingdon, 1965), 76-95.

reflection on the methods of theology arrived at just about the same place as had the Congregationalists and Presbyterians. This was the case with the Canadian Nathanael Burwash when he began to lecture on theology in the 1860s and 1870s:

> We study not words nor formal definitions, not second-hand observa-
> tions however perfect or excellent, but wherever possible, the things
> themselves. Hence we must get at, not volumes of theology constructed
> to hand, not creeds and dogmatic canons, but the original facts with
> which theology deals: — the living sin, the living Christ, the living God
> himself. . . . Where shall we find our facts as to these? In the Bible and
> in the heart of humanity.[52]

And it became a prominent feature in the systematic reasoning of John Miley, who, writing in 1892, sounded very much like Charles Hodge:

> A system of theology is a combination of doctrines in scientific ac-
> cord. . . . Through a careful study of the facts of geology the doctrines
> of the science are reached and verified, while in turn they illuminate
> the facts. . . . So must systematic theology study the elements of doctri-
> nal truth, whether furnished in the book of nature or the book of
> revelation, and in a scientific mode combine them in doctrines.[53]

Such attitudes were by no means limited to the established denominations with reputations to protect. A recent study of Alexander Campbell and the Restorationist movement, which led to the founding of the Disciples of Christ, the Churches of Christ, and the Christian Churches, argues convincingly that "the Campbell movement was as clear an expression of the spirit of Common Sense rationalism as one could hope to find in American religion in the early nineteenth century."[54] Nowhere does that rationalism appear more evidently than in Restorationist use of Scripture. At [Francis] Bacon College, which Disciples founded in 1836, Camp-

---

52. Nathanael Burwash, notes for "A System of Inductive Theology," as quoted in Marguerite Van Die, *An Evangelical Mind: Nathanael Burwash and the Methodist Tradition in Canada, 1839-1918* (Kingston and Montreal: McGill-Queen's University Press, 1989), 98.

53. John Miley, *Systematic Theology* (New York: Methodist Book Concern, 1892), 5.

54. Richard T. Hughes and C. Leonard Allen, *Illusions of Innocence: Protestant Primitivism in America, 1639-1875* (Chicago: University of Chicago Press, 1988), 143.

bell told how he studied the Bible: "I have endeavored to read the Scriptures as though no one had read them before me." Other Restorationist leaders, like Tolbert Fanning, expressed the boundless methodological confidence of the age when he asserted that "the Scriptures fairly translated need no explanation." Another Restorationist, James S. Lamar, published in 1859 his *Organon of Scripture: Or, the Inductive Method of Biblical Interpretation,* in which the impress of the Enlightenment was unmistakable: "the Scriptures admit of being studied and expounded upon the principles of the inductive method; and . . . when thus interpreted they speak to us in a voice as certain and unmistakeable as the language of nature heard in the experiments and observations of science."[55]

Such views of method were so widespread in antebellum America as to constitute a national faith every bit as dominant as confidence in Scripture itself. In fact, the two were indistinguishable. Only a very occasional critic protested. John W. Nevin, weaned from scientific rationalism by the influence of pious German romanticism, thought the self-delusion of this biblicism was very clear: "The liberty of the sect consists . . . in thinking its particular notions, shouting its shibboleths and passwords, dancing its religious hornpipes, and reading the Bible only through its theological goggles."[56] But antebellum Protestants paid about as much attention to Nevin as they did to John Henry Newman hurrying his way toward Rome. Nevin was free to speak, but since he challenged the prevailing interpretive system, his voice would not be heard until, much later, the hegemony of theistic Enlightenment science began to disintegrate.

In sum, before the Civil War, Protestants mastered not just the media of communications but also the dominant interpretive system of the day. Evangelical Protestantism flourished because its message was heard everywhere and because its message was spoken with concepts that Americans could understand.

At this point, however, it is pertinent to ask about connections between media and interpretations. Antebellum evangelicals mastered both, and their message had great effect. But were mastery of media and mastery of interpretation linked organically — did the spread of evangelical Christianity depend upon their fruitful union? Or were they linked only adventitiously — would evangelicalism have exerted such force if the

55. Quoted in Hughes and Allen, *Illusions of Innocence,* 157, 161, 156.
56. John W. Nevin, "The Sect System," as quoted in Hatch, *Democratization of American Christianity,* 183.

dual mastery had not been present? If answers to these questions are possible, they will likely come from the history of the Methodists. That denomination led the evangelical charge, but its history also differs in important respects from that of other evangelical bodies. It is obvious that Methodists mastered the powerful print media available in the new American nation, but they were not leaders in such work. Early on, as Donald Mathews points out, "American Wesleyans relied much less on the written word than that which was spoken."[57] Although by 1828 a Methodist periodical, the *Christian Advocate and Journal,* had become one of the widest circulating weeklies in the world, it was only ten years earlier that the Methodists had founded their first successful journal.[58] Only gradually did Methodists show a great concern for mastering the theistic Enlightenment science that was the new nation's dominant interpretive system. It is not as though early Methodists of Francis Asbury's generation were antagonistic to theistic Enlightenment science, for when Methodists did finally devote time in the 1830s and 1840s to formal learning and the formal defense of their convictions, they were all but indistinguishable from other American evangelicals. That is, they appealed to the facts of moral experience and championed the sovereignty of Baconian method almost as ably as the Presbyterians.[59] The difference is that Methodists did not seem much interested in such matters during the first decades of the century — precisely at the time when they were fueling the evangelical surge. At least into the 1830s, Methodists seemed more content with mastering the flow of communication. Later, in the transition from enthusiasm to intellectual order, they too took up the burden of deploying theistic Enlightenment science for the Christian cause.[60] Did the

57. Donald G. Mathews, "Evangelical America — The Methodist Ideology," in *Rethinking Methodist History: A Bicentennial Historical Consultation,* ed. Russell E. Richey and Kenneth E. Rowe (Nashville: Kingswood, 1985), 92.

58. Hatch, *Democratization of American Christianity,* 142-43; Leland Scott, "The Message of Early American Methodism," in *The History of American Methodism: Volume I* (New York: Abingdon, 1964), 331.

59. For Methodist similarities to other proponents of theistic Enlightenment science, see Holifield, *Gentlemen Theologians,* passim; Van Die, *An Evangelical Mind,* 89-113. According to Scott, "Message of Early American Methodism," 353, the first year of the *Methodist Magazine* (1818) included extracts from James Beattie's "Essay on Truth" (a popularization of Thomas Reid's commonsense ethics) and from Stanhope Smith's *Lectures on Moral Philosophy* (the most sophisticated American distillation of Scottish thought in the first decades of the nineteenth century).

60. A fine recent study on that transition is William Westfall, *Two Worlds: The*

Methodists change? Were they simply responding in new ways appropriate to changes in the culture? Their experience is enough to raise questions about whether it was necessary to master both media and interpretation in order to make the gospel meaningful in an age, but it is not enough — at least not enough for one with my knowledge about the Methodists — to answer them.

In the event, the passing of evangelical hegemony after the Civil War seems more closely related to problems of interpretation than to problems of media. Evangelicals would never again dominate the media as they had in the early part of the century, but they would remain a creative force, alike in the days of Chautauqua as in the ages of radio and television.[61] Perhaps evangelical mastery of antebellum media did present difficulties when media technologies evolved after the Civil War. Whatever the situation of the media, that evangelical mastery of the prevailing antebellum interpretive system had definite results. By the last third of the nineteenth century, that mastery had become an incubus rather than an assist.

## IV

Theistic Enlightenment science grew to dominance with great speed in revolutionary America. Less than a century later, it vanished even more rapidly. The end of its hegemony was, in Perry Miller's words, "one of the most radical revolutions in the history of the American mind," when "the philosophy and the philosophers of Scottish Realism vanished from the American colleges, leaving not even a rack behind."[62] Just as a war, along with the social, political, and cultural circumstances attending a war, had been responsible for its rise, so war and attendant cultural changes may have been responsible for its demise.

---

*Protestant Culture of Nineteenth-Century Ontario* (Kingston and Montreal: McGill-Queen's University Press, 1989), which describes a process whereby Methodistic religion of experience came to resemble the Anglican religion of order.

61. See, e.g., Quentin J. Schultze, "Evangelical Radio and the Rise of the Electronic Church, 1921-1948," *Journal of Broadcasting and Electronic Media* 32 (Summer 1988): 289-306; and Larry K. Eskridge, "Evangelical Broadcasting: Its Meaning for Evangelicals," in *Transforming Faith: The Sacred and the Secular in Modern American History,* ed. M. L. Bradbury and J. B. Gilbert (New York: Greenwood, 1989), 127-39.

62. Perry Miller, *American Thought: Civil War to World War I* (New York: Rinehart, 1954), ix.

In the revolutionary period it had not been developments in theology, philosophy, or the zeitgeist that converted Americans from the idealism, Augustinianism, and conversionist ethics of Puritanism to the realism, optimism, and universalistic ethics of theistic Enlightenment science. It was rather that the Scottish Enlightenment offered Americans exactly what they seemed to require to master the tumults of the Revolution. As Norman Fiering has put it, the "moral philosophy" of the eighteenth-century Scottish Enlightenment "was uniquely suited to the needs of an era still strongly committed to traditional religious values and yet searching for alternative modes of justification for those values."[63]

In like manner, the fall of theistic Enlightenment science took place when the Civil War and the changes it accelerated in the nation's political economy altered the environment in which theistic Enlightenment science had once flourished. During the antebellum period, theistic Enlightenment science had contributed massively to a series of ongoing political arguments about the nature of the Union, the rights of the states, and the imperatives of republicanism. After the war and the securing of the Union, there was little call in national politics for a philosophy of justice that was concerned about the nature of virtue. Armies, not arguments, had settled the issue of what a republic is and how its parts should fit together. American politics then entered into a long period, from which it has not yet emerged, in which material interests and debates over the role of government — but not arguments over first principles — defined the horizon of public debate. In such a political situation, theistic Enlightenment science was irrelevant.[64]

Something similar may be said about social order. Abraham Lincoln to the contrary notwithstanding, the Civil War heralded the final triumph of laissez-faire liberalism over nostalgic republicanism, of Adam Smith over Francis Hutcheson, of philosophies geared toward competition and therapeutic care of the self over philosophies geared toward community and

63. Norman Fiering, *Moral Philosophy at Seventeenth-Century Harvard: A Discipline in Transition* (Chapel Hill: University of North Carolina Press, 1981), 300.

64. I do not know enough about the effects of the Civil War to pontificate in this fashion. Nonetheless, the notions explored here arise from reading books such as Daniel Walker Howe, *The Political Culture of the American Whigs* (Chicago: University of Chicago Press, 1979); Anne Norton, *Alternative Americas: A Reading of Antebellum Political Culture* (Chicago: University of Chicago Press, 1986); and James M. McPherson, *Battle Cry of Freedom: The Civil War Era* (New York: Oxford University Press, 1988); and from pondering the approach of historians such as James R. Moore, Douglas Frank, George Rawlyk, Jackson Lears, and Burton Bledstein to the cultural frameworks of belief.

the sacrificial pursuit of fame. In such a world the public-spirited constraints of Christian altruism that theistic Enlightenment science attempted to inculcate had almost no meaning.

What, then, of the hereditary Protestant bond with theistic Enlightenment science after the Civil War? When political and social conditions arose for which theistic Enlightenment science was no longer useful, Christian allegiance to commonsense reasoning became problematic. Protestants might still want to rely on the Scottish philosophy, but when they did so they were now increasingly out of sync with the perceived political and social needs of the time. So, although Protestants might cling to theistic Enlightenment science, it was rapidly becoming a ticket *out* of the discussion and *off* the fast track of the rising American empire. In these circumstances, caused or at least stimulated by the War between the States, theistic Enlightenment science gave way, and other contenders arose to take its place as the public's dominant interpretive system.

One of the contenders was a revived form of the humanities, which savants such as Charles Eliot Norton promoted at Harvard by systematically infusing old vocabulary with new meaning. Like Matthew Arnold, Norton and like-minded aesthetes "preached" to their students, urged upon them the "inspiration" that comes from studying great art, and beckoned them to a "chapel" of modern humanistic learning.[65] But an even more powerful challenger now seemed to offer a mystical, ennobling, suprahuman, and world-integrating potential to its devotees. That rival was, of course, science. As the humanities bloomed as substitutes for theistic Enlightenment science, so too did the new naturalistic science. If there was a religion of literature, philosophy, and art in the late nineteenth century, so also was there now a religion of science.[66]

By 1900, in other words, we can see two contenders in American intellectual life for the functions exercised in antebellum America by the ideology of the evangelicals: scientism and aestheticism, both equipped with full metaphysical, ethical, and epistemological ambitions. But why were there just these two contenders? Why, with the collapse of theistic

65. For the use of these terms in a new way, see James Turner, "Secularization and Sacralization: Speculations on Some Religious Origins of the Secular Humanities Curriculum, 1850-1900," in *The Secularization of the Academy,* ed. George M. Marsden and Bradley J. Longfield (New York: Oxford University Press, 1992), 74-106.

66. For one example of a vast literature, see Alexandra Oleson and John Vos, eds., *The Organization of Knowledge in Modern America, 1860-1920* (Baltimore: Johns Hopkins University Press, 1979).

mental science, do we not see other contenders — such as, for example, the kind of traditionalism that was then being promoted in Catholic circles through the influence of Pius IX, the First Vatican Council, and a revival of Thomism? Even more, why were both aestheticism and scientism so a-Christian or anti-Christian?

The answer lies in the history of the theistic Enlightenment science from which this scientism and this aestheticism emerged. These were the two claimants because they were both descendents of prominent elements in the project of antebellum moral philosophy.

In the early United States, theistic Enlightenment science had been a singularly creative way of holding together humanistic (subjective) and scientific (objective) learning. As America's leading educators (who were also among America's leading Protestants) described it, *intuition* provided the axioms and data from which moral philosophy could be constructed by means of *scientific induction.* At a time when both enthusiasm and the new science were thought to threaten social order, political stability, and the Christian faith, theistic Enlightenment science had achieved something magical. It had joined the intuitive explanatory powers of self-conscious-ness to the skyrocketing reputation of Newton in such a way as to support rather than undercut social order, political stability, and Christianity. To put it in different terms, theistic Enlightenment science had not only concocted a brew out of supposedly irreconcilable ingredients from the Enlightenment and Romanticism, but it had alchemized this potentially fatal mix into a life-giving elixir for the new republic.

But when the maturing republic, its constitutional crisis settled at last and its eyes now fixed on the prize of wealth for all, no longer required such an elixir, it turned out that the elixir had perhaps not been so magical after all. For one thing, aestheticism and scientism emerged quite directly from the subjective and objective elements that Enlightenment mental science had attempted to fuse. Aestheticism as the successor of self-consciousness and scientism as the successor of Baconianism occupied positions in intellectual life that had been defined by fault lines within theistic mental science.[67]

From the vantage point of the 1880s, the elixir also turned out to be as much a poison to Christianity as a tonic for it. Modern unbelief,

---

67. For a particularly full description of the earlier capacity to straddle the later divide, see Lefferts A. Loetscher, *Facing the Enlightenment and Pietism: Archibald Alexander and the Founding of Princeton Theological Seminary* (Westport, CT: Greenwood, 1983).

James Turner has argued persuasively, "resulted from the decisions that influential church leaders — lay writers, theologians, ministers — made about how to confront the modern pressures upon religious belief. . . . [Their] choices, taken together, boiled down to a decision to deal with modernity by embracing it — to defuse modern threats to the traditional bases of belief by bringing God into line with modernity."[68] In American terms, although theistic Enlightenment science had once proved useful in supporting Christianity, it nonetheless promoted lines of reasoning and conceptions of morality that were eventually antagonistic to the faith. That is, mastering the interpretive system of one era hampered the ability of its advocates to master the changing intellectual circumstances of a succeeding age.

The depths to which Protestants were pushed by the late-century consequences of mastering the early-century interpretive system are well illustrated by struggles to come to terms with the higher criticism of Scripture. The consensus that had once prevailed among Protestants on the nature of the Bible began to change during the last third of the nineteenth century.[69] Conclusions from both "textual criticism" and "higher criticism" were calling settled opinions into question. The appearance of new views on the American scene corresponded with a surge of professionalization in the country's universities. In the 1870s and 1880s, graduate study on the European model began to be offered at older universities such as Harvard and newer ones such as Johns Hopkins. At such centers objectivist science was exalted as the royal road to truth, and the new professional academics reacted scornfully to what were perceived as parochial, uninformed, and outmoded scholarship. All fields, including the study of the Bible, were to be unfettered for free inquiry. In keeping with newer intellectual fashions, this scholarship relied heavily upon evolutionary notions; histories, stories, and writings all evolved over time, as did religious consciousness itself. It also tended to be skeptical about the

68. James Turner, *Without God, Without Creed: The Origins of Unbelief in America* (Baltimore: Johns Hopkins University Press, 1985), 266.
69. On that consensus, see John D. Woodbridge, *Biblical Authority: A Critique of the Rogers-McKim Proposal* (Grand Rapids: Zondervan, 1982), as supplemented by Jack B. Rogers and Donald K. McKim, *The Authority and Interpretation of the Bible: An Historical Approach* (San Francisco: Harper & Row, 1979). The paragraphs that follow draw on Mark A. Noll, *Between Faith and Criticism: Evangelicals, Scholarship, and the Bible* (San Francisco: Harper & Row, 1986); "Review Essay: The Bible in America," *Journal of Biblical Literature* 106 (1987): 493-509; and "Biblical Interpretation," in *Dictionary of Christianity in America,* ed. Daniel G. Reid (Downers Grove, IL: InterVarsity Press, 1990), 146-50.

miraculous and to reflect the view that the religious experience of the Jews and Christians was not essentially different from that of other peoples in the ancient world.

For our purposes the salient feature of Protestant responses to the new views of the Bible was their uniformly scientific character. To new questions Protestants brought old habits of thought. An inaugural public discussion of the new views occurred between Presbyterian conservatives and moderates from 1881 to 1883 in the pages of the *Presbyterian Review*. Both sides tried, as would almost all who followed in their train, as if by instinct to secure for themselves the high ground of scientific credibility. The moderates, led by Charles A. Briggs, were committed to "the principles of Scientific Induction." Since Old Testament studies had "been greatly enlarged by the advances in linguistic and historical science which mark our century," it was only proper to take this new evidence into account. To these Presbyterian intellectuals, the situation, as Briggs saw it, was clear: "The great majority of professional Biblical scholars in the various Universities and Theological Halls of the world, embracing those of the greatest learning, industry, and piety, demand a revision of traditional theories of the Bible on account of a large induction of new facts from the Bible and history."[70]

The conservatives were just as determined to enlist science on their side. As A. A. Hodge and Benjamin B. Warfield put it at the start of the exchange,

> [We] are sincerely convinced of the perfect soundness of the great Catholic doctine of Biblical Inspiration . . . and hence that all their elements and all their affirmations are absolutely errorless, and binding the faith and obedience of men. Nevertheless we admit that the question between ourselves and the advocates of [modern criticism], is one of fact, to be decided only by an exhaustive and impartial examination of all the sources of evidence, i.e., the claims and the phenomena of the Scriptures themselves.

Their colleague, William Henry Green, chose not to examine W. Robertson Smith's "presumptions" that led him to adopt critical views of the Old

---

70. Charles A. Briggs, "Critical Theories of the Sacred Scriptures in Relation to Their Inspiration," *Presbyterian Review* 2 (July 1881): 558; Henry Preserved Smith, "The Critical Theories of Julius Wellhausen," *Presbyterian Review* 3 (Apr. 1882): 386; and Briggs, "Critical Theories," 557.

Testament, but rather chose the way of induction: "We shall concern ourselves simply with duly certified facts." And Willis J. Beecher contended that the "mere hypotheses" of the new views proved nothing. "Without some element of positive evidence, a hypothesis or a hundred hypotheses fail of themselves. . . . Any author is uncritical if he indulges in assertions which are based on mere hypotheses."[71] In this debate, both sides recognized the role of presuppositions — they were what kept the other side from seeing the truth.

Once the terms of the debate were set in this scientific form, there was little deviation. On the right, the singularly evangelical type of the populist scholar continued without hesitation to apply standards of the early American Enlightenment to the Bible. R. A. Torrey's *What the Bible Teaches,* for example, provided in 1898 a book whose method was "rigidly inductive," where "the methods of modern science are applied to Bible study — thorough analysis followed by careful synthesis." The result was "a careful, unbiased, systematic, thorough-going, *inductive* study and statement of Bible truth."[72] More academic conservatives followed the same path. Robert Dick Wilson of Princeton Seminary, for instance, published in 1926 a work entitled *A Scientific Investigation of the Old Testament* in which he chose not to use prophecy or miracles to support his traditional conclusions about the Old Testament. Rather, he would use "the evidential method . . . the Laws of Evidence as applied to documents admitted in our courts of law . . . the evidence of manuscripts and versions and of the Egyptian, Babylonian, and other documents outside the Bible" to demonstrate the truth of traditional opinions.[73]

For their part, defenders of the new views were no less committed to the authority of detached scientific effort, although, of course, science in the new mode instead of the old. Shirley Jackson Case at the University of Chicago justified renovation of older views of Scripture because of the demands of science. Secular and religious historians alike employed a "method of procedure which is strictly inductive; all [their] conclusions are to be derived from concrete and empirically verifiable data." A true

71. A. A. Hodge and Benjamin B. Warfield, "Inspiration," *Presbyterian Review* 2 (Apr. 1881): 237; William Henry Green, "Professor W. Robertson Smith on the Pentateuch," *Presbyterian Review* 3 (Jan. 1882): 111; Willis J. Beecher, "The Logical Methods of Professor Kuenen," *Presbyterian Review* 3 (Oct. 1882): 706.
72. R. A. Torrey, *What the Bible Teaches* (Chicago: Fleming H. Revell, 1898), 1.
73. Robert Dick Wilson, *A Scientific Investigation of the Old Testament* (Philadelphia: The Sunday School Times, 1926), 6-7.

scholar sticks to "experimentally ascertainable facts," shuns "metaphysical speculation and worships at the shrine of empiricism." The best way of proceeding is "under the conviction that religion can be best understood by giving first attention, not to its theoretical aspects, but to its actual historical manifestations, and when speculative interpretations and historical research meet on common grounds he will insist that all hypotheses be judged at the bar of his science."[74]

A special irony attended the sway of the Enlightenment among at least some of those who promoted new views of the Bible. In the early years of critical scholarship, Case and his colleague Shailer Mathews at the University of Chicago were especially important influences. But although they promoted new views, they did so with traditional attitudes toward method. What William J. Hynes has called an "anti-metaphysical and anti-philosophical bias" characterized their work. Influenced first by Albrecht Ritschl and later by the scientific ideal of the "socio-historical" method, both scholars, again in Hynes's words, seemed to "prefer that philosophical questions be bracketed with respect to Christianity and theological methods."[75] Case and Mathews made no secret of their desire to replace fundamentalist views of the Bible with scientific, enlightened views. But the irony of their situation is that their aversion to philosophical self-consciousness followed exactly the path of nineteenth-century traditionalists who were also proud of having no preconceptions and simply letting the facts speak for themselves. At Chicago, the content of biblical interpretation shifted dramatically from previous patterns, but the power of Enlightenment assumptions about method remained pretty much the same.

In the end, therefore, questions about biblical criticism divided Protestants. But they remained struggles over facts (and also over control of schools and denominations) that did not upset hereditary Protestant confidence in Enlightenment rationality. Because it was an age of unquestioned hegemony for science — an age that fully embodied the optimism, this-worldliness, and scientific confidence of the early theistic Enlightenment science — and because Protestants for a century had known no other world, it was second nature to address new problems with the old certainties of the first American Enlightenment: form for the moderates, form

74. As quoted in William J. Hynes, *Shirley Jackson Case and the Chicago School* (Chico, CA: Scholars Press, 1981), 80.

75. Hynes, *Shirley Jackson Case*, 119.

and content for the conservatives. To put it another way, authority in America since 1776 had been self-generating. In the early years of the republic, Protestants had been able to unite a commitment to authority from the people with a commitment to authority from science. In response to shifting intellectual conditions after the Civil War, fundamentalists tried to retain the old populist science, while modernists opted instead for an elite new science over against the old populism; but both, along with the multitudes in between, did not challenge the older conceptions of self-justifying authority. Mastering the antebellum interpretive system stood squarely in the way of mastering the postbellum interpretive systems.

## V

The evangelical Enlightenment was a momentous creation. Side by side with the evangelical media, the two bestrode American civilization for its first seventy-five years. If the Christian America they created was a flawed, hypocritical, incomplete, and presumptuous triumph, it was still a triumph. Evangelical control of media provided the means; evangelical control of interpretation provided the rationale; evangelical energy drove both media and interpretation. However one may evaluate mastery of the media, mastery of the interpretive system was not enough. Or at least mastery of the sort found in this era was not enough. Without a point of evaluation outside the interpretive system — or at least without the awareness of the need to strive for a point outside the interpretive system — the temptation was irresistible to think of the gospel expressed in terms of theistic Enlightenment science as the only possible expression of the gospel. Theological education, in its broadest aspect, needed to go beyond mastery *of* the interpretive system to struggle *with* the interpretive system. By and large, this wrestling did not take place, and so the heady security of one age gave birth to the shaking insecurities of the next. Still, it had been a breathtaking attempt.

The task of theological education is ideally a reflection of the gospel, of the Word becoming flesh and dwelling among us. To be effective, the Word must really dwell among us, as in antebellum America the labor of so many itinerants and Sunday school teachers, colporteurs and printers, purveyors of tracts and printers of Bibles insured that it would. But in addition it must really be the Word that dwells among us. The evangelical Protestants who mastered the interpretive system of antebellum America did their job well, perhaps too well. Admiration for their achievement and charity arising from an awareness of the flaccidity that has followed should mitigate censure, but they cannot hide the fact that these worthy predecessors, who, in wrestling with the prevailing interpretive system of their age, aimed at incarnation, nonetheless arrived at enculturation, and did not notice when they passed from one to the other.

# Preaching to the "Faith" of America

## David G. Buttrick

When preachers preach, they do not address a congregation of empty heads waiting to be crammed with the word of the gospel. No, the common mind of any congregation is already packed full of all kinds of convictions, from political dreams to primitive theologies, from pop-psychology to undernourished notions of life, death, and destiny. Because preaching addresses a particular mind, it employs a carefully calculated language; homiletics is always street-smart strategy. So, if we are to discuss contemporary homiletics, we must venture some analysis of the changing American religious mind.

The American experience slices some three hundred years from the human history book — three hundred years filled with almost every form of piety possible to imagine. Is there any way to muddle meaning out of an American religious history that has included Puritan "hanging sermons," Mormon polygamy, African-American gospel music, Swedenborgian temples, Quaker silences, camp meeting hoopla, exotic celebrations of "La Conqui" in the Southwest, not to forget gurus in Aspen, laced Anglicans, straight-laced Presbyterians, Pat Boone's white shoes, and the National Conference of Catholic Bishops at prayer? We must either wallow in pluralism or find some framework to make sense of America's odd religious history. Let us probe the three-hundred-year span during which different models of God and humankind have danced with grave and/or graceful steps across the American mind.

## Faith and Formulation

When scholars chatter about the three hundred years coinciding with the colonization of America to the present day, they tend to use different labels. Some have called the period a "Protestant Era" while others bundle the centuries together and tag them "Enlightenment."[1] Please note that they are using two terms to refer to the same time period. The conjunction of terms makes sense if we remember that the rise of a Protestant empire in America was matched by the spiraling up of a cultural formulation dedicated to enshrined reason.[2] At the same time as Methodist circuit riders were galloping the frontier with handout salvation, a way of looking at life was striding ever more deeply into the penumbral fringes of the American cultural mind. Is it possible that the secret of American religiousness involves interaction between a system of belief and a burgeoning cultural formulation: the Protestant Era and the Age of Enlightenment?

The wonderful thing about a cultural formulation is that it offers what might be termed the comforts of correspondence. By "correspondence" I mean the idea that there is some sort of connection, some correspondence, between our "here and now" and beyond, between the human world we live in and some realm of transcendent reality. To sum it up simply one could say, "There's something out there like us," there is something beyond us that is nevertheless analogous to us, a higher world of which our world is a pale mirror image. If you chase your way through the past, taking a peek at the "great ages" in Western history, you'll find that each embraced a cultural formulation based on some notion of correspondence. The Greek mind after Plato conceived a transcendent world of eternal "forms," related to the dim encaved images of our earthly world. Likewise, medieval men and women believed in hierarchies of heaven related to hierarchies of earth, a "City of

1. The term "Protestant Era" is drawn from Paul Tillich, *The Protestant Era*, trans. J. L. Adams (Chicago: University of Chicago Press, 1948). The term "Enlightenment" is used by Crane Brinton in *A History of Western Morals* (New York: Harcourt, Brace, and Co., 1959) for the "mind-set" of the past three hundred years. See also the monumental work by Peter Gay, *The Enlightenment: An Interpretation*, 2 vols. (New York: Alfred Knopf, 1966, 1969). A fine study of the interaction between early-day Calvinism and Enlightenment is Alan Heimert's *Religion and the American Mind* (Cambridge, MA: Harvard University Press, 1966).

2. I borrow the term "cultural formulation" from Brinton, *History of Western Morals*. By cultural formulation I mean the convictional system, often tacit, of a given cultural era — ideas of human being, world, destiny, and God, not to mention values, social styles, notions of heroism, etc.

God" and a human city bound by bridges of analogy. In the eighteenth century, folk were dazzled by a similar notion of correspondence. You find it lurking in the Deism of a Ben Franklin or a Thomas Jefferson; you hear it echoing in sermons or political oratory with sweet talk of natural law, divine reason, and harmony; you can even sing it in the measured stanzas of "The Spacious Firmament on High," scribbled by Addison in 1712.[3] The eighteenth century looked not to heaven for transcendence but to the heavens, to Nature spelled with a capital "N." In nature's Grand Design they read patterns of order that, to them, displayed divine reason. Since human being was a child of nature, humanity was also aglow with divinity, embodying a holy rational spirit. For the eighteenth century, the key word was *reason* — divine reason disclosed in patterns of creation, divine reason enlightening the human mind. No wonder brash Tom Paine could toss aside his Bible: "Are we to have no word of God," he demanded rhetorically. "I answer . . . the word of God is the creation we behold."[4] Do you get the picture of correspondence? Creation is good, rational, lawful, benevolent, and its glory reflects in human beings.

Now take note: Developed cultural formulations are a comfort indeed. They give us a sense of belonging in the world, not to mention some hint of extension beyond the world — "intimations of immortality."[5] Eugène Ionesco catches the mood when he has his stage hero, Bérenger, declaim: "Gardens, blue sky, or the spring which corresponds to the universe inside . . . a smiling being in a smiling world . . . I couldn't die."[6] Cultural formulations are clearly satisfying; they warm the soul. More than that, if you mix a little religion into a cultural formulation, you can provide what Peter Berger has called "a sacred canopy," a structure of civil religion to justify and even ennoble society.[7] Of course, the only trouble with cultural formulations is that, once the cognitive props are kicked out, they can come tumbling down like a house of cards — or, better, like a tower of Babel, leaving societies in a confusion of tongues.

3. Joseph Addison's "The Spacious Firmament on High," based on Psalm 19:1-6, was first published in No. 465 of *The Spectator*, 23 August 1712, at the end of "an essay on the proper means of strengthening and confirming faith in the mind of man [sic]."

4. Thomas Paine, *The Age of Reason*, Part I, p. 24, in *The Great Works of Thomas Paine* (New York: D. M. Bennett, 1877).

5. From the title of William Wordsworth's famous "Ode: Intimations of Immortality from Recollections of Early Childhood," published in 1807 as a corrective to Coleridge's "Ode on Dejection." Coleridge was, of course, a better theologian.

6. Eugène Ionesco, *The Killer and Other Plays* (New York: Grove Press, 1960), 19.

7. Peter L. Berger, *The Sacred Canopy* (Garden City, NY: Doubleday and Co., 1967).

They are glorious, gleaming constructs that offer social stability and vertical piety, but when they crumble you are apt to get cultural chaos or sometimes a "death of God" theology. So much by way of introduction to the cultural formulation we call Enlightenment.

What about the "Protestant Era," that other label frequently pasted on the American experience? Certainly the first two hundred years in America were marked by Protestant expansion. As late as the first quarter of the nineteenth century, less than five percent of the religious population was made up of anything other than nominal Protestants.[8] At the start of things, America was essentially a Protestant land.

Moreover, the first colonists who ventured to America were not only Protestants; for nearly one hundred years they were Protestants of Calvinist persuasion. Shaped by the rigor of post-Reformation scholasticism, they bowed before the awful Sovereignty of God, brooded over their Total Depravity, rejoiced in Election, and puzzled over the ways and means of a destining Providence. They brought to America not only a Bible but also respect for the laws of God and a growing suspicion that, oddly enough, they were God's new Israel transplanted in a somewhat alien promised land.

So much for our dramatis personae — a religion and a cultural formulation, the Protestant Era and the Age of Enlightenment. Let us raise the curtain on an American drama.

## An American Drama

### Act I: Pilgrim Piety[9]

When Pilgrims stepped onto the rocky shore of Massachusetts, they brought along a book, the Bible, and from the book a story, the story of God and Israel. The story gave meaning to their lives, for it seemed to match up marvelously with their peculiar experience. Were they not covenanting people set free from European oppression, walking in a lush new land of promise? They saw themselves as a new Israel in the wilderness. Egypt, the corrupt courts of Pharaoh, was behind them across a sea that God had miraculously opened. Now they were standing on the edge of a land of milk and honey, not to mention berries and maize corn. Just as

8. Martin E. Marty, *Righteous Empire* (New York: Dial, 1970), 16.
9. Please remember that "pilgrim" can be both a noun and an adjective.

God had given the law to the children of Israel, so they had received the new covenant law through Jesus Christ, God's second Moses. And just as God had destined Israel, providentially guiding her holy wanderings, so they saw the hand of God managing their destiny. God's story was their story — no doubt about it at all.[10]

Not only did the colonists have a story, they had theology as well, namely Calvinism of the post-Reformation period. In their theology, the glory of sovereign God stood blazing like the noonday sun above them. Sovereign God had elected them covenant people and by holy law would weigh their lives. Their duty was clear: to be holy as God was holy. So the Puritans were heavily into sanctification, a sanctification to be accomplished by the preaching of God's Law and the inward grafting of God's Word on their hearts by the working of the Holy Spirit.[11] But sanctification was more; it was understood as a story, an inward story, a "Pilgrim's Progress" of the heart from Adam's bondage to amendment of life by regeneration and to eventual heavenly rest. The Pilgrims set out quite deliberately to become God's "visible saints."[12]

For one hundred years the American spirit was shaped by Calvinism; American piety was manufactured in New England and bore a Puritan trademark. At worst, it may have been legalistic and stifling, bent on taming an old Adam heart — the kind of piety ridiculed by the Hugh Hefners of our more modern age. At best, however, it was a piety of story written on three levels at once: a story of God, a story of God's new people, and a story of sanctification — a Pilgrim's Progress of the heart. As long as narrative informed devotion, all life had meaning, not only public events but also private traumas. Oscar Hardin catches the mood:

> Every event had a deep meaning. . . . Indeed nothing that occurred in the world was simply a random event . . . life was filled with signs and

---

10. See Sydney E. Ahlstrom, *A Religious History of the American People* (New Haven: Yale University Press, 1972), chap. 8; Daniel J. Boorstin, *The Americans: The Colonial Experience* (New York: Random House, 1958), 3-31; and M. Walzer, *The Revolution of the Saints* (New York: Atheneum, 1968).

11. On Puritan preaching, there are many studies, but few as comprehensive as Harry S. Stout, *The New England Soul* (New York: Oxford University Press, 1986); see also T. Toulouse, *The Art of Prophesying: New England Sermons and the Shaping of Belief* (Atlanta: University of Georgia, 1987); and E. White, *Puritan Rhetoric* (Carbondale: Southern Illinois University Press, 1972).

12. Edmund S. Morgan, *Visible Saints: The History of a Puritan Idea* (New York: New York University Press, 1963).

portents. . . . In the pilgrimage of life, man [sic] cautiously made his way, examining every incident for clues to his destiny.[13]

To our modern, wised-up age, such talk sounds suspiciously like paranoia, yet for Puritan selves it was faith, because all the "signs" they read were interpreted in light of a story. America's native piety then was a sense of destiny, social and personal, within the storied purposes of God; it was pilgrim (adjective) piety.

Let the curtain fall on Act I.

### Act II: The Perils of Courtship

Two hundred years after the Pilgrims blew ashore in New England, their brand of Calvinism had come unglued. Calvinism still haunted the post-Puritan characters in Hawthorne's novels, but otherwise it had been compromised, fatally weakened, and all but lost. Emerson in an atypically nostalgic moment could glance back at the Puritan world and ask plaintively, "What is to replace for us [their] piety . . . it glides away from us day by day."[14] By mid-nineteenth century, it had clearly glided away from that dear blither-head Emerson, if not from the American scene.

So what happened? How did colonial Calvinism lose its grip on the American mind? Puritanism didn't lose its grip; it let go. It let go in order to chase that gaudy creature "Enlightenment." Bluntly, Puritan faith bedded down with a cultural formulation and in the process conceived the sometimes sanctimonious child we call "civil religion." Oh, the courtship was strained, to say the least; as lovers they argued, spat, backed off, made up — worthies such as Jonathan Edwards, Samuel Hopkins, Charles Chauncy, and William Channing chronicled the story;[15] but, as everyone knows, stormy courtships can a marriage make. The marriage of religion and a cultural formulation, consummated in the eighteenth century, created an American "synthesis" and gave America

13. Oscar Hardin, *The Americans* (Boston: Little, Brown, and Co., 1963), quoted by Martin E. Marty, "The Spirit's Holy Errand," *Daedalus* (Winter 1967): 105.

14. Ralph Waldo Emerson, "The Method of Nature," *The American Transcendentalists*, ed. Perry Miller (Garden City, NY: Doubleday and Co., 1957), quoted in Marty, "Spirit's Holy Errand," 105.

15. See Joseph Haroutunian, *Piety versus Moralism: The Passing of the New England Theology* (Hamden, CT: Archon Press, 1964).

a common mind, even if as a result there was a loss of narrative meaning.[16]

How could sturdy Puritanism succumb to the wiles of a cultural formulation? Puritanism succumbed because of a flawed hermeneutic. While the Puritans had a biblical story, they were woefully short on hi*story*. Yes, they embraced the story of Israel and their own New World experience, but nothing in between; they lost track of twenty centuries between Scripture and the immediacies of experience because their binary typology simply annihilated history. After all, Puritans saw themselves as the new Israel, liberated from the decadent Egypt of European history; they were God's new communal Adam and, therefore, cast behind the history of the old Adam. In a way the Puritans typify the flaw of most American Protestant communities, for in clinging to Scripture and experience they lost sight of tradition, and in losing tradition they forgot about historical consciousness.[17] How hard it is to hold onto a story when you lose a sense of hi*story!*

In still another way, Puritanism was set up for the blandishments of Enlightenment. The Puritan mind bowed before an immutable God — a God remote, eternal, and above all unchanging.[18] So the Puritan God was fixed as a tablet of stone, as unmoving as a throne room. (Clearly, the Puritans were not much into process theology!) Well, if your God is a fixed point, it's mighty hard to hold onto a sense of pilgrimage; for unless God has some kind of "history," it is almost impossible for God's people to have history.

16. Though I may seem to distinguish Christian faith as separate from cultural formulation, it is not. The idea of an "essence of Christianity" that can be distilled from its many cultural expressions is surely a fancy. Nevertheless, there are times when Christians are conscious of having to contend with a budding cultural formulation and other times when faith seems in evident tension with its cultural context. For a recent discussion of the issue, see Stephen Sykes, *The Identity of Christianity: Theologians and the Essence of Christianity from Schleiermacher to Barth* (Philadelphia: Fortress Press, 1984), esp. chaps. 1 and 9.

17. This is a criticism of Protestant hermeneutics suggested by E. Schillebeeckx, "Toward a Catholic Use of Hermeneutics," *God the Future of Man* (New York: Sheed and Ward, 1968), 3-49.

18. The one word that occurs twice in the Westminster Confession's famous definition of God is the word "immutable": "There is but one living and true God, who is infinite in being and perfection, a most pure spirit, invisible, without body, parts, or passions, *immutable,* immense, eternal, incomprehensible, almighty, most wise, most holy, most free, most absolute, working all things according to his [sic] own *immutable* and most righteous will . . ." *The Westminster Confession of Faith* (1647), chap. 2, sec. 1; emphasis added.

An immutable God is a God of fixed principles, laws, and virtues, but scarcely a God of story. You can adore an unchanging, unmoving God and align your life with the divine will ("getting right with God"), but you cannot *go along* with God. So an odd combination of hermeneutic flaw and static theology led to the weakening of the Puritan mind.

When colonial Calvinism forgot hi*story*, it was easily taken in by the cultural formulation we have termed "Enlightenment." Enlightenment was unhistorical, as are all cultural formulations. Remember, the genius of a cultural formulation is that it lives in the mind like a two-sided mirror, earth reflecting heaven and heaven reflecting earth in a glass called analogy. The motions of history are always a threat to the static vertical construct implicit in a cultural formulation; historical movement can shatter glass. Instead, cultural formulations are at home with fixed principles, natural laws, and the like, and resist the relativities of mobile historical conscious-ness. The "gods" of cultural formulation — divine reason, for example — are static and will always attempt to hold back an ongoing story. Put Puritan theology together with a fixed cultural formulation and what do you get? You get the death of what Brian Wicker has called the "story-shaped world."[19] So when Puritanism became engaged to Enlightenment, there was a loss of narrative meaning, and America was storyless; the mythos structure dissolved.[20] No wonder we have been left to console ourselves with those incredible fables about George Washington and Tom Jefferson given to us in our childhood.[21]

What exactly happened to the American religious mind? Deprived of story, of horizontal "pilgrim" meaning, it gave itself to what might be termed "vertical pieties" — namely, faith *sans* history. American religion became either a vertical "this nation under God" moralism, or a vertical "this self under God" pietist-revivalism, one or the other. Now make no mistake, such religion was productive; it was pragmatically useful in Amer-ica as the frontier wilderness was populated with villages. When communi-ties appeared, "this nation under God" built churches and ordered public morality, while "this self under God" one by one converted an exploding population. Vertical piety "worked," even if its God became more and

19. Brian Wicker, *The Story-Shaped World* (South Bend: University of Notre Dame Press, 1975).

20. See the argument in Hans W. Frei, *The Eclipse of Biblical Narrative: A Study of Eighteenth and Nineteenth Century Hermeneutics* (New Haven: Yale University Press, 1974).

21. For a fascinating account of the rise of national legends, see Daniel Boorstin, *The Americans: The National Experience* (New York: Random House, 1965), part 7.

more either the vague sanction of political rhetoric or a private secret in the saved heart. So much for Act II, which, after all, might be retitled "the triumph of a vertical piety."

### Act III: The Post-Protestant Era

Here we are in Act III. The curtain has gone up, and guess who's standing in center stage? We are. The scenery around us? A tumbled-down cathedral and shards of stained glass that crunch like dry bones beneath our feet. Some call us a "post-Christian" era, but Christian faith has not disappeared. What has happened is that the synthesis between Protestantism and Enlightenment has broken down. Like a top-heavy tower of Babel, the cultural formulation has tumbled; it has been brought down by the hand of God or, if you prefer, by vagaries of history — World War I, a Great Depression, World War II, Korea, Vietnam, three assassinations, Watergate, and that living symbol of American narcissism, Ronald Reagan. The old "god," enthroned reason, reflecting harmony in human affairs, hasn't held up too well — or may have been a hoax all along.[22] Of course, if people confuse Christian faith with the Enlightenment synthesis, they may suppose that God is dead and may shed dry tears or scurry in a kind of desperate frenzy trying to prop up vertical piety all over again for the good of the nation, seeking to restore the glory gone from New Israel. Here we are, center stage, Act III, and "Henny Penny, the sky has fallen." We are refugees from the death of an age, or a "god," we've forgotten just which. Here we are trying to figure out how to function in a post-Protestant era.

There are people today who cling tenaciously to the vertical pieties of the past. They seek to shore up civil religion or to breathe life into absent-minded personal faith: prayer breakfasts in the White House or still another banner announcing "Revival." Perhaps the aging Dr. Billy Graham is a symbol for the endeavor, for in his heyday he seemed to represent a fusion of civil religion and personal renewal, "this nation under God" and "this self under God."[23] And perhaps Dr. Graham epitomized

---

22. Back in the late fifties, I recall watching on television a Saturday morning children's cartoon in which a white-coated scientist, pointer in hand, stood describing a live ape. As he spoke, the ape reached out and started pummeling him, twisting his arms and legs into a pretzel shape. The scientist, though all but crushed by the ungoverned ape, kept on objectively remarking features of the animal's performance. So much for objective reason!

23. So argues Marshall Frady, *Billy Graham* (Boston: Little, Brown and Co., 1979).

the flaws of both forms of vertical piety: civil religion without a sense of corporate evil, and individual salvation without a social context. Vertical piety, however, cannot be refurbished, for such piety is erected on the scaffolding of cultural formulation, and the cultural formulation is now in shambles. Nevertheless, the grip of nostalgia and the longing for social stability are intense, so there are many nowadays who would build their backyard patios out of bricks from a fallen Tower of Babel, the American religious synthesis.

There are others who are committed to vertical piety: the twentieth-century "mystery cults." Denying history, they grope for a lost God. Picture their predicament. Back in the fifties and early sixties, a kind of all but unnoticed nihilism swept the American mind. Because the god of cultural synthesis seemed dead, we suffered an acute loss of correspondence; there appeared to be nothing "out there." Then gradually, as Peter Berger has observed, "a rumor of angels" seemed to spread through the land.[24] We recovered, however slightly, some sense of unnamed transcendence and with it the resurgent, if romantic, religiousness of the seventies. Thus vertical piety attached itself to unnamed transcendent mystery, producing a clatch of mystery cults: Transcendental Meditation, pop-Zen, Krishna Consciousness, "Moonies," New Age enthusiasts — you name it, we've got it.[25] The mystery cults have managed to erect a vertical piety of mysterious ritual in correspondence with mystery unnamed, but without myth or narrative meaning to sustain their poignant enterprise.

What of "mainline" Protestantism and the Catholic Church in America? The Protestant synthesis has collapsed, and of course the Catholic synthesis tumbled down centuries earlier. Triumphalist nostalgia is still around, however, for there are many people in both Protestant and Catholic camps who long for vertical piety, who mourn the passing of the tridentine Mass, the loss of stately cadences from King James English, or the old oaken-bucket faith of frontier days, Hee Haw religion. But nostalgia is unbecoming to Christian communities in any age — "Let us go back to Egypt" — and cultural syntheses cannot be patched once they have torn apart. In between the ages, mainline Christian communions

24. Peter L. Berger, *A Rumor of Angels* (Garden City, NY: Doubleday and Co., 1969).

25. Robert S. Ellwood, Jr., *Religious and Spiritual Groups in Modern America* (Englewood Cliffs, NJ: Prentice-Hall, 1973). For an odd critique, see Harvey Cox, *Turning East* (New York: Simon and Schuster, 1977).

pathetically seem to be into self-preservation, clutching identity for dear life in the absence of any cultural presence of God.[26]

## "Media as Epistemology"

Until recently, our American religious narrative has been mostly a Protestant story. Not only has the American religious scene been predominantly Protestant, it has been bookish to boot: "Protestantism was born with printing and has been the religion in which printing — the printed Bible, the Catechism, newspapers, and journals — has played a vital part."[27] We have noted that when the *Mayflower* nudged onto the shores of New England, there were books on board — the Bible, of course, but also Captain John Smith's *Description of New England,* and some others as well. American religious history began with a migration of books.

Though moveable type for printing was invented in Europe by Johann Gutenberg sometime in the mid-1400s, book production did not catch up with technology for more than a century. In our own age we have witnessed much the same delay. The basic technology for "electronic media" was invented by Samuel F. B. Morse just prior to the middle of the nineteenth century; and Louis Daguerre developed the "daguerreotype" around the same time. Yet it has taken nearly a century and a half for extra TV sets to fill our bedrooms and for computer screens to flicker in our family dens. Similarly, there was no widespread distribution of books until the late seventeenth century. Thus the colonization of America coincided with an expanded marketing of books. Enlightenment Protestantism was a typological movement.

How hard it is to grasp the impact of publishing on the American religious mind. In New England, from 1650 on, most communities required the maintenance of a "reading and writing" school.[28] Education

26. See the overall analysis in Robert Wuthnow, *The Restructuring of American Religion* (Princeton: Princeton University Press, 1988). See also the insightful diagnosis in Edward Farley, "The Presbyterian Heritage as Modernism: Reaffirming a Forgotten Past in Hard Times," in *The Presbyterian Predicament: Six Perspectives,* ed. M. J. Mulder and L. B. Weeks (Louisville: Westminster/John Knox, 1990).

27. Richard Molard, *Horizons protestants* (June 1975), 3. Cited in Pierre Babin with Mercedes Iannone, *The New Era in Religious Communication,* trans. David Smith (Minneapolis: Fortress Press, 1990), 25.

28. Kenneth Lockridge, "Literacy in America, 1650-1800," in *Literacy and Social Development in the West: A Reader,* ed. Harvey J. McGraff (New York: Cambridge University Press, 1981), 184.

was egalitarian; everyone read. Thus the hunger for books was truly astonishing. Neil Postman observes that Thomas Paine's *Common Sense,* published in January of 1776, sold more than 100,000 copies in a little less
than three months. Of course, the population was smaller then. Nowadays,
a book would have to sell more than eight million copies in about eight
weeks to duplicate the impact of the earlier work. Postman goes on to
suggest that if *Common Sense* sold 400,000 volumes in total, it would be
equivalent to sales of 24,000,000 today.[29] Americans also read newspapers
and polemic pamphlets and almost anything else they could lay their hands
on. William Cobbett, writing in 1795, testified: "There are very few really
ignorant men in America of native growth. Every farmer is more or less a
reader. . . . They have been readers from their youth up; and there are few
subjects upon which they cannot converse with you, whether of a political
or scientific nature."[30] America was a remarkably literate land.

With the printing of books, America did not cease speaking. Public
oratory flourished in law courts, on the political stump, and, above all, in
the pulpit. But, please notice, public discourse was decidedly bookish.
Speakers' language sounded written.[31] For example, notice the complex
clausal language spoken by Abraham Lincoln in Freeport, Illinois, during
the Lincoln-Douglas debates:

> It will readily occur to you that I cannot, in half an hour, notice all the
> things that so able a man as Judge Douglas can say in an hour and a
> half; and hope, therefore, if there be anything that he has said upon
> which you would like to hear something from me, but which I omit to
> comment upon, you will bear in mind that it would be expecting an
> impossibility for me to cover his whole ground.[32]

People not only read books; they sounded like the books they read. They
spoke a literate, linear language. Their speeches were above all rational,

29. Neil Postman, *Amusing Ourselves to Death: Public Discourse in the Age of Show
Business* (New York: Viking Penguin, 1985), 34-35.
30. William Cobbett, *A Year's Residence in the United States of America,* 3 vols. (1819
ed.; Montclair, NJ: Thomas Kelley, 1969), sec. 356.
31. These days, the language used in ordinary speech is quite different from written
prose. Therefore, it is exceedingly difficult to employ quoted material in oral presentations.
See my *Homiletic* (Philadelphia: Fortress Press, 1987), 143-45.
32. Postman, *Amusing Ourselves to Death,* 45. Were the transcriptions of the debate
accurate? Did Robert Hitt, who transcribed the debates, correct Lincoln's "illiteracies" as
some political critics insisted? Hitt denied that he had "doctored" any of the speeches.

involving a sequential development of arguments, the coherent arrangement of ideas, and a clear, studied presentation of concepts. By the beginning of the nineteenth century, America thought like a book!

Neil Postman, something of a curmudgeon on the subject of communication, does have a helpful title phrase: "Media as Epistemology."[33] Postman means by the phrase that media tend to provide a kind of pervasive metaphor for understanding. In oral cultures, wisdom is conveyed by proverbs, and contracts are arranged by word of mouth and sealed with oaths. In typographic cultures, truth is literal, and contracts are written out in precise legal language. But notice, the differences are not merely "either/or" options — either writing or speaking. Rather, they are differences of mind; two very disparate ways of thinking are involved. If a conflict must be resolved in an oral culture, some wise Solomon type may speak a proverb that can inform both sides and thus lead to resolution. But in a typographical culture, lawyers will cite written precedent cases in adjudicating a dispute. In a bookish culture, people speak, but their speech is shaped by linear assumptions; printed language — what Marshall McLuhan labeled "The Gutenberg Galaxy" — has become a kind of epistemology.[34]

We have traced a pattern in American religious history involving Protestantism and Enlightenment. In many ways, writing was the "epistemology" that presided over the three-hundred-year period; it characterized both the Enlightenment and the Protestant era and was perhaps the form of their synthesis. Part of the confusion of our time is that we struggle between the ages, between the age of the written word and the new, as yet barely ventured, age of electronic communication. In the new age of electronic media, people will still speak and preachers will still preach. But what kind of speaking will we hear? And how will electronic media reshape the configurations of the American religious scene?

## Switching on the Gospel

At the outset, let us recognize that media are neither neutral nor interchangeable. We should not suppose that the gospel can be preached orally

---

33. Postman, *Amusing Ourselves to Death,* chap. 2.

34. Marshall McLuhan, *The Gutenberg Galaxy* (Toronto: University of Toronto Press, 1962).

or visually or even tactually and that "it's all a matter of choice." No, as Walter Ong noted some years ago, different media accomplish rather different ends.[35] Thus, for example, a single voice addressing an audience will foster unity, whereas a film is apt to isolate viewers in their separate subjectivities.[36] Likewise, speaking seems to align with our processes of inner understanding, whereas visual presentations are apt to impress pre-cognitively and may separate us from our self-awareness; Jenny Nelson terms television watching a "prereflective passive activity."[37] Speech may well be a singularly appropriate medium for the proclamation of the gospel, for, in preaching, a word of God addresses our common understanding. Of course, we can present the gospel in many ways — by TV programs or computerized texts or whatever — and we should, but preaching may still be a most satisfactory way of spreading the good news. Even though speech may be particularly suited to the gospel message, all our speaking will be shaped by the "epistemological metaphor" of the electronic media. So we will preach; but, of course, we will preach very differently in an electronic age.

Already we have seen homiletic conventions changing under the impact of electronic communication. People we see on television are simply unknown faces until they supply identity, usually by some form of narrative. Thus, more and more, we hear preachers becoming personal raconteurs — telling their stories in sermons. Inasmuch as congregations presumably know something about their preachers, personal narration in sermons may be superfluous and even homiletically unfortunate.[38] But the current self-narrative tendency in preaching is rather clearly a carryover from visual presentations, which all but demand some sort of storied information to sustain visual images.[39]

35. Walter Ong, S.J., *The Presence of the Word: Some Prolegomena for Cultural and Religious History* (New Haven: Yale University Press, 1967), chaps. 4 and 5.
36. Note that films may well appeal to a religion of the heart. After a movie, even when we are with friends, we are apt to remain silent for a while because we are still "in" the world of the film. After we adjust, we can discuss our shared experience of the film. But even in discussion, we are bringing our separate subjectivities into play.
37. Jenny Nelson, "Eyes Out of Your Head: On Television Experience," *Critical Studies in Mass Communication* 6, 4 (Dec. 1989): 387-403.
38. See my *Homiletic,* 141-43.
39. The current flap over narrative preaching must be critically weighed. If we simply retell *our* story for the sake of identity preservation — a strategy that I believe is being urged by William H. Willimon and Stanley Hauerwas — we will reinforce the church's current provincialism. The only story worth telling is the story of God and *humanity,* a

Likewise, more and more, preachers are dealing in visual images; they are talking about seeing different things and describing the process — particularly in relation to subjective feelings produced by the image. The convention is again a carryover from television. Things appear on the TV screen and, particularly in the irritation of advertising, voices describe objects and give them value in terms of personal gain or personal affect. Now, it is likely that people do grasp meaning these days by juxtaposing image and idea. But the current convention showing up in sermons seems preoccupied with the process of visualizing and may not be altogether helpful.

Of course, because the visual tends to relate to affect, television favors attractive people who will appeal to an audience's feelings; an audience must feel good if Nielsen ratings are to rise. No wonder news anchor types must always be photogenic. So we can entertain a rather frightening vision of the future in which happy, carefully groomed, comely preachers will tell their personal religious stories or, alternately, offer object-lesson sermons to promote a Christian gospel "product," perhaps accompanied by leggy Christian chorus-line singers crooning familiar hymns. When religion becomes "show biz," sermons can turn into trivia — and, of late, they frequently have![40]

## On Learning How to Speak — Again!

There have been some homiletic changes that are directly connected with the impact of electronic media and that are of substantial importance for preachers. Let us take note.

### Rhetorical Logic

When human beings speak, the topics they cover are put together by some kind of logic, philosophical or rhetorical.[41] Sometimes topics are assembled by nothing more than a process of addition, one topic after another; in effect, topics are connected by an "and" — topic A *and* then topic B *and*

much bigger story than that of the Christian community or any of its denominational subdivisions.

40. See Postman, *Amusing Ourselves to Death,* chaps. 6 and 8.

41. On the kinds of logic, see discussion in Chaim Perelman, *The Realm of Rhetoric,* trans. W. Kluback (Notre Dame: University of Notre Dame Press, 1982).

then topic C, etc. The logic that connects ideas in a talk can be much more sophisticated, though even sophisticated logic can usually be represented by a conjunction — "but," "because," "yet," "though," etc.

Lately another form of logic seems to be emerging, something we might term a "logic of consciousness." For example, in a talk on ecology it might be possible to describe a woodland hacked by unrestricted lumbering in one paragraph and then, in a following paragraph, to describe the same forest tract in its original unspoiled condition before the lumber camps arrived. The connective logic might be represented by "but," though a speaker would likely add the word "imagine": "but *imagine* the tract before lumbering began." The logic is actually a visual logic, a logic of consciousness. For in consciousness we can visualize the lumbered forest and then, in an instant, imagine the same forest lands in pristine, untouched beauty. The visual logic is not dissimilar to the way in which images can be connected in TV presentations (which themselves may duplicate a language of consciousness). Lately, our speaking assembles on the basis of a fairly sophisticated perceptival logic, the same logic employed by electronic media.[42]

### Point of View

If we look at transcripts of sermons preached around 1830, we will notice that their language is a language of observation. Speakers talked about ideas, they described feelings, they made "points" — all from the same third-person observational stance. Of course, such sermons were not exceptional; landscapes were painted with the same perspective, and scientific discourse by common convention was always third-person objective. People seemed to see their world with a kind of fixed camera lens built into consciousness.

Times have changed, and so, apparently, has human consciousness. We look at movies from early in our century and laugh at their stilted, fixed-camera unreality. Nowadays a single scene in a television drama may involve hundreds of different camera angles from cameras mounted on moving booms. We view the product and remark its realism. The electronic media are a product of a changed, highly complex human consciousness and, in turn, act on the consciousness of the age.

The way in which language forms in consciousness these days is

---

42. See my *Homiletic,* chap. 5, for further discussion.

multiperspectival. Sections of speeches seem to come at us from different angles of vision and to be representing different perspectives, slants, or opinions. One of the reasons why even well-crafted sermons may seem strangely tedious these days is that some may still be written from a fixed perspective with third-person observational language.[43]

### Mobility and Plot

Years ago, students of literature began to notice shifts in traditional story-telling. Usual stories began at a beginning and proceeded chronologically to an ending. But some novels — for example, those by William Faulkner — seemed to develop plotlines that transcended normal sequences of time and space. The difference could be grasped: In the world "out there" time and space were fixed, but in the world of consciousness different times could be recalled and depicted in a very different order or even juxtaposed. In consciousness, an event could be entered mid-action and then later a beginning recalled by "flashback." In other words, plots could be constructed as sequences in consciousness rather than chronologies governed by time and place. In consciousness, there is a kind of simultaneity of experience.

Obviously simultaneity characterizes the electronic media. The evening news on television will draw in images from all over the world, and sometimes not only from different places but from different eras as well. We are no longer bound by the linear logic of the typographical age.[44] Thus, future preachers will plot their sermons in very different ways than preachers use now. Such homiletic revision is already beginning to happen.[45]

Notice that we have used the word "plot" and have avoided the term "outline." We have remarked that cultural formulations tend to be static; they resist temporal movement. But now, in a time of cultural breakdown, a sense of movement has returned to modern consciousness. Do we not discuss "process theology" and "narrative theology"?[46] Sermons that put

43. See my *Homiletic,* chap. 4, for further discussion.

44. See my *Homiletic,* particularly chap. 18.

45. For discussion of recent changes in homiletic theory, see Richard L. Eslinger, *A New Hearing: Living Options in Homiletic Method* (Nashville: Abingdon, 1987).

46. The turn to narrative has been prompted in part by Frei, *The Eclipse of Biblical Narrative.* As a result, there are capable theorists who advocate narrative preaching. Edmund A. Steimle, M. J. Niedenthal, and Charles L. Rice, *Preaching the Story* (Philadelphia: Fortress, 1980), as well as Eugene Lowry, *The Homiletical Plot* (Atlanta: John Knox, 1980)

forth a precept or fixed idea and then rally rhetorical support to establish truth are rare these days. Is the change related to the advent of electronic media? Perhaps. Television thrives on movement, on dramatic plot and visual narration; television does not tolerate static, unchanging images. So lately, sermons are plotted in sequences characterized by movement; their logic is mobile.[47]

## People of the Book?

Now let us raise some odd theological questions. We have suggested that, during the past three hundred years, American religious life has been conducted under the rubric of Enlightenment Protestantism. Rather obviously, the religious synthesis between Protestantism and Enlightenment has come unglued. These days we speak of living in a "postmodern" world, which, not surprisingly, is also regarded as a post-Protestant world.[48] What held the synthesis between Protestantism and Enlightenment together? The synthesis was based on rationality, a correspondence between divine and human reason. But clearly eighteenth-century rationalism, typographical rationalism, has crumbled. A type of preaching that distilled rational precepts from biblical texts is also now passé. And yet, culturally, we are beyond mere nihilism — which is obviously the opposite of synthesis. Perhaps in the late fifties there was a negative correspondence between *Deus Absconditus* and T. S. Eliot's "hollow men." In an age when electronic media may offer a metaphor for understanding, perhaps the future will be built on some sort of correspondence of consciousness. Perhaps, religiously, we have to do with a Consciousness that is conscious of us — a Consciousness revealed not so much in historical event as by social symbols in common consciousness.

---

and *Doing Time in the Pulpit* (Nashville: Abingdon, 1985), represent homiletic theory related to narrative theology. For some criticism of the position, see my *Homiletic*, chap. 1.

47. In my *Homiletic*, I have deliberately replaced the traditional rationalist term "points" with the term "moves." Sermons may be designed as a series of "moves" sustained by kinds of narrative plotting or by a visual logic of consciousness.

48. The neologism "postmodern" seems to mean two different things. For some, "postmodern" has a conservative meaning: let us give up foolish modernism and revert to tradition once more. For others, the term seems to mean something else: let us go beyond modern cosmetic modifications of the past so as to embrace new paradigms. We are apparently living in a split-level culture.

A more serious matter is this: We have seen that in American religious history a typographically oriented formulation, Enlightenment, has been aligned with Protestantism, a biblical faith uniquely related to book learning. What will happen to a religion of book in an age dominated by the epistemology of the electronic media? Obviously the whole notion of biblical authority will not wash in an electronic age. Current cultural fundamentalism, thriving in a reactionary, frightened America, cannot survive for long as more and more electronic media provide the metaphors of understanding. Though fundamentalism has taken to the TV screen, it is an obvious mismatch — a bookish literalism is scarcely photogenic. But what will replace that Protestant bulwark, biblical authority? Will personal authority, forms of religious shamanism, arise? Possibly. In the long run, however, a more likely scenario will see authority built on a juxtaposition of interpretation and image to establish "truth" in consciousness. The crucial question is this: What happens to Protestantism, a religion of the book, in an electronic age?[49]

The church does seem to be caught in a kind of cultural impasse. The American religious synthesis is in tatters; a typographical age is ending. In such a time, the church is in a quandary. There are voices urging us to "master" the media; there are others — for example, Neil Postman — who grouch against change for fear of losing Protestantism's devotion to rationality. Obviously, we are called to a profound act of reconceptualization. We are changing. Biblical studies have moved away from the historical paradigm, and theology is revisionist. Electronic media are impacting our lives. Perhaps now we can at least begin with awareness.

---

49. On biblical authority, see the argument in Edward Farley, *Ecclesial Reflection* (Philadelphia: Fortress Press, 1982), part 1; and also my *Homiletic*, chap. 15.

# Oral Roberts: Religious Media Pioneer

David Edwin Harrell, Jr.

Historically, pentecostals have sustained a love-hate relationship with modern technology. Every pentecostal youngster learned early that Hollywood was synonymous with Sodom and Gomorrah and that going to the movies led inexorably from excommunication to hell. Generally speaking, however, pentecostals did not object to modern inventions; technology was guilty by association. In many ways, they embraced invention with far more enthusiasm than their more respectable religious neighbors. The neon signs outside their rustic churches became to them bright signals that they were no longer in the backwater.

Radio particularly captured the fancy of pentecostals. By the 1930s, crackling hallelujahs, Stamps-Baxter quartets, and gasping pentecostal preachers crowded the airwaves. There was status in being a "radio preacher"; with a little faith and fervor any pentecostal pastor could sustain a local broadcast by soliciting freewill offerings from his listening audience. To a degree, the whole pentecostal community gained status by sharing the airwaves with the Baptists and Methodists.

Evangelistic fervor, rather than status, was the primary magnet that drew pentecostals to radio. Within five years of the licensing of KDKA in Pittsburgh, over fifty radio stations in America were owned and operated by religious organizations. In 1924, Aimee Semple McPherson observed that it had become "possible to stand in the pulpit, and speaking in a normal voice, reach hundreds of thousands of listeners," carrying on "the winged feet of the winds, the story of hope, the words of joy, of comfort, of salvation."[1] McPherson's radio program made her the first widely recognized pentecostal evangelist and a national celebrity. Her success set a goal for future generations of pentecostal evangelists who believed that God had called them to touch the world. In the years after World War II, no one heard that call more clearly, and obeyed it more successfully, than Granville Oral Roberts.

Oral Roberts was born in 1918 in Pontotoc County, Oklahoma, the son of a poor pentecostal preacher.[2] He carried through life the brand of the Holy Roller, with all that such scars do to one's psyche. Oral's grandfather parceled out small farms to each of his seven sons, but after a few years of scratching a feeble subsistence from the red sandy hills of Pontotoc County, Ellis Roberts and his wife Claudius, Oral's parents, felt a call from above. In an old-time shouting, brush arbor meeting they were baptized in the Holy Ghost. Ellis sold his farm (missing the subsequent oil boom), bought a portable organ, and preached pentecost all over southeastern Oklahoma. A gentle man, he walked to his meetings, trusting the Lord for his support. Claudius and the children worked in the neighbors' fields and came to know hunger — depression Okies.

Oral's two older brothers rebelled against their pentecostal upbringing — disgusted by the grinding poverty imposed on the family by their equally desperate supporters and cut by the snickers of city sophisticates in Ada. Oral tried to escape; at the age of fifteen he ran away to Atoka to finish high school, study law, become governor, and play basketball for the Atoka High Waumpus Cats. He collapsed during a game and was taken home and diagnosed as tubercular. The rest of the story is hagiography, told by Oral thousands of times and published millions: the despondent youth was bedridden for 163 days thinking he would die; he underwent a conversion experience in which his father was transformed into the image of Jesus, and then he experienced a miraculous healing under a tent in Ada.

On the evening of his healing, while Oral was riding to the tent, God spoke audibly to him, as he was to do from time to time in the years ahead, and said that Oral would bring healing to his generation. After about a year

1. Quoted in William Martin, "Mass Communication," in *Encyclopedia of the American Religious Experience,* ed. Charles H. Lippy and Peter W. Wiliams (New York: Scribner, 1988), 1715.
2. See David Edwin Harrell, Jr., *Oral Roberts: An American Life* (Bloomington: Indiana University Press, 1985).

of recuperation (Oral's healing was instant but his recovery was gradual), he spent twelve years preaching in the small Pentecostal Holiness church in the South. Then, in 1947, in a step that required audacity and faith, he resigned his pastorate and launched an independent revivalistic ministry. During the next twenty years he preached healing and deliverance from Miami to Tacoma, from San Diego to Bangor, on Indian reservations, in Israel, and in over fifty other nations. His big tents (seating 3,000 in 1948 and 18,000 in 1968) crisscrossed the nation like Barnum and Bailey. Night after night Oral called sinners to repentance with astonishing results; at his peak, over one million souls sought the Lord under Oral's tents each year. About 10:30 each evening, in the incandescent canvas haze, Oral began to lay his throbbing right hand on the sick, sometimes gently, but more often violently, vice-like, commanding the foul demons of fear and disease to come out. Sometimes fifty, sometimes three hundred, sometimes — stretching far into the morning hours, broken by periods when Oral retired backstage to wait on the Lord and have a chocolate milk, not a soul leaving the enchanted premises — as many as 5,000 sought wholeness through his healing touch. In two decades about a million people passed across the platform to receive a healing touch.

By the middle of the 1960s, Oral Roberts had taken healing evangelism to new heights, far outdistancing his pentecostal competitors and winning the admiration of his evangelical contemporary, Billy Graham. Partly, Roberts's success was built on his preaching skills and his charismatic presence in the healing line. Partly, it was a tribute to his managerial ability. But his lasting success, and his survival as a celebrity preacher when the healing revival slowly ended in the 1960s, was the result of his innovative uses of radio, television, and direct mail.

Several months before he launched his independent ministry in June 1947, Roberts initiated a radio broadcast, "Healing Waters," on station KCRC in Enid, Oklahoma. Oral announced that his radio program would reach out to "all people of all churches," but in fact for fifteen years he preached sermons designed to attract pentecostal supporters. The general format of Oral's radio program was much like that used by hundreds of local pentecostal evangelists. But his message was sufficiently bold to pique the interests of the most jaded pentecostal. Each program began with a recitation of Oral's divine call:

> Hello, neighbors. This is Oral Roberts, your partner for deliverance. God marked me from my mother's womb and chose me to bring His healing power to lost and suffering humanity. God has spoken to me

three times. I was told God's healing power would be felt in my right hand. The Lord is healing thousands through my humble prayers. Neighbor, I am sent of God today to bring God's healing power into your life by faith. So believe and turn your faith loose.

The broadcasts closed with a healing prayer, Oral placing his healing hand on the microphone and instructing his listeners to touch their radios:

I lay my hand over this microphone, and, lo, I am laying it upon you there in your home. Now, Father, I come to Thee in the name of Thy son, Jesus of Nazareth. Grant me this miracle according to Thy will in heaven. . . . And now, Father, I meet sickness and disease. I meet sin and despair, and fear and demon oppression through the authority of God. And I charge you, Satan, to loose suffering humanity. I command thee to let them go free today. . . . Heal those dads and mothers, and these precious ones who are gathering around their radios now. In Jesus' name, I command their diseases to go. Now, neighbor, rise and be made whole by the power of God. Only believe.[3]

Oral's radio network expanded rapidly; by 1949 he was on twenty-five stations and a year later the number was nearing 100. He reached 200 stations by 1953, but building a radio network of independent stations was cumbersome, and it was not until he negotiated a contract with the American Broadcasting Company (ABC) in the summer of 1953 that Oral was able to reach his target of 500 stations. The addition of ABC not only gave his program broad coverage; it was also a trophy to be displayed to his growing body of financial supporters. Oral's radio network remained about the same size for over a decade; he toyed with plans to build his own stations in the United States and abroad, but those ideas, like many of his other divine leadings, were superseded by later directions.

Radio was the most effective tool in the early expansion of the Roberts ministry beyond the tent. The radio broadcasts produced far more healing testimonials than the crusades and literally hundreds of thousands of letters telling of conversions to Christ — in 1959, there were 364,448 such professions. The radio program also added thousands of "prayer warriors" willing to share the expenses of the mushrooming ministry. These

3. See Healing Waters Broadcast Tapes, Oral Roberts University Archives, Tulsa, Oklahoma; Oral Roberts, "The Story Behind Healing Waters," *Healing Waters* (June 1952): 15.

"Partners for Deliverance" accepted the challenge to "have a part in every soul being saved, every captive being delivered from sickness, affliction or demon-possession, . . . and in every constructive effort made during these times of great need."[4]

In part, Roberts's radio success was a product of his growing organizational skills. His radio programs meshed well with his crusade ministry, providing advance advertisement and continued contact with the people who attended his crusades. Even more important, Oral worked to establish mail contact with his listeners, creating a permanent tie with them. He constantly offered incentives on his radio programs to persuade people to write to him — ranging from free copies of his books to anointed handkerchiefs. And he tirelessly sought efficient ways to handle the truckloads of letters that became the financial and spiritual lifeline of his ministry. In the early 1960s he computerized his direct mail operation with the latest IBM equipment; his office was used by the company as a showroom. The Roberts ministry perfected many of the techniques that became the foundation for direct mail operations in the 1980s. By the mid-1980s, the ministry received over 5,000,000 letters a year, about half of them including contributions. In return, the organization mailed around 50,000,000 pieces per year at a cost of over two million dollars. A letter received by the association would usually be answered within three days.[5]

Oral built his radio network with great patience and skill, bringing a degree of unity to the millions of pentecostals who had long been divided into bickering sects. He wanted above all to bring authenticity to each broadcast, to somehow transfer the tent atmosphere to the airwaves. He sought the "anointing of the Lord" before he preached and prayed, as he did before every crusade service. Roberts particularly disliked uttering his concluding healing prayer without a subject before him to touch; aides would scour the studio to find someone for Oral to touch — preferably a worker or aide with a cold or a corn that needed attention. In short, Oral tried to transmit to the radio the intensity of belief and experience that drove the crusades.

Television presented a more formidable challenge. Oral was fascinated by the medium and was impressed by Billy Graham's early airings of his crusades. But in the early 1950s he was neither financially nor

4. Oral Roberts, *If You Need Healing — Do These Things,* 2nd ed. (Tulsa, 1949), 129.

5. See Harrell, *Oral Roberts,* 411-21.

artistically prepared to take his message on television. Instead, in 1952 he produced a movie based on a crusade in Birmingham, Alabama, *Venture in Faith,* and it was widely shown in churches around the world. At the same time, he informed his partners that "the Lord is pressing me about TV," insisting that "the devil must not steal this great medium from God's people."[6] Launching a television ministry was such an expensive undertaking that few pentecostal evangelists could have entertained the idea, but Oral dangled the challenge before his growing body of partners in 1952 and 1953 and the financial roadblock was easily overcome.

More difficult was the task of capturing the charged atmosphere of the healing revivals on television. In 1954, Oral and his wife, Evelyn, filmed twenty-six thirty-minute programs in a Hollywood studio. The programs followed the format of the radio program, but Oral was stilted and uncomfortable in the studio, and the programs flopped when they were aired. After six months, Roberts abandoned television, though he remained convinced that "more souls can be reached through TV than through any other means."[7] Oral was still searching for an adequate way to show the power of his revivals on television during a 1954 crusade in Akron, Ohio. His friend Rex Humbard convinced him to film three of the crusade services. The tent services were very difficult to film, but Oral was ecstatic about the results. The filming included not only his sermons but also the "altar calls, healing lines, actual miracles, the coming and going of the great crowds, the reaction of the congregations."[8] He now had the means to introduce the nation to the remarkable healing revival that had gripped the pentecostal subculture for nearly a decade.

Oral's television program was an immediate success. By 1957 it was being shown on 135 of the nation's 500 television stations and reached eighty percent of the nation's potential television audience. Money and healing testimonials poured into Tulsa. By 1959, the ministry reported more than 500,000 yearly converts attributed to the television program. The ministry mailing list soared to over a million names of people who had written to get and give help.

The Roberts television program solidified him as the premier evangelist of the pentecostal healing revival and made his name synonymous

6. H. Montgomery, "Looking Forward with Oral Roberts," *Healing Waters* (Jan. 1952): 13.

7. "TV News," *America's Healing Magazine* (June 1954): 12.

8. G. H. Montgomery, "The March of Deliverance," *America's Healing Magazine* (Sept. 1954): 4.

with faith healing. Television critics and many religious leaders were offended by the program; in the mid-1950s Roberts became the focus of an unsuccessful campaign to limit religious broadcasting on television. *New York Times* columnist Jack Gould protested: "If Brother Roberts wishes to exploit hysteria and ignorance by putting up his hands and yelling 'Heal,' that is his affair. But it hardly seems within the public interest, convenience and necessity, for the TV industry to go along with him."[9] The *Christian Century* warned that "the Oral Roberts sort of thing" would do harm to the "cause of vital religion"; the National Council of Churches, the chief recipient of free television time, lobbied throughout 1956 for legislation restricting the purchase of television time for religious programming.[10] In short, Oral's early use of television won widespread support from pentecostals and outraged millions of other Americans.

By the mid-1960s Oral Roberts's ministry had stagnated. It continued to be supported by the base of partners that had been accumulated through decades of crusading and broadcasting on radio and television, but the pentecostal world was entering a period of dynamic change. The beginning of the charismatic movement in mainstream Protestantism, signaled by the publicity surrounding the tongues-speaking experience of Episcopalian priest Dennis Bennett in 1960, and the student charismatic revival at Notre Dame in 1966 were omens that spoke loudly to Oral Roberts. Roberts had long been on the cutting edge of the move to take the Holy Spirit to broader audiences; he contributed to the development of a new charismatic theology and carefully cultivated the new tongues speakers. Since the late 1950s, Oral had noted that his crusades and healing lines included increasing percentages of non-pentecostals.

Roberts brooded and prayed about the new developments, wondering where he would fit into the emerging scheme of things. Beginning in 1967, he made a stunning series of changes in his ministry that would reinvigorate it and carry it to new heights. In 1967 he canceled his television program, and the following year he packed away the big tent and ended his crusade ministry. In the spring of 1968, in the most controversial act of his career, he left the Pentecostal Holiness church to become a Methodist.

9. "Letters Commenting on Oral Roberts and the Article by Times' Critic," *New York Times,* 4 March 1956.

10. See "Oklahoma Faith Healer Draws a Following," *Christian Century* (29 June 1955): 749-50.

In the mid-1960s, Roberts spent several traumatic years "waiting on the Lord," but by 1968 he had a plan. His new media strategy, in combination with the university he had begun in the early sixties, would allow him to carry his healing message to a world far wider than he had ever dreamed. By the fall of 1968, Roberts was preparing to return to television in prime-time specials produced in an entertainment format.

The scheme that Oral settled on was a high-stakes gamble — a plan to take his program out of the Sunday morning religious ghetto. Television had changed drastically since Roberts had first used the medium in 1954; in 1969 an estimated 190 million Americans had access to TV sets. "A whole new generation has come up not knowing God," Oral wrote to his partners, "spitting on the church, and the government, and even on one another."[11] How could those people be reached? Television, he believed, was the answer: "To reach them we have to go where they are, because they are not coming where we are."[12]

The risks were huge. The plan hammered out in the fall of 1968 called for a new weekly series on Sundays and the production of four one-hour specials to be aired in prime time. The cost was staggering — about $3,000,000 a year. But Roberts's partners responded to the idea, and ministry contributions began to rise even before the new programs were aired.

Cost was only the most obvious of the risks posed by the new television series. A religious special designed for prime time posed novel production and marketing problems. Who would watch such a production? How could television stations be persuaded to air it?

The catalytic figure in assembling the artistic team for the new programs was Ralph Carmichael, a talented musical writer, director, and arranger who had scored many television specials for some of the nation's most popular singers. Carmichael was widely known for his work in the field of religious music; he had done some work on Oral's radio programs, and in 1968 the two began discussing Oral's ideas about a new approach to religious programming. Roberts explained to Carmichael that he wanted to recast his message in a popular, entertaining format, building around the musical talents of the Oral Roberts University students who would be featured as the World Action Singers. It was a dream come true for

11. Oral Roberts, "Back on Television," *Abundant Life* (March 1969): 3.

12. Oral Roberts, Chapel Transcript, 14 March 1969, p. 17, Oral Roberts University Archives.

Carmichael, who had wanted to "do music like that all his life and nobody paid any attention to him."[13]

Carmichael introduced Roberts to Dick Ross, who had produced programs for Billy Graham and Kathryn Kuhlman, as well as such non-religious programs as George Jessel's "Here Come the Stars." To Ross fell the "challenge" of amending "his star's healing, preaching, soul-cleansing image."[14] At a breakfast meeting in the Roosevelt Hotel in Hollywood, the team made its final commitments; it was agreed to produce the first program in Burbank in December.

Carmichael came to Tulsa in September to begin working with the World Action Singers and with Richard Roberts, who had joined the ministry to be a featured singer on the new programs. While Carmichael worked "day after day" with Richard and the other singers "to produce a new sound in gospel music," Dick Ross created a show that featured not only Richard and the World Action Singers (clad in shockingly modish dress) but also guest star Mahalia Jackson. Oral preached a short sermon entitled "Touching Someone" and led a prayer; he was given seven minutes. The program was light, upbeat, and innovative. "It was not outstanding, but it was good," observed one critic, and better was on the way.[15]

With product in hand, the last challenge was to persuade television stations to air the Oral Roberts special in prime time. The fact that the show had been produced professionally in NBC's studios was enough to get it accepted by some stations, but with others, especially in the major market areas, the selling task was formidable. Oral dispatched one of his talented young lieutenants, Al Bush, to tour the nation's major cities, showing the tape to independent station managers and purchasing time wherever he could. In New York City, Bush presented the owner of a station with a computerized printout of "contributors from Manhattan only," about 50,000 names, promising not only to prepay but also to "bring you an audience."[16] The first show was aired in March 1969; three other specials followed during the year, featuring guest stars Pat Boone, Dale Evans, and Anita Bryant.

13. Interview with Wayne Robinson, 14 April 1983.
14. Mary Begley, "Christmas Show Next," *Los Angeles Times,* 18 December 1969, p. 14.
15. See Oral Roberts, "We Are Returning to Television," *Abundant Life* (Feb. 1969): 2-6; Bill Donaldson, "Showcase," *Tulsa Tribune,* 22 March 1969, p. 21; interview with Albert E. Bush, 11 February 1983.
16. Bush interview.

In early 1969, Oral and his television team waited anxiously for the returns on the experiment. When Roberts first asked Dick Ross to join the team, the producer had been noncommittal. He later explained: "Only when I saw that he was interested in changing his whole approach and was courageous enough to stand up in front of his old constituents, did I respond."[17] How would his old constituents respond? Oral waited uneasily, and his fears were well founded. *Christianity Today* prudishly questioned the "animated singing and slithering of the World Action Singers";[18] Robert's old-time pentecostal supporters were dismayed. "He's gone into orbit," commented a Pentecostal Holiness church leader; the barrage of epithets that greeted the specials included "Hollywoodizing," "flesh," and "compromise."[19]

It did not take long, however, to learn that the television gamble had resulted in a victory of unanticipated proportions. Rating services estimated that nearly 10,000,000 people viewed the first special, and ratings continued to rise for several years. By the end of 1969, the ministry's mail was soaring, setting "all-time highs" every month. By January 1970 the number of inquiries from prospective students at Oral Roberts University had doubled. By the fall of 1970, Oral was euphoric. The most recent special had been followed by over 500,000 letters, most of them, Oral believed, from people who "don't darken the door of a church, don't even know religious terms." The results validated Oral's bold risk. "That's worth something to me," he exulted. "I'm willing to stick my neck out."[20] The success story continued. In 1973, the spring special attracted an estimated audience of over 37,000,000 viewers; in its wake, the ministry's mail reached an astonishing all-time monthly high of about 760,000 letters. In the judgment of Oral's old friend, Rex Humbard, it had become clear that "Oral Roberts is reaching more non-church people than any man in America. Because he has taken a new approach and he's not afraid of criticism of church people."[21]

Even more unexpected was the critical acclaim the program won in

17. Begley, "Christmas Show Next," 14.
18. "Roberts Ratings: Rising," *Christianity Today* (16 January 1970): 36.
19. Interviews with J. A. Synan and L. C. Synan, 16 April 1983; interview with Juanita Coe Hope, 6 December 1973; Evelyn Roberts, *His Darling Wife, Evelyn* (New York: Dial Press, 1976), 230.
20. Oral Roberts, Chapel Transcript, 23 September 1970, p. 12, Oral Roberts University Archives. See Harrell, *Oral Roberts,* 267-75.
21. Chapel Transcript, 13 October 1971, p. 11, Oral Roberts University Archives.

the early 1970s. The 1969 judgment of a Tulsa television critic that Oral had a "hit on his hands" was true artistically as well as in the ratings.[22] In 1971, the Roberts Valentine special received Emmy nominations in the categories of art direction and scenic design and lighting direction. By the end of 1972, the specials were being broadcast on more than four hundred stations. "That means a lot to me," Oral told his partners, "that . . . after four years we have won the confidence of the television industry."[23] The Roberts productions quickly became the model for religious telecasting. In a conversation with Merv Griffin at the end of 1974, Roberts reflected on the criticism he had received: "Merv, when we went on television about seven years ago, we had methods of choreography and so on that turned a lot of church people off, but now there are 111 religious shows or programs on television that came on since we went on and most of them have adopted many of our methods."[24] The modern electronic church was born with the airing of Oral's first special in March 1969.

In the years from 1969 to 1975 Oral's television specials paraded before the cameras an impressive array of Hollywood talent. The early shows featured stars with recognizable religious connections, but the programs increasingly took on the character of variety shows, with commensurately elevating production costs. Included among Roberts's visiting celebrities were Jimmy Durante, Jerry Lewis, Lou Rawls, Kay Starr, Roger Williams, and Johnny Cash. The Hollywood talent appearing on Oral's programs was joined by a parade of political figures, who welcomed Oral to their areas for on-location productions, and by Billy Graham, who joined Oral for an interview on a 1972 special.

In spite of the remarkable success of his programs, by the mid-1970s Oral had grown fidgety about the format. Partly, he began to feel the pressure of competition from his emulators, but he also wanted greater creative control over the content of the programs. He moved the production of the programs to the campus of Oral Roberts University, building state-of-the-art production facilities in Tulsa, to help him "feel the anointing of the Spirit on the program."[25]

22. John Hamill, "Evangelist Roberts Has Hit in 'Contact,'" *Tulsa Tribune*, 27 August 1969, p. 18-D.

23. Oral Roberts Evangelistic Association Transcript, 1 December 1972, Oral Roberts University Archives.

24. Chapel Transcript, 14 November 1974, p. 18, Oral Roberts University Archives.

25. Oral Roberts, "February 9th Was a New Day for Us on Television," *Abundant Life* (March 1975): 2-3.

The creative changes instituted in the 1970s underscored Roberts's spiritual intentions and objectives in his television ministry — a motive that had been questioned by many of his critics. At times it had appeared that Oral's message was almost lost amid the glitter of the Hollywood productions, and Oral himself seemed enamored of the trappings of stardom. But he was never completely captured; he was uncomfortable with most of his guest stars, and he was impatient to include more preaching in his programs. For several years he restively preached sermonettes in the most inoffensive language he could muster, hoping that his audience of religious illiterates would want more.

Roberts imagined that he could use television to reestablish "one-to-one" contact with people — the same relationship that he had perfected under the tent. He insisted that his message and his intent were the same: "I'm married to principles but I'm not married to methods. I'd change my method tomorrow if I could find a better one. But I'll never change a principle. . . . Now I lay hands in my view a hundred times more than I did because I've got a hundred times bigger crowds. Television is where it's at, where the people are."[26]

Beginning in the fall of 1972, when a special was filmed in Tulsa featuring a conversation between Oral and Billy Graham, the production team felt that the program could include more "spiritual emphasis." "We feel that the American public is beginning to accept us for what we are," Richard Roberts told a student reporter, "and we're becoming bolder in our witness for Christ. America is more ready now for fewer guests and entertainment and more of the basics of what we believe."[27] In a candid meeting with the student body in December 1972, Oral bared his feelings about the tactics he had used in his specials, believing that the ministry was about to "turn a corner." The early programs "had to be done" the way they were because "the news media almost singled me out as if they took their spite out on me." So he played a lesser role in the early productions: "What we did to get around that is to bring big performers in . . . and now we have won the industry. If I had let out . . . they wouldn't have sold me the time. So I'd rather have half a loaf than no loaf at all."[28]

26. Oral Roberts, My Own Personal Testimony Transcript, October 1970, p. 14, Oral Roberts University Archives.

27. Renee Colwill, "Television Special Uses Mabee Center Setting," *Oracle* (23 Oct. 1972): 1.

28. Chapel Transcript, 6 December 1972, pp. 6-7, Oral Roberts University Archives.

Throughout the 1970s Oral's television specials continued to receive good ratings; the spillover from the specials kept his Sunday morning program "Oral Roberts and You" solidly in first place in religious programming. Nonetheless, at the end of 1979, Oral stopped the production of the hour-long specials. There were no demanding reasons for making the decision; ratings had declined slightly, but not markedly, and they fluctuated depending on the popularity of the guest stars. Costs had not escalated dramatically — although the general austerity measures put in place during a ministry financial crisis in 1979 contributed to the decision to cut television expenses. But by and large, Oral simply felt, after ten years, that the specials had "run their course"; God was leading him in other directions.[29]

By 1980 Oral Roberts's days as a media pioneer appeared to be drawing to an end. He tried one last prime-time experiment with a puppet special produced by Sid and Marty Krofft, attempting once again to find a format that would separate him from the competition, but Oral soon concluded that the shows were a "serious mistake."[30] Richard Roberts began a daily talk show program in an effort to expand the ministry's audience in 1985, but the program made no major inroads in that competitive market and remained a financial liability to the ministry. By the 1980s other television innovators, including Pat Robertson, Jim Bakker, and Jimmy Swaggart, were using the medium more effectively in reaching broad audiences than Roberts.

Oral's media decline after 1975 was not caused entirely by competition, however; it was the result of the evangelist's changing interests. By 1975 Roberts had decided to expand his university, adding graduate schools in seven areas, including law and medicine, and in 1977 he announced plans to build a huge hospital and medical research center in Tulsa. During the next decade, those projects, construed by Roberts to be the fulfillment of his divine calling, sapped the energies and assets of the ministry. During those years, Oral raised hundreds of millions of dollars to support his ill-fated educational and medical ventures.

In one sense, Roberts used television more effectively than ever during these years — this time as a fund-raising tool. The sequence of supernatural visitations that began with a vision of a 900-foot-tall Jesus, and included a premonition of death unless his partners responded with

29. Interview with Ron Smith, 24 May 1984.
30. Interview with Richard Roberts, 31 March 1983.

$8,000,000, subjected Roberts to a new series of indictments accusing him of "hucksterish tactics."[31] Roberts's fund-raising tactics in the 1980s were not new, however; they were very much like the appeals made under the big tent in the 1950s. They were delivered in the language of the pentecostal subculture, and they were remarkably successful, raising around half a billion dollars in contributions in the decade of the 1980s.

Oral's financial problems in the 1980s forced him to use television in new ways that may have signaled the direction likely to be taken by the electronic church in the 1990s. He adopted a narrow-casting philosophy, securing firmly the loyalty of his partners and winning a deeper financial commitment from them. Roberts's messages in the 1980s vexed outsiders and probably estranged marginal supporters of the electronic church, but they spurred to action the core supporters of his ministry. In the 1990s, strategies for developing strong core constituencies may be the key to survival.

Is Oral Roberts finished as a media innovator? At the end of the eighties, Oral finally abandoned his scheme to finance a medical school and hospital. That burden lifted, he was free to look again for new challenges. The Oral Roberts ministry bid over $6,000,000 to gain control of the PTL Network, only to be outbid, unexpectedly, by second-echelon evangelist Morris Cerullo. It may have been Oral's last chance as a media innovator; the days of building cable networks from the ground up, as Pat Robertson and Jim Bakker did in the 1960s and 1970s, appear to be past. But out in Tulsa, Oral is waiting on the Lord, and he is as fascinated as ever by the miracles of modern technology.

Oral Roberts's striking success with the media, ranging from direct mail to radio and television, was partly a product of the times. He was the most visible and admired spokesman of a post–World War II pentecostalism that craved respectability. Oral spoke their language; he explained to outsiders their faith in the mysterious and the miraculous; he preached in person to millions; and he personally touched and prayed for hundreds of thousands. These believers provided him with a base of supporters that supplied the hundreds of millions of dollars he needed to experiment. He made countless mistakes, but his successes were historically important.

Roberts's media successes came as a result of his tireless search for authenticity. He sought techniques that would allow him to appear to

31. Jack Mobley, "Pastor Isn't Buying Hard Sell on Radio, TV," *Chicago Tribune,* 7 October 1980, p. 17.

communicate personally with his far-flung body of partners, and with sinners. Oral and his wife Evelyn labored over the written paragraphs that were selected by the hundreds of ministry employees to answer the millions of questions and prayer requests received in Tulsa. He struggled to bring the atmosphere of the tent into the radio studio and to the television screen. Even during the prime-time specials, Oral prayerfully sought God's anointing before he preached. When he was stirring public outrage with his fund-raising appeals in the 1980s, Oral was probably at his best in sharing with his partners the spiritual trauma that he was experiencing.

Roberts succeeded also because he brought to the mass media a disarmingly simple and appealing message, presenting it with uncommon consistency for over forty years. Oral's theology was upbeat and hopeful — it was captured in the series of slogans that became a litany for his audiences: "God is a good God"; "Something good is going to happen to you"; "Expect a miracle"; "Greater is He that is in you than he that is in the world." Roberts never made the mistake of trying to communicate complex ideas on television. His message was simple, it was understandable, and it was helpful.

Finally, Oral was always willing to innovate. His introduction of the entertainment format to religious programming in prime time was a dangerous gamble. He knew that he would offend some of his pentecostal supporters; indeed, he left the Pentecostal Holiness church partly because he feared official sanctions from the church once the programs aired (being reasonably sure that Methodists would not be shocked by skirts that revealed women's kneecaps). Oral took the same kind of gamble when he began his unpopular financial appeals in 1980, realizing that he would offend some of his supporters and that he would incur the ridicule of the press. In a sense, both of those major innovations worked, though his calculated turn to a smaller clientele left him with a battered public image and made him a smaller player in the broader religious television picture.

# From New Thought to New Vision: The Shamanic Paradigm in Contemporary Spirituality

Catherine L. Albanese

In 1886, according to her own account, Myrtle Fillmore was dying in Kansas City. She claimed that she had inherited tuberculosis, and now, said her biographer, it had flared up along with malarial complications. Drugs of the age failed to help, and prospects seemed bleak. Then, a Dr. E. B. Weeks, a student of Emma Curtis Hopkins — herself a former disciple of Mary Baker Eddy — appeared in Kansas City. Weeks lectured, and Fillmore listened. The lecture, she testified, was a turning point on her road to recovery. As Fillmore recalled the event:

> I was supposed to be dying, or very close to it, of tuberculosis, a disease that was supposed to belong to my father's family. My first teacher spoke the word: "One is your Father, even God. He is your heredity parentage — only what belongs to God belongs to you." The truth came to me — a great revelation, showing me that I am a child of the one whole and perfect mind, created to express the health that God is.[1]

Fillmore went on to begin, with Charles Fillmore, the Unity School of Christianity, and her healing became foundational in the New Thought theology her followers affirmed. As the healing was transformed into sacred lore, the recollection of it assumed paradigmatic form. Thomas Wither-spoon's devotional biography suggests its tenor:

1. Myrtle Fillmore, as quoted in Thomas E. Witherspoon, *Myrtle Fillmore: Mother of Unity* (Unity Village, MO: Unity Books, 1977), 39.

As she left his [Week's] lecture that night, one sentence illumined the very depths of her soul: *"I am a child of God and therefore I do not inherit sickness."* Slowly she let this Truth sink into her conscious mind and take hold. It was her last straw, and she grasped it with both hands and all her strength, and she would not let it go.[2]

The incantational quality of Fillmore's new thought — as Unity remembered it — is still more apparent in other devotional accounts. Here, for example, is James Dillet Freeman:

As she walked from the hall, one statement repeated itself over and over in her mind:
*I am a child of God and therefore I do not inherit sickness.*
Over and over in her mind the words tolled like a bell:
*I am a child of God and therefore I do not inherit sickness.*
. . . Even as she stepped out of the doors of the hall, this new, this divine realization was working in her, not only in her mind but in the very cells of her body:
*I am a child of God and therefore I do not inherit sickness.*[3]

Here spirituality was focused in a declaration of the desired condition — stated, though, as actually now existing. And the formulaic account became the charter for the Unity tradition of New Thought affirmation. The Marcus Bach version of the Fillmore story points to the process:

At this gathering [the Weeks lecture] the speaker included a "healing affirmation" in his lecture and suggested it be used as a working therapy to be taken faithfully, believed in implicitly, and realized fully. The words were: *I am a child of God and therefore I do not inherit sickness.*
For Myrtle it was a moment in which the meeting, the speaker, and the affirmation had irrefutably been established just for her.[4]

The affirmation was meant to draw full mental and emotional attention to a desired state, to rivet person, as it were, to goal. Here Reformation emphasis on the word in the Bible had metamorphosed to a

2. Witherspoon, *Myrtle Fillmore*, 38.
3. James Dillet Freeman, *The Story of Unity*, rev. ed. (Unity Village, MO: Unity Books, 1978), 44-45.
4. Marcus Bach, *The Unity Way* (Unity Village, MO: Unity Books, 1982), 30.

particularly American incarnation as the central ritual of New Thought spirituality. The new *sola scriptura* was solitary, self-generating, and tailor-made for New World space, time, and circumstance. In the formulaic repetitions of the prayer, with the desired condition invoked as actually present, the word became magical instrument and sacramental tool. The word, in short, was vested with power. And religion used the word to order the world as humans, in their best moments, wanted it to be.

Through the trajectory that New Thought traveled on its twentieth-century road, it enjoyed success more by cultural influence than by organizational strength. Its incantational spirituality spread beyond its boundaries to become the property of numerous other Americans. And by the early seventies, New Thought was not only maintaining its own tradition but was also providing material for the emerging New Age movement. Still, New Thought was already becoming old thought, and its spirituality was being eclipsed by new forms. In the paradigm that was swiftly gaining ascendancy, the religion of the Word — even in what may have been its final American form — was being supplanted by a new imagistic spirituality. I call this new form of religion shamanic spirituality, and I see its increasing presence as an important and insufficiently noticed cultural shift.

Shamanism, we are told by historian of religions Mircea Eliade, is a "technique of ecstasy." It involves a "magical specialty," the central feature of which is a form of magic flight in which, during trance, the shaman's "soul" is "believed to leave his body and ascend to the sky or descend to the underworld." Comparative religionist Åke Hultkrantz from his own perspective calls a shaman an "inspired visionary" and notes that shamanic experiences "are connected with the appearance of ghosts, spirits, and gods." A shaman, says Hultkrantz, "visits the realms of the heavenly powers and the land of the dead, and is in his turn visited by spirits." Meanwhile, anthropologist and present-day shamanic teacher Michael Harner speaks of shamans as persons who journey in "nonordinary reality" to Upper, Lower, and Middle worlds.[5]

To be sure, there are other aspects to shamanism besides the visionary journey — its social matrix that makes of the shaman the emissary of a community, its mastery over fire and other physical substances, its healing

5. Mircea Eliade, *Shamanism: Archaic Techniques of Ecstasy,* trans. Willard R. Trask, Bollingen Series LXXVI (Princeton: Princeton University Press, 1964), 4-5; Åke Hultkrantz, "Shamanism: A Religious Phenomenon?" in *Shaman's Path: Healing, Personal Growth, and Empowerment,* comp. and ed. Gary Doore (Boston: Shambhala, 1988), 34-35; Michael Harner, "What Is a Shaman?" in *Shaman's Path,* 8.

and sacrificial functions. Here, though, I single out what is arguably its clearest hallmark and most important identifying sign. And I do so, not so much to contribute to the technical study of shamanism, but to find a language to describe an emerging form of American spirituality. Shamanic spirituality, as I understand it, is spirituality that substitutes image for word, using the resources of the pictorial imagination to journey to places and times that modify everyday reality. Like the New Thought affirmation of this century's beginning, the shamanic vision-journey focuses mental and emotional faculties. Like the New Thought affirmation, it channels personal resources to meet challenges and transform circumstances toward desired ends. But unlike New Thought, the vehicle of transformation is no longer verbal and abstract. It comes, instead, as an expression of the resources of image and sight.

Let me explain more clearly what I have in mind. The parameters I propose for the shamanic model are wide. On one side, it includes simple visualizations and heightened dream states. Beyond these, the model describes the classic shamanism of conscious mental journeys seeking wisdom and power. But it refers also to other forms of vision, especially, in our time, to sightings of unidentified flying objects and abductions by their crews. And the shamanic model encompasses, finally, physical journeys or pilgrimages to sacred sites where, as in journeys to nonordinary reality, vision, it is hoped, will transform life.

Emphasis on sight and vision is hardly new in the history of religions. One need only think, within the Christian tradition, of the iconic spirituality of Eastern Orthodoxy, of the mysticism of light in both Eastern and Western Christendom, of the richly visual texture of the Western church throughout the Middle Ages. Yet, important for the early modern period and the settling of America, the Reformation had exalted the biblical word. The Reformers had initiated changes in the Protestant order of service that, notably in the continental Calvinist and free-church traditions and later and derivatively in the English Puritan tradition, brought a measure of visual austerity to the church. More than that, the Enlightenment — for all its reported hostility to religion — in actuality proved more damaging to Roman Catholic than to Protestant forms of spirituality. Enlightenment privileging of reason could merge with forms of Calvinist, Anabaptist, and English Protestantism to become a kind of biblical rationalism, an elevation of verbal form and order to religious prominence. The central placement of the pulpit in the classic colonial New England meetinghouse suggests the power of the transformation.

Still, the evangelical revivals that swept the nation in the nineteenth century undercut the rationalism of the word. New religious forms stressed the emotional and experiential component of religion, and as they did so they moved from Calvinist emphasis on divine sovereignty to Arminian notions of human ability. The strong emotion unleashed by a culture of religious awakenings kept the word for a time but eroded its reasonableness. New Thought was one result, its thoroughly Arminian and emotionally toned word a synthesis of what the times offered religiously. By the late twentieth century, however, even the New Thought word was being supplanted, and the visual was reentering American religion with its own brand of triumph.

Let a brief sampling of the literature of shamanic spirituality suffice to illustrate. Take, for example, the homiletic advice offered by Shakti Gawain in her book *Creative Visualization*. "In creative visualization," she explains, "you use your imagination to create a clear image of something you wish to manifest. Then you continue to focus on the idea or picture regularly, giving it positive energy until it becomes objective reality." Nor does Gawain have qualms about naming the process she encourages. "Creative visualization is magic in the truest and highest meaning of the word," she writes. "It involves understanding and aligning yourself with the natural principles that govern the workings of our universe, and learning to use these principles in the most conscious and creative way." Beyond "the very limited type of education our rational minds have received," creative visualization can bring results that in their own way seem miraculous. They are, however, "perfectly understandable once we learn and practice with the underlying concepts involved."[6]

For her part, performer-become-spiritual-teacher Shirley MacLaine is not reluctant to demonstrate what practice may entail. In her book *Going Within* MacLaine describes an elaborate process of chakra meditation that correlates distinct identifying colors with each of the seven classical Indian chakras, or invisible energy centers, within the body. "I lie in bed and begin with the base chakra," she says. "I visualize it as red and spin the wheel that I 'know' is there." "Sometimes," MacLaine confesses, "I 'see' the red of the energy center. Sometimes I don't. Whether I do or not, I accept that it exists and so, proceeding with my own acceptance, I spin the red chakra until sometimes I can feel the crimson heat of accel-

6. Shakti Gawain, *Creative Visualization* (San Rafael, CA: New World Library, 1978), 14, 16.

eration in the center of the base of my spine." MacLaine goes on to elaborate how she uses the red spinning chakra as a way to come to terms with emotional and spiritual blockages.

> Some days I just simply "see" red and have to relax my anger by meditating on the red of the base chakra. When I come into alignment with it, the anger dissipates. If I'm having a problem with my kidneys, I meditate longer and spin the chakra faster because the base chakra governs the kidneys. If I feel sluggish and lacking in energy, I picture the adrenal glands and spin red energy to them because I know that the base chakra externalizes as the adrenals.[7]

For MacLaine, chakra meditation is not an end in itself, for the chakras connect body and personality to the soul or Higher Self. And MacLaine writes, too, of visualizing as the way to a felt realization of this Higher Self. Lying on a table as she worked with a "spiritual acupuncturist" in New Mexico, she followed a train of pictures as they unfolded in her mind. She thought she was making the pictures up, but then, she reported, the scenes grew slower and "something akin to a form shrouded in a golden copper hue came into view in the center of my being." It was MacLaine's Higher Self, she claimed, and she beheld it with imagistic precision: "The figure was very tall, an androgynous being with long arms and the kindest face I had ever seen. The hair was reddish gold and the features aquiline. The figure lifted its arms and welcomed me to recognize it, saying 'I am the real you!' "[8]

MacLaine's waking reverie suggests the unraveling of a dream sequence. So with shamanic spirituality in general. Dreams of the day fold back into dreams of the night, and creative visualization becomes creative dreaming. Patricia L. Garfield provides an appropriate example. Enthusiastically introduced to Sigmund Freud and Carl G. Jung in her teenage years by her mother, Garfield later earned a doctorate in clinical psychology from Temple University. By 1974 her first book appeared, filled with advice on controlling dreams and maintaining lucidity during their course. "As you become conscious in your dreams," she urged, "you can have limitless positive dream adventures, as well as turn off negative dream happenings."

7. Shirley MacLaine, *Going Within: A Guide for Inner Transformation* (New York: Bantam Books, 1989), 113-14.
    8. MacLaine, *Going Within*, 73.

Delightful things can happen to you without dream consciousness — you can see a beautiful painting, get a brilliant idea for reorganizing the office, experience waves of passion, observe strange animals and people, or fly to a different land. However, when you become conscious in your dreams, your range of choice is multiplied a thousandfold.[9]

Such conscious dreaming required focused work on the dreamer's part, including strong intentionality and technical assists such as a dream diary. But the rewards were evidently worth the effort, as Garfield recounted in her "Great Steering Wheel" dream. In it Garfield was driving her car down a San Francisco street until she became aware that it was "*not* an ordinary day, place, or feeling."

> *I am in a dream.* Still driving, I command, "Up"! and my body lifts from the ground. The car is gone. I now whiz through the air as I lie on my stomach about ten or fifteen feet above the earth. I'm no longer driving but I still grasp the upper part of the steering wheel, which has become huge, a great circle. I hold the top rim, and the lower part rests on my thighs, above the knees. I feel the sun and the wind. I see the pavement clearly as I sail along. Everything is sharp, bright. It's a glorious sensation. I ask myself, "Are you happy?" and I know that I am. "And you know that you're dreaming?" and I know that I am.[10]

As surely as any shaman from a traditional society, Garfield was experiencing magic flight. By 1979, however, she was ready to go further in image and claim. In the first edition of her book *Pathway to Ecstasy,* dream work became mandala work.[11] Like a Tibetan adept, Garfield sought to come to terms with female deities who ruled different quadrants of her dream mandala and, finally, to meet and merge with a Branching Woman, goddess of the center. Psychology had merged, too, with soul and spirit, and dream work had become an important source of revelation.

Garfield was not alone in the religious resonances of her work. In an insightful study that includes a wide range of dream-related material,

9. Patricia L. Garfield, *Creative Dreaming* (New York: Ballantine Books, 1974), 206.
10. Patricia Garfield, "The Great Steering Wheel" (29 May 1974), in Garfield, *Pathway to Ecstasy: The Way of the Dream Mandala,* 2nd ed. (New York: Prentice Hall Press, 1989), 4-5.
11. Patricia Garfield, *Pathway to Ecstasy: The Way of the Dream Mandala* (New York: Holt, Rinehart and Winston, 1979).

Lucy Bregman suggests the religious overtones of contemporary popular psychological literature on dreaming. Dreams are perceived in psychological literature, Bregman tells us, as "minirevelations." They are understood as "messages or gifts from a 'Whence'" that are "seen as binding and more or less authoritative for the dreamer alone." Finding sources for this view in folk tradition and an Americanized form of Jungian psychology, Bregman surveys the results in a literature of "trustful receptivity" of the Whence.[12] Writes one of her dreamers: "Thank you, dream power, for the dream of the island (or whatever) you sent last night. I feel it's an important dream, but despite all my efforts, I'm still unable to get the message. Please send me another dream tonight putting the same message in a way I can understand." Or again: "As we have learned to give our conscious selves over to God, and trust our thought, so we can also commit our unconscious to Him for His protection of His message through dreams."[13]

Dreams that are conscious and lucid, dreams that issue from a Whence, dreams that inspire trust and receiving, all of these suggest the possibility of translation back from night to day in classic shamanic journeying. Already Garfield's "Great Steering Wheel" told of shamanic flight, entered apparently spontaneously through the doorway of sleep. But attempts to exert greater control of dreams are paralleled by other attempts to allow greater freedom to the imagination of the sacred in daytime mental journeying. Dreamscapes become magic landscapes that play out to an active imagination — but an active imagination that "trusts" and "receives" more than commands and dominates. What separates the magic journey from creative visualization is the journey itself — and the relinquishment of the conscious mind's leadership in arranging the vision.

Perhaps the most well-known contemporary teacher of shamanic journeying techniques is anthropologist Michael Harner. From 1956 to 1957 and from 1960 to 1961, Harner lived among the Jivaro and Conibo Indians of South America. This extensive fieldwork introduced him firsthand to the powerful and dangerous hallucinogens that the Indians used to enter trance states for shamanic journeying. His own experiments with these materials convinced him of the seriousness of the risks involved. By 1980, however,

12. Lucy Bregman, *The Rediscovery of Inner Experience* (Chicago: Nelson-Hall, 1982), 17, 13-31.

13. Ann Faraday, *The Dream Game* (New York: Harper & Row, 1974), 142, and Herman H. Riffel, *A Living, Loving Way* (Minneapolis: Bethany Fellowship, 1973), 67, quoted in Bregman, *Rediscovery of Inner Experience,* 21.

Harner's *Way of the Shaman* appeared.[14] Directed to a popular audience, the small and highly successful book owed a debt to Carlos Castaneda's *Teachings of Don Juan* and its language of "ordinary" and "nonordinary reality."[15] But unlike the Don Juan of Castaneda's book, with the Indian shaman's use of plant hallucinogens, Harner promoted his Harner Method for shamanic journeying. In the Harner Method, sonic driving (drumming) instead of medicine plants induced an altered state of consciousness. The swift beat of the drum in a patterned rhythm invited the would-be shaman to enter the Lower or Upper World. The slower, steady beat of the drum provided accompaniment for the journey. And the altered, speeded beat of the drum, again in a patterned rhythm, commanded the journeyer to return to ordinary space and time.

Using his method, Harner claimed, contemporary Americans could benefit from visionary journeys similar to those that the shamanic elites of traditional societies had undertaken. His book detailed case after case, from his own growing workshop activity, to document his claims. Visually rich and complex, the journeys as interpreted by Harner brought power and knowledge and helped to heal both physical and mental complaints. Harner suggested methods of entering and leaving the Lower World and described the acquisition of power animals or guardian spirits. He cautioned against certain forms of behavior and encounters while on the journey, and he encouraged symbolic elaboration on the part of journeyers. Consider, for instance, this partial account of a first shamanic journey transcribed in Harner's book:

> I was just moving very quickly, flying all the way through. When I got to sort of the center, there were all these nature spirits, very ethereal-type bodies everywhere. At first they were just standing around and then they all started dancing to the beat of the drum. They were all going the same way at the same time and I was seeing different ones. There was a frog one that had big eyes and looked really strange, and a tree one that was very tall. They were all moving to the drum beat. Then I just returned when you said to come back.[16]

14. Michael Harner, *The Way of the Shaman: A Guide to Power and Healing* (New York: Harper & Row, 1980).

15. Carlos Castaneda, *The Teachings of Don Juan: A Yaqui Way of Knowledge* (Berkeley: University of California Press, 1968).

16. Michael Harner, *The Way of the Shaman: A Guide to Power and Healing* (New York: Bantam Books, 1982), 48.

Harner's Center — and later Foundation — for Shamanic Studies
aimed to provide an institutional base for his work. Meanwhile, Harner
emphasized the worldwide (and not exclusively Indian) nature of shamanism and also experimented with tape recorders and cassettes instead
of actual drums. Drumming groups sprang up in various places where
Harner or his associates had conducted workshops, and shamanic visionary
journeying was encouraged as a regular and disciplined spiritual activity.
At the same time, a small group of shamanic counselors trained by Harner
began to offer professional services.

Nor was Harner alone in his promotion of modern or "urban"
shamanism. Other teachers proliferated, and the lavishly illustrated and
anthropologically sophisticated journal *Shaman's Drum* appeared. Among
the teachers, Serge Kahili King taught a version of Hawaiian healing
shamanism that he claimed he had inherited, and he regularly continued to
initiate Americans into shamanic techniques in a series of graduated workshops. King's Aloha International published a regular newsletter for workshop graduates *(The Aloha News),* and by 1990 his concept of the urban
shaman had provided the title for one of his latest books.[17] Meanwhile, Brant
Secunda with his Dance of the Deer Foundation fostered the Huichol
shamanism of his adoptive father, don Jose Matsuwa, who by 1990 was said
to have reached 110 years. Works on shamanism multiplied in the popular
press, and even Santa Claus was claimed in one journal to be a shaman:

> In the world of childhood, Santa Claus is the master of ecstasy. With
> his sacred flying reindeer, he makes his journey through the heavens,
> descends through the blazing hearth to our mundane reality, and leaves
> behind a gift. The journey, the reindeer, the passing between worlds,
> the mastery over fire, the healing gifts — all belong to the realm of the
> shaman.[18]

17. Serge Kahili King, *Urban Shaman: A Handbook for Personal and Planetary
Transformation Based on the Hawaiian Way of the Adventurer* (New York: Simon & Schuster,
1990).
    18. Jim Hanna, "Centering: Santa Claus as Shaman," *Yoga Journal* 95 (Nov./Dec.
1990): 112. Among the spate of recent titles on shamanism that I have not previously
cited are the following: Jeanne Achterberg, *Imagery in Healing: Shamanism and Modern
Medicine* (Boston: Shambhala, New Science Library, 1985); Cynthia Bend and Tayja Wiger,
*Birth of a Modern Shaman: A Documented Journey and Guide to Personal Transformation*
(St. Paul: Llewellyn Publications, 1988); Joan Halifax, *Shamanic Voices: A Survey of Visionary
Narratives* (New York: E. P. Dutton, 1979); Holger Kalweit, *Dreamtime and Inner Space:
The World of the Shaman,* trans. Werner Wunsche (Boston: Shambhala, 1988); Shirley

But as the shamanic paradigm spread, magical flying reindeer had already yielded place, for some, to magical transport that moved beyond power animals to technology. Moreover, these flying objects moved out of the classic shaman's inducted journey and, some said, into the space and time of ordinary reality. Waking visions and encounters with the extraordinary were reported by numbers of modern-day Americans; and among them claims of contact with unidentified flying objects (UFOs) may be cited. Indeed, the general structure of contact stories — with accounts of meetings with space beings, travel in their spacecrafts, and messages from them to humanity — bore similarities to traditional shamanic lore.

Present-day fascination with UFOs may be dated to 1947 and the reported encounter of a private pilot, Kenneth Arnold, with nine mysterious objects, silver-colored and crescent-shaped, over Mount Rainier. But almost as quickly as the Arnold report became known, a split developed among those who accepted it. Some saw the space objects as scientific challenges, demands for greater knowledge of the universe and its occupants. Others, more metaphysically inclined, regarded the objects as vehicles of moral communication, the technological conveyances of "Space Brothers," or — as Carl G. Jung called them — of "technological angels," who sought to warn humans against their own evil.[19] It is the second group who concern me here.

Already before the end of the forties, occultist George Adamski was sharing with California metaphysical groups his photographs of what he claimed were spacecraft. In 1953, Adamski's book, with senior author Desmond Leslie, appeared. *Flying Saucers Have Landed* detailed an alleged 1952 encounter between Adamski and a Venusian known as Orthon. Other books followed, reporting further contacts with Venusians, Mar-

Nicholson, comp., *Shamanism: An Expanded View of Reality* (Wheaton, IL: Theosophical Publishing House, 1987); Gini Graham Scott, *The Shaman Warrior* (Phoenix: Falcon Press, 1988); Jose Stevens and Lena S. Stevens, *Secrets of Shamanism: Tapping the Spirit Power within You* (New York: Avon Books, 1988); Roger N. Walsh, *The Spirit of Shamanism* (Los Angeles: Jeremy P. Tarcher, 1990). One might add, too, the works of adoptive Australian Nevill Drury, which are readily available in bookstores in the United States: *The Elements of Shamanism* (Longmead, Shaftesbury, Dorset: Element Books, 1989), and *Vision Quest: A Personal Journey through Magic and Shamanism,* rev. ed. (Bridport, Dorset: Prism Press and Lindfield, NSW: Unity Press, 1989).

19. See Jerome Clark, "UFOs in the New Age," in J. Gordon Melton, with Jerome Clark and Aidan A. Kelly, *New Age Encyclopedia* (Detroit: Gale Research, 1990), 476-77. For Carl G. Jung on "technological angels" and flying saucers, see his *Flying Saucers: A Modern Myth of Things Seen in the Skies* (1959; repr. New York: Signet Books, 1969).

tians, and Saturnians. At the same time, in their commentary on Venusians, Adamski's books showed their debt to Helena Blavatsky, cofounder of the Theosophical Society.[20]

Meanwhile, other contactees, such as Truman Bethurum, Carl Anderson, and George Van Tassel, claimed they flew in the craft piloted by the extraterrestrial visitors. Acknowledging such claims, Robert Ellwood and Harry Partin explain in some detail the formulaic structure of the reported encounters with space beings:

> These extraterrestrials communicate with the human, perhaps by telepathy, take him aboard their spacecraft and perhaps take him for a ride. The technology of the spacecraft and of space travel is explained. He also learns of the superior civilization from which the visitors have come. . . . He receives also a prediction of dire events soon to occur on earth because of the failure of humans and their civilization (atomic testing, wars, inequalities, etc.). Life on other planets is said to be affected by the activities of earthlings (e.g., radiation from atomic testing). The contactee is given a mission. Its success is crucial, for it will allow earthlings to avert catastrophe and to live in peace and plenty.[21]

On the other hand, even as space beings are seen as warning the human race as a collectivity, encounters reported by individuals can also be distinctly private and addressed to issues of personal transformation. Consider, for example, the case of Merry Lynn Noble, who attended at least one of a series of Rocky Mountain Conferences on UFO Investigation that took place in the eighties. In an experience that changed her life, the former call girl, alcoholic, and drug addict, sitting with her parents in a car in 1982, declared she believed God was "connected with UFOs." Then, she recounted:

> There was a *whoosh* sound and the car was covered with white light. I tried to look out the window but the light was too bright. I did get a glimpse, no more than a few seconds, of a saucer-shaped outline, a dark gray disc. . . . Then I felt my astral body rising through the roof of the

20. Desmond Leslie and George Adamski, *Flying Saucers Have Landed* (New York: British Book Center, 1953); George Adamski, *Inside the Space Ships* [ghost-written by Charlotte Blodgett] (New York: Abeland-Schuman, 1955); and George Adamski, *Flying Saucer Farewell* (New York: Abelard-Schuman, 1961).

21. Robert S. Ellwood and Harry B. Partin, *Religious and Spiritual Groups in Modern America,* 2nd ed. (Englewood Cliffs, NJ: Prentice Hall, 1988), 113.

car. I felt a sense of freedom that I'd never felt before. The light was no longer blinding. I began communicating telepathically with a source inside the UFO — a Presence.[22]

The Presence in the light became a Voice to whom Noble spoke and from whom she received an answer: "I put my hands up and said, 'Thy will be done.' The Voice said, 'That's all I wanted to hear.'" The results, as she told them, were as extraordinary. "My old soul went on," she said, and "a new soul came into my body, with new energy, new humility."[23] A Colorado housewife and a reformed alcoholic when she gave her account, Noble had clearly been transformed by whatever happened to her as she sat in the automobile.

Beyond the technological domain of the UFO contactee testimonials, however, extraordinary sightings may be found among Americans in more traditional religious contexts. Visions, for example, have come to public religious figures of clearly Christian provenance, and the imagistic power of the visions has become, in the contemporary context, one more sign of the prevalence of shamanic spirituality. There is, in one well-known case, Oral Roberts's account of a vision he claimed to have experienced as he was beset with financial difficulties in building his City of Faith hospital. On 25 May 1980, Roberts reported, as he looked at the still-unfinished structure, he experienced an "unusual feeling" and sensed "an overwhelming holy presence." He opened his eyes, he said, to the figure of Jesus "some 900 feet tall, looking at me." This was, Roberts pointed out, "a full 300 feet taller than the 600 foot tall City of Faith."

There I was face to face with Jesus Christ, the Son of the Living God. I have only seen Jesus once before, but here I was face to face with the King of Kings. He stared at me without saying a word; Oh! I will never forget those eyes! And then, He reached down, put his Hands under the City of Faith, lifted it, and said to me, "See how easy it is for Me to lift it!"[24]

Or, in another instance, there is Jim Bakker's widely known claim of a vision that led to the building of his Heritage Village. After Bakker

22. Jerome Clark, "Contactees," in *The UFO Encyclopedia,* vol. 1: *UFOs in the 1980s* (Detroit: Apogee Books, 1990), 54.

23. Clark, "Contactees," 54.

24. Oral Roberts, September 1980, quoted in David Edwin Harrell, Jr., *Oral Roberts: An American Life* (Bloomington: Indiana University Press, 1985), 415.

presided over the purchase of some twenty-five acres of land in Charlotte,
North Carolina, not quite knowing what its use would be, he sought divine
guidance. During a sleepless night, "somewhere around three o-clock in
the morning," he recounted, "the Lord began answering." But the answer,
as Bakker reported it, was startling in its visual definition. God wanted a
village, Bakker said, " 'a miniature version of Colonial Williamsburg.' "
"God had imprinted a blueprint of the building in my head. I got out of
bed and began drawing it just as I had seen it."[25]

In their reported experiences, both Roberts and Bakker move us well
beyond classical shamanism, but elements of magical vision and self-
empowerment suggest continuity with the shamanic model. The same may
be said, too, for the religious sightings that come, not through inward
journeying or other mentalistic phenomena, but through the outward
travel that is pilgrimage. Journeys to the "center out there," as Victor
Turner argued, are not unrelated to forms of mysticism. With Edith Turner
he thought that "if mysticism is an interior pilgrimage, pilgrimage is
exteriorized mysticism."[26] (And, it might be added, the analogy is still
more persuasive in the case of shamanic journeying.) The Turners observed,
too, that journeys of pilgrimage are often perilous.

> For many pilgrims the journey itself is something of a penance. Not
> only may the way be long, it is also hazardous, beset by robbers, thieves,
> and confidence men aplenty (as many pilgrim records attest), as well as
> by natural dangers and epidemics. But these fresh and unpredictable
> troubles represent, at the same time, a release from the ingrown ills of
> home. They are not one's own fault, though they may be sent by the
> Almighty to try one's moral mettle.[27]

Almost, it seems, pilgrims undergo hazards and ambiguous encounters that echo those of the shaman during the nonordinary journey to the
Lower World. What is as important here, though, is that there has been
a remarkable growth in the practice of pilgrimage in recent times. The
Turners were able to document the phenomenon in Lourdes, France, from

25. Jim Bakker with Robert Paul Lamb, *Move That Mountain!* (Plainfield, NJ: Logos
International, 1976), 170-71.

26. Victor Turner, "The Center Out There: Pilgrim's Goal," *History of Religions* 12
(1973): 191-230; Victor Turner and Edith Turner, *Image and Pilgrimage in Christian
Culture: Anthropological Perspectives* (New York: Columbia University Press, 1978), 7.

27. Turner and Turner, *Image and Pilgrimage*, 7.

the fifties to the early seventies. There were, according to the Turners, 1.6 million Lourdes pilgrims in 1950; 5 million in 1958 (the centenary of the reported apparitions of the Virgin Mary that led to the construction of the shrine); 3.1 million in 1970; and 3.5 million in 1972. And the trend continued. In a more recent study (1989), Mary Lee Nolan and Sidney Nolan estimated the number of annual pilgrims and "religiously motivated travelers" at Lourdes as above 4 million.

Nor was the pattern at Lourdes exceptional. "One fact is certain and striking," the Turners noted. "The numbers of pilgrims at the world's major shrines are still increasing." The phenomenon, they argued, was "not due merely to tourism," and they cited as evidence the huge literature published at major pilgrimage centers. "The papers, journals, and annuals of these centers abound with devout articles, fervent religious poetry, and news about visits to the shrine by organized pilgrimages and celebrities of church and state." Moreover, observed the Turners, feast-day sermons of distinguished bishops and other preachers were duly printed, and there were "lively correspondence columns on questions of doctrine and on the social role of the Church." More than a decade later, the Nolan study described a scene that was similar. "At present," the authors wrote, "Western Europe's more than 6,000 pilgrimage centers generate a conservatively estimated 60 to 70 million religiously motivated visits per year."[28]

And if increasing numbers of Americans and others were journeying to behold traditional Christian pilgrimage sites, by the eighties nontraditional pilgrimages to sacred places were also on the increase. For example, the Harmonic Convergence of 16-17 August 1987 provided one occasion. Responding to the planetary patterns art historian Jose Arguelles claimed to have found in the Mayan calendar, Americans organized to spend the peak days during August 1987 at sites considered to possess heightened spiritual energy. Places like Mount Shasta in northern California, the mesa lands of the Hopi Indians, Serpent Mound in Ohio, the Arizona desert at Sedona, and other locations throughout the world (Stonehenge, Jerusalem, and Machu Picchu in Peru among them) became centers to be seen and contemplated.

28. Turner and Turner, *Image and Pilgrimage,* 230, 38; Mary Lee Nolan and Sidney Nolan, *Christian Pilgrimage in Modern Western Europe,* Studies in Religion (Chapel Hill: University of North Carolina Press, 1989), 26, 1. Ellwood and Partin note the similarities between "myths of origin of pilgrimages of the apparitional type" and the stories of UFO contactees in *Religious and Spiritual Groups in Modern America,* 113.

Meanwhile, a continuing pattern of shamanic pilgrimage was noticeable. Brant Secunda regularly led shamanic seekers to Puerto Vallarta, where they could learn Huichol shamanism. Other teachers brought students to Mount Shasta, to places in Hawaii considered sacred, and to numbers of South and Central American locations. The periodical *Shaman's Drum* continued to publish advertisements for pilgrimages and worried sometimes in its editorial columns and letters to the editor about exploitation of Indian peoples and their traditions. Others, like Sacred Earth Tours, promised "spiritual" and "metaphysical" journeys to sites in Egypt, Mexico, Peru, Australia, England, Greece, Arizona, and Hawaii. And Action Travel publicized its "Magical Mystery Tour of Varanasi, Sarnath, Bodhgaya, Tantric Temples of Khajuraho, Ellora and Ajanta Caves."[29]

While I know of no study comparable to that of the Turners that documents the number of Americans who visit these and similar pilgrimage places, impressionistic evidence suggests that the journeys are popular and that the numbers who search for vision in these locations are growing. The pilgrims visit, they insist, because of the energetic properties of the particular place, because sight is mingled with other forms of perception that dissolve the visual in an intensified energy field. They seek, through the visual and the sensible, an experience of oneness with the universe and harmony with the planet and its peoples. My expression of the views of such contemporary pilgrims in these terms is an appropriate gloss on the short tour of shamanic spirituality I have offered. For the language of "energy" and "field" brings me to the threshold of an explanation for this imagistic spirituality.

In comparative perspective, of course, it is clear that shamanic spirituality frees the power of the unconscious to a greater degree than does the earlier, verbal model of New Thought. Comparison suggests, too, that the shamanic "power to make things happen" taps into more-than-ordinary human resources by its access to imagination. With less ego control of the result of the ritual process, flexibility is greater, and outcomes may be transformative in ways not originally foreseen. The would-be "shaman" may experience pain as well as pleasure and end in places that he or she did not intend.

But beyond the strictly formal questions of comparison, there are,

29. I take these illustrations from the classified section of *Yoga Journal* 95 (Nov./Dec. 1990): 110.

for an American religious historian, other questions that are equally compelling. How do we explain the growing prominence of shamanic spirituality in our time? How did the shamanic paradigm come to achieve its
current importance in our culture? What is it that establishes a set of
cultural preconditions that make this imagistic spirituality plausible and
desirable? Surely no single explanation can provide an adequate answer to
this set of questions; and the religious historian can, even at first glance,
point to a series of contributing factors that help toward explanation. A
theosophical past, media attention to unconventional spirituality, the new
visibility of American Indian traditions, the availability of efficient means
of travel at prices affordable for the middle class, the unabashed quest for
miracles among evangelicals and others — these are only a few. But why,
even in the web of all these preconditions, the preference for the visual?
What is it that makes the spirituality of our time more and more privilege
sight?

Here, especially, the language of "energy" and "field" that I cited
above offers important clues. Both terms suggest electromagnetic phenomena, and that is indeed a major part of their provenance. But it is important
to notice, too, that "energy" and "field" represent key connectors across
the divide between the world of physical science and the world of spirit.
The language of energy functions to bring mysticism and science together,
to render spiritual claims and concerns as authoritative in some circles as
those of science. Moreover, the language of energy does so, first, through
its invocation of the new, or quantum, physics, and second, through its
symmetry with contemporary electronic purveyors of images.

At the dawn of this century, one of Thomas Kuhn's momentous
paradigm shifts occurred in the physical sciences when quantum mechanics
had its birth.[30] Physical light, long understood to be a wave phenomenon,
now appeared to be emitted and absorbed in discrete and unconnected
energy packets that came to be called quanta. Thus, in the subatomic
world of electrons, matter was thought to behave sometimes as if it were
composed of particles and sometimes as if it were made up of waves. With
the growing authority of the new science and its heroes — men like Max
Planck, Albert Einstein, and Werner Heisenberg — quantum physics
could provide raw material for powerful metaphor. And such metaphor

30. For Kuhn's concept of the paradigm shift, see Thomas S. Kuhn, *The Structure
of Scientific Revolutions,* 2nd ed., International Encyclopedia of Unified Science (Chicago:
University of Chicago Press, 1970), esp. 111-35.

moved beyond claims for the subatomic constitution of matter to function in socioreligious contexts in important ways.[31] Nearly any one of the texts of the new shamanic spirituality will serve to illustrate.

Shakti Gawain, for example, announces that "the scientific world is beginning to discover what metaphysical and spiritual teachers have known for centuries. Our physical universe is not really composed of any 'matter' at all; its basic component is a kind of force or essence which we can call *energy.*" And Shirley MacLaine in *Going Within* weaves a "scientific" sub-text throughout. MacLaine consciously invokes a "new Soul Physics," finds "science and spirituality" to be "converging," and declares the universe to be "a gigantic, multidimensional web of influences, or information, light particles, energy patterns, and electromagnetic 'fields of reality.' " Nor does Michael Harner hesitate to cite "new medical evidence that in an altered state of consciousness the mind may be able to will the body's immune system into action through the hypothalamus."[32]

Gary Zukav, whose popular book on the new physics entitled *The Dancing Wu Li Masters* enjoyed a wide reading, in another work states his case for the science-spirituality connection. "Thinking of the Universe in terms of light, frequencies, and energies of different frequencies," he declares, is "a natural and powerful way to think of the Universe because physical light is a reflection of nonphysical Light." Zukav goes on to explain that, like visible light with its "graduated frequencies" extending "below and above what the eye can see," light that is nonphysical "extends below and above, so to speak, the frequency range in which the human exists."

The human experience is a particular frequency range in the continuum of nonphysical Light in the same way that visible light is a particular frequency range in the continuum of physical light.

Other intelligences inhabit other ranges of frequency. These forms of Life do not exist elsewhere from us. . . . The Life forms that are characterized by different frequency ranges of nonphysical Light coexist with us, but are invisible to us. In the place that you now sit exist many different beings, or groups of beings, each active and

31. For a somewhat more extensive discussion of the new physics and its implications for spirituality, see Catherine L. Albanese, *Nature Religion in America: From the Algonkian Indians to the New Age,* Chicago History of American Religion (Chicago: University of Chicago Press, 1990), 150-52.

32. Gawain, *Creative Visualization,* 17; MacLaine, *Going Within,* 49, 82, 85; Harner, *Way of the Shaman* (1982 ed.), 175.

evolving in its own reality and in its own way. These realities co-mingle with yours in the same way that microwave radiation exists alongside of visible light, but is undetectable to the human eye.[33]

All that is required in order to apprehend these "realities," for Zukav, is the natural evolution of humans so that they can respond to "another, higher range of frequency."[34] In short, all that is required is that the visual and visionary be subsumed into the domain of energy. This, shamanic authors as a group are consistently willing to do. That willingness suggests a predisposition, a context, a surrounding ambience, if you will, that invites contemporary spiritual seekers to a series of interpretive moves. Present-day pilgrims of the visual live in a world that has seen the dramatic replacement of the word by the image through photograph, film, and television. Significantly, all three of these are visual *and* energetic phenomena. All three carry the subtext of the electromagnetic universe and its mysteries, of the ultimate conflation of matter and energy (read "spirit").

Robert Jewett and John Shelton Lawrence have pointed to the mythic power of the image in film and television dramas, and Gregor T. Goethels has underscored the sacramental function of television. "These images that reach us through television may in some strange, perhaps perverse, way confirm us as basically nomic creatures," Goethels writes.[35] Here, however, I move past myth and sacramental symbol, both of them products of the content mediated by the screen. I notice more the frame for the content, the structure of the medium or media. And I notice that the content (whatever it may be) comes in imagistic form, in waves of light that strike receptor human retinas and that are organized by human beings as knowledge. I notice, in short, a symmetry between the "ghosts" of the electromagnetic image and the visions of the shamanic spirituality I have documented. My argument is a simple one. It is in some — and considerable — measure because of the ubiquitousness of electromagnetically derived images in our society that individuals can turn easily to shamanic spirituality. And it is because of the cultural authority of these images and the

33. Gary Zukav, *The Seat of the Soul* (New York: Simon & Schuster, Fireside Book, 1990), 96-97. Zukav's earlier work, on the new physics, was *The Dancing Wu Li Masters: An Overview of the New Physics* (New York: Bantam Books, 1980).

34. Zukav, *Seat of the Soul,* 97.

35. Robert Jewett and John Shelton Lawrence, *The American Monomyth,* 2nd ed. (Lanham, MD: University Press of America, 1988); Gregor T. Goethels, *The TV Ritual: Worship at the Video Altar* (Boston: Beacon Press, 1981), 4.

technology that brings them that individuals are predisposed to find in shamanic spirituality resources for transformation.

On one level, just as the media can magically shift reality, sweeping away one illusion with the introduction of another, so the new urban shaman can, with the power of the interior or exteriorized image, shift and reorder the details of life. On a deeper level, just as the visual presentations of the media dissolve in a bath of energy and electromagnetic transformation, the American urban shaman can create light and rearrange the dark. In sum, the urban shaman can alter reality as magical vision suggests because he or she has already seen it happen before — on television and in the movies.

Supported, then, by its symmetries with an electronic culture, shamanic spirituality will likely continue to be a strong suit. In its restoration of ancient and traditional modes of spiritual practice, the shamanic paradigm finds its own endorsement in the sophisticated science of the day. Indeed, the shamanic restoration possesses an inescapable millennial ring, for shamanic spirituality understands itself to be the wave-and-particle phenomenon of the time to come. Thus, the path from New Thought to new vision shifts the spiritual ground on which many Americans stand — and travel. And the structure of their spiritual practice, like the structure of Kuhn's science, has shown itself subject to upheaval.[36]

36. I wish to express my gratitude to J. Gordon Melton, Director of the Institute for the Study of American Religion at the Library of the University of California, Santa Barbara, for his help in locating and providing materials for this study.

# American Christianity and the History of Communication: A Bibliographic Probe

Elmer J. O'Brien

## I. Bibliographical Sources

Albaugh, Gaylord P. *History and Annotated Bibliography of American Religious Periodicals and Newspapers, 1730-1830, With Library Locations and Microform Sources: [Also With Sketches of Changes of Title after 1830 to Time of Discontinuance, or to Date]*. Hamilton, Ontario: McMaster Divinity College, McMaster University, 1990; mss. publication forthcoming.

This work helps to document the growth in the United States of the periodical press during its first century. It provides seventeen elements of description for each of 590 distinct religious journals, involving in their several histories the use of 867 titles, known to have been founded in what are now the United States; "another 124 titles are known to have been proposed for publication but apparently never actually published." Title entries are arranged alphabetically, and to each title are appended library holdings and microform sources. Appendices provide a chronological list of titles by years of founding, a geographical list of titles by states and cities or towns of publication, titles arranged by major religious interest, a bibliography of microform listings used, and an index of editors, publishers, printers, illustrators, and engravers.

*Annual Bibliography of the History of the Printed Book and Libraries*. The Hague: Martinus Nijhoff, v. 1–; 1973–.

International in coverage, "this bibliography aims at recording all books and articles of scholarly value which relate to the history of the printed book, to the history of the arts, crafts, techniques and equipment, and of the economic, social and cultural environment, involved in its production, distribution, conservation, and description." Especially helpful for religious communication are the sections on general works; book trade, publishing; libraries; newspapers, journalism; and the sub-section on religion under secondary subjects.

Batsel, John D., and Lyda K. Batsel. *Union List of United Methodist Serials, 1773-1973*. Evanston, IL: Commission on Archives and History of the United Methodist Church and Garrett Theological Seminary, 1974.

"The purpose of this list is to provide as accurately as possible bibliographical and holdings data for the serial publications, with the exception of board reports and local publications, of the main branches of American Episcopal Methodism and the Evangelical United Brethren Church and its predecessors. The geographical area is limited to the United States" (introduction). It includes the holdings of 103 reporting libraries and archives. Together with Kenneth E. Rowe's *Methodist Union Catalog*, it provides comprehensive data on the script of a major American denomination.

Bishop, Selma L., comp. *Isaac Watts's Hymns and Spiritual Songs (1707): A Publishing History and a Bibliography*. Ann Arbor, MI: Pierian Press, 1974.

A bibliography studying "every edition known anywhere in America or in Europe . . . has been the aim of this work." Includes imprints of 672 editions published between 1707 and 1962. Watts's hymns, together with those of John and Charles Wesley, dominated American hymnody in the eighteenth and early nineteenth centuries. While Watts is popularly credited with having displaced the earlier use of psalmody, Bishop notes, "the present world seems unaware that the greatest of Watts's hymnal compositions are not hymns but Psalms" (p. xxi). For generations, Americans relied upon British presses for their hymns, but once publication began in the New World Watts's hymnbooks rolled off the presses by the millions. "Proof that Watts's *Hymns and Spiritual Songs* adjusted to all levels of Christians is doubtless, since Watts admitted special effort to lower the language of his Hymns for less intellectual people, seeing that they did not grasp Psalmic phraseology. After all, Watts soon became a household word in Britain as also in America" (p. ix). Each entry provides format, title page, decor, physical description, pagination, signatures, and name of the holding library or owner. See also the study by Richard Crawford, "Watts for Singing" (listed in Section IV).

Bowe, Forrest. *List of Additions and Corrections to Early Catholic Americana: Contribution of French Translations (1724-1820)*. New York: Franco-Americana, 1952.

This volume "gives only translations from the French which were printed in the United States through the year 1820 and which are omitted in Father [Wilfrid] Parsons's *Early Catholic Americana*" (p. 2). Of Parsons's 660 items through 1820, 155 are translations from the French. With Bowe's compilation of 236 new editions, a combined list of 391 editions is possible. The author includes numerous corrections of Parsons. Parts of this work were previously published in *Catholic Historical Review* 27 (1942): 229-47.

Braude, Ann. "News from the Spirit World: A Checklist of American Spiritualist Periodicals, 1847-1900." *Proceedings of the American Antiquarian Society* 99 (1990): 399-462.
    This work lists 214 titles with geographic, editor-publisher, and chronological indexes. Each listing provides title, place of publication, frequency, dates of publication, names of editors, subtitles, and notes about the nature or content of the publication. Also listed are Library of Congress location symbols for libraries that hold examples of the title. The author gives a description of the popular Spiritualist movement, which, "emphasizing freedom of conscience and direct inspiration over religious authority, . . . became a magnet for social radicals, especially advocates of women's rights and abolition" (p. 399). Spiritualist periodicals provide information about a movement that, because of its abhorrence for organization, can be otherwise difficult to chart. Books on spiritualism contain philosophical accounts and spirit messages; periodicals abound with information about Spiritualist practices and practitioners.

Brigham, Clarence Saunders. *History and Bibliography of American Newspapers, 1690-1820.* Worcester, MA: American Antiquarian Society, 1947.
    Arranged alphabetically by state and town, Brigham lists 2,120 newspapers with indication of files in all parts of the country. Historical notes are given for each title, including dates, title changes, frequency of publication, names of editors and publishers, etc. An index of titles and printers is included.

Bristol, Roger Pattrell. *Supplement to Charles Evans' American Bibliography.* Charlottesville: University Press of Virginia for the Bibliographical Society of the University of Virginia, 1970.
    This work adds some 11,200 entries to Charles Evans's *American Bibliography* (see below).

———. *Index to the Supplement* . . . Charlottesville: University Press of Virginia for the Bibliographical Society of America and the Bibliographical Society of the University of Virginia, 1971.

Britton, Allen Perdue; Irving Lowens; and Richard Crawford. *American Sacred Music Imprints 1698-1810: A Bibliography.* Worcester, MA: American Antiquarian Society, 1990.
    This bibliography lists collections of sacred music, compiled by 141

men, over a 112-year period. These collections are represented by 545 entries under the name of the compiler, or, if a collection is not identified with an individual compiler, by the agency that issued it. Variant issues of a title or edition receive a subordinate letter designation (e.g., 5a). Each item is described by nineteen elements, but chiefly by title page, pagination, size, method of printing, engraver, musical notation, date, contents, copies located, and other descriptive elements. Appended to the bibliography are five appendices: "Chronological List of Music"; "Sacred Sheet Music, 1790-1810"; "List of Composers and Sources"; "The Core Repertory"; "The 101 Sacred Compositions Most Frequently Printed in America During the Period Covered by the Bibliography"; and a "Geographical Directory of Engravers, Printers, Publishers, and Booksellers." The Introduction by Richard Crawford (pp. 1-45) is a valuable discussion of nine topics: compilers and compiling, composers and composing, poets and sacred poetry, teachers and teaching, performers and performance, publishers and publishing, engravers and engraving, printers and printing, and sellers and selling. The product of three authors, spanning a period of forty-three years, this is the most comprehensive bibliography of early American sacred music available and, therefore, indispensable for documenting a genre of literature that deeply influenced church life as well as being a powerful cultural influence.

Cadbury, Henry Joel. "Harvard College Library and the Libraries of the Mathers." *Proceedings of the American Antiquarian Society* 50 (1941): 20-48.

A historical and bibliographical essay detailing Mather books in the possession of Harvard University. See the earlier essay by J. H. Tuttle, "The Libraries of the Mathers" (listed below).

Campbell, Richard H., and Michael R. Pitts. *The Bible on Film: A Checklist 1897-1980.* Metuchen, NJ: Scarecrow Press, 1981.

"*The Bible on Film* is divided into three sections: The Films of the Old Testament, The Films of the New Testament, and Selected Television Programs based on both the testaments. . . . In listing the individual films, the following information is included where possible: title, release year, country of origin, release company, running time, and whether in color or black and white" (p. viii). The films are arranged by year of issue, then alphabetically when there is more than one entry in a given year.

Capo, James A. "Annotated Bibliography on Electronic Media." *Religious Education* 82 (1987): 304-32.

A critically annotated bibliography of 74 books, essays, journal titles and articles, and dissertations published since 1948 "classified to shed the most light on relationship between television and those concerned with theological education." Entries include publishing information and are enriched with indications of whether the work includes references to other discussions about the subject, footnotes, endnotes, bibliography, and/or appendices. Annotations offer judgments about the appropriate audience and relative importance of each work, whether directed to a specialized, scholarly audience or a more general audience. This bibliography is especially useful for relating religious concerns and issues to public policy and to developments in the television industry.

Crandall, Marjorie Lyle. *Confederate Imprints: A Check List Based Principally on the Collection of the Boston Athenaeum.* 2 vols. Boston: Athenaeum, 1955.

Part 5 of volume 2, "Religious Publications," lists 825 titles of sermons, Bibles, devotionals, hymnbooks, catechisms and Bible study, miscellaneous religious writings, church publications, and tracts. This two-volume work lists 2,391 official publications, 2,730 unofficial publications, besides 181 newspapers and periodicals. See also T. Michael Parrish and Robert M. Willingham, *Confederate Imprints* (listed below).

Danky, James P., ed. *Native American Periodicals and Newspapers, 1828-1982: Bibliography, Publishing Record, and Holdings.* Compiled by Maureen E. Hady. Westport, CT: Greenwood Press, 1984.

A guide to the holdings and locations of 1,164 periodical and newspaper titles by and about Native Americans developed from a detailed description of the holdings of the State Historical Society of Wisconsin's Library, 873 of which are held by the Society. Listings are by title, with subject, editor, publisher, geographic area, catchword, and subtitle; chronological indexes are included. Includes religious and denominational newspapers and periodicals. See also the bibliography by Francis Paul Prucha (listed below).

Degroot, Alfred E., and Enos E. Dowling. *The Literature of the Disciples of Christ.* Advance, IN: Hustler Print, 1933.

This bibliography includes approximately 1,000 titles of books and periodicals. Each book entry includes author's name, short title, pagination, name of publisher, and date of publication. Data for periodicals includes short title, place of publication, name of publisher, and the beginning date of publication. See also the bibliography by Leslie R. Galbraith and Heather F. Day (listed below).

Dexter, Henry M. *The Congregationalism of the Last Three Hundred Years as Seen in Its Literature . . . With a Bibliographical Appendix.* New York: Harper, 1880.

Over a century old, this groundbreaking study is based on an extensive bibliography that documents the origins of New England, particularly its

religious foundations in Anglican sixteenth-century England and as expressed
in the Martin Marprelate controversy, the Puritan exodus to Holland, the life
of the Leyden congregation, and the formative process of the Congregational
way. The American phase is included in two sections on New England Congregationalism and on ecclesiastical councils. The appendix, "Collections
Toward a Bibliography of Congregationalism," contains entries covering the
years 1546 through 1876. Throughout the text the author cites, quotes, and
analyzes this literature.

Dick, Donald. "Religious Broadcasting: 1920-1965: A Bibliography." *Journal of
Broadcasting* 9 (1964/65): 249-79; 10 (1965/66): 163-80; 257-76.
    A comprehensive listing of both primary and secondary sources including
books, pamphlets, theses, dissertations, documents, addresses, unpublished
mimeographed and other miscellaneous materials, and periodical articles on
religious broadcasting. "The major portion of this bibliography was compiled as
a part of the author's Ph.D. dissertation, completed in 1965 in the Department of
Speech of Michigan State University. . . . It has been updated and corrected to July
1965." This bibliography is published in three sections. Section one includes
sources, theses and dissertations, books and pamphlets, and unpublished and
miscellaneous materials; sections two (A-J) and three (K-Z) list periodical articles.

Drake, Milton, comp. *Almanacs of the United States.* New York: Scarecrow Press,
1962.
    This comprehensive bibliography of American almanacs contains over
14,000 entries. The almanac was, prior to 1850, usually the first local publication a printer would issue. "The profit from its sale usually covered his
expenses well into the following year." The seventeenth-century almanacs often
contained an ecclesiastical calendar, and by the nineteenth century there were
sectarian almanacs: *Baptist Almanac, Metropolitan Catholic Almanac, Clergyman's Almanack,* etc. Next to the Bible, it was the most often consulted book
in the American home prior to 1850. Entries are arranged geographically by
place of publication (state), chronologically by year of title, and alphabetically
by year. Library holding symbols are given.

Eames, Wilberforce. *Early New England Catechisms: A Bibliographical Account of
Some Catechisms Published Before the Year 1800, for Use in New England.* New
York: Burt Franklin, 1965(?).
    This bibliography relates chiefly to some of the catechisms for children
and older persons that were used in the seventeenth and eighteenth centuries.
As forerunners of the *New England Primer* they provide insight into the
education of children as well as being examples of popular religious literature
available in most homes. Introductory comments and detailed bibliographic

descriptions are given for many entries. Sample questions and answers from the catechisms are included. Originally published in *Proceedings of the American Antiquarian Society* n.s. 12 (October 1897): 76-182.

Edgar, Neal L. *A History and Bibliography of American Magazines, 1810-1820.* Metuchen, NJ: Scarecrow Press, 1975.

Chapter four, "The Magazines and Religion" (pp. 60-70), discusses sixty-five titles issued for the decade. The bibliography section of this work includes 223 titles and provides such details as title, place(s) and dates of publication, editors, frequency, size, availability, etc. A third section contains appendices: exclusions, a chronological list of magazines, and a register of printers, publishers, editors, and engravers.

Ellis, John T. "Old Catholic Newspapers in Some Eastern Catholic Libraries." *Catholic Historical Review* 33 (1947/48): 302-5.

Catholic newspapers, largely American, held by five libraries, are listed by short title and place of publication. Holdings are also given. This list supplements and enriches the earlier list published by Thomas F. Meehan in 1937 (see below).

Evans, Charles. *American Bibliography: A Chronological Dictionary of All the Books, Pamphlets and Periodical Publications Printed in the United States of America from the Genesis of Printing in 1639 Down to and Including the Year 1800; With Bibliographical and Biographical Notes.* Chicago: Printed for the Author, 1903-59; repr. New York: Peter Smith, 1941-67.

This is the most important bibliography of colonial publications. A large proportion of the titles are theological, making this an indispensable reference source for Puritan and early American religious history. Arranged chronologically, it includes all types of publications and gives location of copies in American libraries. The classified subject indexes are helpful in identifying genres of theological literature, such as sermons, catechisms, tracts, etc. Includes indexes of authors, printers, and publishers. See also the supplement by Bristol (listed above).

Finotti, Joseph Maria. *Bibliographia Catholica Americana: A List of Works Written by Catholic Authors and Published in the United States . . . from 1784 to 1820 Inclusive.* New York: Catholic Publication House, 1872.

Entries are arranged alphabetically by author/title and are largely English language, with numerous French but no German titles. Not all entries provide complete bibliographical description, while others do and are enriched with extensive notes. Originally projected to be issued in several volumes, this is the only part to have appeared.

Galbraith, Leslie R., and Heather F. Day. *The Disciples and American Culture: A Bibliography of Works by Disciples of Christ Members 1866-1984.* ATLA Bibliography Series, no. 26. Metuchen, NJ: Scarecrow Press, 1990.

A comprehensive bibliography of 4,750 book titles by Christian Church (Disciples of Christ) members, organized in subject sections by author's last name. A general literature section lists 508 titles of periodical and general literature by and about Disciples. Each entry provides the author's full name with birth and death dates, indication of the author's profession, book title, name of publisher, and date of publication. Nearly half the entries (2,471) constitute the section on theology. This bibliography helps to document the influence of this denomination and its members upon American culture. See also the bibliography by Degroot (listed above).

Graff, Harvey J. *Literacy in History: An Interdisciplinary Research Bibliography.* New York: Garland Publishing, 1981.

This bibliography organizes the available book and serial literature on literacy according to an ideal type and brings into focus systematic historical studies, which have increased dramatically since 1968. It includes a section on historical and theoretical studies of religion, which Graff views as having a dual importance: "religion has been, and continues to be, one of the primary sources and influences in the spread of mass literacy in modern societies . . . and, literacy alone was quite often seen as potentially dangerous: it had to be controlled and structured by moral values which derive from religion." The citations are predominantly European, with minimal attention to the sociology and anthropology of religion. An author index is included.

Hallenbeck, Chester T. "A Colonial Reading List from the Union Library of Hatboro, Pennsylvania." *Pennsylvania Magazine of History and Biography* 56 (1932): 289-340.

A transcription of loans, 1762-1774, from the Hatboro, Pennsylvania, Public Library (originally a subscription library), which indicates books borrowed from this rural library twenty miles from Philadelphia. Includes a bibliography identifying 211 titles listed in the loan register. Religion titles appear in the list. This list is significant since the majority of colonial subscription libraries were limited to urban centers.

Harris, Michael H. "A Methodist Minister's Library in Mid-Nineteenth Century Illinois." *Wesleyan Quarterly Review* 4 (1967): 210-19.

A listing of 156 volumes, based on probate records of the Rev. John Winteringham's estate, showing "a well rounded working collection with commentaries, church histories, hand-books, hymnals and dictionaries in profusion." Bibliographic identification of entries is provided when available.

Harwell, Richard. *More Confederate Imprints.* Richmond: Virginia State Library, 1957.

This work supplements Marjorie L. Crandall's *Confederate Imprints,* listing 1,773 additional titles published in the Confederate States of America. Part five, "Religious Publications," includes 319 titles of sermons, Bibles, devotionals, hymnbooks, catechisms and Bible study, miscellaneous religious writings, church publications, and tracts. Full bibliographic descriptions are given, with holding library symbols attached.

Heartman, Charles F. *The New-England Primer Issued Prior to 1830: A Bibliographical Check-List for the More Easy Attaining the True Knowledge of This Book* . . . New York: R. R. Bowker, 1934.

This checklist estimates that six to eight million copies of this primer were printed between the years 1680 and 1830. "It was practically an institution. It was, next to the Bible, the 'stock book' in the bookshops of the towns and the general stores of the village" (p. xviii). This list greatly expands Paul L. Ford's bibliography (see Section III), listing 457 variations with locations for 915 copies.

Hill, George H., and Lenwood Davis. *Religious Broadcasting, 1920-1983: A Selectively Annotated Bibliography.* New York: Garland Publishing Co, 1984.

"Intended for the 'seasoned' researcher as well as for the student doing his first term paper," this bibliography provides an introduction to work in religious radio and television, listing 1,644 books, dissertations, and articles. Annotations are given for books and dissertations but not for periodical articles. Articles tend to be those appearing in popular magazines.

Kennett, White. *The Primordia of Bishop White Kennett, the First English Bibliography on America, Introductory Study by Frederick R. Goff.* Washington, DC: Pan American Union, 1959.

This volume contains a facsimile reprint of Bishop White's *Bibliothecae Americanae Primordia* of 1713, designed toward laying the foundation of an American library and given to the Society for Propagation of the Gospel in Foreign Parts. As such, it represents the Church of England's missionary interest in the New World. This bibliography comprises some 1,216 books, broadsides, and manuscripts dating from 1170, all relating to the discovery, exploration, and evangelization of America. For related materials and developments, see entries by Thomas Bray (listed in Section IV).

Lippy, Charles H., ed. *Religious Periodicals of the United States: Academic and Scholarly Journals.* New York: Greenwood Press, 1986.

Of the 2,500 religious periodicals in print in the United States in 1985, "this book concentrates on a sampling of those (ca. 100) that focus on academic and scholarly concerns." Each title is profiled and includes a capsule history, discusses some of the materials that have appeared in the periodical, provides an assessment of the contribution an individual title has made within its own field, gives suggestions for further reading, identifies index sources for the periodical under review, whether reprint or microform editions are available, and selected libraries that contain the periodical in their collection.

Marsden, R. G. "A Virginia Minister's Library, 1635." *American Historical Review* 11 (1905/1906): 328-32.

A schedule of books belonging to a minister of the Church of England, which provides a concrete example of the contents of a library brought to America by a clergyman. It contains biblical texts, commentaries, concordances, Psalm books, theological treatises, lexicons, grammars, devotional manuals, classical authors, and secular works. Nearly all the titles are identified.

McKay, George L., and Clarence S. Brigham, comps. *American Book Auction Catalogues, 1713-1934: A Union List.* New York: New York Public Library, 1937.

"This list of some ten thousand American auction catalogues covers the period from 1713 through 1934, and is limited to auction catalogues, issued in what is now the United States, that list books, pamphlets, broadsides, newspapers, manuscripts, autographs, and bookplates" (preface). Auctions constitute a significant segment of the book trade. A considerable number of entries represent libraries of clergy offered at auction, making it possible to identify the specific contents of such libraries. A thirty-seven page introduction, "History of Book Auctions in America," by Clarence S. Brigham reviews auctions held in Boston, New York, and Philadelphia, with brief notes about other cities.

Meehan, Thomas F. "Early Catholic Weeklies." *United States Catholic Historical Society. Historical Records and Studies* 28 (1937): 237-55.

Nineteenth-century Catholic weeklies in the libraries of Georgetown University and Villanova College are listed with title, place of publication, and library holdings given. The author provides some historical commentary on the titles. At the end of the article is included a list of fifty anti-Catholic books and pamphlets maintained by the U.S. Catholic Historical Society at Dunwoodie Seminary. For an updating of this list see John T. Ellis's "Old Catholic Newspapers" (listed above).

Merrill, William S. "Catholic Authorship in the American Colonies Before 1784." *Catholic Historical Review* 3 (1917): 308-25.

This work contains a list of 47 titles, with full bibliographic descriptions, by Catholic authors printed before 1784. It serves as a valuable addition to Finotti's *Bibliographia Catholica Americana* (see above), which covers the period 1784 to 1820. In accompanying comments the author discusses the question of Catholic authorship and explains his methodology of locating qualifying authors and their titles.

Metcalf, Frank J., comp. *American Psalmody or Titles of Books Containing Tunes Printed in America from 1721 to 1820.* New intro. by Harry Eskew. New York: DeCapo Press, 1968.

"*American Psalmody* is a bibliography listing the short titles and library locations of more than two hundred books containing sacred music which were published in America in the eighteenth and early nineteenth centuries." The books listed here feature the manuals of singing schools, which were founded in the early eighteenth century to promote the reform of singing in New England. These tunebooks are not limited to settings of metrical psalms as the title implies. Useful as a complement to Britton et al., *American Sacred Music Imprints* (see above).

Montgomery, Michael S., comp. *American Puritan Studies: An Annotated Bibliography of Dissertations, 1882-1981.* Bibliographies and Indexes in American History, no. 1. Westport, CT: Greenwood Press, 1984.

"This bibliography comprises 940 American, British, Canadian and German doctoral dissertations and published monographs based on them relating to the American Puritans from 1882, the year the first thesis was accepted, through 1981." The Puritan period is defined as extending from 1620 to 1730 and includes all aspects of Puritan life: history, law, education, economics, music, etc. The scope of religion includes: "The history of the Congregational Church and its Platforms; biographies of Puritanism's prominent religious figures; the Puritan's Bible, its exegesis, and the uses of typology; doctrinal theology; practical theology; pastoral theology; sectarians, schismatics, and heretics; demonology and witchcraft." For related materials see also Henry M. Dexter's *Congregationalism* (listed above) and Edward J. Gallagher and Thomas Werge's *Early Puritan Writers* (listed in Section III).

Norton, L. Wesley. *Religious Newspapers in the Old Northwest to 1861: A History, Bibliography and Record of Opinion.* Athens, OH: Ohio University Press, 1977.

As the Old Northwest grew and developed, the religious denominations employed newspapers to develop and support consensus. While coping with growing religious diversity, the newspapers did not hesitate to promote morals and manners. The advocacy of such policies as national development, educational reform, and an aggressive foreign policy paved the way for dealing with the most controversial subject of all: slavery. The religious newspapers of the Old Northwest prior to the Civil War are viewed as having largely succeeded in their efforts to sanctify the secular, but they also reflect the challenges of an expanding and tumultuous society. This work includes a "Bibliography of Religious Newspapers with Library Holdings," pp. 161-78.

Parks, Roger, ed. *New England: A Bibliography of Its History.* Hanover, NH: University Press of New England, 1989.

This work contains a historiographic essay by David D. Hall and Alan Taylor. Organized by subject, some 4,200 entries are listed, including books, periodicals (about 50 percent), and dissertations. The works cited were written by academic scholars, professional writers, and amateur historians. Listings "provide uniform bibliographic data: name of author, full title of the work, place and date of publication, and pagination." Library locations are provided. Well indexed by author, editor, and compiler names as well as by subject and place. Subject sections include "Religion" (573 entries) and "Literature, Language, and the Printed Word" (488 entries).

Parrish, T. Michael, and Robert M. Willingham. *Confederate Imprints: A Bibliography of Southern Publications from Secession to Surrender (Expanding and Revising the Earlier Works of Marjorie Crandall and Richard Harwell).* Austin: Jenkins Publishing; Katonah, NH: Gary A. Foster, 1987.

Containing 9,497 titles gleaned from over one thousand libraries, this is the most comprehensive bibliography of Confederate imprints available. Included are books, pamphlets, broadsides, maps, sheet music, and pictorial prints. Newspapers are excluded. The religion section (including fraternal organizations) lists 1,516 titles, with holding library symbols attached. A major feature of this work is the index, which provides access by title, author, corporate name, printer, geographic area, and subject. See also Marjorie L. Crandall's *Confederate Imprints* and Richard Harwell's *More Confederate Imprints* (listed above).

Parsons, Wilfrid. *Early Catholic Americana: A List of Books and Other Works by Catholic Authors in the United States, 1729-1830.* New York: Macmillan, 1939.

This bibliography lists chronologically, then alphabetically within each year, over 600 titles, represented by 1,187 entries, of any book written by a Catholic published in the United States between 1729 and 1830. Full bibliographic descriptions are provided, with library locations indicated. Brief historical notes are given for many entries. Appendix II contains "A List of Periodicals Edited or Published by Catholics in the United States, 1785-1830," pp. 261-63. This bibliography greatly expands the earlier effort by Joseph Finotti, *Bibliographia Catholica Americana* (1872); see also the bibliography by Forrest Bowe (both listed above).

Prucha, Francis Paul. *A Bibliographical Guide to the History of Indian-White Relations in the United States.* Chicago: Center for the History of the American Indian of the Newberry Library and the University of Chicago Press, 1977.

"This volume lists and discusses more than nine thousand items, including materials in the national Archives, indexes of printed and archival government documents, guides to manuscripts, and other references. The main section, an extensive classified bibliography, includes books, journal articles, pamphlets, and dissertations. . . . Spanning the period from colonial days to the present this compendium includes introductions which provide a schematic overview of each section of the history of Indian-White relationships" (blurb). Especially helpful to communications researchers are Part One, chapters 1 through 4, "Guide to Sources," and Part Two, chapter 11, "Missions and Missionaries." Includes a detailed and extensive index of names and subjects.

Riley, Sam G., comp. *Index to Southern Periodicals.* New York: Greenwood Press, 1986.

Riley lists roughly 7,000 periodicals for the period 1764-1984, 1,800 of which are non-newspaper periodicals founded prior to 1900, with each entry arranged by title; place or places of publication; dates of publication; any title changes; absorptions or continuances; and a sample of libraries that hold files of the periodical's back issues.

Rowe, Kenneth E., ed. *Methodist Union Catalog: Pre-1976 Imprints.* Metuchen, NJ: Scarecrow Press, 1975–.

Vols. 1-6, A-I published to date. A bibliography "of the cataloged holdings of more than 200 libraries that have been reported to the editor or recorded in printed catalogs" (Introduction). Includes works on Methodist history, biography, doctrine, polity, missions, education, and sermons published as books, pamphlets, or theses. "The *MUC* is arranged as a cumulative author list in one alphabet. One entry per title, edition or issue, including full author and title, place, date, publisher, paging and series if any, is given" (p. iv). Gives location of copies in reporting libraries. Represents the script of a major American denomination. For the serial publications of Methodism, see John D. Batsel and Lydia K. Batsel, *Union List of United Methodist Serials* (listed above).

Seybolt, Robert F. "Student Libraries at Harvard, 1763-1764." *Publications of the Colonial Society of Massachusetts* 28 (1935): 449-61.

Based on inventories of student losses in the Harvard fire of 1764, a list of titles is compiled that reflects the college's program of studies and the reading of leisure hours. Theology and rhetoric are present, but much less so than in the preceding century, for which see the study by Arthur Norton (Section III).

Shea, John Dawson Gilmary. *A Bibliographical Account of Catholic Bibles, Testaments and Other Portions of Scripture, Translated from the Vulgate and Printed in the United States.* New York: Craimosy Press, 1859.

A basic, authoritative list of early American Catholic Scriptures, 1790-1859.

Smith, Joseph. *A Descriptive Catalogue of Friends' Books, or Books Written by Members of the Society of Friends, Commonly Called Quakers.* London: Joseph Smith, 1867.

Entries are listed alphabetically by author of books and periodical articles on all subjects written by Quakers. Full titles and imprints are given with notes and extracts from reviews. Author entries include dates and/or residence, and in some cases biographical notices are added. Includes British, American, and other imprints.

————. *Supplement to a Descriptive Catalogue of Friends' Books, or Books Written by Members of the Society of Friends, Commonly Called Quakers.* London: Edward Hicks, 1893.

Soukup, Paul A., comp. *Christian Communication: A Bibliographical Survey.* Bibliographies and Indexes in Religious Studies, no. 14. New York: Greenwood Press, 1989.

"Christian communication refers both to any communication used by the Christian churches and to a style of communication consistent with Christian ethics and practices." This annotated bibliography, international in scope and multilingual in character, contains books, journal articles, essays, pamphlets, and dissertations. The entries are largely those extracted from electronic databases, supplemented by manual searching. Containing 1,311 entries, this is the most comprehensive attempt yet undertaken to bring this broad discipline under bibliographic control. The most extensive section, with 470 entries, covers mass or social communication — primarily the press, film, radio, and television. Homiletics, however, receives limited coverage since it is adequately covered in other works. Some 100 entries constitute a section of historical materials. The first section of this volume contains an introductory chapter that surveys and discusses the history, issues, and approaches of the field. The second section provides a listing of resources that enlarge and extend the discussion of introductory matters and issues. Other chapters cover more specific areas of the discipline: communication theory, history, rhetoric, interpersonal communication, mass communication, intercultural communication, and other media, followed by name, title, and subject indexes. This bibliography is by no means exhaustive, as the author states, but is rather introductory in nature. It will be especially useful to those new to the field and to those who wish to integrate and relate Christian communication to other disciplines. Special attention is given to the need for a theology of communication.

Stroupe, Henry S. *The Religious Press in the South Atlantic States, 1802-1865: An Annotated Bibliography with Historical Introduction and Notes.* Historical Papers of the Trinity College Historical Society, Series 32. Durham, NC: Duke University Press, 1956.

> "The area studied consists of Virginia, the Carolinas, Georgia and Florida, and West Virginia before 1861. . . . 'Historical Introduction' narrates briefly the founding of the leading periodicals, explains why they were started, and analyzes their problems, their objectives and their relations with each other. . . . In the annotated bibliography, arranged alphabetically by title, each of the 159 publications known to have appeared in the South Atlantic States before 1865 is described. Nine others that were proposed but apparently not published are listed . . . each sketch locates extant files, either by references to published works in which they are listed or to libraries holding them" (pp. vii-viii).

Swift, Lindsay. "The Massachusetts Election Sermons." *Publications of the Colonial Society of Massachusetts, Volume I, Transactions, 1892-1894.* Pp. 388-451. Boston: The Society, 1895.

> Extended discussion, year by year, of the election sermons. Good detail on publication.

Tanselle, George Thomas. *Guide to the Study of United States Imprints.* 2 vols. Cambridge, MA: Belknap Press of Harvard University Press, 1971.

> This work records the basic titles needed to study United States publishing history. The genre lists in the first volume detail denominational studies such as Catholic Americana, Baptist Americana, et al. The second volume provides the bibliography of histories of religious publishing houses.

Trinterud, Leonard J., comp. *A Bibliography of American Presbyterianism During the Colonial Period.* Presbyterian Historical Society Publications, 8. Philadelphia: Presbyterian Historical Society, 1968.

> This work contains 1,129 entries for printed sources issued prior to 1800 that are by or identified with one of the twelve autonomous Presbyterian bodies in colonial America. It includes items published abroad and also lists items by non-Presbyterians who dealt with Presbyterianism in some significant way. Entries are keyed to Charles Evans's *American Bibliography* (see above), which this bibliography supplements.

Tuttle, Julius Herbert. "The Libraries of the Mathers." *Proceedings of the American Antiquarian Society* 20 (1910): 269-356.

The libraries of the Mathers (Richard, Increase, Cotton, Samuel [2]) are discussed in the context of early libraries in the Massachusetts Colony. Catalogs of the libraries are provided: Increase (1664); Mather books in the Massachusetts Historical Society; Mather books in other libraries; and the Mather library in the American Antiquarian Society, the latter obtained by Isaiah Thomas.

Vail, Robert W. G. "A Check List of New England Election Sermons." *Proceedings of the American Antiquarian Society* 45 (October 1936): 233-66.

Provides authors and titles of the sermons, together with holdings symbols referring to 30 depositories, for the colonies and/or states of Connecticut (1674-1830); Massachusetts (1634-1884); New Plymouth (1669, 1674); New Hampshire (1784-1831, 1861); and Vermont (1777-1834, 1856-1858).

Watts, Isaac. *Divine Songs Attempted in Easy Language for the Use of Children . . . With an Introduction and Bibliography by J. H. P. Pafford.* London: Oxford University Press, 1971.

First published in 1715, this book, popularly known as *Divine and Moral Songs,* went through at least 667 editions and sold over eight million copies in Britain and America. Didactic by design, almost propagandistic, it supplied, together with his catechism for children and youth, a system of worship for childhood. Ironically, Watts's fame as a hymnologist rests on his other works, but much of his popularity can be attributed to the *Divine Songs.* Among recognized authors, the work is known to have influenced Alexander Pope, William Blake, and Lewis Carroll. "The book was used by and for children, in homes, schools, and Sunday schools, in many parts of Britain and America for over a hundred years" (p. 89). This edition contains a facsimile reproduction of the first edition of 1715, and an illustrated edition, circa 1840.

Wolf, Edwin II. *The Book Culture of a Colonial American City: Philadelphia Books, Bookmen, and Booksellers.* Lyell Lectures in Bibliography, 1985-86. Oxford: Clarendon Press, 1988.

The purpose of this study is "to present a method for documenting the existence of certain books in a specific locality within a specific time span" (p. vii). The pattern of research is bibliographical. Chapter 1, " 'Sundry Printed Books,' " includes general remarks on theological titles, and Chapter 2, "Books for Large People and Small," includes more specific details on Bibles, psalters, and prayer-books. Other theological works are not treated. Basing his research on library catalogs, newspaper advertisements, and book inventories in wills at Philadelphia, Wolf believes that the titles identified here are valid "for the rest of the North American British colonies, and, indeed for middle-class Great Britain" (p. vi).

Wright, John. *Early Bibles of America; Being a Descriptive Account of Bibles Published in the United States, Mexico and Canada.* New York: Thomas Whittaker, 1894.

This source provides brief histories and commentaries on Bible versions printed in America through the early nineteenth century.

## II. General Studies

Baumgartner, Appolinaris W. *Catholic Journalism: A Study of Its Development in the United States, 1789-1930.* New York: Columbia University Press, 1931.

A chronological review of Catholic newspapers, their founding, their development, and the general conditions under which they appeared. The study is limited primarily to English language organs with some remarks on the journalism of the foreign language groups among American Catholics. One chapter discusses Catholic journalistic education for the period 1910-1930. A list of Catholic weekly papers published in the United States is given, while an appendix lists journals of record published prior to 1892, the dates of whose foundations are unknown.

Bronner, Edwin B. "Distributing the Printed Word: The Tract Association of Friends, 1816-1966." *Pennsylvania Magazine of History and Biography* 91 (1967): 342-54.

This article provides the basic historical facts concerning the establishment and development of this Quaker tract society whose program and activities are similar to those of other tract societies.

Brown, Herment Ross. *The Sentimental Novel in America, 1789-1960.* Durham, NC: Duke University Press, 1940.

Novels on temperance, slavery, domestic concerns, and religious-moral themes are discussed and analyzed in detail. As the old Calvinism, with its stern moral demands and cold theology, was displaced by the more evangelical zeal of the antinomians, the "sentimentalizing of reality is to be found at every point at which these novelists touched life" (p. 365). In this context, religion becomes a stepping-stone to success, and heaven is only the extension of the material blessings enjoyed here in this life. Reprinted 1959 by Pageant Books, New York.

Bullock, Penelope L. *The Afro-American Periodical Press, 1838-1909.* Baton Rouge: Louisiana State University Press, 1981.

"Presents a narrative history of the beginnings and early development of periodical publishing among black Americans, discusses the individuals and institutions responsible for the magazines, and suggests the circumstances in

American history and culture that helped to shape this press" (p. xi). This study includes ninety-seven titles, restricting periodicals sponsored by religious organizations to publications at the national level, such as the *African Methodist Episcopal Church Magazine, Repository of Religion and Literature and of Science and Art,* and the *A.M.E. Church Review.* Appendices give publication data and selected finding list, chronology, and geography of the periodicals.

Cavanaugh, Mary Stephana. "Catholic Book Publishing History in the United States, 1784-1850." Master's thesis, University of Illinois, 1937.

This study traces the origin, scope, and progress of early Catholic book publishing in the United States. "The biographical method is used and an attempt is made to answer such questions as: Who were these Catholic publishers? What factors in their education and environment prepared them for their work? What important books did they make available to American Catholics? What contribution was made by each to Catholic life and thought?" (p. 1). Attention is largely limited to that part of the United States east of the Mississippi River.

Commission on Freedom of the Press. *A Free and Responsible Press; A General Report on Mass Communication: Newspapers, Radio, Motion Pictures, Magazines, and Books . . .* Chicago: University of Chicago Press, 1947.

Defines free press "to include all means of communicating to the public news and opinions, emotions and beliefs, whether by newspapers, magazines, or books, by radio broadcasts, by television or by films" (p. 109). The report advocates a free press that is responsible and accountable. Chapter six, "What Can be Done," gives thirteen recommendations issued by the Commission, grouped according to the sources from which action must come: (1) government, (2) press, (3) public. See also the study by Fred S. Siebert (listed below).

Dobbins, Gaines Stanley. "Southern Baptist Journalism." D.Th. diss., Southern Baptist Theological Seminary, 1914.

A historical study based primarily on sixty-three United States Baptist newspapers and periodicals associated with the Southern Baptist Convention, a list of which is included in the bibliography.

Drury, Clifford M. "Presbyterian Journalism on the Pacific Coast." *Pacific Historical Review* 9 (1940): 461-69.

This article reviews the publication of some twenty Presbyterian newspapers and periodicals for the period 1843-1940. While most were published on the Pacific Coast, at least one journal was published at Salt Lake City and another at Denver.

Ellinwood, Leonard. "Religious Music in America." In *Religious Perspectives in American Culture,* ed. James W. Smith, pp. 289-359. Princeton: Princeton University Press, 1961.

Hymnody has played a significant role in American life from the beginning, with hymnals and songbooks constituting one of the most popular genres of religious literature. Ellinwood delineates the history of hymnody from Native American music and colonial psalmody down to modern choirs, stressing its oral-aural characteristics as well as its communal aspects.

"From Revivalism to Rock and Roll: Youth and Media Historically Considered." In *Dancing in the Dark: Youth, Popular Culture, and the Electronic Media,* ed. Quentin J. Schultze et al., pp. 14-45. Grand Rapids: Eerdmans, 1991.

This chapter examines the conjunction between restless youth, new media, and new entertainment. The conjunction is studied in relation to modernization, which is interpreted as a cyclical social process recurring since the eighteenth century in the following periods: youth and revival discipline (1740-1790); revival discipline in the young republic (1790-1840); youth and Victorian nurture (1840-1890); the 1890s; and the 1920s. In each period of contest between freedom and control, communication technology constitutes the chief means of exchange.

Gerbner, George. "Mass Media and Human Communication Theory." In *Human Communication Theory,* ed. Frank E. X. Dance, pp. 40-60. New York: Holt, Rinehart and Winston, 1967.

This study places the development of mass media in a historically conditioned context that lends itself to religious and mythic interpretations. After exploring the definition of terms and concepts, the author summarizes the work of political scientists and others concerned with the public policy functions of mass media and concludes by summarizing some of his own notions about a theory of mass media and mass communications. A bibliography of ninety titles is included.

Grimstead, David. "Books and Culture: Canned, Canonized, and Neglected." *Proceedings of the American Antiquarian Society* 94 (1984): 297-335.

This study deals with the particular areas and topics where books and popular culture might be drawn together and, in so doing, argues for "the benefits of closer ties between respectable books, representing the canonized lineage of humane scholarship, and the burgeoning if somewhat declasse field of popular or canned culture" (pp. 298-99). Grimstead's statement is significant because he raises serious questions about the rigidities and inadequacies of works such as Ray Billington's *Protestant Crusade* and Ann Douglas's *The Feminization of American Culture.* Grimstead calls for more historically connected studies of such literature as hymns and an exploration of social convictions of mainline Protestant and Catholic journals. Roger Chartier responds to Grimstead's article in pp. 336-42 of the issue.

Hall, David D. "Introduction: The Uses of Literacy in New England, 1600-1850." In *Printing and Society in Early America,* ed. William L. Joyce et al., pp. 1-47. Worcester, MA: American Antiquarian Society, 1983.

This essay contains significant data on the relationship between books and readers and delineates the distinction between "verbal" and "oral" modes of culture. New England, with a traditional literacy, was characterized by an intense relationship between book and reader. The steady sellers (books of devotional instruction and piety) encompassed four great crises or rites of passage: conversion, self-scrutiny when receiving communion, the experience of "remarkable" afflictions, and the art of dying well.

Hudson, Frederic. *Journalism in the United States from 1690 to 1872.* New York: Harper, 1873.

While ranging broadly over the field of journalism, chapter 19 is devoted to the religious press, and chapter 30 briefly surveys female journalists. Its contents are largely anecdotal, statistical, and biographical, but it does contain historical data compiled from many sources organized in topical and outline form.

Joyce, Donald Franklin. *Gatekeepers of Black Culture: Black-Owned Book Publishing in the United States, 1817-1981.* Westport, CT: Greenwood Press, 1983.

Chapter 4, on book-publishing activities of black religious publishers, 1900-1959, and Appendix C, with profiles of sixty-six black publishers and two printers identified as engaging in black-owned book publishing, 1917-1981, include religious publishers and provide profiles with (1) dates of existence, (2) major officers with dates of tenure, (3) major publications citing author, title, and publication date for books and titles for periodicals with opening and closing dates, (4) type of business structure, (5) categories of books published, and (6) publishing objectives.

Lacy, Creighton. *The Word Carrying Giant: The Growth of the American Bible Society (1816-1966).* South Pasadena, CA: William Carey Library, 1977.

A compact history of the American Bible Society, founded in 1816, which documents the development of Bible printing and distribution on a mass scale. Chapter 3, "Auxiliaries and Agents," and chapter 4, "The General Supply," are especially helpful in detailing the development of printing, distribution, and organization.

Lankard, Frank G. *History of the American Sunday School Curriculum.* Abingdon Religious Education Texts. New York: Abingdon Press, 1927.

    This study relates "the history of the religious curriculum found in the Sunday schools of America during the National Period (1800-1925)." Beginning with the hornbook and the *New England Primer,* the author uses the term "curriculum" to denote the materials in printed form used in Protestant Sunday schools. These materials, used in the various periods of the history of the Sunday school, are examined, with examples, to illustrate the objectives and major emphases of the field. An extensive bibliography of original and secondary sources is included, as well as tables of curriculum plans.

Lehmann-Haupt, Helmut; Lawrence C. Wroth; and Rollo G. Silver, eds. *The Book in America: A History of the Making and Selling of Books in the United States.* New York: R. R. Bowker Co., 1951.

    A solid, well-organized, balanced history of printing, publishing, selling, and distribution of books in the United States from colonial times to 1950. It represents a significant effort at cultural history, noting that the book industry has been a highly important factor in national development, with the church, school, and press intimately involved in structuring the new nation. The religious press, as well as the role of religion in American life, is given succinct but sympathetic treatment. The study pulls together information from many sources to provide an integrated survey of the book in America.

Levine, Lawrence W. *Black Culture and Black Consciousness: Afro-American Folk Thought from Slavery to Freedom.* New York: Oxford University Press, 1977.

    See especially chapter 1, "The Sacred World of Black Slaves," and chapter 3, "Freedom, Culture, and Religion," pp. 136-89, with sections on the language of freedom, the fate of the sacred world, and the development of gospel song. Levine directly challenges the view expressed by Gunnar Myrdal and others that black culture was characterized, not by any degree of cultural distinctiveness, but by unhealthy deviance. Levine finds that "again and again oral expressive culture reveals a pattern of simultaneous acculturation and revitalization. From the first African captives, through the years of slavery, and into the present century black Americans kept alive important strands of African consciousness and verbal art in their humor, songs, dance, speech, tales, games, folk beliefs, and aphorisms" (p. 444).

Lynn, Robert W., and Eliot Wright. *The Big Little School: Two Hundred Years of the Sunday School.* Nashville: Abingdon Press, 1980.

    This study includes the development of the Sunday school unions of the early nineteenth century, which labored on the frontier and in the isolated areas of the United States. Also included are the revitalization and great

expansion of Sunday school work, particularly after the Civil War. In the first
instance, the tract, books, and libraries were pervasive; in the latter, the Uniform Lesson Series and the development of curriculum materials assumed
massive proportions. With a circulation of literature in the millions, it remains
even today a defining feature of Protestantism. In this study hymnody is
considered essential to an understanding of the institution.

Miller, Glenn T. *Piety and Intellect: The Aims and Purposes of Ante-Bellum Theological Education.* Atlanta: Scholars Press, 1990.
        The first of a two-volume work that explores the motives of the persons
and denominations who founded theological seminaries in the United States
prior to the Civil War. In the eighteenth century ministers were trained through
reading programs and tutoring, and in the nineteenth century through both
public and private colleges. By 1850 theological seminaries were formed to
teach theology and to combat heresy. Such schools as Andover, Harvard, and
Princeton defined the programs and standards that other schools replicated,
and they provided a home for theology. The seminaries, through their faculties
and libraries, succeeded in transmitting the best theological and biblical research to new generations. "A related achievement was their publication of
scholarly journals" (p. 451). American scholars read and reviewed European
scholarship, which established critical, historical, and scientific principles for
the development of American scholarly theology. This is the most careful study
to date that probes the origins of contemporary theological education.

Miller, Russell E. *The Larger Hope.* Boston: Unitarian Universalist Association,
1979-85.
        Volume 1: *The First Century of the Universalist Church in America,
1770-1870.* Chapter 13, "The Newspaper Press" (pp. 285-319), chronicles
and evaluates the publishing enterprises of this comparatively small denomination, which issued, in the period 1793-1886, 182 periodical titles and
thousands of books. A section on "Southern Denominational Journalism" is
included, and abolition and slavery are discussed. Volume 2: *The Second
Century of the Universalist Church in America, 1870-1970.* Chapter 14, "Publications and Scholarship" (pp. 230-52), details the history of the Universalist
Publishing House, founded in 1871, which issued twelve periodical titles and
numerous books during the century.

Morehouse, Clifford P. "Almanacs and Year Books of the Episcopal Church."
*Historical Magazine of the Protestant Episcopal Church* 10 (1941): 330-53.
        This article traces the evolution of *The Living Church Annual,* a current
publication combining features of the almanac and yearbook, over a period of
more than two and a half centuries. This publication and its predecessors have

enjoyed an honorable history since they document the ecclesiastical calendar and lectionary while also featuring statistics, biography, historical records of the church, and current data about the clergy, dioceses, institutions, and organizations of the church.

―――――. "Origins of the Episcopal Church Press from Colonial Days to 1840." *Historical Magazine of the Protestant Episcopal Church* 11 (1942): 199-318.

In this article Morehouse traces the history of the earliest periodicals, the first church weeklies, and the monthlies, quarterlies, and children's magazines. Separate sections are devoted to three titles published for over a century: *The Churchman* (1831–); *The Southern Churchman* (1835–); and *The Spirit of Missions* (1836–). It includes a bibliography and index of periodicals and also an index of persons.

Mott, Frank Luther. *Golden Multitudes: The Story of Best Sellers in the United States.* New York: Macmillan, 1947.

The first comprehensive and scholarly effort to define, analyze, and study best-selling books in America from colonial times through 1945. Part of the author's interest is to delineate "the workings of a democratic society concerned with the mass impact of so much reading matter upon the public" (p. 5). The analysis contained in this study is largely literary and historical rather than sociological and political. Chapters on religion, publishing in the colonies, Bibles, books for children, Harriet Beecher Stowe, Charles M. Sheldon, and Howard Bell Wright all touch on the immense popularity of religious books. Appendices contain lists of best sellers from 1662 through 1945.

―――――. *A History of American Magazines.* Cambridge, MA: Belknap Press of Harvard University Press, 1957-68.

The standard general five-volume history covering the period 1741-1930. Up to 1850, religious journals are identified as being sectarian, with their content given over to controversy. In the period 1850-1865, denominational magazines rise to prominence, although the religious press was not of the highest character either as journalism or as religion. In the period 1865-1885 two kinds of journals appear: (1) reviews, monthly or quarterly, devoted largely to theology and scholarship; and (2) the weeklies with general news. For the years 1885-1905 the author extends his coverage to include papers featuring agnosticism, the Ethical Culture Movement, Christian Socialism, New Thought, Christian Science and faith healing, theosophy, the YMCA, and the Salvation Army. Volumes 1-3 include descriptive, historical sketches of important journals for each period, including religious titles. Volume 5, spanning the years 1905-1930, contains sketches of 21 magazines, none of which is religious. This volume also includes a cumulative index to the five volumes. See also the study by Lyon N. Richardson (listed below in Section IV).

Moyer, Jane. "The Making of Many Books: 125 Years of Presbyterian Publishing, 1838-1963." *Journal of Presbyterian History* 41 (1963): 124-40.

This article sketches the development of the publishing house of the United Presbyterian Church in the U.S.A. known today as the Westminster/John Knox Press, one of the major Protestant publishing concerns in the United States. Titles of books and periodicals issued by the press are noted together with descriptions of various needs to which the publishing house has responded through the years.

Ness, John H. *One Hundred Fifty Years: A History of the Publishing in the Evangelical United Brethren Church.* Dayton: Board of Publication of the Evangelical United Brethren Church, 1966.

This study includes the publishing history of the Evangelical United Brethren Church (1946-66) and its predecessor bodies, the Evangelical Church (1816-1946) and the Church of the United Brethren in Christ (1834-1946). The presses of these three denominations devoted much of their efforts to publishing tracts, hymnbooks, catechisms, disciplines, church papers, conference minutes, Sunday school literature, and other religious literature. These publishing houses, complete with proprietary bookstore outlets, were multi-million-dollar enterprises by the twentieth century, with professional management and employing hundreds of workers. Like most Protestant denominational publishing houses, these publishing enterprises fulfilled both an evangelizing function, printing and distributing literature promoting salvation for the masses, and an institutional function, promoting and sustaining an organized Christian denomination. Also included is a brief history of publishing by these denominations through their European publishing houses.

Nichols, Charles L. "Notes on the Almanacs of Massachusetts." *Proceedings of the American Antiquarian Society* 22 (1912): 15-134.

William Pierce's almanac for 1639 was the first book printed in British America (no copy survives). The almanacs issued through 1700 were distinctly religious. The almanac was one of the books nearly every seventeenth-century household possessed. This article includes a "Chronological List of Massachusetts Almanacs, 1639-1850."

Nystrom, Daniel. *A Ministry of Printing: History of the Publication House of Augustana Lutheran Church, 1889-1962.* Rock Island, IL: Augustana Press, 1962.

This study covers earlier publishing enterprises, 1850-1869, including those of the Swedish Lutheran Publication Society, the Augustana Book Concern, and others. It provides a description of church periodicals, books published, annuals and quarterlies, and the Augustana tract program. See also Ernst W. Olson (listed below).

O'Brien, Elmer J. "The *Methodist Quarterly Review:* Reflections on a Methodist Periodical." *Methodist History* 25 (1987): 76-90.

This essay describes the project to index articles and book reviews in five scholarly journals published by American Methodists from 1818 to 1985, which, under the generic name of *Methodist Quarterly Review,* had a longer life than any other religious publication in America. Historical, theological, denominational, and social developments that influenced and shaped the journals are discussed. The essay concludes with some reflections on themes, issues, and concerns that have characterized these titles over the past 167 years.

Olson, Ernst W. *The Augustana Book Concern: A History of the Synodical Publishing House with Introductory Account of Earlier Publishing Enterprises.* Rock Island, IL: Augustana Book Concern, 1934.

Like that of many denominational publishing houses, the primary purpose of this Lutheran concern, founded in 1851, was to promote spiritual culture. However, intellectual and aesthetic requirements were not neglected. See also Daniel Nystrom (listed above).

Ong, Walter J. *Orality and Literacy: The Technologizing of the Word.* New York: Methuen, 1982.

This study posits a dual approach to the study of orality-literacy controls and writing cultures that coexist at a given period of time, diachronically or historically, by comparing successive periods with one another. Attention is given to printing as an extension of literacy and electronic processing of the word and of thought because it is only since the electronic age that we have become sensitized to the contrast between writing and orality. The author assesses the intellectual, literary, and social effects of writing, as well as the effects of print and electronic technology.

———. *The Presence of the Word: Some Prolegomena for Cultural and Religious History.* New Haven: Yale University Press, 1967.

A history of communication, including the religious state, focused around a succession of difficult and often traumatic reorientations of the human psyche in which, as the word moves into space, it restructures itself and the sensorium is reorganized. The history of the Hebrew-Christian tradition is probed to identify these shifts in communication that demand a reorganization and restructuring of human experience. In this view the present era is post-typographical, "incorporating an individualized self-consciousness developed with the aid of writing and print and possessed of more reflectiveness, historical sense, and organized purposefulness than was possible in preliterate oral cultures" (p. 302). Ong's exegesis invites a new vantage point from which to interpret the human experience as it is affected by rapid technological and social change, especially that occasioned by media.

Parsons, Paul F. "Dangers of Libeling the Clergy." *Journalism Quarterly* 62 (1985): 528-32, 539.

　　"This article traces the evolution of libel law involving the clergy as plaintiff and the news media as defendant" (p. 528). While it is true that clergy once retained nearly blanket immunity from libel, the changing nature of libel law "has greatly eroded the special protection that existed for members of the clergy earlier in the nation's history and has fully eliminated it when the minister becomes active in a public or political issue" (p. 539).

Pilkington, James Penn. *The Methodist Publishing House: A History.* Volume 1: *Beginning to 1870.* Nashville: Abingdon Press, 1968.

　　This study includes history of the publishing concerns of the Methodist Episcopal Church, the Methodist Episcopal Church, South, and the Methodist Protestant Church. Reflecting on the growth of Methodism in America's first century, the author attributes part of the growth to American Methodist publishing. "The Methodist publishing houses grew because the churches grew, and at least in part, the Methodist churches grew because of their publishing houses. . . . Here it should be recalled that the secular publishing business in America was really successor to rather than antecedent of the religious publishing business. Actually, therefore, in America's first hundred years the secular publishers, it might be said, caught up with the denominational publishers" (p. 500). For volume 2, see Walter Newton Vernon (listed below).

Plimpton, George A. "The Hornbook and Its Use in America." *Proceedings of the American Antiquarian Society* 26 (1916): 264-72.

　　Indirect evidence indicates that the hornbook was used in the American colonies as a favorite device for teaching children to read. As late as the first quarter of the nineteenth century, the hornbook was flourishing. With print and paper coming into plentiful supply, this simple technology was displaced.

Rice, Edwin Wilbur. *The Sunday-School Movement, 1780-1917, and the American Sunday-School Union, 1817-1917.* Philadelphia: American Sunday-School Union, 1917; repr. New York: Arno Press, 1971.

　　A substantive history of Sunday school work, more especially of the American Sunday-School Union (ASSU). The chapters describing the creation of juvenile literature (the ASSU was a pioneer in this effort); Uniform Bible Lessons; missionary work, which included the employment of theological students; International Lessons (1872-1925); and general comments on the production, distribution, and sale of literature are especially valuable. The Union succeeded in becoming an agency for the mass production and distribution of popular religious literature.

Richmond, Peggy J. Z. "Afro-American Printers and Book Publishers, 1650-1865." Master's thesis, University of Chicago, 1970.

Contains a chapter on the press of the African Methodist Episcopal Church, the oldest continuous black church press in the United States, established in 1818 (pp. 100-121). While its output prior to the Civil War was very limited, it pioneered in publishing that was followed by other black organizations and established one of the few ways in which blacks could express themselves and communicate their concerns.

Rogal, Samuel J. "Major Hymnals Published in America: 1640-1900." *Princeton Seminary Bulletin* 61 (1968): 77-92.

A listing of hymnals, grouped by denomination and/or sponsoring organization, which documents the three major stages in the growth and development of American hymnody: "(1) psalters, or metrical versions of the psalms, 1620-1728; (2) the age of Isaac Watts and the Wesleys, 1729-1824; and (3) the rise and dominance of evangelical hymnody and gospel songs, 1824-1900" (p. 77). Author name, short title, and place and date of publication are given for each title.

Schick, Frank L. *The Paperbound Book in America: The History of Paperbacks and Their European Background.* New York: R. R. Bowker, 1958.

This study "covers the history of paperbacks from 1639 to 1939 in survey form and serves as a general introduction to the current phase. . . . The histories of individual firms are arranged by chapters according to the specialization of their activities (textbook, university presses, religious paperbacks, etc.) as they relate to paperback production and within each chapter, chronologically according to the dates of the release of the first paperbacks of significance to the contemporary development" (p. viii). Religious publishers entered the contemporary development of the paperback relatively late (1950).

Schneider, Louis, and Sanford M. Dornbusch. *Popular Religion: Inspirational Books in America.* Chicago: University of Chicago Press, 1958.

Through sociological analysis, employing the technique of content analysis, inspirational religious books are examined. Forty-six best-sellers published during the years 1875 to 1955 were chosen for analysis. This study evaluates the literature as part of mass culture and locates it as one element in a vast market of commodities and ideologies. "This material, produced for everyday people with the avowed aim of helping them meet their everyday problems, is obviously dependent on a mass market for its sales and consumption. It employs a language addressed to the masses and not adapted to the uses of a spiritual or literacy or any other kind of elite" (p. 133).

Shera, Jesse H. *Foundations of the Public Library: The Origins of the Public Library Movement in New England, 1629-1855.* University of Chicago Studies in Library Science. Chicago: University of Chicago Press, 1949.

This study views the early development of libraries in New England as "a record of transition from a narrowly conservational function to a broad program directed toward the advance of popular education," and it regards the public library as a social agency, as a derivative of social patterns, rather than as a social institution. The author touches on the influence that the church and religion, as one of New England's established institutions, had on libraries and the public library movement. This study stands as one of the best social interpretations of American library development.

Shewmaker, William O. "The Training of the Protestant Ministry in the United States of America, Before the Establishment of the Theological Seminaries." *American Society of Church History. Papers,* 2nd series, 6 (1921): 71-202.

A general overview of ministerial training in the American colonies for the New England Puritans, Anglicans, and Presbyterians during the seventeenth and eighteenth centuries. Three aspects of training are discussed: (1) collegiate and university, (2) the private teaching of theology, and (3) the beginnings of seminaries. The methods of instruction and the importance of books are noted, along with comments on the manner of delivering sermons. During this period there was a consistent expectation and demand that the ministry be maintained as a "learned profession."

Siebert, Fred S.; Theodore Peterson; and Wilbur Schramm. *Four Theories of the Press: The Authoritarian, Libertarian, Social Responsibility, and Soviet Communist Concepts of What the Press Should Be and Do.* Urbana: University of Illinois Press, 1963.

The original edition was published in 1956. "These essays were prepared in connection with a study of the social responsibilities of mass communicators which Dr. Schramm conducted for the Department of the Church and Economic Life of the National Council of Churches. The thesis of this volume is that the press always takes on the form and coloration of the social and political structures within which it operates." The social responsibility theory, which has been widely accepted by the churches, is based on the study conducted by the Commission on Freedom of the Press (listed above).

Soltow, Lee, and Edward Stevens. *The Rise of Literacy and the Common School in the United States: A Socioeconomic Analysis to 1870.* Chicago: University of Chicago Press, 1981.

This study builds on Kenneth Lockridge's study of New England literacy to examine literacy in other areas, notably in Ohio for the period 1790-1870. Three major vehicles for cultural transmission are identified: newspapers, the library, and book trade. The common school is seen as instrumental in three shifts during the period: (1) the teaching of basic reading skills so as to instill biblical values and improve individual social behavior, (2) the shift from a religious-literacy framework to a nation-building framework, and (3) school reform, a product of Victorian didacticism, which shifted the literacy framework to emphasize an individual, internalized sense of obligation and of self-control. These shifts resulted in the firm establishment of a meritocratic social structure grounded in literacy and residual Protestant moral, ethical values.

Stevens, Daniel Gurden, and E. M. Stephenson. *The First Hundred Years of the American Baptist Publication Society.* Philadelphia: American Baptist Publication Society, n.d.

Founded in 1824, the society grew out of the ferment roused in the religious world by the missionary idea. An immediate denominational need that also gave impetus to its organization was the desire for Baptist tracts. Over the century the society prospered and expanded its activities to service Sunday schools, issue periodicals, publish books, and carry on extensive evangelistic work employing the railroads and the automobile.

Tebbel, John. *A History of Book Publishing in the United States.* 4 vols. New York: R. R. Bowker, 1972-81.

In brief sections each of the four volumes of this history traces the rise, development, and expansion of religious book publishing from 1630 to 1980. The seventeenth century saw the rise of religious publishing with the issue of sermons and tracts and the appearance of John Eliot's Indian Bible. The eighteenth and nineteenth centuries witnessed the establishment and expansion of both denominational and nondenominational publishing houses. Bible publication dominated both the sectarian and the general markets of the period. In the current century there has been a major expansion of religious book publishing, characterized by a golden age of growth (1920-1940). Protestant, Catholic, and Jewish publishers shared in large increases in publishing, while Bible sales continued as a lucrative market. Trade publishers greatly expanded the issuance of religious titles beginning in the 1930s. In recent years Protestant publishing has experienced unprecedented growth, especially on the part of evangelical publishers. Tebbel provides a general if restricted overview of religious book publishing interpreted as centering in Bible publication and the development of major denominational publishing houses.

Thompson, Ernest Trice. *Presbyterians in the South. Volume Two: 1861-1890.* Richmond: John Knox Press, 1973.

The Executive Committee on Publication was authorized by the first General Assembly in 1861. It began publication of tracts, Sunday school papers, army hymnbooks, and other titles. It also put into circulation volumes secured from England. During the Civil War, "Chaplains and missionaries reported a hunger for the printed word — for religious tracts, for religious papers, and for copies of the Scriptures" (p. 45). Distributed in the army were the following: *Central Presbyterian,* 2,000 copies weekly; *Christian Observer,* 3,000 copies weekly; *Southern Presbyterian,* 4,000 copies weekly. "Most eagerly sought (by soldiers) were copies of the New Testament" (p. 45). In chapter 14, "The Educational Foundation," see the section on publication, pp. 332-38, especially the discussion of the colportage system.

Thorn, William J. "The History and Role of the Catholic Press." In *Reporting Religion: Facts and Faith,* ed. Benjamin J. Hubbard, pp. 81-107. Sonoma, CA: Polebridge Press, 1990.

"The Catholic press serves the Catholic subculture as an interpreter of the American experience; it also speaks to American society about the Catholic vision of life" (p. 83). The Catholic press is viewed as having moved through five major stages: (1) immigrant (1789-1884); (2) consolidation and institutionalization (1884-1945); (3) professionalization (1945-65); (4) Vatican II exploration (1965-70); and (5) reinstitutionalization (1970 to the present).

Thorp, Willard. "The Religious Novel as Best Seller in America." In *Religious Perspectives in American Culture,* ed. James W. Smith, pp. 195-242. Princeton: Princeton University Press, 1961.

This essay analyzes the plots and themes used by the authors of American religious novels during the first century (1837-1940) of the religious novel's development. These novels succeeded as best-sellers because they brought reassurance and comfort to millions of readers. The piety in them is genuine, and many were written by clergymen who were converting their most dramatic sermons into novels. Some of the more recent novels have also been made into motion pictures.

Vernon, Walter Newton. *The United Methodist Publishing House: A History.* Volume 2: *1870-1988.* Nashville: Abingdon Press, 1989.

This study details the second century of the history of this major religious publisher, which has evolved today into a "print–electronic software–video–satellite communicating religious publishing and distributing agency which reaches out to the general society, cooperatively serves many other denominations, and extends its services to more than 20 foreign countries and U.S. military chapels around the world" (p. vii). During the past century, the United Methodist Church has become a diverse body of people. To maximize its role as a service agency of the denomination, the publishing house has seen its main task as an educational one: "seeking to change the mind of the church through reading, teaching, study, meditation, and discussion, rather than through direct action or crusade" (pp. 587-88). In recent years the publishing house has expanded its programs beyond the production of print resources to include the development of educational services and the production of films, videos, software, and other media resources. For volume 1 see James Penn Pilkington (listed above).

White, Eugene E. "Puritan Preaching and the Authority of God." In *Preaching in American History: Selected Issues in the American Pulpit, 1630-1967,* ed. DeWitte Holland, pp. 36-73. Nashville: Abingdon Press, 1969.

This essay traces the following: covenant theology, Protestant thought, and the needs of humankind; the social covenant; church covenant; covenant of grace; and the divine platform, imitable by the creature. In two sections (pp. 49-51 and 55-59) White deals with rhetoric and preaching.

White, Llewellyn. *The American Radio.* Chicago: University of Chicago Press, 1947.

The Commission on the Freedom of the Press, building on its general report, *A Free and Responsible Press* (see above), extends the concept of social responsibility to the area of radio-television broadcasting. Eight recommendations are framed, together with a set of conclusions and proposals, to suggest ways in which the public, the communication industry, and the government can insure a socially responsible improvement and reform of radio-television broadcasting.

Woodson, Carter G. *Negro Orators and Their Orations.* Washington, DC: Associated Publishers, 1925.

To Aristotle's three classes of oratory — judicial, deliberative, and epideictic — Woodson adds a fourth: pulpit oratory, in which the African-American has excelled and by means of which the doctrine of the Christian church has been popularized. The orations in this compilation, and the author's comments, are organized around the American anti-slavery controversy, the speeches of African-American congressmen during the Reconstruction period, and the black struggle for justice and equal opportunity in the early twentieth century.

Wright, John. *Early Prayer Books of America*. St. Paul: n.p., 1896.

This study represents the first systematic attempt to treat prayer book literature, particularly that of the American Episcopal Church. It clearly illustrates that nearly all the larger bodies of Christians had adopted liturgies by the nineteenth century and that during the century there was great enrichment and expansion of liturgical forms. Appendix C lists prayer books, and portions thereof, published in Mexico, Canada, and the United States, prior to 1861.

## III. Colonial Period: 1640-1689

Axtell, James. "The Power of Print in the Eastern Woodlands." *William and Mary Quarterly*, 3rd series, 44 (1987): 300-309.

"The Protestant failure to capitalize on the power of print helped the Jesuits to win the contest of cultures in colonial North America" (p. 309). The Native Americans, with their oral culture and shamanistic religion, were greatly impressed with literacy and books. The Jesuits were culturally more flexible than the Puritans and insinuated themselves into Native American society. "The magic of literacy rather than the touch of cold theology led the Indians to Christianity" (p. 306).

Bercovitch, Sacvan. *The American Jeremiad*. Madison: University of Wisconsin Press, 1978.

A major study of the jeremiad, or the political sermon, of the New England Puritans and its role in fashioning the myth of America, particularly in the seventeenth and eighteenth centuries. A wide range of literature is examined — doctrinal treatises, histories, poems, biographies, and personal narratives, "in order to place the jeremiad within the larger context of Puritan rhetoric, and, in later chapters, the much larger context of American rhetoric, ritual and society through the eighteenth and nineteenth centuries" (p. xiv). Bercovitch judges the strength of the Puritans to have been in their command of the art of suggestive, provocative, poetic speech rather than in their mastery of argument through reason.

Boorstin, Daniel J. *The Americans: The Colonial Experience*. New York: Random House, 1958.

The colonial experience was varied and diffuse in the four colonies considered: Massachusetts Bay, Pennsylvania, Georgia, and Virginia. Viewpoints and institutions are examined with respect to education, the professions, medicine, and science. The third section, "Language and the Printed Word," contains perceptive insights concerning uniformity of American speech, the development of the American press (which, while economically and culturally conservative, was politically radical), and the democratic character of American culture. Religion, as a dominant ingredient in colonial times, figures prominently in this study. Boorstin notes that for Americans printed matter is treated less as literature and more as communication.

Bosco, Ronald A. "Lectures at the Pillory: The Early American Execution Sermon." *American Quarterly* 30 (1978): 156-76.

    From 1674 to the end of the eighteenth century, seventy execution sermons were published, and even as late as 1772 one of these sermons went through nine printings. The author directs most of his attention to the sermons published in New England between 1674 and 1750. These sermons variously emphasize conversion, declension from the true New England way, and admonition to the young. "Of the great variety of literary forms and sermon types introduced to and developed in New England by the early Puritan settlers, the execution sermon was one of the few to survive the disintegration of Puritan faith during the mid-eighteenth century" (p. 172). See also the study by Wayne C. Mimmick (listed below).

Bremer, Francis J. "Increase Mather's Friends: The Trans-Atlantic Congregational Network of the Seventeenth Century." *Proceedings of the American Antiquarian Society* 94 (1984): 59-96.

    Utilizing an anthropological network-analysis methodology, the author examines the network of friends developed by Increase Mather during the seventeenth century. This network provided "the news, advice, and tangible forms of aid, moving both ways across the ocean, that strengthened bonds of support and helped to insure that Puritans in both countries marched in cadence into the eighteenth century" (p. 92). A bibliography of references for illustrations is included.

Butler, Jon. "Magic, Astrology and the Early American Religious Heritage, 1600-1760." *American Historical Review* 84 (1979): 317-46.

    This essay identifies evidence that documents the widespread ownership of occult books in the American colonies. The library of the Reverend Thomas Teackle, a Virginia Anglican minister, is cited as an example of such ownership. Almanacs were popular partly because of the occult materials they contained. After 1700 occult religious practices declined for a number of reasons, among which was a scarcity of such reading material in America. In addition, official religion, represented by denominations and the state, refused to recognize noninstitutional religious practices as legitimate.

Caldwell, Patricia. *The Puritan Conversion Narrative: The Beginnings of American Expression.* Cambridge Studies in American Literature and Culture. Cambridge: Cambridge University Press, 1983.

This study traces the best of American literature back to the Puritan conversion narrative or confession that contains an expression of personal experience in the New World. This study is based on a close examination of the fifty-one "confessions" given at the First Church of Cambridge, Massachusetts, between 1637 and 1645, and recorded by the minister of the church, Thomas Shepard. The confession was set in the context of a church founded on a written covenant subscribed to by all. The next step was admission to membership in this covenanted community, which required an auricular confession in the presence of a priesthood of literate believers. These American narratives are characterized by ambivalence, uncertainty, and tension about the validity of the New World experiment. The expression of this ambivalence and experience through vital language "has ever since been the cause not only of New England but of the best of American literature."

Cotton, John. *Spiritual Milk for Babes.* 1584-1652.

One of the earliest Pilgrim catechisms, issued in London in 1646, famous for more than two generations. Cotton Mather called it "The Catechism of New England," and fifty years after its issue he said, "The children of New England are to this day most usually fed with this excellent catechism." The catechism contained sixty questions and answers. It formed a part of the New England Primer in the next century, thus continuing its popularity for more than 100 years.

Crawford, Richard. "A Historian's Introduction to Early American Music." *Proceedings of the American Antiquarian Society* 89 (1979): 261-98.

This essay examines music in the English-speaking colonies and states prior to 1801. It hypothesizes "that Protestant psalmody was never intended to be a purely written tradition but was designed instead to be flexible, that is accessible to written and oral practice alike" (p. 280). The essay includes statistics on issuance of sacred music 1698 to 1810.

Dexter, Franklin B. "Early Private Libraries in New England." *Proceedings of the American Antiquarian Society* 18 (1907): 135-47.

A study of "more detailed inventories filed in the Probate Courts in connection with the settlement of estates" (p. 135) is used to gain an assessment of what printed books the original settlers brought with them and what books the early generations used. In most cases inventories mention no titles, but of those that do, titles in theology predominate.

Elliott, Emory. "The Development of the Puritan Funeral Sermon and Elegy, 1660-1750." *Early American Literature* 15 (1980/81): 151-64.

     Basing his study on a reading of all the printed American funeral sermons and elegies of the period, Elliott compares the development of these two genres and attempts "to establish the connections between these literary changes and the new social conditions that may have produced them." He challenges the opinion that the clergy devalued their position in society compared to earlier times or that they promoted feminization of the culture. The clergy did respond, however, to the demands of a more heterogeneous society and crafted their sermons to accommodate a larger audience and community of hearers/readers.

Fogel, Howard H. "Colonial Theocracy and a Secular Press." *Journalism Quarterly* 37 (1960): 525-32.

     "The American colonial press won its freedom from interference by religious authorities in a gradual process, highlighted by the experiences of William Bradford in Pennsylvania and of James Franklin in Massachusetts." By 1721 the newspaper had become an effective voice for freedom, and the colonial theocracy had lost its power to impose restrictions on the press.

Ford, Paul Leicester, ed. *The New-England Primer: A History of Its Origin and Development* . . . New York: Dodd, Mead, 1897.

     The introduction gives a general history and brief literary analysis of the primer. Facsimiles of the first extant American edition (1727), *The New English Tutor* (1702-1714?), John Rogers's *Exhortation* (1559), Cotton Mather's *Views on Catechising* (1708), Rev. Dorus Clarke's *Saying the Catechism* (1878), *Bibliography of the New England Primer* (1727-1799), and a *Variorum of the New England Primer* (1685-1775) complete the volume. Various catechisms were incorporated in the primer, the most notable of which is John Cotton's *Milk for Babes.* The primer reigned for 150 years as a best-seller. For a more complete bibliography, see Charles F. Heartman (listed above in Section I).

Ford, Worthington C. *The Boston Book Market, 1679-1700.* Boston: Club of Odd Volumes, 1917.

     Based largely on original sources, this study of Boston booksellers and their business confirms the predominance of religious titles in their trade. The study also includes significant data on readers, censorship, and publishing. The clergy figured prominently in this period as authors, readers, and consumers.

Foster, Stephen. "The Godly in Transit: English Popular Protestantism and the Creation of a Puritan Establishment in America." In *Seventeenth-Century New England,* ed. David D. Hall and David Grayson Allen, pp. 185-238. Publications of the Colonial Society of Massachusetts, 63. Boston: Colonial Society of Massachusetts, 1984.

> This essay views the transformation of popular Protestantism into a genuinely Puritan establishment whereby the clergy gained power, especially over words. They "gave the ceremonial addresses on public days, wrote the tracts the presses turned out, came to be identified as the source of all schooling above the most rudimentary" (p. 237). This ministerial vision permeates the historiography of New England to this day. After 1660 the clergy had solidified its grip on the social order, and personal piety was presided over by a standing clerical order.

Franklin, Benjamin (1939–), ed. *Boston Printers, Publishers and Booksellers, 1640-1800.* Boston: G. K. Hall, 1980.

> Documenting the first 160 years of printing and publishing in Boston, this volume provides "succinct professional histories of every person known to have appeared in a Boston (including Cambridge) imprint through the year 1800. Each entry for a significant figure includes an essay preceded by an introductory paragraph, a list of major authors he published, and, when applicable, names of publishers he served." Includes a name and title index.

Gallagher, Edward J., and Thomas Werge. *Early Puritan Writers: A Reference Guide: William Bradford, John Cotton, Thomas Hooker, Edward Johnson, Richard Mather and Thomas Shepard.* Reference Guides to Literature, no. 10. Boston: G. K. Hall, 1976.

> The author has tried "to cite all significant twentieth-century writings about each of the six authors" and has "also included substantive material from the seventeenth, eighteenth and nineteenth centuries." Each entry is furnished with critical annotation. This guide is helpful in delineating the status of American Puritan studies relating to the key individuals included.

Hall, David D. *The Faithful Shepherd: A History of the New England Ministry in the Seventeenth Century.* Chapel Hill: University of North Carolina Press, for the Institute of Early American History and Culture, Williamsburg, VA, 1972.

> The author argues, in distinction from Sidney E. Mead, that the Puritans imported their evangelical understanding of the ministry. Chapters 1-3 lay out a frame of reference that goes back to Calvin and the Bible. The later chapters examine the rhetoric that the colonists used to describe their situation. "I have tried to view the preachers' rhetoric from within, to reconstruct the way they saw themselves and their values in relation to society" (p. xi). Hall deals with

the social setting, definitions of the church and of the preachers' status, their social role, and, finally, the nature of evangelism.

―――. "Toward a History of Popular Religion in Early New England." *William and Mary Quarterly,* 3rd series, 41 (1984): 49-55.

A response to George Selement's argument, based on a study of Thomas Shepard's "Confessions," that only a third of the population in early New England was literate. Selement concludes from this that ministerial publishing produced a certain mentality. Hall contests this, arguing that "the seventeenth century [was] a time when a vernacular literature addressed to everyday readers was becoming more decisive in the making of religion, though still a time when reading was powerfully complemented by listening to sermons. The very process of becoming literate began by hearing others read or recite from books" (pp. 51-52). See George Selement, "The Meeting of Elite and Popular Minds . . . " (listed below).

―――. "The World of Print and Collective Mentality in Seventeenth-Century New England." In *New Directions in American Intellectual History,* ed. John Higham and Paul K. Conkin, pp. 166-80. Baltimore: Johns Hopkins University Press, 1979.

Challenging the view that seventeenth-century New England can be divided up intellectually on the basis of social class or literacy, Hall indicates that "we can move from the world of print, with its fluid boundaries and rhythms of long duration, to an understanding of intellectual history as itself having wider boundaries than many social historians seem willing to recognize" (p. 177). Books of history, romance, and religion constituted a special kind of literary culture characterized by slower cultural rhythms and a marketplace where formulas were more traditional.

―――. *Worlds of Wonder, Days of Judgment: Popular Religious Belief in Early New England.* New York: Alfred A. Knopf, 1989.

Chapter 1, "The Uses of Literacy," describes and interprets the significance of a "communications circuit that ran from writers and the printing press to publishers and readers" (p. 89). This circuit operated in a society that was highly literate and that drew on the Protestant tradition of scriptural authority.

Hall, Michael G. *The Last American Puritan: The Life of Increase Mather, 1639-1723.* Middletown, CT: Wesleyan University Press, 1988.

The first major biography of this remarkable Puritan divine in over fifty years. Mather wrote continuously for the press over a period of fifty-eight years, from 1663 to 1723, exerting a powerful influence both in the colonies and in

England. Hall sets Mather's writings in their religious, political, and social context to weave a rich cultural background on which he limns a sensitive, critical, yet sympathetic portrait of this complex human being. Mather emerges as the chief exponent and defender of the original Puritan way, which he tirelessly proclaimed by both the spoken and the written word.

Hambrick-Stowe, Charles E. *The Practice of Piety: Puritan Devotional Disciplines in Seventeenth-Century New England.* Chapel Hill: University of North Carolina Press for the Institute of Early American History and Culture, Williamsburg, VA, 1982.

In contrast to studies that place great emphasis on the orality of Puritan preaching and worship, this study, while not discounting orality, stresses the great reliance the Puritans placed on the Bible and meditative reading, the use of devotional manuals and writing. It also locates Puritan spirituality within a continuum that is linked historically with medieval practices and Christian antiquity. From a close examination of devotional manuals and individual diaries, the author shows that "public worship and the characteristic private devotional exercises were what made a Puritan a Puritan. Devotional manuals were an important part of the Puritan movement from the late sixteenth century onward, a product of the demand for pious reading matter that widespread Protestant literacy created" (p. viii).

Herget, Winfried. "Writing After the Ministers: The Significance of Sermon Notes." In *Studies in New England Puritanism,* ed. Winfried Herget, pp. 113-39. Studien und Texte zur Amerikanistik: Texte, 9. Frankfurt am Main: Verlag Peter Lang, 1983.

A representative study of "more than 5,000 notations of sermons preached in and around Boston between 1670 and 1700 extant in various New England libraries" (p. 116). These source materials are judged to be important to understanding the New England mind, since Puritan preaching was primarily an oral form (few sermons were printed) and the most important duty that the minister exercised. These sermons are found to be consistent structurally, to follow a pattern of *lectio continua* (series of sermons on the same Scripture), with the greatest number of sermon texts being found in the Epistles. Notes and printed sermons are found to be generally concordant.

Holifield, E. Brooks. *The Covenant Sealed: The Development of Puritan Sacramental Theology in Old and New England, 1570-1720.* New Haven: Yale University Press, 1974.

A concentrated study "on the debates about baptism and the Lord's Supper, and the devotional writings, that illuminate the variety of efforts in the large century stream of seventeenth-century Puritanism to combine Reformed theology and a vital sacramental piety" (p. x). At first reluctant to accept visible symbols, the New England Puritans by 1700 had spiritualized the sacraments and given them symbolic associations. This sacramental renaissance was eclipsed and inhibited by the Great Awakening and subsequent revivals after 1740. By the mid-nineteenth century American Protestants looked upon baptism and the Lord's Supper as inferior to conversion and other religious experiences.

—————. *Era of Persuasion: American Thought and Culture, 1521-1680.* Boston: Twayne Publishers, 1989.

European society supported scholars through institutional wealth and complexity. European princes, the church, the courts, and patrons all sustained scholars in their research and study. "Persuasive discourse in Europe often reflected the force of an imbedded intellectual tradition" (p. 5). Seventeenth-century America, by contrast, was culturally pluralistic, with Indians, Africans, Puritans, Catholics, and numerous national groups present. Ideas and concepts, including religious thought, made their way among and were influenced by these competing groups and the various ideologies they articulated.

Jones, Phyllis. "Biblical Rhetoric and the Pulpit in Early New England." *Early American Literature* 11 (1976-77): 245-58.

The author maintains that while "existing scholarship enables students of this literature (i.e., sermons) to assume the practice of the plain style and the methods of preaching . . . [w]hat needs emphasis is that the Bible was one of the greatest influences on the pulpit rhetoric of early New England" (p. 245). Jones argues that for the first generation of New England preachers, "a minister did not find a passage (of scripture) to strengthen his message; rather, a text seized him and made clear its meaning, dictating and controlling the ensuing doctrines and applications" (p. 246).

Kellaway, William. *The New England Company, 1649-1776; Missionary Society to the American Indians.* New York: Barnes & Noble, 1962.

This study details the work of the society, which is still in existence, whose purpose in the American colonies was to evangelize the Native Americans. Part of the society's program to educate the native inhabitants was concentrated in teaching and publishing. Chapter 6, "The Indian Library" (pp. 122-65), covers the work of John Eliot and others to produce literature in the Algonquin language, including the famous Eliot Indian Bible. Other publications, consisting largely of materials to explain and elicit support for its work, are also discussed, as well as the work of missionaries employed by the company.

Levy, Babette May. *Preaching in the First Half Century of New England History.* Hartford: American Society of Church History, 1945.

This study surveys pulpit oratory, both its content and its style, during the early period of settlement when Puritanism prevailed as the only religious identification of consequence in New England. The background and preparation of the preachers is examined, together with the doctrine they preached. The message of faith that was preached was delivered by preachers who spoke from their hearts to listening sinners. Their teachings also touched the larger issues of life such as politics and war. The Puritan ministers' ability to communicate effectively is best seen in the form of the sermons, their use of similitudes, and the simplicity of their pulpit style. A final chapter treats the reception of the sermons. This study is noteworthy for trying to get beyond and behind the printed sermon to the forms and means of communication used by the early Puritan preachers.

Martin, Howard H. "Puritan Preachers on Preaching: Notes on American Colonial Rhetoric." *Quarterly Journal of Speech* 50 (1964): 285-92.

A survey of some fifty ordination sermons published between 1639 and 1773 in an attempt to secure direct evidence on the best manner of preparing and delivering sermons. "The most frequent comments on preaching manner made in ordination sermons touched on the need for 'plainness' and simplicity" (p. 291). The author concludes that, apart from general comments, the ordination sermons contain a minimum of rhetorical guidance or advice.

Miller, Lillian B. "The Puritan Portrait: Its Function in Old and New England." In *Seventeenth-Century New England,* ed. David D. Hall and David Grayson Allen, pp. 153-84. Publications of the Colonial Society of Massachusetts, 63. Boston: Colonial Society of Massachusetts, 1984.

While the Puritans were strongly iconoclastic, they did endorse the art of portraiture, a disposition reflecting their interest in history and biography. Seventeenth-century American portraits are modeled on fifteenth- and sixteenth-century English portraits, reflecting a tradition going back to medieval times. "Despite their greater familiarity with language as a vehicle for imaginative expression, New Englanders, like their compatriots who remained at home, were not fearful of and did not completely reject the visual arts. . . . Puritan portraits are testimony to the power of the painted as well as the written word" (pp. 183-84).

Miller, Perry. *The New England Mind: The Seventeenth Century.* New York: Macmillan, 1939.

A preliminary survey and topical analysis of the intellectual terrain of the seventeenth century that defines and classifies the principal concepts of the

Puritan mind in New England. It is based on the premise that the first three generations in New England paid almost unbroken allegiance to a unified body of thought. The survey is divided into four sections: religion and learning; cosmology; anthropology; and sociology. Chapters on rhetoric and plain style deal with the Puritan sermon and its delivery. Bibliographies on the logic of Peter Ramus and the Federal School of Theology are included. (For discussion of this book, see George Selement, "Perry Miller," listed below.)

————. "The Religious Impulse in the Founding of Virginia: Religion and Society in the Early Literature." *William and Mary Quarterly*, 3rd series, 5 (1948): 493-522.

In this essay Miller argues that in many of the documents written about the founding and settlement of Virginia there reside affinities to Calvin and Loyola as well as to wealth and commerce. "The cosmos expounded in the Virginia pamphlets is one where the principal human concern is neither the rate of interest nor the discovery of gold, but the will of God. . . . For the men of 1600 to 1625, the new land was redemption even as it was also riches, and the working out of the society and the institutions cannot be understood (and it has not been understood), except as an effort toward salvation. Religion, in short, was the really energizing power in this settlement, as in others" (p. 493). This material is reprinted in chapter 4, "Religion and Society in the Early Literature of Virginia," in Miller's *Errand into the Wilderness* (New York: Cambridge University Press, 1956), pp. 99-140.

————. "Religion and Society in the Early Literature: The Religious Impulse in the Founding of Virginia." *William and Mary Quarterly*, 3rd series, 6 (1949): 24-41.

In 1624, King James I dissolved the Virginia Company to place the colony under the crown and to end the chaotic state of affairs there. In sermons and pamphlets there was enunciated the ideal of religious authoritarianism coupled with a corporate social hierarchy. However, by this date the old medieval synthesis was broken and "church and state would be separated, reason would usurp the place of revelation, and physics would become a better expositor of the divine mind than theology" (p. 41). The government of Virginia would feature the General Assembly where the organized rights of Englishmen could be exercised and protected. Virginia was changed from a holy experiment to a commercial plantation. This material is reprinted in chapter 4, "Religion and Society in the Early Literature of Virginia," in Miller's *Errand into the Wilderness* (New York: Cambridge University Press, 1956), pp. 99-140.

Mimmick, Wayne C. "The New England Execution Sermon, 1639-1800." *Speech Monographs* 35 (March 1968): 77-89.

Sixty-seven printed texts of this genre are analyzed. Their authors represent the best-educated and most influential ministers of New England. Since thousands assembled to witness executions, preachers addressed many more persons there than in the church, and through the published sermon they reached a potential audience of other thousands. The function of the sermon was, in Daniel Boorstin's words, "the ritual application of theology to community building and to the tasks and trials of everyday life." See the study by Ronald A. Bosco, *Lectures at the Pillory* (listed above).

Morison, Samuel E. *Harvard College in the Seventeenth Century.* Cambridge, MA: Harvard University Press, 1936.

Chapters on curriculum, library, and the study of divinity provide the fullest available description of theological training for the first century of settlement in New England. The study of rhetoric (based on Peter Ramus), preaching, languages, and theology was basic. This history provides clear evidence that Harvard was founded primarily for the training of the learned ministry and, from its inception, strove to maintain high academic standards.

Murdock, Kenneth B. "Clio in the Wilderness: History and Biography in Puritan New England." *Church History* 24 (1955): 221-38.

The New England Puritan's use of history and biography is here lodged in both the Christian and humanist traditions. For the Puritans, biography supplemented prayer and Bible reading in the quest for holiness, tormented as they were by the critical nature of their earthly adventure. Historically, "the New Englanders are a new army called up by Christ; New England is their training camp; and the campaign they are destined for is led by Christ against his enemies" (p. 231). In their writing of history and biography, the Puritans, especially in times of crisis, sought to appropriate both personal and objective resources to justify their journey into the New England wilderness and to assuage their loneliness and isolation.

Norton, Arthur O. "Harvard Text-Books and Reference Books of the Seventeenth Century." *Publications of the Colonial Society of Massachusetts* 28 (1935): 361-438.

Some 228 book titles are identified, together with some miscellaneous titles, as having been used as text or reference books by Harvard students in the seventeenth century, based on a study of the subjects taught at the college and of student signatures in volumes from the period. This study confirms the view that Harvard College was founded primarily for the education of clergy, and this listing also confirms studies by Perry Miller, Walter Ong, and others concerning early Puritan education.

Ong, Walter J. *Ramus: Method, and the Decay of Dialogue from the Art of Discourse to the Art of Reason.* Cambridge, MA: Harvard University Press, 1958.

This study provides essential analysis for understanding the shift in communication from being grounded in discourse prior to the invention of printing to the development of a typographically oriented culture. Special location and the visual replaced the aural experiences of the earlier oral culture. Pierre Ramus and his many followers reconstructed the intellectual framework of antiquity and scholasticism to develop the notion of "method" by which knowledge could be organized in discrete units. Ramism became a formative influence in Western thought during the sixteenth and seventeenth centuries, exercising a decisive role in shaping New England thought. The Puritan educational method, the use of plain style in preaching, and the employment of a simplified rhetoric are brought into sharper focus when viewed from Ong's wide-ranging and detailed scrutiny.

Pead, Deuel. "A Sermon Preached at James City in Virginia the 23d of April 1686." *William and Mary Quarterly,* 3rd series, 17 (1960): 371-94.

One of the few southern colonial sermons of the seventeenth century to have survived, it is rough in style and plain but crafted to "imply in these Virginians who heard him a relatively high quality of literacy, even modest learning" (p. 377). Preached on the first anniversary of James II's coronation, the text shows Pead to be a staunch supporter of the status quo, with loyalty to the church equated with loyalty to the crown.

Plumstead, A. W., ed. *The Wall and the Garden: Selected Massachusetts Election Sermons 1670-1775.* Minneapolis: University of Minnesota Press, 1968.

A collection of nine sermons chosen as the best based on literary excellence and ideas and points of style relevant to later developments in American literature and history. "In a general introduction, Professor Plumstead provides background information about the history and significance of the election sermons." See the earlier compilation by John W. Thornton (listed below in Section IV).

Powell, William S. "Books in the Virginia Colony Before 1624." *William and Mary Quarterly,* 3rd series, 5 (1948): 177-84.

A review of existing records specifies books sent to and requested for use in Virginia during the earliest years of the colony. These included a good number of theological works: Bibles, prayer books, catechisms, sermons, and general theological titles.

Rosenmeier, Jesper. " 'Clearing the Medium': A Reevaluation of the Puritan Plain Style in Light of John Cotton's *A Practicall Commentary Upon the First Epistle*

*Generall of John* [published in London, 1656]." *William and Mary Quarterly,* 3rd series, 37 (1980): 577-91.

As one of the first preachers to develop and use the "Puritan plain style" of rhetoric, Cotton broke with the old Anglican rhetoric characterized by indirect, impersonal objective speech. Rosenmeier argues "that Cotton conceived of verbal relationships as analogous to personal ones, and that he held his analogy between word and person to rest in the Christian view of the Trinity" (p. 577). The new plain style of rhetoric and communication helps to explain not only how this language and manner of speaking led to personal conversion but also to the renewal of society. A new communion or fellowship is established that generates a Christian society. For a fuller discussion of rhetoric and plain style, see Perry Miller's *New England Mind* (listed above).

Rutman, Darrett B. *American Puritanism: Faith and Practice.* Philadelphia: J. B. Lippincott, 1970.

Rutman defines Puritanism as a particular "Christian fellowship" of ministers who communicated an evangelical-theological dialectic of election, vocation, justification, sanctification, and glorification. The audience consisted of the gentry, the peasants, the townspeople or urban middle class, and a fourth group not influenced by the preachers. In the New World this audience accepted the clergy's evangelical doctrine as ideology, while the clergy came to institutionalize the values of fellowship in ways that combined against the original evangelical thrust. Rutman's work is significant for the questions it raises about audience and communication.

————. "New England as Idea and Society Revisited." *William and Mary Quarterly,* 3rd series, 41 (1984): 56-61.

A response to George Selement's argument, based on a study of Thomas Shepard's "Confessions," concerning his concept of "collective mentalities" to explain the relationship between the minister and his audience. Rutman articulates the need to move beyond speaker and audience to establish the effect(s) the message had upon the subsequent experiences of the hearers. This synthesis is seen as bridging the gap between the intellectual historian and the social historian. See George Selement, "Meeting of Elite and Popular Minds . . ." (listed below).

Salisbury, Neal. "Red Puritans: The 'Praying Indians' of Massachusetts Bay and John Eliot." *William and Mary Quarterly,* 3rd series, 31 (1974): 27-54.

Having failed to evangelize the Native Americans as part of their mission in the New World, the Puritans in 1646 provided for the establishment of missions as a part of their Indian policy. John Eliot and other missionaries developed a program that included praying towns where Indians could be controlled and "civilized," the formation of praying Indian congregations, the establishment of an educational program to teach literacy and instruct school children, and the production of books in the Algonquin languages. In the end, Eliot's simplistic program and efforts failed, but they "provided the postwar [King Philip's War, 1675] government with a precedent for the waging of cultural warfare and for the management of a powerless minority" (p. 54).

Seaver, Paul S. *The Puritan Lectureships: The Politics of Religious Dissent, 1560-1662.* Stanford, CA: Stanford University Press, 1970.

Chapter 1, "The Importance of Preaching" (pp. 15-54), provides the historical context for English Puritan preaching, which, by the 1630s when Massachusetts Bay Colony was established, was well developed. Preaching, not the sacraments, came to be viewed as the means of conveying saving knowledge to the masses. The laity, through control of the lectureships, succeeded in circumventing ecclesiastical discipline. "By constantly preaching the need for reformation the Puritan ministers undoubtedly encouraged the laity to assert themselves in ecclesiastical affairs" (p. 49). These developments in England provide the background for understanding the Thursday lectures and other sermons preached in addition to those on the Sabbath in New England.

Selement, George. "The Meeting of Elite and Popular Minds at Cambridge, New England, 1638-1645." *William and Mary Quarterly*, 3rd series, 41 (1984): 32-48.

A detailed analysis of the Reverend Thomas Shepard's "Confessions," which contains testimonies of faith by 51 persons applying for membership at First Church, Cambridge. Selement's appraisal includes literacy evaluation, occupational and community status, as well as an extensive theological analysis comparing the doctrinal content of the testimonies against those of Shepard. He concludes that the "Confessions" demonstrate close affinities between Shepard's preaching and the faith of his church members.

————. "Perry Miller: A Note on His Sources in 'The New England Mind': The Seventeenth Century." *William and Mary Quarterly*, 3rd series, 31 (1974): 453-64.

Selement challenges the widely held assumption "that Miller read, comprehended, and utilized all or, at least, the overwhelming majority of New England materials. Actually, the converse is closer to the truth. Miller utilized a limited and extremely selective number of authors in formulating his version of the New England mind" (p. 155). In questioning Miller's use of sources, Selement at the same time calls into question his portrait of Puritan orthodoxy.

————. "Publication and the Puritan Divine." *William and Mary Quarterly,* 3rd series, 37 (1980): 219-41.

"The data about ministerial publication . . . indicate that publishing was seldom more than a small part of a preacher's work and was in the majority of cases eschewed altogether" (p. 240). Only five percent of the clergy from 1561 to 1703 published ten or more tracts during their lives. Data include tables on publishing by ministers and types of works published by prolific and nonprolific ministers.

Shea, Daniel B. *Spiritual Autobiography in Early America.* Princeton: Princeton University Press, 1968.

Shea discusses and analyzes twenty Quaker and Puritan autobiographies written prior to 1800. As the common property of English Protestantism, spiritual autobiography was widely employed in early America. Shea probes the autobiographies to reveal their distinctions rather than stressing their homogeneity. There are sections devoted to John Woolman, Increase Mather, Cotton Mather, Jonathan Edwards, and Benjamin Franklin.

Silver, Rollo G. "Financing the Publication of Early New England Sermons." *Studies in Bibliography* 11 (1958): 163-78.

In the seventeenth and eighteenth centuries New England sermons, besides being theological, "also marked important political occasions, memorialized the dead, and sometimes functioned as a newspaper in reporting and editorializing on current events" (p. 163). The economics of present-day publishing of sermons is remarkably similar to that in our early history, ranging from guaranteed success to vanity publishing. Silver examines Cotton Mather's sermons in some detail, supplying a table with examples of sponsorship for his sermons.

Sprunger, Keith L. "Ames, Ramus, and the Method of Puritan Theology." *Harvard Theological Review* 59 (1966): 133-51.

A careful and succinct overview of theological methodology formulated by Peter Ramus, the French Protestant philosopher and logician. William Ames, the leading seventeenth-century exponent of Ramist theology, laid the basis for New England Puritan theology in his *Marrow of Divinity.* "The *Marrow,* one of the most frequently printed Protestant theological treatises of the seventeenth century, was renowned both among Puritans and Continental Calvinists" (p. 141). See also Walter Ong's *Ramus* and Perry Miller's *New England Mind* (both listed above).

St. George, Robert. " 'Heated' Speech and Literacy in Seventeenth-Century New England." In *Seventeenth-Century New England,* ed. David D. Hall and David

Grayson Allen, pp. 275-322. Publications of the Colonial Society of Massachusetts, 63. Boston: Colonial Society of Massachusetts, 1984.

A detailed analysis of the court records of Essex County, Massachusetts, between 1640 and 1680 (in which 363 offensive speech cases are listed) "helps lead to a systematic and unified conception of literacy in past life by suggesting connections between the social meanings of spoken and written communications" (p. 278). The Puritans viewed heated speech as a sign in the ongoing battle between God and Satan, belching forth the flames of hell. They recognized that spoken words had the power to convey God's truth but that they could also rebuke and socially damage individuals. This study underlines the importance of cultural transitions. In this case the transition is from oral, agonistic culture to written, objective culture.

Stewart, Randall. "Puritan Literature and the Flowering of New England." *William and Mary Quarterly,* 3rd series, 3 (1946): 319-42.

"The literature of early New England was important not only in itself but in its influence on later times, particularly the period of the 'flowering'" (p. 338), as contained in the writings of Emerson, Hawthorne, Thoreau, Longfellow, Lowell, and Holmes. Influenced by the Bible and humanism, the early Puritans expressed themselves vividly in histories, diaries, and accounts of nature, but "the literary productions of greatest contemporary interest in seventeenth-century New England were the sermons" (p. 329). "Rarely has the mind worked with greater vigor and penetration than in the early New England community; rarely has the written word been used more effectively; rarely has the human spirit burned with an intenser, brighter flame" (p. 342).

Stout, Harry S. *The New England Soul: Preaching and Religious Culture in Colonial New England.* New York: Oxford University Press, 1986.

Stout contends that Sunday sermons, which were unpublished, consistently extolled God's saving power and demanded Christian liberty to secure a purified commonwealth. Stout maintains that 2,000 sermons (1630-1776) that he examined set out gospel commonplaces that thrilled the Puritans. There was a continuity in the Sunday sermons, unlike the special sermons, which dealt with unusual natural occurrences, fast days, etc. The special sermons often made it into print, whereas the Sunday sermons did not.

————. "Word and Order in Colonial New England." In *The Bible in America: Essays in Cultural History,* ed. Nathan O. Hatch and Mark A. Noll, pp. 19-38. New York: Oxford University Press, 1982.

The Authorized/King James Bible of 1611 replaced the earlier Geneva translation as the foundational Scripture for New England Puritans. "Throughout the colonial period the vernacular Bible interpreted by a learned

ministry remained the mainstay of New England culture." The New World
settlement raised questions of national policy and social order. These were
partially answered through adoption of the Authorized Version as the New
England vernacular text.

Taylor, Edward. *Upon the Types of the Old Testament.* Ed. Charles W. Mignon.
Lincoln: University of Nebraska Press, 1989.

"This edition comprises the text of a holograph manuscript 'Upon the
Types of the Old Testament' — a sequence of sermons on the theme of
Christian typology — by the seventeenth-century colonial poet and gospel
minister, Edward Taylor." This critical edition makes available the uses of
typology, a prominent feature of Puritan preaching, developed over the career
of a seventeenth-century divine.

Toulouse, Teresa. *The Art of Prophesying: New England Sermons and the Shaping
of Belief.* Athens: University of Georgia Press, 1987.

The purpose of this study "is to trace the interrelations among ideas of
faith, their presentation, and their audiences, and to suggest possible cultural
implications of these interrelations" (p. 1). Four New England ministers and
the structures of their sermons are examined: John Cotton, Benjamin Colman,
William Ellery Channing, and Ralph Waldo Emerson. The two chief strengths
of this approach are its concentration on audience and its relation of sermon
structure to the conveyed message. It vividly demonstrates that the job of
communicating faith is complex, sometimes frustrating, in the dynamic interplay between belief and believers.

Upshur, Anne F., and Ralph T. Whitelaw. "Library of the Rev. Thomas Teackle."
*William and Mary Quarterly,* 2nd series, 23 (1943): 298-308.

A short title and author list of books in English and Latin from the
inventory of Teackle's estate, recorded February 11, 1696/7, Accomack County,
Virginia. Theological and classical authors are well represented.

Weber, Donald. *Rhetoric and History in Revolutionary New England.* New York:
Oxford University Press, 1988.

Drawing together the methodologies of literary criticism, symbolic anthropology, and narrative theory, Weber examines the sermonic discourses of
five New England patriot preachers to understand how they experienced the
Revolution and how they translated that experience from their pulpits to their
people. Weber clearly shows how the homiletic style of these ministers, under
the influence of the Great Awakening, changed from that of linear narrative
discourse to that of a fragmented oral culture rooted in the radical evangelicalism of the Awakening. Coupled with the publication of revolutionary pam-

phlets during the same period, the foundations of mass media, which would emerge in the nineteenth century, were laid.

Westerkamp, Marilyn J. *Triumph of the Laity: Scots-Irish Piety and the Great Awakening, 1625-1760.* New York: Oxford University Press, 1988.

This study treats the Great Awakening out of a definition of religious systems. "This definition sets up an analytical structure that divides religious systems with four distinct, interdependent components: shared beliefs; common rituals; institutional manifestations, and participants. . . . The defining characteristic of the Great Awakening is ritual. . . . The history of these rituals has been the focus of my research" (p. 8). Westerkamp studies the colonial Presbyterian Church in southern New York, New Jersey, Pennsylvania, Delaware, and the Chesapeake area, tracing Presbyterians back to Northern Ireland and Scotland. Westerkamp lists the following characteristics of revival: size — must be larger than normal religious services; duration of the meeting — revival must last three to four days; intense emotional response; purpose of the ritual — to free participants from guilt, shame, and sin and to experience conversion (p. 10). "The Great Awakening in the middle colonies represented neither innovative religious behavior nor a statement of challenge to the establishment. Rather, that revivalism, first observed in the colonies during the time, was actually part of the Scots-Irish religiosity, a tradition that flourished under the encouragement afforded by the colonial ministers" (p. 14).

White, Eugene E. "Cotton Mather's *Manductio Ad Ministerium.*" *Quarterly Journal of Speech* 49 (1963): 308-19.

The *Manductio,* first published in 1726, has been widely regarded as one of the first manuals of instruction for ministerial candidates produced in America. While it also served more subjective purposes, White examines "Mather's advice to young men entering the ministry, the central function of which he considered to be oral communication" (p. 309). Mather advocates a humane religion of love and service to be proclaimed by his "ideal preacher: a learned, pious, zealous, and — for that era — tolerant man — speaking well" (p. 319).

―――. *Puritan Rhetoric: The Issue of Emotion in Religion.* Carbondale: Southern Illinois University Press, 1972.

The Puritan theory of preaching matched the Puritan system of the covenants. The system of covenants was modified and disrupted by the Great Awakening and allied events. The Puritan system failed both theologically and rhetorically. "A requirement of the Puritan sermon was orality. It had to sound personal and immediately direct. It had to provide for instant comprehension.

Nothing should be permitted to come between the listener and his contact with the Word of God — not the learning of the preacher" (p. 191).

————. "Solomon Stoddard's Theories of Persuasion." *Speech Monographs* 29 (1962): 235-59.

Long recognized as the "pope" of the Connecticut River Valley, the Reverend Solomon Stoddard depended upon persuasion to convince, shape, and control his church at Northampton, Massachusetts, and to guide other clergy. Through careful analysis of Stoddard's view of human nature and of rhetorical invention, White credits him with having initiated revivalism in America and for laying the foundations of the Great Awakening, which his grandson, Jonathan Edwards, would help to launch in 1734-35 and 1741-42. Stoddard induced the Awakening "by employing an adequate pen, personal magnetism, and 'plain and powerful' preaching" (p. 259).

Wigglesworth, Michael. *The Poems of Michael Wigglesworth,* ed. Ronald A. Bosco. Lanham, NY: University Press of America, 1989.

This volume contains texts of Wigglesworth's two most popular poems, *The Day of Doom* and *Meat Out of the Eater.* Composed in the years 1661 to 1669, these verses were accepted by his Puritan audience as the speaking of a spiritual father. Rivaled only by the Bible and the *Bay Psalm Book, The Day of Doom* went through five American editions, three English editions, and innumerable reprints into the nineteenth century; it is a document that brings together in a single text the preacher, poet, and vigorous defender of the old "New England way." *Meat Out of the Eater,* published in 1717, went through at least five editions.

Wright, Louis B. "Pious Reading in Colonial Virginia." *Journal of Southern History* 6 (1940): 382-92.

The colonial libraries of the so-called cavaliers — the great planters who made up the ruling class — contained significant proportions of religious works. Titles on piety and practical ethics were more popular than theological and controversial works. Evidence, including specific titles of books, is examined to show that "the books on religion that a Virginia gentleman collected in his library were as necessary to him as books on history, politics, or law" (p. 392).

————. "The Prestige of Learning in Early America." *Proceedings of the American Antiquarian Society* 83 (1973): 15-27.

Wright notes that the Renaissance ideal of education, translated to colonial America, helps to explain the qualities of the intellectual and more unselfish leaders of the Revolutionary era. Books are identified as highly prized and esteemed sources of education, with religious books having influenced mores profoundly.

─────. "The Purposeful Reading of Our Colonial Ancestors." *ELH, A Journal of English Literary History* 4 (1937): 85-111.

The early colonists brought books with them to the New World as well as collecting them once here. While belles lettres was scarce in seventeenth-century America, the colonists read widely on many subjects, including religion. Their reading matter was practical to aid them in affairs of agriculture as well as in government; it was cultural to perpetuate learning, to keep alive the desire for knowledge. "In the seventeenth century, colonists of varied sectarian beliefs drew inspiration and instruction from so many of the same literary sources" (p. 111). Their reading, while it did not produce an urbane school of letters, was purposeful and helped the colonists to establish themselves in the New World.

## IV. Colonial Period, Religious Ferment, and the New Nation: 1690-1799

Abelove, Henry, and Jonathan Edwards. "Jonathan Edwards's Letter of Invitation to George Whitefield." *William and Mary Quarterly,* 3rd series, 29 (1972): 487-89.

Abelove gives the text of Edwards's letter, dated Northampton, February 12, 1739/40, which was previously unpublished and can be found in the Methodist Archive and Research Center, John Rylands Library, Manchester, England. Whitefield preached and stayed in Northampton October 17-20, 1740. Some months later, Northampton exploded into a period of intense revivalism.

Adams, Willi Paul. "The Colonial German-language Press and the American Revolution." In *The Press and the American Revolution,* ed. Bernard Bailyn and John B. Hench, pp. 151-228. Worcester, MA: American Antiquarian Society, 1980.

Through careful analysis of the political content of the German-language press at the eve of the Revolution, Adams concludes in part that "the image of [Christopher] Sauer the pietist, the pacifist prayer book printer, needs to be revised. Sauer was a journalist who used the modern instrument of the press to influence social conditions and to hold accountable those in positions of authority" (p. 155).

Baldwin, Alice M. "Sowers of Sedition: The Political Theories of Some of the New Light Presbyterian Clergy of Virginia and North Carolina." *William and Mary Quarterly,* 3rd series, 5 (1948): 52-76.

Baldwin seeks to show that certain New Light Presbyterian clergy in Virginia and North Carolina played a part in the political thinking of the people and in the development of political institutions. The sources of the theories of government they expounded were these: the Bible and its equalitarian impulse as understood by George Whitefield and others; the teachers under whom they studied and the books they read; and, in some cases, the doctrines of the Scottish Covenanters. In the South, as in New England, the clergy were active in making known to the common people the basic principles on which the Revolution was fought and the government founded.

Bercovitch, Sacvan. "Cotton Mather." In *Major Writers of Early American Literature,* ed. Everett Emerson, pp. 93-149. Madison: University of Wisconsin Press, 1972.

A major literary assessment of Mather's writings with particular attention given to the diaries and *Magnalia Christi Americana.* Having written and published over four hundred books, sermons, treatises, and tracts, Mather was one of America's most prolific authors. In this essay, Bercovitch shows that the nineteenth-century stereotype of Mather as strident, bigoted, judgmental, and reactionary is misleading. He notes that the great Puritan divine was a person of remarkable achievements, many of them revealed in his writings.

————. "The Typology of America's Mission." *American Quarterly* 30 (1978): 135-55.

In this essay Bercovitch examines the role of the Edwardsean revivals in the development of the concept of America's mission. Unlike his Puritan predecessors, Jonathan Edwards couched his view of history in terms of continuous and indefinite enlargement, asserting that the story of America was intrinsic to sacred history. In a "host of civic as well as clerical writings, treatises, orations, pamphlets . . . sound an urgent summons for covenant renewal and concert of prayer" (p. 150), invoking and affirming the typology of mission: the Hebrew exodus, New England's errand, America's destiny. The revivals helped to define this typology, which would be fulfilled in the Revolution and the founding of the United States of America.

Botein, Stephen. "The Anglo-American Book Trade Before 1776: Personnel and Strategies." In *Printing and Society in Early America,* ed. William L. Joyce et al., pp. 48-82. Worcester, MA: American Antiquarian Society, 1983.

Religious commitments and family ties were instrumental in the formation of the Anglo-American book trade. In the early eighteenth century the colonial market was underdeveloped. New trade strategies emerged in the 1750s and 1760s, only to be interrupted by the Revolution. The essay includes biography of book dealers and data on sale of religious titles.

Bray, Thomas. *An Essay Towards Promoting All Necessary and Useful Knowledge in all Parts of His Majesty's Dominions, Both at Home and Abroad . . .* Boston: G. K. Hall, 1967.

    Facsimile reprint of the London 1697 edition, containing Bray's proposal "for purchasing lending libraries in all the Deaneries of England, and parochial libraries for Maryland, Virginia, and other of the foreign plantations," and also containing the catalog of books for lending libraries for the use of clergy, schoolmasters, and gentlemen. For a discussion of Bray's and related activities in establishing colonial libraries, see the entries by John F. Hurst (listed below) and White Kennett (Section I).

————. *The Reverend Thomas Bray: His Life and Selected Works Relating to Maryland.* Baltimore: Printed by J. Murphy, 1901.

    This volume contains documents pertaining to Bray's work in the colony of Maryland, including Richard Rawlinson's *Life of Thomas Bray,* Bray's *Apostolick Charity,* and his treatises on the value of books and reading. It gives a list of titles of a lending library for the use of the laity (pp. 153-56) and his *Bibliotheca Parochialis* (1697, pp. 191-205), a plan for establishing libraries in the American colonies. For a discussion of Bray's and related activities in establishing libraries, see the entries by John F. Hurst (listed below) and White Kennett (Section I).

Bridenbaugh, Carl. *Mitre and Sceptre: Transatlantic Faiths, Ideas, Personalities, and Politics, 1689-1775.* New York: Oxford University Press, 1962.

    For eighty-five years a transatlantic controversy raged over efforts by the Church of England to install bishops in America, a development that the Puritans saw as an attempt at state control of religion. Many facets of this struggle were waged in the press in the effort to influence public opinion. Sermons, tracts, letters, pamphlets, and books were used to turn ideas into common currency. This fine study supplements and updates the earlier work of Arthur L. Cross, *The Anglican Episcopate* (listed below).

————. "The Press and the Book in Eighteenth Century Philadelphia." *Pennsylvania Magazine of History and Biography* 65 (1941): 1-30.

    A close examination of reading habits in the Middle Colonies in the four decades prior to the American Revolution. A vigorous colonial press, the expansion of the printing trade, the operation of bookstores, the development of private and social libraries (including religious denominational libraries), and the spread of elementary and secondary education all contributed to a literate public that read widely. Both in politics and in religion, these developments helped to establish strong democratic principles among all classes of people.

Brown, Richard D. *Knowledge Is Power: The Diffusion of Information in Early America, 1700-1865*. New York: Oxford University Press, 1989.

This study "explores America's first communication revolution — the revolution that made printed goods and public oratory widely available and, by means of the steamboat, railroad, and telegraph, sharply accelerated the pace at which information traveled." Brown focuses considerable attention on the clergy, beginning with their strategic position in the communication system early in the eighteenth century and moving on to their changed role as denominational advocates in the mid-nineteenth century. This careful study on the infusion and diffusion of information limns the change from a hierarchically based communication system to a democratically based one. In this process the clergy changed from being powerful authoritative figures to partisan figures competing to make their message heard.

————. "Spreading the Word: Rural Clergymen and the Communication Network of 18th-Century New England." *Proceedings of the Massachusetts Historical Society* 94 (1982): 1-14.

"In most rural parishes the clergy occupied a special place in New England's communication system and exercised a significant influence on the flow of information into and within a community" (p. 2). By 1800 an abundance of newspapers, periodicals, books, and professional persons informed people in rural areas. Clergy became denominational advocates rather than community oracles as in earlier times.

Butler, Jon. *Awash in a Sea of Faith: Christianizing the American People*. Cambridge, MA: Harvard University Press, 1990.

Challenging traditional interpretations of American church history, Butler asserts that the Puritans brought the instability of religion in Europe with them to the New World. This instability, rather than eclipsing denominational development, spawned creative tensions between pulpit and pew. The churches emerged after 1800 as powerful institutions using authority, coercion, and persuasion to advance religious commitment to levels never equaled in Europe in modern times. Drawing on popular sources, including those of occultism and folk magic, the author completes a picture that shows that laypeople were instrumental, during the period 1700 to 1865, in creating enduring religious patterns that ensured the success of lay Christianization in America. For a related but somewhat different interpretation, see Nathan Hatch's *The Democratization of American Christianity* (listed below).

————. *Power, Authority, and the Origins of American Denominational Order: The English Churches in the Delaware Valley, 1680-1730*. Transactions of the American Philosophical Society, 68, pt. 2, 1978. Philadelphia: American Philosophical Society, 1978.

Butler challenges the often held view that American religious life is primarily rooted in democracy. He shows that the English peoples, Presbyterians, Quakers, and Baptists held on to the hierarchical, clergy-oriented system transported from England well into the late eighteenth century. "Consequently, Dissenters all found in the colonial relationship itself a supple and efficient vehicle for transferring their English past overseas and for succeeding there after they had arrived. And because they developed in America in this way, rather than by overthrowing their European past, their experience in the Delaware Valley again demonstrates the continuing centrality of Old World tradition in the shaping of New World Society" (p. 78).

Case, Leland D. "Origins of Methodist Publishing in America." *Papers of the Bibliographical Society of America* 59 (1965): 12-27.

Case presents evidence that the commonly accepted date for the founding of the Methodist Publishing House, 1789, was preceded by publishing and bookselling activity prior to that date. The early American Methodists adhered to the wishes of their founder, John Wesley, that his followers purchase and read books, tracts, and magazines.

Crawford, Richard. "Watts for Singing: Metrical Poetry in American Sacred Tunebooks, 1761-1785." *Early American Literature* 11 (1976): 139-46.

A review of the sacred tunebooks published in the twenty-five years surrounding the American Revolution, a period when "the traditions of sacred-music making in America brought into print a substantial musical repertory by native American composers" (p. 145). The poetry used by these composers is drawn, to a large extent, from Isaac Watts, whose collections attained a near-literary status. See Selma L. Bishop for Watts bibliography (listed in Section I).

Crawford, Richard, and D. W. Krummel. "Early American Music Printing and Publishing." In *Printing and Society in Early America,* ed. William L. Joyce et al., pp. 186-227. Worcester, MA: American Antiquarian Society, 1983.

This essay examines the development of religious and secular music publishing in colonial America. "The role of printing in sacred music is brought into focus by examining three issues: the introduction of notation into an essentially oral practice; the economic support of sacred music publication; and the changing technology of early American sacred music publishing" (p. 189). Isaiah Thomas's *The Worcester Collection* (1786) is examined in detail, and analysis is made of the contents of early tunebooks.

Cross, Arthur L. *The Anglican Episcopate and the American Colonies.* New York: Longmans, Green, 1902; repr. Hamden, CT: Archon Books, 1964.

The controversy over episcopal jurisdiction in the colonies, which extended from 1609 until after independence, was for a century and a half an ecclesiastical affair, until the newspaper controversy of 1768-69, when it became a public and political issue as well. This is a prime example of the significance of the rise of the press, which became influential in both molding and reflecting public opinion, for which see chapter 8. See also the studies by George W. Pilcher (listed below).

Davis, Richard Beale. *A Colonial Southern Book Shelf: Reading in the Eighteenth Century.* Mercer University Lamar Memorial Lectures, 21. Athens: University of Georgia Press, 1979.

Davis challenges Kenneth Lockridge's assessment of literacy in Virginia and the South, believing literacy to have been widespread. A chapter devoted to religion discusses in detail the possession of books and the reading of specific titles. Bibles, Testaments, Books of Common Prayer, printed sermons, catechisms, psalters, and devotional manuals were widely used. "The theological and religious reading of those southern eighteenth-century men and women, represented by titles in their libraries and what they themselves wrote on Christianity, covers a fairly wide spectrum of belief and speculation" (p. 89). There is some discussion of the Bethesda Orphanage library, George Whitefield, and his popularity as an author.

―――. *Intellectual Life in the Colonial South, 1585-1763.* 3 vols. Knoxville: University of Tennessee Press, 1978.

As the most extended analysis and record of the early southern mind, this study gives major attention to religion and to the part both education and the printed word played in its development. Volume 1 includes formal education, institutional and individual, with extensive comments on lay and clerical theories and philosophies of education. Volume 2 is devoted to (1) books and libraries, reading and printing; (2) religion — established, evangelical, and individual; and (3) the sermon and the religious tract. Volume 3 discusses the fine arts in the life of the southern colonist. Davis is able to document and demonstrate convincingly that settlers in the South and their descendants, as in New England, brought books to the New World with them, that merchants imported books, that there was local printing, and that libraries flourished. Sermons — Anglican, Presbyterian, and evangelical — were characterized by plain style and were crafted to persuade as well as teach, convert, and remonstrate. This study is a rich, meaty supplement — and, in some respects, a corrective — to the studies of Perry Miller, Alan Heimert, and other American historians. Extensive bibliographies and notes are included for each chapter.

———. "Samuel Davies: Poet of the Great Awakening." In *Literature and Society in Early Virginia 1608-1840,* ed. Richard Beale Davis, pp. 133-48. Baton Rouge: Louisiana State University Press, 1973.

Usually cited as the earliest hymn writer of colonial Presbyterianism, Davies has also been judged "the foremost southern pulpit orator of the period." His poems and hymns "were bought and read by stout Anglicans as well as Presbyterians . . . and they were copied in newspapers and early magazines from South Carolina to New Hampshire" (p. 147). Davis judges Davies's poetry to have been the rhymed representation of the Great Awakening and credits him with having brought sacred poetry, much of it based on Watts and Doddridge, before the American public.

Endy, Melvin B. "Just War, Holy War, and Millennialism in Revolutionary America." *William and Mary Quarterly,* 3rd series, 42 (1985): 3-25.

"The thesis of this article is that the large majority of ministers who published sermons during the Revolutionary era justified the war effort by a rationale that was more political than religious" (p. 3). This view, that the Revolution falls into the just war tradition of the Christian church, is in contrast to those of historians such as Sacvan Bercovitch, Nathan Hatch, Catherine Albanese, and Alan Heimert, who have traced the development of the holy war perspective on the Revolution.

England, J. Merton. "The Democratic Faith in American Schoolbooks, 1783-1860." *American Quarterly* 15 (Summer 1963): 191-99.

The schoolbooks of the period reflected, transmitted, and shaped popular culture. Among other things "they perpetuated the secular ethic of Puritanism, emphasizing work, thrift and earnestness . . . they intensified the concern of the age with individual morality, under the guidance of religion, and the belief in man's capacity and responsibility to do good" (p. 199).

Farren, Donald. *Subscription: A Study of the Eighteenth-Century American Book Trade.* Ann Arbor: University Microfilms International, 1983.

While books sold by subscription "were not a dominant factor in the production and distribution of books in eighteenth-century America, they were a constant and pervasive factor" (abstract). For purposes of examination, Connecticut is taken as a microcosm of eighteenth-century British North America. Farren found that about ten percent of books published by subscription were for special interest groups and that they "are to an overwhelming extent works connected with a church or otherwise of religious subject matter" (p. 116). Sacred tunebooks, in addition to general titles in religion and theology, receive specific treatment and analysis.

Fiering, Norma S. "The Transatlantic Republic of Letters: A Note on the Circulation of Learned Periodicals to Early Eighteenth-Century America." *William and Mary Quarterly,* 3rd series, 33 (1976): 642-60.

 This article demonstrates that such notable Americans as Cotton Mather, Samuel Johnson of Connecticut, Jonathan Edwards, and James Logan relied upon English learned periodicals to keep them informed about current scholarship and publications of the period. It also helps to document the fact that ideas were transmitted to America through various genres of literature.

Flory, John S. *Literary Activity of the German Baptist Brethren in the Eighteenth Century.* Elgin, IL: Brethren Publishing House, 1908.

 More than half of this account is devoted to the work of Christopher Sauer, the establishment of his press, and the Bibles and periodicals he issued. Also discussed are the literary products of other eighteenth-century Dunker writers. An appendix lists all the work produced, either written or printed, by the German Baptists during the century. Originally a Ph.D. dissertation, University of Virginia.

Foster, Charles I. *An Errand of Mercy: The Evangelical United Front, 1790-1837.* Chapel Hill: University of North Carolina, 1960.

 Faced with the social tensions occasioned by rapid expansion and growth, church people in the United States turned to Great Britain to appropriate the means of adjustment necessary to promote stability in the nation. The adjustment was generated through the formation of benevolent societies, which promoted Bible and tract distribution, the formation of Sunday schools, temperance, the colonization of African-Americans, and education. These nondenominational Protestant societies formed an interlocking network of effort in which clergy and laity cooperated to establish evangelical social control. For a contrasting view of these developments, see Fred Hood's *Reformed America* (listed below).

Gilmore, William J. *Reading Becomes a Necessity of Life: Material and Cultural Life in Rural New England, 1780-1835.* Knoxville: University of Tennessee Press, 1989.

 Focusing on the Windsor District of Vermont (11 towns), this study examines the transformation of a traditional agricultural region into a commercial one. The cultural, social, and economic links involved in this transformation also included an ideological commitment to reading and learning. Part 2, "Print Communications and Cultural Exchange," contains a detailed and explicit analysis of the shift from a predominantly oral to a print-centered culture. Gilmore carefully places the Bible, theological works, devotional literature, and family and social libraries in the matrix of these changes that occurred in the fifty years following the American Revolution to establish a *mentalités* that underlies the cultural transformation of "modern life" in America. For a somewhat different but related interpretation, see Richard Brown's *Knowledge Is Power* (listed above).

Goddard, Delano A. "The Pulpit, Press, and Literature of the Revolution." In *The Memorial History of Boston. Including Suffolk County, Massachusetts, 1630-1880,* ed. Justin Winsor, pp. 119-48. Boston: J. R. Osgood, 1881.

    This essay discusses the pulpit ministries of the clergy who served Boston's eighteen churches and religious societies from 1750 to 1776, with brief comments on their literary activities.

Greene, Jack P. "A Mirror of Virtue for a Declining Land: John Camm's Funeral Sermon for William Nelson." In *Essays in Early Virginia Literature Honoring Richard Beale Davis,* ed. J. A. Leo Lemay, pp. 181-201. New York: Burt Franklin, 1977.

    This sermon, preached and published about November 1772, is the only known extant colonial funeral sermon to have been published outside New England. "The sermon was entirely conventional: it does not seem to have deviated in either tone or thrust from the common run of Anglican funeral sermons in contemporary England" (p. 182). However, just as the New England Puritans extolled the lives of worthy men, Camm extols Nelson as a "pattern to succeeding generations."

Hatch, Nathan O. *The Democratization of American Christianity.* New Haven: Yale University Press, 1989.

    Focusing attention on the period 1780-1830, Hatch examines "the cultural and religious history of the early American republic." He argues that a wave of popular religious movements challenged the established churches, spread revivalism, and democratized American society. Section 3 on "Audience" describes and analyzes the combined forces of the written and spoken word as expressed through vernacular preaching, new forms of religious music, and the creation of a mass religious culture in print. These changes altered the networks of religious communication in America by deposing the clergy as the authoritative sources of information and by stimulating an explosion of popular printed material.

Hatchett, Marion J. *The Making of the First American Book of Common Prayer, 1776-1789.* New York: Seabury Press, 1982.

    While centered on the liturgical, theological, and historical issues involved in the compilation of the first Episcopal prayer book in America, this richly detailed study provides the literary background of a significant liturgical landmark. As the prototype for all subsequent revisions of the prayer book, this first effort was foundational. Based on the author's 1972 thesis, General Theological Seminary.

Henderson-Howat, A. M. D. "Christian Literature in the Eighteenth Century." *Historical Magazine of the Protestant Episcopal Church* 30 (1961): 24-34.

This article briefly outlines the work of the Society for the Promotion of Christian Knowledge (SPCK) and of the Reverend Thomas Bray in securing and distributing literature for the American colonies. It discusses some of the authors and titles of works printed by the SPCK and sent to America.

Holifield, E. Brooks. "The Renaissance of Sacramental Piety in Colonial New England." *William and Mary Quarterly,* 3rd series, 29 (1972): 33-48.

Puritan sacramental piety was inaugurated in 1690 with the publication of Cotton Mather's *A Companion for Communicants.* Prior to that date no sacramental manual had been printed in New England, but between 1690 and 1738 twenty-one editions of communion manuals were produced. Holifield surveys this literature and interprets it as "evangelistic sacramental piety," an attempt to assist the faithful saints, but also as instruction, admonition, and exhortation to unregenerate baptized Christians, urging them to partake of the sacrament. Sacramental piety fell into eclipse with the advent of the Great Awakening. Only eight manuals were printed between 1739 and 1790.

Hood, Fred J. *Reformed America: The Middle and Southern States, 1783-1837.* University, AL: University of Alabama Press, 1980.

The Reformed tradition, defined as persons or groups in the theological tradition of John Calvin, is viewed as having been highly influential in the middle and southern states as well as nationally, especially in the period 1783-1837. The Reformed joined in the activities of the benevolent societies, attempting to bring problems of poverty, population explosion, and suffrage under social control. Hood sees these efforts as having failed, with revivalism emerging as salvation for the individual and for the republic. Religion was moved beyond the dominance of any conglomerate of institutions. The book crusade of the reform movement is carefully delineated.

Houlette, William D. "Parish Libraries and the Work of the Reverend Thomas Bray." *Library Quarterly* 4 (1934): 583-609.

Parochial libraries were especially valued in the southern colonies. Houlette describes and explains the work of the Reverend Thomas Bray, Commissary of the Bishop of London, in setting up libraries in the three colonies of Maryland, North Carolina, and South Carolina. Part of Bray's design in developing parish libraries was to encourage "studious and sober" men to serve as clergy in the colonies.

Hurst, John Fletcher. "Parochial Libraries in the Colonial Period." In *Papers of the American Society of Church History*, ed. Samuel Macauley Jackson, vol. 2, pt. 1, pp. 37-50. New York: G. P. Putnam's Sons, 1890.

This essay details the work of Rev. Thomas Bray, Commissary of the Bishop of London, who worked in Maryland. He divided ten counties into thirty-one parishes. His labors resulted in the establishment of thirty-nine parish libraries throughout Maryland and the other colonies. To some parishes over 1,000 volumes were given. Books were of two classes: one for the use of clergy, the rest of them for the laity. Books also were to be loaned. Also included is a complete list of the Library of Herring Creek, Anne Arundel County, Maryland (1698). The Revolution marks the close of the foreign interest in colonial parish libraries.

Isaac, Rhys. "Books and Social Authority of Learning: The Case of Mid-Eighteenth-Century Virginia." In *Printing and Society in Early America,* ed. William L. Joyce et al., pp. 228-49. Worcester, MA: American Antiquarian Society, 1983.

A study of the authority of the written word and its symbolic significance in society with both oral-dramatic and script-typographic media of communication. The Reverend Devereux Jarratt's "recollections of the processes by which he acquired, first, common literacy, and then access to higher learning, provide outlines of the relationship between popular culture — with its large oral component — and the authoritative realm of great books" (p. 233).

————. "Preachers and Patriots: Popular Culture and the Revolution in Virginia." In *The American Revolution: Explorations in the History of American Radicalism,* ed. Alfred F. Young, pp. 125-56. DeKalb: Northern Illinois University Press, 1976.

Isaac concludes that while the revolutionary evangelical movement represented a sharp challenge to the style and values of the traditional society of the gentry, at the same time the patriot movement infused traditional styles and values with meetings, elections, committees, and resolutions. Both movements, however, were powerfully shaped by the ability to communicate in popular style the passion for a truly moral order.

————. *The Transformation of Virginia, 1740-1790.* Chapel Hill: University of North Carolina Press, 1982.

A detailed and nuanced review of the social-cultural context of the double revolution in religious and political thought that took place in the second half of the eighteenth century. Drawing upon both art and social science, Isaac uses the device of dramaturgy to suggest a way of looking at the important communications included in patterns of action. Popular movements of religious dissent, notably Baptist and Methodist, rose to challenge and ultimately displace that of the Anglican/gentry class. Much of this struggle is viewed in the tensions between an orally oriented populace and a gentry more closely identified with a typographically scripted bias.

Jarratt, Devereux. *The Life of the Reverend Devereux Jarratt.* New York: Arno Press & The New York Times, 1969.

Jarratt's autobiography is considered the most interesting autobiography written in eighteenth-century Virginia. It is also a significant social document because in it Jarratt recalls the process by which he acquired literacy and access to higher learning. These achievements enabled him to acquire social status and prestige. The story of this process of self-education, the relation between popular culture, largely oral, and the realm of great books, is effectively told by one who experienced the transition. This is a reprint of the Baltimore 1806 edition covering the years 1732-1797. Text of the same edition for the years 1732-1763, with an introduction and notes by Douglass Adair, was published in *William and Mary Quarterly,* 3rd series, 9 (1952): 346-93.

Johnson, Thomas H. "Jonathan Edwards' Background of Reading." *Publications of the Colonial Society of Massachusetts* 28 (1935): 193-222.

This study of Edwards's reading, based on a study of his education, his letters, his access to libraries, references and notes in his treatises, and a surviving catalog containing some five hundred itemized book titles, reveals that for a provincial colonial clergyman associated with democratic and local developments his literary acquaintance was phenomenal. From this study Johnson has compiled a list of authors and their works as an example of Edwards's professional reading.

Kerr, Harry P. "The Election Sermon: Primer for Revolutionaries." *Speech Monographs* 29 (1962): 13-22.

"Rhetorical analysis of occasion, audience, speaker, and speech is applied to a type of speaking that was popular in America between 1763 and 1783. The resulting portrait provides background which can enrich the study of a particular election sermon. It demonstrates, moreover, that the annual sermons followed a distinct pattern, and that in so doing, they popularized and reinforced by repetition the major philosophical underpinnings of the Revolution."

———. "Politics and Religion in Colonial Fast and Thanksgiving Sermons, 1763-1783." *Quarterly Journal of Speech* 46 (1960): 372-82.

Convinced that "much of the oratory which enlisted and stimulated support for the American Revolution originated in colonial pulpits," Kerr concludes that "the sermons preached on these holydays were more effective instruments of mass persuasion than any other political sermons delivered during the period, and rank almost on a par with newspapers, pamphlets, and quasi-legal organizations as mainstays of the war of words which preceded and accompanied the American Revolution" (p. 382).

Klingbero, Frank J. "The Anglican Minority in Colonial Pennsylvania, With Particular Reference to the Indians." *Pennsylvania Magazine of History and Biography* 65 (1941): 276-99.

This article emphasizes the part played by the Society for the Propagation of the Gospel in Pennsylvania before the Revolution, particularly focusing upon the Anglican work with Native Americans centering in education and evangelization. "The pioneer missionary, acting as a religious and humanitarian lookout on the frontier, wrote to his central body in London from many stations. . . . The disposition of these missionary consuls [was] read, discussed, codified, digested and enriched with theory and accumulated philosophical insight by men of perspective, who then sent fresh instructions, from the general pool of reports, out to all the network, thus maintaining a continual chain of ideas in transit, throughout the century" (p. 299).

Kraus, H. P., publishing firm (New York). *The Reverend Thomas Bray D.D. 1656-1730 Founder of the American Public Library System, the Society for the Propagation of the Gospel in Foreign Parts and the Society for Promoting Christian Knowledge: A Selection from his Papers together with a Group of American Manuscripts.* Catalogue 152. New York: H. P. Kraus, 1978.

A sale catalog of seventy-nine sequentially numbered entries, sixty of which are books, pamphlets, or manuscript letters written by Bray or relating to him. Part I contains entries 1-22 of "Papers relating to the libraries established in America and elsewhere by Bray"; Part II, entries 23-47, "Letters and papers of Bray and others regarding religious and civil affairs in the American Colonies"; Part III, entries 48-50, "The (S.P.G.) and (S.P.C.K)"; Part IV, entries 51-57, "Printed material by Bray" (and one other piece); Part V, entries 58-60, "Miscellanea"; and Part VI, entries 61-79, "American Manuscripts, Letters and Documents." Each entry has a full bibliographic description and annotation providing a historical and contextual placement of the document in American colonial history. The catalog includes facsimiles of pages from selected documents.

Kraus, Michael. *The Atlantic Civilization: Eighteenth-Century Origins.* Ithaca, NY: Cornell University Press, 1949; repr. New York: Russell and Russell, 1961.

This study surveys the cultural interchange between America and Europe in many fields, including communications, religious relations, and books and learning. Kraus emphasizes the impact of the New World upon the Old, believing that the American colonies contributed their share to the synthesis called "the Atlantic civilization." The Great Awakening and analogous revivals in Britain kept presses on both sides of the Atlantic busy telling of the religious revival. This survey clearly outlines the linkage among the colonies, the mother country, and Europe. At times it was mutually beneficial, at other times anxious, but always vital and influential, especially prior to the American Revolution.

Kroeger, Karl. "Isaiah Thomas as a Music Publisher." *Proceedings of the American Antiquarian Society* 86 (1976): 321-41.

Music publishing during the seventeenth and eighteenth centuries consisted almost entirely in collections of psalm tunes and instruction books designed to aid in the singing of psalms. Isaiah Thomas entered the music publishing field in 1786 with the appearance of *The Worcester Collection of Sacred Harmony* in two volumes, which, over a period of seventeen years and eight editions, established him as the major publisher of sacred vocal music in America.

Laugher, Charles T. *Thomas Bray's Grand Design: Libraries of the Church of England in America, 1695-1785.* ACRL Publications in Librarianship, no. 35. Chicago: American Library Association, 1973.

Based on the use of archival sources previously unexploited, this is the fullest description and most extensive analysis of the work of the Reverend Thomas Bray, the Society for the Propagation of the Gospel in Foreign Parts, and the Bray Associates in founding and supporting libraries in the American colonies. Bray and these societies began work in 1695, and in nearly a century of effort they sent hundreds of missionaries and thousands of books and religious tracts to the New World. Appendixes give a listing of the libraries founded and the catalogs of five collections.

Lemay, J. A. Leo. "The Rev. Samuel Davies' Essay Series: *The Virginia Centinel, 1756-1757.*" In *Essays in Early Virginia Literature Honoring Richard Beale Davis,* ed. J. A. Leo Lemay, pp. 121-63. New York: Burt Franklin, 1977.

This essay attempts to prove that Rev. Samuel Davies, a New Light Presbyterian minister who wrote and published extensively during his career, is the author of some nineteen essays that appeared anonymously in the *Virginia Centinel* newspaper. These essays are complementary to a series of sermons Davies published urging young Virginians to join the militia, to be brave, and to defeat the French and Indians, who in 1757 challenged British control of the colony. See also the study by Elizabeth I. Nybakken (listed below).

Lydenberg, Henry M. "The Problem of the Pre-1776 American Bible." *Bibliographic Society of America. Papers* 48 (1954): 183-94.

    This article continues the debate about the Baskett Bible of 1752, reviewing the evidence and debate down to the present. It concludes that Thomas Baskett did publish a Bible in America in 1752.

Mather, Cotton. *Magnalia Christi Americana.* Ed. Kenneth B. Murdock with the assistance of Elizabeth W. Miller. Cambridge, MA: Belknap Press of Harvard University Press, 1977–.

    Judged by Sacvan Bercovitch as the "literary summa of the New England Way," Mather's *Magnalia* is his largest and greatest book, first published in 1702. Labeled a huge, undigested mass of biographies, sermons, narratives, and theology, it stands as the great American epic, infused with biblical typology and apocalyptic thrust. The tension between promise and fulfillment that it contains still permeates much of American historiography. The biographical genre Mather developed, identifying New England's progress with the private, interior movement of grace, was to become standardized for a century and a half. Interestingly, Mather identified the printing press and the Reformation as the two most significant contributions of modern civilization and the heaven-inspired navigation to the New World as a specimen of the thousand-year reign of the saints.

McCulloch, Samuel C. "Dr. Thomas Bray's Commissary Work in London, 1696-1699." *William and Mary Quarterly,* 3rd series, 2 (1945): 333-48.

    This essay sets the work of the Reverend Thomas Bray, Commissary for the Bishop of London to the Maryland Colony, in an educational, missiological context: "He strove to better education through charity schools, to found libraries, to reform prisons, and to propagate the gospel among white and colored alike in England and the colonies" (p. 333). More specifically, Bray's efforts to provide the colonial parishes with libraries is detailed. "From 1696 to 1699, Bray had revealed a remarkable driving energy, a keen intelligence, and an unusual executive ability" (p. 348).

Mixon, Harold D. "Boston's Artillery Election Sermons and the American Revolution." *Speech Monographs* 34 (1967): 43-50.

    Mixon concludes that revered and respected ministers, in these sermons, "reiterated not new ideas but familiar concepts which the colonists also heard on other occasions." These sermons were part of a larger stream of discourse, "promoting patterns of thought which prepared the colonies for the ideas of the revolutionists."

Nash, Gary B. "The American Clergy and the French Revolution." *William and Mary Quarterly*, 3rd series, 22 (1965): 392-412.

> Up until 1795, American clergy steadfastly supported the French Revolution, but then they turned against it. In May 1798, Jedidiah Morse electrified his parishioners and others with the charge that "Agents of a secret European organization dedicated to the destruction of all civil and ecclesiastical authority . . . had invaded the United States" (p. 392). This organization, The Illuminati, was the final corrupt result of the Revolution. Newspaper editors, clergy, politicians, and citizens took up the cry, and in editorials, sermons, pamphlets, and books they affirmed the need for social unity, conservative government, and a revival of religion. Events in America such as the rise of Deism and threats of war and social unrest, more than events in Europe, help to account for these changes in attitude.

Nerone, John C. "The Press and Popular Culture in the Early Republic: Cincinnati, 1793-1843." Ph.D diss., University of Notre Dame, 1982.

> A local study posited on "a framework of democratization of mind and the generation of a popular culture in print" (p. 16). The introduction is particularly helpful in sketching the role and power of the press for the period. A chapter on religious and literary periodicals outlines the development of religious journalism and how this idea changed over time. "Popularization was the crucial factor in the development of religious journalism" (p. 205).

Nord, David Paul. "The Authority of Truth: Religion and the John Peter Zenger Case." *Journalism Quarterly* 62 (1985): 227-35.

> While the overt issues in the trial of John Peter Zenger, charged with publishing seditious libels, were political and legal, this study argues that, "in essence, the Zenger case was a disputation on truth, and on how truth is revealed to men" (p. 227). The trial, which took place in 1735, is viewed in conjunction with the Great Awakening of the same period as touching on the great question of how God's truth can be discerned by humankind. Thus, freedom of expression is seen as having important religious roots, and Americans still retain an ambivalent attitude toward the dichotomy between authoritarian religion and libertarianism.

Nybakken, Elizabeth I., ed. *The Centinel: Warnings of a Revolution.* Newark: University of Delaware Press, 1980.

> This study contains the texts of nineteen installments of the "Centinel,"

published March 24 through July 28 of 1768 in the *Pennsylvania Journal and Weekly Advertiser.* These pieces were written "to alert Pennsylvanians of the movement to introduce an Anglican bishopric into the colonies and to warn them of the pernicious effects of such an innovation" (p. 13). Also included are two texts of the "Anti-Centinel" (June and September 1768) and four texts of the "Remonstrant" (October and November 1768), which extend the discussion. These documents are significant for having appeared in a newspaper and for signaling the transformation of a religious controversy into a political one. See also the studies by George W. Pilcher (listed below) and J. A. Leo Lemay (listed above).

Parsons, Wilfrid. "Early Catholic Publishers of Philadelphia." *Catholic Historical Review* 24 (July 1938): 141-52.
    "Up to the year 1816 . . . Philadelphia was the sole Catholic publishing center of the United States." The careers and printing activities of the Philadelphia Catholic publishers are sketched, including those of Mathew Carey, Bernard Dorin, and Eugene Cumminskey. With very few exceptions the printing activities of these publishers were confined to "reprints from books written or published in England or Ireland, or translations from the French or Italian. Most of their production was religious."

Pilcher, George W. "The Pamphlet War on the Proposed Virginia Anglican Episcopate, 1767-1775." *Historical Magazine of the Protestant Episcopal Church* 30 (1961): 266-79.
    A review of the pamphlet literature, both pro and con, concerning the establishment of Church of England bishops in Virginia. In 1767 the Reverend Thomas Bradbury Chandler, a missionary of the Society for the Propagation of the Gospel in Foreign Parts, formulated the basic "seven arguments which became the basis for many future demands of the pro-Episcopal party" (p. 267). In 1774 Chandler issued two more pamphlets before returning to England. The outbreak of the Revolution brought the pamphlet war to an end.

————. "Virginia Newspapers and the Dispute Over the Proposed Colonial Episcopate, 1771-1772." *Historian* 23 (1960): 98-113.
    In May and June 1771 the Virginia Anglican clergy attempted to secure a bishop for the colony through a proposed petition to King George III. This action provoked a lively debate pro and con in Purdie and Dixon's *Virginia Gazette* and other newspapers. See also the study by Arthur L. Cross (listed above).

Reilly, Elizabeth Carroll. "The Wages of Piety: The Boston Book Trade of Jeremy

Condy." In *Printing and Society in Early America,* ed. William L. Joyce et al., pp. 83-131. Worcester, MA: American Antiquarian Society, 1983.

Jeremy Condy, sometime controversial minister of First Baptist Church in Boston, built a substantial portion of his trade on "the immense popularity of books that were religious in nature and devotional in mode" (p. 118). He also ventured into publishing on a modest scale, including reprints of English works and the issuance of sermons by Jonathan Mayhew.

Richardson, Lyon N. *A History of Early American Magazines, 1741-1789.* New York: Thomas Nelson and Sons, 1931.

A richly detailed study that greatly augments Frank Luther Mott's *History of American Magazines.* Richardson discusses such well-known religious titles as *The Christian History,* Christopher Sauers's *Ein geistliches Magazien,* and *Arminian Magazine.* As Richardson notes, "The contents of the thirty-seven periodicals I have included for study, the incidents in the lives of the men involved with respect to their publications, the general circumstances of publishing, and the literary and historical trends of the period have been my special interest" (p. ix). See also Frank L. Mott, *A History of American Magazines* (listed in Section II).

Sachse, Julius Friedrich. *The German Sectarians of Pennsylvania, 1708-1800: A Critical and Legendary History of the Ephrata Cloister and the Dunkers.* Philadelphia: Author, 1899-1900.

This study contains considerable discussion on the printing activities of Christopher Sauer and the Ephrata and Kloster presses. It also details Sauer's relationship with the Lutheran pietists and the Cansteinsche Bibel Anstalt (Canstein Bible Institution), for whom he served as a distributor of their Bibles, tracts, and other publications.

Schmidt, Leigh Eric. "'A Second and Glorious Reformation': The New Light Extremism of Andrew Croswell." *William and Mary Quarterly,* 3rd series, 43 (1986): 214-44.

Schmidt examines the career and influence of Andrew Croswell, who has been neglected by historians but who by some estimates deserves ranking with George Whitefield, James Davenport, and Gilbert Tennent as a spiritual hero of the Great Awakening. "Croswell was more persistent and visible, provoked more controversies, itinerated longer, and published more tracts than any other incendiary New Light, including James Davenport. In his writings one finds the fullest articulation of the theology and spirituality of the radical awakening" (p. 214).

Seidensticker, Oswald. *The First Century of German Printing in America, 1728-1830: Preceded by a Notice of the Literary Work of F. D. Pastorius.* Philadelphia: Schaefer and Koradi, 1893.

The American German press, like that of other national groups, was in its early history dominated by religious sectarianism. Titles by mystic transcendentalists, inspirationists, Dunkers, and theosophists predominated and were followed by those of the Lutherans, Moravians, and others.

Silver, Rollo G. "Publishing in Boston, 1726-1757: The Accounts of Daniel Henchman." *Proceedings of the American Antiquarian Society* 66 (1956): 17-29.

Daniel Henchman, although known primarily as a book merchant, was also a publisher who issued many sermons and other religious titles. This account details titles published, production costs, press runs, sales figures, and the rudiments of author royalties. It provides an intimate glimpse into the trade of the bookseller-publisher who had "the most effective method of communication in his time" (p. 18).

Smith, Peter H. "Politics and Sainthood: Biography by Cotton Mather." *William and Mary Quarterly,* 3rd series, 20 (1963): 186-206.

Cotton Mather wrote many biographies conforming to the conventional Puritan literary canon and structured "according to the processes of divine election, conversion, vocation, justification, and sanctification. . . . Mather's deference to the traditional biographical form was not only pious, however, it was also functional" (pp. 186-87). Two of his biographical works, *Magnalia Christi Americana* and *Johannes in Eremo,* are examined in some detail to show that Mather's purpose was to promote his political interests. His intention in doing so was to call the wayward descendants of New England's seventeenth-century orthodoxy back to the saintly practices of earlier generations.

Smith, Wilson. "William Paley's Theological Utilitarianism in America." *William and Mary Quarterly,* 3rd series, 11 (1954): 402-24.

"The books on moral philosophy and natural theology by William Paley were once as well known in American colleges as were the readers and spellers of William McGuffey and Noah Webster in the elementary schools" (p. 402). Paley's utilitarian ethics reigned supreme in American academia during the first three decades of the nineteenth century. "And the welcoming committee was headed by the moral philosophers of the educating community, men who believed in the individual conscience as the source of right social action" (p. 423). Down to the close of the century Paley's texts and ideas were still appearing in theology classes, although by the time of the Civil War Paleyism waned and was replaced by a more powerful evangelical absolutism.

Solberg, Winton U. "Cotton Mather, *The Christian Philosopher* and the Classics." *Proceedings of the American Antiquarian Society* 96 (1987): 323-66.

Mather's work, issued in 1721 and recognized as a major intellectual achievement of the colonial period, is the best example of the way in which Newtonian science was first disseminated in British America. It contains references to 415 authors. Solberg traces Mather's reliance on the literature of classical and Christian antiquity in producing *The Christian Philosopher.*

Stout, Harry S. "Religion, Communications, and the Ideological Origins of the American Revolution." *William and Mary Quarterly,* 3rd series, 34 (1977): 519-41.

A reexamination of evangelical oratory, exemplified in the Great Awakening, which established patterns of communication spilling over into political life. "Evangelical rhetoric performed a dual function: it proclaimed the power of the spoken word directly to every individual who would hear, and it confirmed a shift in authority by organizing voluntary popular meetings and justifying them in the religious vocabulary of the day" (p. 530). The revivals set the pattern of oral address and mass meetings that was to characterize the Revolutionary period of American history.

Tanselle, George Thomas. "Some Statistics on American Printing, 1764-1783." In *The Press and the American Revolution,* ed. Bernard Bailyn and John B. Hench, pp. 315-63. Worcester, MA: American Antiquarian Society, 1980.

In a brief section that characterizes output of the press by type of materials (pp. 326-30), based on a tabulation of the number of entries Charles Evans lists under subject headings, Tanselle shows that output for theology, while dominant, declined from twenty-nine to nineteen percent over the twenty years studied.

Thornton, John W., ed. *The Pulpit of the American Revolution; or, The Political Sermons of the Period of 1776.* Boston: Gould and Lincoln, 1860.

This volume contains seven election sermons, one Thanksgiving sermon, and one regular sermon that "presents examples of the politico-theological phase of the conflict for American Independence" (p. ix). Pulpit and press are viewed as having been closely allied in the struggle for independence. Election sermons were first printed for circulation to other clergy and then circulated far and wide by means of newspapers.

Tichi, Cecelia. "Spiritual Biography and the 'Lords Remembrancers.'" *William and Mary Quarterly,* 3rd series, 28 (1971): 64-85.

Thomas Prince, in his *Chronological History of New England* (1736), abandoned the traditional biographical form to embrace a chronological approach more in keeping with a society that was heterogeneous and no longer tribal. Tichi reviews the histories written prior to 1730, those of the "Lords Remembrancers," with their reliance on the typology of pilgrimage and wilderness, to explain their spiritualizing of biography and history. However, this theme of social quest remains firmly imbedded in Prince and later historians; "its tradition in American literature was founded in the spiritual biographies of the 'Lords Remembrancers'" (p. 85).

Van de Wetering, John E. "The *Christian History* of the Great Awakening." *Journal of Presbyterian History* 44 (June 1966): 122-29.

This article views the *Christian History*, which reported events of the Great Awakening in New England, as presenting a "partisan view of the revival." Thomas Prince, Sr., is identified as the force behind its publication, with the junior Prince, its editor, having no more "than a mechanical share in the production of the publication." The senior Prince sought to appeal to the authority of New England's ancestors and even to events abroad as justification for the revival. By 1745 the momentum of the revival had cooled and Prince's efforts to publicize and justify the revival had provoked powerful opposition. After nearly two years of publication (March 1743 through February 1745) and 104 numbers, the *Christian History* had run its course.

Warch, Richard. *School of the Prophets: Yale College, 1701-1740*. New Haven: Yale University Press, 1973.

An account of the early years of Yale College, this book deals primarily with the religious dimensions of the school and the society surrounding it in the years before the Great Awakening (blurb). "What follows is intended to be both a record of Yale's first forty years and a story of the college as intellectual history. Samuel Eliot Morrison's three-volume study of seventeenth-century Harvard has demonstrated the validity and value of this approach and I have tried to extend it to the history of Yale" (pp. ix-x). See the index for entries on the curriculum of Yale College, theology, rhetoric, implications for religion, etc. See pp. 113-14 for remarks about the Yale library.

————. "The Shepherd's Tent: Education and Enthusiasm in the Great Awakening." *American Quarterly* 30 (1978): 177-98.

The Shepherd's Tent that existed in New London, Connecticut, in 1742-43 was an early attempt on the part of New Light disaffected clergy to establish a private school or seminary of learning for the training of clergy. Attempts to suppress the school by opponents of the Great Awakening were largely unsuccessful. It was the excesses of a revelation received by students and tutors in March 1743 that led to the burning of books "suppos'd by them to be tinctured with Arminianism & opposed to the work of God's spirit in the Land." The next day, clothes, symbolizing idolized worldly items, were also burned. More moderate and rational New Light clergy, including Jonathan Edwards, condemned the sensational behavior and the mentality that prompted it. One significance of the Tent was that it challenged the presumed compatibility of church, state, and academy.

Whitehill, Walter M. "The King's Chapel Library." *Publications of the Colonial Society of Massachusetts, Transactions* 38 (1959): 274-89.

The library given to King's Chapel, Boston, by King William of England in 1698 "contained ninety-two folios, eighteen quartos, and ninety smaller works, including Walton's great *Biblia Polyglotta,* lexicons, and commentaries, fine editions of the Church Fathers, Bodies of Divinity, works on Doctrine and Duty, the sermons of the great preachers of the English Church, historical works . . . , Controversial and Philological Treatises" (p. 275). This article includes a short-title catalog of the library, which has been housed since 1823 at the Boston Athenaeum.

Williams, Robert V. "George Whitefield's Bethesda: The Orphanage, the College and the Library." In *Library History Seminar No. 3, Proceedings, 1968,* ed. Martha Jane K. Zachert, pp. 47-72. Tallahassee: Florida State University Press, 1968.

This essay gives a brief history of the library, which compares not unfavorably with college libraries of the period, and an analysis of its content. About seventy-five percent (900 volumes) of the books in the library were of a religious nature. An exact inventory of the library exists, although it is not a part of this study.

Wilson, James Southall. "Best-Sellers in Jefferson's Day." *Virginia Quarterly Review* 36 (1960): 222-37.

Drawn from the records of the *Virginia Gazette,* the newspaper for the colony of Virginia before the American Revolution (1750 to 1765), this study describes and records book titles sold by the firm to specific individuals. Sermons and political pamphlets sold well, and titles are mentioned for some religious works, with the richest detail devoted to politics, literature, the classics, and journals. The author concludes, "This cosmopolitanism of taste had its part in preparing colonial gentlemen who could take their places easily with the best minds and manners of England and France" (p. 237).

Yodelis, Mary Ann. "Boston's First Major Newspaper War: A 'Great Awakening' of Freedom." *Journalism Quarterly* 51 (1974): 207-12.

"A study of the printers, particularly Thomas Fleet, during the revival period [i.e., Great Awakening (1740-45)] indicates that the seeds of some free press concepts traditionally described as those embodied in the First Amendment perhaps were planted in religious controversy well before Boston became the cradle of the political revolution of 1763" (p. 207). While most printers favored the revival, Fleet led the opposition press, through the pages of the *Boston Evening Post,* with criticism of George Whitefield.

————. *Who Paid the Piper? Publishing Economics in Boston, 1763-1775.* Journalism Monographs, no. 28. Lexington, KY: Association for Education in Journalism, 1975.

　　Earlier studies by historians and journalists have suggested that printers owed their existence to government subsidy. Through economic analysis of the revolutionary period in Boston, "this study shows that publications with a religious orientation were a more significant source of revenue for many printers than government printing. There generally was three to four times as much religious as government printing in Boston" (p. 1).

Youngs, J. William T., Jr. *God's Messengers: Religious Leadership in Colonial New England, 1700-1750.* Baltimore: Johns Hopkins University Press, 1976.

　　Three periods of New England religious leadership are identified: (1) ministers were admired religious leaders of a relatively harmonious society; (2) ministers sought to establish a quasi-aristocratic control over a society of contending factions; and (3) ministers based their leadership upon a principle of consent. In moving from stage one to stage three the ministry was transformed. Clergy changed from being authority figures to being democratic leaders whose leadership depended on their ability to relate religious doctrine to the needs of their people. The key event in this transformation was the Great Awakening in the 1740s. This study, based on clergy diaries and sermons, not only documents this social shift but also provides good detail on the minister's calling, education, and work.

## V. Growth of the Nation: 1800-1860

Altick, Richard D. *The English Common Reader: A Social History of the Mass Reading Public 1800-1900.* Chicago: University of Chicago Press, 1957.

　　Many of the same forces and influences that generated a mass reading public in America in the nineteenth century were also at work in England, usually preceding the same developments in the United States. As one of the two most potent influences upon the social and cultural tone of nineteenth-century England, evangelical religion is given careful consideration in this excellent study. Appendices contain a "Chronology of the Mass Reading Public 1774-1900," a "List of Best Sellers," and "Periodical and Newspaper Circulation."

Andrews, Charles Wesley. *Religious Novels: An Argument Against Their Use.* New York: Anson D. F. Randolph, 1856.

A critique of religious novels, which at that time were being widely discussed in the religious press, pro and con. Andrews objects to these novels because they are not true, are unauthorized by Scripture, and are uncalled for in the lawful exercise of the imagination. Andrews attacks the use of fictitious literature in Sunday schools, pointing out that oral instruction is superior to other methods of teaching.

Banks, Loy O. "The Role of Mormon Journalism in the Death of Joseph Smith." *Journalism Quarterly* 27 (1950): 268-81.

Suppression of the Nauvoo, Illinois, *Expositor,* an apostate journal published by a group of dissenting Mormons, in 1844 by the Nauvoo mayor, Joseph Smith, and the city council led to the indictment, arrest, jailing, and subsequent mob-murder of Hyrum and Joseph Smith at Carthage, Illinois. Other Mormon newspapers were also involved in the dissension that led to the events surrounding Joseph Smith's death.

Barnes, Elizabeth. "The 'Panoplist': 19th Century Religious Magazine." *Journalism Quarterly* 36 (1959): 321-25.

"The Rev. Jedediah Morse stood stern-faced against the growing liberalism in New England after 1800 which was to crystallize as Unitarianism. Morse began a magazine which vainly espoused his views, but which also carried material of interest to literary historians." The *Panoplist,* while failing in its mission to stem liberalism, is a record of transitional events in American history and a rich source on cultural development.

Barnett, Suzanne Wilson, and John King Fairbank, eds. *Christianity in China: Early Protestant Missionary Writings.* Cambridge, MA: Harvard University Press, 1985.

A study based on the archives of the American Board of Commissioners for Foreign Missions, housed at the Houghton Rare Book Library (mss.) and the Harvard-Yenching Library of East Asian materials. From the early nineteenth century through the late 1920s, missionaries in the field regularly sent their tracts and other writings back to Boston. "Missionaries wrote almost as much as they preached. Their American constituency back home was, in some ways, even more important to them than their Chinese converts, and sometimes received almost equal attention" (pp. 2-3). "Christian tracts were a principal feature of mission work. Since the early Protestant missionaries often lacked the linguistic capacity and the opportunity for preaching, they resorted to the preparation and distribution of moral writings" (p. 13).

Barrett, John Pressley, ed. *The Centennial of Religious Journalism.* Dayton, OH: Christian Publishing Association, 1908.

About half of this work commemorates the founding of the *Herald of Gospel Liberty*, the first religious newspaper in America, giving details relating to its beginnings and subsequent publication. The remainder of the book concentrates on the history and work of the Christian Church.

————, ed. *Modern Light Bearers: Addresses Celebrating the Centennial of Religious Journalism.* Dayton, OH: Christian Publishing Association, 1908.

Seventeen addresses, about half of which focus on the founding of the *Herald of Gospel Liberty* by Elias Smith in 1808, the other half focusing on denominational journalism, exhibiting the flavor and style of religious journalism in the early twentieth century.

Baumgartner, A. M. " 'The Lyceum Is My Pulpit': Homiletics in Emerson's Early Lectures." *American Literature* 34 (January 1963): 477-86.

Baumgartner argues that Ralph Waldo Emerson's methodology and success as the most popular lyceum lecturer of his time can be traced to his homiletical training at Harvard. Upon examination of the lyceum lectures, it is found that they correspond to the rhetorical methods in Hugh Blair's *Lectures on Rhetoric,* while Emerson's use of rich imagery is traced to Jeremy Taylor. This approach "was similar in theory to what has come to be known as 'the stream of consciousness' or multiple point of view — Gertrude Stein, Faulkner, Richardson, Joyce, Virginia Woolf" (p. 485). Emerson's style, pragmatic and idealistic, became very popular.

Baym, Nina. *Novels, Readers, and Reviewers: Responses to Fiction in Antebellum America.* Ithaca, NY: Cornell University Press, 1984.

This study focuses attention on a form of writing seldom studied but of immense proportions in nineteenth-century periodicals, the book review. More specifically, the author has selected reviews of individual novels "that appeared in major American periodicals, chiefly between 1840 and 1860" (p. 14). Reviews from twenty-one periodicals are drawn upon, and at least two of them are sectarian journals that figure prominently in this study: the *Christian Examiner* (Unitarian) and the *Ladies' Repository* (Methodist). Chapters on "Morality and Moral Tendency" and "Classes of Novels" help to classify and to explain religious novels of the period.

Billington, Ray A. *The Protestant Crusade, 1800-1860: A Study of the Origins of American Nativism.* New York: Macmillan, 1938.

Through the formation of voluntary associations and a torrent of literature, the American Protestant establishment and sectarian groups waged a crusade against Roman Catholicism in particular and against foreign immigrants generally. The author meticulously documents the organization of these groups and the literature they issued. These developments are related to the concurrent political debates and issues of the period.

Bledstein, Burton J. *The Culture of Professionalism: The Middle Class and the Development of Higher Education in America.* New York: W. W. Norton, 1976.

 Chapter 2, "Space and Words" (pp. 46-79), sketches the technological and social changes that contributed to alterations in the concepts of space and words in the nineteenth century. "Describing the outer structure of the visible universe, Mid-Victorians believed that they also described the inner structure of the invisible one" (p. 55). In a discussion of words and the communications revolution, Bledstein notes that "words rather than face-to-face or direct human contact became the favorite medium of social exchange" (p. 65). In this view the church is a specialized place where the clergy are experts using special words shared only by other experts. More schools of theology were founded in the nineteenth century than any other type of professional school.

Bode, Carl. *The American Lyceum: Town Meeting of the Mind.* New York: Oxford University Press, 1956.

 A study of the first major adult education movement, begun in the late 1820s, which flourished in the 1830s and 1840s and declined in the 1850s. "Along with promoting adult education the lyceums advocated better public schools and better teacher-training and helped to lay the groundwork for the public library movement." The lyceum also helped to lay the groundwork for the Chautauqua movement. Clergy found the lecture platform congenial. "The organization, length, style of the lyceum lecture closely resembled that of the religious homily" (p. 31). The lecturing was sometimes referred to as "Lay Preaching" and the lectures as "Lay Sermons." For comments on connections between lyceum and books/magazines, see pp. 34-37.

Briggs, F. Allen. "Sunday School Libraries in the 19th Century." *Library Quarterly* 31 (1961): 166-77.

 An overview and analysis of Sunday school libraries based on catalogs, manuals, and reports. "The Sunday-school library, which had its beginnings about 1825 as an economical means of circulating information and awarding prizes to worthy pupils, by 1850 became the leading medium for distributing didactic literature in America; it continued to grow into the third quarter of the century but fell into disrepute and disuse by the end of the century" (pp. 176-77). See also the study by Frank K. Walter (listed below).

Buddenbaum, Judith M. "'Judge . . . What Their Acts Will Justify': The Religion Journalism of James Gordon Bennett." *Journalism History* 14 (1987): 54-67.

 Founder of the *New York Herald,* Bennett is credited with beginning religious news coverage (1836) in a newspaper intended for a general audience. In 1840, other newspapers, business leaders, and clergy combined in a moral war against Bennett and the *Herald*. "This study is based primarily on a content analysis of a constructed month of issues of the *Herald* during 1836 . . . and at two-year intervals through 1844" (p. 56). Attention to religion varied over this period and coverage did change, but more in response to economic factors than in response to the effects of the moral war. While Bennett's coverage of religion provided an easy avenue of attack for his critics, he succeeded in making religion a subject of discussion for the masses via the newspaper.

Buell, Lawrence. "The Unitarian Movement and the Art of Preaching in 19th Century America." *American Quarterly* 24 (1972): 166-90.

"Seminaries, the press and popular demand conspired to encourage a greater attention to preaching as an art" (p. 174), with the Unitarians beginning to advocate in the early nineteenth century a higher literary standard in preaching. The scope of preaching was broadened beyond doctrinal concerns, and scriptural texts were handled more freely and creatively. The retelling of the Bible story and the reconstruction of a biblical character's psychology became standard. The Unitarians hesitated to innovate beyond this, and their influence in expanding the frontiers of preaching ceased in 1842 with the death of William Ellery Channing, one of their finest pulpiteers.

Canary, Robert H. "The Sunday School as Popular Culture." *Midcontinent American Studies Journal* 9, 2 (Fall 1968): 5-13.

This article investigates two aspects of the Sunday school: "as a vehicle for the professed ideals of society, and the history of the Sunday school movement as an example of the effects of institutionalization and centralization of American popular culture." Sunday school literature, which is likened "to the works of our great theologians as the dime novel is to the works of Hawthorne and Melville," is examined for its representative values.

Carleton, William G. "The Celebrity Cult of a Century Ago." *Georgia Review* 14 (1960): 133-42.

Carleton reviews the golden age of American oratory, 1830-1860, a tradition that ended in 1925 with the death of William Jennings Bryan. "Throughout most of American history, the folk hero has been the jury lawyer, the hortatory minister, and the political orator. Until the turn of the century the most important American folk art was oratory." The celebrities of the golden age were the entertainers of the courtrooms, the camp meeting, the stump, and the political forum. "Today, it is the entertainer of radio, television, and the motion-picture world" (p. 133).

Clark, Clifford E. "The Changing Nature of Protestantism in Mid-Nineteenth Century America: Henry Ward Beecher's *Seven Lectures to Young Men.*" *Journal of American History* 57 (1971): 832-46.

First published in 1844, these lectures went through two editions and ten printings. Through his extensive activities as newspaper editor, lyceum lecturer, author, and preacher, Beecher reached an audience of thousands and helped to shape their views on religious and social questions. These lectures document how the outlook of American Protestantism underwent "a change from an other-worldly perspective to a largely uncritical acceptance of the status quo." Doctrine gave way to ethics, and "by 1880 the process of secularization had become virtually complete."

Cook, R. S. *Home Evangelization: A View of the Wants and Prospects of Our Country, Based on the Facts and Relations of Colportage.* By one of the secretaries of the American Tract Society. New York: American Tract Society, 1850(?).

This study provides a description of the colportage system for distributing tracts and literature as developed by the Tract Society over a seven-year period. This system succeeded in providing for distribution on a mass scale over an immense geographical area. The use of steam power, electricity, magnetism, the railroads, and technological improvements in printing contributed to this success. The Tract Society kept as one of its purposes the diffusion of oral as well as printed truth. Colporteurs were required to hold public meetings and to give oral instruction and testimony. Students of theological seminaries were employed as colporteurs, figuring significantly in the society's work. See also the article by Mark Hopkins (listed below).

Douglas, Ann. *The Feminization of America.* New York: Knopf, 1977.

Douglas examines Protestant clerics and sentimental women authors for the period 1820-1875. This cultural subgroup, lacking social power, sought to extend their "influence" through literature, which was in the process of becoming a mass medium. With the advancement of industrialization and the disestablishment of the churches, this group "attempted to stabilize and advertise in their work the values that cast their recessive position in the most favorable light." By popularizing piety, morals, and domestic concerns, they exercised an enormously conservative influence on their society. Reading had become a feminine preoccupation by mid-century, and these authors, particularly the liberal ministers, "preached, talked and acted, largely for women" (p. 103). The bond between author and reader, producer and consumer, was forged, and the basis of mass culture was solidified.

———. "Heaven Our Home: Consolation Literature in the United States, 1830-1880." *American Quarterly* 26 (1974): 496-515.

"Liberal clergymen and devout women were the principal authors of the mourner's manuals, lachrymose verse, obituary fiction and necrophilic biographies popular at the time" (p. 498). The locus of earthly concern about death changed from concern with the kind of life a believer must live to warrant heaven to that of heaven as home, very much akin to the domestic scene the deceased had always known. By 1868 Elizabeth Stuart Phelps in her best-selling novel *Gates Ajar* would describe heaven in detail as a domestic realm of children, women, and ministers (i.e., angels). Heaven became a realm "scaled to their domestic and pastoral proportions, as a place where they would dominate rather than be dominated" (p. 515).

Edmonds, Albert S. "The Henkels, Early Printers in New Market, Virginia, With a Bibliography." *William and Mary Quarterly,* 2nd series, 18 (1938): 174-95.

The German Lutheran family Henkel settled in the Shenandoah Valley in 1782, and from this family sprang printers, translators, and publishers who, over a 130-year span, published more English language Lutheran theological works than any other similar publishing house in the country. The press was founded in 1806 by Ambrose Henkel (1786-1870), to whom belongs the credit of establishing the first German-language printing press south of the Mason-Dixon line. A bibliography of titles issued by the press, with full detail, is provided.

England, Martha Winburn. "Emily Dickinson and Isaac Watts: Puritan Hymnodists." *Bulletin of the New York Public Library* 69 (February 1965): 83-116.

A fascinating excursion into the poetry of Emily Dickinson that shows the powerful influence of Isaac Watts's hymnody upon her, though she consistently denied any such influence. "The formal influence in all her poetry is the hymn. When music is considered along with hymn texts, that influence is seen as pervasive. Her poetry was written as Watts's was written, as most hymns are written, par-odia, to an existing tune" (p. 88). An excellent example of how hymnody — or popular, devotional literature — becomes culturally integrated.

Frankiel, Sandra Sizer. *California's Spiritual Frontiers: Religious Alternatives in Anglo-Protestantism, 1850-1910.* Berkeley: University of California Press, 1988.

Drawing heavily on newspapers, sermons, and other popular sources, the author reconstructs the religious history of California following the discovery of gold. She concentrates attention on Protestant evangelicalism with its voluntaristic, revivalistic aim to shape American civilization along moral lines. Much of the struggle to plant traditional Protestantism in California, its encounter with alternative religious groups, and the development of denominational networks was articulated in the press, both secular and religious.

Griffin, Clifford S. *Their Brothers' Keepers: Moral Stewardship in the United States, 1800-1865*. New Brunswick: Rutgers University Press, 1960.

From 1800 to 1865 powerful social and religious forces combined to prompt the organization and institutionalization of a program for American moral reform. Protestant laymen and clergy founded a series of interlocking voluntary associations designed to Christianize the country and bring social discord and unrest under control. These associations, such as the American Bible Society and the American Sunday School Union, established publishing programs that flooded the country with millions of books, periodicals, manuals, and tracts. These groups pioneered the mass production and distribution of the printed word. A section entitled "Essay on the Sources," pp. 302-21, gives an excellent description of both primary and secondary sources, with depository identifications, of materials relating to the benevolent associations.

Harris, Michael H. " 'Spiritual Cakes Upon the Waters': The Church as a Disseminator of the Printed Word on the Ohio Valley Frontier to 1850." In *Getting the Books Out: Papers of the Chicago Conference on the Book in 19th-Century America*, ed. Michael Hackenberg, pp. 98-120. Washington, DC: Library of Congress, 1987.

Delivery of the printed word to the West, accomplished largely through voluntary organizations — missionary, tract, Bible, and Sunday school associations — was as significant, if not more significant, than the delivery of missionaries. Itinerant preachers labored with zeal and dedication to distribute the printed word on the frontier in the certain belief that it had the power to reshape social reality.

Hatch, Nathan O. "Elias Smith and the Rise of Religious Journalism in the Early Republic." In *Printing and Society in Early America*, ed. William L. Joyce et al., pp. 250-77. Worcester, MA: American Antiquarian Society, 1983.

Smith, who launched the *Herald of Gospel Liberty* in 1808, the first religious newspaper in America, was an indefatigable publisher of radical opinion. His communication strategies, in conjunction with freedom of the press as popularly understood and practiced, "accelerated a process by which democratic forms of religion came to resonate powerfully within American popular culture" (p. 276).

Havas, John M. "Commerce and Calvinism: The *Journal of Commerce*, 1827-65." *Journalism History* 38 (1961): 84-86.

Arthur Tappan, a successful businessman who promoted Protestant reform through philanthropy, founded "the *New York Journal of Commerce* in 1827 with the twin objectives of publishing a daily newspaper of general interest for businessmen and spreading moral enlightenment." Ironically, while

Tappan was himself an abolitionist, the paper failed in 1865, after his death, because of its pro-slavery stance.

Holland, Harold Edward. "Religious Periodicals in the Development of Nashville, Tennessee, as a Regional Publishing Center, 1830-1880." D.L.S. diss., Columbia University, 1976.

This study identifies and gives the history of seventy-seven religious periodicals published in Nashville. "They include religious newspapers, aids to the ministry, magazines for women and children, Sunday school papers, temperance journals, and missions papers." By 1880 publishing and printing constituted the leading industry of Nashville, much of it related to religious publishing. Detailed attention is given to periodicals issued by the Baptists, Disciples of Christ, Methodists, and Presbyterians.

Hopkins, Mark. "Colportage by Theological Students." *American Messenger* 6, 6 (June 1848): 22.

The president of Williams College remarks on the training of ministerial students by the theological seminaries at the theoretical level, concluding that experience in colportage provides students with valuable practical experience and that the agency and power of the press is second only to that of the ministry itself. See also the study by R. S. Cook (listed above).

Horst, Irvin B. "Joseph Funk, Early Mennonite Printer and Publisher." *Mennonite Quarterly Review* 31 (October 1957): 260-77.

One of the first Mennonite printers and publishers to use English almost exclusively in his publications, Funk was active as an author, printer, and publisher from 1816 to 1862, issuing ten titles as an author, compiler, or translator and forty-nine imprints as a publisher-printer. Funk printed fifteen titles pertaining to music, fifteen on the Evangelical Lutheran Synods of Virginia and Tennessee, and eight items of a distinctly Mennonite character. This article includes a bibliography of works by Funk.

Hovet, Theodore R. "Principles of the Hidden Life: *Uncle Tom's Cabin* and the Myth of the Inward Quest in Nineteenth-Century American Culture." *Journal of American Culture* 2 (1979/80): 265-70.

The author views Harriet Beecher Stowe's *Uncle Tom's Cabin* (1851) as a model "which would encourage the Christian to set out on a life-long quest for spiritual growth" (p. 265). Phoebe Palmer, Thomas C. Upham, and Horace Bushnell, who became spokespersons for the "holiness movement," also sought to create such a model through theological writing and sermons. In creating the fictional hero Tom and in drawing on landscape terminology, Stowe discovered images, types, and symbols that would express the spiritual processes hidden within the individual. Stowe created a model that still strongly pervades American culture and American Protestantism.

"The Inauguration of the *United States Catholic Miscellany* of Charleston, June 6, 1822." In *Documents of American Catholic History: Volume I: 1493-1865,* ed. John Tracy Ellis, pp. 227-29. Wilmington, DE: Michael Glazier, 1987.

 The prospectus for the first American Catholic newspaper. Its inauguration in 1822 is widely considered the birth of American Catholic journalism.

Johnson, James E. "Charles G. Finney and a Theology of Revivalism." *Church History* 38 (1969): 338-58.

 A good review of Finney's basic writings as well as of those who opposed his theological views. Seen together with Timothy Dwight and Nathaniel Taylor as having repudiated the main tenets of Calvinism, Finney aroused a furious opposition on the part of the Old School Presbyterians and the Unitarians and Universalists. Much of the controversy was aired in the press, especially in sermons and lectures that were later published. Like many ministers, Finney "probably felt more comfortable in the pulpit than in the study for he possessed a power over a crowd which was somewhat diminished when he put his ideas in print" (p. 358).

Keller, Ralph A. "Methodist Newspapers and the Fugitive Slave Law: A New Perspective for the Slavery Crisis in the North." *Church History* 43 (1974): 319-39.

 "A look at response in the five official papers of the Methodist Episcopal Church (the Northern wing of Methodism after the sectional split of 1844) to the new fugitive slave bill in 1850" (p. 320). These Methodist papers enjoyed large circulations, representing as they did the largest and most widely dispersed denomination of the time. The five preacher-journalist editors of the papers differed in their approaches to the intense controversy that surrounded the fugitive slave law. Keller concludes that these papers and their editors accurately reflected a deeply held and widespread opposition to the bill. This study helps to document the depth of clergy opposition to slavery and corrects the views of Allan Nevins, Stanley Campbell, and other historians who see the clergy as having been silent on slavery. It also shows that the papers expressed opinions that were widely held by the public, especially in the North. See also the study by L. Wesley Norton (listed below).

Kubler, George A. *A New History of Stereotyping.* New York: [J. J. Little & Ives], 1941.

 This study contains much valuable and informative history of the craft of stereotyping, especially as it is related to newspaper publishing. Bibles and schoolbooks were the first publications to be stereotyped.

Lattimore, R. Burt. "A Survey of William Brownlow's Criticism of the Mormons, 1841-1857." *Tennessee Historical Quarterly* 27 (1968): 249-56.

> William G. Brownlow, a Methodist minister who during Reconstruction was also governor of Tennessee and a United States senator, was editor of the *Jonesboro* (Tennessee) *Whig and Independent Journal* from 1839 to 1849. When Mormons moved into Eastern Tennessee, Brownlow published highly critical attacks on them and helped to stir up political agitation condemning them. This is an interesting example of how a clergyman-editor could influence public opinion and how politics and religion were mixed during this period.

Lee, Robert E. "Timothy Dwight and the Boston *Palladium*." *New England Quarterly* 35 (1962): 229-39.

> In 1800 Dwight and other Federalists purchased control of the New England *Palladium* to counteract Jacksonian democracy and to launch a conservative revolt against the American and French Revolutions. Dwight was joined by other clergy — John Thornton Kirkland, Eliphalet Pearson, Jedediah Morse, and David Tappen — in writing biting, satirical attacks on Deism. Dwight dropped his sponsorship of the newspaper after 1802, having shown that a powerful clergyman could, by attacking irreligion, also propagate the Federalist system of politics and delay in Connecticut the democratizing forces then sweeping the nation.

Marraro, Howard R. "Rome and the Catholic Church in Eighteenth-Century American Magazines." *Catholic Historical Review* 32 (1946): 157-89.

> Based on an examination of "about ninety of the more important literary and political reviews, magazines, and newspapers of the period for various years" (p. 158), these are examined to identify articles that influenced opinions and attitudes toward the Catholics, which, "in turn, might serve to explain the difficulties and the struggles the early Catholic missions encountered in this country" (p. 158). Anti-Catholic feeling was especially strong before the Revolution and continued in a somewhat mitigated form through the remainder of the century.

McLaws, Monte B. "The Mormon *Deseret News:* Unique Frontier Newspaper." *Journal of the West* 19, 2 (April 1980): 30-39.

> "The history of the *Deseret News* [founded in 1850] is the history in miniature of frontier journalism, with one significant difference. It was financed, not by political faction nor ambitious individuals, but by the Mormon Church." The *Deseret News* has been described by Frank Luther Mott, the dean of newspaper historians, as the "first successful religious daily newspaper in the English language."

————. *Spokesman for the Kingdom: Early Mormon Journalism and the "Deseret News," 1830-1898.* Provo, UT: Brigham Young University Press, 1977.

"This study concentrates on the nineteenth-century life of the *Deseret News,* chief official organ of the Mormons, emphasizing the paper's role as an active agent in Mormondom. However, it is also an interpretive account of local and foreign Mormon journalism from 1830, and also treats gentile newspapers inside Utah and out as their pages related to the Mormons. It deals with press power, reliability, and tactics as well as censorship and control in a theocratic frontier government" (p. xii).

McLoughlin, William G. "Charles Grandison Finney: The Revivalist as Folk Hero." *Journal of American Culture* 5, 2 (Summer 1982): 80-90.

Relying upon Finney's own words, taken largely from his autobiography, the author argues that the evangelist's stature as a cultural hero was established prior to the 1830-31 revival in Rochester, New York. A large part of Finney's success as a hero was due to his ability to persuade an audience. "When Finney stood up to preach, the Spirit of God shot forth, people fell off their seats 'struck' by God's power" (p. 86). Along with Andrew Jackson, Finney gave the nation a new definition of America's future: the Westerner would help save the nation.

————. *The Meaning of Henry Ward Beecher: An Essay on the Shifting Values of Mid-Victorian America, 1840-1870.* New York: Alfred A. Knopf, 1970.

An "essay" on, not a biography of, a Congregationalist minister, who for thirty years emerged as the most popular orator in America. "He was far more than a pastor of a well-to-do suburban church. He was for much of his life an editor and weekly columnist of religion and secular newspapers with hundreds of thousands of readers. He published over thirty books" (p. x). McLoughlin examines Beecher's novel *Norwood* to define and explain the clergyman's views, which expressed the popular Protestantism of the middle decades of the nineteenth century. While this study provides significant insights concerning Beecher's views and the sources of his influence, it contains very little about audience. Beecher is well known as the quintessential representative of liberal, romantic Christianity, which rose to such importance in the early twentieth century.

Mishra, Vishwa M. "The *Lutheran Standard:* 125 Years of Denominational Journalism." *Journalism Quarterly* 45 (1968): 71-76.

"In this historical case study of three distinctive phases in the magazine's publication, the author traces the emergence of a modernized journal of the American Lutheran Church."

Nir, Yeshayahu. "Cultural Predispositions in Early Photography: The Case of the Holy Land." *Journal of Communication* 35, 3 (Summer 1985): 32-50.

Photographs of the Holy Land were among the first to appear in books and were immensely popular. A study of French and British photography confirms the general view that "behind the lens and eye were cultural predispositions of a religious nature" (p. 49). The French tended to photograph "monuments," a tendency linked to the Catholic tradition in which the figurative and decorative arts are dominant, while the British Anglicans tended to photograph landscapes and biblical sites, a tendency linked to a tradition that is more ascetic.

Nord, David Paul. *The Evangelical Origins of Mass Media in America, 1815-1835.* Journalism Monographs, no. 88. Columbia, SC: Association for Education in Journalism and Mass Communications, 1984.

This study examines "the evangelical Christian publicists in the Bible and tract societies who first dreamed of a genuinely mass medium — that is, they proposed to deliver the same printed message to everyone in America. To this end, these organizations helped to develop, in the very earliest stages, the modern printing and distribution techniques associated with the reading revolution in the 19th century. . . . By 1830 in some sections of the country — long before the success of the penny press or the dime novel or the cheap magazine — they had nearly achieved their goal of delivering their message to everyone" (p. 2). See also the study by Lawrance Thompson (listed below).

Norton, L. Wesley. " 'Like a Thousand Preachers Flying': Religious Newspapers on the Pacific Coast to 1865." *California Historical Society Quarterly* 56 (1977): 194-209.

Norton reviews the origins of twenty-eight broad-appeal religious papers published on the Pacific Coast between 1848 and 1865. While all the papers were evangelistic in tone and sought to "build and maintain denomination identity and cohesion amid the weakening pressures of the frontier," the editors catered to the secular interests of their subscribers by including a large variety of news. Some of the papers expressed clear opinions on civil rights questions and politics. A bibliography of the twenty-eight papers is included, with library holdings indicated.

————. "The Religious Press and the Compromise of 1850: A Study of the Relationship of the Methodist, Baptist, and Presbyterian Press to the Slavery Controversy, 1846-1851." Ph.D. diss., University of Illinois, 1959.

"The object of the present study is a systematic review of the discussion of slavery in the denominational press, North and South, from 1846, when the Wilmot Proviso was introduced, to 1851, when the controversy over the extension of slavery into the territories subsided temporarily with the Compromise in late 1850. The author has selected for detailed examination twenty-one of the most widely circulated denominational weeklies of the period" (preface). These widely circulated weekly journals of the popular churches were vigorous exponents of anti-slavery doctrines and disseminated their views to a large circle of readers. See also the study by Ralph A. Keller (listed above).

————. "Religious Newspapers on the American Frontier." *Journal of the West* 19, 2 (April 1980): 16-21.

In this essay Norton "surveys the religious journals of the West, showing that although the preacher-editor exhorted his readers to salvation — a newspaper editorial was worth a thousand sermons, his journal nevertheless contained news and was generally conducted like its secular counterpart." The West, as discussed here, includes the Old Northwest and later the Pacific Coast and Texas.

O'Connor, Lillian. *Pioneer Women Orators: Rhetoric in the Ante-bellum Reform Movement.* New York: Columbia University Press, 1956.

In an examination of 145 extant speeches, O'Connor found that "the majority of the women speakers presented a wealth of facts, statistics, and chains of reasoning, both deductive and inductive. They used copious quotation from the most accepted authority of the time, the Bible. Moreover, they detailed narrative and anecdotal material relevant to their theses, chosen chiefly from history, sacred and profane" (p. 229). While the oratory of these early platform speakers used arguments falling within the Aristotelian categories of ethos, pathos, and logos, their rhetoric more nearly conforms to nineteenth-century standards.

Olasky, Marvin. "Democracy and the Secularization of the American Press." In *American Evangelicals and the Mass Media: Perspectives on the Relationship Between American Evangelicals and the Mass Media,* ed. Quentin J. Schultze, pp. 47-67. Grand Rapids: Academie Books, Zondervan Publishing House, 1990.

The *Boston Recorder,* launched in 1816, was a highly successful newspaper of the early nineteenth century that attempted to combine journalism, Christianity, and democracy. Olasky uses the *Recorder* as a test case to imply that "instead of preserving the future developing democracy in coverage and style while maintaining its theocentrism, it tried to quasi-democratize in theology as well" (p. 63). Olasky posits the genesis of this American experience with a "brief excursion into . . . early journalism history, beginning in England during the sixteenth and seventeenth centuries" (p. 53). He concludes that by minimizing theological distinctions, such newspapers as the *Recorder* contributed to the demise of significant religious journalism in the United States.

Peckham, Howard H. "Books and Reading on the Ohio Valley Frontier." *Missis-sippi Valley Historical Review* 44 (1958): 649-63.

In 1810 there were three sources of supply for books on the frontier: migrants who brought books with them; early merchants who imported books; and Ohio Valley printers who published locally. Between 1812 and 1840 libraries "spread like a rash." Religious literature figured prominently in the reading material of the period. The activities of printers and the establishment of libraries in Ohio, Indiana, Kentucky, western Pennsylvania, and Illinois are treated. While the isolated farmer's cabin contained few books, "frontier communities . . . offered a much wider range of reading matter."

Reynolds, David S. *Faith in Fiction: The Emergence of Religious Literature in America.* Cambridge, MA: Harvard University Press, 1981.

Documenting the triumph of the religious novel as a highly popular literary form, Reynolds analyzes the content of these novels to show that "the rise of religious tolerance and diversity in nineteenth-century America was accompanied by an increasingly widespread tendency to embellish religion with diverting narrative." Popular authors and clergy employed fiction as the most appropriate literary mode for accommodating secularism and the antitheological tenor of a nation that had radically changed since the demise of Puritanism in the eighteenth century. Popular religion, embellished in this milieu of wish fulfillment and fantasy, clearly distinguished itself from theology and the demands of incarnational faith. A "Chronology of Fiction" is included.

———. "From Doctrine to Narrative: The Rise of Pulpit Story-Telling in America." *American Quarterly* 32 (1980): 479-98.

By 1850 doctrinal preaching had given way to a more popular style of sermon in which storytelling figured prominently. "The post–Civil War American preacher was competing with newspapers and novels for public attention, and they braved conservative charges of sacrilege and sensationalism by preaching entertaining sermons with mass appeal in an increasingly secular culture." By the late nineteenth century, American preachers felt morally obliged to damn the secular press, but they also exploited it to reach millions, thereby anticipating the use of the mass media by twentieth-century popular preachers.

Ryan, Thomas R. *Orestes A. Brownson: A Definitive Biography.* Huntington, IN: Our Sunday Visitor, 1976.

As the leading Roman Catholic journalist of the nineteenth century, Brownson exerted a wide-ranging influence on American thought. His intellectual powers and firm convictions helped Catholics to discard their self-deprecatory stance and take their place in the mainstream of American life. This extensive biography richly details Brownson's literary efforts, paying attention to the many audiences or publics he addressed.

Schaffer, Ellen. "The Children's Books of the American Sunday-School Union." *American Book Collector* 17 (1966): 21-28.

Founded in 1817 as the Sunday and Adult School Union, this nondenominational organization grew rapidly to become the leading publisher of children's literature. "By 1830 the Union had published 6,000,000 books and had 400,000 scholars in its schools" (p. 23). It pioneered in developing lesson books, magazines for young people, series, annuals, and storybooks, employing some of the best artists as illustrators.

Scott, David M. "Print and the Public Lecture System, 1840-60." In *Printing and Society in Early America,* ed. William L. Joyce et al., pp. 278-99. Worcester, MA: American Antiquarian Society, 1983.

Scott focuses on the "popular lecture system" that emerged as an organized, national system centering on a core of professional lecturers. While the "popular" lecture was explicitly a public occasion, it was in many respects a creation of the world of print of mid-nineteenth-century America. The new oral medium of the lecture emerged "firmly rooted in both the revolutionary new world of 'cheap literature' and in the older modes of oratorical discourse" (p. 299).

Sizer, Sandra S. *Gospel Hymns and Social Religion: The Rhetoric of 19th Century Revivalism.* Philadelphia: Temple University Press, 1978.

The author attempts to relate texts, in this instance gospel hymns, to a general social situation — namely, nineteenth-century revivalism as a form of evangelization and social control. The texts achieved a tremendous popularity, with sales in the millions, and became a staple feature of urban revivalism, which persists today in the Billy Graham Crusade. Rhetorical analysis of the hymns reveals them to have become popular because they built community identity around an ideology of "'evangelical domesticity': of home and woman as primary vehicles of redemptive power, as embodiments of a pure community of feeling" (p. 87). Sizer's methodology is based on an interdisciplinary fusion of history, anthropology, and literary criticism.

Spring, Gardiner. *Memoirs of the Rev. Samuel J. Mills, Late Missionary to the South Western Section of the United States, and Agent of the American Colonization Society, Deputed to Explore the Coast of Africa.* New York: New York Evangelical Missionary Society, 1820.

Mills estimated that the western and southern territories of the nation contained more than a million inhabitants, soon to be increased by a flood of emigration. Seventy-six thousand families were destitute of the Bible, and the larger need was for half a million Bibles. After two tours of this vast region he appealed for missionaries and religious literature to be sent.

Stange, Douglas C. "Benjamin Kurtz of the *Lutheran Observer* and the Slavery Crisis." *Maryland Historical Magazine* 62 (1967): 285-99.

Over a twenty-five-year (1833-1858) career as editor of the *Lutheran Observer,* "the most important Lutheran periodical in ante-bellum America," Kurtz steered an editorial policy of neutrality on the question of slavery. This policy offered little guidance to his readers, either political or moral, but the church remained united at a time when other denominations were split apart. This study tends to verify the influential and powerful role that editors of nineteenth-century religious journals exercised.

Stearns, Bertha-Monica. "Reform Periodicals and Female Reformers, 1830-1860." *American Historical Review* 37 (1931/32): 678-99.

The author discusses women reformers and the papers they founded and published. While all urged some reform of American society and promoted improvement in women's conditions, the particular causes chosen and the means of reform advocated varied widely. The earlier papers carried unmistakable religious conviction, and clergymen as well as church women were instrumental in their founding and operation. On the other hand, the clergy were not infrequently rebuked for their passivity and lack of sensitivity to women's conditions. After the Civil War these early efforts, largely individualistic, were usurped by reform organizations and by periodicals that became business enterprises.

Sutton, Walter. *The Western Book Trade: Cincinnati as a Nineteenth Century Publishing and Book Trade Center . . .* Columbus: Ohio State University Press, 1961.

Cincinnati was, prior to the Civil War, the fourth largest publishing center in the United States and the leading center of western publishing. This study "focuses attention upon the leading center of the western trade and attempts to trace the development of its regional publishing industry from its pioneer beginnings, through its period of greatest importance, into its decline in the years following the Civil War" (preface). The Swedenborgians, Episcopalians, Methodists, Presbyterians, and Catholics all had western agencies for the distribution of their publications. Chapter 12, "The Western Methodist Book Concern" (pp. 150-65), details the history of religious publications, with major attention given to the largest of these operations run by the Methodists.

Thompson, Lawrance. "The Printing and Publishing Activities of the American Tract Society from 1825 to 1850." *Papers of the American Bibliographic Society* 35 (1941): 81-114.

> A succinct view of the society from its origins in local tract societies, with modest publishing programs, to its development as a national organization and one of the nation's first mass media institutions. See also David Paul Nord's study *Evangelical Origins* (listed above).

Thorp, Willard. "Catholic Novelists in Defense of Their Faith, 1829-1865." *Proceedings of the American Antiquarian Society* 78 (1968): 25-117.

> Anti-Catholicism ran high in the early nineteenth century and was often expressed in the Protestant press. Catholic writers turned to novel writing as one way of presenting a positive view of their faith. This study discusses some fifty pro-Catholic novels on American themes published both domestically and abroad.

Venable, William H. *Beginnings of Literary Culture in the Ohio Valley: Historical and Biographical Sketches.* Cincinnati: Robert Clarke, 1891.

> "The Voice of the Preacher and the Clash of Creeds" is more biographically oriented than literary, but it does provide an overview of religious writings in the first half of the nineteenth century. Sermons, debates, and sectarian discourse, both oral and written, "had an immense influence in shaping the literature of the Ohio Valley 'in the beginning'" (p. 226).

Walter, Frank K. "A Poor But Respectable Relation: The Sunday School Library." *Library Quarterly* 12 (1942): 731-39.

> A study on the origins and development of Sunday school libraries during the nineteenth century as predecessors to the public library. These efforts were directed toward children. "In the years preceding the Civil War, rising tides of temperance and antislavery sentiments, as well as religious evangelism, added support to the Sunday school library. . . . During the War, extension of these libraries was retarded in the South, but their growth and use in the North continued." After the war they became more secular, gradually faded into disuse, and were displaced, in part, by the development of public libraries. See also the study by F. Allen Briggs (listed above).

Webster, George Sidney. *The Seamen's Friend: A Sketch of the American Seamen's Friend Society.* New York: American Seamen's Friend Society, 1932.

> Organized in 1828, the Society has, as part of its purpose, the promotion in every port of libraries, reading rooms, and schools so as to improve the social and moral condition of seamen. Its activities as a publisher are detailed in a chapter on publications. Libraries in ports and on ships are reviewed in

another chapter on loan libraries. From 1859 to 1932, the society sent to sea 13,543 new libraries "and the reshipment of the same 17,187, making in the aggregate 30,730" (p. 93).

Weiss, Harry B. "Hannah More's Cheap Repository Tracts in America." *Bulletin of the New York Public Library* 50 (1946): 539-49, 632-41.

The Cheap Repository Tracts, as a serial, made their appearance in America in 1800 at Philadelphia after having gained great popularity in England. "The series of tracts published by B. & J. Johnson were direct approaches and even though not sponsored by a religious group, they constitute, as far as I know, the first organized distribution of tracts in America" (p. 547). Their popularity continued for many years, and they were used frequently, mainly by various tract societies. Includes "A Preliminary Check List of Cheap Repository Tracts Published in America, 1797-1826," with location of copies in libraries.

## VI. The Civil War and Rapid Technological Development: 1861-1919

"The Bishops and the Catholic Press, October 21, 1866." In *Documents of American Catholic History: Volume 2, 1866 to 1966,* ed. John Tracy Ellis, pp. 387-89. Wilmington, DE: Michael Glazier, 1987.

Noting that "the power of the press is one of the most striking features of modern society," the seven archbishops and thirty-eight bishops attending the Second Plenary Council of Baltimore exhort the laity to support the press and the newly established Catholic Publication Society.

Carroll, Henry King. "The Relation of Editors of Religious Journals to Foreign Missions." *Report of the Sixth Conference of Officers and Representatives of the Foreign Missions Boards and Societies in the United States and Canada,* pp. 38-44. New York: Foreign Missions Library, 1898.

This report advocates a proactive stance of editors to promote the cause of missions.

Caudill, Ed. "A Content Analysis of Press Views of Darwin's Evolution Theory, 1860-1925." *Journalism Quarterly* 64 (1987): 782-86, 946.

Stories about Charles Darwin and his evolution theory in the press between 1860 and 1925 centered on the conflict of science and religion. "Even though press opinions about the theory changed . . . the press' orientation to conflict did not. Only the conflict changed — from the challenge of evolution to religion, to the challenge of religion to scientific fact" (p. 946).

Coleman, Earle. "Edward Everett Hale: Preacher as Publisher." *Bibliographic Society of America Papers* 46 (1952): 139-50.

      Hale felt the need to disseminate his ideas to an audience larger than his churches, and this led him to write for the press, to undertake the publication of his own sermons, and to edit monthlies and weeklies. "As a businessman and publisher he was not a notable success. As a preacher and publisher his success is indeterminate" (p. 150).

Daniel, W. Harrison. "Biblical Publication and Procurement in the Confederacy." *Journal of Southern History* 24 (1958): 191-201.

      Attempts to meet the demand for Bibles in the South included publication, formation of the Bible Society of the Confederate States of America, importation from England, and procurement from the North. These efforts were frustrated by shortages of paper, uncertain mail runs, Federal raids, the naval blockade, and rising inflation. "Thousands of copies of Scripture were acquired and distributed, but never enough to supply the need."

————. "The Southern Baptists in the Confederacy." *Civil War History* 6 (1960): 389-401.

      This essay reviews the stance of the Southern Baptist press on the questions of secession from the Union and Confederate government conduct of the war. It also details cooperation with other Christian groups, especially efforts to provide religious reading for the Confederacy: the Bible Society of the Confederate States of America, the Evangelical Tract Society, the South Carolina Tract Society, and the Tract Society of Houston, Texas. On the denominational level the Sunday School and Publication Board at Richmond directed its work to the publication and distribution of literature to the armed forces.

Delp, Robert W. "The Southern Press and the Rise of American Spiritualism, 1847-1860." *Journal of American Culture* 7, 3 (Fall 1984): 88-95.

      Prior to the Civil War, the South "set up an intellectual blockade or *cordon sanitaire* to protect itself against the contamination of radical reform movements originating in the North. The southern press, an important element in that defensive mechanism, attacked the major threat of abolitionism, women's rights and other movements to rehabilitate society by linking them with spiritualism" (p. 88). Methodist, Baptist, and Presbyterian journals were especially vocal in warning their readers about the unscriptural dangers of spiritualism.

Ferre, John P. *A Social Gospel for Millions: The Religious Bestsellers of Charles Sheldon, Charles Gordon, and Harold Bell Wright.* Bowling Green, OH: Bowling Green State University Press, 1988.

"*In His Steps* by Charles Sheldon, *Black Rock* by Ralph Connor (Charles Gordon), and *The Shepherd of the Hills* and *The Calling of Dan Matthews* by Harold Bell Wright outsold almost every other book of the generation before World War I, religious or not. The analysis of these bestselling religious novels in *A Social Gospel for Millions* illustrates a way to understand the meaning of historical and contemporary mass media in American culture" (blurb). See also the study by Gary Scott Smith (listed below).

Getz, Gene A. *MBI: The Story of Moody Bible Institute.* Chicago: Moody Press, 1969.

Part 5, on the "Origin, Development and Outreach of the Literature Ministries of Moody Bible Institute," discusses the Bible Institute Colportage Association, Moody Press, Moody Literature Mission, and *Moody Monthly.* Part 6 devotes chapters to broadcasting, radio, and films. With sales in the millions, the Colportage Association and Moody Press publications reach a large audience both domestically and abroad. Spin-offs of the Moody enterprises include the Christian Booksellers Association, which is the largest network of evangelical publishers in the United States, and the radio department at MBI is considered the pacemaker for several hundred stations that call themselves Christian.

Hackett, Alice P. *70 Years of Best Sellers, 1895-1965.* New York: R. R. Bowker, 1967.

The purpose of this book is "to present as completely as possible the facts and figures about American best sellers during the period in which their records have been preserved, to interpret and comment to some extent upon the statistics and the trends, but not to evaluate them from a literary point of view." It contains a section on religion.

Haggard, Fred Porter. "Missionary Magazines: Their Value to the Societies, Make-up and Distribution." In *Twelfth Conference Foreign Mission Boards, United States and Canada, 1905,* pp. 61-75. New York: Foreign Missions Library, 1905.

Missionary magazines have a threefold value: as organs, as records, and as advertising and educational media. The greatest value of the magazine is seen in the fulfillment of its function as advertising and educational media. The newspaper is seen as giving way to the magazine in popularity. Clubs as means for circulating the missionary magazine are identified as the most effective method in churches, as opposed to direct appeal to subscribers used by the secular press.

Henry, James O. "The United States Christian Commission in the Civil War." *Civil War History* 6 (1960): 374-88.

The Christian Commission, a voluntary association, sent some 5,000 delegates and permanent agents to the battlefields, hospitals, and camps. It was organized by evangelical clergy and laity to aid surgeons, cooperate with chaplains, visit hospitals, distribute reading matter, bury the dead, etc. "Collectively they distributed among the Federal armies the contents of 95,000 packages of stores and publications, which included nearly 1,500,000 Scriptures, more than 1,000,000 hymnbooks, and over 39,000,000 pages of tracts."

Kaser, David. *Books and Libraries in Camp and Battle: The Civil War Experience.* Westport, CT: Greenwood Press, 1984.

This study reviews the reading of soldiers during the Civil War. Three factors are considered: "the degree of literacy prevalent . . . , the amount of reading material easily at hand, and the availability of time to read" (p. 3). Also considered are the sources of soldiers' reading matter. There are sections on "Religious Reading" (pp. 21-26) and "Religious and Charitable Sources" (pp. 98-114). Considerable effort was made in both the North and the South to place religious books, hymnals, and tracts into the hands of soldiers, and they were eagerly read. This book is also interesting as a study of what men were reading in the nineteenth century.

Malin, James C. "William Sutton White, Swedenborgian Publicist, Editor of the *Wichita Beacon,* 1875-1887 and Philosopher Extraordinary." *Kansas Historical Quarterly* 24 (1958): 68-103; 25 (1959): 197-227.

An extended examination of the philosophical and religious views of William S. White, editor for eleven years of the *Wichita Beacon.* Philosophically a follower of Herbert Spencer and religiously a follower of Emanuel Swedenborg, White based his press comments on their writings and thought. He commented extensively on such subjects as church doctrine as applied to life, the pulpit and secular press, inter- and intra-cultural relations, theology and science, revivalist methods, science and technology, and humankind, freedom, and use. As a civil libertarian in advance of his time, White held that schools, libraries, and churches should be supported by private associations of their patrons. This Swedenborgian editor stands as an example of a journalist who, through his conviction that religion relates to life, compelled his readers "to re-examine the whole of society, its ideals and procedures, in fresh perspectives."

Marvin, Carolyn. *When Old Technologies Were New: Thinking About Electric Communication in the Late Nineteenth Century.* New York: Oxford University Press, 1988.

This study "argues that the early history of electric media (last quarter of the nineteenth century) is less the evolution of technical efficiencies in communication than a series of arenas for negotiating issues crucial to the conduct of social life; among them, who is inside and outside, who may speak, who may not, and who has authority and may be believed" (p. 4). This historical interpretation centers on the human body as a delimiting line between nature and culture; the immediate community of family, professional group, gender, etc.; and the unfamiliar community. Though religion is given minimal attention, this study is one of the few to push back the history of twentieth-century mass media to its nineteenth-century roots.

Nicholl, Grier. "The Image of the Protestant Minister in the Christian Social Novel." *Church History* 37 (1968): 319-34.

This article surveys "the image of the social gospel clergyman in the Christian social novel between 1865 and 1918. . . . Christian social novelists aimed to project an idealized image of a minister who could lead the faltering church out of the morass of conservatism, outdated creeds, and worldliness and show a concern for urban and industrial problems. . . . Although it is difficult to determine whether these suggested roles of the social gospel minister had any influence at all, they served in their own way to stem the waning influence and image of the Protestant clergy, tarnished by their own failures, and by criticisms in the press and literature of the day" (p. 333).

Olasky, Marvin. "Late 19th-Century Texas Sensationalism: Hypocrisy or Biblical Morality?" *Journalism History* 12 (1985): 96-100.

While Texas newspapers, in the period 1880-1900, used sensationalism in reporting, their reasons may have been based in biblical morality as much as in profiteering. In examining the context of the reporting, "there is no reason to assume hypocrisy. There is every reason for us to refrain from condemning sensationalism in general. Instead we should examine context and underlying morality" (p. 99).

Quimby, Rollin W. "Recurrent Themes and Purposes in the Sermons of the Union Army Chaplains." *Speech Monographs* 31 (1964): 425-36.

Civil War sermons delivered by Union Army chaplains to the troops — whether delivered as departure, field, evangelistic, or special addresses — were Protestant and usually featured two themes: (1) love of God and country, urging the soldiers to be brave, reverential, strong, and righteous, and (2) "What must I do to be saved?" with an urgent appeal to conversion under the threat of death that war imposed. Evidence suggests that the chaplains were partially successful in communicating their message, in circumstances alien to their prior experience, to appreciative soldiers.

————, and Robert H. Billigmeier. "The Varying Role of Revivalistic Preaching in American Protestant Evangelism." *Speech Monographs* 26 (1959): 217-28.

"The purpose of this paper [is] to consider the shifting role of evangelistic preaching of the type associated with Moody, Sunday, and Graham between 1875 and 1955" (p. 217). The revivalistic preaching of the late nineteenth century was rejected by the churches after World War I and replaced by visitation evangelism, which in turn saw the return of evangelistic preaching in modified form after World War II.

Ripley, John W. "Another Look at the Rev. Charles M. Sheldon's Christian Daily Newspaper." *Kansas Historical Quarterly* 31 (1965): 1-40.

A detailed reconstruction of the 1900 experiment of the Topeka, Kansas, *Daily Capital* newspaper to appoint Rev. Charles M. Sheldon editor for one week, during which time the clergyman and noted author would publish the daily paper as he thought Jesus would. This account differs in many respects from Rev. Sheldon's remembrance of the events in his auto-biography, where "there is not a hint of the intrastaff squabble brought on by his experiment" (p. 5). The experiment created difficulties for the many persons involved, and even brought indifference and criticism from the religious press and others.

Sandeen, Ernest R. "*The Fundamentals:* The Last Flowering of the Millenarian-Conservative Alliance." *Journal of Presbyterian History* 47 (1969): 55-73.

This study interprets the publication of a series of twelve volumes, *The Fundamentals,* 1910-1915, the cost underwritten by Lyman and Milton Stewart, to "reflect the last positive thrust of an alliance between millenarians and conservative Calvinists which characterized the waning years of the nineteenth century" (p. 56). Over three million copies were published, but the extent of their influence is problematical. "*The Fundamentals* plainly failed in their primary purpose — that of checking the spread of Modernism" (p. 73). They foreshadowed the modernist-fundamentalist controversy of the twenties but clearly reflected the concerns of an earlier era.

Shiffler, Harrold C. "The Chicago Church-Theater Controversy of 1881-1882." *Journal of the Illinois State Historical Society* 52 (1960): 361-75.

This article reviews the fierce debate in the press concerning the alleged immorality of the theater in Chicago. Two of the chief antagonists were James H. McVicker, the "dean" of Chicago's legitimate theater, and Dr. Herrick Johnson, pastor of the Fourth Presbyterian Church. This illustrates a kind of controversy not unusual in America during the nineteenth century, which generated extensive press coverage.

Smith, Gary Scott. "Charles M. Sheldon's *In His Steps* in the Context of Religion and Culture in Late Nineteenth Century America." *Fides et Historia, Journal of the Conference on Faith and History* 22 (Summer 1990): 47-69.

Sheldon's social gospel novel *In His Steps* was translated into more than twenty languages, presented as a lantern slide "pictureplay" (1900), as a published play in 1910, as a silent movie in 1916, as a "talkie" in 1936, and as a syndicated radio serial of twenty-six transcribed half-hour shows in 1947-48. This article includes important bibliographic notes on novel publication, etc. See also the study by John P. Ferre (listed above).

Spillers, Hortense J. "Moving on Down the Line." *American Quarterly* 40 (1988): 83-109.

This essay analyzes the texts of several African-American sermons, published prior to 1917 and prior to the electronically recorded sermon. "These sermons provide a demonstration of the rhetoric of admonition" (p. 96). Spillers maintains that the audience of these sermons in the process of hearing/reading them understands that there is only one conclusion possible: history as process guarantees, as does the gospel, that on the other side of this disaster is resurrection, a "good time coming." There is an extensive analysis of two sermons by the Reverend J. W. E. Bowen, pastor of the Asbury Methodist Episcopal Church in Washington, DC. The passion to remember and to repeat the narratives of African-American history stands as a contract between preacher and audience, a means of cultural management expressed both orally and in print.

Stern, Madeleine B. *Books and Book People in 19th-Century America.* New York: R. R. Bowker, 1978.

This volume includes a chapter entitled "The First Feminist Bible: The Alderney Edition, 1876" that gives the history of this Bible's publication by Julia Evelina Smith, who is credited with being "the only woman in the world's history to translate the entire Bible into any language." This Bible was published at Hartford, Connecticut, by the American Publishing Co., with a print run of 1,000 copies.

Stewart, Charles J. "The Pulpit and the Assassination of Lincoln." *Quarterly Journal of Speech* 50 (1964): 299-307.

A detailed study of 372 northern Protestant sermons delivered between April 16 and June 1, 1865, by 332 ministers, which were occasioned by the assassination of President Abraham Lincoln. The thousands of persons who attended churches heard "inordinately emotional discourses describing the intense grief and sorrow of the occasion, calling for love of Lincoln, arousing hatred and anger toward the South, and appealing to hope in the future. In short, the pulpit reacted in the same manner as the general public" (p. 306).

Suderman, Elmer F. "The Social-Gospel Novelists' Criticisms of American Society." *Midcontinent American Studies Journal* 7 (1966): 45-60.

This study analyzes sixty-two novels written by forty-three authors of the social-gospel novel that flourished from 1882 to 1915. These novels, which had a wide circulation, "were propagandistic rather than literary in purpose, [and they] were one of the most spectacular and effective methods of acquainting Americans with social Christianity" (p. 45). The novels are classified, in part, with the larger genre of American economic novels. A bibliography of social-gospel novels is included.

Theisen, Lee Scott. " 'My God, Did I Set All This in Motion?': General Lew Wallace and *Ben Hur.*" *Journal of Popular Culture* 18, 2 (Fall 1984): 33-41.

First published in 1880, the famous novel on the life of Christ sold in the millions, became a stage play in 1899, was made into a motion picture in 1921, and in 1971 drew over 85 million television viewers. *Ben Hur* "broke down the last prejudices in the American public to the novel and made acceptable to many the stage and then the motion picture" (p. 39). Along with Harriet Beecher Stowe's *Uncle Tom's Cabin,* it stands as one of the most popular novels written in America.


## VII. The Modern Electronic Era: 1920 to the Present

Austin, Charles. "The History and Role of the Protestant Press." In *Religious Reporting: Facts and Faith,* ed. Benjamin J. Hubbard, pp. 108-17. Sonoma, CA: Polebridge Press, 1990.

The author views the Protestant press as having "had a distinguished history, paralleling the steady influence of Protestantism on the development of American society" (p. 108). This essay gives only a cursory bow to history, focusing primarily on the role of the press today.

Baker, Carlos. "The Place of the Bible in American Fiction." In *Religious Perspectives in American Culture,* ed. James W. Smith, pp. 243-72. Princeton: Princeton University Press, 1961.

Baker identifies the Bible, especially the King James Version, as the greatest English classic, which has exerted and continues to exert a pervasive influence on American novelists. While the stylistic influence of the Bible has declined in recent years, "the present-day critic can discover a very ample use of Biblical metaphors, symbols and mythological stories in recent American fiction" (p. 269). The forms and visual images of these ancient mythologies and ideas are powerfully present in contemporary culture because they deal with the whole soul and are "inexhaustible to meditation."

Baldwin, Carolyn W. "Denominational Publishing: A Study of Major Church-Owned Publishing Houses in the United States." M.A. thesis, University of Chicago, 1971.

A study of nine Protestant denominational publishing houses, with significant trade book production, based on interviews with editors and the study of their catalogs and other literature. Seven questions were addressed to each editor. There is a separate chapter on each publishing house, "including a general statement of policy with appropriate examples of titles to illustrate." The author concludes that significant books, not limited to apologetic or narrow denominational concerns, are being issued by these presses. Publishing houses studied include Abingdon, Broadman, Judson, Augsburg, Fortress, Pilgrim, Seabury, and Westminster.

Barnhart, Joe E., and Steven Winzenburg. *Jim and Tammy: Charismatic Intrigue Inside PTL.* Buffalo, NY: Prometheus Books, 1988.

A gossipy review of the 1986-88 "Gospelgate" scandals, which touched TV evangelists such as Jim and Tammy Bakker, Jimmy Swaggart, and Oral Roberts. Chapter 7 is particularly interesting because it details the twelve-year war of words between PTL and the *Charlotte* (Virginia) *Observer.*

Berkman, Dave. "Long Before Falwell: Early Radio and Religion — As Reported by the Nation's Periodical Press." *Journal of Popular Culture* 21, 4 (Spring 1988): 1-11.

This article reviews the reporting, in the periodical press of the 1920s, of religion and radio's "coming together." Initial fears that "listening to religion" would come to replace attendance at religious services gave way by 1924 to accommodation and acceptance of the new media. The press helped to inform both clergy and laity about this new extension of religion into the home.

Betten, Neil. "Catholic Periodicals in Response to Two Divergent Decades." *Journalism Quarterly* 47 (1970): 303-8.

An analysis of major Catholic journals during the 1920s and 1930s shows that those periodicals "neither followed a party line nor were static in their views." They reflected not only the concerns but also the general tendencies of these periods, particularly on economic and social issues. "At the same time, the journals provided different answers to the problems of the day, illustrating the independence of Catholic publications" (p. 308).

Bluem, A. William. *Religious Television Programs: A Study of Relevance.* New York: Hastings House, 1969.

A study based on a "detailed questionnaire which was sent to all TV stations in the U.S.A. in 1966. Stations were asked to provide specific information concerning their religious program activity during the year July 1, 1964 to June 30, 1965, as well as to enter descriptions of their own locally created programs. Over 430 individual stations responded to the survey" (p. 25); the stations are identified on pp. 193-200. Chapters 2 and 3 cover religious television programming in America, 1965-66, together with brief descriptions of syndicated, network, and local programming. The book includes "A Short History of Religious Broadcasting," by William F. Fore (pp. 203-22).

Boyd, Malcolm. *Crisis in Communication: A Christian Examination of the Mass Media.* New York: Doubleday, 1957.

One of the first books to bring a Christian judgment to bear on the general use made of the mass media: radio, TV, movies, and public relations. The author views mass media from the perspective of the age of publicity. Chapter titles include the following: chapter 1, "The Age of Publicity"; chapter 2: "Religious Communication by the Mass Media"; chapter 3: "Point of Contact." The author argues, "It is the difficult task of the Church both to employ the implements and techniques of public relations and publicity in doing its missionary work — and, as a part of its mission in the world, to stand in judgment upon these implements and techniques" (p. 21).

————. "How Does the Secular Press Interpret Religious Movies?" *Religion in Life* 27 (1958): 276-85.

In an appraisal of religious movie reviews in the 1950s, the author concludes, "The press on the one hand accentuates or magnifies existing popular, or mass media, stereotypes; and, on the other hand, creates new stereotypes, sometimes by publicizing new mass media portrayals. Religiosity is rooted in mass culture — and the gentlemen and ladies of the press, in reporting and interpreting mass culture, wield a powerful influence."

Brack, Harold A. "Ernest Fremont Tittle: A Pulpit Critic of the American Social Order." *Quarterly Journal of Speech* 52 (1966): 364-70.

A critique of Tittle's thirty-one-year preaching career at First Methodist Church, Evanston, Illinois. Tittle consistently advocated a theologically grounded critique of the American social order on such issues as war and peace, racism, free speech, patriotism, civil rights, and slum clearance. Twice (1932 and 1940) his effectiveness as an articulate pulpiteer was recognized by the invitation to give the Lyman-Beecher lectures on preaching at Yale University.

Brown, James A. "Selling Airtime for Controversy: NAB Self-Regulation and Father Coughlin." *Journal of Broadcasting* 24 (1980): 199-224.

This article reviews the radio broadcast activities of the controversial priest Charles E. Coughlin, who established a network of stations to carry his addresses in the 1930s. National audiences multiplied until his series was one of the most popular on American radio. However, his strident attacks on President Franklin Roosevelt and on international bankers and his anti-Semitism provoked a storm of protest and demands that he be silenced. It was a ban on Coughlin's broadcasts by the National Association of Broadcasters, not the Roman Catholic hierarchy, that forced Coughlin off the air.

Browne, Benjamin P., ed. *Christian Journalism for Today: A Resource Book for Writers and Editors.* Philadelphia: Judson Press, 1952.

This volume contains forty-one addresses delivered at the Christian Writers and Editors' Conferences, Philadelphia and Green Lake, Wisconsin, 1948-51, organized in six parts: (1) what is it all about? (2) what do you have to say? (3) for whom do you write? (4) how to do the job; (5) from behind the editor's desk; and (6) where to sell it. Written by the leading editors and publishers of religious literature, prominent educators, and successful authors, this collection is a good state-of-the-art view of religious journalism following World War II. It is broadly ecumenical.

Buchstein, Frederick D. "The Role of the News Media in the 'Death of God' Controversy." *Journalism Quarterly* 49 (1972): 79-85.

Buchstein surveys news media coverage of this controversy, which gained widespread attention in 1965-66. He concludes, "The news media fulfilled their traditional responsibilities of collecting and distributing information concerning the ideas and events of this controversy and of acting as a forum for the exchange of comment and criticism" (p. 83). This article contains excerpts of replies received from four Death of God theologians when queried about the controversy.

Buddenbaum, Judith M. "An Analysis of Religion News Coverage in Three Major Newspapers." *Journalism Quarterly* 63 (1986): 600-606.

"This study found there were similarities in the religion news coverage in the *New York Times, Minneapolis Star,* and *Richmond Times-Dispatch* during the summer of 1981. These similarities were, in general, consistent with the findings of previous studies of religion news, which suggest that religion news stories are longer, broader in scope and more issue-oriented than they once were" (p. 605).

Burton, Laurel Arthur. "Close Encounters of a Religious Kind." *Journal of Popular Culture* 17, 3 (Winter 1983): 141-45.

Burton maintains that "the mass media have constructed an amazing message of salvation which fits the American belief system perfectly" (p. 141). All three commercial television networks and the producers of movies promote this religious belief system, which is centered in a shared concern with the doctrines of evil, eschatology, and salvation.

*The Church in the Sky.* New York: Federal Council of Churches of Christ in America, 1938.

A stenographic report of the proceedings commemorating the fifteenth anniversary of national religious radio under the auspices of the Council by eighteen persons prominent in religious radio broadcasting: Ralph Sockman, Norman Vincent Peale, Harry Emerson Fosdick, Daniel A. Poling, David Sarnoff, and others.

Cogley, John. *A Canterbury Tale: Experiences and Reflections, 1916-1976.* New York: Seabury Press, 1976.

The memoirs of a prominent Roman Catholic journalist who "tells of his early years with the Catholic Worker movement and as a journalist with *Today, Commonweal, The New York Times, Center Magazine* and the *National Catholic Reporter*." At the Center for the Study of Democratic Institutions, he directed a study of blacklisting in radio, television, and motion pictures during the McCarthy era (late 1950s). As the first religious news editor of *The New York Times,* he covered the final session of Vatican Council II in Rome. His growing doubts about the future of Roman Catholicism led him to join the Episcopal Church in 1973. This volume recounts Cogley's involvement in significant religious and political events from World War II through the post–Vietnam War era.

*The Community and the Motion Picture: Report of National Conference on Motion Pictures . . . Sept. 24-27, 1929.* [n.p.]: Motion Picture Producers and Distributors of America, 1929; repr. Jerome S. Ozer, Publisher, 1971.

Four recommendations came from this conference at which representatives of many churches and religious and social organizations were represented. One of the recommendations was the "Appointment by the Conference of a Committee to study the use of films in religious education with a view to listing such films as are in existence and crystallizing opinions as to the kind of special pictures needed in their field" (p. 13).

Cornell, George W. "The Evolution of the Religion Beat." In *Reporting Religion: Facts and Faith,* ed. Benjamin J. Hubbard, pp. 20-35. Sonoma, CA: Polebridge Press, 1990.

> This essay documents and substantiates the claim that religion news reporting in the secular press has grown and increased since 1950. The transition from limited to very widespread growth in religion news reporting has been spurred by the rise of the ecumenical movement, the Roman Catholic reforms of Vatican Council II, the civil rights movement, "the upheavals abroad generated by religious passions, the emergence of religious right-wingers into the political arena . . . and the latter-day TV preacher scandals" (p. 21).

Cox, Kenneth. "The FCC, the Constitution, and Religious Broadcast Programming." *George Washington Law Review* 34 (1965/66): 196-218.

> The author maintains "that regulation of broadcasting in the public interest requires — regrettably perhaps — that the Commission concern itself with programming, including that designed to serve the religious needs of the public" (p. 196). FCC Commissioner Cox believes that the Commission must consider programming since it was established to serve the public interest, which includes the expression of religious views. For a contrary view, see the study by Lee Loevinger (listed below).

Day, Dorothy. "Dorothy Day Describes the Launching of *The Catholic Worker* and the Movement Behind It, May, 1933." In *Documents of American Catholic History, Volume 2: 1866-1966,* ed. John Tracy Ellis, pp. 625-29. Wilmington, DE: Michael Glazier, 1987.

> This essay recounts the beginnings of the Catholic Worker's best-known publication.

*The Drive for Decency in Print: Report of the Bishops' Committee Sponsoring the National Organization for Decent Literature.* Huntington, IN: Our Sunday Visitor Press, 1939.

> A lengthy report of the first year's work of the National Organization for Decent Literature, organized by the United States Catholic Bishops. It contains a detailed survey of periodical and brochure publishers and of objectionable materials issued by them. It details plans and strategies, including legal remedies, for local organizations (diocesan level) to combat indecent literature. It documents negotiations with publishers to revise their publications and lists titles of magazines that failed to meet the NODL's standards of decency. It is estimated that in 1938 fifteen million copies of these objectionable publications were reaching a readership of sixty million each month (p. 188). NODL also took its campaign to the nation in a series of four radio broadcasts over the CBS network.

Dugan, George; Caspar H. Hannes; and R. Marshall Stross. *RPRC: A 50-Year Reflection*. New York: Religious Public Relations Council, 1979.

A brief history of the Religious Public Relations Council, an interfaith organization founded in 1929, whose membership is made up of professional public relations persons who work for a religious communion, organization, or agency accredited by its Board of Governors. In 1979 it had an international membership of over seven hundred persons. An important aspect of the RPRC's program has been the discussion and debate among its members of the relationship of the churches to the media. An addendum includes a list of charter members, a roster of RPRC presidents, and brief sketches of public relations work in fourteen denominations.

Duke, Judith S. *Religious Publishing and Communications*. White Plains, NY: Knowledge Industry Publications, 1981.

"This report aims to analyze the structure of the religious communications industry as it is today — the demographic, economic and social trends affecting the industry — and the economics of the industry itself. Second, it intends to analyze trends within the markets for Jewish books, Bibles and general religious books, and to discuss the book club, record, magazine and broadcasting markets. Finally, it will attempt, from an outsider's point of view, to arrive at some conclusions about the direction in which the industry appears to be heading and the challenges it faces in coming years" (p. 2).

Durgnat, Raymond, and Scott Simon. "Six Creeds That Won the Western." *Film Comment* 16 (Sept.-Oct. 1980): 61-70.

Western movies, featuring the universal cowboy, "far from being apolitical and nonhistorical, are myths in the sense of being saturated with ideologies and assumptions" (p. 61). These myths, solidified into creeds, form a national "essence" of political, philosophical, and religious ideologies. The predominant religious ideology is that of the reclusive inner-directed Puritan. "His in-tensity forms a Puritan-like figure with spring-loaded inner awareness and an exterior calm, shunning emotionalism and casual intimacies" (p. 62). Other creeds examined are these: Hobbesian nature (secularized Calvinism); democratic, rural ur-democracy; possessive individualism; social Darwinism (evolutionary, expansionist progress); and populism (small farmer).

Ellens, Jay H. "Program Format in Religious Television: A History and Analysis of Program Format in Nationally Distributed Denominational Religious Television Broadcasting in the United States of America: 1950-1970." Ph.D. dissertation, Wayne State University, 1970.

This study contains "a history and analysis of program format in nationally distributed Protestant denominational religious broadcasting in the United States: 1950-1970." It focuses on the relative significance of seven influential factors in the shaping of program format. Three of these are philosophical: the church's concept of its role in society, the church's communication policy, and the church's broadcasting objectives. Four are not philosophical but sociological, technological, administrative, and economic in character. Transcripts of interviews with seventeen denominational media directors are included.

Elvy, Peter. *Buying Time: The Foundations of the Electronic Church.* Mystic, CT: Twenty-third Publications, 1987.

This study was commissioned by "concerned Christian church, publishing, and industry leaders apprehensive about the advent of electronic religious broadcasting in the United Kingdom and Europe" (blurb). Elvy, a European clergyman and researcher, presents the economic, political, and religious influence the electronic church exercises in the United States. The study helps to document the rise to power and dominance of the Christian broadcasting industry by independent fundamentalist preachers, who in the past forty years have formed political and economic alliances that feature superstar preachers aspiring to be candidates for national office or who plan to influence election campaigns. The study includes basic historical information on the development of religious broadcasting.

Evans, James F. "What the Church Tells Children in Story and Song." *Journalism Quarterly* 44 (1967): 513-19.

"A look at content of lesson books and hymnals used in Presbyterian Sunday schools shows that while they help explain society and the church, they emphasize firm social and religious control."

Fackler, Mark. "A Short History of Evangelical Scholarship in Communication Studies." In *American Evangelicals and the Mass Media: Perspectives on the Relationship Between American Evangelicals and the Mass Media,* ed. Quentin J. Schultze, pp. 357-71. Grand Rapids: Academia Books, Zondervan Publishing House, 1990.

A bibliographic essay on the primary sources for the study of American religious communication from an evangelical perspective.

Fadley, Dean, and Ronald Green. "A Man, A Prophet, A Dream." In *The God Pumpers: Religion in the Electronic Age,* ed. Marshall Fishwick and Ray B. Browne, pp. 75-86. Bowling Green, OH: Bowling Green State University Popular Press, 1987.

An analysis of Martin Luther King, Jr.'s use of rhetoric in his *Letter from Birmingham Jail.* His rhetoric is shown to have been effective because he utilized the technique of shifting from a fact or truth statement, "mediated with a transitional metaphor, and argued from a value stance" (p. 81).

Federal Communications Commission. *Reports,* 2nd series, 54 (1975): 941-51.

Rulemaking, Number RM-2493, December 1974, the so-called "Petition Against God" proposal, which requested "a 'freeze' on all applications by religious 'Bible,' Christian, and other sectarian schools, colleges, and institutes for reserved educational FM and TV channels" (p. 941). The petition, which generated over 700,000 letters of protest in nine months, was mistakenly attributed to Madalyn Murray O'Hair and was erroneously thought to propose a ban on the broadcast of all religious programs. The FCC denied the petition in this Rulemaking issued August 1, 1975.

Ferre, John P. "Denominational Biases in the American Press." *Review of Religious Research* 21 (1979/80): 276-83.

"Because biased religion coverage in the elite press affects the sociopolitical role denominations play in society, a study of the 1977 coverage of denominations in the *New York Times* and the *Washington Post* was conducted. The results show that numerical biases were present: establishment denominations tended to receive inordinate coverage and prominent placement, while evangelical groups were slighted. The numerical biases probably resulted to a large degree from the issues which were reported most often" (p. 276).

Ford, James E. "Battlestar Gallactica and Mormon Theology." *Journal of Popular Culture* 17, 2 (Fall 1983): 83-87.

This article surveys the television program by focusing on Mormon-derived elements of *Battlestar Gallactica.* "These doctrines are generalized and 'philosophized' enough to lose any direct identification with Mormon theology" (p. 87). The public's enthusiastic acceptance of programs solidly grounded in theology suggests that audiences will view substantive programming in prime time.

Fore, William F. "A Short History of Religious Broadcasting." In *Religious Television Programs: A Study of Relevance,* ed. A. William Bluem, pp. 203-11. New York: Hastings House, 1969.

Fore gives specific information on programs as well as summarizing trends.

Forshey, Gerald E. "American Religious and Biblical Spectacular Films, 1932-1973." Ph.D. diss., University of Chicago, 1978.

Forshey examines the cultural significance of spectacular religious and biblical movies — "their conventions, their internal structure, the cultural influences which shaped them, and how the public received them — in order to assess their importance and to understand how popular culture uses religion" (pp. 1-2). Problems treated in these movies include science and religion, the difficulties in sustaining national purpose, and theological ethics (duty preferable to pleasure). These problems continue to trouble Americans, but they are now treated in other ways that are less mythical and closer to everyday experience.

Fox, Matthew T. *Religion USA: An Inquiry into Religion and Culture by Way of TIME Magazine.* Dubuque, IA: Listening Press, 1971.

A phenomenologically and pastorally oriented approach, utilizing religion coverage in *Time* magazine. All issues for the year 1958 were included as primary data. A dialectical conclusion is researched, namely, "that religion is or can be anywhere and everywhere in a culture — either positively (living religion . . .) or negatively (dying religion) and that the latter can pose as religion anywhere and everywhere within a culture under either of its two guises, manipulated or hypocritical religion" (p. 399). This is one of the most extensive studies ever undertaken to analyze the religion content of an American mass circulation secular publication.

France, Inez. "Radio and Television Stations Owned by Religious Bodies." *Journalism Quarterly* 32 (1955): 356, 385.

France reports that "there are at least 22 stations, including the five new ones, owned by religious bodies today."

Frankl, Razelle. *Televangelism: The Marketing of Popular Religion.* Carbondale: Southern Illinois University Press, 1987.

"This study examines the general sociological development of the electric church as a social institution (ideal type), the nature of its relationships with other institutions, its political goals, and the influence of television on its messages" (p. 9). This study has two parts: (1) a historical analysis of urban revivalism pioneered by Charles G. Finney, Dwight L. Moody, and Billy Sunday, who developed a new institution to be modified and transformed by television, and (2) the results of content analysis of religious television programs. Frankl concludes that the televangelists are employing broadcasting "as a means of social control, of transmitting their own ideology" (p. 154). This study represents one of the few attempts to trace the roots of modern televangelism to nineteenth-century urban revivalism.

Goethals, Gregor T. *The Electronic Golden Calf: Images, Religion and the Making of Meaning.* Cambridge, MA: Cowley Publications, 1990.

Focusing on the role of images in the communication of religious meanings, this study selects from "certain historical periods illustrations which show both the impulse to construct world views in visual terms and the fragility of such construction" (p. 1). This historical background is used to help analyze and explain the presence of visual symbols on American television and in art that are used to convey religious meanings. Images, long eschewed by the church, satisfy a deep aesthetic and sacramental need to communicate and have been taken over by the secular culture. Goethals helps us understand this process both historically and contemporaneously, explaining how the mass media, particularly television, possess a capacity to give material form to invisible faith. As Goethals explains, "This book is an attempt to understand the transformation and dispersal of the sacramental functions of images in a secular and pluralistic society" (p. 1).

Goethals, Gregor T. "Religious Communication and Popular Piety." *Journal of Communication* 35, 1 (Winter 1985): 149-56.

 Popular piety is being communicated by persuasive evangelical preachers who emphasize the conversion experience but who also, ironically, rely upon image and object to convey grace, a means vehemently rejected by historic Protestantism. A complementary expression of popular piety is "popular" or "civic" religion. Sports events, the nightly news, soap operas, presidential press conferences, etc. are ritualistic forms of communication that blend elements from political and denominational sources. The former seeks to convert, the latter to confirm time-honored values.

Gottlieb, Bob, and Peter Wiley. "Static in Zion." *Columbia Journalism Review* 18 (1979): 59-62.

 Efforts by Mormon media producers to reach the eighteen-to-thirty-four-year-old audience have resulted in intervention and revision of programming by church officials. Beyond reporting these controversies, this article provides a succinct sketch of the Mormon media organizations, which include interests in radio, television, film production, broadcast consulting, computer services, public relations, and publishing.

Greif, Edward L. "Communications: The New Ministry." In *Crisis in the Church: Essays in Honor of Truman B. Douglass,* ed. Everett C. Parker, pp. 85-95. Philadelphia: Pilgrim Press, 1968.

 A layman in public relations work challenges the church to make a new commitment to mass communication and urges it "to train theologians to develop the basis for a ministry of communications, not only to see how the new technologies apply to the church, but for the statement of the moral and legal codes which must adhere to the control of the new media, both by secular groups and the church" (p. 94).

Hamlin, Fred. *S. Parkes Cadman: Pioneer Radio Minister.* New York: Harper, 1930.

Chapter 10 of this popularly written biography outlines Cadman's use of radio to broadcast Sunday afternoon YMCA meetings in Brooklyn, New York. These grew in 1927 to become regularly broadcast Sunday afternoon services from the Cathedral Studio of the National Broadcasting Company, New York City, under the auspices of the Federal Council of the Churches of Christ in America. Together with Harry Emerson Fosdick, Cadman was one of the first ministers to broadcast over a national radio network.

Harding, Susan. "The World of the Born-Again Telescandals." *Michigan Quarterly Review* 27 (1988): 525-40.

Reflecting on Ted Koppel's post-Swaggart special reports on televangelism, "The Billion Dollar Pie," aired in May 1988, Harding discusses the Christian identity industries: Jerry Falwell's empire, Jim and Tammy Faye Bakker's empire, and the PTL scandal. Harding views these developments as a struggle on the part of aging evangelists to retain/secure economic control of a Christian identity industry and the opening of a new world where the old fundamentalist, pentecostal, evangelical divisions are giving way to "preposterous categorical hodgepodges and antic criss-crossings of social boundaries" (p. 539). In this new configuration churches become businesses, faith-healers build ultramodern hospitals, creationism calls itself a science, and fictions come true.

Harrell, David E. *Oral Roberts: An American Life.* Bloomington: Indiana University Press, 1985.

Based on extensive use of the Oral Roberts archives and on interviews with Roberts and many of his associates, this study comes close to being an authorized biography with rich detail concerning his life. Harrell believes that "no one had done more to bring the pentecostal message to respectability and visibility in America" (p. 494). Harrell also asserts that "Roberts has influenced the course of modern Christianity as profoundly as any American religious leader" (p. vii) and that one way in which he has done this stems from his innovative use of the media. Because it covers every facet of Roberts's life, this biography is valuable for placing his radio, television, and publishing efforts into the larger context of his ministry. The "Bibliographical Essay" (pp. 499-504) discusses both primary and secondary sources.

Hart, James D. "Platitudes of Piety: Religion and the Popular Modern Novel." *American Quarterly* 6 (1954): 311-22.

Originally condemned as immoral, novels did not gain respectability until nineteenth-century authors began to fill them with piety and preachment. Beginning with the Christian social fiction of Charles Sheldon and others, the religious novel gained huge popularity. By the 1950s, preachment had given way to a happy fusing of psychiatry and theology that produced a dramatic tale of spiritual struggle that, when read by believers, reinforced their piety and, for the alienated or strayed, provided the "relish of salvation."

Hart, Roderick P.; Kathleen J. Turner; and Ralph E. Knupp. "Religion and the Rhetoric of Mass Media." *Review of Religious Research* 21 (1979/80): 256-75.

"Using content-analytic procedures, the authors investigate how American religion has been defined, described, and given 'social reality' via mass communication. Six hundred and forty-eight religion sections appearing in *Time* magazine between 1947 and 1976 were analyzed in several ways. Statistical treatment of the data revealed that (1) religion is depicted as a conflict-ridden human enterprise, (2) denominational stereotypes and geographical biases affect media coverage of religion, and (3) media-based portrayals of religion differ sharply from demographic and sociological facts. Five conventional explanations of these data are discussed, but a sixth — a rhetorical understanding of mass communication activities — is preferred" (p. 256).

Hefley, J. Theodore. "Freedom Upheld: The Civil Liberties Stance of the *Christian Century* Between the Wars." *Church History* 37 (1968): 174-94.

Judged by *Newsweek* magazine in 1947 to be "the most important organ of Protestant opinion in the world today," the *Christian Century* rose to this eminence under the editorship of Charles Clayton Morrison, who consistently executed a pro–civil rights policy, especially noteworthy during his tenure, 1908 to 1947, an era dominated by the big red scare (communism), the rise of fascism, and the suppression of rights for blacks and other minorities. "The *Century*'s tone during the twenties and thirties was consistently critical of America in terms of potential unfulfilled; but at the same time it was optimistic in terms of the country's vitality and historic determination to make a more socially and economically just democracy" (p. 194).

Hess, J. Daniel. "The Religious Journals' Image of the Mass Media." *Journalism Quarterly* 41 (1964): 106-8.

After analyzing over five hundred references in the 1962 issues of four prominent religious journals, the author concludes that "the charges that religious journals are not ardent admirers and supporters of the mass media, seem not altogether unfounded."

Hynds, Ernest C. "Large Daily Newspapers Have Improved Coverage of Religion." *Journalism Quarterly* 64 (1987): 444-48.

Coverage of religion in large newspapers in the United States (with circulations of 100,000 or more) appears to be growing both in quantity and in quality, based on a comparison with a similar study by the same author ten years previously (p. 448). Most of the newspapers select and use religion throughout the paper and periodically run a page or section of religious news.

————. "News Coverage of Religion Is Growing." *Editor & Publisher* 108, 42 (18 Oct. 1975): 15, 38.

"It appears that daily newspapers today are continuing a trend, developed gradually over 25 years, of expanding their coverage of religion" (p. 38). Analysis, largely statistical, is summarized under five headings: space allocations, types of coverage, personnel, growing interest, and readership.

Inbody, Tyron, ed. *Changing Channels: The Church and the Television Revolution.* Dayton, OH: Whaleprints, 1990.

A collection of eight essays, most by faculty members of United Theological Seminary, which challenge Catholic, Orthodox, Anglican, mainstream Protestant, and some evangelicals to consider ways in which they can use electronic communications to proclaim the faith. Professors of church history, Bible, theology, religious education, and missiology address the challenge from their respective disciplines. Two other authors evaluate the place of television in the church's communication and the use of television in interpretive communities. A foreword by Martin E. Marty reflects on the response of theological education to the television revolution, while Gregor Goethals suggests in an afterword that "seminaries may use their resources to create alternative symbols of faith and to offer a critique of cultural values and ideologies." A four-page bibliography of further readings is included.

Jacobs, Hayes B. "Oral Roberts: High Priest of Faith Healing." *Harper's* 224 (February 1962): 37-43.

A freelance journalist's portrait of Oral Roberts and his healing ministry, based partially on interviews with the evangelist, who at the time had established a national reputation for his crusades and radio-television ministry. Jacobs is critical of Roberts's fund-raising techniques and of his critical attitudes toward the press.

Jeansonne, Glen. "Religious Bigotry and the Press: The Treatment of Gerald L. K. Smith." In *Reporting Religion: Facts and Faith,* ed. Benjamin J. Hubbard, pp. 177-91. Sonoma, CA: Polebridge Press, 1990.

Gerald L. K. Smith (1898-1976) was a "depression-era religious leader who won millions of followers through media coverage" of his demagogic appeals (pp. 177-78). Early attempts by Jews and leftists, whom Smith regularly attacked, to disrupt his meetings and curb his activities failed. A new strategy of silence, of persuading the press to ignore Smith, was successful. By the late

1940s the blackout had curtailed Smith's influence and hate-mongering. Jeansonne concludes that for the future, the activities of threatening figures "should be described in their complexity, and the potential dangers they pose should be discussed realistically" (p. 190).

Johnstone, Ronald L. "Who Listens to Religious Radio Broadcasts Anymore?" *Journal of Broadcasting* 16 (1971/72): 91-102.

Johnstone reports the results of a "national survey conducted in 1970 by the Lutheran Council in the U.S.A. concerning the 'image of Lutheranism'" (p. 91). It found that "religious radio broadcasting tends to reach those who have already been reached in the sense of already having formal association with religious institutions" (p. 101). *The Lutheran Hour* radio program was congruent with this general finding and consequently was found to serve primarily a reinforcement function.

Keyser, Lester J., and Barbara Keyser. *Hollywood and the Catholic Church: The Image of Roman Catholicism in American Movies.* Chicago: Loyola University Press, 1984.

This study "surveys the American movies from 1916 to the present which center on Catholic issues or topics. The authors have selected movies from different genres in order to analyze how Hollywood has portrayed Catholic clergy, religious, and laity, ethnic immigrants, saints and sinners, as well as the patriotic and sexual attitudes of Catholics" (blurb). "Church and cinema co-exist, commingle, and frequently compete in modern life" (p. xii). The authors speak about the tension between secular entertainment and spiritual enlightenment.

Kinkead, Joyce. "The Western Sermons of Harold Bell Wright." *Journal of American Culture* 7, 3 (Fall 1984): 85-87.

Wright wrote nineteen best-selling novels, most of them composed after he moved to California and after he resigned the ministry to form the lucrative Book Supply Company. Strongly flavored with a social gospel motif, "thematically and structurally in these western novels Wright is clearly the preacher" (p. 87).

Lacey, Linda J. "The Electronic Church: An FCC Established Institution?" *Federal Communications Law Journal* 31 (1978): 235-75.

A detailed examination of the legal questions posed by religious broadcasts and the role of the Federal Communications Commission's regulatory policies as related to the first amendment of the U.S. Constitution. "It concludes that a strong argument can be made that the FCC's actions do constitute establishment clause violations, and that it is time for the Commission and interested onlookers to devote serious thought and attention to the 'Electric Church' and its first amendment implications" (p. 236).

Larson, Cedric. "Religious Freedom as a Theme of the Voice of America." *Journalism Quarterly* 29 (1952): 187-93.

"An agency of the United States government, the Voice of America (VOA), is carried in 46 languages to areas having a potential audience of 300 million" (p. 187). Although a secular organization, VOA has consistently emphasized in its programming freedom of religion and the spiritual and moral values on which American democracy is founded.

Larson, Robert E. "An Accreditation Program for Contact Teleministries USA." D.Min. diss., Lancaster Theological Seminary, 1986.

This study "addresses the problem of maintaining uniform standards of identity and service delivery within a national network of ministries designed to provide telephone help to persons in distress." It is related entirely to the program and situation of Contact Teleministries USA, a national organization that accredits some one hundred centers of teleministry.

Loevinger, Lee. "Religious Liberty and Broadcasting." *George Washington Law Review* 33 (1964/65): 631-59.

"Communications attorneys have long questioned the authority of the Federal Communications Commission to fix what it considers desirable elements of programming; they claim it is violative of the first amendment. Here, a member of the Commission itself reviews the law and suggests, "that it may be unconstitutional for the FCC to consider any religious programming proposals in awarding licenses" (p. 631). For a contrary view, see the study by Kenneth Cox (listed above). A condensed version of this article appeared as "Broadcasting and Religious Liberty" in the *Journal of Broadcasting* 9 (1964/65): 3-23.

Marty, Martin E. *The Improper Opinion: Mass Media and the Christian Faith.* Westminster Studies in Christian Communication. Philadelphia: Westminster Press, 1967.

Marty proposes that Christianity could best communicate through mass media by masking its message. Mass media direct messages that are widely acceptable, non-threatening to a mass audience, that are proper opinions. Protestant Christianity can communicate authentically when it presents the gospel by portraying lives and events in which the invitatory power of sacrifice and service are made clear. This stumbling block or scandal is the central message, the improper opinion that the church and Christians are challenged to proclaim.

————, et al. *The Religious Press in America*. New York: Holt, Rinehart and Winston, 1963.

    A sustained analysis of the religious press (Protestant, Catholic, and Jewish), which at the time when this volume was written had a total circulation of fifty million. The contributors provide historical perspective for their branches of American religious journalism and also provide both descriptive material and prescriptive analysis. "They are unanimous in criticizing the way in which key issues of religious concern are often either ignored or made to appear trivial" (p. viii). Written before television or the advent of the computer, these studies reflect a previous era, but to their credit, they incorporate a pluralistic consciousness that is now taken for granted.

Martz, Larry, and Ginny Carroll. *Ministry of Greed: The Inside Story of the Televangelists and Their Holy Wars*. New York: Weidenfeld & Nicholson, 1988.

    A detailed account of the scandals that involved prominent televangelists in the late 1980s, especially as focused in the struggles surrounding control of the PTL empire. The study is based largely on files and information gathered by *Newsweek* magazine. This was one of the top news stories in 1987. As the authors point out, the battle between the evangelists was played out in the press and "the warring evangelists used Ted Koppel, CNN's Larry King, and other television shows as gun platforms to wage their battle." They conclude by observing that "religious broadcasting of some sort will not only survive but almost surely grow as a cultural force" (p. 244).

Maynard, Edwin H. *Keeping Up With a Revolution: The Story of United Methodist Communications*. Nashville: United Methodist Communications, 1990.

    This volume was written and published to celebrate the fiftieth anniversary of institutional communication work in a major Protestant denomination. From the beginning, the communication agencies of the church provided a news reporting function, quickly developed training in public relations to support a corp of public relations specialists, and later assumed the responsibility for promoting denominational programs. These functions have been supported by agencies issuing filmstrips, radio and television programming, and other productions. Operating on limited budgets and always struggling with the tension between news reporting and denominational promotion, the church has worked energetically and intensively to keep pace with developments in the media, ranging from print communication to communication by satellite and computer.

McChesney, Robert W. "Crusade Against Mammon: Father Harney, WLWL and the Debate Over Radio in the 1930s." *Journalism History* 14 (1987): 118-30.
    In May 1934, the U.S. Senate defeated the Wagner-Hatfield amend-

ment, which would have reformed the oligopolistic and commercially sub-sidized nature of American broadcasting by, among other provisions, requiring the FCC to allocate a minimum of twenty-five percent of the channels to nonprofit and educational broadcasters. "By all accounts, the person most responsible for getting the Wagner-Hatfield amendment to the floor of the Senate and, indeed, to near passage was the Very Reverend John B. Harney, the superior general of the Missionary Society of St. Paul the Apostle" (p. 118). This case confirms an important precedent for media reformers interested in a more democratic press, especially in reference to educational and nonprofit groups.

Miller, Robert Moats. *Harry Emerson Fosdick: Preacher, Pastor, Prophet.* New York: Oxford University Press, 1985.

A highly detailed, largely sympathetic biography of "the era's leading homiletician." Chapter 20, "The Dean of All Ministers of the Air: Radio's 'National Vespers Hour' Reaches Millions" (pp. 379-88), recounts Fosdick's radio ministry from 1924 through 1946. Fosdick was unable to completely shake off his hold on the past and open himself to the future when it came to acceptance of the theatre in relation to his own disposition and in relation to his childhood standards of bourgeois nineteenth-century culture. "Confirm-ing his cries to the twenties alone one hears him assert that the American theater is in a 'deplorable condition,' having largely 'fallen into the hands of commercial panders who fed the populace on rottenness'" (pp. 436-37). Fosdick also had his reservations about movies, dancing, and much contem-porary literature (pp. 437-40).

Miller, Spencer. "Radio and Religion." *Annals of the American Academy of Political and Social Science* 177 (January 1935): 135-40.

This essay recounts the early history of religious broadcasting, the poli-cies of the National Broadcasting Company and the Columbia Broadcasting System, and explains their ecumenical nature in involving Protestants, Cath-olics, and Jews. It includes an interview of Rev. Edwin Van Etten, rector of Calvary Episcopal Church in Pittsburgh — site of the first religious broadcast. The author concludes, "Radio is here to stay — a part of the matrix of our complex civilization."

Montgomery, Edrene S. "Bruce Barton's *The Man Nobody Knows:* A Popular Advertising Illusion." *Journal of Popular Culture* 19, 3 (Winter 1985): 21-34.

Montgomery places Barton's best-seller (over one million copies) in the category of a "secularized portrait of Christ, which reinforced the culturally sacred values of economic activity, success and material gain, [and which] satisfied the spiritual needs of his generation" (p. 28). Barton, using the techniques of advertising, succeeded in projecting an image of Jesus as real that was, in fact, fictional. Barton's book was serialized, translated into many languages, and issued as a motion picture.

Niebuhr, Reinhold. "Introduction." In *Responsibility in Mass Communication,* pp. xi-xxiii. New York: Harper, 1957.

Niebuhr discusses the norms of conduct/duty as contrasted with the problem of grace, arguing that "secularized grace" is best manifested in the communication industry through the grace of imagination. "In the communications industry, in which news and entertainment are variously compounded, imagination is necessary in interpreting the news, and even more in projecting the various art forms. . . . Here the Church must modestly realize and confess that it is not by moral censoriousness but by inspiring the imagination and by gratefully acknowledging the greatness of a creative imagination, wherever manifested, that it best serves the spiritual values in a technical culture" (p. xxi).

Niebuhr, Richard R. *Experiential Religion.* New York: Harper & Row, 1972.

In the foreword (pp. xii-xiii), Niebuhr uses the analogy of the "radial man," one who is shaped by listening to the radio. "But what is clear is that the radio listener lives in a radial world of energy, and the device itself is but one of the instruments that are transforming him into, and reminding him that he is, a being for whom immediate reality is power: power driving and moving him, distracting and destroying him, healing and shaping him. He is a radial man in a radial world" (p. xiii). The radio analogy is originally from Rudolf Bultmann, *Kerygma and Myth* (New York: Harper Torchbook, 1961), p. 5. Today's "listener symbolizes the modern human situation Christianly as well as scientifically understood" (p. xiv).

Ogles, Robert M., and Herbert H. Howard. "Father Coughlin in the Periodical Press." *Journalism Quarterly* 61 (1984): 280-86, 363.

The controversial "radio priest" Father Charles Coughlin became during the 1930s "one of the most influential individuals ever to use the mass media." An analysis of news coverage in the periodical press about Father Coughlin during the period 1931-1942 reveals that selected representative journals of wide appeal published negative assessments of him. Themes of pro-Nazism, pro-Facism, demagoguery, and anti-Semitism, attributed to Coughlin, are analyzed and summarized. Because of changes in the media and in American society, "it would be almost impossible for a person to attain a mass audience proportional to Coughlin's in today's fragmented broadcast marketplace" (p. 363).

Orbison, Charley. " 'Fighting Bob Shuler': Early Radio Crusader." *Journal of Broadcasting* 21 (1977): 459-72.

Orbison reviews the case of the Reverend Bob Shuler, crusading Los Angeles Methodist pastor, who owned and operated a radio station from 1926 to 1931. Shuler's relentless crusading against corruption in the city provoked his enemies into contesting renewal of the station's license in 1930. The FCC revoked the station's license, a decision upheld by the Supreme Court. The Shuler case was the first to identify the authority of the Federal Radio Commission to consider past program performance at renewal time, "to deal directly with the constitutional issue of freedom of speech over the air and one of the first to raise the issue of deprivation of property without due process of law" (p. 459).

Ostling, Richard N. "Evangelical Publishing and Broadcasting." In *Evangelicalism and Modern America*, ed. George Marsden, pp. 46-55. Grand Rapids: Eerdmans, 1984.

Ostling identifies the communication media as being the core of evangelicalism's success in putting together a network of denominational and parachurch agencies to promote their beliefs and programs. He contrasts the approach of mainline Protestant denominations with that of the evangelicals concerning use of radio and television in particular. This essay provides basic information on the founding and purposes of parachurch media groups.

————. "Reporting Religion: The Religion Newswriters Association." *Theology Today* 31 (1974): 236-42.

A brief history of developments and controversies in the Religion Newswriters Association since its founding in May 1949. As the association entered its second quarter-century, the author identified three trends in secular press coverage of religion: (1) independence — taking an independent, critical stance toward the organizations and personalities covered; (2) investigation — reporters are devoting more effort to the art of investigation; and (3) interpretation — newspaper people are likely to offer opinions on the events, organizations, and personalities they are covering.

————. *Secrecy in the Church: A Reporter's Case for the Christian Right to Know.* New York: Harper & Row, 1974.

Ostling, himself a journalist, examines the Roman Catholic Church practice of maintaining secrecy about ecclesiastical matters, particularly by withholding information. This tradition, as known in modern times, "started, perhaps, with the discovery of the printing press and the beginnings of mass culture" (p. 79) and reached its apex in 1864 with the promulgation of the

*Syllabus of Errors.* Beginning with Pope Pius XII, the church has moved toward a policy of responsible exchange of freely held and expressed opinion. Ostling, in a brief chapter, also examines secrecy in Protestant churches.

Parker, Everett C. "Big Business in Religious Radio." *The Chicago Theological Seminary Register* 34 (1944): 21-24.

   Parker estimates that the annual contributions to commercial radio religious programs in 1943 was $200,000,000, most of it "contributed directly to the backers of the hundreds of religious programs which buy time and which seek funds for their work, either by appeals over the air or by other means." In view of free time provided by the major radio networks, Parker questions the validity of indiscriminate giving and advocates contributing to responsible religious bodies and educational institutions that can produce quality programming. Appended to the article are recommendations for religious broadcasting adopted by the Religious Work-Study Group Institute for Education by Radio in 1942.

Paulson, Steven K. "Printed Advertisements as Indicators of Christian Institutional Secularization." *Review of Religious Research* 19 (1977/78): 78-83.

   "The purpose of this paper is to demonstrate the use of commercial advertisements in religious publications[;] unobtrusive measures of American Christian institutional secularization are reviewed and advertisements found in major Christian publications are analyzed in terms of their economic, administrative and religious claims for the period 1921-1971. The trend, as partially suggested in other literature, is from predominately religious to predominately economic and administrative" (p. 78).

Peters, Charles C. *Motion Pictures and the Standards of Morality.* New York: Arno Press, 1970.

   One of a series of twelve Payne Fund studies on motion pictures and youth employing sociological and psychological methodology. Peters undertook to compare the content of motion pictures with the accepted standards of American morality in the 1930s. Using a wide variety of individuals, he devised rating scales measuring reactions to the following: aggressiveness of women in lovemaking, kissing, democratic attitudes and practices, and the treatment of children by parents. This study is distinguished as a scientific attempt to measure the social and moral content of movies at a time when American religious communities were raising major concerns about the influence of motion pictures, especially as they affected youth.

Peterson, Richard G. "Electric Sisters." In *The God Pumpers: Religion in the Electronic Age,* ed. Marshall Fishwick and Ray B. Browne. Bowling Green, OH: Bowling Green State University Popular Press, 1987.

Thumbnail sketches of women televangelists of conservative Protestantism, who either have or have had their own ministries or who are part of a
husband-and-wife team. The biographical sketches range from Aimee Semple
McPherson (1890-1944) to Anne Giminez and Beverly LaHaye.

————. "Stained Glass Television: A Female Evangelist Joins the Electronic
Church." *Journal of Popular Culture* 19, 4 (Spring 1986): 95-105.

This article discusses the rise of Terry Cole-Whittaker as founder of the
Science of Mind International Church and media personality whose ministry
is centered in southern California. Peterson interprets Cole-Whittaker's success
in terms of David Riesman's concept of "privatization": a quasi-obsession with
personal achievement and self-fulfillment. Her message stresses personal responsibility and managing one's own life.

Peterson, Theodore. "*Playboy* and the Preachers." *Columbia Journalism Review* 5
(Spring 1966): 32-35.

Peterson reflects particularly on the twenty-four installments of *Playboy*
magazine written by founder Hugh Hefner to explain his philosophy and sexual
attitudes, which initiated a dialogue, at various levels, between Hefner and
clergy and laity. The dialogue included a radio show, direct mailings to clergy,
and exchanges between Hefner and Harvard theologian Harvey Cox. Peterson
finds that the religious press treated Hefner more charitably than the secular
press.

Pointer, Michael. "Good Gods and Bad: From DeMille to Kubrick." *American
Film* 1, 1 (September 1976): 60-64.

Pointer views Hollywood-produced religious films as primarily commercial ventures designed to entertain the masses. The cinema has largely avoided
depicting God on the screen, but when it has, the topic has been kept at arm's
length and has been treated superficially. "Despite the occasional uplifting
experience, the cinema is too transient and ephemeral a medium to advance
any particular religious faith. The durability of the printed word, with its ease
of repeated reference, and the need for participation would make the film a
poor competitor in any systematized presentation of religion" (p. 63).

Powers, Mary L. "The Contribution of American Catholic Commercial Publishers, 1930-1942." Ph.D. diss., University of Chicago, 1945.

Thirteen publishers, each identified as Catholic or as "one whose output,
for the most part, treated of Catholic subjects and/or general subjects from a
Catholic viewpoint," are included. A list of nearly 2,000 titles issued by these
firms over the thirteen-year period were studied. These titles were classified
according to the Lynn scheme, with the result that religion and theology

predominate as subject matter. Qualitatively, criteria of excellence revealed "the superiority of the general publishers over the Catholic publishers in the production of effective and successful Catholic literature." A digest of this thesis was published as "Catholic Commercial Publishing in the United States," *Catholic Library World,* April-May 1946.

Real, Michael R. "Trends in Structure and Policy in the American Catholic Press." *Journalism Quarterly* 52 (1975): 265-71.

This article gives a brief historical sketch of the Catholic press in America down to 1960, when its circulation had grown to 26 million. During the sixties, a professionally trained press reflected a more libertarian spirit, only to come under criticism and more assertive control by the church hierarchy by the end of the decade. Generally, however, "the Catholic newspaper press has tended to follow its secular counterparts in theoretically explaining its policy as that of a free press with libertarian roots but concretely organizing its structure as one of hierarchical economic institutions with authoritarian roots" (p. 271).

Sandoval, Moises. "All We, Like Sheep." *Columbia Journalism Review* 18, 1 (May-June 1979): 44-47.

A critical assessment of the press coverage given Pope John Paul II at the Third Hemispheric Conference of Latin American bishops in Puebla, Mexico, where the pope addressed the question of liberation. The *New York Times* interpreted the pope's statements as being critical of liberation theology, a position that other papers adopted but that has since proven to be misleading and insubstantial. Sandoval is critical of the secular press for bungling religious news coverage, stating that "an American secular press apparently finds it difficult to credit the power that faith wields around the world" (p. 47).

Schramm, Wilbur. *Responsibility in Mass Communication.* New York: Harper, 1957.

"This book is one of a series on ethics and economic life originated by a study committee of the Federal Council of Churches subsequently merged in the National Council of Churches." It includes historical background from the invention of printing through the power press, telegraph, movies, radio, and television. It discusses the four major concepts of communication: authoritarian, totalitarian, libertarian, and social responsibility.

Schultze, Quentin J. "Evangelical Radio and the Rise of the Electronic Church, 1921-1948." *Journal of Broadcasting and Electronic Media* 32 (Summer 1988): 289-306.

"Evangelicals in the U.S. used radio extensively between the wars to preach their old-fashioned gospel and to enhance their social status in the expanding industrial nation. They were among the earliest station owners and operators and, despite restrictive network and regulatory policies, built audiences through creative and entertaining programming. National radio preachers such as Charles Fuller and Walter Maier became symbols of the rising influence and growing public acceptability of twentieth century American evangelicalism. They proved that evangelical broadcasting was commercially viable, setting the scene for the rise of the electronic church on U.S. television" (abstract).

————. "The Wireless Gospel: The Story of Evangelical Radio Puts Televangelism into Perspective." *Christianity Today* 32 (January 1988): 18-23.

Evangelicals were among the first to utilize radio as a means of communicating their programs and beliefs to a mass audience. Schultze sketches some of the early history of the medium, showing that the basic methods and personality types of televangelism now used were originally developed sixty years ago.

Sellers, James E. *The Outsider and the Word of God: A Study in Christian Communication.* New York: Abingdon Press, 1961.

"It is the task of the minister and the Christian educator to examine the means of religious communication with the 'outsider,' particularly the utilization of mass media, such as film, print, radio and television, and discussion. Dr. Sellers discusses at length the communicative techniques evolved by the mass media, emphasizing their limits and potential for communicating the word of God to the 'outsider'" (blurb). Theologically, Sellers relates communication to the thought of Søren Kierkegaard and Paul Tillich in particular.

————. "Religious Journalism in Theological Seminaries." *Journalism Quarterly* 35 (1958): 464-68.

This article provides a summary of a survey on training for religious journalism in sixty theological seminaries and forty-eight schools and departments of journalism in universities and colleges. Journalism is defined broadly to include course offerings in public relations, radio, and television as well as journalism per se.

Smith, Robert R. "Broadcasting and Religious Freedom." *Journal of Broadcasting* 13 (1968/69): 1-12.

Smith argues that "the Commission's [FCC's] past practices, based upon religious liberty and market community rather than religious freedom and interest community, are not adequate to solve the problems confronted by the broadcaster in his current religious programming" (p. 5). Smith proposes an alternative approach that accounts for new impulses in religion and society which emphasize new understandings of community, religious freedom, and commitment. This article was written as a response to Lee Loevinger's "Religious Liberty and Broadcasting" (listed above).

Sonenschein, David. "Sharing the Good News: The Evangelical Tract." *Journal of American Culture* 5, 1 (Spring 1982): 107-21.

A descriptive report of tract "publishers active today who responded to a brief questionnaire [and who] have been in the business for some years. . . . The total number of titles given by all the producers shows over 4,000 with total printings well into the billions" (p. 107). Authorship, the ideology of evangelism, visuals/graphics, publications for children, and means of distribution are all discussed. The report is well documented with twenty-six bibliographic notes.

Stitzinger, Michael F. "Evangelical Religious Publishing: An Examination, Analysis, and Comparison of Selected Publishing of Evangelical Materials." Master's thesis, University of Chicago, 1984.

Stitzinger investigates key factors that led to the success of evangelical publishing during the sixties and seventies. Thirty-four publishers of evangelical materials were queried, via a questionnaire-survey, about publishing trends. The data and publishing opinions concerning success are summarized and discussed. The development of evangelical publishing over two decades is examined, and consideration is given to sales and output figures for religious publishing as a whole. Finally, the situations of evangelical and general trade houses that produce evangelical religious titles are analyzed.

*Symposium on the Contemporary Catholic Book Trade.* Washington, DC: Catholic University of America, 1952-53.

These transcriptions from tapes of presentations and discussions held at two national meetings of Catholic booksellers, publishers, and librarians provide a snapshot view of challenges facing these professions/trades during the era that saw the rise of paperback publishing, the impact of television, and the need to define/identify the role of sectarian publishing.

Thaman, Mary P. *Manners and Morals of the 1920's: A Survey of the Religious Press.* New York: Bookman Associates, 1954(?).

Thaman analyzes the opinions contained in fifteen periodicals of the period representing the Baptist, Roman Catholic, Methodist, Jewish, Lutheran, and Unitarian religious press. Six thousand five hundred issues of these journals, which are officially recognized representatives of their respective religious denominations, were examined to produce chapters commenting on the automobile, sports, dancing, fashions and fads, the cinema, crime, marriage, birth control, and divorce. This study reveals "that the religious editors and spokesmen were keenly alerted to the shiftings in the contemporary scene, and in their journals have reconstructed for future generations a picture of their day" (p. 167).

Tweedie, Stephen W. "Viewing the Bible Belt." *Journal of Popular Culture* 11 (1978): 865-76.
    Contending that previous studies relying on interviews and church membership and attendance records are inadequate methods for defining the Bible Belt, Tweedie uses television audience estimates for popular evangelical, fundamentalist religious programs as a more reliable indicator. "The Baptist South certainly is a major part of this Bible Belt, but areas of strength also include parts of the Methodist dominated Midwest as well as portions of the predominantly Lutheran Dakotas" (p. 875). Tables, diagrams, and statistics are included.

Van Driel, Barend, and James T. Richardson. "Print Media Coverage of New Religious Movements: A Longitudinal Study." *Journal of Communication* 38, 2 (Summer 1988): 37-61.
    Four newspapers and three newsweeklies during the period May 1972 to May 1984 were analyzed for their coverage of new religious movements (NRMs). During this period NRMs were "placed on the societal agenda as serious social problems . . . and have been portrayed as a less than integral part of U.S. society, as not really belonging" (pp. 55, 58). The mass media are seen in this study as being an agency of social control, strongly influencing the various religious parties involved.

Vatican Council II. "Decree on the Instruments of Social Communication *(Inter Mirifica)*." In *The Documents of Vatican II,* ed. Walter M. Abbott, pp. 317-35. New York: Herder and Herder; Association Press, 1966.
    This decree asserts the church's claim "as a birthright [to] the use and possession of all instruments of this kind [of social communication]," directing that both clergy and laity be "trained to bring the necessary skills to the apostolic use of these instruments." While not a very progressive or visionary statement, this decree is significant since it is the first time a general council of the Catholic Church addressed itself to the problem of communication.

Voskuil, Dennis N. "The Power of the Air: Evangelicals and the Rise of Religious Broadcasting." In *American Evangelicals and the Mass Media: Perspectives on the Relationship Between American Evangelicals and the Mass Media,* ed. Quentin J. Schultze, pp. 69-95. Grand Rapids: Academie Books, Zondervan Publishing House, 1990.

This essay outlines the development of religious radio broadcasting by Protestant evangelicals from the 1920s until the late 1970s, when, expanding into television, they came to dominate broadcasting and usher in the era of the electronic church. Voskuil reviews the formation of the National Religious Broadcasters, the conflict between the Federal and National Council of Churches and the evangelicals, and the ways in which "broadcasting contributed to the institutional growth and unity of the evangelical movement" (p. 91).

Wakin, Edward. "The Catholic Press: Parochialism to Professionalism." *Journalism Quarterly* 43 (1966): 117-20.

Wakin sees Catholic journalism, in the period following World War II, developing more editorial freedom and more professionalism for a religious press of 151 Catholic weeklies and 408 Catholic magazines with a total circulation of twenty-eight million.

Weimann, Gabriel. "Mass-Mediated Occultism: The Role of the Media in the Occult Revival." *Journal of Popular Culture* 18, 4 (Spring 1985): 81-88.

Occultism relies on the mass media — magazines, newspapers, radio, and television — as channels of information and influence. The occult satisfies many of the attributes of news. The effects of media coverage of occultism tend to demonstrate the place of occultism as a deviant variable in daily life.

Whalen, James W. "The *Catholic Digest:* Experiment in Courage." *Journalism Quarterly* 41 (1964): 343-52.

This article relates the story of the founding, growth, and stature of this unique reprint and digest magazine, which in 1964 had a circulation of 650,000. Founded in 1936 by the Reverend Louis A. Gales on good will and with tenuous financial resources, it grew to be, against many predictions of failure, a mass circulation publication.

Wills, Gary. "Greatest Story Ever Told." *Columbia Journalism Review* 18 (1980): 25-33.

Wills, himself a journalist and author, reviews press coverage of Pope John Paul II's October 1979 visit to the United States. Historically the visit marked the first time a pope had been formally received by an American president at the White House, an event that marked the end of American nativism. The press is judged to have abrogated its duty to inform, debate, and question the event and its impact. "The press did not choose to explore the event, to reflect it and reflect on it; it became an unthinking part of the event, joining in all moods rather than deepening them, trivializing with empty acclaim" (p. 33).

Wright, J. Elwin. *The Old Fashioned Revival Hour and the Broadcasters.* New York: Garland Publishing, 1988; reprint of the Boston 1940 edition.

A popularly written account of the early years of a radio program by Charles E. Fuller (1887-1968), a fundamentalist Baptist preacher from California. Begun locally in Los Angeles in May 1933, the program by 1940 was nationally distributed and broadcast over the Mutual Broadcasting System. Also by 1940, 152 radio stations provided coverage to North and South America, the Islands of the Pacific, and parts of Asia, reaching a weekly audience estimated at several million. Considerable attention is given to listener response; excerpts from letters received by the broadcast are included.

# Contributors

**Catherine L. Albanese** — Professor of Religious Studies, University of California, Santa Barbara

**David G. Buttrick** — Professor of Homiletics and Liturgics, Divinity School of Vanderbilt University

**Charles E. Hambrick-Stowe** — Adjunct Professor of Church History, Lancaster Theological Seminary, and Pastor, Church of the Apostles, Lancaster, Pennsylvania

**David Edwin Harrell, Jr.** — Breeden Eminent Scholar in the Humanities, Auburn University

**Martin E. Marty** — Fairfax M. Cone Distinguished Service Professor of the History of Modern Christianity, University of Chicago

**Glenn T. Miller** — Professor of Church History and Academic Dean, Bangor Theological Seminary

**James H. Moorhead** — Mary McIntosh Bridge Professor of American Church History, Princeton Theological Seminary

**Mark A. Noll** — Professor of History, Wheaton College

**David Paul Nord** — Professor, School of Journalism, Indiana University

**Elmer J. O'Brien** — Director of Library Information and Service and

Professor of Theological Bibliography and Research, United Theological Seminary

**A. Gregory Schneider** — Professor, Department of Behavioral Science, Pacific Union College

**Harry S. Stout** — Professor of American Religious History, Yale Divinity School, and John B. Madden Master, Berkeley College

**Leonard I. Sweet** — Professor of Church History and Chancellor, United Theological Seminary

**Ronald J. Zboray** — Assistant Professor of History, Georgia State University